Speaking of Sexuality

Interdisciplinary Readings

J. Kenneth Davidson, Sr.
University of Wisconsin–Eau Claire

Nelwyn B. Moore
Southwest Texas State University

Foreword by
John D. DeLamater
University of Wisconsin–Madison

Roxbury Publishing Company
Los Angeles, California

Library of Congress Cataloging-in-Publication Data

Speaking of Sexuality: Interdisciplinary Readings/ J. Kenneth Davidson, Sr.
Nelwyn B. Moore.
p. cm.
Includes bibliographical references.
ISBN 1-891487-33-7
1. Sex. 2. Sex (Psychology). 3. Hygiene, Sexual. I. Moore, Nelwyn B. II. Title.
HQ21.D29 2001
306.7–dc21

99-35447
CIP

Publisher: Claude Teweles
Managing Editor: Dawn VanDercreek
Production Editor: Carla Max-Ryan
Assistant Editor: Monica Gomez
Typography: Synergistic Data Systems
Cover Design: Marnie Kenney

Printed on acid-free paper in the United States of America. This paper meets the standards for recycling of the Environmental Protection Agency.

ISBN 1-891487-33-7

Roxbury Publishing Company
P.O. Box 491044
Los Angeles, California 90049-9044
Tel.: (310) 473-3312 • Fax: (310) 473-4490
E-mail: roxbury@roxbury.net
Web site: www.roxbury.net

*We dedicate this book to the countless
thousands of students who have touched our
lives in more years than we care to count . . .*

*And to our professional colleagues with whom
we share
a common passion,
teaching and a common illusion,
a belief that we know more about the subject
of sexuality than do the students.*

—J. Kenneth Davidson, Sr.
and
Nelwyn B. Moore

Contents

Part I: Historical and Theoretical Perspectives on Sexuality

Ira L. Reiss and Harriet M. Reiss
The authors delineate the reasons for the emergence of two sexual revolutions in the late twentieth century and propose a pluralistic approach to sexuality: individual choices guided by the values of honesty, equality, and responsibility (HER).

Anne Bolin and Patricia Whelehan
This historical account traces the contributions of such early notables as Mead, Malinowski, and Beach and Ford, exploring the anthropological perspective in the study of human sexuality.

Vern L. Bullough
Bullough chronicles the life and career of Alfred Kinsey from biologist to renowned sex researcher, and offers numerous insights into why his work continues to be controversial.

Vern L. Bullough
This brief history of Masters and Johnson's research documents their clinical measurements of physiological sexual response that led to their often-cited, arbitrary four-stage division of the sexual response.

Part II: Sexuality and the Life Cycle: Childhood and Adolescence

Part III: Sexuality and the Life Cycle: Young Adulthood

Part IV: Sexuality and the Life Cycle: Middle and Later Adulthood

Part V: Physiology, Sexual Desire, and Sexual Response

Part VI: Birth Control and Sexually Transmitted Diseases

Part VII: Sexual Orientation

  Ritch C. Savin-Williams
  The author portrays the situation confronting gay, lesbian, and bisexual youths as they seek to develop intimate, romantic relationships through dating.

Part VIII: Sexual Victimization

  David Finkelhor, Gerald Hotaling, I. A. Lewis, and Christine Smith
  This first national survey of adults regarding their childhood sexual abuse history has become the benchmark for establishing the prevalence of child sexual abuse in American society.

  Gordon C. Nagayama Hall, Amy K. Windover, and Gloria Gia Maramba
  Hall et al. discuss risk factors for sexual aggression toward Asian American women and protective factors unique to the Asian culture.

  Charlene L. Muehlenhard and Carie S. Rodgers
  Candid accounts of actual dating situations among college women and men are used to address the controversial issue of token resistance to sex, i.e., "Does no mean yes?" through candid accounts of actual dating situations among college women and men.

  Judith A. Richman, Kathleen M. Rospenda, Stephanie J. Nawyn, Joseph A. Flaherty, Michael Fendrich, Melinda L. Drum, and Timothy P. Johnson
  These researchers reveal the prevalence of sexual harassment and generalized workplace abuse in a university-employee setting.

  Al Cooper, David L. Delmonico, and Ron Burg
  Cooper et al. investigate cybersex use and abuse, and quantitatively assess the primary methods and locations for obtaining sexual material.

Part IX: Legal and Educational Issues

Foreword

A visitor to the United States in the year 2001 would probably conclude that it is a completely open society with regard to sexuality. Every one of us is surrounded by sexual materials and information. Sexual behavior and relationships are portrayed in prime-time television programs and soap operas; "news stories" about sex fill our daily papers, news magazines, and TV news. Feature films display a wide range of sexual behaviors and lifestyles. Advertisers use images of sexually attractive men and women to sell us everything from cosmetics, beer, and wine to automobiles and vacations. And then there is explicit pornography, the largest single category on the Internet.

Unfortunately, the person who attempts to fashion his or her sexual expression and lifestyle using these media depictions is not likely to find fulfillment and lasting relationships. The portrayals we see on prime-time television and in films are unrealistic; they feature young, attractive people who aren't married to each other, a group that does not include most Americans. Further, the plots of soap operas and news stories often focus on the dangers associated with sexuality, dangers such as unwanted pregnancy and sexually transmitted diseases (STDs).

Fortunately, we have much better sources of information available to us. Scientific research on human sexuality dates back at least to the 1890s and the pioneering work of Sigmund Freud. Over the years, many social and behavioral scientists have contributed to our understanding of sexuality. Textbooks written by knowledgeable scientists and anthologies of professional readings are readily available. For example, this collection of articles is designed to introduce sexuality research and writings by scientists, psychologists, social psychologists, sociologists, and anthropologists. The editors have carefully selected these readings to reflect the variety of materials published in this field. They have also edited the readings to make them more interesting and informative.

The selections introduce you to important influences on your sexual thoughts, emotions, and behavior. Biological development and aging, parents, friends, sexuality education, religion, and culture all affect sexuality throughout a person's life. Such complex influences can lead to emotionally and sexually satisfying relationships and behavior. They can also lead to frustrating and painful outcomes, such as loneliness, sexual problems or dysfunctions, STDs, and forms of sexual victimization. Reading the articles in this book, you can learn about the influences on your sexuality, and gain a sense of agency and control, enabling you to avoid undesirable outcomes and making it more likely that you will experience positive outcomes.

As you read, consider how the content relates to you and your relationships. For example, if the article is about factors that contribute to sexual harassment, consider whether your attitudes and behavior make you more or less likely to be a victim. If you find a particular reading especially interesting and want more information, you can consult the sources listed in the References, or your textbook.

I have been teaching human sexuality for 26 years. Many of my students have told me that it was the single most important course that they took, because they gained a greater understanding of their sexuality and of our society. I hope these readings contribute to your own achievement of this understanding.

—John D. DeLamater
Professor of Sociology
University of Wisconsin–Madison

Preface

Overview

No aspect of human life seethes with so many unexorcised demons as does sex. No human activity is so hexed by superstition, so haunted by residual tribal lore, and so harassed by socially induced fear.

—Harvey Cox

The captivating words by noted theologian Harvey Cox alluding to the unstateable state of the subject of this anthology, sexuality, are less than rhetorical. They portend that all is not well in the real world of sexuality. We agree. But neither is all lost. This latter belief is the basis of the paradigm for this work.

By choosing to reframe many of today's considered-to-be sexuality issues, we hope to dispel a number of sexual myths that have been formed from society's free-floating sexual anxieties. To accomplish this feat, we called upon academicians—women and men of letters in the fields of medicine, theology, sexology, sociology, marriage and family therapy, psychology, social work, psychiatry, and family studies. Most have spoken with empirical authority, based on their own research. Some few by virtue of the respect gained over a lifetime of work in the field of sexology were selected for their accumulated acumen. For balance, a number of challenging selections were included from writers in lay sources such as *Harper's*, *Newsweek*, and *The New York Times Magazine*.

English educator Robert Grimm once said that if you want to know what individuals are really like at their very core, look at the way they use their sexuality. If, for you, this book has a voice, you may well hear it ask, "How are we, as a part of humankind, collectively using our sexuality?" We invite you to accompany us into the pages of this book in order that we may all more authoritatively answer this question.

About the Anthology

At last, an alternative is provided for instructors of human sexuality courses who prefer a student-friendly, yet more rigorous, less sensationalized book of readings than any currently on the market. This anthology presents an array of personal and societal sexuality issues at a scholarly level that previous works have failed to achieve. In so doing, the subject of human sexuality is addressed from a position of strength, one that is realistic as well as sex-positive. Vestiges of numerous theories can be traced throughout the carefully selected entries, all of which fit into a health-promoting framework, spanning the life cycle from birth to death. From this perspective, sexuality is viewed as an inseparable part of a person's personality, with great potential for fulfillment. The authors' core belief that a healthy sexual script is a realistic goal for every person is the book's bottom-line rationale. Further, respect for the integrity of the professor and the student has guided this professional endeavor. Because we believe that professors bring their own personality to the process of facilitating learning and that students are both interested in and capable of learning, the narrative in this anthology is purposefully classic in format, challenging in content, and devoid of jargon.

To enable the reader to encounter leading sexuality authorities, past and present, seminal works in sexuality research and theory are included. A balance achieved by also offering articles that reveal popular treatment of today's timely topics enables students to become more discriminating and, thus, better consumers of sexuality materials in the mass media, essential skills in a sex-saturated society. To this end, the selections included in *Speaking of Sexuality* explore the following areas of sexuality: historical and theoretical perspectives on sexuality; sexuality and life cycle issues during childhood and adolescence, young adulthood, and middle and late adulthood; physiology, sexual desire, and sexual response; birth control and sexually transmitted diseases; sexual orientation; sexual victimization; and legal and educational issues.

With every product, there is a parallel process story. In this case, negotiating the sometimes slippery slope between a sociologist/researcher and a family scientist/family therapist was not always an easy task. However, we feel the results are considerably stronger because of our team efforts. Together, we have interwoven complex phenomena from fields known for their diversity of theories, concepts, and issues. The final product is an anthology with professional integrity and pragmatic pedagogical purposes—to provoke critical thinking and to motivate future learning.

Instructor's Manual

A full-scale *Instructor's Manual* is available to provide assistance when integrating the anthology material into sexuality courses and when evaluating student achievement. The components for each entry include general summarizing statements, key points, and general conclusions. Additionally, there are multiple choice, true/false, and essay questions for student evaluation. Finally, the following pedagogical tools are provided: a Topical Matrix, based on current sexuality texts; an Article Review Form, a one-page document, that can be reproduced as needed; and Web site addresses, which focus on sexuality and sexual health issues and topics.

Acknowledgments

First among persons acknowledged for contributions to this book must be those thousands who shall remain nameless: students who over many years of teaching have taught us far more valuable lessons about life and humanity than we ourselves have taught. And, the many family professionals along the way who have served as mentors may be unaware of their influence in our lives, but it is present just the same. Some are names instantly recognizable, such as Gerald R. Leslie (JKD) and James Leslie McCary (NBM), but not all. Some are no longer with us, some retired, while still others remain in our current networks of professional colleagues. Many of those who have touched our lives significantly and kept us true to our purpose are today's promising young scholars.

Our faith in the review process has been strengthened by the significant contributions made by our colleagues who served as reviewers for this work. We express sincere appreciation to these consummate professionals, without whose numerous comments and recommendations this anthology would not be as pragmatic, student friendly, or interesting. They are: Carol V. Apt, South Carolina State; M. Betsy Bergen, Kansas State University; Clive M. Davis, Syracuse University; Patricia H. Dyk, University of Kentucky; John W. Engel, University of Hawaii; Terri D. Fisher, Ohio State University–Mansfield; G. David Johnson, University of South Alabama; David Knox, East Carolina University; Dan Landis, University of Mississippi; Marsha McGee, Northeast Louisiana University; Robert H. Pollock, University of Georgia; David Przybyla, Denison University; Marie Saracino, Stephen F. Austin State University; Michael R. Stevenson, Ball State University; David L. Weis, Bowling Green State University; and Colin J. Williams, Indiana University/Purdue University–Indianapolis.

We are indebted to Claude Teweles, Publisher, Roxbury Publishing Company, without whose persistence, perseverance, and patience this sexuality anthology would never have come to fruition. In addition, we want to acknowledge the numerous helpful suggestions and cordial assistance provided by Carla Max-Ryan at Roxbury. Further, we thank Ann West for her expert copyediting, which has made our anthology a more concise and tightly written work.

Without the capable support of research assistants, this work would not have been developed and brought to completion. Kristin Wanish Salisbury helped to compile the large pool of resources from which these selections were made and conducted a detailed analysis of the reviewers' comments. Tiffany E. Collins spent many hours typing and revising numerous drafts as well as conducting library research. Heather Carden made invaluable contributions with her typing, proofreading, and editorial suggestions. Finally, John Curtis Copeland deserves special recognition for his myriad management contributions. He set up and managed the word processing files, contributor files, and copyright permission files while also assisting with the typing and proofreading.

Finally, without the loving support of our families, Jo, John, Lisa, John III, and Stephen (JKD) and Jerry, Jay, Amy, Madeleine, and Max (NBM), this project would not have been possible. They have understood and accepted our passion for completing what has proven to be an infinitely more complex and time-consuming task than originally perceived.

—J. Kenneth Davidson, Sr.
Nelwyn B. Moore

About the Contributors

Paul R. Abramson, Professor of Psychology at the University of California, Los Angeles (UCLA), has research interests in the epidemiology of HIV and sex and the law. His recent books include *With Pleasure: Thoughts on the Nature of Human Sexuality* (1995) and *A House Divided: Suspicions of Mother-Daughter Incest* (2000).

Joseph Adelson is a retired professor of psychology at the University of Michigan.

Nancy E. Adler is Professor of Psychology at the University of California, San Francisco, with research interests in the causes and consequences of unwanted pregnancy and the prevention of sexually transmitted diseases. She is coeditor of *Health Psychology* (1979) and *Socioeconomic Status and Health in Industrialized Nations* (1999).

Sevgi O. Aral works in the division of Sexually Transmitted Disease Prevention at the Centers for Disease Control.

J. Michael Bailey, Professor of Psychology at Northwestern University, conducts research on sexual orientation.

Lessie A. Bass is Assistant Professor in the School of Social Work at East Carolina University.

Leah Beardsley holds an appointment in the Department of Epidemiology and Social Medicine at the Albert Einstein College of Medicine.

Sharon L. Begley serves as Senior Science Editor at *Newsweek*. She is the author of *The Hand of God* (1999).

Robert Bierman works in the Rutgers University Student Health Service.

Kimberly Black works as a counselor at Safe Place: Domestic Violence and Sexual Assault Survival Center, in Austin, Texas, focusing her attention on the sexuality issues of spinal-cord injured women and sexual assault victims.

Anne Bolin, Professor of Anthropology at Elon College, has research interests in sport ethnography, body building, human sexuality, and gender variance. She has authored *In Search of Eve: Transsexual Rites of Passage* (1987) and coauthored *Perspectives on Human Sexuality*.

Vern L. Bullough currently is Clinical Professor of Nursing at the University of Southern California and Distinguished Professor Emeritus at the State University of New York at Buffalo. A prolific writer, he has authored, coauthored, or edited twenty books on sexual topics, including *Science in the Bedroom: A History of Sex Research* (1994).

Ron Burg holds an appointment as a psychologist at Stanford University, where he researches Internet sexuality and sexual orientation.

Robert D. Burk, Professor of Pediatrics at Albert Einstein College of Medicine, has primary research interests in the genital human papillomavirus infection (HPV), especially in young women.

William M. Byne holds an appointment as Assistant Professor of Psychiatry in the Mt. Sinai School of Medicine, with primary research interests in sexual orientation.

Janis M. Byrd is a physician specializing in family practice at Physicians Plus in Columbus, Wisconsin.

Al Cooper, Staff Psychologist at Stanford University and Director, San Jose Mental and Sexuality Centre, conducts research on Internet sexuality and compulsivity.

Daniel Daley is a contributing editor at the Sexuality Information and Education Council of the United States (SIECUS).

Henry P. David is Director of the Transnational Family Research Institute in Bethesda, Maryland.

J. Kenneth Davidson, Sr. is Professor of Sociology and Coordinator of Family

Studies at the University of Wisconsin–Eau Claire. His research interests include sexual attitudes and behavior of college students, the Grafenburg spot and female ejaculation, sexual fantasies, and orgasm among women. He is coauthor of *Marriage and Family* (1992) and *Marriage and Family: Change and Continuity* (1996) and coeditor of *Cultural Diversity and Families* (1992).

John D. DeLamater is Professor of Sociology at the University of Wisconsin—Madison, with primary research interests in sexuality and the life cycle. He is coauthor of *Premarital Sexuality* (1974) and *Understanding Sexuality*, 7th edition (2000).

David L. Delmonico serves as Associate Professor of Counseling at Duquesne University and has research interests in sexual addiction and Internet sexuality.

Melinda L. Drum is a research associate in biostatistics/health studies at the University of Chicago.

Marion A. Eppler serves as Assistant Professor of Psychology at East Carolina University.

Julia A. Ericksen, Professor of Sociology at Temple University, has research interests in sexuality and gender, with a current focus on the study of breasts and breast cancer. She is coauthor of *Kiss and Tell: Surveying Sex in the Twentieth Century* (1999).

Pamela I. Erickson, Associate Professor of Anthropology at the University of Connecticut, has research and writing interests in adolescent sexual and reproductive behavior. She is author of *Latina Adolescent Childbearing in East Los Angeles* (1998).

Michael Fendrich is Associate Professor of Psychiatry at the University of Illinois at Chicago, specializing in research on gender differences in substance use disclosure.

David Finkelhor is Director of the Crimes Against Children Research Center and Research Professor of Sociology at the University of New Hampshire, where he continues his research interests in family violence, sexual behavior, and victimology. He is author of *Sexually Victimized Children* (1979) and coauthor of *Theory-Based Assessment, Treatment, and Prevention of Sexual Aggression* (1996).

Joseph A. Flaherty holds an appointment as Professor and Head of the Department of Psychiatry at the University of Illinois at Chicago. His research focuses on gender differences in psychopathology. He is the author of *Psychiatric Diagnosis and Treatment* (1997).

Kathleen Ford is a research scientist in the Department of Epidemiology at the University of Michigan, where her interests center on reproduction and the social epidemiology of sexually transmitted diseases, including AIDS.

Robert T. Francoeur, Professor Emeritus of Biology and Psychology at Fairleigh Dickinson University, has research and writing interests in cross-cultural studies of sexual attitudes, values, and behavior. His coedited books include the *International Encyclopedia of Sexuality* (1997); *Sexuality in America* (1998); and *Sex, Love, and Marriage in the 21st Century* (1999).

John H. Gagnon is Professor of Sociology at the State University of New York at Stony Brook and past president of the International Academy of Sex Research. His coauthored books, which reflect his research interests in sexual conduct, include *The Social Organization of Sexuality* (1994), *Sex in America* (1994), *Sexual Conduct* (1973), and *Conceiving Sexuality* (1994).

Deirdre Giesen is a statistical researcher at Statistics Netherlands.

Susan E. Golombok is Professor of Psychology at City University, London, with research interests in gender development and lesbian-mother families. She is author of *Parenting: What Really Counts* (2000) and coauthor of *Bottling It Up* (1985), *Gender Development* (1996), and *Growing Up in a Lesbian Family: Effects on Child Development* (1997).

Gordon C. Nagayama Hall has an appointment as Professor of Psychology at Pennsylvania State University, with a special interest in sexual aggression. He is coauthor of *Theory-Based Assessment, Treatment, and Prevention of Sexual Aggression* (1996).

Gloria Y. F. Ho is affiliated with the Department of Microbiology and Immunology at the Albert Einstein College of Medicine.

Gerald Hotaling is a professor in the Department of Criminal Justice at the University of Massachusetts at Lowell.

Janet Shibley Hyde, whose research includes the study of gender and sexuality, is the Helen Thompson Woolley Professor of Psychology and Women's Studies at the University of Wisconsin—Madison. She is coauthor of *Understanding Human Sexuality,* 7th Edition (2000).

Timothy P. Johnson, Associate Professor with the Survey Research Laboratory at the University of Illinois at Chicago, specializes in the measurement of sensitive behaviors.

Sheryl A. Kingsberg, Assistant Professor in the Department of Reproductive Biology and Psychiatry at Case Western University School of Medicine, has research interests in the psychological aspects of infertility, menopause, and female sexuality.

Patricia Barthalow Koch holds an appointment as Associate Professor of Behavioral Health at Pennsylvania State University, specializing in sexual health, women's sexuality, and sexuality education. She is the author of *Exploring Sexuality: An Interactive Text* (1995) and coeditor of *Sexuality in America: Understanding Our Sexual Values and Behavior* (1998).

Lewis H. Lapham works as a staff writer for *Harper's Magazine.*

Edward O. Laumann, George Herbert Mead Distinguished Service Professor, is Chairman of the Department of Sociology and Director of the Ogburn Stouffer Center for Population and Social Organization at the University of Chicago, where his major research interests include social stratification, sociology of the professions, and sociology of human sexuality. He has authored or coauthored twelve books, including *The Social Organization of Sexuality* (1994), *Sex in America* (1994), *Prestige and Association in an Urban Community* (1966), and *The Organization of State* (1988).

Michele Lempa is affiliated with the Rutgers University Student Health Service.

I. A. Lewis conducted polls as a staff member for the *Los Angeles Times.*

Brenda N. Major holds an appointment in the Department of Psychology at the University of California, Santa Barbara, where her primary research interests center on preabortion conflict and postabortion adjustment.

Gloria Gia Maramba is affiliated with Kent State University.

Barry W. McCarthy, whose writing interests are related to sexual dysfunction, serves as a Professor of Psychology at American University. He is coauthor of *Couple Sexual Awareness* (1998).

Robert T. Michael serves as the Eliakim Hastings More Distinguished Service Professor of Public Policy Studies at the University of Chicago. He has coauthored *Sex in America* (1994) and *The Social Organization of Sexuality* (1994) and authored *Pay Equity* (1989).

Stuart Michaels, a researcher at the University of Chicago, was Project Manager for the National Health and Social Life Survey (NHSLS), leading to the Laumann et al. study and the subsequent publication of *The Social Organization of Sexuality* (1994) and *Sex in America* (1994).

Nelwyn B. Moore is Professor Emeritus of Family and Child Studies at Southwest Texas State University and a certified marriage and family therapist. Her research interests include sexual attitudes and behavior, teen pregnancy, and cross-cultural sexuality education. She is coauthor of *Marriage and Family* (1992) and *Marriage and Family: Change and Continuity* (1996), and coeditor of *Cultural Diversity and Families* (1992).

Charlene L. Muehlenhard is Professor of Psychology and Women's Studies at the University of Kansas, with research interests in rape and other forms of sex and coercion, sexual consent, and communication and miscommunication about sexuality issues.

Stephanie J. Nawyn is a graduate student in sociology at Loyola University, Chicago, with research interests in the social construction of sexuality.

Anne E. Norris serves as Associate Professor of Nursing at Boston College with research interests in sexual abstinence, sexual risk taking, pregnancy, and sexually transmitted diseases.

Paul Okami, a post-doctoral scholar in psychology at the University of California, Los Angeles (UCLA), has research interests in sex differences in behavior, childhood sexuality, and the evolution of sexuality.

Richard Olmstead, Assistant Research Psychologist at the University of California, Los Angeles (UCLA), has research interests in addiction from a biobehavioral perspective.

Susie Orenstein works as a contributing author for the Sexuality Information and Education Council of the United States (SIECUS).

Laura Pendleton is a graduate student in the Department of Psychology at the University of California, Los Angeles (UCLA).

Michael Peters works in the Rutgers University Student Health Service.

Richard C. Pillard, Professor of Psychology at Boston University, has primary research interests in sexual orientation.

E. Ashby Plant, whose research interests include the social psychology of prejudice, is Assistant Professor of Psychology at Florida State University.

Ronald L. Poulson serves as Associate Professor of Psychology at East Carolina University.

Pamela C. Regan, Associate Professor of Psychology and Director, Social Relations Laboratory at California State Los Angeles, has research interests in sexual attraction. She is coauthor of *Lust: What We Know About Human Sexual Desire* (1999).

Harriet M. Reiss is a retired social worker with research and writing interests in premarital sexuality.

Ira L. Reiss, Professor Emeritus at the University of Minnesota, has authored numerous publications on sexuality, gender, and the family. He is the author of twelve books, including *Premarital Sexual Standards in America* (1960); *The Social Context of Premarital Sexual Permissiveness* (1967); *Journey Into Sexuality* (1986); and *Solving America's Sexual Crisis* (1997).

Judith A. Richman, Professor of Psychiatry at the University of Illinois at Chicago, conducts research on the mental health and alcohol-related consequences of sexual harassment.

Carie S. Rodgers holds an appointment as a post-doctoral fellow in clinical psychology at the University of California, San Diego, and the San Diego Veterans Administration Medical Center, and has research interests in the psychology of women, gender-role development, and treatment of sexual trauma.

Kathleen M. Rospenda serves as Assistant Professor in Psychiatry at the University of Illinois at Chicago and has research interests in the mental health, physical health, and job-related outcomes of sexual harassment.

Susan H. Roth is Professor of Psychology at Duke University, specializing in research about regret and abortion.

Nancy Felipe Russo, Professor of Psychology at Arizona State University, has primary research interests in the relationship of abortion to psychological well-being.

Tammy N. Satterwhite is a graduate student in psychology at East Carolina University.

Ritch C. Savin-Williams is Professor of Developmental and Clinical Psychology at Cornell University, with primary research interests in same-sex attractions, behavior, and identity. He is the author of ". . . And I Became Gay": Young Men's Stories* (1998) and *Mom, Dad. I'm Gay: How Families Negotiate Coming Out* (2001).

David M. Schnarch, a certified sex therapist and clinical member of the American Association of Marriage and Family Therapists, is Director of the Marriage and Family Health Center, in Evergreen, Colorado, where he focuses on the treatment of sexual desire problems. He is the author of *Constructing the Sexual Crucible* (1991) and *Passionate Marriage* (1997).

Marca L. Sipski, Associate Professor of Neurologic Surgery in the University of Miami School of Medicine, specializes in the sexual functioning of spinal-cord injured women. She is coeditor of *Sexual*

Function in People With Disability and Chronic Illness (1997).

Christine Smith is a staff member of Abt Associates, Cambridge, Massachusetts.

Susan Sprecher, Professor of Sociology at Illinois State University, has research interests in the sexual attitudes and behavior of college students.

Sally A. Steffen, who is an associate in Ballard, Spahr, Andrews, and Ingersoll, LLP, is coauthor of *Kiss and Tell: Surveying Sex in the Twentieth Century.*

Ron Stodghill II serves as a contributing correspondent for *Time.*

Susanne S. Strauss works as a social worker at the New Jersey Medical School in the Department of Physical Medicine and Rehabilitation.

Margaret Talbot is a staff writer for *The New York Times Magazine.*

Koray Tanfer, Senior Research Scientist at Battele Centers for Public Health Research and Evaluation, concentrates on sexually transmitted diseases, high-risk behaviors, and sexual behavior as social interaction.

Fiona L. Tasker is Senior Lecturer at Birkbeck College, University of London, with major research interests in lesbian-mother families, gay-father families, and family therapy of sexual identity. She is co-author of *Growing Up in a Lesbian Family* (1997).

Judith Treas is Professor of Sociology at the University of California, Irvine, with primary research interests in attitudes toward nonmarital sex.

Patricia Whelehan teaches in the Department of Anthropology at the State University of New York at Potsdam. She is coauthor of *Perspectives on Human Sexuality.*

Michael W. Wiederman, Associate Professor of Psychology at Columbia College, focuses his research interests on extra-dyadic sex, gender differences, and jealousy. He is the author of *Guide to Graduate School Admission: Psychology, Counseling, and Related Professions* (2000) and *Understanding Sexuality Research* (2001).

Amy K. Windover is affiliated with Kent State University.

Vivian Wong serves as a contributing author for the Sexuality Information and Education Council of the United States (SIECUS).

Lore K. Wright holds an appointment as Professor and Department Chair of Nursing at the Medical College of Georgia, with research interests in aging and sexuality. She is the author of *Alzheimer's Disease and Marriage* (1993).

Karl L. Wuensch serves as Associate Professor of Psychology at East Columbia University.

Gail E. Wyatt, whose current research interests are directed toward first sexual intercourse and risky sexual practices, holds an appointment in the Department of Psychiatry and Behavioral Sciences at the University of California, Los Angeles (UCLA). ✦

About the Editors

J. Kenneth Davidson, Sr., a nationally recognized authority in the field of human sexuality, has taught a course in the sociology of human sexuality for the past 27 years. His selected teaching materials appear in *The Sociology of Sexuality and Sexual Orientation: Syllabi and Teaching Materials* (1997). He is also one of the most widely published researchers in the area of human sexuality, with numerous papers in professional journals concerning premarital sexual attitudes and behavior of college women and men, the female sexual response and sexual satisfaction, the Grafenberg spot and female ejaculation, and sexual fantasies. In addition, Davidson is coauthor of *Marriage and Family* (1992) and *Marriage and Family: Change and Continuity* (1996), and coeditor of *Cultural Diversity and Families* (1992).

Nelwyn B. Moore has taught courses in marriage and family for 37 years. She is a licensed marriage and family therapist and a licensed professional counselor with professional training in the area of human sexuality. Moore is recognized for her contributions in sexuality education as well as her publications in professional journals on sexual attitudes and behavior of college women and men, family life education, child development and guidance, curriculum design, and family and interpersonal relations. She is coauthor of *Marriage and Family* (1992) and *Marriage and Family: Change and Continuity* (1996) and coeditor of *Cultural Diversity and Families* (1992). ✦

Part I

Historical and Theoretical Perspectives on Sexuality

As the most ambitious of the offerings in this anthology, Part I almost assumes a life of its own. Most of the selections were purposely chosen because they reflect seminal works in the field of sexuality research. Names like Kinsey, Masters and Johnson, Lauman, Gagnon, and Reiss are instantly recognizable as standard-bearers in the field of sexuality research, yesterday and today. Although most students may not be primarily interested in the theory and history of sexuality research, they will be fascinated with the insights furnished by the authors. For example, historian Bullough not only records interesting facts, but also reveals the colorful personalities of three key players—Kinsey and Masters and Johnson. This prolific writer's unbiased treatment of the life and work of these giants in the field of sexuality research documents their singular, rare contributions, while also acknowledging their shortcomings as researchers.

The selections in Part I introduce readers to highly detailed portraits of American sexuality—who does what, with whom, how, and how many times—a feat certainly more easily accomplished with the click of a mouse to browse the Internet. But the difference between Internet browsing and mining the minds of the century's giants in the field of sexuality research is immeasurable. With their scientific orientation to the study of sexual behavior and attitudes,

each of the authors here helps students reframe the issues to fit into broader social contexts. The picture that emerges for avid readers is a sum that is truly greater than the individual parts.

As a young professional, Ira Reiss was one of the first observers on the American scene to predict the last sexual revolution, which began in the 1960s. He presents a logical argument that another sexual revolution supporting pluralism of sexual morality is needed. With a careful review of this entry, students may be better prepared to formulate their own opinions about troubling issues in American sexuality. Why, for example, as Reiss points out, does the United States, a leader in the Western world, remain the nation with the highest rates of virtually every sexual problem: teen pregnancy, rape, child sexual abuse, and AIDS? Perhaps, students reading about previous sexual revolutions will be motivated to become twenty-first century sexuality researchers and help resolve this apparent national paradox.

From its inception in the nineteenth century, anthropology has examined the role of human sexuality—in evolution and in the organization of culture. Differentiating culture-specific sexual behavior from that which is shared as a species, this approach places sexual behavior in a larger context, one that precludes norm-based judgments about this complex phenomenon. The anthropological perspective of sexuality, introduced by Bolin and Whelehan in Part I, is one that incorporates both the biological and cultural approaches. While defining the patterning of human sexuality as biocultural, the authors do not exclude the psychological dimension but regard it as a part of the culture that shapes personalities.

Ericksen's provocative history of sex surveys in the United States is a revealing account of the social construction of sexuality and scientific knowledge. The author's excellent discussion of how a researcher's "agenda" may influence the choice and wording of questions helps to explain some of the nonrepresentative, biased data and even "incorrect" findings that may surface in researchland. For example, she clearly delineates how men studying female sexuality can derive incorrect conclusions, due to male assumptions about gendered sexuality.

Various aspects of gendered sexuality are a common thread woven throughout the history of sexuality research. A recent *New York Times* (Kolata, 1998) feature, titled "Women and Sex: On This Topic, Science Blushes," serves to illustrate this point. Do women become sexually excited by talk of love and romance or are they turned on by explicit talk of sexual activity itself? This interesting question was posed by Julia Heiman, a psychologist who directs the Reproductive and Sexual Medicine Clinic at the University of Washington. To discover answers, she asked college women to wear a tampon-like device that detects blood flow to the vagina while alternately listening to romantic tape recordings and erotic ones. The results indicated that, if blood flow to the vagina is an accurate measure of sexual excitement, women, like men, are sexually excited by erotic talk, not romance (Heiman, 1975).

What makes this study unique? It occurred in the early 1970s and, for all of the medical advances in the past 30 years, Julia Heiman's study still represents the state of the art. When the recent Viagra rush occurred for men, drug-company scientists asked academic scientists what was known

about women's sexual responses; not much, came the reply. Although every survey invariably finds that many more women than men complain of sexual difficulties, the dearth of female sexuality research suggests that there is a resistance to understanding women's sexual responses.

The Laumann et al. and Adelson selections stand alone, but students will miss an interesting exercise in analyzing and synthesizing if they fail to read both. Hailed by *Time* (Elmer-Dewitt, 1994) as probably the "First truly scientific study of sexuality in America," the Laumann et al. study published as *The Social Organization of Sexuality*, exploded many myths of sexuality. Whether the findings were received as reassuring or alarming depended upon one's personal agenda. The first chapter is included here as a significant piece of work in that it clarifies the rationale and theoretical base of the study.

Joseph Adelson's treatment of the Laumann et al. data in "Sex Among the Americans" is at once compelling and practical. Students will enjoy the fast read with its astonishing facts, guaranteed to shatter at least some myths about Americans and sexuality. Adelson's critique points to the authors' avoidance of a value construct and their questionable choice of social networks and the sexual marketplace as theoretical structures. He is troubled by the authors' lack of consideration of the "inner world," the motives and character that influence sexual behavior and attitudes. He does conclude, however, that the data have great value. This offering, more than most, will motivate students to move closer to their own position statement about sexuality in America.

References

Elmer-Dewitt, P. (1994, October 17). "Now for the Truth About Americans and Sex." *Time*, pp. 62–66, 68, 70.

Heiman, J. R. (1975). The Physiology of Erotica: Women's Sexual Arousal. *Psychology Today, 8*, 90–94.

Kolata, G. (1998, June 21). Women and Sex: On This Topic, Science Blushes. *New York Times*, p. A3. ✦

Chapter 1
The Stalled Sexual Revolutions of This Century

Ira L. Reiss
Harriet M. Reiss

In *a professional lifetime devoted to the study of sexuality, sociologist Ira Reiss has long evoked reason in the often murky waters of emotion surrounding the subject of sexuality. As one of the few voices predicting the second sexual revolution of the twentieth century that occurred in the 1960s, Reiss seems eminently qualified to analyze the unfolding of twentieth-century sexuality in America. Drawing upon the parallels that propelled the sexual revolutions of the 1920s and the 1960s, he uses words such as* intolerance, *in*equity, *and* dogmatism *to argue convincingly for far more complex causes of these grassroots uprisings than merely the revolutionary power of the pill or of women in the workforce.*

"Shaping Our Next Sexual Revolution" is a fitting subtitle to the book An End to Shame, *in which a pluralistic approach to sexuality is proposed: individual choices, guided by the values of honesty, equality, and responsibility (HER). Against a backdrop of twentieth-century sexuality, readers are left to ponder a number of salient points raised by Reiss: Are we, as fellow travelers with women and men of the Western world, really traveling in the same direction in our move toward gender equality and sexual permissiveness? Is the price to pay for every societal arrangement always self-evident? If social customs are not built on principles of fairness, what are their basic premises? What should they be? If the homosexual revolution that began in 1969 led to more tolerance for gays and les-*

bians, why does American society, in general, continue to engage in repression of homosexuality? And, finally, if as suggested, the two sexual revolutions of the last century were only stalled, partial revolutions, what might the sexual script be like for a successful twenty-first century sexual revolution?

Readers will undoubtedly gain an important historical perspective from this work. More personally, such insight may spark a reassessment of their own sexual script. If so, pluralism will, it is hoped, be the criterion of choice.

Revolutions: One Isn't Enough

One day back in 1973 historian Carl Degler was sifting through the materials in the archives of Stanford University's library. To his surprise he found a manuscript by a medical doctor who had started a study of the sexual lives of married women in the year 1892! The author was Clelia Duel Mosher, M.D., born in 1863. She began her research as a student of biology at the University of Wisconsin and finished it at Stanford University. She never published her story and just tucked it away in Stanford University's archives at the end of her life in 1940. When it was discovered thirty-three years later, it was indeed like an archaeological find—the oldest recorded study of sexual practices in America, gathering dust in the archives at Stanford!

Most of the forty-five women Mosher interviewed were, like herself, born before 1870. They were highly educated women for their times; over three quarters of them had been to college or normal school. When Stanford historian Carl Degler read Dr. Mosher's findings, he was taken aback by the strength of the sexual interests of these Victorian women. Over 40 percent of these wives reported that they usually or always had orgasm in sexual intercourse and only one-third reported that they rarely or never had orgasm during sexual intercourse. Their rate of sexual intercourse was five times a month—not so low even by today's averages of almost seven times a month.[1]

There were clear signs that, at least for these women, Victorian restraints were not fully dominating their sexuality. They were, of course, more sexually constrained than we are today, but they also showed that even a century ago sexual intercourse in marriage was for many women far more than just a "wifely duty."

Later in her career, when she was sixty-three years old, Dr. Mosher taught a class in Personal Hygiene at Stanford University. It was the 1920s and "the times they were a-changin'." The premarital sexual escapades of this generation far exceeded the moderate pursuit of marital sexual pleasure by her nineteenth-century sample of women. This new generation was born in the first decade of the twentieth century and came to maturity in the 1920s.[2] Dr. Mosher was lecturing to the "flaming youth" of the 1920s. This century's first sexual revolution was in progress. According to the data gathered by Kinsey, the percentage of women born between 1900 and 1909 who had intercourse before marriage doubled from 25 percent to 50 percent! The premarital nonvirginity rate for men in that same birth cohort held relatively stable at about 80 percent.[3] It may shock today's baby boomers to realize that these were their grandparents!

Still, despite some sensationalized reporting, the 1920s were not a time of orgiastic sexuality. Most of the increased sexuality occurred in stable, affectionate relationships. Men moved more toward intercourse with women for whom they cared rather than with prostitutes or casual sexual partners. During the 1920s, these young revolutionaries fashioned a more egalitarian version of courtship and sexuality—one that continued to evolve during the rest of the century.[4]

The 1920s were a turning point in our society. As University of California historian Paula Fass sees it: "The twenties [were] a critical juncture between the strict double standard of the age of Victoria and the permissive sexuality of the age of Freud."[5] Fass describes the overall spirit of the 1920s:

> Did the young use sex and morals as a basis for conscious generational revolt?

On the whole the answer would appear to be no, although their sexual attitudes and practices did distinguish them from their elders and made them appear rebellious. They welcomed the lingering naughtiness of which they were accused, but more in the spirit of play than with any serious display of anger. As eager capitalists, the young were anything but rebellious in social and political questions.[6]

There are some remarkable similarities in the social forces that propelled the sexual revolution of the 1920s and those involved in the second sexual revolution which began in the late 1960s. Both revolutions involved a major war, a dramatic rise in divorce, and increased equality between men and women.

World War I ended in 1918. It was the first war in which American troops had been sent to Europe. The war provided a more panoramic view of the world to millions of American men and women. "How you gonna keep 'em down on the farm after they've seen Paree" was not just a line from a World War I song. It reflected the realization that the war had enlarged our awareness of possible lifestyles and that the nineteenth-century wall of Victorianism had started to crumble.

The Vietnam war, starting in the mid-1960s, helped to propel us into the *second* sexual revolution of this century. That war produced a profound disruption of our customary ways of viewing the world. It was the most unpopular war in our history, and young people felt justified in criticizing our involvement. Anyone over thirty can recall the scores of protests, often followed by violent confrontations with police and national guardsmen. The tragedy at Kent State epitomized the public turmoil in that war:

> On April 30, 1970, President Nixon announced that American and South Vietnamese forces were moving against enemy sanctuaries in Cambodia. Minutes after this announcement, student-organized protest demonstrations were under way. . . . On May 2, the ROTC building at Kent State was set afire. On May 4, Kent State students congregated on

the University Commons and defied an order by the Guard to disperse. Guardsmen proceeded to disperse the crowd. The students then began to taunt Guard units and to throw rocks . . . the three ranking officers on the hill all said no order to fire was given. . . . Twenty-eight guardsmen have acknowledged firing from Blanket Hill . . . the firing . . . lasted approximately 13 seconds. The time of the shooting was approximately 12:25 p.m. Four persons were killed and nine were wounded.[7]

The Vietnam war increased our willingness to criticize our society. Our view of what was right and wrong was changing. Many people reasoned that if our country could be wrong about Vietnam, then it could be wrong about other things like family, religion, and certainly sexuality. This critical stance helped prepare the fertile soil in which the second and much more angry sexual revolution was starting to grow.

The 1920s' sexual revolution set the direction of change, which during the next few decades transformed the public view of sexuality, and helped to clear the path for the sexual revolution of the late 1960s. But as I have noted, there were significant differences in the tone of these two sexual revolutions. One shorthand way to grasp the difference is to listen to the popular music of each time period. For example, the lyrics of Cole Porter's 1928 hit "Let's Do It (Let's Fall in Love)" portray the jocular sexual atmosphere of the 1920s in comments about the birds and the bees and springtime. Contrast that with the Beatles hit of 1968 "Why Don't We Do It in the Road."[8] The Beatles were not talking about birds or bees or springtime. They were directly talking about "doing it." The mood and type of emotion involved in these two revolutions are revealingly written into these contrasting popular tunes of the two eras.

In both the 1920s' and the 1960s' sexual revolutions, there was a move toward greater equality between men and women. In 1920 the Nineteenth Amendment enfranchised women after more than seventy years of political struggle. Women were entering the labor force in growing numbers

and their incomes slowly began to increase their social power. In addition, women were going to college in greater numbers than ever before, and that, too, was destined to increase their influence and change the image of the "gentler sex." Most of us have forgotten that it was during the 1920s that feminists made their first unsuccessful attempt to pass an Equal Rights Amendment granting legal equality to women. By the end of the 1920s the feminist movement declined somewhat in influence. But it was only a pause, not an ending. The rush into the labor force by women, which started in World War II and continued into the 1960s, reignited the drive for greater female power and aided the revival of the feminist movement in this country. The 1960s, like the 1920s, also showed a sharp rise in the percentage of women in our colleges. The expectations men and women held for each other continued to alter in accordance with the new opportunities to meet and to get to know one another on the campuses and in the workplaces in our country.

Gender Equality: The Mother of Change

Each sexual revolution moved us closer to an egalitarian relationship between men and women in all spheres of life. Still we must admit that even in the late 1990s we've got a long way to go before even coming into sight of full equality between the genders. Evidence of this is that women in 1997, in the last few years of the twentieth century, comprise only 11 percent of Congress and at work earn 30 percent less pay than men do; furthermore, there are very few female rabbis or ministers and there are no female priests. Finally, even in nurturing institutions like the family, men still dominate.

But we have made some progress in gender equality. As an example of political changes in gender attitudes, in 1972 only 74 percent of a national sample representative of the country said they would vote for a woman president. But by 1996 that percentage had risen to 93 percent. All these findings document the fact that sizable changes in attitudes have occurred and these trends seem to be continuing at the present time.[9]

When male and female roles change rapidly, there is always a price to pay. Major changes in the divorce rate are almost always an unambiguous sign of rapid social change. In both sexual revolutions, the divorce rate soared skywards. Between 1915 and 1920 our divorce rate increased 50 percent. That is a relatively moderate increase compared to what has happened recently—between 1963 and 1979 our divorce rate more than doubled![10] When there are extensive changes in the way men and women relate in the workplace, the schools, and elsewhere, they can no longer depend on conventional ways of interacting with each other in marriage. Each couple must privately negotiate new ways of getting along. That process is often accompanied by conflict, and more than occasionally it breaks down and ends in divorce.

Divorce rates have been stable or slightly down during the entire decade of the 1980s and in the 1990s have dropped a bit more. Maybe we are getting better at our new marital negotiations and expectations. But new problems have arisen. As sociologist Lenore Weitzman has pointed out in her award-winning book *The Divorce Revolution*, the new "no fault" divorce laws did not take into account the sacrifices made by wives for their husbands' careers.[11] After a divorce, a husband still has his career, but his wife often has a house that she can no longer afford to keep. This situation has pressured women to prepare better for their economic futures just in case a divorce does occur. Seeking economic independence has an impact on many parts of the female role—including the sexual. Economic autonomy reduces dependence on others and makes sexual assertiveness a much less risky procedure.

The family may still be the number one priority for most women, but the ability to earn money is running a close second. Given the poor record of child-support payments, being employable becomes essential. One divorced wife in California described her economic plight to sociologist Lenore Weitzman this way: "There is no way I can make up for twenty-five years out of the labor force.... No one wants to make me president of the company just because I was president of the PTA."[12]

High divorce rates have given many people more years during which they are not married and thus more time to rethink their sexual standards. And thought is the enemy of habitual ways of behaving in sex and everything else. Divorced people are more open in acknowledging their sexual interests and are more aware of what they do and don't like in dating. Sexual standards often change after a divorce. For both men and women it is common after a divorce to have a period of time during which sex takes over center stage.

Sociologist Robert Weiss studied the transition to being single again. He reports what one of his divorced men told him:

> At first I went around screwing everything I could get my hands on. You go through that stage. And then you ask yourself why you did that. And then you realize that sex isn't all you want out of a relationship. And then you can start having normal relationships with people. But it took me a year, a year and a half.[13]

Divorce adds a variety of new family forms—single parents, stepparents, and even parents who marry each other a second time. About half of today's children will at some time in their lives live with only one parent. These experiences change our conception of marriage and the family. People are more likely to think about the possibility of having more than one marriage, for they know that half of those who marry today will divorce.

About 10 percent of our young people will never marry—most of them by choice. Another 10 percent will most likely never have children—some by choice and some due to repeated postponements that exceeded the time on the biological clock. The average age at first marriage has increased from twenty for women and twenty-three for men in the early 1960s to over twenty-four for women and twenty-six for men in

1996—the oldest age at marriage in the twentieth century!

All these changes do not mean that young people don't want to marry, that they don't want to have children, or that they don't value marriage. What the sexual revolutions did was increase the value of other choices and legitimize a wider range of choices relating to marriage. But almost all young people continue to expect to marry someday and have children someday.

Nevertheless, there is more than one script to read from today. Young people can now think about whether they want to marry, have children, remarry, live together, focus on a career, or just put off deciding anything. The age of pluralism is arriving in our gender roles. It makes life more interesting and exciting but also less secure and less predictable. Choices increase the ability to find a rewarding fit between lifestyle and personal values, but they also increase the need for awareness, understanding, and hopefully a bit of luck in making those choices. Sexual practices have also become more pluralistic. One prime example is cohabitation. Young people now feel they have the right to live together without being married if they so choose. In the late 1960s there were about five hundred thousand unmarried couples living together in America. By the mid-1990s that number had reached three and a half million.

Premarital sexual intercourse changed dramatically during the last sexual revolution. During the 1970s the percentage of women having intercourse before they married rose sharply from the 50 percent level that had been reached in the 1920s' sexual revolution. Since the late 1970s the percentage of women having premarital intercourse has surpassed the 80 percent mark and is now approaching 90 percent. For men, over 90 percent had premarital intercourse, only a small rise from the 80 percent figure prevalent in the 1920s.[14] In addition, women were starting to have intercourse at much earlier ages.

Sexual attitudes, too, had changed a great deal. In a national study I conducted in 1963, only 23 percent of Americans ac-cepted premarital intercourse under some conditions, but by 1975 that percentage had risen to over 70 percent and in 1996 it was 76 percent.[15] Choice had become legitimate in the area of premarital sexual intercourse. Sexual attitudes on extramarital sexuality change much more slowly, but here too there seems to have been some change: more people feel that if a married couple is in the process of divorcing or if they have an agreement to accept affairs, then extramarital sexuality may not always be wrong.[16]

During most of this century, the entire Western world has been moving in the same direction toward gender equality and sexual permissiveness. The greatest amount of equality has occurred in Sweden and Denmark and the least in Spain and Ireland. We [fall] somewhere in between in our degree of progress toward overall sexual and gender equality. But we are all together, traveling in the same direction; only the speed of movement varies.

The Leadership Role of the Baby Boomers

The pacesetters of the sexual revolution of the late 1960s were the so-called baby boomers. They are the progeny of the millions of men and women who after World War II produced large families so quickly that startlingly high birth rates resulted. Our families had been getting smaller for over one hundred years, but from 1946 to 1964 American women gave birth to an average of four million babies a year. That amounts to almost twice as many babies for each woman of childbearing age as are born today. This dramatic rise in birth rate is what has come to be known as the baby boom. There are seventy-six million baby boomers, and if you were born between 1946 and 1964, you are one of them.

When the massive baby-boomer cohorts began to reach adolescence in the 1960s, they changed our outlook on youth. Politicians very quickly recognized a large potential constituency and in 1971 passed the Twenty-Sixth Amendment to the Constitution dropping the voting age to eighteen.

These early baby boomers were joined year after year by more fellow baby boomers like wave after wave, crashing against the shore of conventions until they permanently transformed the shape of our lifestyles.

The mothers of these baby boomers were themselves changing in ways that helped prepare their children for their future revolutionary role. During the 1950s and especially the 1960s, the mothers of the baby boomers joined the labor force in unprecedented numbers.[17] There were many reasons for this change—money for their larger families, interests in the world outside the home, the desire to be more economically independent, the desire to have a higher standard of living, and the availability of jobs in our expanding economy—all were motivations for change. Day care centers began to grow all over the country and grandparents filled in when needed. It is remarkable that in 1950 just 12 percent of the mothers of preschoolers were employed, whereas today the figure is about 60 percent. The employment of mothers of preschoolers indicates there has been a significant change in the way people conceive of a woman's role. It shows that motherhood, though still of primary importance, can be modified because of the desire to work outside the home. That alteration decreased the difference between men and women. Men have long been allowed both family and employment as acceptable parts of their gender role.

The Victorian family with its dominant husband and full-time housewife had ironically been dealt a lethal blow at the very time that we were glorifying parenthood in the baby-boom years. It certainly isn't easy for women to combine parenthood and full-time employment, but neither was it easy to meet the demand that every woman be a full-time mother regardless of her ability or interest in doing so and despite whatever career interests she might have. Of course, pluralism would allow a woman to choose for herself to be a full-time housewife or any other lifestyle. There is a price to pay for every societal arrangement, but at least now a woman has more choice in her lifestyle.

The employed mother played a key role in the sexual revolution that began in the late 1960s. For one thing, her employment meant that her child probably had a greater variety of role models. Children were exposed to other adults who gave them choices that parents alone might not. Accordingly, such children were likely to become more autonomous—more desirous of running their own lives. In particular, those children had a more varied model of the role of mothers. That more flexible view of mothers expanded the acceptance by both boys and girls of female autonomy—the freedom of women to choose what they wish to do with their lives. Now, despite Sigmund Freud, autonomy rather than anatomy was becoming destiny for women!

The increased autonomy of baby boomers themselves meant that they did not simply pass on the traditions of their parents but were more likely to be innovative and to scrutinize their traditions carefully. They experimented with new sexual scripts—some wisely and some not so wisely—but they strove for a much higher degree of overall equality between men and women. The baby boomers were the generation for which our second sexual revolution was waiting. They took another giant step away from our Victorian traditions. But they were a charismatic generation that established changes for younger and older Americans and energized our entire society. They redesigned our concepts of sexuality and gender equality in their own image. But, unfortunately they never really finished the job. They left us as "liberated Victorians"—not fully able to enjoy our liberation or to escape our Victorianism. But they set the stage for the third sexual revolution.

The Mythical Place of the Pill in the 1960s Revolution

The media and even many experts have spread the word and convinced many people that changes in gender equality and the autonomy that those changes brought were not the key causes of our sexual revolution.

Here are the words of historian Bradley Smith:

> The event that was to have the greatest effect upon sexuality in the United States and, ultimately, in the world was the release of the birth control pill. . . . Young women who would never before take a chance on sex with their boyfriends for fear of pregnancy . . . adopted new attitudes towards sex. . . . The resulting freedom changed the sex habits of the nation.[18]

Smith is thus arguing that gender equality and autonomy were themselves the consequences of the development of the contraceptive pill. In this view, the pill is seen as the central force that produced the sexual revolution and the related changes in our society. The reasoning is that with the pill available the main reason blocking women from sexual equality was removed. We have also had support for this view from the famous sex therapists Masters, Johnson, and Kolodny:

> The pill made premarital sex considerably safer and permitted millions to think of sex as relational or recreational rather than procreative . . . the availability of the pill provided a sense of freedom for many women and probably contributed more to changing sexual behavior than has generally been imagined.[19]

Lots of people believe this explanation and it sounds persuasive. But let me indicate why it's really not a very accurate picture of what happened.

Those who believe in the revolutionary power of the pill are presuming that before the sexual revolution of the 1960s women were ready and willing to have intercourse if only their worries about pregnancy were alleviated. That makes female sexual motivations much like a car with an engine running but blocked from movement by one obstacle, fear of pregnancy. Just remove that road block and it will surely push forward. But the major block for women was not their fear of pregnancy. Women throughout this century have been subjected to a restrictive sexual upbringing.

Accordingly, they have been programmed by society to start premarital sexuality, if at all, cautiously and only with the justification of serious emotional commitment. The evidence indicates that this upbringing and not the fear of pregnancy is the basic cause of female sexual resistance.

The Kinsey data gathered mostly in the 1940s supports my perspective. In the Kinsey sample the primary reason for women restricting premarital coitus was "moral objections." That was cited as a "definite reason" by 80 percent of his sample, whereas fear of pregnancy was cited as such by only 21 percent of his sample. I should add that 32 percent of the women said that lack of sexual responsiveness was a reason for restricting coitus.[20] This lack of primary emphasis upon pregnancy doesn't mean that it was not a concern and unimportant. But for most women, whether virginal or not, moral objections drilled into them by our society were by far the more important reasons for their reluctance to have sex.

Another way to see the flaws in the "powerful pill" view of our last sexual revolution is to ask, what if the pill did launch the last sexual revolution? If so, then today, thirty years later, we should surely find that most women starting to have premarital coitus would be on the pill. But if that were the case, we wouldn't have the Western world's highest rate of unwanted pregnancy. There is far from universal use even today. The latest data from the National Survey of Family Growth (1995) showed that only 15 percent of the women having first sexual intercourse in the 1990s were on the pill.[21]

Reluctance to have uncommitted premarital intercourse was instilled in women throughout this century by their parents and by our patriarchal traditions. In a formal sense both men and women were supposed to be abstinent before marriage, but in reality the harsher restraints and punishments were imposed upon women. Limiting the sexual experience of women gave husbands more confidence that their wives and girlfriends would be loyal and faithful to them. In effect this was an expression of the power of men over women. Of course, wives in our male-dominant society would not have the power to insist on equivalent behavior from their husbands.

But insisting that women be chaste doesn't stop men from having sex. Men would simply persuade some women to violate their standards and then blame the women for the transgression. That practice is the heart of the ancient double standard. The sexual revolution of the 1960s did somewhat mute the difference in sexual restrictions between men and women, but the difference is still very real even for young women in the 1990s. Unfair? Of course, but social customs are not built on the principle of fairness—they are based far more on who has power. Just ask Blacks, Jews, Hispanics, Catholics, or any other minority group about that.

Women even today feel that they cannot be as free as men for they must avoid the appearance of being too cavalier about sex. We don't live in isolation from our fellow humans. Their opinions of us and especially the wishes of those close to us influence us more than does a new contraceptive advance. A changed attitude of acceptance of sexuality among the key people in one's life makes it far easier to accept sex than does the advent of a new contraceptive technique. The revolutionaries of the 1920s and the 1960s did not have to wait for effective contraceptive methods. If they wanted to use them, they were already here. What they needed in order to be sexually freer was a change in the equality and autonomy our basic social institutions granted to women. Accompanying such egalitarian changes is the acceptance by one's friends and family of the right to have sex. That group support is the vital element needed for any lasting change in sexual behavior.

'Swept Away': The Escape from 'Being Used'

Even today women don't fully accept their right to have sex. Dr. Carol Cassell, a well-known sex educator, has written in depth about the ways in which women in our society have been trained to feel the need to be "swept away" by passionate, romantic feelings in order not to feel "used" and to justify their sexual interests. That need was built into women by our society. I call our society's approach the "dirty glass of water" view of sexuality. Sexuality is perceived as too dirty for women to ingest unless they add a magical elixir that will purify it. The magical potion that can make the sexual water digestible is called passionate romantic love. It is mainly women who are seen as needing this special purification. In accord with my own views, Cassell describes the sexual plight of all too many women even today:

> Despite the sexual revolution, the pill, slogans of sisterhood, and media assurance that "we've come a long way," we are still not sexually free or emotionally satisfied. . . . Swept Away is a sexual strategy, a coping mechanism, which allows women to be sexual in a society that is, at best, still ambivalent about, and at worst, condemnatory of female sexuality. It is a tactic, employed unconsciously by women to get what they want—a man, sexual pleasure—without having to pay the price of being labeled wanton or promiscuous. Swept Away is, consequently, a counterfeit emotion, a fraud, a disguise of our true erotic feelings which we've been socialized to describe as romance.[22]

The persistence of the "swept away" phenomenon tells us that equality in sexuality is very hard to achieve in a society where the power of men and women is still unequal.[23] To be sure, we have moved somewhat toward greater overall gender equality and accordingly there are more women today who feel that they do not need to be swept away in order to justify their sexuality. They may require love or friendship or just physical attraction, but in all these cases they take responsibility for their choices and do not feel the need for the excuse that they were emotionally swept away.

Surely many more women would pursue sexual pleasures if they were treated as equals by men and therefore did not have to be concerned so much about whether their sexual behaviors might alienate some men. However, women would still have their requirements for a good sexual relationship beyond the physical. We all want women and men to act responsibly and honestly with each other. But if we want to achieve that important goal, we will have to equalize the distribution of power between men and women. That involves far more than simply giving women greater rights to have sex. Many women have learned that they can be free sexually but will still not be treated equally by men. Several feminist writers have noted the clash between sexual equality and inequality in social power:

> For women, sexual equality with men has become a concrete possibility, while economic and social parity remains elusive. We believe it is this fact, beyond all others, that has shaped the possibilities and politics of women's sexual liberation.[24]

As long as women have less power they will feel the need somehow to please and attach themselves to these more powerful creatures called men, and sex will serve as a commodity in that pursuit. Inequality can easily lead to distrust, force, and manipulation between men and women. Women will see sex as a service to men as long as they are doing sex "his way and for him." When they have the feeling of power to pursue sex for their own satisfaction and not just for their partner's satisfactions, then the concept of sex as a service and being used will become rarities.

Some readers, no doubt, may still be skeptical and think that sexual differences between men and women are just "natural." Well, come with me on an imaginary journey to a mythical society and I think I'll convince you otherwise. Picture yourself in a society called *Matriarchia* in which women dominate in every major institution—they hold the top political offices; they are the religious leaders; they are the leaders in the economy; they even are expected to lead in their marriages. Men are raised knowing that they have less power than the women with whom they will eventually mate. Women are the initiators in sex

just as they are in every area because they are the most powerful group.

How many men reading this account would like to live in this type of society? The mirror image of that society is the heritage of women in most cultures in the world. It is not the "nature" of women to be less sexually assertive. Rather, it is the nature of human beings with little social power to be generally less assertive.

If we want women and men to have equal rights to sexual expression, then we must work to create equality in the overall society between women and men. Gender equality can bring into being the values that should go with sexuality: honesty, equality, and responsibility.

The Homosexual Revolution: Out of the Closet and into the Streets

Contrary to what many people think, we did not have only a heterosexual revolution in the late 1960s. There was also a very important revolution involving homosexual men and women. There were some moderate gay right movements in the 1950s and 1960s, but they only laid the foundation for what was to come. The significant gay liberation revolt began with the Stonewall riot in New York City in 1969. At that time it was routine to harass the patrons in gay bars, but something different happened that summer night in Greenwich Village. As historian John D'Emilio describes it:

> On Friday, June 27, 1969, shortly before midnight, two detectives from Manhattan's Sixth Precinct set off with a few other officers to raid the Stonewall Inn, a gay bar on Christopher Street in the heart of Greenwich Village.... Patrons of the Stonewall tended to be young and nonwhite. Many were drag queens and many came from the burgeoning ghetto of runaways living across town in the East Village. As the police released them one by one from inside the bar, a crowd accumulated on the street. Jeers and catcalls arose from the onlookers when a paddy wagon departed with the bartender, the Stonewall's bouncer, and three drag queens. A few minutes later, the scene became ex-

plosive. Almost by signal the crowd erupted into cobblestone and bottle heaving. . . . From nowhere came an up-rooted parking meter used as a batter-ing ram on the Stonewall door. I heard several cries of "Let's get some gas," but the blaze of flame which soon appeared in the window of the Stonewall was still a shock. . . . Rioting continued far into the night, with Puerto Rican transves-tites and young street people leading charges against rows of uniformed po-lice officers and then withdrawing to re-group in Village alleys and side streets. By the following night, graffiti calling for "Gay Power" had appeared along Christopher Street. . . . After the second night of disturbances, the anger that had erupted into street fighting was channeled into intense discussion of what many had begun to memorialize as the first gay riot in history. . . . Before the end of July, women and men in New York had formed the Gay Liberation Front. . . . Word of the Stonewall riot and GLF spread rapidly among the net-works of young radicals scattered across the county and within a year lib-eration groups had sprung into exis-tence on college campuses and in cities around the nation.[25]

The gay liberation movement built up the identification of gays with one another. The conflict unified homosexuals, gave them a sense of belonging, and thereby a sense of common identity. Historian John D'Emilio summed it up by noting that: "Gay liberation transformed homosexual-ity from a stigma that one kept carefully hidden into an identity that signified mem-bership in a community organizing for freedom."[26]

In the 1970s thousands of young gay men and lesbian women left their small towns and headed for the cities. Pulitzer Prize–winning author Frances FitzGerald described the changing scene, particularly in San Francisco, in this way:

The gay liberationists called upon ho-mosexuals to make an open avowal of their sexual identity. "Coming out" sym-bolized the shedding of self-hatred, but it was also a political act directed to-ward the society as a whole. . . . "We're

the *first* generation to live openly as ho-mosexuals," Randy Shilts said. "We have no role models. We have to find new ways to live."[27]

Gay organizations and publications grew in many cities, but nowhere did they flourish as in San Francisco. In the 1970s gay men by the tens of thousands migrated to the city by the bay. It is estimated today that about a third of the adult men in San Francisco are gay. When the AIDS epi-demic hit, San Francisco had a politically powerful gay community that fought its way through the conflicts of those early epi-demic years and came out with an orga-nized way of coping. In contrast, cities like New York with larger gay populations but with less open gay identity were much less effective in the early handling of the AIDS crisis.[28]

It is important to note that it was not until the late nineteenth century that the term homosexual was applied as a label for a "type of person." Until then homosexual behavior was simply an act that violated Christian teaching—similar to adultery, masturbation, or fornication. It was not be-lieved that it took a special type of person to do any of those acts. We need to regain that belief because there is no one type of homo-sexual person. A homosexual orientation, important as it may be, is but a part of a per-son's makeup. The same is, of course, true of heterosexuals. One doesn't really learn very much about a person by being told that he or she is a heterosexual. Things like our social class, politics, religion, job, and basic values determine much more about what kind of person we are than whether we are heterosexual or homosexual.

In homosexuality, as in heterosexuality, our society's gender roles are a powerful de-terminant of behavior. Many gay males tend to orient themselves to sexuality just as heterosexual men do—emphasizing physical pleasure—whereas a great many lesbians approach sexuality like heterosex-ual women do—emphasizing emotional in-volvement with each other. But, especially during the last ten years gay males have radically changed their behaviors and les-bian females today do not fit so neatly into any one "feminine" pattern. Therapist Margaret Nichols notes:

> Tastes in erotica became more varied and not limited to "warm" sex and many women began to prefer sex that included activities heretofore considered to be outside the boundaries of "normal" female sexuality: rough sex, "dirty" sex, role-polarized sex, "promiscuity," anonymous sex, sex without love, and sadomasochistic sex. By the mid-1980s, some women were producing pornographic magazines for lesbians such as *On Our Backs* (a takeoff on a well-known feminist newspaper called *Off Our Backs*).[29]

For lesbians the broader societal influence was visible in the fusion for many women of lesbian identity with feminism. Sisterhood was often more important than erotic pleasures, and the bond to women and the freedom from men was primary. Lesbianism, in this sense, developed the "male-free" potential of women. In contrast, the middle-class, college-educated women who founded the National Organization for Women (NOW) in 1966 were mostly heterosexually oriented feminists. Most feminists are not lesbians, but a great many lesbians do identify as feminists.

The lesbian feminist position is well put by Lillian Faderman:

> There is a good deal on which lesbian-feminists disagree. . . . But they all agree that men have waged constant battle against women, committed atrocities or at best injustices against them, reduced them to grown-up children, and . . . a feminist ought not to sleep in the enemy camp.[30]

Lesbian feminists want to see a dramatic change in men's treatment of women before they will be willing to sanction heterosexuality. Many other feminists believe that "sleeping in the enemy camp" is an advantage that can encourage change toward greater gender equality.

It seems that just as straight women sought equality in the heterosexual revolution, the goal of the homosexual revolution was for homosexuality to be recognized as a legitimate option and for homosexuals to be treated as equals rather than as inferiors. In this sense, for both homosexuals and heterosexuals, the last sexual revolution was a movement toward greater social equality with sexuality serving as one of the lead vehicles in that pursuit.

The Deadly Mixture of Victorianism and Liberation

The rapidity of change during the sexual revolutions of this century left many with the illusion of being sexually liberated from the past. After this roller-coaster ride of social upheaval, we might well feel that everything has indeed changed. In reality the sexual revolutions of the 1920s and 1960s, instead of destroying our Victorian heritage, suppressed large segments of it in our collective psyche. The two revolutions were partial revolutions—what one might call "stalled revolutions" waiting to be finished. Without a doubt, there was considerable change, but much remains the same. The excitement of increased sexual liberation has blinded us to the sex-negative Victorian feelings residing within us. By and large, we have retained our dogmatic stance against gender equality, homosexuality, and teenage sexuality, and we continue to harbor remnants of an overall degrading and fearful view of sexuality.[31]

Each new sexual problem that arises, like teen pregnancy or date rape, breathes new life into those Victorian feelings about the degrading, demeaning, and dehumanizing qualities of sexuality. As a result instead of a reasoned response, each new crisis panics millions of Americans into emotionally running away from their newly won sexual freedoms. We have become a nation of fair-weather sexual liberals. At the first sign of a sexual storm we retreat to a more traditional position. Victorianism, though weakened, is far from dead in America. Why else would so many Americans at the end of the 1990s still think that homosexuality is immoral and so many women feel the need to justify their sexuality by being "swept away"?

Changes in sexual behavior and attitudes take time to be fully digested and to become a natural part of our lives. It is one thing to accept a new behavior intellectually and quite another to accept it emotionally. The forty years between our two sexual revolutions were a time for consolidation of our thinking, feeling, and acting in the sexual realm.[32] The dramatic changes of the last sexual revolution left us with a new consolidation problem. The sexual revolution ended in the late 1970s and only moderate changes have occurred in sexual behavior or attitudes during the decade of the 1980s. Both the remnants of our Victorianism and the societal inequalities between men and women have blocked our making further progress toward the goal of pluralism.

The Victorian sexual philosophy in America is part of a traditional approach to life in which male dominance is accepted and the inequality between men and women is considered proper. One basic reason why Victorianism is so difficult to eradicate is that it has the support of those who endorse the traditional philosophy in our country. But, the 1990s offered a major opportunity for promoting a more gender-equal lifestyle and strengthening our new sexual philosophy of pluralism. The widely shared values of HER (honesty, equality, and responsibility) can guide our sexual acts in this pluralistic context.

Many Americans have allegiances to both our traditional *and* our pluralistic sexual philosophies. Because of this internal conflict we have fallen behind most other Western nations in gaining control over our sexual problems. One thing is clear: we need a more pluralistic view of sexuality. We need to broaden, not narrow, our sexual choices and we need to empower, not restrict, ourselves. Our freedom to make wise choices depends on our moving in this direction. Despite our two sexual revolutions, many Americans are still uncomfortable in dealing with their sexuality. We are in a sense "liberated Victorians." In today's world that can be a fatal mixture.

Notes

1. Edward Laumann, John Gagnon, Robert Michael, and Stuart Michaels, *The Social Organization of Sexuality* (Chicago: University of Chicago Press, 1994), p. 98.

2. Clelia Duel Mosher, *The Mosher Survey: Sexual attitudes of 45 Victorian Women* (New York: Arno Press, 1980), p. xviii.

3. See Alfred C. Kinsey, W. Pomeroy, C. Martin, and P. Gebhard, *Sexual Behavior in the Human Female* (Philadelphia: Saunders, 1952), Ch. 8, and Alfred C. Kinsey, W. Pomeroy, and C. Martin, *Sexual Behavior in the Human Male* (Philadelphia: Saunders, 1948), Ch. 8.

4. See Ira L. Reiss, *Premarital Sexual Standards in America* (New York: The Free Press of Macmillan, 1960), and *The Social Context of Premarital Sexual Permissiveness* (New York: Holt, Rinehart and Winston, Inc., 1967).

5. Paula Fass, *The Damned and the Beautiful: American Youth in the 1920's* (New York: Oxford University Press, 1977), p. 260.

6. Ibid., p. 326.

7. William A. Williams, T. McCormick, L. Gardner, and W. LaFeber (eds.), *America in Vietnam: A Documentary History* (New York: Anchor Books, 1985), pp. 288–289.

8. Cole Porter, "Let's Do It (Let's Fall in Love)," copyright 1928 by Harms, Inc. John Lennon and Paul McCartney, "Why Don't We Do It in the Road," by The Beatles, Apple Records, copyright 1968 Northern Songs, BMI.

9. Arland Thornton, "Changing Attitudes Toward Family Issues in the United States," *Journal of Marriage and the Family* 51 (November 1989): 873–93, Table 1; National Opinion Research Center, *General Social Surveys, 1972–1996* (Chicago: NORC, 1996), p. 204.

10. Ira L. Reiss and Gary R. Lee, *Family Systems in America*, 4th ed. (New York: Holt, Rinehart and Winston, Inc., 1988), Chs. 7 and 12.

11. Lenore J. Weitzman, *The Divorce Revolution: The Unexpected Social and Economic Consequences for Women and Children in America* (New York: The Free Press of Macmillan, 1985), especially Ch. 11.

12. Ibid., p. 209.

13. Robert S. Weiss, *Marital Separation: Coping with the End of a Marriage and the Transition to Being Single Again* (New York: Basic Books, 1975), p. 288.

14. The 1995 National Survey of Family Growth reported 89 percent of unmarried women aged twenty-five to twenty-nine had experienced intercourse.

15. National Opinion Research Center, *General Social Survey, 1972–1996*, p. 215.

16. See Ira L. Reiss, "Sexual Behavior," pp. 828–30, in George T. Kurian and Graham T. T. Molitor, eds., *Encyclopedia of the Future*, Vol. 2 (New York: Macmillan Publishers, 1996). On extramarital sexual attitudes and behavior see Edward Laumann, John Gagnon, Robert Michael, and Stuart Michaels, *The Social Organization of Sexuality* (Chicago: University of Chicago Press, 1994), p. 216. See also Philip Blumstein and Pepper Schwartz, *American Couples* (New York: William Morrow, 1983), pp. 289 and 585.

17. Steven D. McLaughlin et al., *The Changing Lives of American Women* (Chapel Hill: The University of North Carolina Press, 1988), Ch. 6.

18. Bradley Smith, *The American Way of Sex: An Informal Illustrated History* (New York: Two Continents Publishing Company, 1978), p. 232.

19. William H. Masters, Virginia E. Johnson, and Robert C. Kolodny, *Masters and Johnson on Sex and Human Loving* (Boston: Little, Brown and Company, 1986), pp. 22–23.

20. The choices add to more than 100 percent because respondents were permitted to check more than one choice. See Kinsey et al., *Sexual Behavior in the Human Female*, p. 344. See Donn Byrne and William A. Fisher, *Adolescents, Sex, and Contraception* (Hillsdale, N.J.: Lawrence, Erlbaun Assoc., 1983), p. 181.

21. National Center for Health Statistics, "Fertility, Family Planning and Women's Health: New Data from the 1995 National Survey of Family Growth," *Vital Health Statistics* 23, No. 19 (May 1997).

22. Carol Cassell, *Swept Away: Why Women Fear Their Own Sexuality* (New York: Simon and Schuster, 1984), pp. 20, 24.

23. In my book, *Journey into Sexuality: An Exploratory Voyage*, I examined the close relationship of power and sexuality not only in Western societies but in 186 non-Western cultures.

24. Barbara Ehrenreich, Elizabeth Hess, and Gloria Jacobs, *Re-making Love: The Feminization of Sex* (Garden City, New York: Anchor Books, 1987), p. 9.

25. John D'Emilio, *Sexual Politics, Sexual Communities: The Making of a Homosexual Minority in the United States, 1940–1970* (Chicago: University of Chicago, 1983), pp. 231–33.

26. Ibid., p. 247.

27. Frances FitzGerald, *Cities on a Hill: A Journey Through Contemporary American Cultures* (New York: Simon and Schuster, 1986), pp. 42, 47. See Jeffrey Weeks, *Invented Moralities: Sexual Values in an Age of Uncertainty* (New York: Columbia University Press, 1995). See also Jeffrey Weeks, *Sexuality and Its Discontents: Meanings, Myths, and Modern Sexualities* (London: Routledge and Kegan Paul, 1985).

28. See Randy Shilts, *And the Band Played On: Politics, People, and the AIDS Epidemic* (New York: St. Martin's Press, 1987).

29. Margaret Nichols, "Sex Therapy with Lesbians, Gay Men, and Bisexuals," in Sandra Leiblum and Raymond Rosen, *Principles and Practice of Sex Therapy*, 2d ed. (New York: The Guilford Press, 1989), p. 276.

30. Lillian Faderman, *Surpassing the Love of Men: Romantic Friendship and Love Between Women from the Renaissance to the Present* (New York: William Morrow, 1981), p. 413. See also Lillian Faderman, *Odd Girls and Twilight Lovers: A History of Lesbian Life in 20th Century America* (New York: Penguin Books, 1991).

31. Albert D. Klassen, Colin J. Williams, and Eugene E. Levitt, *Sex and Morality in the United States: An Empirical Enquiry Under the Auspices of the Kinsey Institute* (Middletown, Conn.: Wesleyan University Press, 1989).

32. John Modell, *Into One's Own: From Youth to Adulthood in the United States 1920–1975* (Berkeley and Los Angeles: University of California Press, 1989).

Chapter 2
Perspectives on Human Sexuality

Anne Bolin
Patricia Whelehan

Today's college students may be surprised to discover the seminal role played by the discipline of anthropology in the study of human sexuality. The biological, psychosocial, psychological, behavioral, clinical, and sociological perspectives are indeed more frequently used to frame today's research on human sexuality. Therefore, these perspectives are more familiar to students than the anthropological approach, with its evolutionary and cultural context.

In tracing the history of the study of human sexuality, Bolin and Whelehan correct this imbalance by recounting the contributions of a number of notables in the field, most of whom were anthropologists. Names like Darwin, Malinowski, Benedict, Mead, and Beach and Ford span the decades of groundbreaking research that contributed significantly to the store of knowledge that exists about human sexuality, especially that within the cultural context. Much of this early twentieth-century work in sexuality was based on ethnographic studies, an anthropological method of participant observation whereby the researchers actually lived among those being observed.

Terminological confusion may be created by the authors' broad definition of sex, which includes all types of sexual activity as well as sentiments, emotions, and perceptions. This possibility is heightened in light of former President Clinton's recently refined definition of "having sex" that excluded oral sex. The fact that two-thirds of Indiana University college students surveyed in 1991 did not classify fellatio or cunnilingus as "having sex" also begs the question of meaning. Does

this new light simply reflect that many persons today are uninformed about the holistic nature of sexuality or are we, in fact, witnessing changing mores? There may, as yet, be no definitive answers to such questions. But understanding the interrelated nature of biology and culture as applied in the field of sexuality will enable students to broaden their worldview, an essential competency for success in the twenty-first century.

Sex as Biology

Confusion about what anthropology is stems from the interdisciplinary nature of the field. An anthropological approach is one that incorporates an understanding of humankind as biological as well as cultural beings. We use the term *bio-cultural* to describe our perspective. While bio-cultural approaches in anthropology may not be appropriate for all the subjects anthropologists might research, for a number of topics such a view lends a fuller and more complete understanding. Bio-cultural perspectives are widespread in fields such as medical anthropology, biological anthropology, and the anthropology of sex and gender, to name just a few of our many specializations.

The term "sex" has many meanings. Sex is part of our biology. It is a behavior that involves a choreography of endocrine functions, muscles, and stages of physical change. It is expressed through the "biological sex" of people classified as male or female (Katchadourian 1979). Despite this physiological component, the act of sex cannot be separated from the cultural context in which it occurs incorporating meanings, symbols, myths, ideals, and values. Sex expresses variation across and within cultures.

An anthropological definition of sex is necessarily a broad one that includes the cultural as well as biological aspects of sex. We shall offer you a definition of sex, but urge you to remember that defining sex is far more complex than our definition suggests. For example, our definition cannot

16

limit sex to only those behaviors resulting in penile-vaginal intercourse, for by doing that we would eliminate a variety of homosexual, bisexual, and heterosexual behaviors that are obviously sexual but not coital. Therefore, we shall define sex as those behaviors, sentiments, emotions, and perceptions related to and resulting in sexual arousal as defined by the society or culture in which it occurs. We qualified our definition by referring to cultural definitions of sexual behaviors since these differ a great deal among ethnic groups and among different cultures. For example, petting as we know it in western society is not universal, that is, it is not necessarily considered a form of arousal among all other peoples of the world. As you read, you will begin to broaden your horizons of understanding yourself, your own society and the multicultural world in which we live.

Anthropological Perspectives on Human Sexuality

The study of human sexuality is a cross-disciplinary one. Six major perspectives dominate the study of human sexuality. Included are: the biological with a focus on physiology; the psychosocial with an emphasis on the developmental aspects of sexuality and the interaction of cognitive and affective states with social variables; the behavioral that stresses behavior over cognitive and emotional states; the clinical with a concern with sexual disorders and dysfunctions; the sociological, with a focus on social structures and the impact of institutions and socioeconomic status factors on sexual behavior; and the anthropological, which includes evolutionary and cultural approaches with emphases on sexual meanings and behaviors within the cultural context. By culture we mean: the skills, attitudes, beliefs, and values underlying behavior. These are learned by observation, imitation, and social learning.

In today's global community it is increasingly important for us to incorporate multicultural perspectives in our knowledge base. Since this approach is at the heart of anthropology, we offer a brief historical

overview of some of the more well-known cultural anthropologists who have shaped the study of human sexuality.

Anthropology as a discipline developed in the nineteenth century. From its inception, anthropologists have been interested in the role of human sexuality in evolution and the organization of culture. Darwin, most well known for the biological theory of evolution, also formulated theories on culture that included ideas on human sexuality. These were presented in *The Descent of Man and Selection in Relation to Sex* (1874, orig. 1871). Darwin argued that morality is what separated humans from animals. In his theory of morality, Darwin regarded the regulation of sexuality as essential to its development. According to Darwin, marriage was the means for controlling sexual jealousy and competition among males. In the course of moral evolution, restrictions of sexuality were first required of married females, then later all females, and finally males restricted their own sexuality to monogamy. Darwin's approach incorporated notions of male sexuality and assertiveness, and female asexuality. These views reflected Darwin's own cultural beliefs about sex and gender (Martin and Voorhies 1975:147–149).

Other nineteenth century anthropologists also produced theories of social evolution that included the regulation of sexuality. John McLennan (1865), John Lubbock (1870) and Louis Henry Morgan (1870) conceived of societies as having evolved through stages. These stages represented increasing restrictions on sexuality as societies progressed from primitive stages of promiscuity to modern civilization characterized by monogamy and patriarchy (Martin and Voorhies 1975:150). These theories were flawed by thinking that esteemed western European culture was superior and viewed social evolution as an unwavering linear trend of "progress."

The twentieth century brought new approaches to the study of human sexuality as anthropology shifted from grand evolutionary schemes with little rigor to empirically oriented studies. This turn led to a new methodology for which anthropology has gained acclaim. Bronislaw Malinowski is the acknowledged parent of this anthropological research method known as ethnography. Ethnography is the research method of participant observation in which the anthropologist becomes entrenched in the lives of the observed. Malinowski is known for his analysis of sex as part of the ethnographic context. His groundbreaking work entitled *The Sexual Life of Savages in North-Western Melanesia: An Ethnographic Account of Courtship, Marriage and Family Life Among the Natives of the Trobriand Islands, British New Guinea* was first published in 1929. While others were writing in the 1920s on the subject of indigenous peoples and their sexuality, unlike Malinowski theirs was not based on firsthand research but rather missionary and travelers' reports or short-term field projects (Weiner 1987:xiii–xiv). Malinowski's two-year-term living with the Melanesian Trobriand Islanders and his scientific and systematic methods of data collection left an important legacy for the field of anthropology and the study of human sexuality.

Malinowski was interested in the relationship of institutions to cultural customs including sexual behaviors. His perspective stressed the importance of the cultural context and emphasized how social rules ordered sexuality among the Trobriand Islanders. What appeared to Europeans as unrestrained sexuality were in actuality highly structured premarital sex rules and taboos based on kinship classification (Weiner 1987:xvii). Malinowski seriously challenged the dominant nineteenth century cultural evolutionism of McLennan, Lubbock, and Morgan. He rejected the notion that early human life was represented by sexual promiscuity. The Trobriand Islanders illustrated that even the most nontechnologically complex peoples regulated their desires through systems of kinship. Rather than promiscuity as a prior condition, Malinowski focused on the ordering of sexual relations in creating the family (Weiner 1987:xiii–xix).

Malinowski was also influenced by another trend impacting anthropology: that of psychoanalysis. He was impressed with the psychoanalytic openness to the study of sex, but was critical of Sigmund Freud's theory of the incest taboo and the Oedipus complex. In a nutshell, Freud's argument is that unconsciously little boys experience a desire to marry/have sex with their mothers and murder their fathers. In *Sex and Repression in Savage Society* (1927), Malinowski " . . . argued that Freud's theory of the universality of the Oedipus complex had to be revised because it was culturally biased. Freud based his theory on the emotional dynamics within the patriarchal western family" (Weiner 1987:xxi). The Trobrianders presented quite a different picture from the western nuclear family because the Trobriand culture is a matrilineal one; that is, people traced descent through their mother's family. This produced different family dynamics so that Malinowski concluded that the Trobrianders were free of the Oedipus complex. Unfortunately his work did not influence the psychoanalytic position to any great degree.

Ruth Benedict and Margaret Mead loom large in the history of anthropology and in their respective contributions to the study of sex. Both were students of Franz Boas, the parent of American anthropology. Benedict's contribution continues to be felt today. Her perspective, in revised form, is embedded in contemporary anthropology in the concepts of ethos (the "approved style of life") and world view (the "assumed structure of reality") (Geertz 1973:126–141). Benedict's *Patterns of Culture* offered an approach in which cultures were regarded as analogous to personalities. She stressed how each culture produced a unique and integrated configuration. This was known as the configurational approach (Benedict 1959:42–45).

That Benedict was light years ahead of her time was demonstrated in her concluding chapter where she reiterated points from her paper "Anthropology and the Abnormal" (1934). She was concerned with individuals whose temperaments were not matched to their cultural configuration and the psychic costs to those such as homosexuals who were "not supported by the institutions of their civilization" (1946:238 in Bock 1988:52). She proposed that "abnormality" was not constant but is rather culturally constituted. She suggested what, at that time, was a radical view: tolerance for non-normative sexual practices such as homosexuality. Implicit in her view was that sexuality was no different than any other social behavior, it was culturally patterned. Benedict challenged prevailing notions of homosexuality as pathology. In 1939, in her "Sex in Primitive Society," she concluded that homosexuality was primarily social in nature, shaped by the meanings of gender and sex roles (Dickermann 1990:7).

For the study of human sexuality, Benedict's major contribution was that sex, which is a part of culture, is patterned, fitting into the larger society, the cultural whole or the gestalt. The configurational approach was certainly not without flaws and anthropology has moved well beyond regarding cultures as personalities. But, Benedict has left an important legacy for anthropology in her emphasis on patterning and cultural holism. For the field of sexology, Benedict was bold and unafraid in her perspective on sexual variation.

Margaret Mead was also an important and powerful figure in anthropology and sexology. Before her death in 1978 she was more widely recognized for her work than any other anthropologist in the world. In numerous books and articles, Mead addressed the subject of sex and gender. While her contributions are many, we shall focus on her first book *Coming of Age in Samoa* (originally 1928) investigated when she was not yet 24 years old.

In *Coming of Age in Samoa*, her commentary addressed female adolescence in Samoa as well as in the United States. She proposed that the turbulence of the American girls' adolescence was not typical of adolescence throughout the world. Mead was responding to a popular biological theory of adolescent stress and storm believed to be caused by the changes in hormones during puberty. Her study of Samoan adolescence provided a very different picture. Unlike American adolescence, for the Samoan

youth, this was not a period of turbulence and high emotion. Based on evidence of a carefree Samoan adolescence, Mead reasoned that the conflict experienced by the American teenagers was due to culture rather than hormones.

In contrast, the Samoan girls' adolescence was conflict free. This was due to Samoan culture, which was relatively homogeneous and casual. So casual that according to Mead the young woman:

> defers marriage through as many years of casual love-making as possible. . . . The adolescent girl's total interest is expended on clandestine sex adventures . . . to live with as many lovers as possible and then to marry into one's village. . . . (Mead 1961:157)

Samoan society was one in which extremes in emotion were culturally discouraged. It was characterized by casualness in a number of spheres including sexuality, parenting, and responsibility. In contrast to western culture, the young Samoan woman's sexuality was experienced without guilt. She concluded that the foundation of this casual approach to sex and painless adolescence could be explained by the following: 1) a lack of deep feeling between relatives and peers, 2) a liberal attitude toward sex and education for life, 3) a lack of conflicting alternatives and 4) a lack of emphasis on individuality. In this work, she established the importance of the study of women when little information was available (Howard 1983:69). She also challenged notions of biological reductionism that even today are all too often used to support status quo politics.

While the approaches of Malinowski, Benedict, and Mead contributed to the creation of the ethnographic study of sexuality with an emphasis on the cultural, Clellan S. Ford and Frank A. Beach's *Patterns of Sexual Behavior* deserves credit for offering the first synthetic study that incorporated biological, cross-cultural, and evolutionary considerations. Their work is distinctive for its inclusion of homosexual and lesbian data. According to Miracle and Suggs (1993:3), Ford and Beach's book is "[t]he single most important and provocative work on sexuality to date. . . . It also provided the intellectual—if not the methodological—foundation for the subsequent work of Masters and Johnson." *Patterns of Sexual Behavior* integrated information from 190 different cultures as well as provided comparative data on different species with an emphasis on the primates (humans, apes, and monkeys). Their work includes an encyclopedic collection of sexual behavior cross-culturally. For example, Ford and Beach offer discussion and information on sexual positions, length (time) of intercourse, locations for intercourse, orgasm experiences, types of foreplay, courting behaviors, frequencies of intercourse, and methods of attracting a partner, among numerous other topics.

Ford and Beach's study relied on ethnographic data that was collected and coded in the HRAF (the Human Relations Area Files), a rigorous classification scheme for information on the world's societies. Categories of information for over 1,000 societies are now coded and available to researchers through HRAF.

The cross-cultural correlational statistical method was subsequently used by Martin and Voorhies in *Female of the Species* (1975). Like Ford and Beach, Martin and Voorhies included evolutionary and biological issues. Their focus was broader in that they were interested in the relationship of human sexuality to gender status/roles, social organization, and type of subsistence (how people make a living). In a sample of 51 foraging societies Martin and Voorhies found that 30 percent of them allowed premarital sexual experimentation (1975:188–189). This pattern was related to matrilineality (where descent is traced through the mother's side of the family) and matrilocality (where the couple resides in the village of the wife's mother). Their studies of horticultural groups also revealed a statistical correlation between matrilineal societies and sexual permissiveness toward premarital sex, while patrilineal (tracing descent through the father's side) societies tended to control female premarital sexual behavior (1975:246–247).

Frayser's *Varieties of Sexual Experience* (1985) is in the tradition spawned by Ford and Beach, incorporating the cross-cultural correlational approach with biological and evolutionary concerns. In regard to evolution, Frayser examines cross-species sexuality, particularly that of our close relatives, the non-human primates. For example, she points out that human sexuality is distinguished by unique sexual and reproductive attributes; these include the ability for sexual arousal that is not limited to estrus ("heat"), and the evolution of the female orgasm. These capabilities are present in our relatives to a limited extent, but emerge full blown in humans and may be linked to extraordinary amounts of non-reproductive sexual behavior among humans in contrast to other animals.

Sex as Culture

The regulation of human sexual expression as to when, where, how, and who may serve diverse socio-cultural goals. George Peter Murdock's pioneering study, *Social Structure* (1949), offers us a classic approach to the different ways that the regulation of sexuality contributes to the organization of cultures. In all societies sexual access among members of a society is regulated. The most obvious example of this is the incest taboo. With an almost universal prevalence, the incest taboo prohibits sexual access between siblings and between siblings and their parents. But, even those societies which have allowed incest have regulations surrounding it that are integrated in the wider social organization and belief system. The exceptions include Hawaiian royalty, kings and queens of ancient Egypt, and Inca emperors. These elites were regarded as so powerful and sacred that only their very close relatives had the equivalent status to qualify as a mate and to perpetuate the lineage. Such sexual unions and marriages were not allowed, however, for the population at large (Murdock 1949:13).

Rules for sexual access also extend beyond the immediate nuclear family. Exogamy is a rule requiring that people marry outside their group, while endogamy specifies marriage within the group (not the immediate family). These rules create kin groups through different kinds of restrictions on sexual access. Rules of exogamy and endogamy are defined by reference to marriage. This illustrates how sexual ideologies are integrated in the social organization of kin groups. One should, however, not make the error that sex and marriage are always equated. This is a mistake often found in the literature on human sexuality, but one seldom made by the people involved in extramarital affairs. "Marriage is a publicly recognized union between two or more people that creates economic rights and obligations within the group . . . and guarantees their offspring rights of inheritance" (Crapo 1987:148). It is regarded as an enduring relationship and includes sexual rights (Ember and Ember 1988:13). Murdock (1949:8) offers clarification:

> Sexual unions without economic co-operation are common, and there are relationships between men and women involving a division of labor without sexual gratification, e.g., between brother and sister, master and maidservant, or employer and secretary, but marriage exists only when the economic and the sexual are united in one relationship, and this combination occurs only in marriage.

Ford and Beach's pioneering *Patterns of Sexual Behavior* (1951) proposed that sexual partnerships consist of two types: mateships, defined in the same way as marriages; and liaisons, ". . . less stable partnerships in which the relationship is more exclusively sexual" (1951:106). Sexologists and anthropologists generally subdivide human liaisons on the basis of their premarital or extramarital character (Ford and Beach 1951:106).

Societies differ as to their tolerance of premarital and extramarital activities and the conditions under which these are acceptable and/or prohibited. According to Broude and Greene's (1976) survey of the cross-cultural record, in 69 percent of the societies studied, men "commonly" participated in extramarital sex while in 57 per-cent of the societies women did so as well. This leads us to another thorny issue for sex researchers, the contrast between ideal and real culture. The ideal culture or normative expectation is that in 54 percent of the societies extramarital sex is allowed only for men, while only 11 percent allow it for women. But the data suggest that many more people actually violate this ideal, particularly in the case of women.

In summary, human sexuality is a central force in the origin of kin groups. In Murdock's words: "All societies have faced the problem of reconciling the need of controlling sex with that of giving it adequate expression" (1949:261). The regulation of sexual relations is the basis for descent and inheritance, critical factors for human societies in the maintenance of social groups. Yet, sex and marriage do not necessarily "go together" like a horse and carriage. Sex is not the central factor in the bonding of two individuals through marriage. To think so is to engage in a bias shaped by recent modern U.S. views of marriage. Sex is indeed critical for kin groups and their perpetuation; and while sex is a right and an obligation in marriage, it is not necessarily the basis upon which marriages are made. Economic cooperation emerges as an important factor in marriage both in evolutionary terms and in the cross-cultural record. This will become more evident in our discussion of "The Patterning of Human Sexuality."

The Patterning of Human Sexuality: The Bio-Cultural Perspective

Human sexuality has a foundation in human biology which provides us with certain inherited potentialities. "The inherited aspects of sex seem to be nearly formless. It is only through culture that sex assumes form and meaning" (Davenport 1976:161).

Our human biological wiring is very different from what we think of as animal instincts. The drive for sex is shaped by culture and is very unlike a mating instinct. When a female animal comes into heat, she automatically (through hormonal mechanisms) becomes sexually responsive and follows her mating instinct. Humans, however, may ignore their drives; for example, Catholic priests and nuns deny their sexuality in order to live in celibacy (Scupin and DeCorse 1992:164). Others delay sexuality until marriage, which may not occur until their twenties or later.

Human biological predispositions are not ". . . rigidly determined. . . . They may orient us in particular directions in pursuing certain goals, but they do not determine our behavior in a mechanical fashion without learned experiences" (Scupin and DeCorse 1992:164). This biological underpinning to our sexuality and other behaviors is part of what is called an open biogram, "an extremely flexible genetic program that is shaped by learning experiences" (Scupin and DeCorse 1992:164). Through socialization humans acquire their culture. This capacity to learn and to adapt to one's environs is a part of our unique bio-cultural evolution as humans. We can say that our biology sustains us as cultural beings by providing us with an unusual capacity to learn.

Sexual behavior is culturally patterned; it is not accidental or random but is integrated within the broader context of culture and is intermeshed in a web of other cultural features as we have seen in our discussion of sex, marriage, and kinship. A number of cultural characteristics are associated with patterns of human sexuality. These may include: the level of technology, population size, religion, economics, political organization, medical practices, kinship structure, degree of acculturation and culture change, gender roles, power and privilege (stratification).

Cultures are integrated systems that exist within particular environmental and historical contexts. We have discussed the biological basis of human sexuality; we offer now an overview of the cultural basis of human sexuality. To comprehend how sexuality is embedded in culture necessitates an understanding of the culture concept. We can think of culture in terms of architecture. The basement represents our biology as humans, including our evolution and physiology. The floor is the foundation for understanding that cultural variation lies in how people have adapted to their environments. This includes how people make a living, their technologies, and economics. There are a number of ways people have found to survive in the world. Anthropologists have classified societies in terms of: foraging, horticulture, agriculture, pastoralism (herding), industrial, and post-industrial adaptations.

Adaptation to the environment impacts the social system, including social organization and social structures, which may be likened to the frame of a house. The social system is the means that people adapt to one another. It includes social organization and its elements including kinship and marriage, various institutions and structures such as religion and political organization. The social system is influenced by how people make a living through demographics, the relations of work such as age, gender, and kinship: who controls the means of production and the power relations of society. Societies have been classified in terms of their social systems as bands, tribes, chiefdoms, pre-industrial states, and industrial states.

The roof of our building may be conceptualized as the ideological value system. This is the system of meanings and beliefs in a culture. It includes expressive elements of culture like art, music, rituals, myths, folklore, cosmology. It is the meanings and beliefs behind and sustaining the patterning of cultures such as marriage norms, gender roles, courtship, etc. The foundation, the frame, and the roof are all interrelated parts of the cultural whole.

Human sexuality is part of that cultural whole. We may first encounter it in the basement in terms of our evolution and our unique human physiology. To grasp human sexuality as part of a cultural matrix we may locate it in any of our architectural levels. For example, in investigating beliefs about human sexuality, we might begin with our roof (ideology and the value system). We may observe that a particular culture has very few restrictions on premarital sex. This culture may regard premarital sex among adolescents as an amusement (Schlegel and Barry 1991:21), as part of an experiential kind of sex education, or perhaps as a way to find a marriage partner. In short, there are numerous meanings and beliefs around premarital permissiveness among cultures which allow and encourage its practice.

We offer this architectural approach to culture and sex to illustrate that culture is a complex whole in which the parts are interrelated. One can begin anywhere in our biocultural architecture and explore human sexuality. Some researchers prefer limiting their research to one area; for example, Masters and Johnson's investigations of human sexual response have focused on the biological. Others, such as the anthropologists cited, may be more interested in the relationship between beliefs and premarital sex practices and how these are related to social organization. Even others may want a bigger picture and explore how premarital sex norms are related to the types of subsistence adaptation. These are the kinds of opportunities for understanding human sexuality offered by a bio-cultural perspective. This approach will allow a greater awareness of selves as sexual beings, a greater understanding of selves as cultural creatures, and an appreciation of our evolutionary past and biological heritage.

References

Benedict, R. 1959. *Patterns of Culture*. New York, NY: The New American Library.

——. 1934. "Anthopology and the Abnormal." *Journal of General Psychology* 10:59–82.

Bock, P. K. 1988. *Rethinking Psychological Anthropology*. New York, NY: W. H. Freeman and Company.

Broude, G. J. and Greene, S. J. 1976. "Cross-Cultural Codes on Twenty Sexual Attitudes and Practices." *Ethnology* 15:409–429.

Crapo, R. H. 1987. *Cultural Anthropology*. Sluice Dock, Guilford, CT: Dushkin Publishers.

Darwin, C. 1874. (Original 1871). *The Descent of Man and Selection in Relation to Sex*. New York, NY: Thomas Y. Crowell.

Davenport, W. H. 1976. "Sex in Cross-Cultural Perspective." *Human Sexuality in Four Perspectives*. Baltimore, MD: The Johns Hopkins University Press: 115–163.

Dickermann, M. 1990. "A Sister Reclaimed. A Review of Ruth Benedict: *Stranger in This Land*." In *Solga Newsletter* 12(2): 5–9.

Ember, C. and Ember, M. 1996. *Anthropology*. 8th edition. Englewood Cliffs, NJ: Prentice Hall.

——. 1988. *Anthropology*. 5th edition. Englewood Cliffs, NJ: Prentice Hall.

Ford, C. and Beach, F. 1951. *Patterns of Sexual Behavior*. New York, NY: Harper Torchbooks.

Frayser, S. 1989. "Sexual and Reproductive Relations: Cross-Cultural Evidence and Biosocial Implications." *Medical Anthropology* 11(4), 385–407.

——. 1985. *Varieties of Sexual Experience: An Anthropological Perspective on Human Sexuality*. New Haven, CT: HRAF.

Geertz, C. 1984, 1973. *The Interpretation of Cultures*. New York, NY: Basic Books.

Howard, J. 1993. "Angry storm over the south seas of Margaret Mead." *Smithsonian*, 14(1):67–74.

Katchadourian, H. A. (ed.). 1979. *Human sexuality: A comparative and developmental perspective*. Berkeley: University of California Press.

Katchadourian, H. A. and Lunde, D. T. 1975. *Fundamentals of Human Sexuality*. New York, NY: Holt, Rinehart, and Winston.

Lubbock, J. 1873. (Original 1870). *The Origin of Civilization and the Primitive Conditions of Man: Mental and Social Condition of Savages*. New York, NY: D. Appleton.

Malinowski, B. 1961. (Original 1927). *Sex and Repression in Savage Society*. Cleveland, OH: World.

——. 1929. *The Sexual Life of Savages in North-Western Melanesia: An Ethnographic Account of Courtship, Marriage and Family Life Among the Natives of the Trobriand Islands, British New Guinea*. London: George Routledge.

Martin, M. K. and Voorhies, B. 1975. *Female of the Species*. Irvington, NY: Columbia University Press.

McLennan, J. 1865. *Primitive Marriage*. Edinburgh: Adam and Charles Black.

Mead, M. 1961. (Original 1928). *Coming of Age in Samoa*. New York, NY: Morrow Quill Paperbacks.

Miracle, A. W. and Suggs, D. N. 1993. "On the Anthropology of Human Sexuality." In *Culture and Human Sexuality: A Reader*. Pacific Grove, CA: Brooks/Cole Publishing Co: 2–6.

Morgan, L. H. 1870. *Systems of Consanguinity and Affinity of the Human Family*. Washington, DC: Smithsonian Institution.

Murdock, G. P. 1949. *Social Structure*. New York, NY: The Free Press.

Schlegel, A. and Barry, H. 1991. *Adolescence: An anthropological inquiry*. New York, New York: The Free Press.

Scupin, R. and DeCorse, C. R. 1992. *Anthropology: A Global Perspective*. Englewood Cliffs, NJ: Prentice Hall.

Weiner, A. B. 1987. "Introduction." In *The Sexual Life of Savages*. Bronislaw Malinowski. Boston, MA: Beacon Press: xiii–xix.

Chapter 3
Alfred Kinsey

Vern L. Bullough

". . .The most influential American sex researcher of the twentieth century." Readers do
not have to be experts in the area of sex research to recognize that this quote refers to
Alfred Kinsey. A biologist turned sexologist,
Kinsey is portrayed in the literature as both a
colorful character and a consummate researcher. Kinsey's advocates and adversaries
alike agree that his controversial life's work
sparked a revolution in sexuality research.

Born on the cusp of the last century in
1894, Kinsey entered the field of sexuality research at a time when two circumstances occurred simultaneously: a growing awareness
of the importance of sexuality and an increasing volume of studies about human sexuality. His study of human males, published in
1948, and his study of females, published in
1952, were hailed as benchmarks for changes
in American society. Perhaps best known for
his distinctive interviewing techniques,
Kinsey's most valuable contribution is said to
be his success in treating the study of sexuality as a scientific discipline.

The directionality of Kinsey's influence
can be questioned, depending upon one's
point of view. Was the greatest significance of
Kinsey's work that it was a marker of changes
at that time as claimed by one historian? Or,
as suggested by others, was his work seminal
because it was instrumental in bringing
about the changes? David Mace, who defined
the 1960s sexual revolution as a grassroots
uprising against organized religion's teachings about sexuality, identified Kinsey along
with Freud and Ellis as highly influential
forces in the sexual revolution because of
their contributions to the knowledge about
human sexuality.

Regardless of the position that one takes
concerning the influence of Kinsey's work,
facts cannot be ignored. The radical changes
in public attitudes that followed his first published report on males in 1948 were precursors of a new discipline of sexology, a new
profession of sex therapy, and new materials
and methodology for sexuality education.

Kinsey has been criticized by many professionals in the field, including a recent director of the Kinsey Institute. Critics point to
problems such as the following:

- His difficulties with sampling and survey research, illustrated by the fact that
  he confused, in some cases, the concepts of random sampling and representativeness.

- His infamous seventeen-hour interview
  with a pedophile, that admittedly was
  the basis for much of his data about the
  onset of childhood sexual activity.

- His use of data collected from an Indiana State Prison for the bulk of his male
  study.

Even detractors, however, recognize many
contributions made by Kinsey to sexuality research:

- His 7-point scale that placed persons
  along a continuum of sexual activity
  from exclusively heterosexual to exclusively homosexual that is still in use today.

- His objectifying the existence of homosexuality and his conclusion that one or
  a few homosexual experiences do not
  classify a person as homosexual.

- His reported data on the percentage of
  the population that is exclusively homosexual is amazingly consistent with
  national probability samples today.

- His data reporting multiple orgasms
  among women were among the first
  and are still cited today.

- His landmark federal court case decided
  after his death resulted in scientists and
  scholars being treated as a "community"; therefore, they can possess obscene materials for scientific purposes.
  Today, the Kinsey Institute at Indiana
  University has the largest collection of
  pornography in the world.

It was in a setting of a growing awareness of the importance of sexuality and an ever-increasing volume of studies on human sexuality that Alfred Kinsey began to do his research. Kinsey was born in 1894 in Hoboken, New Jersey; he was at the height of his career in 1938 when he shifted from the study of gall wasps to the study of human sexuality. He probably also was going through what might be called a midlife crisis, hunting for new fields to conquer. In the summer of that year, Indiana University began to teach a course in marriage, one of the many colleges and universities to venture into this new area. Because no professor on the faculty was considered qualified to teach it singlehandedly, teachers (all men) were gathered together from the departments of law, economics, sociology, philosophy, medicine, and biology to do so. Kinsey ended up as coordinator of the course.

To add to his own knowledge, he soon began taking histories of the students, many of whom came to him for counseling. He sought information on age at first premarital intercourse, the frequency of sexual activity, the number of partners, and similar data. Gradually, he amplified his search for information by including questions about prostitutes, the age of the partner with whom the subject had his or her first intercourse, the percentage of partners who were married, and so forth. Kinsey, a compulsive data gatherer, began an extensive reading program into all aspects of sexual behavior. This led him to build up a personal library, since serious studies on sex were difficult to find in most public or university libraries. To extend his collection of data beyond the classroom, Kinsey took a field trip to Chicago in June 1939 to conduct interviews. About this time, he also began working with inmates at the Indiana State Penal Farm and their families, compiling their sexual histories. All of this he did in consultation with the university officials, who had ruled that the histories were to be kept completely confidential. His students apparently trusted him, and many of them who had taken the class continued to write Kinsey about their sexual problems long after they had graduated.

Kinsey's expanding research into human sexuality was not without controversy, and one of his most persistent critics was Thurman Rice, a bacteriology professor at the university who had written extensively on sex, primarily from the point of view of eugenics. Rice had long given the sex lecture that was part of a required course in hygiene at the university and for which males were separated from females. Rice was typical of an earlier generation of sex experts, in that he considered moral education a part of sex education. He believed masturbation was harmful, condemned premarital intercourse, and was fearful that Kinsey's course on marriage was a perversion of academic standards. He charged Kinsey with, among other things, asking some of the women students about the length of their clitorises, and then demanded the names of students in the class so he could verify such classroom voyeurism. Rice totally opposed Kinsey's questioning in general, because he believed that sexual behavior could not be analyzed by scientific methods as it was a moral subject, not a scientific one. Some parents also objected to the specific sexual data given in the course, and university president Herman Wells, a personal friend of Kinsey, offered him the alternative of either continuing to teach the course or to conduct his sex research.[1] In any case, Kinsey would continue to teach in the biology department. He elected to do the research and dropped his participation in the marriage course.

Kinsey was not only interested but well prepared. As a bench scientist, he felt the researcher had to be directly involved in the project. He was somewhat disdainful of the work of most of his predecessors in sex research. He was appalled at how Freud and the early analysts, still under the influence of Krafft-Ebing, had looked on masturbation as a sickness. He was also concerned that Freud relied on subjective impressions and did not test them. Similarly, he disagreed with Stekel and, ultimately, with the whole psychoanalytic approach. He had no use for Krafft-Ebing's unscientific cataloging of sexual behavior. Kinsey believed that American psychologists and American followers of Freud were not objective scientists and were too highly influenced by traditional moral codes. Though he had good words to say about Ellis, his esteem dwindled when he learned that the British researcher was so timid about his work that he could not talk to his subjects face to face and depended entirely on letters written to him. Kinsey was also offended by Hirschfeld's open proclamation of his own homosexuality, which led him to regard Hirschfeld as a special pleader and not an objective scientist. Similarly, he was disdainful of Malinowski because in his mind Malinowski was not only afraid of sex but had been taken in by the islanders. He and Mead disagreed publicly, because Mead accused him of talking only about sex per se and not about such things as maternal behavior. Kinsey thought they were different things and said he wanted to study sex, not love. Obviously, Kinsey was a strong-minded individual—some might call him arrogant; he was critical of most of his predecessors, although he was always careful to cite them in his work if they had broken new ground. Moreover, in spite of his criticism, he recognized that some, particularly Freud and Ellis, had made important contributions for their time. They just fell short of what Kinsey felt was necessary, namely the study of human sexual activity in as detached and scientific a way as possible. He had the commitment and the temperament to do so, since he thought he had to be rigorously neutral and nonjudgmental and let his data speak for him.[2]

In short, after years of skirting around the subject of human sexuality, the CRPS (Committee for Research in the Problems of Sex) jumped in with full support for Kinsey. The result was a revolution in sex research. Aiding this revolution was what for a time was believed to be the elimination of the threat of venereal diseases, or as the Centers for Disease Control began to call them, sexually transmitted diseases.[3]

The first big step in this direction was the discovery of sulfa drugs in 1935, and this was followed by the development of a commercial process for making penicillin during World War II. Sulfa proved effective against gonorrhea, while penicillin was effective against both gonorrhea and syphilis. Other new antibiotics soon appeared in the postwar period, and for a time at least, the fear of sexually transmitted diseases was no longer an issue and, more important, no longer an inhibitor, in sexual relations. In sum, Americans, who had been among the most sexually inhibited, proved to be a receptive audience for the new findings about human sexuality.

The two decades following the appearance of the first Kinsey report in 1948 saw a radical change in public attitudes about sexuality spurred both by the development of the oral contraceptive and by new studies in human sexuality, including additional ones by Kinsey and his team and by William Masters and Virginia Johnson. The results of these studies included the establishment of a new discipline, sexology; the emergence of a new helping profession, sex therapist; and a reorientation of the way sex was taught. Individually and collectively, there was also a changing attitude, more positive if you will, toward sexuality.

Kinsey's Research

Kinsey is a good marker of these changes because, unlike almost all previous American sex researchers, Kinsey emphasized the sex part of sex research and held that sex was as legitimate a subject to study as any other. He recognized the many facets of sexual behavior from biology to history and gathered together one of the great resource libraries of the world devoted entirely to sex. He openly challenged the traditional medical dominance of sexual topics and, in the process, opened up the field to many other disciplines. Though some of his statistics can be challenged, it was the combination of all his contributions that make him the most influential American sex researcher of the twentieth century.

His two major works, the male study in 1948 and the female study in 1952, serve as effective indicators of the change taking place in American society.[4] Though Kinsey is known for his diligent interviewing and summation of data, his work is most significant because of his attempt to treat the study of sex as a scientific discipline, compiling and examining the data and drawing conclusions from them without moralizing.

The Kinsey Interview

The key to Kinsey's studies was the interview, since Kinsey was convinced that it was only through this means that accurate data could be compiled. His interview technique included a number of checks for consistency, and if inconsistencies appeared, either from attempts to deceive or from faulty memory, the interviewer probed deeper until the apparent disagreement could be explained or eliminated. Kinsey strongly believed he could detect fraudulent answers, and certainly his ingenious coding system was designed to detect the most obvious ones.

Exaggeration proved almost impossible in the system in which questions were asked rapidly and in detail, because few subjects could give consistent answers. Though he recognized that some subjects might not remember accurately, he felt errors resulting from false memories would be offset by errors other subjects made in an opposite direction. A deliberate cover-up was a more serious problem, but he felt his numerous cross-checks made it difficult. If histories were taken of a husband and wife, the two were cross-checked to see how they conformed; some retakes were conducted after a minimum interval of two years and an average interval of four years to see if people would give the same basic answers.

Kinsey was also concerned with potential bias by the interviewer, and he sought to overcome this by limiting the number of interviewers to four: himself, Wardell Pomeroy, Clyde Martin, and eventually Paul Gebhard. These men engaged in discussion sessions after a series of interviews to see if they agreed on the coding of certain kinds of responses. Collaboratively, the four interviewed some eighteen thousand individuals: eight thousand each by Kinsey and Pomeroy and two thousand by Martin and Gebhard.[5] Kinsey actually hoped to get one hundred thousand sexual histories, but his death ended this long-term plan.

The interview covered a basic minimum of about 350 items, and these items remained almost unchanged throughout all the interviews. A maximum history covered 521 items, and whenever there was any indication of sexual activity beyond what the basic questions covered, the interviewer could go as far as he thought necessary to get the material. All the questions had been memorized by the interviewers, and there was no referral to any question sheet. Questions were asked directly and without apology, and the interviewer waited for a response from the subject. Initial questions were simply informational ones about the informant's age, birthplace, educational experience, marital status, and children. These were followed by questions on religion, personal health, hobbies, special interests, and so on. It was not until 20 minutes into the interview that sex questions appeared, and these started with sex education, proceeded to ages when a person first became aware of where babies came from, and then on to menstruation and growth of pubic hair and various anatomical changes. From here, the questions went on to early sex experiences, including age at first masturbation. Techniques of masturbation were investigated for both men and women. There were questions on erotic fantasies during masturbation and about erotic responses, and next was a series of questions about actual sex practices. The answers to the basic 350 questions could be coded on one page; Pomeroy estimated that the code sheet provided information equivalent to twenty-five typewritten pages.[6]

Before any specific questions about homosexuality were asked, twelve preliminary inquiries were scattered throughout the early questions, the answers to which would give the interviewer hints about the subject's sexual preference in partners. If the interviewer thought the subject was not being honest, he told the person so and generally refused to finish the interview. In some cases, the interview continued, but at the end the interviewer then told the subject that he wanted to go through some questions again, so that the subject could answer accurately questions that he or she had not been honest about the first time. In general, the interview ran from 1.5 hours to 2 hours. Children were also interviewed, but a different approach was used and at least one parent was always present.

Some individuals were interviewed for much longer periods of time. For example, those individuals who had extensive homosexual experiences were asked more questions than those who did not; subjects who had engaged in prostitution were also asked more questions. The longest interview was of a pedophile. It took some 17 hours and involved both Pomeroy and Kinsey. This man was sought out because he was known to have kept accurate written records of his sexual activity, a not uncommon occurrence among pedophiles. The man had sexual relations with six hundred preadolescent males and two hundred preadolescent females, as well as intercourse with countless adults of both sexes and with animals of many species. He had developed elaborate techniques of masturbation and reported that his grandmother had introduced him to heterosexual intercourse and that his first homosexual experience was with his father.

His notes on his sexual relations with preadolescents furnished much of the information on childhood activity that Kinsey reported, since it included the length of time it took the child to be aroused, the child's response, and other such data. Kinsey's use of these data has been much criticized,[7] in part because Kinsey did not report his subject to the authorities. During the interview, the man was boastful about his ability to masturbate to ejaculation in 10 seconds from a flaccid start, and when Kinsey and Pomeroy openly expressed their disbelief at such a statement, the man effectively demonstrated his ability to them then and there. Pomeroy added that this was the only sexual demonstration that took place dur-

ing the eighteen thousand interview sessions.[8] There were, however, laboratory observations from which data were derived, but these were separate from the interview and did not necessarily include the same individuals.

Kinsey and Statistics

One of the major criticisms of Kinsey was the way in which he drew his sample. Two difficulties were at the heart of the criticism: (1) it was not random, and (2) it depended on volunteers. His critics urged him to undertake at least a small interviewing project on randomly selected individuals to test the validity of his findings,[9] but he refused. His reason for the refusal is that he believed some of those chosen randomly would not consent to answering the questions, and thus he argued it would no longer be a random sample. Though sampling techniques when Kinsey began in the 1930s were not as advanced as they later became, the issue of Kinsey's sampling concerned the Committee for Research in the Problems of Sex very early in their support. They had concluded, however, that the cluster method he advocated was as good as could be expected.[10] After the first Kinsey volume was published, Kinsey took greater care to explain his sampling method in his second book, and also eliminated some of the more controversial data gathered from interviews with prisoners.[11]

Kinsey's sample is clearly overrepresented in some areas; for example, there are too many midwesterners, particularly from Indiana, and in the male study there is a disproportionate number of prison inmates and perhaps also of homosexuals.[12] Critics also charged that those who volunteered for the project were among the less inhibited members of society, and this gave an erroneous picture of the American public. There probably is some truth in this charge, but Kinsey tried to guard against it through what he called 100 percent sampling. When he turned to organized groups to obtain subjects, all members had to agree to be interviewed about their sexual histories, whether the group was a college fraternity, a woman's club, or the residents of a particular building. About a quarter of his sample was picked this way, and since he found few significant differences between the reports of those who belonged to groups and those he contacted in other ways, he felt he was able to establish the representativeness of his sample. Though this was an ingenious resolution to the problem, his sample was, by any definition, not a cross-sample of the total population.[13]

One of the problems with any statistical summary of sex life is what is reported and how it is reported. Kinsey, for example, put sexual activity on a 7-point continuum that ranged from 0 to 6; exclusively heterosexual behavior was on one end (0) and exclusively homosexual or lesbian behavior was on the other (6). The effect of this was to emphasize the variety of sexual activity and to demonstrate that homosexuality and lesbianism were more or less a natural aspect of human behavior. This was a partial solution to an impossible question: What is homosexuality, or for that matter what is heterosexuality? Kinsey avoided these questions by defining sex in terms of outlet, any activity that resulted in orgasm. This was something that could be measured with his 7-point bipolar scale.

At the time Kinsey began his research, 5-, 6-, and 7-point scales seem to have been the most popular, and he probably adopted such a scale for this reason. Although the Kinsey scale can be improved on and although it does not measure all the things that many researchers would now want to measure, it did two things of great importance. It offered comfort to both homosexuals and heterosexuals. Kinsey, in effect, demonstrated that homosexual activity was widespread in the American population: 37 percent of his American male sample had at least one homosexual experience to orgasm sometime between adolescence and old age.[14] This statistic gave assurance to many worried heterosexuals who had experimented briefly with same-sex activities that they were not homosexuals and could relax in their normality.

Homosexuals, on the other hand, found that they were more numerous than the general public (and perhaps they themselves) realized and that many heterosexuals had experimented with homosexuality. It also led many writers on homosexuality to claim a higher percentage of homosexuals in society than probably existed. Reports of the proportion of gays in the population ranged from one person in twenty to one person in ten to even higher ratios, depending on which Kinsey statistic was used.[15] However, only 4 percent of Kinsey's subjects could be labeled as exclusively homosexual; this percentage is close to what has been found in more recent studies. Kinsey noted that the proportion of women engaging in same-sex activity was less than half that of the men.

Kinsey's Definitions and Homosexuality

Kinsey's insistence on a behavioral definition of homosexuality has led to speculation about his own potential homosexuality,[16] a question that seems to arise about almost every investigator of homosexuality. There is no evidence for this, but Kinsey did not condemn homosexuality, which might have been the basis for the charge. He also rejected the popular stereotype of the homosexual as effeminate, temperamental, and artistic; instead, he held there were wide variations among homosexuals. To gauge this he turned to measuring sexual activity. He did, however, believe that homosexual relations were characterized by promiscuity and instability, a statement somewhat contrary to his own data, as homosexual contacts accounted for only 6 to 7 percent of all male orgasms.[17]

Undoubtedly, Kinsey's findings and the publicity about homosexuality were valuable in assuring many a parent and many a client that one experience does not a homosexual make. On the other hand, his conclusion that a significant percentage of his sample was exclusively homosexual or almost exclusively homosexual allowed American society to come to terms with the facts of life and to recognize the widespread existence of this phenomenon. These are extremely important contributions, and the modern gay movement would probably not have come into being without them, at least it the time it did. Kinsey, in effect, accepted the bisexual potential of humans as a reality and this in itself was a major challenge to existing concepts in the psychoanalytic community, which tended to argue that bisexuals were really homosexuals trying to adjust to societal norms.[18] Kinsey's emphasis on outlet and his bipolar scale not only challenged traditional attitudes about sex but undermined them.

Other Findings

Kinsey was also important in emphasizing that there are class distinctions in sexual practices, that highly educated individuals have a different history of sexual activity than do the less educated, and the affluent have patterns that are different from the poor. This finding basically challenged the validity of most of the studies that had gone before his, which for the most part were based on college-educated or upper-middle-class samples. He also found that the younger generation in his male study was less likely to visit prostitutes than the older, suggesting not only that there was a generational change, but that age cohorts also must be taken into account. Kinsey was not the first to recognize generational change; it had been much commented on by others, including Terman, even though the phenomenon had not been measured effectively by his predecessors.

Kinsey challenged all sorts of myths about sexuality. One such challenge had to do with female frigidity, or what is now called anorgasmia. A total of 49 percent of the females he studied had experienced orgasm within the first month of marriage, 67 percent by the first six months, and 75 percent by the end of the first year. More remarkable was the fact that nearly 25 percent of the women in the sample recalled experiencing orgasm by the age of fifteen, and more than 50 percent by the age of

twenty and 64 percent before marriage. The orgasms occurred through masturbation (40 percent), through heterosexual petting without penetration (24 percent), and through premarital coitus (10 percent). For 3 percent it was through a homosexual experience.[19]

Women varied enormously in the frequency of their orgasmic responses, with some reporting only one or two orgasms during their entire lives, while some 40 to 50 percent responded being orgasmic almost every time they had coitus. Still, 10 percent of his sample who had been married at least fifteen years had never had an orgasm. He also reported cases in which women failed to reach orgasm until after twenty years of marital intercourse. He also documented (as had others) the female ability to achieve multiple orgasm. Some 14 percent of the females in his sample responded that they had multiple orgasms. Several managed to have a dozen or more orgasms while their husbands ejaculated only once.[20] He concluded from his data that the human female, like the human male, is an "orgasm experiencing animal."[21]

Sometimes Kinsey seemed deliberately to flaunt the differences between widely held beliefs about traditional conduct and reality. He showed that fewer than half of the orgasms achieved by American males were derived from intercourse with their wives, which meant, he said, that more than half were derived from sources that were "socially disapproved and in large part illegal and punishable under the criminal codes."[22] He seemed to imply that premarital abstinence was unnatural and argued that nearly all cultures other than those in the Judeo-Christian tradition made allowance for sexual intercourse before marriage.[23] Similarly, he found that nearly 50 percent of the women in his sample had coitus before they were married, although in a "considerable portion" it had been confined to their fiancé and had taken place within one or two years preceding marriage.[24] He also argued that his data did not justify the general opinion then existing that premarital coitus was of necessity "more hurried and consequently less satisfactory than coitus usually is in marriage."[25] Kinsey, in effect, ended up defending premarital intercourse just as he had masturbation and petting, arguing that premarital experience contributed to sexual success in marriage.[26]

The two reports hit different emotional responses in the American public. For the male study it was the incidence of homosexuality that received much of the headlines, while for the female study it was the generalized premarital and even extramarital activity of the women. Some 26 percent of the women had engaged in extramarital coitus,[27] and about 50 percent of the married male population had.[28] Still, it was the case of the women "adulteress" that roused public opinion.

Kinsey reported that 50 percent of the males who remained single until age thirty-five had overt homosexual experiences, and some 13 percent of his sample had more homosexual than heterosexual experiences between the ages of sixteen and fifty-five, and Kinsey noted that between 4 and 5 percent of the male population were exclusively homosexual.[29] This figure corresponds to some of Hirschfeld's figures and, as indicated, tends to be supported by more recent data. Women in his sample reported considerably fewer homosexual contacts than the men. Some 28 percent had reported homosexual arousal by age forty-five, but only 13 percent had actually reached orgasm.[30] The homosexual pattern, however, differed between men and women by social class. Among men it was the lower socioeconomic class that had more homosexual experiences, whereas among women, it was the upper class, better-educated group that had more homosexual activity.[31] He did not really explain this difference, which might well have been due to the ability of the upper-class women to have more choices in their partners and the economic capability to be independent of a man.

Kinsey openly and willingly challenged many basic societal beliefs. Though there is considerable evidence of Kinsey's commitment to marriage, and he demanded that his interviewers be happily married,[32] his data seemed to many to undermine the belief in marriage and traditional family. Kinsey had questioned the assumption that extramarital intercourse always undermined the stability of marriage and held that the full story was more complex than the most highly publicized cases led one to assume. He seemed to feel that the most appropriate extramarital affair, from the standpoint of preserving a marriage, was an alliance in which neither party became overly involved emotionally. He was, however, more cautious in the female book and conceded that extramarital affairs probably contributed to divorces in more ways and to "a greater extent than the subjects themselves realized."[33] Inevitably, his ideas came under attack, because he seemed to be assaulting traditional religious teachings.[34]

Interestingly, Kinsey ignored what might be called sexual adventure, paying almost no attention to swinging, group sex, and alternate lifestyles as well as such phenomena as sadism, masochism, transvestism, voyeurism, and exhibitionism. He justified this neglect by arguing that such practices were statistically insignificant. But the real answer is probably that Kinsey was not interested in them. He was also not particularly interested in pregnancy[35] or sexually transmitted diseases. What he did, however, was to demystify discussions of sex as much as it was possible to do so. Sex, to him, became just another aspect of human behavior, albeit an important part. He made Americans and the world at large aware of just how big a part human sexuality played in the life cycle of the individual and how widespread many kinds of heterosexual and homosexual activity were.

Criticism

Though the general public accepted the importance of the study,[36] many people attacked it, including Harold W. Dodds, president of Princeton University, and the Reverend Henry P. Van Dusen, president of Union Theological Seminary as well as a member of the Rockefeller Foundation.[37]

While a significant proportion of the more serious criticisms was based on the sampling method and the statistical reliability of the data, the vast majority of criticism was based on what can only be called moralism and prudery. Kinsey was surprised and upset by the criticism, but since he basically had challenged much of psychoanalytic thinking, disagreed with and criticized the findings of many of his predecessors in the social sciences, and stated that much of Western moral teaching ignored reality, it is difficult to understand why he did not expect severe criticism. Moreover, as Lionel Trilling reported, in spite of Kinsey's scientific stance, his book was "full of assumptions and conclusions; it makes very positive statements on highly debatable matters, and it editorializes very freely."[38] This made criticism easier than it might have been if he had not, either consciously or unconsciously, engaged in editorializing.

Though in terms of serious criticism, he had as many defenders as he did hostile critics, most of his defenders also had some criticism not only of his results but of his plans.[39] Despite the criticisms of the first report, the CRPS continued to fund Kinsey.

Because the response to the first volume had made it a best-seller, the press had eagerly anticipated the publication of the second volume on the female. By the time the book was ready to appear, the advance interest was so great that Kinsey and coworkers were literally besieged by the press, which was engaging in what has since come to be called a frenzy. The center of the assault on the female volume was essentially by the moralists, particularly by the clergy, who seemed to feel that Kinsey had undermined the virginal status of American womanhood. Some who had supported the first study, such as Karl Menninger, joined in the denunciation of the second. In part, some of the criticism was a turf war. For example, Menninger said, "Kinsey's compulsion to force human sexual behavior into a zoological frame of reference leads him to repudiate or neglect human psychology, and to see normality as that which is natural in the sense that it is what is practiced by animals."[40]

For public relations purposes, it was announced that Kinsey's support was not renewed because he had failed to request support, but there is ample evidence in the Rockefeller Archives that he did. Some of the slack in funding for Kinsey was taken up by Indiana University through the effort of its president, Wells. The scope of the project, however, was severely curtailed. Kinsey continued to try to gain funding from the Rockefeller Foundation. He continued to pursue his research and tried desperately to raise more funds, up until his death on August 25, 1956. In spite of the trauma of his last years and the serious and legitimate criticism of his studies, he was probably the major figure in transforming American public attitudes about sex, helping Americans to come to terms with the existence of real sexual behaviors that had been previously ignored.[41]

Kinsey and Censorship

Kinsey also broke new legal ground in disseminating information about sex. This was because he was nothing if not thorough, and typical of his research was his attempt to survey exhaustively the literature about human sexuality. This, among other things, involved collecting materials from all over the world. Inevitably, he ran into difficulty with postal and customs officials. Alden H. Baker, Collector of Customs at Indianapolis, called some of the incoming materials, "Damned dirty stuff," and held in 1950 it was inadmissible. Kinsey believed that the law specifically granted exceptions to scientists and medical individuals in matters dealing with possible obscenity, and he argued, it was under this category that the materials should be admitted. Washington, D.C. customs officials said there was nothing in the materials that was of intrinsic value or that made it valuable to scientists. Rather than destroy the material outright, as they held was their right, they agreed to wait for final court adjudication.[42] The case, *U.S. v. 31 Photographs*, was finally decided after Kinsey's death in the Federal Court of New York.[43] Judge Edmund L. Palmieri, ruling in

Kinsey's favor, stated that there was no warrant for either custom officials or the court to sit in review of the decisions of scholars as to the bypaths of learning on which they would tread. The legal question was narrowly defined, whether among those persons who sought to see the material, there was a reasonable probability that it would appeal to prurient interest.[44] In this case, Palmieri decided it would not. The important aspect of the case was that the court, in determining community standards for defining whether a material was obscene, recognized those scientists and scholars interested in studying human sexuality as a community when it could be shown that this was the audience for which the material was intended. Customs decided not to appeal the ruling, and this has allowed various institutions and professionals to collect materials essential for sex research.

Kinsey was determined to make the study of sex a science and had projected a number of projects and book-length reports. Though some of these studies on which data had been collected were brought to fruition by his successors in Indiana and other new projects were initiated, Kinsey's death led to a greater dispersion of sex research across the United States than might have been the case had he lived.

A good example is the study of the biological factors involved in sexual behavior, for which Kinsey had been gathering data. At his death, his collection included, among other things, more than four thousand sets of measurements of penises made by subjects who gave their case histories, and another twelve thousand measurements made by a person who turned his records over to Kinsey. In the Kinsey files, the longest authenticated measurement of a penis was 10.5 inches in erection, although there were unofficial reports of longer ones. The average length was nearly 6.5 inches.

Kinsey had also attempted to measure clitorises, but this was more complicated because the amount of fleshy material and the position of the material in the prepuce. Still, clitorises that measured as long as 3 inches were reported (primarily in black women), and Kinsey noted that peep shows had exhibited women with 4-inch clitorises. Kinsey also turned to gynecologists to determine the extent to which women were aware of tactile and heavier stimulation in every part of the genitalia. He thought that clitoral stimulation was the key to female orgasm.[45] Kinsey, ever the entrepreneur, had grand plans to do much more in this area and had requested funds for a physiologist, a neurologist, and a specialist in the sexual behavior of lower animals, but nothing had come of these requests. Instead, William Masters and Virginia Johnson were the pioneers in this area.

Notes

1. Wardell B. Pomeroy, *Dr. Kinsey and the Institute for Sex Research* (New York: Harper & Row, 1972). Judith Reisman has charged that Kinsey was not simply chosen for the university's new marriage course but that he had maneuvered for many years to gain approval for the course and to be able to direct it. See Judith A. Reisman and Edward W. Eichel, *Kinsey, Sex and Fraud: The Indoctrination of a People* (Lafayette, LA.: Lochinvar-Huntington House, 1990).

2. George W. Corner, *The Seven Ages of a Medical Scientist* (Philadelphia: University of Pennsylvania Press, 1981), 314.

3. Ibid., 268.

4. Alfred Kinsey, Wardell Pomeroy, and Clyde Martin, *Sexual Behavior in the Human Male* (Philadelphia: Saunders, 1948); and Alfred Kinsey, Wardell Pomeroy, Clyde Martin, and Paul Gebhard, *Sexual Behavior in the Human Female* (Philadelphia: Saunders, 1953).

5. Wardell B. Pomeroy, *Dr. Kinsey and the Institute for Sex Research* (New York: Harper & Row, 1972).

6. Ibid., 121; and Wardell Pomeroy, personal communication.

7. See Judith A. Reisman and Edward W. Eichel, in *Kinsey, Sex, and Fraud*, ed. J. Gordon Muir and John H. Court (Lafayette, LA.: Lochinvar-Huntington House, 1990). This is a badly written and poorly edited book, in which Kinsey is described as unscientific for relying on either the memory of older subjects or data gathered from a pedophile. See the reply from Gebhard, "Dr.

Paul Gebhard's Letter to Dr. Judith Reisman Regarding Kinsey Research Subjects and Data" (March 11, 1981) [Appendix B], in *Kinsey, Sex, and Fraud*, 223.

8. Ibid., 122–3.

9. William G. Cochran, Frederick Mosteller, and John W. Tukey, *Statistical Problems of the Kinsey Report* (Washington, D.C.: American Statistical Association, 1954), 23.

10. See "Report" Foundation 1, Ser. 200, Box 41, Rockefeller Foundation Archives, Pocantico Hills, North Tarrytown, New York.

11. George W. Corner, *The Seven Ages of a Medical Scientist: An Autobiography* (Philadelphia: University of Pennsylvania Press, 1981), 315–6.

12. Pomeroy, *Dr. Kinsey*, 464.

13. See Kinsey et al., *Sexual Behavior in the Human Female*, 28–31.

14. Kinsey et al., *Sexual Behavior in the Human Male*, 161, 610–50.

15. See Vern L. Bullough, "The Kinsey Scale in Historical Perspective," in *Homosexuality/Heterosexuality: Concepts of Sexual Orientation*, ed. David P. McWhirter, Stephanie A. Sanders, and June Machover Reinisch (New York: Oxford University Press, 1990), 3–14.

16. See Pomeroy, *Dr. Kinsey*, 46; and Paul Robinson, "Dr. Kinsey and the Institute for Sex Research," *Atlantic* 229 (May 1972): 99–102.

17. Kinsey et al., *Sexual Behavior in the Human Male*, 610, 633–6. This is the explanation advanced by Paul Robinson, *The Modernization of Sex* (New York: Harper & Row, 1976), 70–71.

18. See Kenneth Lewes, *The Psychoanalytic Theory of Male Homosexuality* (New York: Simon & Schuster, 1988).

19. Kinsey et al., *Sexual Behavior in the Human Female*, 375–408.

20. Ibid., 377, 383.

21. Edward M. Brecher, *The Sex Researchers* (Boston: Little, Brown, 1969), 124.

22. Ibid., 568.

23. Ibid., 547, 549, 559; and Kinsey et al., *Sexual Behavior in the Human Female*, 284.

24. Ibid., 186.

25. Ibid., 311.

26. Ibid., 328.

27. Ibid., 416.

28. Kinsey et al., *Sexual Behavior in the Human Male*, 585.

29. Ibid., 650–1.

30. Kinsey et al., *Sexual Behavior in the Human Female*, 450–1.

31. Ibid., 460.

32. Pomeroy, *Dr. Kinsey*, 101.

33. Kinsey et al., *Sexual Behavior in the Human Female*, 435–6.

34. See Reinhold Niebuhr, "Kinsey and the Moral Problems of Man's Sexual Life," in *An Analysis of the Kinsey Reports*, ed. Donald Porter Geddes (New York: New American Library, 1954), 62–70.

35. Actually, he had collected data on pregnancy, birth, and abortion, which appeared in Paul H. Gebhard, Wardell B. Pomeroy, Clyde E. Martin, and Cornelia V. Christenson, *Pregnancy, Birth, and Abortion* (New York: Harper, 1958).

36. A Gallup poll following the book's publication found that 58 percent of the men and 55 percent of the women thought Kinsey's research was a good thing; only 10 and 14 percent, respectively, thought it a bad thing. See Pomeroy, *Dr. Kinsey*, 283–4.

37. Dodds went so far as to meet with officials of the Rockefeller Foundation to express his unhappiness and that of Van Dusen. See Memo of June 28, 1948, Foundation Ser. 200, Box 40, Rockefeller Foundation Archives.

38. Lionel Trilling, *The Liberal Imagination* (1950; reprint, New York: Viking, 1957), 218.

39. Pomeroy, *Dr. Kinsey*, 298–9.

40. Quoted in Ibid., 367.

41. Corner, *Seven Ages of a Medical Scientist*, 316–7.

42. *The New York Times*, "U.S. Customs Refuses to Pass Obscene European Photos," November 18, 1950, n18, 9:5, and in *Indianapolis Star-News*, December 8, 1950. See Foundation Records [National Research Council] Ser. 200, Box 41, 463, Rockefeller Foundation Archives.

43. *United States v. 31 Photographs*, 156 F. Supp. 350 (S.D.N.Y., 1957).

44. Morris L. Ernst and Alan U. Schwartz, *Censorship: The Search for the Obscene* (New York: Macmillan, 1964), 125.

45. Pomeroy, *Dr. Kinsey*, 317–9.

Chapter 4
Masters and Johnson

Vern L. Bullough

of the treatment for sexual dysfunction. By moving the focus to the medical model, they expanded treatment options to include obstetrics and gynecology, urology, and, later, sex therapy. Today, medical and behavioral professionals across many disciplines can more competently address the problems of sexual dysfunction because of the remarkable work of this research team.

Although Alfred Kinsey pioneered the use of *case histories to study human sexuality, Masters and Johnson were the first to use clinical techniques of observing, measuring, and recording actual sexual behaviors in a laboratory setting. Technological advances made after the Kinsey data were collected, such as the development of an artificial coital device with a miniature camera and intrauterine electrodes, enabled the latter research team to achieve their goal of replacing many of the "phallic fallacies" with facts.*

Building on a baseline of Kinsey's sociological data about patterns of sexual behavior, Masters and Johnson emphasized the application of clinical scientific methods in studying the physiology of sexual response in women and men. Through such methods, they clearly delineated varied physiological responses to sexual stimulation in women and to a lesser degree in men. For example, they clinically documented multiple orgasms in women and discovered the source of vaginal lubrication during sexual arousal to be the walls of the vagina, rather than the Glands of Bartholin as previously believed. Even though they clinically verified Kinsey's findings concerning the similarity of the anatomy and physiology of the sexual response in females and males, they rejected his claim that the differences were centered in the brain's capacity to respond to psychological stimuli. Masters and Johnson are perhaps best recognized for their arbitrary four-stage division of the sexual response cycle still in use today: the excitement, plateau, orgasmic, and resolution stages.

Masters and Johnson were the first to challenge the assumption that psychiatry and psychoanalysis should be the sole providers

William Masters and Virginia Johnson from the first were much more practice oriented than Kinsey. Masters was a physician who was concerned with helping his patients overcome their problems. Together, Masters and Johnson thought of themselves as therapists, which meant they accepted the world as they saw it existing and wanted to help their clients adjust to it. Kinsey, on the other hand, was a scientist, describing the world as it existed but also emphasizing the contradictions between actuality and accepted standards. Masters and Johnson conducted their research for a reason that was entirely different from Kinsey's.

When the laboratory program for the investigation in human sexual functioning was designed in 1954, the greatest handicap to successful treatment of sexual inadequacy was a lack of reliable physiological information in the area of human sexual response. It was presumed that definitive laboratory effort would develop material of clinical consequence that could be used by professionals in the field to improve methodology of therapeutic approach to sexual inadequacy.[1]

Just as Kinsey had challenged, sometimes with considerable hostility, the psychiatric monopoly on sexual treatment and research, Masters and Johnson offered whole new areas for the gynecologist, urologist, and other medical specialists to extend their services. Ultimately, Masters and Johnson also helped establish a whole new profession, the sex therapist, which was no longer restricted to the psychiatrist but included nurses, psychologists, social workers, and counselors. It should be added, however, that the initial promise of nonevasive therapeutic techniques for problems of sexual inadequacy was oversold by some therapists and that, as the years passed, the balance between medical intervention and nonintrusive therapy changed. The basic teaching techniques pioneered by Masters and Johnson and their contemporaries, however, still remain important.

Masters was a native of Cleveland and was born to a well-to-do family in 1915. He attended Lawrenceville Prep School and went on to Hamilton College, where he received his bachelor's degree in 1938. He then entered the University of Rochester School of Medicine and Dentistry, where he worked in Corner's laboratory. Interestingly, Corner had three of the leaders in what he called "the practical application of scientific thought to problems of human sex behavior" as students: Guttmacher, who became internationally prominent in the family planning movement; Mary Steichen Calderone, co-founder of the Sex Information and Educational Council of the United States (SIECUS); and Masters.[2]

Masters, who had always been more interested in medical research than in the practice of medicine, decided he would like to do sex research when he completed his degree, and went to Corner for advice. Corner essentially gave him three general principles to follow in pursuing sex research: (1) he should establish a scientific reputation in some other scientific field first, (2) he should secure the sponsorship of a major medical school or university, and (3) he should be at least forty years of age.[3]

Masters followed the advice almost to the letter, although he did start his research into sexuality at the age of thirty-eight. After graduation from medical school, he accepted a position at Washington University in St. Louis. Willard Allen, another of Corner's students and an active researcher in endocrinology, helped Masters get the appointment as an intern in obstetrics and gynecology. Masters moved up the ladder through resident to assistant professor and associate professor. He married and had two children. Masters also published a number of papers covering a variety of obstetrical and gynecological topics, although the majority dealt with hormone-replacement therapy for aging and aged women, a treatment that he strongly advocated[4] and that is widely used today.

The Beginnings

Gradually, Masters turned to studying the sexual act itself. The pioneer in this respect had been the French physician Félix Roubaud, who had published his account of the female response cycle in 1855.[5] Kinsey had called Roubaud's description unsurpassed,[6] even though the Frenchman had been mistaken on two points, namely the claim that there was direct frictional contact between the penis and the clitoris, and that the semen was sucked up through the cervix.

Just as Masters was actively beginning to plan his own program, G. Klumbies and H. Kleinsorge, two physicians at the University Clinic in Jena, Germany reported on a patient who was capable of fantasizing to orgasm, a fact that made it possible to distinguish the direct effects of orgasm from the muscular exertion that ordinarily preceded it or accompanied it. With the aid of an electrocardiograph and a blood pressure recorder, Klumbies and Kleinsorge recorded physiological changes, including pulse rate, systolic and diastolic blood pressure, rhythm of heart chamber contractions, respiratory volume, and muscle irritability. The woman identified some of her orgasms as more intense than others, and Klumbies and Kleinsorge noted that the intensity of the orgasm as subjectively reported showed a close relation to the acuteness of the blood pressure peak.[7] Another investigator, Abraham Mosovich, recorded electroencephalograms (brain wave patterns) during sexual arousal and orgasm.[8]

The best and most complete observations made before Masters and Johnson's studies were Kinsey's. He reported that he had access to a considerable body "of observed data on the involvement of the entire body in the spasms following orgasm."[9] Actually, most of the observations had been made on volunteers by Kinsey or his staff, independent of the interview portion of his research.

When Masters began his studies in 1954, he interviewed at length and in depth 118 female and 37 male prostitutes. Of these, 8 of the women and 3 of the men then participated as experimental subjects in a preliminary series of laboratory studies. Suggestions of this select group of techniques for support and control of the human male and female in situations of direct sexual response proved invaluable. They described many methods for elevating or controlling sexual tensions and demonstrated innumerable variations in stimulative technique. Ultimately many of these techniques have been found to have direct application in therapy of male and female sexual inadequacy and have been integrated into the clinical programs.[10]

Ultimately, however, the experimental results derived from the prostitute population were not included in the final published results, because Masters and Johnson wanted a baseline of what they regarded as "anatomic normalcy." To get this, they turned to patient populations and volunteers for data. It was during this phase that Virginia Johnson joined Masters's team, because Masters strongly believed that a woman should be involved in his research. Born Virginia Eshelman in Missouri in 1925, she had studied music at Drury College and later attended the University of Missouri. In 1950, Johnson married and had a son and daughter before separating from her husband in the late 1950s. Masters was seeking a woman to assist in research interviewing and had specified that he wanted a woman who had experience and interest in working with people. The Bureau sent Johnson, and she was hired. The two later married, but were divorced in 1992.

Johnson's work was particularly important in the first two books but played a lesser part in later studies. The fact that Masters and Johnson were a male-female team separates them from Kinsey. Though Kinsey had added a woman to his team shortly before he died, he seems to have not felt it necessary to do so before. Masters, in general, gave more emphasis to the female than to the male not only in his team but in his studies. In the discussion of physiology, for example, the female is mentioned first. Masters seems to have emphasized that the female is not just an inferior imitation of the male, an attitude widely prevalent even at the time of his research.

Sexual Response Cycle

Masters and Johnson held that the sexual response cycle involved much more than a penis and vagina, and they sought to measure heart rate, respiratory functions, muscle tension, breast response, and any other physiological measurement they could think of. A key element in the ability of Masters and Johnson to break new ground was technological. Advances in the miniaturization of cameras and electronic devices meant that they could be used inside of a plastic phallus. This allowed Masters and Johnson to record what took place inside the vagina during orgasm, and they could observe the phenomena in some detail. This new technology permitted them to give definitive answers to some of the questions about which there had been arguments or on which there had only been subjective data. It allowed Masters and Johnson to determine that there was a moistening of the vaginal lining with lubricating fluid within 10 to 30 seconds of the onset of erotic stimulation and to note that this fluid came from the coalescence of a "sweating" of the vagina's walls. They emphasized that neither the Bartholin's glands nor the cervix, previously believed to be the source of the lubrication, contributed to the fluid. Rather the sweating resulted from the increased blood supply and the engorgement of vaginal tissues.[11]

Masters and Johnson also noted a lengthening and distension of the vaginal walls, while the cervix and the uterus are pulled slowly back and up into the false pelvis (the part of the pelvis above the hip joint). The vagina's walls also undergo a distinct coloration change, from purplish red to a darker purple, as a result of vasocongestion, and the wrinkled or corrugated aspects of the vaginal wall (technically called the rugal pattern) are flattened. Gradually, the outer third of the vagina becomes grossly distended with venous blood, and the vasocongestion is so marked that the central lumen (interior) of the outer third of the vaginal barrel wall is reduced by a least a third. All this takes place during what Masters and Johnson called the plateau phase, or second phase of the sexual response cycle.

This is followed by the orgasmic phase, during which much of physiologic activity is confined to what Masters and Johnson called the orgasm platform in the upper third of the vagina. Here there are strong contractions at 0.8 second intervals, which recur within a normal range of three to five and up to ten to fifteen times per individual orgasm. The uterus elevates and contracts rhythmically with each contraction, beginning at the upper end of the uterus and moving like a wave through the mid-zone and down to the lower or cervical end. These uterine contractions had been long associated with the idea that the cervix sucks up sperm. Masters and Johnson, however, theorized that contractions in such a direction would, if anything, expel sperm. They then proceeded to demonstrate the uterine contractions could not possibly lead to a sucking up of the sperm into the uterus. They prepared a tight-fitting cervical cup that they filled with a semen-like liquid in a radiopaque base. Masters and Johnson then made radiograms during the orgasmic experience and found no such sucking action.[12]

To describe what took place during intercourse, Masters and Johnson developed a four-phase description: (1) excitement, (2) plateau, (3) orgasm, and (4) resolution. They found that men responded in terms of basic physiological changes along the same lines as women; in both sexes, there was an increase in heart rate, blood pressure, and muscle tension, and in the majority of both men and women a "sex flush" (a rosy measlelike rash over the chest, neck, face, shoulders, arms, and thighs) is observable. At orgasm the heart and respiratory rates are at a maximum and the sex flush at its peak, although the male has what are called ejaculatory contractions during the orgasm. The orgasm phase is followed by the resolution phase in which there is a return to conditions as they were before the sexual excitement phase began. Women were found to have a wider variety of orgasmic responses and many could have multiple orgasms.

Masters and Johnson criticized what they called the "phallic fallacy" of comparing the clitoris with the penis. They emphasized that even though the clitoris might be the anatomical analogue of the penis, it reacts to sexual stimulation in a manner quite different from the penis. It does not become erect during arousal but instead withdraws beneath its protective foreskin, and in fact, its length is reduced by at least half as orgasm approaches. When it is retracted, however, it responds to generalized pressure on the labial hood.[13]

Patient concerns were always present in Masters and Johnson's minds. For example, they reported that the average flaccid measurement of a penis was 7.5 centimeters (about 3 inches) and during erection the penis more than doubled in length. However, they recognized that not all men had the same size penis.[14] To allay the qualms of their readers, they emphasized that the vagina was a "potential rather than an actual space," and was "infinitely distensible."[15] Interestingly, however, there is no evidence that they ever asked any of their female subjects whether penis size made a difference, or if they did, the answer was not recorded.

Sample

All told, 694 individuals, including 276 married couples, participated in the Masters and Johnson laboratory program. Of these, 142 were unmarried but 44 had been previously married. The men ranged in age from twenty-one to eighty-nine and the women, from eighteen to seventy-eight. Volunteers for the laboratory research program were involved in masturbation by hand, fingers, or a mechanical vibrator; in sexual intercourse with the woman on her back, with the male on his back; and in artificial coition with a transparent probe. Also studied were the anatomy and physiology of the aging male and aging female, although the data were not as complete as for the younger ages. Masters and Johnson emphasized, however, that if opportunity for regularity of coitus exists, the elderly woman will retain a far higher capacity for sexual performance than her female counterpart who does not have similar coital opportunity. They reported that even though the postmenopausal woman has lost some of her hormone output, the psyche is as important, if not more important, in determining the sex drive.[16] Similarly, while in the aging male the entire ejaculatory process undergoes a reduction in physiological efficiency, the sexual response remains. Masters and Johnson concluded,

> There is every reason to believe that maintained regularity of sexual expression coupled with adequate physical well-being and healthy mental orientation to the aging process will combine to provide a sexually stimulative climate within a marriage. This climate will, in turn, improve sexual tension and provide a capacity for sexual performance that frequently may extend to and beyond the 80-year level.[17]

Sexual Dysfunction

A natural follow-up to the physiological studies of the human sexual response was treatment for dysfunctional clients. For this purpose, Masters and Johnson developed a sex therapy team (a woman and a man) and a methodology through which they said they were treating the "marriage," since the basic foundation of their treatment was that both the husband and wife in a sexually dysfunctional marriage be treated.[18] Such a statement emphasizes Masters and Johnson's marital orientation, something that probably contributed to their widespread acceptance on the American scene. Although a significant proportion of their clients were unmarried, most came to therapy accompanied by a partner.

Because Masters and Johnson always emphasized the therapeutic nature of their research, their aim in effect had always been the development of treatment modalities. In their treatment, they concentrated on specific symptoms rather than generalized disorders. In a way, they adopted some of the concepts of the behavioral psychologists who had begun treating sexual problems in the 1950s,[19] but in the process, they popularized sex therapy and systematized it on a physiological base.

One result was the development of a new specialty in the helping professions, that of sex therapist. Before their entrance on the scene, the predominant treatment of sexual dysfunction, at least in the United States, was through psychoanalysis. What Masters and Johnson essentially did was challenge perhaps the final bastion of the control that psychiatry, and particularly psychoanalysis, had over the sex field. Kinsey had basically undermined many of the assumptions that psychiatry had made about sexual behavior and furnished a new kind of database. With Masters and Johnson, even the treatment option, which psychiatry had dominated, was now redirected to other specialists, many of whom were not physicians. The result was to increase the number of individuals who were not only professionally but economically interested in sex. Kinsey, in effect, had reestablished the concept of sexology. Although sexological research was a somewhat limited field, the rise of sex therapy gave sexology enough other professionals to justify separate sexological societies and journals.

Masters and Johnson were also important because they, although in a much gentler form than Kinsey, emphasized the importance of sex education. For example, in their discussion of the anorgasmic female, they stated that women in general were victims of the double standard, because they more than men had been taught to repress their sexual feelings. Masters and Johnson concluded that repression, in the form of historical and psychological experience, was the most important factor in the development of frigidity.[20] Ignorance and superstition about sex were and remain the major problems in an inadequate sexual response, and when the sexual partners manage to have their prejudices, misconceptions, and misunderstandings of natural sexual functioning exposed, then and only then can "a firm basis for mutual security in sexual expression" be established.[21] In short, for marriage to reach its full potential, and Masters and Johnson were always concerned with marriage, knowledge of sex was essential. This message was seized on not only by a new generation of sex educators to bring about reforms in sex education but by the public in general, who seemed to grow ever more interested in how to have a better marriage, which they believed was highly dependent on sexual performance.

The largest component of the expanding group of sex professionals in the 1960s was the sex therapist, the number of which grew rapidly. Masters and Johnson had established a two-week basic program that involved a male and female sex therapist and a client couple; this program served as the initial model. Masters and Johnson reported that the two-week session eliminated sexual difficulties for 80 percent of their clients. Not content with these immediate results, they followed up these studies five years later and stated that of those they were able to recontact, only 7 percent reported recurrence of the dysfunctions for which they originally had sought treatment.[22] The result of such claims was a demand by the public for help with sexual problems and an awareness by the various kinds of professionals that they could expand their client base if they could gain some expertise in sex.

Many would-be sex therapists went to St. Louis to take special training sessions with Masters and Johnson. Professionals who entered sex therapy from a slightly different background also offered special seminars. On the West Coast, for example, William Hartman and Marilyn Fithian, who had included sexual therapy as part of their marriage and family counseling, had begun to carry out their own set of experiments on the sexual response in their Long Beach, California, center. As the demand for sex therapists grew, Hartman and Fithian conducted training seminars not only in Long Beach but all over the country, introducing would-be professionals to new trends in sex therapy.

Another important early sex therapist was Helen Singer Kaplan, who tried to combine some of the insights and techniques of psychoanalysis with behavioral methods. She questioned Masters and Johnson's use of two therapists and felt that one therapist of either sex would be sufficient,[23] a finding made by others.[24] Kaplan agreed that many sexual difficulties stemmed from superficial causes, but she believed that when unconscious conflict was at the heart of the problem and involved deep-seated emotional problems the therapist should use more analytic approaches. As a result, her approach is designated as psychosexual therapy to distinguish it from sex therapy, and her entry into the field emphasizes how psychoanalysts themselves gradually adjusted to the new sex therapy techniques.

In the afterglow of success, the sex therapy originally presented by Masters and Johnson did not seem to hold true for a growing number of therapists as the field rapidly expanded. This was perhaps because of not only the existence of deep-seated emotional problems in some clients, as Kaplan had pointed out, but the presence of basic physiological problems such as diabetes. The result was an attack on the success claims of Masters and Johnson, as an increasing number of studies reported much higher failure rates.[25]

The difference in success rates, however, is probably the result of both the changing nature of clients and the differing methods of client selection. Many of the original problems presented by the early clients of Masters and Johnson resulted from a lack of knowledge of basic sexual activity, something that was comparatively easy to overcome. The very success of the books by Masters and Johnson made such clients increasingly less likely to seek the help of a therapist, since they could read about the sources of human sexual inadequacy and adjust their own practices. On the other hand, the physical exam required by Masters and Johnson for their patients undoubtedly eliminated many of those with physiological difficulties that other, less knowledgeable therapists attempted to treat and failed to help. The major result of the criticism of Masters and Johnson was to emphasize that sex therapy at its best involved a team, not only of therapists but of medical professionals, particularly the urologist and gynecologist.

Notes

1. William H. Masters and Virginia E. Johnson, *Human Sexual Inadequacy* (Boston: Little, Brown, 1970), 1. The therapeutic intent is not emphasized in their first study, William H. Masters and Virginia E. Johnson, *Human Sexual Response* (Boston: Little, Brown, 1966).

2. George W. Corner, *The Seven Ages of a Medical Scientist* (Philadelphia: University of Pennsylvania Press, 1981), 212.

3. Corner, *The Seven Ages of a Medical Scientist*, 213.

4. Among his articles are W. H. Masters, "Long Range Sex Steroid Replacement: Target Organ Regeneration," *Journal of Gerontology* 8 (1953): 33–39; W. H. Masters, "Endocrine Therapy in the Aging Individual," *Obstetrics and Gynecology* 8 (1956): 61–67; and W. H. Masters, "Sex Steroid Influence on the Aging Process," *American Journal of Obstetrics and Gynecology* 74 (1957): 733–46.

5. Félix Roubaud, *Trait de l'Impuissance et de la Sterilité chez l'Homme et chez la Femme* (1855; reprint, Paris: Baillière, 1876).

6. Alfred E. Kinsey, Wardell B. Pomeroy, and Clyde Martin, *Sexual Behavior in the Human Female* (Philadelphia: Saunders, 1953).

7. G. Klumbies and H. Kleinsorge, "Das Herz in Orgasmus," *Medizinische Klinik* 45 (1950): 952–8; and G. Klumbies and H. Kleinsorge, "Circulatory Dangers and Prophylaxis During Orgasm," *International Journal of Sexology* 4 (1950): 61–66.

8. Kinsey et al., *Sexual Behavior in the Human Female*, 630, fig. 140.

9. Ibid., 631, n. 46.

10. Masters and Johnson, *Human Sexual Response*, 10.

11. Ibid., 300.

12. Ibid., 124.

13. Ibid., 57–61.

14. Ibid., 192.

15. Ibid., 194–5.

16. Ibid., 242.

17. Ibid., 270.

18. Masters and Johnson, *Human Sexual Inadequacy*, 3.

19. Joseph Wolpe, *Psychotherapy by Reciprocal Inhibition* (Stanford, Calif.: Stanford University Press, 1958).

20. Ibid., 214–8, 222–6.

21. Ibid., 62.

22. Masters and Johnson, *Human Sexual Inadequacy*, 366, tab. 11 B.

23. Helen Singer Kaplan, *The New Sex Therapy* (New York: Brunner/Mazel, 1974).

24. Joseph LoPiccolo, J. R. Heiman, D. R. Hogan, and C. W. Roberts, "Effectiveness of Single Therapists Versus Cotherapy Teams in Sex Therapy," *Journal of Counsulting and Clinical Psychology* 53 (1985): 287–94.

25. S. Schumacher and C. W. Lloyd, "Physiology and Psychological Factors in Impotence," *Journal of Sex Research* 17 (1981): 40–53; and B. Zilbergeld and M. Evans, "The Inadequacy of Masters and Johnson," *Psychology Today* 14 (1980): 29–43.

Chapter 5
The Social Organization of Sexuality

Edward O. Laumann
John H. Gagnon
Robert T. Michael
Stuart Michaels

Following the work of Kinsey and of Masters and Johnson, little sexuality research was conducted in the United States from the mid-1950s to the mid-1960s. And even in the period of permissiveness that evolved during the sexual revolution, most of the survey research was retrieved on samples from college students. By the early 1970s, it was evident that significant changes were occurring in sexual behavior and attitudes: rising percentages of young people were having premarital sexual intercourse, and the gay/lesbian movement and the feminist movement were in full swing.

Sex became a household word as the mass media contributed to the widespread belief that everyone, youth and adult, was actively involved in premarital sex and postmarital sexual affairs. Publications such as Playboy and Redbook disseminated information from reader surveys of sexual behavior via "tear out and mail in" questionnaires. Shere Hite reported, in her controversial bestseller, The Hite Report, that 70 percent of married persons were having extramarital affairs within the first five years of marriage. Her claim was based on a survey of 100,000 women, which had a return rate of 3 percent. Her somewhat politicized sample included members of the National Organization for Women (NOW), the American Association of University Women (AAUW), and abortion rights groups. Scholars, lamenting that bad data are worse than no data, concluded that the ability of mass media to produce their own facts is a fact of life that even researchers must learn to live with. By the 1980s, it became apparent that not only were people looking at bad data, they also were looking backward at old data for answers.

It was into such a world in the late 1980s that Laumann, Gagnon, Michael, and Michaels, a research team from the University of Chicago and the State University of New York at Stony Brook, launched their National Health and Social Life Survey, the goal of which was to develop a social scientific theory of sexual conduct. The $1.7 million study was financed in 1992 by eight private foundations after conservative senators had killed federal funding of the research project in 1991.

Although studies in the previous decades had chronicled changes in sexual behavior, the researchers of earlier periods had neglected the construction of theories to explain human sexual behavior. Because sexual behavior is social, the theorists proposed that it must be studied within relationships to explain it as a social phenomenon. Psychological studies invariably center on an individualistic approach to the study of sexuality, but sociological studies focus on the social, the external, the relational, and the public dimensions. Thus, social logic was suggested to be a missing variable in the study of sexuality and, therefore, chosen as a theoretical framework for the National Health and Social Life Survey.

The nation's most comprehensive, representative survey of sexual behavior in the general population to date, the Laumann et al. study utilized face-to-face, 90-minute interviews with subjects from a randomly selected sample of 3,432 American women and men between the ages of 18 and 59. The results of the survey led to a better understanding of how sexual behavior is organized in American society and its broad-ranging public policy implications. Two books were published with the findings: The Social Organization of Sexuality: Sexual Practices in the United States, which included extensive statistical analyses for academic readers, and

Sex Practices in America: A Definitive Work, *intended for general readership.*

As chapter 1 from their scholarly book shows, the theoretical background for this study is carefully constructed from three theories: scripting theory to explain sexual conduct; choice theory to explain sexual decision making; and network theory to explain the sexual dyad. Together, they form at least a middle-range theoretical basis for construction of a social-scientific approach to sexuality. With a careful review of the following selection, readers may gain insight into the Laumann et al. study. More significantly, they can broaden their awareness of theory construction and its importance in survey research.

Human sexual behavior is a diverse phenomenon. It occurs in different physical locations and social contexts, consists of a wide range of specific activities, and is perceived differently by different people. An individual engages in sexual activity on the basis of a complex set of motivations and organizes that activity on the basis of numerous external factors and influences. Thus, it is unlikely that the tools and concepts from any single scientific discipline will suffice to answer all or even most of the questions one might ask about sexual behavior. This [narrative] introduces the several approaches that we have found especially helpful in formulating what we hope will prove to be a more comprehensive social scientific understanding of sexuality.

A Social Scientific Approach to Sexuality

Much of the previous scientific research on sexuality has been conducted by biologists and psychologists and has thus focused on sexual behavior purely as an "individual level" phenomenon. Thus, such research has defined sexual activity to be the physical actions that a person performs (or the thoughts and feelings that a person experiences) and has sought to explain individual variation in these actions in terms of processes endogenous to the individual. A good example of this approach is the study of sexual "drives" or "instincts." In drive theories, people are assumed to experience a buildup of "sexual tension" or "sexual need" during periods of deprivation or during particularly erotic environmental stimulation. When sexual activity is experienced, the drive is satiated and the need reduced. Such cycles of increased drive and its resultant satiation are often used to explain hunger and thirst and, by analogy, sexual conduct. Differences in drives across individuals are generally assumed to result from underlying biological or psychological differences in those individuals.

The major shortcoming of such studiously individualistic approaches is that they are able (at most) to explain only a very small part of the story. This is because, unlike the sexual behavior of certain animal species (e.g., salmon, who are genetically programmed to swim upstream at the appropriate time to spawn), human sexual behavior is only partly determined by factors originating within the individual. In addition, a person's socialization into a particular culture, his or her interaction with sex partners, and the constraints imposed on him or her become extremely important in determining his or her other sexual activities. This observation is perhaps obvious, yet research on social processes represents a disproportionately small amount of the extant scientific literature on human sexuality.

This does not mean that there have been no social scientific studies of sexual behavior. One prominent researcher, Ira Reiss (1990), recently enumerated more than a dozen national surveys of sexual attitudes and practices since Kinsey and his associates' work appeared in the late 1940s. Previous national studies of sexual behavior have targeted specific subpopulations or have focused on a relatively narrow range of sexual conduct. For example, Zelnik and Kantner (1972; 1980) conducted three national studies of pregnancy-related behavior among adolescents. Subsequently, Sonenstein, Pleck, and Ku (1991) conducted a more comprehensive study of sexual practices among adolescent males, and the CDC (1992) reported on a limited number of sexual behaviors among a national sample of high school students.

With regard to adults, the first nationally representative data were collected by Reiss in 1963. Later, Klassen, Williams, and Levitt (1989) conducted a study of adults age twenty-one and older (the data were collected in 1970) that focused primarily on sexual attitudes. In addition, the National Survey of Family Growth (Mosher and McNally 1991) asked its fifteen- to forty-four-year-old female respondents a limited number of questions about sexual behavior, and Tanfer's study of twenty- to twenty-nine-year-old women (Tanfer 1992) focused on a much broader range of sexual behaviors, relationships, and attitudes. These studies were followed in 1991 by a well-publicized study conducted by the Batelle Institute of twenty- to thirty-nine-year-old men that collected data on a wide range of sexual conduct (Billy et al. 1993). Finally, the National AIDS Behavioral Surveys (Peterson et al. 1993) collected behavioral data relevant to the transmission of AIDS from respondents in twenty-three "high-risk" U.S. cities. While these studies provide information on several important issues, few have attended seriously to the fact that sexual activity occurs in the context of a relationship (Blumstein and Schwartz 1983) or the epidemiological consequences of the structure of sexual networks.

We thus have in hand a number of important indications of where to look for the effects that social factors have on sexual behavior. One example is the persistent finding that a person's social class ("working" vs. "middle") is correlated with certain aspects of sexual behavior (Weinberg and Williams 1980), although there is some evidence that the strength of this association is diminishing with time (DeLamater 1981). Another persistent finding comes from the relatively large literature on adolescent sexuality (Brookman 1990).

Sociologists have found that adolescents involved in religious activities tend to delay first intercourse longer than those who are

not (DeLamater and MacCorquodale 1979). These and other essentially descriptive findings are certainly interesting, yet, without a systematic theoretical framework within which to interpret them, they cannot help us understand how and why specific social processes or circumstances affect sexual behavior.

Biological and psychological studies of sexual behavior focus solely on the individual as the relevant "unit of analysis." That is, the objective of such research is to answer questions about why an individual exhibits certain sexual behaviors. But this line of inquiry can reveal only part of the story. Most sexual behavior is not performed by an individual alone and in the absence of others. Instead, sexual behavior is social in the sense that it involves two people (or more). Sex involves negotiation and interplay, the expectation and experience of compromise. There is competition; there is cooperation. The relationships between the partners and between their mutual actions make the sexual partnership or dyad an essential analytic unit in the study of sexuality. This focus on the social, the external, the relational, and the public dimensions is what distinguishes our inquiry from the psychological and biological orientations that have characterized much sex research in the past.

Although little progress has been made in the social sciences toward developing systematic theories about the social processes involved in sexual behavior, social psychology, sociology, and economics have each developed persuasive theories explaining other spheres of social behavior. Therefore, it seems sensible to draw on such theories in attempting to formulate a social scientific theory of sexual conduct. We have begun with three theoretical traditions—scripting theory, choice theory, and social network theory—each addressing certain aspects of sexual behavior.

Scripting Theory: Explaining Sexual Content

Previous researchers have generally adopted the perspective that there is an inevitable negative conflict between the biological nature of human beings and the cultures in which they are reared. With regard to sexual behavior, this implies that social factors function solely to inhibit or constrain people's intrinsic sexual desires and urges. For example, it is assumed that biologically mature adolescents will naturally have intercourse (that they both want to and have the opportunity to do so) and that those who do not are simply better at "controlling their urges." We reject this perspective, not because it allows for the influence of biological effects on sexual behavior, but because it takes a narrow view of the role of social processes as merely constraining sexual conduct. We argue that sociocultural processes play a fundamental role in determining what we perceive to be "sexual" and how we construct and interpret our sexual fantasies and thoughts. Thus, although biological factors may indeed affect sexual behavior, they play at most a small role in determining what those specific behaviors will be and how they will be interpreted.

Scripting theories of sexual conduct address exactly these types of questions. The starting point for these theories can be expressed in terms of several assumptions about the ways in which specific sexual patterns are acquired and expressed. First, they assume that patterns of sexual conduct in a culture are locally derived (i.e., that what is sexual and what sex means differ in different cultures). Second, they assume either that human beings possess no biological instincts about how to act sexually or that the effects of such instincts are minor in comparison with the effects of an individual's socially determined scripts for conduct. People may vary biologically in activity level and temperament, but there are no direct links between this variation and what they will do sexually as adults. Third, they assume that, through a process of acculturation lasting from birth to death, individuals acquire patterns of sexual conduct that are appropriate to their culture (including those patterns that are thought to deviate from the norms of the culture). Fourth, they assume that people may not enact the scripts provided by their culture exactly but instead may make minor adaptations to suit their own needs. In complex and contradictory cultures, such individual adaptations will be very diverse.

On the basis of these four principles, sexual scripts specify with whom people have sex, when and where they should have sex, what they should do sexually, and why they should do sexual things. These scripts embody what the intersubjective culture treats as sexuality (cultural scenarios) and what the individual believes to be the domain of sexuality. Individuals improvise on the basis of the cultural scenarios and in the process change the sexual culture of the society. In this way, individual sexual actors as well as those who create representations of sexual life (e.g., the mass media, religious leaders, educators, and researchers) are constantly reproducing and transforming sexual life in a society. For example, introducing condoms into sexual activity as part of an AIDS education and prevention program requires changing scripts for sexual conduct on the part of individuals. If large numbers of individuals adopt this new script, they will change the effects that sexual activity has on health by reducing unwanted pregnancies, abortions, and the spread of sexually transmitted diseases.

The scripting perspective distinguishes between cultural scenarios (the instructions for sexual and other conduct that are embedded in the cultural narratives that are provided as guides or instructions for all conduct), interpersonal scripts (the structured patterns of interaction in which individuals as actors engage in everyday interpersonal conduct), and intrapsychic scripts (the plans and fantasies by which individuals guide and reflect on their past, current, or future conduct) (Gagnon and Simon 1987; Gagnon 1991).

Several studies provide evidence for the importance of sexual scripts in shaping both perception and behavior (Geer and Brussard 1990; Castillo and Geer 1993). For example, in one study, male subjects listened to one of two different narratives, during which time their level of sexual arousal was monitored. Both narratives began with identical stories describing a young woman getting into her car and driving to a building, where she goes into a room, closes the door, and removes her clothes. At this point, a man enters the room; he is identified in the first narrative as the woman's gynecologist, in the second as her boyfriend. Predictably, subjects hearing the first narrative experienced significantly less arousal than those who heard the second, despite the similarity of the two narratives. Since the physician was not part of the subjects' sexual scripts, they had to reevaluate their perceptions of the situation.

With regard to the effects of scripts on actual behavior, research among adolescents has repeatedly demonstrated the existence of a general pattern of activities that young people follow as they acquire sexual experience (DeLamater and MacCorquodale 1979). The pattern begins with kissing, proceeding first to necking and then to the male fondling the female's breast (first over the clothing, then underneath). Next occurs fondling of each other's genitals, first by the male, then by the female. This is followed by genital-genital contact and then by vaginal intercourse. Only after intercourse do adolescents go on to try oral sex, again first by the male, then by the female. What this means is that those who have had vaginal intercourse are also likely to have engaged in kissing, necking, fondling, and apposition. Similarly, those who have not yet engaged in "heavy petting" are unlikely to move directly to intercourse. Of course, not all adolescents complete the entire program or, to use the especially apt euphemism, "go all the way." Moreover, any single interaction is subject to practical considerations (such as being restricted to the backseat of a car) that may result in temporary deviations from the script.

Choice Theory: Sexual Decision Making

While scripting theories are useful in explaining the range of activities (or scripts) available to an individual, they tell us little about how the individual chooses among

these various possibilities. For example, an individual may have different scripts for how to act toward different partners (e.g., a new partner, a "one-night stand," and a spouse) and in different situations; however, the content of these scripts alone tells us little about why that individual may choose to pursue certain types of relationships to the exclusion of others. In order to address this important issue, we turn to an economic approach to decision making. Essentially, economic choice theory is concerned with how people utilize the resources available to them in the pursuit of one or more specific goals. Since one's resources are generally limited, choices arise regarding how these resources should be apportioned among various activities leading to one or another goal. Were there no scarcity of the necessary resources, there would be no constraint on the achievement of one's goals and no need for choices to be made. However, the necessary resources (i.e., time, money, emotional and physical energy, personal reputation) required to engage in sexual behavior are limited, and choices must therefore be made.

It is important to recognize that an economic approach presumes the existence of a goal or a set of goals. Thus, in order to utilize this approach, we must first identify what those goals (or at least some of them) are. For example, the goals of sexual behavior may include sexual pleasure itself, the emotional satisfaction that results from being intimately involved with someone toward whom one feels affection, having children, and acquiring a "good reputation" among one's friends. So we have listed four goals that may motivate a person to use his or her limited money, time, and energy to achieve one or another of these goals.

People differ in the importance that they accord these various goals and in their capacities to achieve them. Choice theory focuses on how these goals and capacities influence behavior. Invariably, the efforts of one person to achieve his or her goals affect the efforts of others. That is what makes this a social science—people's efforts do not take place in isolation. When it comes to selecting a sex partner, for example, if one person succeeds in attracting a partner, that person is "taken," or "spoken for," and is no longer available to anyone else. This social dimension of sexual behavior is less obvious but no less real when it comes to most other activities, from using contraception to selecting a "sexy" outfit to wear to a party.

In order to make our discussion more concrete, suppose that we are interested in explaining why people have the number of sex partners that they do. Our research shows that 71 percent of adults (aged eighteen to fifty-nine) report having only one sex partner during the previous year and that 53 percent report having only one sex partner over the previous five years. These data suggest that most people change sex partners relatively infrequently, choosing instead to remain in long-term, sexually exclusive relationships. As we stated above, we will assume that most people desire some amount of sexual stimulation and that this, together with other goals, leads them to pursue sexual relationships with one or more partners. Yet securing partners is not without cost; one must expend time, money, emotional energy, and social resources in order to meet people and negotiate a sexual relationship. Solely on the basis of this consideration, it would seem to be more cost effective to fulfill one's sexual needs by remaining in a long-term relationship than by constantly searching for new partners. One might "look around" and perhaps even fantasize about potential partners, but the costs involved in actually pursuing them relative to simply maintaining one's current relationship may be too high. Only those whose objectives explicitly include having sex with many partners (perhaps because of the excitement and uncertainty) will frequently choose to incur such costs.

In this example, an individual spends resources and engages in activities for the purpose of achieving sexual pleasure, in much the same way as an industrial firm manufactures a product in order to make a profit; both may be described as productive activities. And, like most productive activities, both can involve the creation of unintended by-products, desirable and undesirable. In the case of having sex with a partner, an unwanted pregnancy, a sexually transmitted infection or disease, a happier, more pleasant personality, and a greater ability to concentrate are examples of possible by-products.

These decisions are often made in the face of uncertainty: about detection, about the nature of the new partnership, and about the risk of disease, pregnancy, and harm. The more information one has about the outcome of a choice, the wiser will be the choice, of course, but then there is the decision about how much information to acquire before making the choice.

Like so many choices we make, choices regarding sexual behavior are often made under uncertainty. It is the case that people have different attitudes toward risk; some enjoy taking risks, while others prefer to avoid risk. One reason that couples discuss their views and their prior sexual histories is to share information about the probabilities of good and bad eventualities from having sex together. Similarly, people use contraception to avoid pregnancy and disease, travel to distant places to carry on affairs in order to avoid detection, and generally treat their decisions about sexual behavior with some degree of strategy and purpose that characterizes their choices in other domains.

While formal models of behavior often assume that risks are perceived accurately, research in psychology has shown that people do a rather poor job of estimating not only the absolute sizes but even the relative sizes of the risks that they encounter. For example, in a study of possible determinants of self-perceived risk for AIDS, Prohaska et al. (1990) found that respondents in those demographic subgroups with the highest prevalence of HIV infection (singles, males, Blacks, and Hispanics) were not more likely to perceive themselves as at risk than other respondents. The study did, however, show higher perceptions of risk among respondents with multiple partners during the past five years as well as among those who knew little or nothing about the previous sexual behavior of their partners. Finally, respondents who reported that they would be ashamed if they contracted AIDS were less likely to perceive themselves as being at risk. Although it is difficult to interpret this last finding, it suggests the possibility that people's emotional and moral reactions to the disease—factors that may have nothing to do with objective risk—may affect their subjective risk assessment.

In addition to risk management, another conceptual tool from economics that can be useful in understanding sexual behavior is that of human capital. Individuals invest in education and skills in order to achieve their objectives. This is obvious in the case of people preparing to enter or reenter the job market. However, there are also types of human capital that facilitate the pursuit of sexual objectives. One example is the skills necessary to attract potential sex partners. These might include a healthy and attractive appearance, good conversational skills, and the like. Clearly, such human capital is most valuable to those who are actively searching for a partner, so these people should be expected to invest more highly in these skills than others who are involved in long-term monogamous relationships. Since skills tend to deteriorate with disuse, people who have been out of the market for a period of time are likely to find their skills rusty on returning. Moreover, new expectations and protocols in dating may require learning the new "rules of the game."

Another type of human capital used to secure sexual activity is the skills necessary for maintaining an existing relationship. These might include the ability to satisfy one's partner physically as well as the ability to accommodate his or her personality and interests, to get along with his or her family and friends, and so forth. Such skills have been the focus of studies that seek to understand why married couples choose to remain married or to divorce. In a marriage (or in any long-term sexual relationship), each partner acquires specific skills that are beneficial in the couple's interactions. Yet these skills are valuable only as long as the couple remains together. This loss of value associated with dissolution provides incentive for couples to remain together.

Thus far, our discussion about choice theory has been oriented around an individual decision maker. However, the decisions of one person (or institution) often impinge on others through the marketplace in which people acquire the resources to achieve their goals. The key factor in determining an item's value in the market is desirability relative to scarcity. Value is determined by the competitive forces of demand (reflecting desirability) and supply (reflecting availability), while it is measured by the commodity's unit price relative to other goods.

Perhaps the most obvious example of a market in the context of sexual behavior is the market for sex partners. In most cases, this market does not involve a product being exchanged for money but consists instead of a barter exchange in which each person both seeks (i.e., demands) a sex partner and offers (i.e., supplies) himself or herself as a partner in exchange. Each prospective partner offers his or her own physical attributes, personality, skills, etc., in exchange for those of a partner of interest to him or her. This exchange is made explicit in advertisements that appear in the personals column of the newspaper, such as "SWM gd looking, seeks F undr 30 for fun/companionship."

Anyone who has participated in the market for sex partners knows that those possessing more of the traits most valued in a particular culture have more opportunities for exchange than those possessing fewer. The majority of these opportunities are likely to involve similarly or less attractive potential partners, from among whom each individual is expected to choose the "best deal" that he or she can get. If there is a disparity between the numbers of males and females on the market, those who are least desirable are likely to be left without a partner altogether. An example of this is the often talked about "marriage squeeze" in which middle-aged and older women lose out to younger women in the competition for an insufficient number of eligible men.

An important aspect of selecting a sex partner is that it involves little prior knowledge of the other's sexual competence. Like many other "products" acquired in the marketplace, one does not know all about the partner's sexual interests, capabilities, and limitations before a match is made. That, of course, is true of the car you buy or the job you accept. Consequently, one relies on reputation, on what you can tell from looking and talking, on the reliability of the broker or grocer. Buyers invest in information about the product, while sellers invest in presentation and persuasion.

In a day when one shunned sexual contact before marriage, the information that partners had about their sexual compatibility was probably far less at the time of the wedding than is the case in a day when most couples have sex with each other before they form marriage bonds. You would think that this more "intensive searching" would lead to more compatible matches and thus lower divorce rates, but that surely has not been the case in the United States over the past three decades.

In the marketplace for sex partners, there is a time of considerable searching and exploring and a time after a selection is made and a partnership formed when the searching stops or is at least greatly diminished. Interest in a new sex partner can be renewed when divorce or separation occurs, and it is during these times of more extensive searching that additional sex partners are more likely to be acquired. Over the lifetime of an individual we should expect to see certain periods of relatively extensive exploration of the sex partner marketplace and other times with little involvement in that marketplace.

When we think about the market for sex partners, despite the strangeness of the concept to some, there are many parallels to other, more familiar marketplaces. We noted above that individuals surely differ in their goals or objectives as they choose a sex partner—recreational sex, an intense companionship, a partner for raising children, for example. Not surprisingly, then, those active in the market will surely place different values on different attributes in prospective partners—some men might value companionship more than physical attractiveness, while others might value earning power or a strong sense of family loyalty in a prospective sex and marriage partner more than any other attribute.

Another aspect of markets is that they have physical dimensions. Geographic distance adds costs to matching just as much as acquiring information does. Most people search in local markets, and the partitioning of the market into the sex partners in the local community—even in the local social networks in which a person is active—reflects the costliness of searching more widely. That, like the fact that information about options is costly, is a reality in most markets.

As individuals, most of us are accustomed to thinking of sexuality in highly personal terms, consisting of our own thoughts and what we do with our partners. For this reason, our choices about which sexual activities to pursue are based on our personal assessments of the benefits and costs involved. However, the private choices that we make about sexual behaviors and attitudes can also have consequences at a collective or societal level. There can be both benefits and costs to society as a whole that are not immediately visible to the individual. Such benefits or costs are called externalities.

In the United States, an externality resulting from fertility, many would argue, is the burden on the welfare system of children whose parents are either unable or unwilling to support them financially. While many couples determine how many children they can afford to support and plan their fertility accordingly, other couples bear children they did not plan or plan children they subsequently cannot afford. Child welfare programs in effect lower the cost of raising a child to the natural or custodial parents and impose these costs on the taxpayer.

Another externality associated with sexual behavior is the possible transmission of diseases such as gonorrhea, chlamydia, and HIV. Such diseases not only threaten an individual's health but also contribute to collective costs such as the provision of subsidized medical care and research and the increased risk of being exposed to the infection as it becomes more widespread.

The choices that individuals make about sexual behavior that exposes them to the risk of unwanted pregnancy or disease are made in the context of the costs of avoiding these outcomes. Since there are negative externalities associated with these outcomes, it seems a sensible strategy to subsidize the costs of avoiding them. That is one rationale for government support of programs that distribute contraceptives and information about how to avoid pregnancy and sexually transmitted disease or infection.

Note how a brief discussion of externalities can quickly become a discussion of government policy or an advocacy of collective action. Choice theory promotes discussion of this nature since it facilitates an articulation of the relation between private choices and public repercussions between individual and collective action.

Network Theory: The Sexual Dyad

So far, we have said little about how the sexual partnership (or dyad) is theoretically significant. Both scripting and choice theories focus on what individuals do, explaining it on the basis of the experiences, circumstances, and decisions of those individuals. However, sexual activity is fundamentally social in that it involves two or more persons either explicitly or implicitly (as in the case of sexual fantasy and masturbation). This simple fact has three important implications. First, since sexual partnerships are a special case of social relationships we may expect these partnerships to conform to certain regularities that have been observed regarding social relationships more generally. This provides a theoretical framework within which to study the dynamics of sexual parnerships— who becomes partners with whom, how these partnerships are maintained, and why some of them eventually dissolve. Second, since sexual activity is negotiated within the context of a social relationship,

the features of the relationship itself become important in determining what activities will occur. This may seem obvious at first; however, such thinking represents a subtle major departure from previous research on sexuality (Sprecher and McKinney 1993). Finally, sexual dyads do not exist in a vacuum but are instead embedded within larger networks of social relationships. Thus, individual dyads are affected by the social networks surrounding them, and this in turn influences the sexual activity of their members. We now turn to a more detailed discussion of each of these implications.

One of the most persistent empirical regularities that has been observed among social relationships is the tendency toward equal status contact, meaning that people tend to initiate and maintain relationships with others who have the same or similar social characteristics as they themselves do. This general pattern of same-status contact has been observed in studies of friendship (Laumann 1966, 1973; Hallinan and Williams 1989), professional relationships (Heinz and Laumann 1982), and relationships among discussion partners (Marsden 1988). Specifically, these studies have shown that such relationships are more likely to exist among persons of the same gender, age, race, education, and religion. Several factors account for these findings, including the fact that our society is geographically and socially segregated in ways that greatly reduce an individual's opportunities to interact with people unlike himself or herself. In addition, some authors have suggested that people prefer to interact with similar others in order to reinforce their own self-identity, to validate their own behaviors and attitudes and, most obviously, because they are more likely to share common interests with such people. Finally, a person's family, friends, and other associates maintain control over the kinds of people with whom that person forms relationships, often decreasing the likelihood that he or she will interact with dissimilar others.

For similar reasons, we also expect sexual relationships to occur more frequently between people with the same or similar characteristics. Research on similarity among married couples seems to confirm this general hypothesis, identifying large amounts of both educational (Mare 1991) and religious (Kalmijn 1991) homogamy (in other words, marriage partners share similar characteristics). More recently, the same has also been found among cohabiting couples (Schoen and Weinick 1993).

Just as the nature of asymmetries has changed over time, we also expect them to differ across different types of sexual relationships. More specifically, we expect the patterns of racial, age, educational, and religious similarity that have been observed in marital relationships to be different in noncohabitational sexual partnerships. An individual interested in pursuing an extramarital relationship, for example, might intentionally locate a socially dissimilar person in order to minimize the possibility of being discovered by his or her spouse, family, and friends.

In sum, sexual relationships differ markedly from other types of relationships with respect to the types of exchanges that occur within them, and these differences lead to different predictions about the occurrence of sexual relationships between persons with different social characteristics. Moreover, we expect the pattern of sex partner choice to differ across the different types of sexual relationships.

The social composition of sexual relationships also affects the type of behavior that occurs within them. These effects are distinct from those that are due to the individual characteristics of the partners; hence, they can be examined only by studying the dyad as whole. For example, we show that oral sex is a largely reciprocated activity, which implies that it is more likely to occur in those relationships where both parties are willing to perform the act.

In addition, other characteristics of respondents' sexual partnerships are likely to affect whether they engage in oral sex. Thus, while more educated people are more likely to have oral sex, it may also be the case that there is something about the types of sexual relationships that these more highly educated respondents have that increases the likelihood that oral sex will occur within them.

There are several elements of sexual relationships that might plausibly affect which sexual behaviors occur within them. We have already identified one of these as being related to the characteristics of the partners involved. This is the nature of the exchange between the two partners. Relationships that, in addition to sexual interaction, involve the exchange of items, such as economic resources, companionship, and other types of support, may place certain constraints on the types of sexual services that one partner can (or is willing to) extract from the other. For example, if a woman perceives that she is getting more from her partner than she is giving, she may feel obligated to correct this imbalance by performing sexual activities that her partner enjoys. Similarly, if a man perceives himself to be dependent on his partner, he might be willing to forgo his own sexual interests in order to please his partner (Emerson 1981). Conversely, people who perceive themselves as giving more than they receive or as being less dependent on their relationships than their partners might be more likely to ask their partners to perform certain activities or refuse to comply with their partner's wishes.

The exchanges that occur within a relationship are not the only features of that relationship that can affect sexual behavior. Another important feature is the way in which the relationship is socially defined and perceived by the participants. Some common examples of socially defined sexual relationships are "high school sweethearts," "lovers," "boyfriend and girlfriend," "husband and wife," and "one-night stand." Clearly, these may be interpreted differently by different people, and it is also possible that culturally distinct subgroups use a different set of definitions. Consequently, we learn and make decisions about what is and is not appropriate sexual behavior within the context of a specific type of relationship, rather than solely in terms of the individual performing the behavior. Thus, some men force their wives to have sex with them because they believe that, within marriage, a husband is owed sex by his wife whenever and however he wants it, even though the same man might consider the exact same behavior directed toward a stranger or even a girlfriend to be rape.

Both scripting and choice theories combine with a network approach to generate more comprehensive explanations of sexual conduct. Although the network approach emphasizes the properties of relationships rather than persons, it cannot by itself be used to explain what goes on within a specific relationship. This requires an understanding of what motivates the individuals in that relationship, such as that provided by scripting and choice theory. Understandings about what is appropriate within the context of a specific relationship are nothing other than scripts—scripts that are specific not only to the persons involved but also to the relationship between those two people. Similarly, exchanges between partners result from the strategically motivated interests of both partners, implying that, if a relationship costs a partner more than it benefits him or her, he or she will withdraw from the exchange. Nevertheless, regardless of people's cultural understandings and their motivations, sexual activity can occur only when two people come together in a relationship. The fundamental contribution of the network approach is in showing how the social networks in which people are embedded affect whether two people will get together to form a sexual relationship and, if they do, which cultural understandings and economic motivations they will bring to that relationship.

Sexual scripts are learned through interaction with others, and this interaction is clearly shaped by the networks in which we are embedded. Most research on this subject has focused on the sexual behavior of adolescents and has generally found that sexually active adolescents tend to have friends who are also sexually active (Billy, Rodgers, and Udry 1984), although it is unclear which causes which. Similarly, the legitimacy of oral sex in youthful sexual relationships is dependent on gendered

support networks that supply different legitimations for these forms of conduct to both male and female adolescents (Gagnon and Simon 1987). Another less common but still convincing illustration of the role of networks is provided by reports among young boys of "circle jerks," an activity in which a group will masturbate to orgasm, often in some competitive fashion (to see who will ejaculate the soonest, who has the largest penis, or how far the semen travels on ejaculation).

We also expect social networks to be important in determining the sexual behavior of adults. To understand these influences, we must specify the interests that third parties have in the occurrence (or nonoccurrence) of certain activities within specific types of partnerships. By third parties we mean people connected to either or both members of a focal sexual dyad by one or more types of social relationship. Thus, parents have interests in the sexual experiences of their children, such as wanting them to refrain from sexual activity until they are "ready," wanting them not to date people whom they consider to be "poor" influences, etc. Similarly, children of divorced parents also have interests in the sexual relationships of their parents since these can claim part of the parent's attention and lead to remarriage. Third-party interests are not limited to relatives; friends too can be interested in each other's happiness in a relationship and be wary of the threat that that relationship might pose for the stability of the friendship.

Probably the best organized of all groups that have an interest in sexuality are stakeholders in reproductive activity. They range from individual parents to large-scale organizations such as Planned Parenthood that supply services, participate in political lobbying, and seek private and government resources and support for their programs. Control of reproduction involves the control of sexual activity, necessarily a complicated relationship. Morally conservative stakeholders attempt to control both sexuality and reproduction through moral instruction, policing the content of school curriculum and of the media, limiting information about contraception and the availability of contraceptive devices, limiting the access of the potentially sexually active to services for the prevention of sexually transmitted infection and disease (including HIV), and so forth. In contrast, liberal stakeholders seek to provide most of these services while remaining (somewhat) indifferent to the sexual expressions of consenting adults over the age of sixteen.

Other highly organized and politically active stakeholders are those who seek either to facilitate or to limit the acceptance of same-gender sexual relationships and the legal provision of the same rights and privileges for these couples as are enjoyed by heterosexual couples (e.g., allowing them to raise children, to show affection in public, etc.). Friends, relatives, and even parents often admonish or outright reject gay individuals because they do not know how to behave or are uncomfortable around them and, more important, because they are forced to justify or deny the individual's behavior in front of their own friends and associates. In fact, intolerance of homosexuality is so ubiquitous in this country that many homosexuals are forced either to conceal their sexual preference or to move to one of the few social environments where being gay is accepted.

An example of a less organized but still powerful third-party interest is that in maintaining exclusivity in established sexual partnerships, especially marriages. Part of this interest stems from the belief that extramarital sex is morally wrong, a belief that is almost universally accepted (roughly 90 percent of adults believe that extramarital sex is either "always wrong" or "almost always wrong"). In keeping with this attitude, our data suggest that the annual incidence of extramarital sexual activity is modest. Although we do not deny the fact that one's own moral and religious beliefs strongly influence the decision to limit oneself to a single partner at a time, we do argue that these beliefs are legitimated and reinforced through interaction with others who share such beliefs and who have concrete interests in the couple's sexual exclusivity. For example, in their attempts to

support one spouse, the relatives and friends of that person are likely to regard any extramarital activity on the part of the other spouse as unjustifiable.

To acknowledge the potential for extramarital activity, even if only by discussing it with a friend, risks both personal temptation and the possibility of being labeled by others as a potential "cheater." This fact increases people's reluctance to address the topic in conversation, thus decreasing the possibility of locating potential partners or social approval for the behavior.

Opportunities to pursue extramarital sexual activity are also limited by the very large proportion of individuals in the society who are already in relationships. Especially after age thirty, the number of uncoupled individuals is small. This is exacerbated by the fact that marriage accustoms a couple to the conversations and activities of the other married couples to whom they usually restrict their associations. Presumably, some fraction of these married individuals might be willing to engage in extramarital sex; however, this number is almost certainly quite small and, more important, very difficult to identify for the reasons discussed above.

Sexual activity is not unique in being motivated and constrained by the interests of third parties. However, unlike other spheres of activity, sexual activity almost always occurs in private and is usually talked about in highly routine and nonrevealing ways. This fact makes the surveillance of the sexual dyad by outsiders remarkably difficult—third parties are privy only to the testimony of the individuals themselves about what happened. This has both positive and negative social consequences—sexual encounters may be conducted entirely by trial and error and independently of regulation, leading to sexual experimentation, or they may be occasions on which the participants deliberately or ignorantly exploit or violate each other.

Interrelations Among the Theories

As we have indicated, each of these three theories is intended to answer different types of questions about sexual activity. However, since these questions are interrelated, so are the theories used to explain them. In most cases, these interrelations take the form of consistent or complementary predictions by the different theories. For example, we have already shown how both scripting and choice theories may be used to explain what occurs within specific relationships identified by the network approach. Occasionally, however, there are inconsistencies in what the theoretical approaches would predict and no clear way of reconciling these differences on the basis of theoretical arguments alone.

The sharpest inconsistency among the three approaches is between scripting and choice theories. As we have already noted, a fundamental assumption in choice theory is that individuals act strategically or rationally in the pursuit of goals. In contrast, scripting theory suggests that individuals model their actions on the basis of a predetermined (although somewhat flexible) set of cultural scenarios. Given the small number of scenarios relative to the number of different circumstances that people encounter, it is likely that certain people will be unable to locate a scenario that represents what would be considered "rational behavior" in their particular case. In such instances, the predictions of the two theories would conflict. Yet there is a more fundamental difference between scripting and choice theories than the existence of discrepant predictions. The two theories assume very different mechanisms underlying people's behavior. Choice theory assumes that individuals are constantly evaluating their situations and making choices, whereas scripting theory assumes that individuals are constrained by a script that they learned from those around them.

At this point, the reader might be wondering how these general theoretical approaches can be used to inform and interpret analyses of the actual data collected in this study. After all, using a survey instrument limits the researcher to asking only those questions that are easy to understand and to answer. Thus, for example, we were unable to measure sex scripts directly since doing so would require a complicated series of questions about numerous specific activities and the order in which they occurred. More important, the fact that ours was a national survey prohibited us from tailoring certain questions to particular locations or subpopulations. This meant that much fine-grained cultural (and, to some extent, regional) variation in these scripts was beyond our grasp. Similarly, our ability to measure people's networks was also quite limited; we could not ask them about specific places or events where they socialized, nor could we ask them about their relationships with specific persons other than their sex partners. For example, it would be very useful to know something about the larger network structures in which respondents are embedded since these structures certainly affect the structure of their sexual networks. Since such structures are unique to particular locations, however, they are beyond the scope of this type of study. Finally, the methods used to study rational decision making also require an intensive set of questions (such as those designed to determine an individual's preference ordering) targeted to a specific situation. These limitations are important ones, forcing us to relegate focused examinations of specific issues to future projects. However, a national study such as this one is a necessary precursor to more specialized work.

References

Billy, John O. G., Joseph Lee Rodgers, and J. Richard Udry. 1984. Adolescent sexual behavior and friendship choice. *Social Forces*, 62:653–78.

Billy, John O. G., Koray Tanfer, William R. Grady, and Daniel H. Klepenger. 1993. The sexual behavior of men in the United States. *Family Planning Perspectives* 25, no. 2:52–60.

Blumstein, Philip, and Pepper Schwartz. 1983. *American Couples*. New York: Morrow.

Brookman, Richard R. 1990. Adolescent sexual behavior. In *Sexually Transmitted Diseases*, eds. King K. Holmes et al. New York: McGraw-Hill.

Castillo, C. O., and J. H. Geer. 1993. Ambiguous stimuli: Sex in the eye of the beholder. *Archives of Sexual Behavior* 22:131–43.

Centers for Disease Control (CDC). 1992. *STD/HIV Prevention 1991 Annual Report*. Atlanta.

DeLamater, John. 1981. The social control of sexuality. *Annual Review of Sociology* 7:263–90.

DeLamater, John, and Patricia MacCorquodale. 1979. *Premarital Sexuality: Attitudes, Relationships, Behavior*. Madison: University of Wisconsin.

Emerson, Richard M. 1981. Social exchange theory. In *Social Psychology: Sociological Perspective*, eds. M. Rosenberg and R. H. Turner. New York: Basic Books.

Gagnon, John H. 1991. The implicit and explicit use of scripts in sex research. In *The Annual Review of Sex Research*, ed. John Bancroft, Clive Davis, and Deborah Weinstein. Mt. Vernon, Iowa: Society for the Scientific Study of Sex.

Gagnon, John H., and William Simon. 1987. The scripting of oral-genital sexual conduct. *Archives of Sexual Behavior* 16, no. 1:1–25.

Geer, J. H., and D. B. Brussard. 1990. Scaling sex behavior and arousal: Consistency and sex differences. *Journal of Personality and Social Psychology* 58:644–71.

Hallinan, Maureen T., and Richard A. Williams. 1989. Interracial freindship choices in secondary schools. *American Sociological Review* 54:67–78.

Heinz, John P., and Edward O. Laumann. 1982. *Chicago Lawyers: The Social Structure of the Bar*. Chicago: Russell Sage Foundation and American Bar Foundation.

Kalick, S. Michael, and Thomas E. Hamilton III. 1986. The matching hypothesis reexamined. *Journal of Personality and Social Psychology* 51, no. 4:673–82.

Kalmijn, Matthijs. 1991. Shifting boundaries: Trends in religious and educational homogany. *American Sociological Review* 57:706–800.

Klassen, A. D., C. J. Williams, and E. E. Levitt. 1989. In *Sex and Morality in the U.S.*, ed. H. J. O'Gorman. Middletown, Conn.: Wesleyan University Press.

Laumann, Edward O. 1966. *Prestige and Association in an Urban Community*. New York: Bobbs-Merrill.

——. 1973. *Bonds of Pluralism: The Form and Substance of Urban Social Networks*. New York: Wiley.

Mare, Robert D. 1991. Five decades of educational assortative mating. *American Sociological Review* 56:15–32.

Marsden, Peter V. 1988. Homogeneity in confiding relations. *Social Networks* 10:57–76.

Mosher, William D., and James W. McNally. 1991. Contraceptive use at first premarital intercourse: United States, 1965–1988. *Family Planning Perspectives* 23, no. 3:108–16.

Peterson, John L., Joseph A. Catania, M. Margaret Dolcini, and Bonnie Faigeles. 1993. Multiple sexual partners among blacks in high risk cities. *Family Planning Perspectives* 25:263–67.

Prohaska, Thomas R., Gay Albrecht, Judith A. Levy, Noreen Sugrue, and Joung-Hwa Kim. 1990. Determinants of self-perceived risk for AIDS. *Journal of Health and Social Behavior* 31:384–94.

Reiss, Ira L. 1990. *An End to Shame: Shaping Our Next Sexual Revolution*. New York: Prometheus Books.

Schoen, Robert, and Robin M. Weinick. 1993. Partner choice in marriages and cohabitations. *Journal of Marriage and Family* 55:408–14.

Sonenstein, F. L., J. H. Pleck, and L. C. Ku. 1991. Levels of sexual activity among adolescent males in the United States. *Family Planning Perspectives* 23, no. 4:162–67.

Sprecher, Susan, and Kathleen McKinney. 1993. *Sexuality*. London: Sage Publications.

Tanfer, Koray. 1992. Coital frequency among single women: Normative constraints and situational opportunities. *Journal of Sex Research* 29:221–50.

Weinberg, Martin S., and Colin J. Williams. 1980. Sexual embourgeoisment? Social class and sexual activity: 1938–1970. *American Sociological Review* 45, no. 1:33–48.

Zelnick, Melvin, and John F. Kantner. 1972. Sexuality, contraception, and pregnancy among young unwed females in the U.S. In *Demographic and Social Aspects of Population Growth*, eds. Charles F. Westoff and R. Parke. Washington, D.C.: U.S. Government Printing Office.

——. 1980. Sexual activity, contraceptive use and pregnancy among metropolitan-area teenagers: 1971–1979. *Family Planning Perspectives* 12:230–37.

Chapter 6
Sex Among the Americans

Joseph Adelson

Juxtaposing the sexually inhibited and the sexually liberated, Joseph Adelson mines the fields of facts generated by the research of Laumann et al. with a 1990s survey that shocked Americans. The cover of Time (October 17, 1994) announced the news: "Sex in America: Surprising News From the Most Important Survey Since the Kinsey Report!" As the news hit the airwaves and the press, Americans were surprised to learn that the hotbed of sex in the '90s was the marriage bed.

Although media "sexperts," such as Cosmopolitan *editor Helen Gurley Brown; Hugh Hefner, founder of* Playboy; *and Bob Guccione, publisher of* Penthouse, *were uttering words like "outrageous," "stupid," "ridiculous," and "come on now," Europeans seemed less surprised by the findings. They were, in fact, parallel with studies in England and France that also had found low rates of homosexuality and high rates of marital fidelity.*

Critics abounded! They decried the absence of women among the study's directors, asking if this could have skewed the questions. Doubts were also raised about whether personal interviews could elicit truly candid answers to intimate questions, for example, about masturbation, or whether the sample was too small to generalize about some groups, like homosexuals. Adelson himself is less than ebullient about some of the interpretations, given the findings by the researchers and the choice of the theories used as a framework for the study. He does, however, praise its technical competence and its findings, which "carry us beyond, and largely discredit, the data of earlier studies." Among those who praised the survey, Ira Reiss, sexuality scholar from the University of Minnesota, de-

clared that of the major sex surveys to date, the Laumann et al. study was probably the best thought out and had the broadest coverage.

As readers today take a retrospective look at the findings that Adelson presents from the Laumann et al. survey, they can add their own cacophony of beliefs and disbeliefs. After all, their ideas will be no less reflective of their own experiential findings than were those of Brown, Hefner, and Guccione.

I teach a seminar for first-year undergraduates on the troubles of adolescence. During a discussion of teenage illegitimacy not too long ago, I mentioned in passing a surprising datum I had just come across: the average American woman, during her lifetime, has two sex partners. The reaction in my classroom was electric—amazement, disbelief. That can't be! It's more than that! They must be lying!

These are youngsters, mind, who can absorb the most horrendous social statistics—that the killing of adolescents has increased fourfold in the last decade, that two-thirds of all black children are born out of wedlock—without batting an eye. They may or may not find such data troubling (it is often hard to tell), but they do not find them shocking. What shocked them was the *not*-shocking—news of modesty, decorum, restraint.

After class, a young man came up to me who wanted to know the data for homosexuality in the source I had referred to. Well, I replied, if self-definition is the criterion, the figures are a bit under 3 percent for males, and between 1 and 2 percent for females. He was furious. I know that literature in detail, he told me. We're studying it in philosophy (!) class; those numbers are not only false but probably falsified, and I'm sure they're being circulated to discourage the gay community, which in fact is growing by leaps and bounds.

Later in the week, thinking these inflamed responses might reflect the passions of youth, I asked several friends and colleagues—each and every one of them (it goes without saying) wise and worldly-wise—to estimate the number of partners American women have over a lifetime. Their guesses ranged from a low of six to a high of twenty. When apprised of the figure I had come across, they, too, reacted with disbelief, in some cases mixed with heavy sarcasm about the pretensions of survey research and what one of them termed "social so-called science."

Where, then, did I get the numbers I had so innocently broadcast? From a recent sociological study, *Sex in America: A Definitive Survey*,[1] published in both a popular and scholarly edition, the latter under the appropriately academic title, *The Social Organization of Sexuality*.[2] This, the publishers tell us, is the "only comprehensive and methodologically sound survey of America's sexual practices and beliefs."

They were drawn to it, they tell us, by dissatisfaction with prior studies of American sexual behavior. At their best, earlier surveys like the famous one done by Alfred Kinsey and his associates in 1948 were well-intentioned but flawed, the most common problem being a reliance on catch-as-catch-can methods of recruiting interviewees. These studies also lacked any means for checking the truthfulness of the responses given, and the worst of them, like the egregious *Hite Report* on female sexuality of 1976, solicited responses from selected and sometimes highly politicized groups. In the case of the *Hite Report* that meant that the data were drawn from members of the National Organization for Women, abortion-rights advocates, and the like; even so, *Hite* managed but a 3-percent response rate, making it certain that the respondents bore little likeness to American women in general.

The authors of *Sex in America* set out to do things right by sampling accurately our adult population (aged 18–60); preparing a carefully pre-tested questionnaire; training their interviewers rigorously; and introducing several methods of checking the veracity of the responses obtained. One may have some serious reservations, as I do, about what went into the questionnaire as well as what was left out, and about the in-

terpretations offered; but the sampling itself is state-of-the-art, and the authors are right to be pleased with themselves. Carrying out a national survey of this scope is extremely expensive ($450 per interview) and requires great technical expertise and a high level of patience and compulsiveness.

As a culture—and my students beautifully represent that culture—we have come to believe that the degree of individual sexual pleasure can be placed on a linear chart extending from "inhibited" at one end to "liberated" at the other. The sexually free are unattached and unencumbered. They have been everywhere and done everything, and are ready for more—more positions, more variations, more partners, more often. At the other extreme are those who have sex only within marriage and then only infrequently, who employ the missionary position, perform the act rapidly, and achieve shallow orgasms or none at all.

Though we might not say so openly, many of us also tend to believe that blacks are more active sexually than whites, and that those belonging to conservative religious denominations are bound to be more inhibited than those without any religious affiliation. And we may also believe that, sooner or later, sex with the same person becomes too familiar and boring, leading us to seek adventure elsewhere. After all, a cardinal rule in matters sexual is that we are drawn to those unlike us, to what is alien or taboo: opposites attract.

What the research gathered in *Sex in America* tells us is that none of the above is true. In fact, American sexuality is marked by moderation and fidelity. Husbands and wives are faithful to each other, and so are those living together though unmarried. Even the unattached rarely wander, and are certainly not promiscuous. As I had accurately reported to my students, one-half of all Americans of both sexes have three or fewer partners in a lifetime; as one might expect, men are more active sexually, but not by a wide margin. (And lest one protest that all this is the baleful legacy of American Puritanism, parallel studies throughout the Western world, in countries Catholic as well as Protestant, yield essentially the same findings.)

American sexual practices are, similarly, conventional. Vaginal intercourse is by far the most appealing mode, almost universally judged exciting and pleasurable. It is followed, at a distance, by the mild voyeurism of "watching partners undress," and then by oral sex. All other sexual practices—group sex, anal sex in its several variations, sadomasochism, the use of sexual toys and devices, homosexuality, sex with strangers, watching strangers have sex—all these are deemed unappealing, in most cases very unappealing, and by all segments of the population, men and women, young and old.

Sex in America (as I told my young student of philosophy) comes up with a dramatically lower figure for homosexual identity and practice. Until quite recently, the standard number was 10 percent, and when cited it was often preceded by the phrase "at least," suggesting that the true figure was higher and was being suppressed either by caution or by shame. Many psychologists and psychiatrists had their doubts about this, believing the true figure to be 5 to 6 percent for men, and half that for women; but for the most part these doubts went unvoiced. We now learn that even the reduced number was too high. Fewer than 3 percent of men identify themselves as homosexual; more inclusive criteria give us no more than 5 percent. Lesbianism is about half as common. European studies provide similar data.

Among the most interesting findings in *Sex in America* are what one might call the absent findings: in particular, the absence of expected variations associated with race, ethnicity, education, religion, and the like. Both the popular and the scholarly editions of this study are glutted with charts and tables illustrating these modest or nonexistent differences. How frequently do men achieve orgasm with their "primary partners"? About three-quarters of men say "always," no matter what their age, marital status, education, or race. Between a quarter to a third of women say the same, again regardless of age, marital status, education,

or race. "How many times do you have sex each month?" Again, little variation: almost always six to seven times a month, for men and women, well-educated or not, of all religious affiliations; the only blip is that those over fifty report a slightly lower rate (four or five times monthly).

To whom do we become attached? Here we come to a central emphasis of this study: we become dear to those who are near, that is, those who are like us and whom we come to know in the daily routines and venues of our lives. Sexual behavior, the authors tell us time and again, is shaped by the social networks we occupy. We choose (and are chosen by) those within our network, those like us in almost all respects—race, religion, education, class. We rarely venture out of these boundaries, and should we try to, those within them signal their disapproval.

If you enjoy wallowing in numbers, the tables in *Sex in America* provide what seem to be small surprises now and again. For example: more conservative Protestant women report always having orgasms than do women of any other religion. Really? Yes, really; but also not really—they do outpace others in the "always" category, but that aside, there are no other important differences by religion. Nor do the occasional variations by race and education add up to a consistent pattern. Blacks, for example, are high on a few measures, but average or low on others.

Still, that figure about conservative Protestant women and their orgasms does point to what is the real bombshell in this study. Not only does it turn out that, in the war between the prudes and the libertines, Americans in general have continued to hold fast on the side of the prudes. It also turns out—horror!—that the prudes are having much more fun.

This study, in fact, is a paean to sexual bonding, to marriage or its near-equivalents. Intimate, exclusive relationships between spouses or committed partners provide, by far, the greatest degree of sexual gratification. More: in a finding that turns the standard scenario of pornography on its head, these books reveal that those without committed partners are far less likely to engage in casual sex during a given period than to do without sex altogether. Twenty-three percent of unattached men report having had no sex, as opposed to less than 1 percent of those married or living with someone; among women, the figures are 32 percent compared to 2 percent. At the other extreme, attached men and women are twice as likely as unattached to have sex two or more times a week. In the pleasure sweepstakes, monogamy counts.

And we are not done. Perhaps the most astonishing single datum reported in these books has to do with those conducting extramarital affairs: they report that they are more gratified sexually by their spouses than by their lovers. To add insult to injury, they also have sex less often than those faithfully married. Among the unmarried, those who have at least two sexual partners are less pleased with their sex lives, emotionally and physically, than those married or living together. For women in particular, a close attachment is essentially a necessity for a gratifying sex life.

Let me sum up, in the authors' own words, the key findings of this research. Whether you count by "adult lifetime or in the past year," nearly all Americans have "a very modest number of partners." This number "varies little with education, race, or religion." Rather, it is determined by marital status or by whether a couple is living together. Once married, people tend to have one and only one partner, and those who are married and living together are almost as likely to be faithful. Sexual practices, moreover, are highly conventional. Only vaginal intercourse is universally attractive, while almost all the *outre* variations are disliked. Finally, when it comes to sexual pleasure, liberation carries a palpable cost, fidelity its own very great reward.

Which leads to a question: if all this is essentially correct, why are my students and my friends and all the rest of us so mistaken? Why do we think of ourselves as a society which has happily (or, for those scandalized by it, sinfully) thrown off most of the constraints of the past, a society in which more and more of us are sexually adventurous both before and during marriage, and are willing and even eager to try out exotic sexual combinations and practices?

Well, for one thing we believe what "empirical science" has taught us to believe. The Kinsey data, initially so shocking, were rather quickly absorbed into the conventional wisdom. The 10-percent "datum" for homosexuality, for example, had its origins in the Kinsey findings. That statistic and others like it were not superseded by more accurate ones, in large part because subsequent studies made the same sorts of sampling error. Kinseyesque findings were thus presumably confirmed and became accepted even by those distressed by what they implied morally. In this connection, it is ironically pertinent that the research in *Sex in America* failed to win federal support because of the opposition of conservative legislators who expected that it would show a high level of deviant behavior.

This in itself tells us that sexual information is not ideologically neutral. Sexuality is important terrain in the cultural wars that divide us, and what we believe to be true about it is conditioned by a larger set of assumptions and expectations about human nature and the social order. In particular, when we read about sex, or see it portrayed in films or on television, we do not see its mundane, quotidian side; we see persons taking dangerous risks to achieve pleasure, or struggling to realize their true selves by means of erotic liberation.

Robert Lichter of the Media Research Center reports that seven out of eight sexual encounters in television dramas involve extramarital relations. No surprise there—the illicit is all but a *sine qua non* of the dramatic. Yet this same partiality is found throughout the public culture. As I write, my local newspaper—small-city, staid, sober in most respects—has helpfully brought us a report of a bright new development in erotic practice called playful sadomasochism, wherein the gestures and rituals of the real thing are mimicked without serious pain being inflicted. My favorite national newspaper, the *Wall Street Journal*, recently ran a front-page story on another bright new trend, this one among women: serial bisexuality, or going back and forth between male and female partners. These accounts have in common the tone and feel of fashion reporting, complete with the tacit assurance to the shy that, however odd it may appear at the moment, this is indeed the coming style.

Missing in all these savvy, wide-eyed reports is any sense of the everyday torments free-lance sexuality imposes on ordinary and (as we glean from *Sex in America*) even not-so-ordinary people. Will he (she) like it? Will she (he) have an orgasm? Is my body attractive? Do I smell badly? Can I keep going long enough? Will he (she) *really* like it? Am I better than he (she) has had before? Am I being too rough? Not rough enough? Too responsive? Not responsive enough? And on, and on. Not everyone is quite so anxious, but as any psychotherapist can testify, a great many are.

Nor does one need therapeutic testimony to confirm the part played in sexual life by self-doubt, shame, and narcissistic injury. Simply visit any good bookstore to find a substantial array of titles offering advice, instruction, encouragement, and spiritual uplift designed to calm your fears, assuage your guilt, overcome your embarrassment, and protect you against humiliation, thus making the sexual act enjoyable, or in some cases simply possible. Media sex, with its incessant stress on triumph and variety, is blind to this side of sexual feeling; one might say it represents a manic defense against it, if not a denial of its existence.

And this leads us to yet another answer to the question of why we were all so mistaken. Those who construct the public image of sexuality in our country—journalists, dramatists, pundits, professors, etc.—occupy quite a special sociological niche within the population at large, and their constructions to a greater or lesser degree tend to mirror their own attitudes and practices. Significantly, only a quarter of the overall survey sample in *Sex in America*—those whom the authors term "recreationals"—see sex in terms of pleasure alone, removed from obligation, devotion,

or moral concern, and these same "recreationals" are four to five times more likely to have committed adultery, and two to three times more likely to have engaged in deviant sex. We learn from the sociological charts provided by the authors that—surprise—these same "recreationals" tend to be without religious affiliation. In which academic and professional precincts they live, and what they do for a living, it is not hard to guess.

As opposed to the "recreationals," a substantial majority of those surveyed in *Sex in America* report that they are guided in their sexual practices by their religious beliefs, or link sex to marriage or a loving attachment. Here we begin to see most clearly how differences in moral outlook play out in behavior. And here, too, we edge close to the realm of values. This is a realm which our authors, for their part, sedulously strive to avoid.

They, after all, are sociologists (with the exception of Gina Kolata, a science journalist), and they bring to their enterprise a fierce belief in the heuristic powers of their discipline. Thus, they inform us quite solemnly that they have employed the "advanced and sophisticated methods of social-science research," the same ones that have worked so well in the study of such topics as "labor-force participation . . . or migration behavior." In analyzing their findings, they rely almost entirely on two quintessentially social-scientific concepts: social networks and the (sexual) marketplace.

They seem unable, however, to grasp how little these concepts explain. In a long discussion of racial barriers, for instance, the authors succeed in demonstrating that only rarely do American blacks and whites become sexual or marital partners. They cite this finding to support their emphasis on the general explanatory power of social networks as cementers of sexual bonds. But whatever the figures may be for whites and blacks, marriages between whites and Asian-Americans have now become commonplace. If race is so important, how did that happen, and why?

Nor do we hear anything from the authors about the Jews, whose rates of intermarriage are now high enough to threaten the group's survival. When I was a boy, one did not marry outside the faith because doing so would mortify one's family. Needless to say, that pattern changed, and rather quickly. Why? Is religion a less powerful barrier than race? Is family less powerful than class or peer group?

In illustrating the efficacy of social networks, the authors provide a fairly long discussion of how the sexes were kept apart on campuses during the 1950's and early 1960's, when colleges acted *in loco parentis* as guardians of sexual boundaries. Then, in the late 60's, they tell us, due to the pressures of the youth movement, these rules disappeared "virtually overnight," and the era of sexual liberation was unloosed. But no matter what was, or was not, happening in the dormitories between one moment and the next, the same tired notion of a social network is brought in to explain it. How can this be? A social network that stops on a dime, completely reverses direction, and still performs the same function, has no value as an explanatory concept. It is simply a piece of jargon.

Consider, finally, the concept of the sexual marketplace, which the authors invoke to explain how people choose mates. Each person in a pair—so the reasoning goes—trades his or her assets to make the most advantageous match available. Among the examples given are those of Ross Perot and Henry Kissinger, both of whom, the second time around, found women younger and more attractive than themselves, trading money and power for youth and beauty. The authors believe that all such calculations are unconscious; "certainly most people are not consciously aware" of them.

To the contrary, most of us are very much aware of them, and some of us can think of nothing else. My Aunt Sadie's truisms on marriage were largely devoted to such observations: "He didn't marry her for her looks, but her father has a nice business." Come to think of it, so are the truisms of Aunt Jane Austen, Uncle Anthony Trollope, and most of the other greats and not-so-greats who have written about what goes into the formation of domestic arrangements.

The concepts of "network" and "marketplace," in other words, allow us to fashion explanations after the fact—*post hoc ergo propter hoc*. They are a capacious umbrella under which we can place everything we already know—but little else. Why are a given network's boundaries sometimes permeable and sometimes not? How does a group's history influence its members? Which networks evolve in expectable directions, and which do not, and why? These questions are never asked by our authors because they cannot be answered with the equipment they have assembled.

Even more troubling is the avoidance of any consideration of the inner world—the world of motives and character—which influences sexual and mental behavior. Some of the findings simply cry out for the insights of sociobiology, a discipline mentioned briefly only to be firmly dismissed. And when it comes to the psychological sources of behavior, the authors are singularly myopic.

A small but revealing example can be found in the index; for the category "shame," the entry reads, "see guilt." But guilt and shame are very different emotions, different not only subjectively but also in origin and effect. Another small example: general happiness, the authors discover, is correlated with a good sex life—but which comes first? Amazingly, they confess to not having a clue.

The most revealing instance of such myopia concerns the treatment of forced sex. The authors find that about one-fifth of women report having been coerced sexually at some time. The coercers are not, as one might assume, strangers or casual pickups; most of them are husbands or loved ones. And it is usually not clear just what the coercion consists of, though it seems not to be physical assault or rape. Now, these same women also report having many problems in sexual response—pains, difficulty in lubricating, lack of pleasure. It would appear they are inhibited about sex, and would prefer to avoid it. But then we also learn that they have many more sexual partners, and engage in more deviant activities. Finally, sex aside, they are unhappy in general.

What does it all mean? The authors dance around, unable to venture a coherent explanation. It is a case of political correctness—a fear of blaming the victim—joined to a *deformation professionelle*, the limitations produced by vocational bias: in this case, an aversion to psychological inferences. They cannot, in short, bring themselves to state the obvious: these are troubled women whose troubles are almost certainly rooted in personality. Here, as elsewhere throughout their study, the authors have built a conceptual cage and locked themselves in.

But I do not want to end on a wholly critical note. Many of the reviews of this study have been negative, at times scathingly so, the burden of complaint being close to that voiced by my first-year undergraduates—that you cannot trust what people tell you in an interview on sex; that the researchers are self-deceived to think otherwise; that we need some objective, independent measures of the truth, otherwise we are at the mercy of those who lie, or fudge, or misremember, or leave things out.

Most psychological research, Freud's included, depends on self-reporting to some degree. It can rarely do independent checks on veracity, and hence it cannot fully guarantee the probity of its findings. This is an old problem—and those who do survey research are, most of them, especially aware of it. They do what can be done, practically speaking, and present their data honestly and modestly. What other choices do we have? Do we declare some topics off-limits to research? If so, we will soon enough substitute our own experience, writ large, or our own imaginings, or our stern beliefs about what ought to be.

That is just what we have done to sexuality—as this study, despite its flaws, allows us to see. Its strength rests on its technical competence and its findings, which carry us beyond, and largely discredit, the data of earlier studies. That is a lot. The rest, which has to do with human happiness and how it is won and lost, lies in the domain of subtler doctors of the soul than sociologists.

But is it not wonderful enough to learn, through graphs, charts, tables, and survey data, that many of the secrets of such human happiness, no matter how obscure they may be to undergraduates and their professors, have not altogether been lost to most men and women?

References

1. Robert T. Michael, John H. Gagnon, Edward O. Laumann, and Gina Kolata. Little, Brown, 300 pp.
2. Edward O. Laumann, John H Gagnon, Robert T. Michael, and Stuart Michaels. University of Chicago Press, 718 pp.

Chapter 7
Kiss and Tell: Surveying Sex in the Twentieth Century

Julia A. Ericksen
with
Sally A. Steffen

"**K**iss and Tell" is an apt title for this carefully choreographed description of the history of sexuality research: a dance including researchers, respondents, funders, and recipients. Although not an exposé of sensationalism as the title might suggest, the treatise challenges readers to define and perhaps refine their own biases relative to sexuality research.

The rationale for this work is based on the authors' core beliefs that the assumptions driving sexuality research help to create the sexuality that the research reveals. This is hardly an arguable premise. In reality, the relationship between assumptions and outcomes may have been best illustrated by the "media myths" created in the last presidential election. Consider the polarities exemplified in two national news personalities, Rush Limbaugh and Dan Rather. Following the authors' line of reasoning, the assumptions driving Limbaugh and Rather in gathering and reporting political news helped to create the very attitudes in their listeners that their news revealed. Marshall McLuhan popularized this phenomenon more than 30 years ago with his slogan, "The media is the message."

Ericksen and Steffen point to the polarities underlying assumptions in sexuality research. They contend that the bulk of sexuality research to date has been based on the assumption that sexuality is innate, while the flip side of the coin, that sexuality is socially created, has only recently been emphasized in the research arena. Readers are reminded that most researchers' assumptions are the products of the larger society, of the positions within that society, and of the findings of their predecessors. Ericksen and Steffen claim that, because over time, social or professional positions about sexuality have changed little, two factors have remained constant in sexuality research: the belief in innate differences between women and men and the fact that most researchers have been men who viewed the world through the eyes of male privilege.

As readers contemplate the significance of such influential perspectives in guiding research outcomes, they may better understand the challenges in defining their own premises about sexuality and underscore the importance of doing so. This thought-provoking treatise encourages readers to think for themselves, a timely virtue in an era characterized by choices.

> *It is both surprising and disturbing how empirically ill informed we as a nation are about important aspects of sexual behavior.*
>
> —Edward Laumann, John Gagnon, Robert Michael, and Stuart Michaels, 1994

In 1977, after reanalyzing findings from the Kinsey Reports of thirty years earlier, Bruce Voeller, the Chair of the National Gay Task Force, declared that 10 percent of the U.S. population was gay.[1] The media accepted and promoted this as fact until the late 1980s, when the figure was challenged by conservative groups as inflated and self-serving, indeed as "Exhibit A in any discussion of media myths created by scientific research."[2] At a gay rights march in Washington, D.C., the Lesbian Avengers and Act Up, two politically militant groups, chanted "10 percent is not enough, Recruit!

Recruit!" while Bob Knight of the conservative Family Research Council insisted that 10 percent was a gross exaggeration. Knight and other conservatives cast aspersions on a proposed national survey of sexual behavior designed to supply updated and more reliable data. They described this proposal as the result of pressure by "the homosexual activist community" to "gather evidence to buttress up the old claim; if not 10 percent, something close to it."

The controversy flared further when researchers at a Seattle-based think tank, the Battelle Research Center, concluded on the basis of a 1991 survey that only 1 percent of men were gay, a figure the press quoted widely.[3] This new finding stunned both gays and conservatives and became a new rallying point. Gay groups were concerned at the depletion of their numbers and suspicious of the survey's methodology; the sample was too small and the questions too few for an accurate measure. Conservatives were jubilant that gays were less than 10 percent of the population, but such a severely diminished adversary might compromise their anti-gay agenda altogether. Only forty years earlier McCarthyite senators had used Kinsey data to argue that the "homosexual menace" was considerably more serious than previously understood.[4]

To most observers, this disagreement about numbers could be easily resolved by a larger, more rigorous, and more comprehensive survey. Or could it? While "facts" appeared to be the basis of the conflict between the National Gay Task Force and the Family Research Council, the fight went far beyond the data. It was a fight over the nature and validity of social science and over the role of surveys in establishing accurate information about sexual behavior. And it quickly became a political battle over the right to define normal behavior and the nature of the evidence to be used in such definitions.

Sexual behavior is a volatile and sensitive topic, and surveys designed to reveal it have both great power and great limits. By revealing the private behavior of others, they provide a way for people to evaluate their own behavior and even the meaning of information the surveys produce. And they provide experts with information they urgently seek to understand society and develop social policy. Social scientists often view surveys as providing hard facts about behavior, yet results are limited by researchers' often unrecognized preconceptions about what the important questions are and also by respondents' ability and willingness to reveal what they have done. Surveyors frequently assume that the facts are ahistorical realities to be tapped by experts rather than transitory events that are open to interpretation. And the "truths" surveys reveal have enormous implications.

As Voeller understood from the first, 10 percent was large enough to represent an attack on heterosexuality as the accepted norm and indeed on the conventional meaning of gender. It implied that at least one gay person existed in almost every extended family in America. It challenged the underlying principle of family life: the "natural" sexual attraction between men and women. No wonder the leaders of the Family Research Council expended enormous energy in challenging this figure at every possible opportunity. The size of the gay population was critical for determining whether being gay constituted a normal identity. Those who believed the answer to be affirmative knew that a large gay population would strengthen demands for social inclusion, while conservatives seeking exclusion strove to prevent "deviants" from claiming normality.

For most of Western history, religion decreed appropriate standards for sexual and social behavior. By the twentieth century, however, secular social scientists had become the experts. Even conservatives like Knight, who want to espouse the cause of religious fundamentalism, defend their arguments not with theology but with statistical data and other scientific evidence. In deciding what is normal, experts have viewed private behavior, particularly sexual behavior, as an important indicator of personal stability and well-being. They have regarded their assessments as scientific but have based them on assumptions about gender, assumptions promoted by biologists as scientific fact.

Biologists have viewed men's and women's different reproductive systems as inevitable sources of difference in all aspects of their lives, making men and women not only different but complementary, in need of each other to be fulfilled.[5] In this view, fundamental gender distinctions find particular expression in sexual activity between men and women, whose intense natural physical attraction to each other is the centerpiece of their relationship and of the societal ideal of the couple. Individuals may deviate widely from this norm, but such assumptions provide powerful incentives toward conformity. To be normal sexually means to do what is natural, that is, heterosexual. If gay sex is shown to be widespread in the population, it challenges the assumption that men and women are natural sexual partners. . . .

The French intellectual Michel Foucault argued that with the development of the modern nation-state sexual identity became a central component of Western identity.[6] This emphasis on sexual identity, he explained, arose as a mechanism for monitoring individual behavior in a world where external authority had declined. . . . If social order was to remain in this new world, people must assume responsibility for their own behavior. . . .

In such a world, Foucault argued, citizens learned to control their own behavior by checking on the normality of their acts. Private behavior became especially vulnerable to personal scrutiny, since its very nature makes it difficult for others to police. As science replaced religion as the source of advice, biology became the basis for determining what constituted normal sexual behavior. Experts deciphered sexual activities, evaluated their normality, and gave advice to potential practitioners. While Foucault wrote little about gender, those influenced by his work have noted that this normal sexual behavior was gendered. As sexologists catalogued sexual types, they described men and women as having fundamentally different sexual desires, re-

sponses, and roles to play in their relationships with each other.

Foucault took issue with the twentieth-century view that the nineteenth century was a period when human sexuality was subjected to a repressed silence. The Victorians, he argued, discussed sexuality obsessively, since they viewed out-of-control sexuality as a threat to social order. In doing so, they created new sexual identities through which to catalogue sexual acts: for example, the child who masturbated or the sexual deviate whose behavior could be interpreted only by experts. The most famous of the early experts, Richard von Krafft-Ebing, classified a huge array of sexual types, providing detailed descriptions of the personalities of those who engaged in various behaviors or displayed various tastes.[7] . . . In this view, sexuality and society were at odds with each other, and social order faced constant threats from an out-of-control sexuality.

. . . Although governments could attempt to legislate morality and police private lives, the cities, in particular, afforded sexual marketplaces with a broad spectrum of flourishing sexual activity. Such an atmosphere occasioned great anxiety about sex and its practice among the general population.[8]

The citizens of villages and towns in earlier times could scrutinize their neighbors' lives more easily. Proximity made shame a potent force for the regulation and repression of illicit sexual activity. Once people could keep aspects of their lives hidden from families and friends, preventing transgressions became a personal rather than a collective responsibility. Guilt, not shame, ensured conformity. Guilt was especially powerful in a country where immigrants from all over the world flaunted different and sometimes frightening behaviors. Concerns about others' most intimate acts exacerbated fears about moral taint and threats to health.

Turn-of-the-century writers still viewed sexuality as in conflict with society rather than as a product of it, but they were more sympathetic to sexual variety. Sigmund Freud was convinced that the normal path to sexual maturity lay in heterosexuality. Yet he assumed that everyone had to repress a variety of other sexual desires in order to achieve this, and he was tolerant of those who took a different path. Freud's contemporary Havelock Ellis went a step further by describing sexual variety itself as part of the natural order of things. Ellis thought scientific sexology would liberate individuals from the constraints of a repressive social system.[9] But even Freud and Ellis helped increase the pervasive sense that the sexual world held dark secrets. The existence of sexology created the possibility of watching for signs of deviant behavior and rooting it out.

During the twentieth century, experts following in the footsteps of Freud and Ellis espoused increasingly liberal views of sexuality and, like Ellis, sought to liberate sexuality from societal repression. . . . Individuals and institutions concerned with the general welfare, including the government, public health officials, the media, and social scientists, continued to worry that private acts threatened public safety.

All those providing sexual advice viewed the family as the bedrock of social stability and the gendered couple as its foundation. For them, women and men occupied separate spheres of control. Men's assertive personalities, symbolized in their role in sexual intercourse, were ideally suited to run public life, while women were keepers of the private sphere who provided sustenance, sexual and otherwise, to those who ran the world. Over the century, despite significant modifications of these assumptions, the gendered nature of private sexual behavior remained central. Likewise, a pervasive sense that sexuality is so inherently unstable and irrational that society must be ever vigilant kept experts busy proffering advice. This fear that private behavior could affect public well-being fed repeated panics about such issues as venereal disease, teenage pregnancy, and indiscriminate sex, while it fostered an interest in expert counsel.

The first sexologists relied on their own insights supplemented by clinical records to document the dangers of sexual excess.

In the twentieth century this task fell to social scientists. Since the Progressive era, American social scientists have viewed their disciplines as capable of furthering human progress by alleviating such panic. They approached this task using scientific methods, in particular statistical methods. In each time of sexual crisis they perceived an urgent need for information. Yet they did not collect data with the scientific disinterest they imagined. Instead, their assumption that men and women differed from each other sexually dictated the form of their questions about the nation's social and sexual health. Believing that solutions start with the facts, the experts produced their urgently needed data through a filter of gendered sexuality.

Given the long-standing American belief that numbers provide factual representations of the world, surveys are an obvious source of information.[10] Since sex is an arena in which what others do is unclear, actual information about sexual behavior had two ready-made audiences: experts concerned that private behavior had a negative impact on public order, and individuals anxious to use hard evidence to evaluate and regulate their own behavior. Since 1892, when the biology student Clelia Mosher started asking upper-middle-class married women whether they liked intercourse, how often they had intercourse, and how often they wanted to have intercourse[11]—information she never had the courage to publish—researchers have asked hundreds of thousands of people about their sexual behavior and *have* published their findings for others to read.

This intense scrutiny created a window into the sexual lives of ordinary women and men that exposed private behavior to professional interpretation. Experts relayed this information to the public in reports and press releases. They evaluated the meaning of the data for what men and women should do, what they should like to do, and what they should fear doing. They not only reported what they believed to be the facts but helped create these facts in line with their own ideological positions, particularly their beliefs about gender.

These facts, in turn, helped create sexual practices in two ways. First, reports about what others were doing suggested to readers that they should model their behavior on those who appeared to represent them. Second, surveys evaluated the behavior of those in the surveys, and this also provided lessons to readers. Thus even reports that accurately described aspects of the behavior of a particular group at a particular time created behavior by acting as guides or warnings to others. Since the most consistent assumption on which the surveys rested was of a gendered sexuality, albeit a changing one, surveys helped sustain a vision of sexuality as innately contained within masculinity and femininity.

The potential impact of such revelations is the reason those who disagree with results find it necessary to discredit them. Since the meanings attributed to the data have political implications beyond the facts, those who conduct sex surveys feel pressure to meet certain social needs. Investigators do not operate in a cultural vacuum. They approach their research holding beliefs about what is normal and what they expect to find, beliefs shaped by their personal experiences and desires, by their social circumstances, and by the findings of earlier researchers. Furthermore, when survey results become public, readers may change their sexual behavior as a result of finding out what others "like them" do, and researchers find themselves influencing what they had merely hoped to record.

Survey researchers, sensitive to charges of subjectivity, claim that as scientists using modern survey methods they can eliminate the effects of the expectations and biases they bring to their research. They concede that, without the advantage of modern techniques, early researchers were less objective, but they insist that today's methodology can take care of such problems. Asking questions of persons one at a time and aggregating the answers appears to reveal reality. Such scientific surveys seem the perfect way to amass information about a variety of social problems—venereal disease, divorce, teen pregnancy, for example—in order to develop informed public policies aimed at alleviating their ill effects.

Modern survey practice evolved throughout the twentieth century but came into its own after the Second World War.[12] Nowadays, letting prior hypotheses influence outcomes is decried as poor technique and a betrayal of the fundamental principles of science. Researchers view the scientific method as demanding hypotheses, or at least research questions, which they test in ways that do not influence the outcome. Although there has been little acknowledgment that the choice of research topic inevitably represents a point of view, four phases of the survey process have been the subjects of methodological studies intended to achieve this goal of objectivity. These are decisions about whom to interview; methods of data collection, including interviewer training; content and structure of the interview schedule; and the analysis of data.

Early researchers did not understand either the importance of interviewing all segments of the target population or that researchers who chose which respondents to interview might influence the results. They consciously surveyed "the better part of the middle class," or those who were "not pathological mentally or physically," in order to present the best possible case for their arguments.[13] The use of random sampling in surveys, a technique that ensures that each person in the target population has an equal, or a known, probability of being selected, developed in the 1930s. In this method, researchers completely remove themselves from decisions about which persons to interview.[14] . . .

While sampling techniques changed survey research, sex researchers were slow to adopt these superior methods. Alfred Kinsey, who undertook his survey when modern sampling was in its infancy, did not believe random sampling was possible in sex surveys, and many subsequent sex surveyors followed his example. Kinsey believed that people contacted at random would refuse to answer personal questions. Unlike his predecessors, Kinsey understood that all segments of the population should be included, so he went to great lengths to represent all sexual tastes. Unfortunately, in his determination to be inclusive, he most likely overestimated less common sexual activities such as same-gender sexual behavior.

Since the 1980s this avoidance of random sampling has ended. A number of recent sexual behavior surveys, for example the Battelle survey, have successfully used random sampling techniques to select respondents. While a 100 percent response rate is unlikely in a random sample, and nonrespondents can bias the results, the use of this method of selecting respondents has improved the reliability of the data immeasurably.

The history of interviewing in sex surveys is more complex, and many issues remain unresolved. From the beginning some researchers insisted on using face-to-face interviews on the grounds that this would create the intimacy and trust necessary for respondents to reveal their sexual secrets. But they did not understand the problems involved when researchers personally conducted the interviews. Gilbert Hamilton, who surveyed the sexual adjustment of married couples in New York in the late 1920s, did all the interviewing himself and imposed his own notions of intimacy and trust idiosyncratically. Commenting that his interviewing technique produced frequent "weeping and trips to the toilet," he maintained scientific objectivity by noting all such occurrences and by tying "the subject's chair to the wall in order to forestall the tendency that most persons have to draw closer to the recipient of confidences as these become more intimate."[15] Kinsey also was too early to understand the importance of using professional interviewers, of keeping the hypotheses from interviewers, and of training interviewers to ask sensitive questions.

By 1955, when the sociologist Ronald Freedman conducted the first national survey of married women's contraceptive practices, he and his colleagues used properly trained and monitored interviewers; and techniques have further improved since then.[16] Today investigators make well-informed decisions on whether to have interviewers ask the questions or to ask them in other ways, such as by computer. Interviewers receive extensive training and are held to rigorous standards. . . . From the beginning some researchers avoided interviews. Instead, they designed self-administered questionnaires for respondents to fill out and return. This method assures respondents of confidentiality and increases their willingness to disclose sexual secrets. But it produces lower response rates and creates problems for respondents who have difficulty reading.

All surveys, regardless of interview method, require some type of questionnaire. Because the researcher holding the hypothesis selects, words, and orders the questions, questionnaire design is particularly vulnerable to researcher bias. In the early years of sex surveys, surveyors did not understand the problem, and, in order to protect themselves from respondent outrage, wrote reassurances that the sexual acts respondents were being asked to describe were normal. Katharine Davis' 1920 mail-in survey of the sexual experiences of middle-class women included a long prefatory statement to her questions on masturbation communicating the opinion—shared by other progressive thinkers in her day—that, in spite of condemnation, masturbation was not harmful for women. Indeed, some experts, she said, maintained that it was "a normal stage in the development of the sex nature and must be passed through if sexual development is to be complete."[17]

Davis expected to find that many women masturbated, and not surprisingly she found this. In modern questionnaires, such reassurance—which may push a respondent in the direction of a particular response—rarely appears. Before the survey takes place, pretesting helps achieve clear, nondirective questions. Careful wording and ordering of questions produce more accurate responses. It is more difficult to examine the effect of turning abstract concepts into terms that respondents can understand, or to ascertain what a respondent might reasonably remember. Even here, however, research has made progress. For example, one source of variation in estimates of the size of the gay population is the questions asked. Not only does asking the gender of respondents' sexual partners produce different results than asking respondents if they are homosexual, bisexual, or heterosexual, but the specific wording of the question makes a difference. It is hard to compare the findings of the Battelle researchers with those of Kinsey because of the differences in the questions.

During the final phase, data analysis, bias was endemic but often unrecognized in early surveys. Indeed, obtaining impartial data and analyzing them in a manner unfettered by the investigator's agenda was not always the aim. Max Exner, who in 1913 embarked on one of the earliest sex surveys, stated that "we are in urgent need of facts which would enable us to speak with reasonable definiteness" about the need for sex education as a way of curbing young men's excessive sexual desires.[18] Although draped in scientific garb, Exner's questions and analysis reveal that for him the survey was not a tool to discover information. He used it to support his preexisting "knowledge" that learning about sex from the street led to unhygienic sexual practices.

Over time, with increasingly rigorous survey methods, such obviously prejudiced practices ceased. Researchers even began to realize that their unconscious biases could influence the outcome. With more sophisticated data analysis techniques, researchers could be more certain of their conclusions and less able to shape them to satisfy an agenda. Yet they remained largely oblivious of the fact that the questions they ask of the data reveal a point of view. The Battelle researchers insisted that the furor over their reported incidence of male homosexuality was misplaced. This, they said, was not the main target of their research, and they did not have sufficient data for accuracy. But they revealed this result in a carefully orchestrated manner that seemed designed to maximize publicity.

Throughout the century, survey researchers interested in sexual behavior viewed their results as improvements on earlier findings. Indeed, this brief description of survey practice suggests that a history of surveys of sexual behavior should be a history of the growing sophistication of researchers and the increasing certainty of their conclusions. In order for this to be the case, two conditions would have to hold. First, researchers would have to be neutral observers of sexual behavior, an unlikely proposition in a world where no one escapes pressure to monitor personal sexual standards and desires. Second, sexual behavior would have to be independent of history and culture. In such a case, questions such as the proportion of gays in the population would be technical, not political or historically specific questions.

In fact, while survey improvements have produced more accurate reflections of historical moments, surveys do not divulge universal truths, only those relative to their time and place. Furthermore, even with the best intentions, researchers have managed their surveys in such a way as to produce findings reflecting their own beliefs about gender and normality and their concerns about the dangers of sex research. Responsible researchers adopted techniques to neutralize the effect of their biases, but their very choice of research topics assumed a certain view of sexuality. When, in 1992, the research team quoted in the epigraph to this [work] finally received funds for a large national survey of American adults, they used the latest survey techniques. Yet they conducted their research in a climate in which sexual coupling, especially with strangers, was perceived as potentially fatal. Their concern over "promiscuity" colored all aspects of the survey.[19]

In addition to researchers and respondents, two other groups had an impact on what information surveys revealed: those who funded surveys and those who interpreted the results for larger audiences. At first sex surveys were commissioned by private organizations interested in promoting a particular point of view. In later years the federal government took over much of the funding. Those who dispensed federal dollars also had a point of view to promote, although they did so in a less directive manner.

In the early years, researchers not only controlled who respondents were and what their answers meant; they also controlled the dissemination of results to other experts and the general public. . . . Once the media began reporting the results of surveys, their goals differed widely from those of the researchers, who often found their results presented in a distorted manner. The Battelle researchers experienced this. They used the media to promote their survey, but they quickly lost control of the debate. As discussion raged over the percentage of men who were gay, the rest of the results, including those of most interest to the researchers, almost disappeared from view.

Do these limits and problems mean we can learn little from surveys of sexual behavior? On the contrary, such surveys teach us a great deal about sexuality in America, about the beliefs that have shaped sexual behavior, and about the concerns that have driven researchers to ask questions. They show the changes in these concerns and in assumptions about sexuality. Tracing these changes reveals the history of sexuality in the twentieth century. Furthermore, as survey practice improved, the ensuing descriptions of sexual practice not only provided a behavioral control but provided comfort and encouraged people to act on their desires.

We tell this story in the belief that sexuality is not a trait with which individuals are born but a crucial aspect of identity that is socially created. Researchers often assumed that sexuality was innate and that their task was to reveal what already existed. In contrast, we believe that the assumptions driving the research helped create the sexuality the research revealed. Researchers' assumptions were the product of the larger society, of the researchers' positions within that society, and of the findings of their predecessors. While the culture changed over time and researchers did not occupy identical social or professional positions, two factors remained almost constant. First, researchers shared general beliefs in the existence of innate differences between men and women and viewed such differences as the basis of sexual attraction. Second, most researchers were men and viewed the world through the eyes of male privilege. They assumed a straightforward male sexuality while puzzling over "the problem of female sexuality." In this, their major concern was that women should satisfy men's needs. Female sexual pleasure was increasingly viewed as a way to make men happy and families secure. It was not until the 1980s, when women began to undertake sex surveys, that the focus began shifting to female pleasure as a woman's concern.

Researchers believed that women become aroused slowly and through love, while men experience constant arousal. These beliefs influenced surveys and were so powerful that researchers did not always know how to handle contrary findings. For example, the few women surveyors in the early decades described a strong female sex drive, more similar to than different from men's.[20] Yet even as male experts reported these women's results they ignored the voices behind them, choosing instead to reinterpret findings to fit conventional assumptions. Furthermore, these assumptions about gender and sexuality differed according to respondents' race, class, and age. Middle-class adults received the most attention because of beliefs that only they had the time or education to achieve sexual bliss. Only during periods of crisis when sexuality became a symbol for concern about other social changes did groups other than the white middle class become the targets of sex research.

Part of the reason for caution over whom to interview involved researchers' need to justify sex surveys while protecting themselves from charges of prurience. Those undertaking sex surveys found them to be a dangerous enterprise. Sex talk, with its forbidden overtones, was often embarrassing because it was exciting. Doing the research involved invading a private sphere. This affected the nature of the research questions and the explanations given for asking them. Surveyors rarely justified sex surveys on the grounds of interest. Instead, they used the urgent social problems of the day as an explanation for their questions. Their justifications had implications for the collection of data, for the questions asked, and for what constituted knowledge. Discomfort over sex talk, even in scientific guise, made sex surveys more vulnerable to personal pressures at every stage of the survey process.

Researchers in many areas claim their results are definitive, but these claims have a particular cast in sex research because worries about criticism often lead to overstatement of the reliability of conclusions. In reaction to the claims of conservative opponents like Senator Jesse Helms that "most Americans resent even being asked to answer questions about how often they engage in sex, with whom, their preferences for sexual partners, and which sex act they prefer,"[21] researchers tended to downplay the methodological and theoretical challenges of their research. In such a climate they were loath to consider the impact of their research on behavior. They tried to convince skeptical audiences that asking questions about sex was easy and the results were trustworthy. Paradoxically, this need for certainty created resistance to research on the methodology of sex surveys, since such research requires an acknowledgment of uncertainty. It also made researchers hesitant to share their experiences with other researchers, which, in turn, slowed the accumulation of knowledge on which to build. This made researchers vulnerable to attack on methodological grounds even from those whose objections were actually political.

Nevertheless, the history of sexual behavior surveys remains a history of the optimism of researchers and of the enlightenment of readers. Living in a culture in which no topic has been considered too difficult or too private for scientific inquiry, and believing that knowledge would further human progress, surveyors saw themselves as pioneers venturing where others dared not go and doing so without fear of personal consequences. Their goal was to delve into the most secret and shame-laden human behavior, and to reveal it for all to see in the hope that the truth would liberate people from ignorance and stigma. In recent years many writers about sexuality have agreed with Foucault's argument that talk about sex does not liberate sex but is merely another way of controlling it. Researchers had a limited understanding of how they shaped the results of surveys. But they showed courage in following their beliefs that social stability is best served by exposing practice rather than by hiding it. Their work reveals an important thread of cultural and sexual history in the twentieth century.

Notes

1. Bruce Voeller, "Some Uses and Abuses of the Kinsey Scale," in David P. McWhirter, Stephanie A. Sanders, and June Machover Reinisch, eds., *Homosexuality/Heterosexuality* (New York: Oxford University Press, 1990).

2. Interview with Robert Knight, May 24, 1993.

3. John O. G. Billy et al., "The Sexual Behavior of Men in the United States," *Family Planning Perspectives* 25, no. 2 (March/April 1993).

4. John D'Emilio, *Sexual Politics, Sexual Communities* (Chicago: University of Chicago Press, 1983).

5. Thomas Laqueur, *Making Sex* (Cambridge, Mass.: Harvard University Press, 1990).

6. Michel Foucault, *The History of Sexuality*, vol. 1 (New York: Random House, 1978).

7. Richard von Krafft-Ebing, *Psychopathia Sexualis* (New York: Physicians and Surgeons Book Co., 1931).

8. John D'Emilio and Estelle B. Freedman, *Intimate Matters: A History of Sexuality in America* (New York: Harper and Row, 1988).

9. Havelock Ellis, *Studies in the Psychology of Sex* (1899; New York: Random House, 1942).

10. Patricia Cline Cohen, *A Calculating People* (Chicago: University of Chicago Press, 1982).

11. James MaHood and Kristine Wenburg, *The Mosher Survey* (New York: Arno, 1980).

12. Bernard Lecuyer and Anthony R. Oberschall, "The Early History of Social Research: Postscript: Research in the United

States at the Turn of the Century," in *International Encyclopedia of Statistics*, eds. William H. Kruskal and Judith M. Tanur (New York: Free Press, 1978).

13. Walter F. Robie, *Rational Sex Ethics* (Boston: Richard G. Badger, 1916), 30; Katharine Bement Davis, *Factors in the Sex Lives of Twenty-Two Hundred Women* (New York: Harper and Row, 1929), x.

14. Morris H. Hansen, William Hurwitz, and William G. Madow, *Sample Survey Methods and Theory*, vol. 1(New York: Wiley, 1953).

15. Gilbert V. Hamilton, *A Research in Marriage* (New York: A. C. Boni, 1929), 17–18.

16. Ronald Freedman, Pascal K. Whelpton, and Arthur A. Campbell, *Family Planning, Sterility and Population Growth* (New York: McGraw-Hill, 1959).

17. Davis, *Factors in the Sex Lives*, 96.

18. Max J. Exner, *Problems and Principles of Sex Education* (New York: Association Press, 1915), 3.

19. Edward O. Laumann et al., *The Social Organization of Sexuality* (Chicago: University of Chicago Press, 1994).

20. Davis, *Factors in the Sex Lives;* Dorothy Dunbar Bromley and Florence Haxton Britten, *Youth and Sex* (New York: Harper, 1938).

21. Jesse Helms, "Debate on Amendment no. 1757 to the 1992 NIH Revitalization Act," *Congressional Record* (April 2, 1992), S4738.

Adapted from Julia A. Ericksen with Sally A. Steffen, *Kiss and Tell: Surveying Sex in the Twentieth Century*, pp.1–13, Cambridge, MA: Harvard University Press. Copyright © 1999 by the President and Fellows of Harvard College. Reprinted by permission of the publisher. ✦

Part II

Sexuality and the Life Cycle: Childhood and Adolescence

All the world's a stage and all the men and women merely players;
They have their exits and their entrances;
And one man in his time plays many parts,
His acts being seven ages.

—William Shakespeare

William Shakespeare is one among many poets, prophets, and priests who have long proclaimed that the essence of life lies in its progression; that as individuals struggle to balance the inevitable intricacies of change and continuity, life is expressed. It was not until the latter part of the twentieth century that the multidisciplinary field of life-span development emerged from the disciplines of child development and developmental psychology. The study of the journey in human sexuality over the life span is the touchstone personally and professionally for those who seek a holistic understanding of sexuality. For students, the life-cycle perspective of sexuality can lend continuity in a day characterized by disconnects.

As the headwaters of life, the childhood and adolescent years are significant in the development of psychosexual scripts. As such, they offer watershed opportunities for promoting healthy attitudes and behaviors about sexuality, a central core that touches every aspect of a person's being. But, conversely, when the headwaters are troubled, it is difficult to calm the downstream flow. For this reason, family life-cycle and developmental theorists focus on the importance of the formative years in their efforts to understand human behavior.

Defining childhood operationally as any time between infancy and the point at which the individual becomes a sexually mature adult, Francoeur broadens his topic beyond what are typically considered to be the childhood years. His thesis that normative religious doctrines—the attitudes, values, and doctrines endorsed by a culture, society, and parents—are central factors in the psychosexual development throughout one's formative years is hardly debatable. However, what he so richly portrays about this topic will leave readers with an informed awareness of the lack of childhood sexual ethics in most religious traditions.

In Part II, a neglected research arena is highlighted with an important study about the long-term effects of early childhood exposure to parental nudity and to the "primal scene." Okami et al. tap into 18 years of longitudinal data from the UCLA Family Lifestyles Project to clarify what clinicians

75

and child development experts have postulated to be potentially harmful experiences in childhood. A major contribution of the Okami et al. study is their review of the research literature that reveals a lack of empirical support for such claims.

Particularly those students who bring an awareness of family systems theory to the Okami et al. reading may be puzzled by the authors' assertion that their specific findings were not predicted by any theory with which they were familiar. Nevertheless, readers who understand developmental theory and psychosexual development throughout the formative years, emphasized in the first selection of Part II, may be better able to formulate questions for future research because of this study. Further, the results of this research may quiet alarmists whose references to phrases like "the emotional incest syndrome," "maternal seductress," and "sexualized attention" feed the paperback tradition of empirically unsubstantiated theories that abound in the popular genre. Then again, perhaps, it will not.

The reporting of research in the article about Latino adolescent mothers differs significantly from what one journal editor has called "endless statistics which accompany endless articles about endless teenage pregnancies." This selection should be of substantial interest to readers specifically because it is a different approach to gathering data; it is based on case studies of life-history interviews with 40 young Latino adolescent mothers and their partners.

Such qualitative data are rare in the literature for several reasons. One, interviews are much more time-consuming than are other methods of data collection, such as surveys. Another difficulty lies in the analysis of qualitative data, with reviewers claiming that "lack of rigor" produces results too "soft" to merit inclusion in professional journals. This argument can frequently be interpreted to mean that there are no "endless statistics" with which to formulate results and conclusions. Although all professionals in the research arena have a responsibility to maintain the highest standards of excellence for self and others in the discipline, students must learn that differences in research studies are not to be mistaken for deficiencies. Instead, acceptance of diversity in methods of research so aptly demonstrated by Erickson affirms the mutual quest for excellence. This is an important lesson for future researchers as well as those who are consumers of research. ✦

Chapter 8
Current Religious Doctrines of Sexual and Erotic Development in Childhood

Robert T. Francoeur

Students who wish to be informed about either religion and sexuality or childhood and sexuality will find Robert Francoeur's combination of the two concepts intriguing. The author, a university teacher of human sexuality with degrees in embryology, theology, and biology, is uniquely qualified to explore the relationship between religious doctrines and childhood sexuality. From his thorough literary review, he synthesizes current knowledge concerning the influence of religious doctrines as they relate to the sexual development of children. In so doing, he cuts a wide path through the doctrines of the major religious traditions in Western societies as they intersect with sexuality and childhood. Those whose interest extends to the Latino cultures of Latin America, the Islamic culture of the Middle East, or the Hindu, Buddhist, and Confucian Taoist cultures of the Far East are referred to the full text of his chapter.

Major points of interest are the various religious views toward sexual behaviors, such as masturbation, premarital sexual intimacy, and homosexuality. But perhaps of more importance to readers, the information may prompt an assessment of their own experiential data, gleaned from "childhood sexuality lessons" via parents and religious leaders. Although a sample of one is admittedly less than scientific, each person is acutely aware of the significance of his/her own experiences in sexual scripting. Extrapolating from the broader context of adult beliefs and values as a model, Francoeur weaves plausible explanations of this scripting. For example, he postulates that parental efforts to prohibit, prevent, or punish natural sexual behavior in childhood and adolescence may vandalize the formation of normophilic lovemaps and promote the formation of paraphilic lovemaps. The review of Money's concept of the crucial periods of psychosexual development, through which the child passes in the preparation of her/his individual lovemap aids such an introspective journey.

Students may especially resonate to the carefully crafted thesis that as sexually mature single persons today, they are a new human subspecies. It is true that young adults today can claim that they had no ancestors to model appropriate sexual behaviors because the day in which they live is so uniquely characterized by socially prolonged adolescence and later marriages.

Though theoretical in nature, much of this information will be perceived as pragmatic, with tables particularly contributing to this end. The range of sexual moralities in different religious traditions, as related to their basic worldviews, are revealed in Table 8.1. In Table 8.2, the dichotomous "Hot and Cool Sex" paradigm, influenced by Western sexual values and behaviors, may strike a familiar chord with the parents of today's college students. Francoeur's earlier work (1974) furnishes a down-to-earth touch to an at times weighty offering. This treasury which traces independently developed paradigms from a variety of religious philosophies is a must-read for serious students of sexuality.

Objective, Definitions, and Premises

The purpose of this work is to summarize the relatively little information available on religious doctrines as they relate to and affect the sexual and erotic development of children in various contemporary cultures. The cultures surveyed are the Judaic, Christian (both Protestant and Catholic) and humanist traditions in Western societies.

Within this purview, certain premises need to be spelled out.

The child. The status of child is operationally and dynamically defined as including those phases of psychosexual development which occur between infancy and that point, somewhere after puberty, when the individual is socially recognized as a sexually mature adult.

Normative religious doctrines. This work assumes that the religious attitudes, values and doctrines endorsed by a culture, society and parents are a central factor in the psychosexual development of the child. Religious values and doctrines, both directly and indirectly, provide major affective and cognitive sources for establishing standards of acceptable and accepted behavior. Even when an individual, parent or society does not adhere to what would be termed a religious value system, as in the humanist tradition, the normative doctrines endorsed are usually articulated against the backdrop of a prevailing religious tradition.

Moreover, there is good evidence, both historical and contemporary, that in times of political and economic upheaval, societies commonly enlist religious doctrines, even to the point of creating new interpretations and rules, as a means of shoring up the status quo (1).

The dearth and derivative character of childhood sexual ethics. Religious traditions have seldom dealt with the sexual and erotic development of children as something of value in its own right. Childhood sexuality is seldom mentioned, let alone discussed in any detail, in religious studies and secular histories of sexuality.

Moreover, whatever is said about childhood sexuality in religious doctrines is, invariably, subordinate to and derived from the broader context of adult beliefs and values which focus on the pivotal adult sexual relationship, marriage. As the concept of marriage has changed in Europe and North America so have the doctrines about childhood sexuality derived from this adult model. When marriage was based on dynastic or political concerns, adolescent sexual relations were judged in terms of paternal property rights, the legitimacy of offspring and the avoidance of sexual behaviors that would complicate social organization. Premarital and extramarital erotic experiences may have been allowed, or even expected in this context. As the procreative function of marital sex decreased and dynastic/political concerns yielded increasingly to a norm of exclusive emotional and romantic bonding within marriage, so did the acceptability of extramarital erotic fulfillment wane (2-4).

The role of adult religious beliefs in sexual scripting. While Money has detailed the crucial periods or "gates" of psychosexual development through which the child passes after birth, a brief recapitulation here will situate our exploration of the role of parental religious beliefs in the psychosexual development of the child.

When parents first observe the sexual anatomy of their newborn infant and respond by assigning it a gender, as boy or girl, that gender of assignment triggers a sexually dimorphic scripting of the infant for masculine or feminine roles which, in part, reflects the religious beliefs and values of the parents and their adult society.

Infants quickly and spontaneously discover the sensuousness of their genitals. They explore their own bodies. They respond to the rhythmic pressure, squeezing, rubbing and touching that bring pleasurable sensations. In the process, many males and fewer females learn to masturbate. Young males also experience episodic nocturnal penile tumescence (NPT) on average three times per night, for a total duration of two to three hours. Later, during puberty, NPT will be enriched and associated with erotic dreams. Casual genital fondling and masturbatory activities are natural and common between ages three and five. Equally natural and common, when not inhibited or repressed by adults, is the tendency of young children to engage in flirtatious rehearsal play with a parent or other older children of the opposite sex.

About age five, as the child's social context enlarges with the beginning of formal schooling, flirtatious play expands to incorporate boyfriend-girlfriend playmate romance. This is also the age when pelvic rocking or thrusting movements against the body of a partner while lying side by side gives way to the rehearsal play of coitus (5). In our repressed society, positioning rehearsal for coitus is frequently reduced to playing doctor and nurse.

In late childhood, prenatally encoded neural pathway tendencies are elaborated on by an unknown and variable combination of childhood and adolescent sexual fantasies, experiences and scriptings to determine the child's sexual orientation (status) and uniquely personal lovemap. At around age eight, pairbonding in a love affair may occur in a type of prepubertal mating rehearsal. Finally, with puberty, secondary sex characteristics make obvious the physical maturation of the child and its new sexual potential.

Parents are frequently oblivious of the many natural and spontaneous experiences of childhood psychosexual development. When, however, these spontaneous explorations are observed, the parents become mentors and scriptors for what they consider sexually appropriate for children. Given the strong antisexual biases of Western societies, these natural explorations, sexual responses and masturbatory activity are frequently short-circuited because the parental religious beliefs judge these activities sinful and forbidden.

Parental efforts to prohibit, prevent or punish this natural behavior may well vandalize the formation of normophilic lovemaps and promote the formation of paraphilic lovemaps in early childhood and preadolescence, when nurturance or the lack of it elaborates on and reinforces neural templates laid down in the brain before birth (6).

A new human subspecies. In non-technological societies, the physical maturation of puberty is commonly marked with a rite of passage to adulthood which confers and celebrates all the sexual rights and responsibilities that status carries in a particular society. In the technological West, this concurrence has been radically disassociated by socioeconomic changes. In the days of Romeo and Juliet, marriages were arranged by the parents before their children entered sexual maturity, which came in the late teens. In this context, the prolonged period of adolescence we know today did not exist. Thus, adolescent sexual relations, premarital sex, were of minor concern to religious thinkers.

As the Industrial Revolution progressed, the length of adolescence was extended and children no longer married in their early teens. From the late nineteenth century on, the growing emphasis on public education reinforced the social prolongation of adolescence and later marriages. In the mid-twentieth century, the advent of effective and convenient contraceptives culminated in the emergence of a new human subspecies, the sexually mature single person. Unfortunately, religious rites of passage which traditionally acknowledged adult status and responsibilities at puberty, Jewish bar (bat) mitzvah and Christian confirmation, remained devoid of any recognition of this new separation of sexual maturation and marriage.

The period of adolescence is a Western phenomenon. In it, the young person is sexuoerotically capable but socially prohibited from entering the marital state where he/she could legitimately express sexual drives and needs. This new subspecies, the sexually mature single and legally dependent adolescent, has created new questions of sexual morality with which religious groups are only just beginning to deal (7-8). The advent of sexuoerotic drives and interests at puberty and the postponement of adult status leaves the adolescent in a state of limbo. The adolescent's growing need for self-actualizing independence, erotic and romantic fantasies, erotic drives and early erotic experiences with self and others is immediate and real.

The tensions of this transition are evident in Piaget's model of moral development as the child moves from a heteronomous stage based on total acceptance of a morality imposed by others to an autonomous stage in which sexual and other norms are internalized in a morality of cooperation. Kohlberg has proposed a similar, more detailed model with a transition from a conventional morality based on conformity to societal and parental norms to the social contract and universal ethical principles of a postconventional morality (9-11). An application of these models to religious institutions appears at the end of the next section.

The Value Spectrum Within Religious Denominational Doctrines

Although religious value systems are quite varied, their doctrines and norms focus primarily on the adult and adult relationships in marriage, the family and the world outside. Children are addressed mainly in terms of initiation rituals such as baptism and their education for adult responsibilities. Because of this, any discussion of religious doctrines related to childhood sexuality must begin with an analysis of adult religious doctrines.

Recent efforts to analyze doctrinal systems have revealed two distinct world philosophies (weltanschauungs) tenuously coexisting for centuries within the Judaic, Christian, Islamic and Hindu traditions. This author is not aware of evidence of a similar coexistent dualism of world views in the other religious traditions examined here, but the conclusion of Mayr is that no greater revolution has occurred in the history of human thought than the radical shift from a fixed cosmology rooted in unchanging archetypes to a dynamic, evolving cosmogenic world view based on populations and individuals (12). While the process or evolutionary world view may be gaining dominance in Western cultures and religious traditions, the Moral Majority and religious New Right in the United States, and the growing vitality of orthodox Judaism provide ample evidence that the fixed world view still has a clear influence in moderating human behavior (13-15).

Ideologically, the fixed and process world views are at the two ends of a continuum or spectrum that includes a wide range of approaches to moral and sexual issues. While individuals often take a fixed position on one issue and a process position on a second issue, these general categories are instructive when examining the impact of religious doctrines on childhood sexuality because individuals generally tend to adopt one or the other approach and maintain a fairly consistent set of intertwined religious values and attitudes.

Religious doctrines, and their adherents, can be divided by the weltanschauung which underlies their religious beliefs and doctrines. Either the world is a completely finished universe in which human nature was created by some supreme being, perfect, complete and unchanging in essence from the beginning, or the world is a universe characterized by continual change with human nature constantly evolving as it struggles to reach its fuller potential or what it is called upon to become by the deity. Either one believes that the first human beings were created by God as unchanging archetypes, thus determining standards of human behavior for all time, or one believes that human nature, behavior and moral standards have been evolving since the beginning of the human race. In the former view, a supreme being created human nature; in the latter view, the deity is creating human nature with human collaboration.

Deriving from these two views of the world and human nature, one finds two distinct views of the origins of evil and sexuality. If one believes that human nature, the purposes of sexuality and the nature of sexual relations were established in the beginning, then one also finds it congenial to believe that evil results from some original sin, a primeval fall of the first humans from a state of perfection and grace. If, on the other hand, one believes in an evolving human nature, then physical and moral evils are viewed as the inevitable, natural growth pains that come as humans struggle toward the fullness of their creation (16).

Divergent world views and sexual value systems in the Roman Catholic, Protestant, Judaic, Islamic, and Humanist religious traditions are illustrated in Table 8.1.

Table 8.1

A Spectrum of Ethical Systems With Typical Adherents in Different Traditions

Tradition Source	A Spectrum	
	Fixed Philosophy of Nature	Process Philosophy of Nature
Roman Catholic natural law tradition	Act-oriented natural law/divine order ethics expressed in formal Vatican pronouncements	Person-oriented, evolving ethics expressed by many contemporary theologians
Protestant Nominalism	Fundamentalism based on a literal interpretation of the Bible, as endorsed by the Moral Majority and the religious New Right: Seventh Day Adventists, Jehovah's Witnesses, Church of the Latter Day Saints	An ethic based on the covenant between Jesus and humankind; examples in the 1970 United Presbyterian document on Sexuality and the Human Community
Humanism	Stoicism and epicurean asceticism	Situation ethics, e.g., the 1976 American Humanist Association: A New Bill of Sexual Rights and Responsibilities
Judaism	Orthodox and Hassidic concern for strict observation of the Torah and Talmudic prescriptions	Liberal and reformed application of moral principles to today's situations

This general dichotomy of world views comes through with a powerful consistency in an analysis of traditional and contemporary Western sexual values, as Table 8.2 shows (17).

The convergence of independently developed value paradigms from a variety of different disciplines confirms the importance and necessity of ascertaining the weltanschauung that supports any religious doctrinal system and its sexual values. Once these premises are understood, the type of influence a particular religious doctrinal system is likely to have on children can be projected with some degree of accuracy. Since so little is available in terms of specific doctrines or moral precepts for childhood sexual development, this insight, however limited, is valuable as a starting point from which one can appreciate better the divergence of sexual values, for both adults and children.

In an adaptation of the moral development models of Piaget, Kohlberg and Gilligan to American religious institutions,

Stayton (Ref. 8, p. 134) sees three institutional types. Corresponding to stage one in moral development are System A religious institutions, which focus on acts of masturbation, homosexuality, abortion or premarital sex. The act is either right or wrong. Absolute obedience to the authority is expected. At the other end of the spectrum are System C religious institutions, for whom acts are neither evil nor good in themselves and the focus is on the nature of relationships and individual responsibilities, as in stages five or six of the moral development models. System B religious institutions are more complex because they can reflect any of stages two to four, and individuals often fluctuate between stages depending on the extent of their personal involvement in a particular issue of sexuality. As Stayton notes,

> The dilemma for many adolescents is that they may be further along in their moral development than the religious institutions to which they belong. The Judaeo-Christian traditions have al-

Table 8.2

A Dichotomous Paradigm Based on Western Sexual Values and Behaviour

Hot Sex	Cool Sex
Definitions	
Reduction of genital sex.	Sexuality coextensive with personality.
Genitally focused feelings.	Diffused sensuality/sexuality.
Time and place arrangements.	Spontaneous.
Value System	
Patriarchal.	Egalitarian.
Male dominance by aggression.	Equal partnership as friends.
Double moral standard.	Single moral standard.
Behavioral Structures	
Closed possessiveness.	Open inclusiveness.
Casual, impersonal.	Involved, intimate.
Physical sex segregated from life, emotions and responsibility.	Sex integrated in whole framework of life.
Concerns	
Orgasm obsessed.	Engaging, pleasuring communications.
Extramarital relations as escape.	Comarital relations a growth of primary bond.
Fear of emotions and senses.	Embracing of emotions and senses.

Source: A.K. Francoeur, R.T. Francoeur (1974) *Hot and Cool Sex: Cultures in Conflict.* Harcourt Brace Jovanovich, New York.

most exclusively interpreted sexual morality from a System A or absolutist position, although most religious groups have modified their positions slightly in the direction of increased sexual liberality, and a few rabbis, priests, and ministers have become considerably more modern in their views. (Ref. 8, p. 134)

Judaic Doctrines of Childhood Sexuality

Judaism exhibits a clear doctrinal range within the fixed/process philosophies spectrum (Table 8.1). On the fixed world view end, Orthodox Judaism and its most conservative sect, Hassidic Judaism, claim to be most faithful to traditional religious principles, beliefs and rituals. On the liberal side of the spectrum, Reformed and humanistic Judaism are the most open and adaptable to insights from modern developmental psychology and sexology. Conservative Judaism represents the middle of the spectrum.

In general, the Jewish tradition has escaped the antisexualism of the neoplatonic dualism of body/soul that has been so influential in Christian thought. The Judaic tradition affirms sexuality as a blessing, a gift from God which grounds and stabilizes the family. Centuries of persecution and enforced emigration, coupled with a strong biblical tradition, have made the patriarchal family central in the Jewish experience. It is assumed that every Jewish man and woman will marry and have children.

The first commandment of the Torah is "You shall be fruitful and multiply." Hence, there is no place for asceticism, sexual or otherwise. Celibacy is condemned and there is little tolerance or understanding of the single life (18).

Male-female dualism is, however, deeply rooted in the Jewish patriarchal family. Particularly in the orthodox sects, women are peripheral Jews. They are excluded from circumcision, the primary sign of Yahweh's covenant with his chosen people, from study of the Torah, and from ritual service as rabbis. Jewish women are honored as devoted wives and play a powerful role as mothers of the family. In orthodoxy, the sexes are segregated in ritual and much of daily life. There is a fear of female sexuality and the power of women to lure men into lascivious thoughts or untoward behavior that distract them from study of the Torah. "Family purity" is a significant concern for both men and women. At their wedding, Hassidic and orthodox women are given manuals providing meticulous directions about menstruation and its consequences. A woman is ritually unclean during menstruation and forbidden to have sexual intercourse or physical contact of any kind with her husband or any male until the evening of the seventh day after the last sign of vaginal discharge, when she immerses herself in a mikveh, or ritual bath (19-20). Most conservative and reformed Jews no longer adhere to the laws of niddah or menstruation and ritual purity.

As might be expected, Orthodox Judaism has made little if any accommodation to the new discoveries in sexology and child development because all that can be said about these issues has been set down in an unchanging tradition centuries ago. Orthodox Judaism adheres to a strict historical and legalistic interpretation of the Torah which views the pleasures of sexual relations as a mutual right and blessing exchanged between husband and wife. Since marriage and procreation are the most important responsibilities, contraception, masturbation, premarital sexual relations, adultery and homosexuality are all rigorously condemned. Single people are expected to avoid masturbation and premarital sex. In this respect, orthodox Judaism has much in common with the sexual restrictions of formal Catholic doctrine and fundamentalist Protestantism. Reformed Jews, and to a lesser extent Conservative Jews, are more flexible, maintaining a loyalty to tradition while emphasizing themes that allow adherents to adapt to new scientific developments and social exigencies.

Christian Doctrines of Childhood Sexuality

A Historical Overview

Underlying the whole of Christian doctrine is the struggle to overcome the consequences of original sin. In attempting to differentiate themselves from the Jews, the early Christians unfortunately lost the positive Judaic view of sexuality. In its place, under the influence of Paul, Jerome, the Desert Fathers, and especially Augustine in the third century, Christianity adopted a pagan dualism from Hellenic and neoplatonic philosophy that has permeated Christian thinking about sexuality until the present. Linked with Judaic patriarchal dualism, this pagan body-versus-soul dualism created a strongly anti-sexual ethic. Men were portrayed as rational, spiritual and good, provided they avoided the contaminating touch of women. Women, for their part, were passionate, earthly, and "the outpost of hell, the gateway of the devil." They could, however, achieve salvation, preferably in virginity, but also through childbearing. A strong ascetic tradition exalted martyrdom, virginity and celibacy.

Early and medieval Christianity was dominated by a sexual morality based on a selective interpretation of the natural order and purpose of things. Marriage and sexual intercourse could be tolerated but only if they were used exclusively for continuation of the human race. Sex for pleasure was not allowed. The result, in medieval Christianity, was a complete catalog of sexual practices based on natural acts which were procreative (marital intercourse, fornication and rape) and those which were unnatural (masturbation, contraceptive intercourse and sodomy). Sex was licit only between husband and wife, and natural only when it was not enjoyed and nothing was done to interfere with its procreative purpose. For centuries, Christianity has struggled with a radical inability to cope theologically and ethically with the issues of self-love, pleasure and play. Spiritual love, agape, was the ideal and physical love, eros, a sinful indulgence in passion (21-22).

Recently, the analysis of Christian sexual ethics has moved beyond this obvious antisexual posture. Gardella (2) argues convincingly that the contemporary American ethic of sexual pleasure resulted in large part from the struggle of Protestants and Catholics to overcome original sin, gain freedom from guilt and find innocent ecstasy. Without the interplay of Catholic and Protestant sexual moralists in the past two centuries, the contemporary American ethic of sexual pleasure and ecstasy would not be what it is. This more positive interpretation, however, does not alter the fact that with rare exception Christian ethics has been quite uncomfortable with sexual pleasure and sexuality, especially outside the marital and heterosexual realms.

From the early Victorian era to the present, Christian morality in America has maintained two contradictory images of the child and its psychosexual development. In one view, the child, though conceived in original sin, enjoyed a period of sublime innocence which the sexual awakening of puberty shattered. Freud's belief in a period of preadolescent sexual latency reinforced this view.

In the second view, the doctrine of original sin emphasized the innate inclinations to evil and depravity in every child. Since original sin was frequently associated with sex, the parents' role was to watch over each child constantly and eradicate any sign of depraved activity, especially any hint of the vile practice of "self-pollution." Despite their seeming difference, the outcome of both religious views was the prohibition and punishment of any and all expressions of the psychosexual rehearsal

behaviors natural to childhood. The Victorian hysteria over masturbation, which lasted well into this century, has been well documented (23).

Contemporary Doctrines

In Catholicism, formal statements from the Vatican continue adhering to the natural law interpretation of sexuality, focusing on acts, and concluding that any sexual activity outside heterosexual marital procreative sex is a gravely sinful, intrinsically evil and disordered act. This view has been balanced in the past decade by the vast majority of contemporary Catholic moralists who have shifted to a person-oriented, process-based moral thinking. On the subject of masturbation, this person-oriented view ranges from statements that "not every deliberately willed act of masturbation necessarily constitutes the grave matter required for mortal sin" to Catholic moralists who maintain that "it must be said once and for all that the masturbation of the child and of the adolescent is a normal act which has no unfavorable consequences, either physical or moral, as long as one does not make the mistake of placing these acts on a moral plane, with which they have nothing to do" (24).

Despite the disagreements of different sects within mainstream Protestant Christianity, sexuality is affirmed as a good gift of the Creator which has been marred and distorted by human sin and alienation. Unlike Catholicism, Protestantism early on abandoned procreation as the primary purpose of marriage and sexual expression. It has also been more open to new empirical knowledge about sex and more willing to move from categories of acts to an interpersonal focus on the meanings of sexual expression (Ref. 25, pp. 364–392). The United Presbyterian Workstudy document of 1970, for instance, clearly states that morally good and evil sexual actions "are not susceptible of being catalogued" (26). This person-oriented approach is evident in a variety of denominational statements compiled by Genne (27). Typical is the following statement from the United Presbyterian Church:

Since masturbation is often one of the earliest pleasurable sexual experiences which is identifiably genital, we consider it essential that the church, through its teachings and through the attitudes it encourages in Christian homes, contribute to a healthy understanding of this experience which will be free of guilt and shame. The ethical significance of masturbation depends entirely on the context in which it takes place. Therefore, we can see no objection to it when it occurs as a normal developmental experience or as a deliberately chosen alternative to inappropriate heterosexual activity. (Ref. 26, pp. 14–15)

On issues of adolescent sexual relations, premarital sexual intercourse and homosexuality, the mainstream Protestant churches have been more cautious in breaking with the traditional heterosexual marital ethics, asking questions rather than taking definitive positions:

In a society where the sexes are moving more and more toward equal status and away from double standards, is it the responsibility of the Church to examine her traditional standards of sexuality for single adults and ask what values would be best to help single men and women to be themselves as whole human beings? (28)

Sexual union as a communicative act has increasingly become associated with the showing of affection both within and without the institution of marriage and herein lies the problem. If we as a church have and do condone sexual union as a communicative act, can we and should we condone it only within the institution of marriage? (29)

Sexual intercourse outside marriage is a growing reality in our time. To state categorically that it is wrong is to come at it legalistically rather than contextually. (30)

The ordination of acknowledged gay men and lesbian women to the ministry by the Episcopal Church and United Church of Christ (Congregational) and debates over this possibility in other Protestant denominations are indicative of a similar shift in sexual values which will inevitably affect childhood sexuality. John Boswell has noted that homosexually oriented children suffer a unique problem because of their "lack of social category" (1). Both secular and religious cultures ignore gay children as non-existent. Gay children fall off the map of human society. It is to be hoped that, as the mainstream Protestant Churches and process-oriented Catholic moralists adjust more to the realities of modern life, this destructive situation will change for the better.

In 1968, an interfaith statement developed by the National Council of Churches, the Synagogue Council of America and the U.S. Catholic Conference called for tolerance and acceptance of differences in school sexuality programs, informed and dignified discussion on all sides of moral questions, and promotion of our potential as human beings (8).

It is obvious from any cursory reading of religious doctrines based on the fixed world view that the conservative judgments of Orthodox Jews, Eastern Orthodox Christians, the Vatican, Jehovah's Witnesses (31–32), the Seventh Day Adventists, the Church of the Latter Day Saints (Mormons) and fundamentalist Moral Majority Protestant groups will remain unalterably opposed to any acceptance of masturbation, homosexual relations and heterosexual expressions of any kind for the unmarried, adolescents, or especially children. As mentioned earlier, Stayton suggests that most institutions within the Judaeo-Christian tradition, particularly recent pronouncements from the Vatican, reflect a moral development which has been arrested at stage one (Ref. 8, p. 134).

A 1987 report prepared by The Task Force on Changing Patterns of Sexuality and Family Life for Study by the Episcopal Diocese of Newark, New Jersey, is the most advanced and liberal document to be issued by any mainstream Christian church. In essence, this document would provide for gay unions "the same recognition and affirmation which nurtures and sustains heterosexual couples in their relationships, including, where appropriate, liturgies which recognize and bless such relationships." While this report calls for "maintaining the sacredness of the marital relationship in the sacrament of Holy Matrimony," it also calls for recognition and acceptance of young adults who choose to engage in premarital sexual relations or nonmarital cohabitation. Moral criteria urged by the report include: "life-enhancing for both partners and exploitative of neither . . . grounded in sexual fidelity and not involving promiscuity . . . founded on love and valued for the strengthening, joy, support and benefit of the couple and those to whom they are related." Recognition of premarital sex should create a most positive and responsible atmosphere for teenagers (33).

The Society of Friends (Quakers) and the Unitarian/Universalist Church have moved beyond stage-one morality, and have openly acknowledged and dealt positively with issues of sexuality in childhood and adolescence (34). In 1971, a nationwide controversy erupted with the release of a very explicit student-centered experiential program sponsored by the Unitarian/Universalist Church, in which sexually explicit filmstrips, student manuals and parent guides, "About Your Sexuality," dealt with a range of topics no church document had previously dared touch (35). For some, it may have been acceptable for a program for adolescents to deal with male and female sexual anatomy and physiology, dating, partner choice, conception and childbirth, but the inclusion of explicit filmstrips and texts dealing with sexual intercourse, same sex behaviors, masturbation, contraception and sexual diseases was unheard of. In some states, criminal prosecutions were threatened against the main author, Deryek Calderwood, and local Unitarian/Universalist Churches which used this program. Fifteen years later, the third updating of "About Your Sexuality" is still too controversial for use in many Christian churches although its preeminent position is widely recognized.

Humanist Doctrines

Drawing on input from 35 leading sexologists, Lester Kirkendall drafted "A New Bill of Sexual Rights and Responsibilities" for the American Humanist Association. Among the nine main points proposed in this statement was one related specifically to children:

Individuals are able to respond positively and affirmatively to sexuality throughout life; this must be acknowledged and accepted. Childhood sexuality is expressed through genital awareness and exploration. This involves self-touching, caressing parts of the body, including the sexual organs. These are learned experiences that help the individual understand his or her body and incorporate sexuality as an integral part of his or her personality. Masturbation is a viable mode of satisfaction for many individuals, young and old, and should be fully accepted. Just as repressive attitudes have prevented us from recognizing the value of childhood sexual response, so have they prevented us from seeing the value of sexuality in the middle and later years . . . (36)

In Christianity and especially in Roman Catholicism, the patriarchal, marital, reproductive symbols of sexuality have dominated, often reinforced by a competitive or dichotomous dualism of body versus soul, a concept of an "original sin" linked in the common mind with sexual sin, and a redemption achieved by subordination and denial of the body with its passions and emotions. In Western sexual archetypes, the male is active and dominant, the female passive. The rational male is clearly superior to the emotional and passionate female. The world view of the early Persian philosopher Zoroaster split the world into a realm of light, goodness and spirit on one side and a world of darkness, evil and body on the other side. This dichotomy flourished in the West, especially in Roman Catholicism (37).

While the doctrines and symbols of the great religions of the world undoubtedly play a substantial normative role in guiding the sexual lives of adults, only scant indirect and inferential conclusions can be made about their impact on childhood sexual development. In the more dualistic Christian tradition, more can be concluded because of the pervading religious concerns expressed about controlling and regulating sexual expression for those who are not married and ready to have a family. Much more research is needed to answer the question of to what extent dysfunctional and paraphilic lovemaps can be traced to which religious doctrines.

References

1. Boswell J. (1980) *Christianity, Social Tolerance and Homosexuality*. University of Chicago Press, Chicago.

2. Gardella P. (1985) *Innocent Ecstasy: How Christianity Gave America an Ethic of Sexual Pleasure*. Oxford University Press, New York.

3. Bullough V.L. (1976) *Sexual Variance in Society and History*. Wiley, New York.

4. Brinton C. (1959) *A History of Western Morals*. Harcourt Brace and Co., New York.

5. Money J., Cawte J.E., Bianchi G.N., Nurcombe B. (1970) Sex training and traditions in Arnhem Land. *Br. J. Med. Psychol*, 43, 383.

6. Money J. (1986) *Lovemaps: Clinical Concepts of Sexual/Erotic Health and Pathology, Paraphilia, and Gender Transposition in Childhood, Adolescence, and Maturity*, pp. xvi and 18. Irvington Press, New York.

7. Francoeur R.T. (1972) *Eve's New Rib: 20 Faces of Sex, Marriage and Family*, pp. 43-64. Harcourt Brace Jovanovich, New York.

8. Stayton W.R. (1985) Religion and adolescent sexuality. *Semin. Adolescent Med.*, 1, 131–137.

9. Piaget J. (1965) *The Moral Judgment of the Child*. Free Press, New York.

10. Hersh R.D., Paolitto D., Reimer J. (1979) *Promoting Moral Growth: From Piaget to Kohlberg*. Longmans, New York.

11. Gilligan C., Kohlberg L. (1974) Moral reasoning and value formation. In Calderone M.S. (Ed), *Sexuality and Human Values*. Association Press, New York.

12. Mayr E. (1963) *Animal Species and Evolution*, p. 5. Harvard University Press, Cambridge, MA.

13. Francoeur R.T. (1965) *Perspectives in Evolution*. Helicon Press, Baltimore.

14. Francoeur R.T. (1970) *Evolving World Converging Man*. Holt Rinehart Winston, New York.

15. Francoeur R.T. (1984) Moral concepts in the year 2020: The individual, the family, and society. In Kirkendall L.A., Gravatt A.E. (Eds), *Marriage and the Family in the Year 2020*. Prometheus Press, Buffalo, NY.

16. Francoeur R.T. (1982) *Becoming a Sexual Person*, Ch. 14. John Wiley, New York.

17. Francoeur A.K., Francoeur R.T. (1974) *Hot and Cool Sex: Cultures in Conflict*. Harcourt Brace Jovanovich, New York.

18. Nelson J.B. (1983) *Between Two Gardens: Reflections on Sexuality and Religious Experience*, pp. 56–59. Pilgrim Press, New York.

19. Schneid H. (1973) *Marriage* (Popular Judaica Library). Keter Books, Jerusalem.

20. Blasz E. (1967) *Code of Jewish Family Purity: A Condensation of the Nidah Laws Committee for the Preservation of Jewish Family Purity*. Brooklyn, NY.

21. Bullough V.L., Brundage J. (1982) *Sexual Practices and the Medieval Church*, pp. 1–12. Prometheus Press, Buffalo, NY.

22. Bullough V.L., Bullough B. (1977) *Sin, Sickness, and Sanity*, Ch. 2. New American Library Meridian, New York.

23. Phipps W.E. (1977) Masturbation: Vice or virtue? *J. Relig. Health*, 16(3), 183.

24. Kosnik A., Carroll W., Cunningham A., Modras R., Schulte J. (1977) *Human Sexuality: New Directions in American Catholic Thought*. A Study Commissioned by The Catholic Theological Society of America, pp. 219–229. Paulist Press, New York.

25. Herz F.M., Rosen E.J. (1982) Jewish families. In McGoldrick M., Pearce J.K., Giordano J. (Eds), *Ethnicity and Family Therapy*, pp. 364–392. Guilford Press, New York.

26. United Presbyterian Church of the U.S. (1977) *Sexuality and the Human Community*, p. 11. U.P.C.U.S.A., Philadelphia.

27. Genne W. H. (Ed) (1970) *A Synoptic of Recent Denominational Statements on Sexuality*. National Council of Churches, New York.

28. *Christianity and Human Sexuality* (No date) p. 50. The Executive Council of the Episcopal Church.

29. A Staff Report of the Work of the Task Force on Sex Ethics (1969) p. 10. The United

Church of Christ, Division of Christian Education, Philadelphia.

30. *Sex, Marriage, and Family: A Contemporary Christian Perspective* (1970) p. 67. Board of Social Ministry of the Lutheran Church in America, New York.

31. Watch Tower Bible and Tract Society of New York (1978) *Making Your Family Life Happy*. Watch Tower Bible and Tract Society of New York, Inc., New York.

32. Watch Tower Bible and Tract Society of New York (1976) *Your Youth: Getting the Best Out of It*. Watch Tower Bible and Tract Society of New York, Inc., New York.

33. Thayer N.S.T. (1987) (March) Report of the Task Force on Changing Patterns of Sexuality and Family Life. Episcopal Diocese, Newark, NJ.

34. Friends (1966) *Towards a Quaker View of Sex*. Friends Home Service Committee, London.

35. Calderwood D. (1971) *About Your Sexuality*. Beacon Press, Boston.

36. Kirkendall L.A. (1976) A new bill of sexual rights and responsibilities. *The Humanist*, 36(1), 4–6.

37. Cousins E.H. (1987) Male-female aspects of the Trinity in Christian Mysticism. In Gupta B. (Ed), *Sexual Archetypes, East and West*, pp. 45–49. Paragon House, New York.

Chapter 9
Early Childhood Exposure to Parental Nudity and Scenes of Parental Sexuality

Paul Okami
Richard Olmstead
Paul R. Abramson
Laura Pendleton

Is exposure of a child to parental nudity or scenes of parental sexual activity a subtle form of sexual abuse as suggested by some researchers and clinicians? According to Okami et al., empirical data on the long-term outcomes of such scenarios are scant, although seemingly authoritative statements alluding to this fact frequently appear in the popular literature. Thus, the authors' investigation of this subject is a welcome addition to the research literature.

Sigmund Freud coined the term "primal scene" to refer to visual or auditory exposure of children to parental sexual intercourse. Psychoanalysts have long related such exposure to mental health problems of children. The researchers conducting this study reasoned that any such harm from exposure to these events would result from interactions with specific ecological variables, such as age or sex of the child. They framed their study with a number of important outcome measures chosen to reflect long-term adjustment in areas of concern to clinicians.

Readers should be aware of some methodological limitations of the Okami et al. study: the sample was not from "average" U.S. families; the sample was limited in size; a non-random sample was used; and there were some problems of measurement. Nevertheless, this study is an important effort among the few other empirical studies that do exist, and readers will be better positioned to discriminate between myth and fact about this controversial topic.

Introduction

Increasing numbers of academic researchers and clinicians have suggested that behaviors such as exposure of a child to parental nudity or scenes of parental sexuality ("primal scenes") constitute subtle forms of sexual abuse that previously have gone unrecognized (Haynes-Seman and Krugman, 1989; Kritsberg, 1993; Krug, 1989). Such subtle sexual abuse—referred to as syndromes like "maternal seductiveness," "emotional incest syndrome," "emotional sexual abuse," "covert sexual abuse," and "sexualized attention"—may also include less easily defined behaviors such as parent "flirtatiousness," or inappropriate and excessive displays of physical affection (Sroufe and Fleeson, 1986).

As Okami (1995) suggested, however, such concern is not new. That is, although these "syndromes" have recently entered the discourse on sexual abuse, some of the behaviors that constitute them have long held positions in the pantheon of improper parenting practices. For example, Esman (1973) observed that just one of these practices—exposure of the child to primal scenes—has been indicted in 75 years of psychoanalytic, psychiatric, and psychological literature as the primary etiologic agent in virtually every form of child and adult pathology. However, Esman concluded that, "One is moved to wonder whether we are here confronted with one of those situations in which a theory, by explaining everything, succeeds in explaining nothing" (pp. 64–65). In the present article we report results of the first longitudinal investigation of long-term correlates of exposure to parental nudity and primal scenes.

Exposure to Parental Nudity

Only three empirical articles have addressed the issue of childhood exposure to parent and other adult nudity: Lewis and Janda (1988); Oleinick et al. (1966); and Story (1979). In several other cases, descriptive, self-report studies of social nudist or other groups practicing casual nudity have been conducted without comparison groups (Berger, 1977; Hartman et al., 1991; Smith and Sparks, 1986). In general, the tone of all of this work is antialarmist, representing childhood exposure to nudity as benign.

Apart from these tentative attempts to collect data, writings on this topic consist of theory-driven clinical opinion and commentaries by child rearing specialists. Clinical writings typically reflect the notion that exposure to nudity may be traumatic as a result of (i) premature and excessive stimulation in a manner controlled by the adult, leaving the child feeling powerless; (ii) the child's unfavorable comparison between his or her own anatomy and the adult's; or (iii) the intensification of Oedipal desires and consequent anxiety (DeCecco and Shively, 1977; Justice and Justice, 1979).

Given the vehemence with which clinicians and child-rearing specialists often condemn childhood exposure to parental nudity, it is paradoxical that their dire predictions are not supported by the (scant) empirical work that does exist. Findings are at worst neutral, or ambiguous as to interpretation, and there is even the implication of possible positive benefits in these studies (particularly for boys) in domains such as self-reported comfort with physical affection (Lewis and Janda, 1988) and positive "body self-concept" (Story, 1979). Although these investigations are methodologically limited, their results are consistent with the view of a smaller group of child-rearing specialists and other commentators who have stressed the potential benefits to children of exposure to nudity in the home, in areas such as later sexual functioning, and capacity for affection and intimacy (Goodson, 1991; Martinson, 1977). Although some of these writers make reference to the cross-cultural ubiquity of childhood exposure to parental nudity—although objecting to alarmist positions taken by Western commentators who fail to provide supportive data—the cross-cultural record is not generally explicit on the question of actual exposure of children to parental nudity. It does, however, present a strong case for the universality of parent-child cosleeping or room sharing (Caudill and Plath, 1966; Lozoff et al., 1984; Morelli et al., 1992). It may tentatively be inferred that under such conditions large numbers of the world's population of children are exposed to parental nudity. Finally, a third group of writers stress the importance on the context in which childhood exposure to nudity takes place, insisting that outcomes are mediated by such contextual variations as gender of child, age of child, family climate, cultural beliefs, and so on (Okami, 1995; Okami et al., 1997).

Exposure to Scenes of Parental Sexuality (Primal Scenes)

Freud and his followers chose the term "primal scenes" to refer to visual or auditory exposure of children to parental intercourse, and subsequent fantasy elaborations on the event (Dahl, 1982). Despite the identification of such exposure by psychoanalysts and others as uniquely dangerous to the mental health of children, there are, once again, scant empirical data bearing on effects of primal scene exposure. We could locate only one prevalence study (Rosenfeld et al., 1980) and two studies of initial response and subsequent adult functioning (Hoyt, 1979, 1979). Of course, numbers of case studies exist, including a very rich psychoanalytic literature describing putative consequences of exposure to primal scenes. These writers have explained the traumatagenic issues by referring to "a) the erotically charged character of the exposure, resulting in undischarged libidinal energy and concomitant anxiety; b) the sadomasochistic content of fantasy misinterpretation of the event; and c) the exacerbation of oedipal desires and resultant castration anxiety or other fears of retaliation" (Okami, 1995, p. 56).

Again, however, the few attempts to validate these notions empirically do not support predictions of harm. For example, Rosenfeld et al. (1980) concluded that the extent of psychological damage has been exaggerated. These investigators arrived at their conclusion by two routes: First, exposure to primal scenes appeared to be rather prevalent, with the most conservative estimates as high as 41 percent. Rosenfeld et al. suggested that given this frequency of occurrence, factors other than the primal scene qua primal scene must be responsible for trauma when it occurs. Second, parents reported largely neutral and noncomprehending responses from their small children (ages 4–6). On the other hand, some children appeared to respond with amusement, giggling, and clear comprehension. Thus, the rather sinister portrait emerging from psychoanalytic literature was largely absent from these parent reports.

Hoyt (1978) queried college students about their childhood exposure to scenes of parental sexuality. He found that although these students reported that their exposure had resulted in largely negative emotional responses at the time, the exposed group did not differ from the nonexposed group on self-report ratings of "current happiness" or frequency of and satisfaction with current sexual relations. Moreover, these subjects recalled exposure primarily at prepubescent and pubertal ages. Given that the mean ages for first exposure reported by parents in the Rosenfeld et al. (1980) studies were between 4 and 6, it is conceivable that subjects in Hoyt's investigations were not reporting their first actual exposure to scenes of parental sexuality. Therefore, findings of exposure at peripubertal ages are of limited value in assessing outcome of exposure to primal scenes generally, because with a few exceptions, primal scenes have been defined in the literature as events of early childhood. That is, responses such as "castration anxiety" and "Oedipal desires" are said to be of most crit-

ical importance in the lives of very young children.

The Present Study

Despite the lack of empirical support, psychoanalytic and family systems theorists continue to stress the potential for harm in exposure to parental nudity and primal scenes. Therefore, longitudinal outcome data are important in beginning to resolve this question. In the present exploratory study, 204 families were enlisted during the mid-1970s as part of a multidisciplinary investigation of emergent family life-styles, UCLA Family Lifestyles Project. Children were followed from birth to the current wave of data collection at ages 17–18. Because there was no indication in the literature that either of the target behaviors is harmful, we hypothesized no deleterious effects of early childhood exposure either to nudity or primal scenes.

Theories based in evolutionary biology, cognitive science, and ethology predict sex differences in psychological mechanisms mediating sexual behavior in humans (Abramson and Pinkerton, 1995; Buss, 1994, 1995). Although most evolutionary theorizing about human sex differences in sexuality has focused on reproductively mature individuals, sex differences in sexuality-related psychological response also have been found among children and early adolescents (Gold and Gold, 1991; Knoth et al., 1988). In their study of adolescents ages 12–18 who were asked to recall their earliest sexual arousal and sexual feelings, Knoth et al., (1988) reported outcomes markedly congruent with evolutionary theory. Specifically, these investigators found that girls, as compared with boys, reported later onset of arousal, less frequency of arousal, less intense arousal, less distracting arousal, and were less likely to have experienced first arousal in response to visual cues. In the study by Gold and Gold (1991), men, relative to women, reported that their boyhood fantasies were more explicit and focused on the sexual acts themselves, more likely to have resulted from visual cues, more likely to have resulted in positive rather than negative affect, and that they were first experienced at an earlier age. Thus, sex differences in sexuality-related psychological responses appear to be present at least from preadolescence.

Method

Outcome measures were chosen to reflect long-term adjustment in a number of areas of concern to clinicians. These areas included: (i) self-acceptance; (ii) relations with parents, peers, and other adults; (iii) drug use; (iv) antisocial and criminal behavior; (v) suicidal ideation; (vi) social "problems" associated with sexual behavior (getting pregnant or having gotten someone pregnant, and getting an STD); and (vii) quality of sexual relationships, attitudes, and beliefs.

The UCLA Family Lifestyles Project (FLS) is a longitudinal investigation founded in 1973 to examine emergent family life-styles of that era. Fifty "conventional" and 154 "nonconventional" families, matched for ethnicity and socieconomic status (SES) according to Hollingshead's four-factor model (Hollingshead, 1975), were enrolled prior to the birth of the target child. All parents were of European American descent and were living in the State of California when recruited.

Conventional families were defined as those in a "married couple relationship" and were referred by a randomly selected sample of obstetricians from the San Francisco, San Diego, and Los Angeles areas. Nonconventional families were recruited through physician referral, birthing office records, alternative media announcements, and referral by already enrolled participants. Nonconventional family forms included intentional single mothers, couples living in communes or other group-living situations, and "social contract" (cohabiting) couples. During the most recent wave of data collection, target children were between the ages of 17 and 18 years.

For boys, exposure to primal scenes predicted reduced likelihood of having gotten an STD, or having gotten someone pregnant. The reverse was the case for girls, who were significantly more likely to have gotten an STD or to have become pregnant. This finding was independent of the extent of sexual behavior engaged in.

To determine extent of exposure to nudity and primal scenes, parents were asked two questions in a face-to-face interview at child's age 3: "Does mother (father) go nude in front of child?" and "Does mother (father) bathe or shower with the child?" The questions were followed by scales anchored by 1 (never) and 4 (regularly) or 1 (never) and 5 (daily). At child's age 6, parents were asked whether they (i) discouraged family nudity, (ii) felt OK about nudity within the family but not with others, or (iii) encouraged nudity within the family and with others.

Exposure to primal scenes was measured by two items. At child's age 3, parents were asked whether their child had ever seen them "have sex." They were offered a 4-point response format anchored by 1 (never) and 4 (regularly). At child's age 6, parents were again asked if their child had observed them having intercourse, and again offered a 4-point scale anchored by 1 (no) and 4 (regularly). Because of shifts in the identity of mothers' male partners for some of the families over the first 6 years, and the greater frequency of fathers working outside of the home and being unavailable for interview, missing data for fathers approach unacceptable levels. Therefore, only mothers' data were used for these analyses.

Results

The principal components analyses yielded five drug-use factors and four antisocial behavior factors. The drug-use factors are hence referred to as Hard Drugs (i) Sedatives, minor tranquilizers; (ii) Marijuana, hashish, psychedelic mushrooms, LSD, "Ecstasy"; (iii) PCP, major tranquilizers, other psychedelics, inhalants; (iv) Amyl nitrate, amphetamines, other narcotics; and (v) Heroin, barbiturates, cocaine, inhalants. The antisocial behavior variables are labeled antisocial behavior: theft, vandalism, felonies and fighting.

Frequencies for exposure to the main variables are as follows: For exposure to primal scenes, 32 percent of the children were exposed (boys, $n = 34$, girls, $n = 39$), whereas 68 percent of the children were not exposed. For exposure to parental nudity, 25 percent of children were not exposed to any parental nudity, 44 percent of children were exposed with moderate frequency, and 31 percent of children (boys, $n = 34$, girls, $n = 27$) were exposed frequently.

A number of trends were found that were significant. Exposure to parental nudity predicted lower likelihood of sexual activity in adolescence, but more positive sexual experiences among that group of participants who were sexually active. Exposure to parental nudity also predicted reduced instances of petty theft and shoplifting, but this was mediated by a sex of participant interaction indicating that this effect was attenuated or absent for women. Similarly, exposure to parental nudity was associated with reduced use of drugs such as marijuana, LSD, Ecstasy, and psychedelic mushrooms, but again, this effect was experienced primarily by men. Indeed, exposed women were very slightly more likely to have used these drugs.

At the level of trend, exposure to primal scenes was associated with higher levels of self-acceptance and improved relations with adults other than parents. There was also a trend for women exposed to primal scenes to have been less likely to use drugs such as PCP, major tranquilizers, inhalants, and psychedelics other than LSD or mushrooms.

Although a number of nonsignificant trends emerged, the only significant finding was that family sexual liberalism was associated with sexual liberalism at adolescence.

Discussion

This study, using a longitudinal design, is the first to examine long-term correlates of early childhood exposure to parental nudity and primal scenes. Consistent with the cross-sectional retrospective literature (and with our expectations), no harmful main effects of these experiences were found at ages 17–18. Indeed, trends in the data did not reach significance. Exposure to parental nudity was associated with positive, rather than negative, sexual experiences in adolescence, but with reduced sexual experience overall. Boys exposed to parental nudity were less likely to have engaged in theft in adolescence or to have used various psychedelic drugs and marijuana.

In the case of primal scenes, exposure was associated with improved relations with adults outside of the family and with higher levels of self-acceptance. Girls exposed to primal scenes were also less likely to have used drugs such as PCP, inhalants, or various psychedelics in adolescence. The one note of caution: males' exposure to primal scenes was associated with reduced risk of social "problems" associated with sexuality, while the opposite was the case for females. Women in our study who had been exposed to primal scenes reported increased instances of STD transmission and pregnancy. All findings were independent of the effects of SES, sex of participant, family stability, pathology, "pronaturalism," and beliefs and attitudes toward sexuality.

Taken as a whole then, effects are few, but generally beneficial in nature. Thus, results of this study add weight to the views of those who have opposed alarmist characterizations of childhood exposure both to nudity and incidental scenes of parental sexuality. Moreover, although the association of higher instance of sexually transmitted diseases and adolescent pregnancy among young women exposed to primal scenes might appear at first glance to represent harm unequivocally, more careful examination renders these findings somewhat ambiguous. In the case of increased instance of pregnancy among these women, for example, it should be noted that over half of those who reported having become pregnant (and almost half of the men who reported impregnating someone) rated their experience "good" rather than "bad." Although it is true that problems— sometimes serious problems—may attend such pregnancies in U.S. society, some data also suggest that these problems have been exaggerated (Stevens-Simon and White, 1991), and may often result more from low SES than from adolescent pregnancy itself (Trussell, 1988). Current treatment of adolescent pregnancy as intrinsically pathological may in part have generalized from an overall tendency to view adolescent sexual behaviors as problematic.

Even findings of increased instances of STD transmission among the women in our study need to be considered carefully. Symons (February 1995, personal communication) pointed out that increased instances of STDs and pregnancy among women exposed to primal scenes might be more parsimoniously understood as decreased use of condoms among the women. Regardless of problematic outcome, decreased use of condoms may be motivated by heightened desire (and capacity) for intimacy or higher levels of trust in partners—as well as by simple lack of sexual responsibility or self-destructive tendencies. In this respect it should be recalled that there was a (nonsignificant) trend toward higher levels of self-acceptance and improved relations with adults among these women.

Several outcome measures in the direction of beneficial correlates for boys were neutral or problematic correlates for girls. One interpretation would be that human males and females process sexuality-related events differently as the result of sexually dysmorphic psychological mechanisms that have evolved through natural and sexual selection (Buss, 1994). Moore (1995) has suggested the possibility that these mechanisms might begin to emerge reliably in childhood.

Other explanations of the gender interactions are also possible. For example, boys and girls are socialized differently throughout the world where sexuality is concerned, with girls being socialized more restrictively (Mead, 1967). Although these socialization procedures may also represent expressions of sexually dysmorphic psychological adaptation by natural and sexual selection, it could be argued that they instead represent temporally specific but worldwide sociocultural or socioeconomic forces related to patriarchal control of female sexuality. A third explanation of our results is more prosaic. These interactions by sex may be entirely artifactual statistical noise.

Additionally, while findings of beneficial outcomes are interesting, specific findings are not predicted by any theory that we know. In our view, then, the importance of the present investigation, apart from the suggestion of interactions by sex, lies not so much in positive findings as in the negative findings for harm—findings that converge on all of the available empirical data. Admittedly, any one set of negative results is not particularly informative. However, given virtually no evidence in this or any other empirical study that the behaviors examined in the current study are unambiguously harmful, the interesting question becomes: Why is it so widely believed in the United States and certain European nations that these practices are uniformly detrimental to the mental health of children? Such notions, certainly where exposure to parental nudity is concerned, are perhaps better conceptualized as myths. Whereas any of these behaviors of course may be experienced in an abusive context—and may also occasion harm under certain circumstances for certain individuals—their appearance per se does not appear to constitute cause for alarm.

Methodological limitations need to be addressed in interpreting results of this study. Most obviously, although the sample contains an interesting assortment of families that permitted the predictor variables to be studied in a number of contexts, these families undoubtedly differ in a number of potentially important ways from the "average" U.S. family. In addition to volunteer bias, the sample is made up entirely of European Americans residing in California at the time of enrollment, and "nonconventional" means exactly what it says—three-fourths of the sample were nonrepresentative of typical American life-style by definition. However, while not representative, the current sample was dedicated and attrition virtually nonexistent. This adds considerably to the meaningfulness of the analysis. Moreover, because the nonconventional families (whose members constituted approximately 75 percent of the total sample) were more likely to adhere to countercultural values supportive of free sexual expression, nudity within the family, and so forth, it is precisely in a data set such as this that one ought to expect to see elevated problems if these practices are in fact deleterious of themselves.

In any event, lack of reliability in the instruments used here would tend to reduce the probability of the type of findings that emerged. Lack of reliability should have produced null findings—not positive findings in a direction directly opposite that proposed by received wisdom. It is therefore difficult to imagine a methodological problem that could have erroneously painted such a consistent portrait of no harm.

Findings of the current study do not resolve the moral (or legal) issue of whether the behaviors we have examined represent "subtle sexual abuse." However, they do address the empirical question of whether these occurrences are harmful, at least within certain domains. Although evidence gathered for the present study is far from conclusive, at this point it is difficult to see the utility of referring to these events a priori as harmful, and even more difficult to see the utility of characterizing them globally as "abusive."

References

Abramson, P. R., and Pinkerton, S. (1995). *Sexual Nature, Sexual Culture*, University of Chicago Press, Chicago.

Berger, B. (1977). Child-rearing research in communes: The extension of adult sexual behavior to young children. In Oremland, E. K., and Oremland, J. D. (eds.), *The Sexual and Gender Development of Young Children: The Role of the Educator*, Ballinger, Cambridge, MA, pp. 159–164.

Buss, D. M. (1994). *The Evolution of Desire*, Basic Books, New York.

Buss, D. M. (1995). Evolutionary psychology: A new paradigm for psychological science. *Psychol. Inq.* 6: 1–30.

Caudhill, W., and Plath, D. W. (1966). Who sleeps by whom? Parent-child involvement in urban Japanese families. *Psychiatry* 29: 344–366.

Dahl, G. (1982). Notes on critical examinations of the primal scene concept. *J. Am. Psychiat. Assoc.* 30: 657–677.

DeCecco, J. P., and Shively, M. G. (1977). Children's development: Social sex-role and the hetero-homosexual orientation. In Oremland, E. K., and Oremland, J. D. (eds.), *The Sexual and Gender Development of Young Children: The Role of the Educator*, Ballinger, Cambridge, MA, pp. 89–90.

Esman, A. H. (1973). The primal scene: A review and a reconsideration. *Psychanal. Quart.* 28: 49–81.

Gold, S. R., and Gold, R. G. (1991). Gender differences in first sexual fantasies. *J. Sex Educ. Ther.* 17: 207–216.

Goodson, A. (1991). *Therapy, Nudity, and Joy*, Elysium Growth Press, Los Angeles.

Hartman, W. E., Fithian, M., and Johnson, D. (1991). *Nudist Society*, 2nd ed., Elysium Growth Press, Los Angeles.

Haynes-Seman, C., and Krugman, R. D. (1989). Sexualized attention: Normal interaction or precursor to sexual abuse? *Am. J Orthopsychiat.* 59: 238–245.

Hollingshead, A. (1975). *Four Factor Index of Social Position*, Yale University, New Haven, CT.

Hoyt, M. F. (1978). Primal scene experiences as recalled and reported by college students. *Psychiatry* 41: 57–71.

Hoyt, M. F. (1979). Primal-scene experiences: Quantitative assessment of an interview study. *Arch. Sex. Behav.* 8: 225–245.

Justice, B., and Justice, R. (1979). *The Broken Taboo*, Human Sciences, New York.

Knoth, R., Boyd, K., and Singer, B. (1988). Empirical tests of sexual selection theory: Predictions of sex differences in onset, intensity, and time course of sexual arousal. *J. Sex Res.* 24: 73–79.

Kritsberg, W. (1993). *The Invisible Wound: A New Approach to Healing Childhood Sexual Trauma*, Bantam, New York.

Krug, R. S. (1989). Adult male report of childhood sexual abuse by mothers: Case descriptions, motivations and long-term consequences. *Child Abuse Neg.* 13: 111–119.

Lewis, R. J., and Janda, L. H. (1988). The relationship between adult sexual adjustment and childhood experiences regarding exposure to nudity, sleeping in the parental bed, and parental attitudes toward sexuality. *Arch. Sex. Behav.* 17: 349–362.

Lozoff, B., Wolf, A. W., and Davis, N. S. (1984). Co-sleeping in urban families with young children in the United States. *Pediatrics* 74:171–182.

Martinson, F. M. (1977). Eroticism in childhood: A sociological perspective. In Oremland, E. K., and Oremland, J. D. (eds.), *The Sexual and Gender Development of Young Children: The Role of the Educator*, Ballinger, Cambridge, MA, pp. 73–82.

Mead, M. (1967). *Male and Female: A Study of the Sexes in a Changing World*, William Morrow, New York.

Moore, M. M. (1995). Courtship signaling and adolescents: "Girls just want to have fun"? *J. Sex Res.* 32: 319–328.

Morelli, G. A., Rogoff, B., Oppenheim, D., and Goldsmith, D. (1992). Culture variations in infant's sleeping arrangements: Questions of independence. *Dev. Psychol.* 28: 604–613.

Okami, P. (1995). Childhood exposure to parental nudity, parent-child co-sleeping, and "primal scenes": A review of clinical opinion and empirical evidence. *J. Sex Res.* 32: 51–64.

Okami, P., Olmstead, R., and Abramson, P. R. (1997). Sexual experiences in early childhood: 18-year data from the UCLA Family Life-styles Project. *J. Sex Res.* 34: 339–347.

Oleinick, M. S., Bahn, A. K., Eisenberg, L., and Lilienfield, A. M. (1966). Early socialization experiences. *Arch. Gen. Psychiat.* 15: 1966.

Rosenfeld, A. A., Smith, C. R., Wenegrat, M. A., Brewster, M. A., and Haavik, D. K. (1980). The primal scene: A study of prevalence. *Anti. J. Psychial.* 137: 1426–1428.

Smith, D. C., and Sparks, W. (1986). *The Naked Child: Growing Up Without Shame*, Elysium Growth Press, Los Angeles.

Sroufe, A. L., and Fleeson, J. (1986). Attachment and the construction of relationships. In Hartup, W. W., and Rubin, Z. (eds.), *Relationships and Development*, Erlbaum, Hillsdale, NJ, pp. 51–71.

Stevens-Simon, C., and White, M. (1991). Adolescent pregnancy. *Pediat. Ann.* 20: 322–331.

Story, M. D. (1979). Factors associated with more positive body self-concepts in preschool children. *J. Soc. Psychol.* 108: 49–56.

Trussell, J. (1988). Teenage pregnancy in the United States. *Fam. Plann. Perspect.* 20: 262–273.

Chapter 10
Negotiation of First Sexual Intercourse Among Latina Adolescent Mothers

Pamela I. Erickson

Pamela Erickson assumes a laborious task as she investigates cultural and social factors affecting the initiation of sexual intercourse among Latina adolescent mothers using the case study method. The data were drawn from life-history interviews with the young mothers and their sexual partners from 1994 to 1997.

The author's careful review of the research literature revealed a number of stereotyped gender behaviors influenced by Latino cultural norms. These patterns included the fact that, in some cases, the female adolescent wants a baby; she has a high incidence of older men or adolescents as sex partners; and her role models are peers, relatives, and/or a mother who experienced teenage pregnancy. However, Erickson suggests that changes in socio-economic realities, such as the emergence of an educated Latino middle class and exposure to more egalitarian gender norms in the United States, have resulted in greater variations in actual gender behavior among Latina adolescents and less stereotypical behavior.

As the case studies in Erickson's research unfold, patterns emerge: scripting of relationships; male pressure and female resistance; the absence of verbal consent; ignorance about sexuality; and male control along with female passivity. Readers are challenged to determine the role of cultural and societal factors in scenarios so deftly drawn by the data. How do these findings differ from those concerning other populations? Do these findings account for the fact that in 1995 the Latina adolescent birth rate surpassed that of African Americans for the first time? Is Erickson correct that Latino adolescent behavior is becoming less stereotypical? There is no lack of interesting questions for interested readers.

In the United States today, adolescent pregnancy and childbearing are perceived as serious health, social, and economic problems [1]. Despite a substantial research literature and numerous intervention programs, teenage childbearing rates have remained high for two decades [2]. The most recent statistics on adolescent birth rates indicate that those of Latina adolescents have now surpassed those of African Americans for the first time, and among Latina teens, birth rates are highest for those of Mexican descent [3]. This article explores the social and cultural context of romantic relationships in which Latina teen pregnancy occurs, using narratives from young mothers and their partners to illustrate experiences surrounding initiation of sexual intercourse and pregnancy.

The literature on teenage motherhood clearly demonstrates that adolescent childbearing is largely a socioeconomic class phenomenon intertwined with issues of race and ethnicity [2, 4]. Although it is commonly believed that teenage childbearing is disadvantageous for both mother and child [5], recent research suggests that adolescent childbearing may be an adaptive response to severe, generational, socioeconomic constraints experienced most acutely by adolescents of color [6–7].

Although political economy is an important factor in race and ethnic differences in adolescent childbearing, cultural expectations may also influence reproductive behavior [8]. In fact, Latina adolescents have distinct sexual behavior patterns. Compared to African-American and White (Non-Hispanic) adolescents, Latina adolescents have the lowest proportion of sexually active females, and they exhibit low use of family planning clinics, low use of contraceptive methods before becoming pregnant, and low use of abortion [9–11]. Latina adolescents may also be more likely to plan their pregnancies. Two surveys of primarily Mexican origin teen mothers in Los Angeles found that the proportion of young mothers who had planned to have a baby had increased from 34 percent in the 1986–87 survey to 58 percent in the 1992–94 survey [4]. In contrast, national data indicate that only 18 percent of pregnancies to adolescents of all races are planned [5]. In addition, greater acculturation has been associated with higher levels of sexual risk taking behavior and higher birth rates among Latina adolescents [9, 13–14].

Religious values are thought to buttress traditional gender role patterns through opposition to contraception and abortion [15]. In fact, however, Latinos are more similar to other Americans regarding both contraceptive use and attitudes about abortion [11, 15–16]. The use of abortion by Latinas actually exceeds that of Whites, although it may be used less often by Latina adolescents [11, 17].

Research and prevention efforts dealing with teenage pregnancy and childbearing have tended to assume three things: 1) that teenage motherhood is socially, economically, and often medically disadvantageous and should be prevented [1, 6]; 2) that all pregnancies should be consciously planned and young women should prevent unintended pregnancy through abstinence or contraception [5]; and 3) that young women have a choice about whether or not to engage in sex and they make decisions about sex and birth control after weighing the opportunity costs [18]. Yet, such a "rational decision-making" model of sex and reproduction seems to be a construct imposed by researchers, health practitioners, and other professionals dealing with adolescent pregnancy and childbearing issues. It is at odds with the emotional, highly inti-

mate context in which sex is initiated by adolescents [19]. In the real world, sexual initiation is affected by a wide range of factors including emotions, sexual desire, coercion, and social, cultural, and moral norms [18–19].

In order to understand high rates of Latina adolescent childbearing it is important to understand how the social and cultural aspects of young Latinas' lives may put them at risk for early pregnancy. Latino culture places high value on family and motherhood, and childbearing occurs at younger ages than is normative in the broader American culture [20–21]. Latino cultural norms also tend to value premarital virginity and non-aggressive, modest, sexually ignorant, and sexually passive young women [21–23]. American cultural norms make young women the sexual gatekeepers in heterosexual relationships [19] and place high value on consciously chosen, responsible, planned motherhood [1, 5]. This non-traditional, essentially middle class, American gender role pattern may be one for which many Latina teens are not prepared.

THE CURRENT STUDY

Forty Latina teen mothers under age eighteen at the time they gave birth were recruited from a public hospital providing care to a low income, Latino population. The partners of the young mothers were also invited to participate subject to her permission. Fourteen male partners agreed to participate.[1]

Life histories of participants were collected during one to five informal interviews of one and two hours in length. Participants were simply asked to tell the story of their lives. Topics probed included neighborhood, school, and family, sex and romantic relationships, pregnancy and delivery, being a parent, school and work, migration history, acculturation, health care, and future life plans and goals.

Narratives are presented for five cases which illustrate the range of experiences surrounding sexual debut for young mothers. The interviews suggest that for these young mothers, it was not really sex that was being negotiated, but the couple's entire relationship.[2] "Rational" decision making regarding sex, contraception, and STD prevention could only become the norm for these young couples after they had been having intercourse for some time.

Eva and Rudy[3]

At age sixteen, Eva moved out of her mother's house because they fought and she thought her mother drank too much, had too many boyfriends, and made her take care of her younger siblings all the time. Eva moved into a small apartment with her sister and another couple, but the situation was strained:

Eva: That's why I ended up living with Rudy.

Interviewer: When you were living with your sister, and you and Rudy were just *novios* (boyfriend/girlfriend)—you weren't really involved sexually yet. Did it happen after you moved in with Rudy?

Eva: After we moved to his house. He would like ask me, you know, if we could be together like. "No, no, no—I don't want it." Like, I didn't wanna go that far, you know: I was, like, scared. So he—well, he respected me. But we had tried for (having intercourse) sometimes, but it was like—oh! I wouldn't even know what to do. So, just forget it, you know. I was scared, so, I was like, no.

After six months of resistance, Eva gave in to Rudy's urging for sex and got pregnant in the first month.

Eva: The first time (we had sex), I was living with him, he just came outside, but I still got pregnant. (Sex) scared me at first because I was never introduced to my body or even a male's body. I didn't even know how my body worked, you know? To me, in my head it (premarital sex) was wrong.

Interviewer: Were you willing to *entregar* (give yourself up, surrender) yourself to him?

Eva: Yeah, because, see like, I really did love him a lot and I really did care for him, but it was just the fact that I was gonna lose my virginity. I mean, for a Hispanic girl, you know, that's like, God, that's a big thing! That's like something precious. And, you know, like, you just have to wait 'til you're married and stuff, you know? I did love him a lot, but I just didn't want to go that far. I didn't even know why. I just didn't want to do it . . . maybe because of what I had been taught. But I did. I didn't like being at home, and maybe it was a better way to stay away from home. So, being with him was better, and eventually I just gave up to it. But I was just looking for comfort, because I wasn't getting it at home.

Interviewer: Was it ever talked about, planned?

Eva: He would always ask me and I would say "No, no, no, no, no, no."

Eva and Rudy never talked about sex or contraception, but they had talked about a baby.

Eva: He had told me before that he wanted a baby, but I told him "I don't. I don't want a baby."

Eva was surprised that she got pregnant because they had only had sex that one time. By the time she realized she was pregnant she was about twelve to thirteen weeks and would not consider an abortion. After her daughter was born, Eva went back to high school and she is now in college. She and Rudy have a rocky relationship. They don't live together now, but he is very involved as a father and takes Sara frequently.

Rudy was born in Los Angeles and dropped out of school in ninth grade about the time his parents separated. He began working construction and met Eva when he was sixteen.

Rudy: . . . I used to mess around with a lot of girls. But not in, you know . . . to put it this way, I was a virgin. I let her think that I—I was a big time player with the girls. And, uh, she was my first one.

Interviewer: So, how did you decide to have sex?

Rudy: Well, to me it wasn't really hard, but you know, for Eva it was. 'cause . . . you know guys always they always leave them, you know. But the girl, like Eva, she was scared.

Interviewer: Was she scared about getting pregnant? Did you guys ever talk about that?

Rudy: She never did talk to me about that.

Interviewer: And were you trying to get her pregnant?

Rudy: Yeah, in a way, I was like . . . how does it feel to have a kid?

Interviewer: Were you in love with Eva?

Rudy: Well, see, I never loved someone, like really loved 'em (sic). You know? I don't know why. I'm just like that. I do like Eva and everything, but like, I miss her, but I don't like, love her, you know. Not yet. I don't know, we share a lot of things together, you know, but, I don't know how to love someone.

Julia and Juan

Juan met Julia in Mexico. He was born and raised in Los Angeles but was visiting his grandparents in Mexico. Julia's family lived in the same neighborhood and they were family friends of his grandparents. She was twelve years old when they first met, but told him she was fifteen. He was sixteen. For two years, he visited whenever he could. He was in love. He wrote her poems and called her on the phone.

Juan: I wasn't doing good (in school) 'cause all the time I was thinking about Julia—all the time . . . from one period to the next. I just couldn't stop. I couldn't help it. I tried not to think of her but I just couldn't stop.

Interviewer: You were really in love with her.

Juan: Yeah, but not—it was more, uh, spiritual, you know than just wanting to kiss her. No, it was true love. So I didn't want to have sex with her. I got tempted

sometimes—when we were kissing so passionately—but I respected her. She was the first girl I respected.

Juan eventually found out that Julia had lied about her age and he agonized over how young she was. He wanted to wait until she was older before going out, to ask permission from her parents to date her, and then to have a long courtship. But when Julia was fourteen and Juan eighteen, her parents sent her to relatives in Los Angeles. She and Juan arranged to meet, and he took her to live with him at his mother's house.

Juan: I decided to steal her with her permission. She was having troubles with her brothers and with her parents. And everybody was trying to talk me out of it because I was too young, but I was really in love with her and didn't want her to go through any more pain. So, when she was here, I stole her. That's when I got on the bad side of her parents. And they really got upset with me and I understood, 'cause that made me feel like less of a man. So, I decided to go ahead and live with her. I didn't want to 'cause I wanted to get married first instead of taking her, because I knew that once she was there, where was she was gonna sleep? So, I just thought I might as well sleep with her, but I swear I wasn't thinking about the physical—the sexual part didn't hit me until a day before (she moved in).

Interviewer: So, did you and Julia talk about it (having sex)?

Juan: No, we just felt so free that it just happened. When you're in love, it's like a sense of freedom—like you could do anything. You feel real positive about things. I couldn't believe it that she was there with me. I mean one time she's in Mexico and the next she's in my room. She was so beautiful. And I was thinking, well, if I'm gonna marry her it might be OK. So, then, it just happened and it was like—we didn't—it wasn't even planned.

Julia was also in love with Juan.

Julia: He respected me a lot, and that day that I came (to live in his house)—I felt that I had to be with him.

Interviewer: Then, you didn't feel like he was pressuring you?

Julia: No, I knew what I was doing. He excites me, makes me happy. This is a love that is beautiful.

Interviewer: You intended to be his wife and have his children?

Julia: Yes.

Julia got pregnant about six months after they began having intercourse. They weren't using birth control because Julia had had an ovarian cyst in Mexico and she thought the doctor had told her she would never be able to have children. Juan and Julia wanted children someday, and they were hoping that Julia had been misdiagnosed, but they had not pursued medical follow-up in the United States. Thus, when she became pregnant, they were both surprised, but also very happy. They thought it was a little early and that they were a little young, but they were happy. Juan and Julia now have two children and they were married shortly after Julia's eighteenth birthday.

Sylvia

Sylvia, twenty years old at the time she was interviewed, was born in a small town in El Salvador. She came to the United States with her partner, Luís, when she was seventeen years old and three months pregnant with their daughter. Sylvia met and fell in love with Luís in El Salvador when she was fifteen. He was thirty. He had already moved to the United States, but had come back to visit relatives. Two years later when he returned to her village, she was still in love with him.

Luís began coming to her house and walking her to work. One day her stepfather caught them kissing, and her family tried to put an end to the relationship because he was so much older than she was. They threatened to call the police and have him put in jail, but Sylvia and Luís kept seeing each other secretly for about three months, and one day:

Sylvia: That's where it all started. He was going to take me to work, and from there we left. And the condemned man took me to a motel. And when I got there and he went in and I got to the door and I see the bed. Ay, I wanted to go but he grabbed me and wouldn't let me go. Well, maybe I wanted to, because then, we went together. I didn't know anything about condoms—nothing. And, I didn't protect myself. When I got pregnant he said: why didn't you take care of yourself (use contraception)?

In a later interview Sylvia continues with this theme:

Sylvia: Nobody educated me, nobody taught me (about sex). I think that's why I got pregnant so young. I'm not going to hide anything so that she (her daughter) can know. She has to know everything so she can choose what she wants to do. I never knew anything and because of that, I think, things happen.

Luís was surprised to find out that Sylvia was pregnant, and for awhile it was not clear what they would do. They finally decided that she would accompany him to the United States, but they have not married and Sylvia feels that their relationship is changing, or, perhaps that she thinks about things differently now.

Sylvia: When I gave in and got pregnant I was head over heels in love with him. Now I don't know. It could be due to the problems we had when we got here. He drank a lot. Maybe I lost a little of all that I felt for him. Now I love him and all, but not like we were before.

Luís would like another child, but Sylvia does not—not yet anyway. Until things get better financially and emotionally she is using the oral contraceptive pill, despite Luís not wanting her to contracept.

Erika

Erika is a U.S.-born Latina who grew up in the housing projects. She was thirteen when she met Junior, who was twenty at the time. She had her first baby at fourteen.

Erika: I met him on Halloween. I was just a Playboy Bunny (her Halloween costume), so I didn't look my age. I was wearing heels and makeup—all of that. In the beginning I didn't really care for him, to tell you the truth. He kept coming and coming, so I guess that is what made me like him because he kept on coming.

Erika and Junior dated for about seven months before they had sex for the first time. Erika did not plan to have sex with Junior, but she was clear that he did not force her into it. She said that she didn't want to do it, but at the same time she wanted to do it. They never talked about having sex or about using birth control. She got pregnant within the first month.

Interviewer: Were you trying to get pregnant, Erika?

Erika: In a way I was, but in a way I was like no, no. It was in between.

Interviewer: So, why did you want to get pregnant?

Erika: The truth, the truth because I didn't want to be older.

Interviewer: You didn't want to be a mother at an old age?

Erika: Uhuh. My friend, she got a baby too, she got pregnant at thirteen. I had her (first baby) at fourteen. But her sister got pregnant at fifteen, had her (child) at sixteen. Everybody I know had a man, you know? Everybody I know has kids. I only know two people that don't have kids from everyone I know.

Erika and Junior are still together and they now have two children.

Cori

Cori came to the United States from Mexico with her mother after her parents' divorce when she was a small child. When Cori was ten, her mother sent her to live with her father in Mexico because she had a new partner and was beginning another family. When Cori turned thirteen she began having problems with her stepmother and came back to East L.A., where she lived with her mother and stepfather until she was sixteen. They lived in a rough

neighborhood with a lot of gang problems, but now Cori lives in an upscale beach community with her new partner. Cori thinks that the old neighborhood is part of the problem.

Cori: My old friends there, a lot of them want to get out. They don't want to live in the neighborhood and they try to get out and it's too hard. They end up like me getting pregnant, but then they just get on welfare and they just say: "Oh well, I get on welfare I won't have to work." They get all those girls pregnant and they just leave, and they don't think of their kids . . . when they need to give them money, to the girl, to take care of the kid, they are not there.

Cori met Carlos, her baby's father, through friends when she was fifteen. He was already eighteen and out of school, and she would ditch school to be with him. They went out for about a year before they had sex for the first time.

Cori: I mean it (sex) just happened. (laughs) We didn't talk about sex. He did once and got—I slapped him really hard. (laughter) He told me because we were six months together and all his friends were having sex and he wanted a girlfriend and a girlfriend was somebody he could sleep with and be with, and you know. I didn't let him, and he tried grabbing my butt, and I punched him so hard, (laughs) and he didn't like that, and he got mad for a while but then we went back together again, and it happened after a year. Then, we kind of broke off for a while and went back together.

Interviewer: So then, you guys went back together . . .

Cori: . . . for like six more months and then we did (had sex).

Interviewer: And how did that happen? Were you ready for it? Did you want to?

Cori: I don't know. I didn't really want to. It just happened, because I left my house. My mom threw me out. I didn't have anywhere to go, and so I stayed (at his house). I felt like I was trapped, and I am not going to say that he forced me but I was trapped. . . . I don't know, we did it for the wrong reasons. I felt like I was so desperate, I had nothing else to live for. (I thought) "I don't care about anything else, you know? Forget it, it's just you (him, Carlos) now." It would get to a point that I really didn't care. Then I let him. I let him but I didn't feel like it. I don't know, afterwards I felt like oh! What did I do? I just, we did it twice, then after that I didn't want to. I thought I was too young for that. (Then) I went to my friend's, I didn't feel comfortable staying there (with Carlos), because he wanted me to sleep with him again, and I just didn't want to, so I left. And then I went to my other friend's house and I was just there with her. She has a baby and she is on welfare. She has been on welfare forever, since I know her. So then I said "I don't want to see myself like that—I don't," and I thought about it and I go "God! I could be pregnant." You know, it could happen. And I never, never let him touch me again. We did it twice or whatever, and he gave me something and got me pregnant. . . . I found out after, when I found out I was pregnant five months later, I had chlamydia. I was so mad. Afterwards, I found out that he was sleeping with my best friend. All my friends were sleeping with him. He was really cute.

Discussion

These case studies reveal the complexity of negotiating sexual behavior within a romantic relationship. Having sex was an act that, in the words of so many of these young people, "just happened." It was not negotiated verbally. The couple did not discuss or plan it. Rather, sexual involvement was negotiated physically through a gradual escalation in the level of intimate sexual contact allowed by the young woman during the times they were together. Verbal negotiation that occurred in the context of sexual passion consisted of little else but "please" and "no, not yet." One young man, Cori's boyfriend, who tried to discuss sexual involvement outside the context of hugging and kissing, was slapped for his efforts. That slap was a signal that conscious discussion about sexual involvement was not appropriate or appreciated.

In all cases the young man was the initiator of sexual involvement, and the young woman was the resistor and controller of passion. This is a familiar sexual "script" in contemporary American culture [19]. Most of the young women were able to resist having intercourse for a considerable length of time (several months to a year) before giving in to their partner's urging and, in many cases their own desire as well. This period of waiting was called respect. The respect the young men had for their girlfriends (pressuring for sex, but not too hard, and allowing her to make the decision about the timing of their first sexual intercourse) is interpreted by the young women as an indication of their partner's emotional involvement in the relationship. It is a sign of the young man's good intentions, a test period during which he proves that he cares for her, is not just after sex, and will stay with her in a committed relationship.

In some cases, as with Julia and Juan, sexual intercourse became a spontaneous symbol of commitment and love within the context of the development of their relationship. As the relationship evolved and they became emotionally closer, they naturally wanted to express this closeness physically. As they fell in love, sex became a natural part of the union of their two selves into one, the much sought after goal of passionate, romantic love [24]. For Cori and Eva, allowing intercourse to occur seemed to be a bid for greater commitment in the relationship, a strategy that ultimately failed for both of them. Erika and Sylvia both had much older partners, and intercourse took them by surprise, but was not unwelcome. Perhaps the powerful feelings inherent in passionate love in combination with cultural expectations about the importance of female virginity and naivete about sex preclude these young women from planning for sex, the circumstances under which it should occur (the timing of the event), and the prevention of pregnancy and STDs (use of contraception and condoms).

One of the more unfortunate precipitators of sexual debut for three of the cases presented here was conflict within the young women's home. Eva and Cori both felt pressure to leave their mothers' homes and said they had nowhere else to go. Julia, too, was having difficulties at home, and was sent to her aunt in the United States. All three of these young women eventually chose to live with their boyfriends. Julia clearly loved Juan and was ready to become his "wife." Eva and Cori both recognized that they were seeking a safe haven and comfort from their partners. Neither was ready to initiate intercourse. Eva thought it was morally wrong, and Cori thought she was too young. Both were also unsure of the depth of their own feelings for their partners—and their partner's feelings for them. Eva eventually came to love Rudy, but she was not in love with him when she moved in with him. She liked Rudy and was sexually attracted to him, but she needed a place to stay. Cori said she was not in love with Carlos. She gave in to sex because she needed a place to stay, because she thought he was cute, and because he was comforting.

An alternative reading of Cori's and Eva's stories, however, suggests that they only used the excuse of having nowhere else to go to justify the initiation of a sexual relationship with their boyfriends. Cori, it turns out, did have somewhere else to go, and Eva had a close school friend to whose family she probably could have turned had she wanted to do so. Instead, both arranged a scenario in which they could be blameless for engaging in sexual relations they felt were taboo.

Another striking chord in these narratives is the extent to which the young women were ignorant about the biology and physiology of human reproduction. Eva and Sylvia, in particular, thought this was a major reason for their unintended pregnancies—fear and ignorance of the mechanics of sex and contraception. For all except Julia, pregnancy was the consequence most feared by these young women. Although Erika wanted to get pregnant, she was somewhat ambivalent and considered abortion at the urging of her mother and Junior's mother, but all her friends had a man and kids, and she wanted to be like them. Junior was amenable to being a fa-

ther and is still with her. Eva, Sylvia, and Cori had unintended pregnancies that changed their lives. Rudy wanted to see what being a father was like. He tried using withdrawal, but the method did not work well for him and Eva. Luís seemed to think pregnancy prevention was Sylvia's responsibility, but took on responsibility for her and their daughter. Carlos seemed to fit the pattern described by Cori in which young men take no responsibility for their sexual behavior at all. Cori contracted chlamydia and became pregnant. She was the only young mother who expressed any anger at her boyfriend's irresponsible behavior and at her own "stupidity." Interestingly, none of the young women talked about fear of STDs as a deterrent to having sex.

The role of older men dating teenage women and fathering children is just beginning to be addressed in the literature on adolescent pregnancy [25]. In the cases presented here, only Eva and Rudy were within two years in age. For the other four cases, age differences were three, four, six, and fifteen years. Certainly there can be knowledge and power differentials in such relationships, especially when the girl is a young teen (e.g., 12 to 15 years old) and the partner is an adult man. Sylvia's and Erika's families expressed concern about their dating much older men, and Juan also recognized it was problematic. In a later interview he said that he often felt more like Julia's father or her teacher than her husband and worried that perhaps he had stolen her girlhood. Despite their own and their families' concerns, they all persisted in their relationships.

Although none of these young women said they were forced into having sex, all, save Julia, did feel pressured by their partners. Cori came closest to describing a forced situation. She said she felt trapped, but it was a trap partly of her own making. The contradictions in some of these narratives both wanting and not wanting sex at the same time suggest the conflict in these young women's minds. For others, like Erika and Sylvia, sex was not unwelcome, but the timing was unexpected. Julia was the only one who seemed to embrace her sexual relationship with Juan, and her narrative stands in stark contrast to the other four, which depict conflicting desires, lack of preparation for sex, and uncertainty about their own or their partner's feelings.

Adult, middle-class health professionals working with adolescents tend to assume that anyone in a romantic relationship can be reasonably sure he or she might have sex and should be prepared to prevent unintended pregnancy and STDs. All of these respondents, however, indicated that their first intercourse experience together was neither expected nor planned. Moreover, almost all respondents, when asked how couples decide to have sex or use birth control, responded like Eva: "How do they decide? (long pause) They don't decide. They don't think about it." When adolescents say that they were not expecting or planning to have sex, even though they were involved in a romantic relationship that could reasonably be expected to include sexual involvement, we must take them at their word. As these cases indicate, both parties might have been thinking about sex, wanting to have sex, wondering when they would have sex, or trying to delay sex, but they were not consciously planning to have sex.

The implications of these findings for the prevention of pregnancy and STDs among young Latinas are not optimistic. The cultural scripting of gender roles in romantic relationships makes it almost certain that sex will be unplanned and unprotected. The young man pressures for sex, but allows his girlfriend to control the timing of the evolution of sexual intimacy within the relationship in order to prove his love and commitment. The young woman resists sex until she is sure of her partner's emotional commitment to her or wants to put it to the test, but she must remain unprepared for sex to be perceived as virtuous. Although this period of respect lasted six months to a year for these couples, abstinence eventually gave way to intercourse. These months were full of sexual uncertainty and emotional risk during which each person tested the other, and frank discussions about having sex, using birth control, or preventing STDs were cul-

turally inappropriate and too emotionally risky for both parties. If either member of the couple violated these rules, he or she ran the risk of losing the partner.

Ironically, the initiation of sexual intercourse seemed to move the couple into another phase of their relationship in which they either broke up or developed mutual trust and affection that allowed for a more "rational" approach to sexual behavior and concern with its consequences. By this time, however, the young women were all pregnant and other decisions had to be made.

Cultural and social norms and values about appropriate sexual behavior, appropriate sexual partners, the importance of virginity, and contraception shape our experience of love and restrict what can be talked about at different stages of involvement in a romantic relationship. A script for romantic love that portrays spontaneous, unplanned, and unprotected sex after a protracted period of resistance by the female allows young women to retain their purity and relinquish their virginity at the same time. This script when enacted in the contemporary world of incurable STDs and the social and economic burdens of teenage motherhood places young women at enormous risk. Young couples will not behave as "rational decision-makers" in their sexual behavior until their society and community expect them to. Currently, as a society, we expect young people in love to behave "irrationally," to value spontaneous, unplanned (and therefore unprotected) sexual initiation. How, then, can we be surprised when they say, despite months of thinking about having sex, that they did not plan or expect to have sex. But, love can also accommodate prevention. Love, after all, is a valuing of the partner above the self. Surely, protection of the partner's health is part of love. We must teach our youth new scripts for falling in love, scripts that include this message.

References

1. R. A. Hatcher, J. Trussell, F. Stewart et al., *Contraceptive Technology*, Irvington Publishers, Inc., New York, 1994.

2. K. Luker, *Dubious Conceptions: The Politics of Teenage Pregnancy, and Childbearing*, Harvard University Press, Cambridge, MA, 1996.

3. T. J. Mathews, S. J. Ventura, S. C. Curtin, and J. A. Martin, Births of Hispanic Origin, 1989–95, *Monthly Vital Statistics Report*, 46:(6 Supplement), pp. 1–28, 1998.

4. P. I. Erickson, *Latina Adolescent Childbearing in East Los Angeles*, University of Texas Press, Austin, 1998.

5. S. S. Brown and L. Eisenberg, *The Best Intentions: Unintended Pregnancy and the Well-Being of Children and Families*, National Academy Press, Washington, D.C., 1995.

6. L. S. Zabin and S. C. Hayward, *Adolescent Sexual Behavior and Childbearing*, Sage Publications, Newbury Park, California, 1993.

7. L. M. Burton, Teenage Childbearing as an Alternative Life Course Strategy in Multigenerational Black Families, *Human Nature*, 1:2, pp. 123–143, 1990.

8. J. B. Lancaster and B. A. Hamburg, *School-Age Pregnancy and Parenthood: Biosocial Dimensions*, Aldine, DeGruyter, New York, 1986.

9. C. S. Aneshensel, E. Fielder, and R. M. Becerra, Fertility and Fertility-Related Behavior among Mexican-American and Non-Hispanic White Female Adolescents, *Journal of Health and Social Behavior*, 30, pp. 56–76, March 1989.

10. R. M. Becerra and D. de Anda, Pregnancy and Motherhood among Mexican American Adolescents, *Health and Social Work*, 9:2, pp. 106–123, 1984.

11. P. I. Erickson and C. P. Kaplan, Latinas and Abortion, in *The New Civil War: The Psychology, Culture and Politics of Abortion* (Chapter 6), L. J. Beckman and S. M. Harvey (eds.), American Psychological Association, Washington, D.C., pp. 133–155, 1998.

12. T. Reynoso, M. E. Felice, and P. Shragg, Does American Acculturation Affect Outcome of Mexican-American Teenage Pregnancy? *Journal of Adolescent Health*, 14:4, pp. 257–261, 1993.

13. P. I. Erickson, Cultural Factors Affecting the Negotiation of First Sexual Intercourse among Latina Adolescent Parents, *International Quarterly of Community Health Education*, 18:1, pp. 119–135, 1998–1999.

14. R. H. DuRant, R. Pendergast, and C. Seymore, Sexual Behavior among Hispanic Female Adolescents in the United States, *Pediatrics*, 85:6, pp. 1051–1058, 1990.

15. H. Amaro, Women in the Mexican American Community: Religion, Culture, and Reproductive Attitudes and Experiences, *Journal of Community Psychology*, 16:1, pp. 6–20, 1988.

16. H. Aviaro, Latina Attitudes towards Abortion, *Nuestro*, 5:6, pp. 43–44, 1981.

17. L. M. Koonin, J. C. Smith, and M. Ramick, Abortion Surveillance—United States, 1991, *Morbidity and Mortality Weekly Report*, 44:SS-2, pp. 23–53, 1995.

18. J. Abma, A. Driscoll, and K. Moore, Young Women's Degree of Control over First Intercourse: An Exploratory Analysis, *Family Planning Perspectives*, 30:1, pp. 12–18, 1998.

19. S. Thompson, *Going All the Way: Teenage Girls' Tales of Sex, Romance, and Pregnancy*, Hill and Wang, New York, 1995.

20. F. D. Bean and M. Tienda, *The Hispanic Population of the United States*, Russell Sage Foundation, New York, 1987.

21. B. R. Flores, *Chiquita's Cocoon: A "Cinderella Complex" for the Latina Woman*, Pepper Vine Press, Inc., Granite Bay, California, 1990.

22. N. Williams, *The Mexican-American Family: Tradition and Change*, General Hall, Inc., New York, 1990.

23. E. G. Pavich, A Chicana Perspective on Mexican Culture and Sexuality, *Journal of Social Work and Human Sexuality*, 4:3, pp. 47–65, 1986.

24. E. S. Person, *Dreams of Love and Fateful Encounters: The Power of Romantic Passion*, Penguin Books, New York, 1988.

25. D. J. Landry and J. D. Forrest, How Old Are U.S. Fathers? *Family Planning Perspectives*, 27:4, pp. 159–161, 1995.

Notes

1. About half of the young women had no partner at the time of recruitment or did not want us to contact him. Many men who were contacted declined due to time constraints of employment.

2. All of the participants were in consensual relationships, and 90 percent had had only one sexual partner in their lifetime. However, about one-third revealed a history of sexual abuse in the past.

3. Names and details that would identify respondents have been changed to protect confidentiality.

Adapted from Pamela I. Erickson, "Cultural Factors Affecting the Negotiation of First Sexual Intercourse Among Latina Adolescent Mothers." *International Quarterly of Community Health Education*, Vol. 18 (1), pp. 121–137. Copyright © 1998, Baywood Publishing Company, Inc. Reprinted by permission. ✦

Part III

Sexuality and the Life Cycle: Young Adulthood

The expanding definition of sexuality to encompass the entire life span is, perhaps, the most significant changing focus in human sexuality today. Sexuality researchers and clinicians who formerly worked to differentiate normative from nonnormative events first for children and, eventually, adolescents are now addressing developmental and transformational issues about sexuality in young adulthood and beyond. The articles in Part III contribute to that process.

"A lot of kids are putting off sex, and not because they can't get a date. They've decided to wait, and they're proud of their chastity, not embarrassed by it. Suddenly, virgin geek is giving way to virgin chic" (Ingrassia, 1994). This 1994 *Newsweek* quote, used to introduce the topic of virginity on college campuses, could aptly be titled "The Morals Revolution on Campuses." Oddly enough, that title belonged instead to a 1964 *Newsweek* story about virginity ("The Morals Revolution," 1964). The article claimed that men no longer expected to marry virgins, but that because sexual intercourse with anyone except "Mr. Right" was suspect, the question for young women should become, how many "Mr. Rights" make a wrong? Thirty years apart, these accounts by the popular media were merely reporting news of the day—one, a

sexual revolution and the other, its counterpart, a sexual retrorevolution. Could it possibly be true, the more things change, the more they stay the same? After reading the Sprecher and Regan selection, students can better discern the meaning of this conundrum.

If, as claimed, emotions are the critical motivational forces promoting life-course individuation, it is prudent to ask, what is the role of emotion in human behavior? Or more basically, what is an emotion? From Socrates to William James to present-day philosophers, such questions have been the subject of debates. For some, emotion has been perceived as being an inferior threat to reason and dismissed as merely an unintelligent feeling. Others viewed emotion as true wisdom, the master of reason (Solomon, 1993). But most have agreed that virtually all emotion gets expressed in behavior and that it has a cognitive dimension.

Although the newborn infant reveals a narrow range of primary emotional behavior, by the third year of life, the range extends to many highly differentiated ones (Lewis, 1993). Guilt is an emotion that emerges later because it requires certain slow-blooming cognitions related to the self. As such it is said to be a self-conscious emotion, affecting the way one thinks or what one thinks about. As a self-conscious, evaluative emotion, guilt involves a set of standards, rules, or goals. When one evaluates personal behavior vis-à-vis such standards and has not lived up to them, guilt results.

Many authorities agree that learning about sex in America is learning about guilt. And, ample evidence shows that sexual guilt can lead to sexual dissatisfaction, inhibited sexual desire, and other sexual dysfunctions. A thorough literary review of the nature and effects of sexual guilt in the Moore and Davidson article may help answer some of the questions raised by the findings of their study about guilt and first intercourse. This selection, more than most, places readers squarely in the middle of the issue as their own sexual scripts are factored into the equation.

Alcohol and sexually transmitted diseases are pressing problems on most college campuses, and recent studies have exposed the relationship between these two variables. Poulson, Eppler, Satterwhite, Wuensch, and Bass add yet another dimension, religious beliefs. The result is a selection that may encourage students to question their own gender and religious biases as well as to rethink some of their assumptions about the effects of alcohol. Although alcohol is a recreational drug that many believe will enhance sexual experience, research has found that high levels of alcohol actually suppress sexual arousal. The effects of alcohol on sexual response fall into three categories: short-term pharmacological effects; expectancy effects; and long-term effects of chronic alcohol abuse (Hyde & DeLamater, 2000). Most college students are not in the chronic alcohol abuse category with risks of sexual disorders (e.g., erectile dysfunction or loss of desire). However, many do experience anticipated effects. Their expectations that alcohol will make them more social and sexually uninhibited interact with the pharmacological effects to produce increased physical and subjective feelings of arousal. But this condition occurs only when a small amount of alcohol is consumed, with larger amounts acting as a depressant of arousal. This article may raise more questions than answers

about this topic of interest to students and administrators on college and university campuses.

McCarthy takes an interesting oppositional stance on the role of intimacy in facilitating sexual desire and functioning. Asserting that increasing intimacy is not the answer for couples, he embarks on a road less traveled in therapy circles. Using Gottman's (1994) four viable marital styles derived from empirical research to frame his thesis, he contends that to facilitate sexual functioning, the quest must be to find a mutually comfortable and agreeable level of intimacy.

Most therapists would agree with McCarthy about the importance of achieving intimacy early in the marriage. In fact, in the first two years of marriage, one of the most important couple-tasks is to work out their relationship rules in the areas of intimacy and power (Lewis, Beavers, Gossett, & Phillips, 1976). However, as the sexual strengths and vulnerabilities of each of Gottman's marital styles are explored, nowhere does the concept of power in relationship to healthy sexual functioning receive more than a passing glance. By contrast, therapist Keith Miller (1997) gives power top rating in his book, *Compelled to Control: Recovering Intimacy in Broken Relationships*. Miller, who portrays sex as the outward sign of intimacy, views power, or the compulsion to control, as the number one enemy of intimacy. He contends that only as the compulsion to control is conquered can healthier strategies be used in dealing with the loneliness, pain, resentment, fear, jealousy, and shame that are often hidden in the privacy of intimate sexual relationships.

One of life's major transitions occurs for young adults as they add yet another role to their lives, parenting. For most couples, this role presupposes a nine-month term of pregnancy and the inevitable first year of adjustments, not only to the new occupant, but also to the accommodations required in their relationship. Hyde, DeLamater, Plante, and Byrd carefully designed their longitudinal study to collect responses from both mothers and fathers about their sexual relationship on four occasions: the second trimester of pregnancy, and at one, four, and twelve months after childbirth. One of their goals was to address the methodological issues concerning the accuracy of self-reports of sexual behavior by comparing wives' and husbands' answers. Findings from the largest sample of women ever studied on this subject will fascinate students who are yet-to-be parents. Those who have already experienced parenthood will be able to reframe some of the issues in light of their own experientially-based knowledge.

Human beings are designed to fall in love. That is the good news. The bad news from evolutionary psychology is that they are not designed to stay there. Further, there are many modern obstacles to monogamy. Life in large cities, with its anonymity, lends itself to extramarital relationships far more than does life in small-town America. Media messages, with their glossy images of playmates, offer alluring alternatives to monogamous devotion. But economic inequality may be the largest obstacle to lasting monogamy and a major player in extramarital sexual involvement. According to evolutionary psychologists, women seek the protection, resources, and genes of successful men, while men seek success to attract women, especially younger ones (Buss, 1994).

Another modern obstacle to monogamous relationships is the changing roles of women and men. Social and occupational contacts with members of the opposite sex occur with increasing frequency among married persons, largely because of the burgeoning number of women working outside the home. In the world of work, women and men are often thrown into contact with attractive members of the opposite sex under conditions that exclude the spouse. As empathy is established in such relationships, sexual interest may surface. Thus, changing roles may explain why middle-aged women are almost as likely as their husbands to have extramarital relationships. As Treas and Giesen approach the subject of infidelity from the vantage point of both marriage and cohabitation, they courageously study an issue about which more than 90 percent of Americans disapprove (Smith, 1994). Readers of the article will be able to add their own opinion on this timely topic.

References

Buss, D. M. (1994). *Evolution of desire: Strategies of human mating.* New York: Basic Books.

Gottman, J. (1994). *Why marriages succeed or fail.* New York: Simon and Schuster.

Hyde, J. S., & DeLamater, J. D. (2000). *Understanding human sexuality* (7th ed). New York: McGraw-Hill.

Ingrassia, M. C. (1994, October 17). Virgin cool. *Newsweek*, pp. 59–62, 64, 69.

Lewis, J. M., Beavers, W. R., Gossett, J. T., & Phillips, W. A. (1976). *No single thread: Psychological health in family systems.* New York: Brunner/Mazel.

Lewis, M. (1993). Self-conscious emotion: Embarrassment, pride, shame, and guilt. In M. Lewis & J. M. Haviland (Eds.), *Handbook of emotions* (pp. 563–573). New York: Guilford.

Miller, J. K. (1997). *Compelled to control: Recovering intimacy in broken relationships.* Deerfield Beach, FL: Health Communications.

The morals revolution on campuses. (1964, April 6). *Newsweek*, p. 52.

Smith, T. W. (1994). Attitudes toward sexual permissiveness: Trends, correlates, and behavioral connections. In A. S. Ross (Ed.), *Sexuality across the life course* (pp. 63–97). Chicago: University of Chicago Press.

Solomon, R. C. (1993). The philosophy of emotions. In M. Lewis & J. M. Haviland (Eds.), *Handbook of emotions* (pp. 3–15). New York: Guilford. ✦

Chapter 11
College Virgins: How Men and Women Perceive Their Sexual Status

Susan Sprecher
Pamela C. Regan

The sexual lives of college students have been the focus of research since 1938 when two female journalists, Dorothy Dunbar Bromley and Florence Haxton Britten, startled readers with a revealing report of sexual activity based on interviews with students at a number of colleges. But, through the years, very little research on college campuses has been concerned with those young adults who have chosen to remain virgins. In Erickson and Steffen's Kiss & Tell *(1999), which chronicles the history of sex surveys in the United States over a century filled with changing sexual mores, it is not surprising that only 10 of the 220 pages even mention the word "virginity." The body of knowledge about virginity that is found in the research literature concerns adolescents, and it generally explores the predictors of virginity status, not affective reactions. And still more rare are research findings about male virginity, a phrase more likely to be considered an oxymoron.*

This well-executed study of the reasons for virginity and the satisfaction with virgin status will provoke thoughtful responses. The more interesting questions may arise from the findings that emerged when differences in perceptions of virginity over time were examined. Why did more recent cohorts of virgins report more pride about their virginity status

than those five years earlier? Does this represent changing mores? Is it really a sign of "virgin chic," as editorialized by Newsweek? *If so, does it challenge some time-worn assumptions? This article is an interesting commentary on campus life circa 2000 that shouldn't be missed.*

After the sexual revolution of the 1960s and the resulting freedom from sexual mores that promoted and glorified abstinence until marriage, it became somewhat socially gauche (and probably more difficult) for young adults to maintain their virginal status during college or the period immediately after high school (Rubin, 1990). Indeed, during the 1980s, a large majority of both males and females had made the transition to nonvirginity by the age of 19 (Miller & Moore, 1990). However, according to the popular media, we are in the midst of a sexual "retrorevolution" in which virginity is perceived as (and actually may be becoming) a more acceptable and popular choice among older adolescents and young adults; consequently, far from being embarrassed by their sexual status, some young adults who have remained virginal are proudly proclaiming their abstinence (Ingrassia, 1994). Interestingly, there have been few empirical attempts to examine systematically this anecdotal evidence about the feelings and reactions that adult virgins have about their sexual status.

Researchers have accumulated an extensive body of knowledge about the sexuality of adolescents, including the correlates of virginal/nonvirginal status and the factors that are associated with the loss of virginity (Gullotta, Adams, & Montemayor, 1993; Miller & Moore, 1990). We know much less about the virginity of adult men and women, perhaps because adult virgins still represent a relatively small proportion of the larger population (Billy, Tanfer, Grady, & Klepinger, 1993; Reinisch, Sanders, Hill, & Ziemba-Davis, 1992). Several researchers have included virginity as one variable among many in their studies of adult sexuality (Murstein & Mercy, 1994; Salts, Seismore, Lindholm, & Smith, 1994). Those few who have focused specifically upon adult virgins, like those who study adolescent virgins, have explored the correlates or predictors of virginity status (Schechterman & Hutchinson, 1991; Young, 1986). In addition, many have used samples composed solely of women (D'Augelli & Cross, 1975; Herold & Goodwin, 1981). Perhaps this is not surprising; after all, literary history is replete with the tales of sexually innocent young women who seek to preserve their premarital virginity and sexually knowledgeable men who seek to take it from them (Richardson, 1740/1971). Furthermore, modern literature and popular culture also have presented adult virginity as a female characteristic (e.g., the virgin protagonists on the primetime television shows *Beverly Hills 90210*, *Blossom*, and *L.A. Law* are women). However, although the majority of men (and women) are sexually active by the time they reach college age (Billy et al., 1993; Reinisch et al., 1992), adult virgins are found among both genders (e.g., Laumann, Gagnon, Michael, & Michaels, 1994).

Reasons for Virginity

By the time they are in college or engaged in a post-high school vocation, most young adults either have had opportunities for sexual intercourse or have considered whether they want the opportunity. Although the first intercourse experience itself is usually unplanned (e.g., Zelnik & Shah, 1983), the decision to make the transition from virgin to nonvirgin is rarely spontaneous (DeLamater, 1989). Young adults weigh several factors while making this important decision about their sexual status, and some decide to postpone the transition (i.e., to remain a virgin). What are the reasons virginal men and women give for their virginity, and do they have the same reasons?

One major factor related to sexual behaviors (to have sex for the first time) is sexual standards or ideology (DeLamater &

MacCorquodale, 1979). Considerable research conducted over the past few decades demonstrates that men hold more permissive attitudes toward casual (i.e., uncommitted) sexual activity than do women, whereas women are more likely than are men to view romantic love, emotional intimacy, and commitment as prerequisites for sexual activity (Sprecher, 1989). This gender difference has been explained from a number of theoretical perspectives. For example, evolutionary psychologists posit that men, whose reproductive success requires maximizing the number of genes passed on to the next generation, seek to engage in intercourse with many fertile partners, whereas women, whose reproductive success requires maximizing an offspring's chances of survival, confine their sexual activity to long-term relationships with partners who control many resources (Buss & Barnes, 1986). Social learning theorists suggest that men have received more reinforcement than have women for seeking sexual activity (Mischel, 1966), and script theorists point to societal norms that dictate that sexuality is tied more to the quality of the relationship for women than for men (Reiss, 1981). To the extent that women are more likely than men to associate sexual activity with such interpersonal phenomena as romantic love and emotional intimacy, women should place greater importance than men on lack of love and/or an appropriate relationship partner as reasons for remaining a virgin (i.e., abstaining from initial coitus).

Indeed, there is evidence to suggest that lack of a loving or committed relationship is a major reason why abstaining women choose not to have sex. In one of the few studies that focused on virgins and their decision-making processes, Herold and Goodwin (1981) asked Canadian college and high school women to indicate the most important reason why they had not engaged in sexual intercourse. A large number of the participants gave the reason that they had not yet met the "right" person. Also rated as important reasons by women were moral or religious beliefs, not being ready to have sexual intercourse, and fear of pregnancy. However, because Herold and Goodwin (1981) did not survey men, we do not know if virgin men have similar reasons.

A study conducted by Christopher and Cate (1985) suggests that young adult men may have different reasons than young adult women for remaining virginal. For part of a larger study (Christopher & Cate, 1984) these researchers asked college age, virgin men and women to indicate how important several factors would be in their decision to have sexual intercourse with an ideal partner for the first time. Women were more likely than men to rate relationship factors (e.g., love for partner) as a salient issue, which suggests that they would be more likely than men to abstain from sex in the absence of a loving relationship.

The first goal for this investigation, then, was to examine the reasons young adults have for maintaining their virginity status and to examine whether virgin men and women have the same reasons. In our investigation, we considered the reasons that were identified in the previous literature (moral or religious beliefs, fear of pregnancy, not being ready, not being in love enough, not having a willing partner). We also considered two other general categories of reasons that we believed might be relevant: fear of contracting AIDS and other sexually transmitted diseases (STDs) and perception of self-deficiency (i.e., the belief that one is not desirable, that one lacks desire for sex, or that one is too shy to initiate sex).

Affective Reactions to Virginity

Various emotions can be experienced as a consequence of engaging in sexual activity. DeLamater (1991) discussed four: sexual satisfaction/dissatisfaction, embarrassment, anxiety/fear, and frustration. Another negative emotion associated with sexual activity is guilt (Mosher & Cross, 1971). These emotions and others (e.g., pride), however, may also occur as a result of *not* having engaged in sexual activity.

Despite the recent media focus on the positive emotions ostensibly associated with virginity (Ingrassia, 1994), very few researchers have focused on how virgin men and women actually feel about their virginity. In an early study on adolescent sexuality, Sorensen (1973) concluded that the sexually inexperienced teenagers were satisfied with their status. He wrote: "They are, in the main, neither defensive nor ashamed of themselves, nor are they frustrated or preoccupied with the fact they do not have sex" (p. 154). Although Sorensen (1973) did not report whether there were gender differences in affective reactions, in a recent study of adolescent males and females, Langer, Zimmerman, and Katz (1995) found that male virgins were more likely than female virgins to report that they would feel better about themselves if they started having sex. In a study of college virgins, Young (1986) found more virgins of both genders were satisfied than frustrated, but a greater proportion of virgin men than of virgin women were frustrated. Furthermore, Walsh (1991) presented indirect evidence that men are more likely than women to experience a negative reaction to their virginity status. Virgin and nonvirgin women did not differ with respect to scores on a self-esteem scale; however, virgin men had significantly lower self-esteem scores than nonvirgin men. Although these studies suggest that gender differences in emotions associated with virginity in young adulthood exist, investigators have not studied how adult virgins react to their virginity status on a variety of both positive and negative emotions (including pride and embarrassment).

Thus, our second major goal was to examine the affective reactions virgins have in response to their virginity status and to examine gender differences in these affective reactions. We considered a number of emotional reactions—both positive (happiness and pride) and negative (anxiety, embarrassment, and guilt) and we hypothesized, based on previous research (Walsh, 1991; Young, 1986), that men would experience less positive and more negative affective reactions to their virginity than would women.

Associations Among Reasons, Affective Reactions, and Other Aspects of Virginity

The reasons young adults have for remaining virgins are likely to be related to their feelings about their virginity status. Young (1986) found that both male and female virgins who were satisfied with their sexual status reported greater religious commitment than did virgins who were frustrated by their sexual status. Perhaps reasons for remaining a virgin that reflect moral and religious beliefs are associated with positive affective reactions to virginity (e.g., pride, happiness), whereas reasons that reflect one's inability to initiate sexual intercourse with a partner or the partner's unwillingness to engage in sexual intercourse are associated with negative affective reactions to virginity (e.g., anxiety, embarrassment).

Furthermore, reasons for virginity and affective reactions to virginity may be related to the perceived likelihood of becoming a nonvirgin in the near future and the amount of support received from others for being a virgin. Virginity generally has been viewed as a discrete variable (i.e., one is either a virgin or not), but some researchers have further classified virgins by their perceived likelihood of becoming a nonvirgin before marriage. D'Augelli and her colleagues (1977) distinguished between "adamant virgins" and "potential nonvirgins." Adamant virgins have decided that they will not engage in premarital sexual intercourse, whereas potential nonvirgins are willing to consider premarital sex should they find themselves in the "right" situation with the "right" partner. These types of virgins are likely to have different reasons for remaining virgins. Herold and Goodwin (1981) classified their sample of high school and college women into adamant virgins and potential nonvirgins and asked them to select from an array of reasons the single most important reason why they had not engaged in intercourse. Half (50 percent) of the adamant virgins but only 2 percent of the potential nonvirgins endorsed the category encompassing moral and religious reasons (i.e., against religion, parental disapproval, premarital intercourse is wrong), whereas 54 percent of the potential nonvirgins but only 16 percent of the adamant virgins endorsed not having met the "right" person as the most important reason for abstaining from sexual intercourse.

The perceived likelihood of remaining a virgin before marriage may be associated with emotional reactions to virginity. Specifically, adamant virgins may have a more positive overall affective reaction to their virginity than do potential nonvirgins and in particular may feel prouder of their sexual status than do potential nonvirgins. Conversely, potential nonvirgins may feel more guilt, anxiety, and embarrassment than do adamant virgins.

Another factor that may push virgins toward having sexual intercourse is external—specifically, social pressure from others to become sexually active. Young adults who receive social pressure from others to become sexually active should be more likely than young adults who do not receive such pressure to perceive that they are likely to have sexual intercourse in the near future (i.e., to be potential nonvirgins). Furthermore, virgins who receive social pressure to remain a virgin should be less likely than virgins who do not receive this pressure to say that they are likely to begin having premarital sex.

Thus, our third goal was to examine the associations between reasons for virginity and affective reactions to virginity and to examine how both are related to other aspects of virginity, including the likelihood of becoming a nonvirgin and social pressure to become sexually active vs. to remain a virgin.

Changes Over Time in Virginity

As societal attitudes about sexuality change, so too should the experiences of young adults who are virginal when most of their cohort has had sexual intercourse. If, as suggested by the popular media, we are in the midst of a sexual "retrorevolution," then feelings and perceptions that adult virgins have about their sexual status should have changed over recent years. More specifically, fear of AIDS as a reason for being a virgin and positive reactions to virginity status have probably increased over time. Thus, our final goal was to explore the possibility that perceptions of virginity have changed.

In sum, scientists have collect very little data from adult virgins about their virginity. The purpose this study was to examine reasons for virginity, affective reactions to virginity, and other perceptions of virginity with a sample of college age, virgin men and women obtained over a six-year period. We were particularly interested in how virgin men and women may differ.

THE CURRENT STUDY
Method

The participants in this study were selected from a nonprobability sample of undergraduate students enrolled at a Midwestern U.S. University who participated in a survey study of sexual attitudes and behaviors. To be classified as a virgin, the participant had to respond to two separate questions that he or she had not had sexual intercourse. There were not enough self-identified homosexual and bisexual virgins in the sample to examine the association between sexual orientation and reasons for and affective reactions to virginity. The final sample of 97 men and 192 women represented 11 percent and 13 percent, respectively, of the larger sample of men and women participants who were self-reported heterosexuals and had their gender identified.

The median age of the virgin participants was approximately 19.5. A majority (89 percent) identified themselves as White. On a question about religious preference, 44 percent identified themselves as Catholic, 19 percent were Protestants, 21 percent chose "other," 12 percent chose "none," and 4 percent described themselves as Jewish.

The virgin participants were presented with a list of 13 reasons "that people may have for not having premarital sexual intercourse." Participants responded to each item on a 1 = *not at all important* to 4 = *very important* response scale. An analysis conducted on the 13 items revealed 4 [major] factors. The first factor was labeled *Personal Beliefs* and included the following four items: "I believe that intercourse before marriage is wrong," "It is against my religious beliefs," "Fear of parental disapproval," and "I do not feel ready to have premarital intercourse." The second factor, labeled *Fear*, included three items: "I worry about contracting AIDS," "I worry about contracting another STD," and "Fear of pregnancy." *Inadequacy/Insecurity* was the third factor, which included four items: "I have been too shy or embarrassed to initiate sex with a partner," "I don't feel physically attractive or desirable," "I lack desire for sex," and "My current (or last) partner is (was) not willing." The final factor, labeled *Not Enough Love*, contained two items: "I have not been in a relationship long enough or been in love enough" and "I have not met a person I wanted to have intercourse with." Four scale scores were created based on the mean of the items loading on each particular factor, the higher the score, the more important the factor.

Participants were asked how *proud, guilty, anxious, embarrassed,* and *happy* they felt about their virginity status. We also created a summary measure, an index of *hedonic emotional tone.* A positive score on this index means that positive emotions were experienced to a greater intensity than were negative emotions; a negative score means that negative emotions were experienced to a greater intensity than were positive emotions.

Participants were also asked questions assessing the likelihood that they would remain a virgin and the social pressure they received to remain a virgin versus to become sexually active. *Likelihood of becoming a nonvirgin* was measured by the following three questions: "If you were in a close relationship with a partner who desired sexual intercourse and the opportunity were available, would you engage in premarital sexual intercourse?"; "How likely are you to engage in sexual intercourse before you get married?"; and "How likely are you to engage in sexual intercourse during the next year?" *Social pressure* was measured by the following two questions: "How much pressure have you received from others (e.g., dating partners, peers) to have sexual intercourse?" and "How much pressure have you received from others (e.g., parents, peers) to remain a virgin?"

Results

Reasons for Remaining a Virgin

Not all reasons for being a virgin were rated as equally important. For the total sample of virgins, the mean importance of the 4 factor scores derived from the 13 reasons were: Not Enough Love ($M = 2.91$), Fear ($M = 2.86$), Personal Beliefs ($M = 2.21$), and Inadequacy/Insecurity ($M = 1.79$). Women scored higher than men on Not Enough Love. Comparisons on the individual items indicated that women placed more importance than men on both items included in this factor (not been in a relationship long enough or been in love enough and not met the right person). Women also scored higher than men on the Personal Beliefs factor. In particular, virgin women, to a greater degree than virgin men, expressed fear of parental disapproval and stated that they were not ready. On the third factor, Fear, women also scored higher. However, women scored significantly higher than men on only one item included in this factor—fear of pregnancy. The only factor having a higher mean for men than for women was Inadequacy/Insecurity. Of the four items in this factor, men scored significantly higher than women on two: too shy or embarrassed to initiate sex and partner not willing.

Affective Reactions to Being a Virgin

In the total sample of virgins, participants reported being both proud and anxious about their virginity status. They also reported some happiness and embarrassment, but little guilt. The hedonic emotional tone index was positive, which indicates that positive emotions were experienced by the participants to a greater degree than were negative emotions.

As hypothesized, however, men and women differed in their emotional reactions to their virginity status. Women to a greater degree than men were proud and happy, and men to a greater degree than women were embarrassed and guilty. No significant gender difference was found on anxiety, although this emotion was experienced by men more than any other emotion (pride was the primary emotion women experienced). The hedonic emotional tone index was negative for men and positive for women; this difference was significant.

Reasons and Affective Reactions to Virginity

As hypothesized, personal beliefs (e.g., religious reasons) for virginity were strongly associated with positive affective reaction for both men and women. For men, interpersonal reasons (i.e., not enough love) were associated with a positive reaction. The fear factor was not associated with emotional reactions.

Men were more likely than women to believe that they would become a nonvirgin in the near future. There was a very strong correlation between the importance of personal beliefs as a reason for virginity and the perceived likelihood of becoming a nonvirgin. More specifically, the more important men and women rated personal beliefs (e.g., religious reasons) for their virginity, the more adamant they were about their virginity (the less likely they were to perceive that they would become a nonvirgin). In addition, for men only, higher scores on the Inadequacy/Insecurity factor were positively associated with the perceived likelihood of becoming a nonvirgin in the near future. Emotional reactions to virginity were also related to the perceived likelihood of becoming a nonvirgin. The men and women who believed it was likely that they would become a nonvirgin in the near future had the most negative and the least positive reaction to their virginity status.

Virgin men and women reported equal degrees of social pressure to begin to have sexual intercourse. However, virgin women reported more pressure to remain a virgin than did virgin men. Social pressure to become sexually active was negatively associated with women's hedonic emotional tone index; that is, social pressure to become sexually active was associated with a negative reaction to virginity. Conversely, social pressure to remain a virgin was associated with a positive reaction for women. For men, a strong association was found between social pressure to remain a virgin and their positive reaction as indicated by hedonic emotional tone; however, social pressure to become sexually active was unrelated to men's emotional reactions to virginity.

Changes in Virginity Over Time

Because our data were collected over a six-year period, we explored the possibility that there were changes over time in the reasons for and affective reactions to virginity. Over time both genders rated worry about contracting AIDS as increasingly important reasons for virginity. The importance rating of fear of pregnancy also became more important for women over time, as did the Inadequacy/Insecurity factor. The specific item that grew in importance for women was current partner is not willing. Some emotional reactions were also found to change significantly, in that over time men experienced greater pride and happiness. And, over time women reported feeling significantly greater pride and anxiety about their virginity.

Discussion

Reasons for Virginity

College virgins do not abstain from sexual intercourse because of lack of sexual desire. The least important reason for virginity for both men and women was "I lack desire for sex." This finding belies the stereotype of the "frigid" virgin and certainly can be used to argue against the common

beliefs that sexual desire is an inherent aspect of the male but not the female experience (Regan & Berscheid, 1995) and that men have stronger and more frequent desires than do women (Richgels, 1992). Apparently, both men and women in our sample desired sex but abstained from it because they required an "appropriate" reason to become sexually active (e.g., the "right" person); sought to avoid some real, potentially negative consequences of sexual intercourse (e.g., unplanned pregnancy, disease); and were attempting to act in service of their personal beliefs. The reasons both men and women rated as most important had to do with not enough love or having not met the right partner. Overall, then, the relative ratings of the reasons were very similar for men and women.

Gender differences were found in the importance ratings given to many reasons. As expected, our virgin women participants were more concerned than their male counterparts with interpersonal reasons for virginity (i.e., not enough love or not having met the right person). These results are in accord with previous research that suggests that both sexually experienced and inexperienced women are more likely than men to associate sexual activity with love and/or committed relationships (Oliver & Hyde, 1993). Virgin women also placed greater importance than virgin men on such personal beliefs as not feeling ready to engage in sexual intercourse and on parental disapproval of premarital sex. The fact that during adolescence girls are more likely than boys to have discussed abstinence and other sexual topics with their parents (Leland & Barth, 1992) may explain why young adult women are more concerned with parental attitudes toward sexual activity (i.e., they may simply be more aware of their parents' views). Not surprisingly, the women in our sample were also more concerned than the men with the potential negative consequences of sexual intercourse (i.e., pregnancy).

However, men rated reasons having to do with inadequacy and insecurity as more important than did women. More specifically, men viewed their feelings of shyness or embarrassment about initiating sexual activity with a partner as a more important reason for their virginity than did women, and men were also more likely to point to their partners' unwillingness to engage in intercourse. A possible explanation for these gender differences is that the virgin men in our sample may have attempted to initiate sexual intercourse with a potential partner more often than did the virgin women; consequently, they may have experienced rejection more often than have women and may feel less inclined to (and more embarrassed about) making further initiation attempts. That is, this finding may stem from differential experiences of virgin men and virgin women. If virgin men and women perceive the male role in sexual interactions as primarily proactive and the female role as primarily reactive (Gagnon & Simon, 1973; Reiss, 1981), it makes sense that men would be more concerned than women with reasons associated with the initiation of sexual activity (e.g., partner's unwillingness, personal feelings of shyness).

Our results also indicate that the reasons young adult virgins maintain their sexual status have changed over time. Specifically, recent cohorts of virgins placed more importance than earlier cohorts on their fears of contracting AIDS and other STDs. Whether young adult virgins consciously decide not to have sex based upon this reason or simply provide it as an explanation for their current sexual status is not clear; however, sexually active individuals also have grown more aware of AIDS over time and appear to have altered their sexual behaviors as a consequence (e.g., are more likely to use condoms). Another reason that became more important over time, at least for women, was "My current (or last) partner is (was) not willing." Although heterosexual partners largely continue to adhere to the traditional script of male initiation of sexual activity (O'Sullivan & Byers, 1992), recent cohorts of women may be more comfortable with the role of sexual initiator and thus more likely to have experienced a partner's refusal to have intercourse. These changes found over a six-year period may indicate that the type of person who remains a virgin is changing and/or may indicate broader changes in societal attitudes about sexuality.

Affective Reactions to Virginity

Male and female virgins reported a variety of both positive and negative emotional responses to their sexual status; however, women's experiences were more positive than negative, whereas men's were more negative than positive. With respect to specific emotional reactions, women felt greater pride and happiness than did men, and men felt greater embarrassment and guilt than did women. These gender differences may be explained by cultural mandates regarding sexual intercourse that teach that sexual experience is an important aspect of masculinity. Virginity—defined here as not yet having engaged in sexual intercourse—therefore may represent a greater stigma for men than for women. Indeed, some people appear to believe that men are born sexually experienced; more than half the respondents in a survey conducted by Berger and Wenger (1973) argued that it made no sense to speak of "male virginity," and those who felt that such a concept did exist disagreed over the activities that constituted the loss of male virginity. It is not surprising, given these sociocultural expectations and beliefs, that virgin men demonstrate a negative response to their virginity. We might also then expect men to feel positively about the first occurrence of sexual intercourse; after all, it removes an undesired stigma. In fact, the feelings that men and women have about their virginity are to some extent the opposite of the reactions that men and women report to the loss of their virginity; that is, men tend to have a more positive emotional reaction to their first intercourse experience than do women (Darling, Davidson, & Passarello, 1992; Sprecher, Barbee, & Schwartz, 1995).

However, affective reactions to virginity, for both men and women, do appear to be changing over time. In particular, although virgin men continue to feel more negatively about their sexual status than do virgin women, more recent cohorts report greater pride and happiness than earlier cohorts. We also found that more recent cohorts of women reported more pride. These changes may reflect the fact that young adults—especially young men—have a greater number of publicly visible, virginal role models to emulate [for example, the group, Athletes for Abstinence includes a number of well-known male athletes (Newman, 1994)].

Associations Between Reasons and Affective Reactions

Men and women had a more positive overall reaction to their virginity if they viewed their sexual status as the result of their personal beliefs or values (i.e., against religious beliefs, believe that premarital sex is wrong, fear parental disapproval, not ready for intercourse). To the extent that virginity represents tangible evidence that one is living according to one's personal convictions, such positive feelings are understandable. Although we expected to find that men and women who choose to remain virgins because they have not found the right partner or been in love enough would feel less positive about their virginity status, no such association was found for women, and for men, such reasons were associated with a more positive overall affective response. Perhaps men who feel "good" about their virginity—and who are violating the stereotype of the unhappy male virgin—are also those men who violate other stereotypes (who, for example, associate sex and love, which is not a stereotypically "male" response; Carroll et al., 1985). In addition, for men, but not women, reasons related to inadequacy/insecurity—a partner's unwillingness to have sex and the perception that one is unable to attract or initiate intercourse with a potential partner—were associated with a negative emotional reaction. To the extent that a man's virginity is not due to personal choice, but rather reflects an inability to overcome various individual (e.g., undesirability) and interpersonal (e.g., partner's refusal) barriers to sexual experience, it appears to engender negative affect.

Perceived Likelihood of Losing One's Virginity

Several researchers have suggested that virginity is not a discrete variable such that one is virginal or one is not virginal, but rather that there may be additional types of virgins. For example, D'Augelli and D'Augelli (1977) distinguished between "adamant virgins" (who believe that they will wait until marriage to have intercourse) and "potential nonvirgins" (who believe that they will have premarital sex under the "right" circumstances). We argue that it may be even more meaningful to conceptualize virginity along a continuum ranging from fully adamant about one's virginity to fully open to the possibility of losing one's virginity (becoming a nonvirgin).

Although the virgin women in our sample were more adamant than the virgin men about their sexual status, the more adamant that *both* genders were, the more importance they placed on personal beliefs for their virginity and the more positive their overall emotional reaction. Specifically, men and women who were more adamant about their virginity were more likely to experience pride and happiness and less likely to feel anxiety and guilt than were men and women who believed that they were likely to become sexually active in the near future. These results suggest that sexual decision making and affective reactions to virginity are inextricably interwoven. However, we do not know from these data whether individuals first make a sexual decision (i.e., to have sex) and then experience emotional reactions based on that decision or whether they have certain emotional reactions to their current situation (i.e., virginity) and then make a decision as a result of those reactions (e.g., a person realizes that he or she is unhappy about his or her sexual status, and this realization contributes to the decision to become a nonvirgin).

Social Pressure

This study represents an important preliminary step toward delineating the role that social pressure may play in informing the sexual attitudes and decisions of young adult virgins. First, we found several gender differences. Virgin men and women reported receiving equal amounts of pressure (presumably from dating partners and peers) to engage in sexual intercourse, but only women reported greater negative affect toward their virginity as the social pressure to have sex increased. Women also experienced greater pressure (presumably from parents) to abstain from intercourse than men, but both men and women felt more positive about their virginity as this type of social pressure increased.

In addition, the amount of social pressure respondents received to remain a virgin was unrelated to the amount of social pressure they received to lose their virginity, which suggests that young adult virgins may get conflicting messages from different network sectors (e.g., parents vs. friends). However, because we did not explicitly examine the different types of external pressure that virgins may experience (i.e., we asked our participants to indicate the amount of pressure they received from others in general rather than from specific subgroups of others), we do not know, for example, whether virgins received more pressure to have sex from their peers than from their parents, or whether gender differences exist such that virgin women received significantly more pressure to become sexually active from their (male) dating partners than virgin men received from their (female) dating partners. We also did not distinguish between overt pressure (e.g., a parent explicitly communicates his or her negative feelings about premarital sex to a child; a person verbally informs his or her dating partner that it is "time" to have sex) and indirect pressure (e.g., a virgin perceives that all of his or her friends are engaging in sex, regardless of their actual behavior) or how the type or quantity of pressure that a person receives from a particular element of his or her social network may change over time and/or with the interpersonal context.

Future Research Directions

We believe that it is important to include other subclassifications of virginity in research on adult virgins; for example, some virgins have engaged in "everything but" sexual intercourse (Rubin, 1990), whereas others have abstained from all intimate sexual activities. It is likely that sexually active but "technical" virgins will have different reasons for and emotional reactions to their sexual status than will virgins with very little sexual experience. A related issue worth examining is the phenomenon of "second virginity." This concept currently espoused by several social groups, refers to the notion that a sexually experienced man or woman can renew or reclaim virgin status by making the decision to discontinue further sexual activity until marriage (Ingrassia, 1994). Some researchers have in fact distinguished between "regretful nonvirgins" (those who had been sexually active but who planned to abstain from sex for a while) and other types of virgins (Schechterman & Hutchinson, 1991).

References

Berger, D. G., & Wenger, M. G. (1973). The ideology of virginity. *Journal of Marriage and the Family*, 35, 666–676.

Berscheid, E., Snyder, M., & Omoto, A. M. (1989). The relationship closeness inventory: Assessing the closeness of interpersonal relationships. *Journal of Personality and Social Psychology*, 57, 792–807.

Billy, J. O. G., Tanfer, K., Grady, W. R., & Klepinger, D. H. (1993). The sexual behavior of men in the United States. *Family Planning Perspectives*, 25, 52–60.

Brooks-Gunn, J., & Furstenberg, F F., Jr. (1989). Adolescent sexual behavior. *American Psychologist*, 44, 249–257.

Buss, D. M., & Barnes, M. (1986). Preferences in human mate selection. *Journal of Personality and Social Psychology*, 50, 559–570.

Carroll, J. L., Volk, K. D., & Hyde, J. S. (1985). Differences between males and females in motives for engaging in sexual intercourse. *Archives of Sexual Behavior*, 14, 131–139.

Christopher, F. S., & Cate, R. M. (1984). Factors involved in premarital sexual decision-making. *The Journal of Sex Research*, 20, 363–376.

Christopher, F. S., & Cate, R. M. (1985). Anticipated influences on sexual decision-making. *Family Relations*, 34, 265–270.

Christopher, F. S., & Roosa, M. W. (1991). Factors affecting sexual decisions in the premarital relationships of adolescents and young adults. In K. McKinney & S. Sprecher (Eds.), *Sexuality in Close Relationships* (pp. 111–133). Hillsdale, NJ: Lawrence Erlbaum.

Darling, C. A., Davidson, J. K, Sr., & Passarello, L. C. (1992). The mystique of first intercourse among college youth: The role of partners, contraceptive practices, and psychological reactions. *Journal of Youth and Adolescence, 21,* 97–117.

D'Augelli, J. F., & Cross, H. L. (1975). Relationship of sex guilt and moral reasoning to premarital sex in college women and in couples. *Journal of Consulting and Clinical Psychology, 43,* 40–47.

D'Augelli, J. F., & D'Augelli, A. R. (1977). Moral reasoning and premarital sexual behavior: Toward reasoning about relationships. *Journal of Social Issues, 33,* 44–66.

DeLamater, J. D. (1989). The social control of human sexuality. In K. McKinney & S. Sprecher (Eds.), *Human Sexuality: The Societal and Interpersonal Context* (pp. 30–62). Norwood, NJ: Ablex.

DeLamater, J. D. (1991). Emotions and sexuality. In K. McKinney & S. Sprecher (Eds.), *Sexuality in Close Relationships* (pp. 49–70). Norwood, NJ: Ablex.

DeLamater, J. D., & MacCorquodale, P. (1979). *Premarital Sexuality: Attitudes, Relationships, Behaviors.* Madison: University of Wisconsin Press.

Fielding, H. (1979). *The History of Tom Jones, a Foundling* (3rd ed.). New York: The New American Library. (Original work published 1749).

Fleming, A. T. (1995, February). Like a virgin, again. *Vogue,* pp. 68, 72.

Gagnon, J. H., & Simon, W. (1973). *Sexual Conduct: The Social Sources of Human Sexuality.* Chicago: Aldine.

Gullotta, T. P., Adams, G. R., & Montemayor, R. (Eds.). (1993). *Adolescent Sexuality.* Newbury Park, CA: Sage.

Herold, E. S., & Goodwin, M. S. (1981). Adamant virgins, potential nonvirgins and nonvirgins. *The Journal of Sex Research, 17,* 97–113.

Ingrassia, M. (1994, October 17). Virgin cool. *Newsweek,* pp. 59–62, 64, 69.

Langer, L. M., Zimmerman, R. S., & Katz, J. A. (1995). Virgins' expectations and nonvirgins' reports: How adolescents feel about themselves. *Journal of Adolescent Research, 10,* 291–306.

Laumann, E. O., Gagnon, J. H., Michael, R. T., & Michaels, S. (1994). *The Social Organization of Sexuality: Sexual Practices in the United States.* Chicago: University of Chicago Press.

Leite, R. M. C., Buoncompagno, E. M., Leite, A. C. C., Mergulhao, E. A., & Battistoni, M. M. M. (1994). Psychosexual characteristics of female university students in Brazil. *Adolescence, 29,* 439–460.

Leland, N. L., & Barth, R. P. (1992). Gender differences in knowledge, intentions, and behaviors concerning pregnancy and sexually transmitted disease prevention among adolescents. *Journal of Adolescent Health, 13,* 589–599.

Lewis, R., & Casto, R. (1978). Developmental transitions in male sexuality. *The Counseling Psychologist, 4,* 15–19.

Miller, B. C., & Moore, K. A. (1990). Adolescent sexual behavior, pregnancy, and parenting: Research through the 1980s. *Journal of Marriage and the Family, 52,* 1025–1044.

Mischel, W. (1966). A social-learning view of sex differences in behavior. In E. E. Maccoby (Ed.), *The Development of Sex Differences* (pp. 56–81). Stanford, CA: Stanford University Press.

Mosher, D. L., & Cross, J. J. (1971). Sex guilt and premarital sexual experience of college students. *Journal of Consulting and Clinical Psychology, 36,* 27–32.

Mosher, W. D., & Pratt, W. F. (1993). AIDS related behavior among women 15–44 years of age: United States, 1988 and 1990. *Advance Data from Vital and Health Statistics, 239.*

Murstein, B. I., & Mercy, T. (1994). Sex, drugs, relationships, contraception, and fears of disease on a college campus over 17 years. *Adolescence, 29,* 303–322.

Newman, J. (1994, June 19). Proud to be a virgin. *New York Times,* pp. 1, 6.

Oliver, M. B., & Hyde, J. S. (1993). Gender differences in sexuality: A meta-analysis. *Psychological Bulletin, 114,* 29–51.

O'Sullivan, L. F., & Byers, E. S. (1992). College students' incorporation of initiator and restrictor roles in sexual dating interactions. *The Journal of Sex Research, 29,* 435–446.

Peplau, L. A., Rubin, Z., & Hill, C. T. (1977). Sexual intimacy in dating relationships. *Journal of Social Issues, 33*(2), 86–109.

Peretti, P. O., Brown, S., & Richards, P. (1978). Female virgin and nonvirgin psychological orientations toward premarital virginity. *Acta Psychiatrica Belgica, 78,* 235–247.

Peretti, P. O., Brown, S., & Richards, R. (1979). Perceived value-orientations toward premarital virginity of female virgins and nonvirgins. *Acta Psychiatrica Belgica*, 79, 321–331.

Regan, P. C., & Berscheid, E. (1995). Gender differences in beliefs about the causes of male and female sexual desire. *Personal Relationships*, 2, 345–350.

Reinisch, J. M., Sanders, S. A., Hill, C. A., & Ziemba-Davis, M. (1992). High-risk sexual behavior among heterosexual undergraduates at a midwestern university. *Family Planning Perspectives*, 24, 116–121, 145.

Reiss, I. L. (1981). Some observations on ideology and sexuality in America. *Journal of Marriage and the Family*, 43, 271–283.

Richardson, S. (1971). *Pamela; or, Virtue Rewarded*. Boston: Houghton Mifflin. (Original work published 1740)

Richgels, P. B. (1992). Hypoactive sexual desire in heterosexual women: A feminist analysis. *Women and Therapy*, 12, 123–135.

Rubin, L. (1990). *Erotic Wars: What Happened to the Sexual Revolution?* New York: HarperCollins.

Salts, C. J., Seismore, M. D., Lindholm, B. W., & Smith, T. A. (1994). Attitudes toward marriage and premarital sexual activity of college freshmen. *Adolescence*, 29, 775–779.

Schechterman, A. L., & Hutchinson, R. L. (1991). Causal attributions, self-monitoring, and gender differences among four virginity status groups. *Adolescence*, 26, 659–678.

Smith, T. W. (1991). Adult sexual behavior in 1989: Number of partners, frequency of intercourse and risk of AIDS. *Family Planning Perspectives*, 23, 102–107.

Sonenstein, F. L., Pleck, J. H., & Ku, L. C. (1989). Sexual activity, condom use and AIDS awareness among adolescent males. *Family Planning Perspectives*, 21, 152–158.

Sorensen, R. C. (1973). *Adolescent Sexuality in Contemporary America*. New York: World.

Sprecher, S. (1989). Premarital sexual standards for different categories of individuals. *The Journal of Sex Research*, 26, 232–248.

Sprecher, S., Barbee, A., & Schwartz, P. (1995). "Was it good for you, too?": Gender differences in first sexual intercourse experiences. *The Journal of Sex Research*, 32, 3–15.

Sprecher, S., & Sedikides, C. (1993). Gender differences in perceptions of emotionality: The case of close, heterosexual relationships. *Sex Roles: A Journal of Research*, 28, 511–530.

Tiefer, L. (1995). *Sex Is Not a Natural Act and Other Essays*. Boulder, CO: Westview Press.

Tolman, D. L. (1991). Adolescent girls, women and sexuality: Discerning dilemmas of desire. *Women and Therapy*, 11, 55–69.

Walsh, A. (1991). Self-esteem and sexual behavior: Exploring gender differences. *Sex Roles*, 25, 441–450.

Young, M. (1986). Religiosity and satisfaction with virginity among college men and women. *Journal of College Student Personnel*, 27, 339–344.

Zelnik, M., & Shah, F. K. (1983). First intercourse among young Americans. *Family Planning Perspectives*, 15, 64–72.

Chapter 12
Guilt About First Intercourse

Nelwyn B. Moore
J. Kenneth Davidson, Sr.

When queried about their sexual script, most college students would probably reply, "what sexual script?" Yet, by adulthood, all persons have one. That there is a complex network of interacting variables within the individual that affects sexual behavior may seem to be a self-evident fact. But, when sexual decisions are close at hand, most individuals seldom consider the influence of family history, their personality make-up, or the culture in which they grew up, all variables that do indeed impact sexual behavior. Of course, the interaction effects of these factors must also be considered for persons who would wish to scientifically analyze their sexual lives, if any such persons exist! And, the fact that this process is dynamic, continuing to evolve throughout life in relationships with others, must also be factored in for accurate appraisal.

Moore and Davidson focus on just one of the aspects of sexual scripting among young adults as they examine the role of guilt feelings about first sexual intercourse and the relationship of these feelings to current sexual satisfaction. Guilt, a developmentally late-appearing emotion, has received little emphasis in the research literature in contrast to other emotions, such as sadness, fear, and anger, that have received considerable attention. This selection does not purport to be an exhaustive study, but it does provide some insight into the role of guilt about first sexual intercourse in sexual decision making. A heightened awareness of the part that guilt might play in their sexual scripts will assist students who may wish to enhance their role as a director in the drama of their own developmental trajectories in life.

First sexual intercourse is often viewed as a rite of passage to adulthood. And while one's initial coital experience may lead to affirmation of self-identity, it is disappointing for many, resulting in feelings of guilt and shame. Such feelings of guilt are believed to emanate from the sense of hurting others, especially one's parent(s), or from having transgressed one's value system.[1] If guilt feelings do emerge, the likelihood of future sexual dissatisfaction is greatly increased. Guilt about first intercourse among college women has been found to be associated with lack of current physiological and psychological sexual satisfaction, guilt about current sexual intercourse, and guilt if no orgasm occurs during sexual intercourse.[2] And theorists have long suggested that sexual guilt could contribute to subsequent sexual dysfunction.[3] Therefore, one's first intercourse experience may lead to emotional turmoil or sexual dysfunction later in life.

An overwhelming majority of sexual problems are believed to be rooted in psychological or attitudinal determinants. In fact, sexual behavior is highly influenced by a person's "sexual script," a complex network of interacting variables within the individual and the relationship.[4] Five factors are believed to be inherent in a sexual script: family history, individual personality dynamics, cultural context, interaction effects of these factors on the individual, and interaction of these factors on the relationship dyad.[5] Although the foundation of one's sexual script is embedded in early childhood experiences, it is a dynamic process that continues to evolve throughout life in relationships with others.[6]

When individual personality dynamics are studied as precursors of sexual scripting, self-image and guilt both surface as influential variables affecting sexual attitudes and behavior. In fact, an impaired sense of self is believed by some authorities to be women's greatest psychological and sexual barrier to intimacy.[7] Lending support for such a hypothesis, present paradigms for female sexuality include a wide range of mental health problems in which sexuality and self-image intersect.[8]

Female Sexual Behavior

Partner-Related Sexual Behavior

A wide range of percentages for premarital sexual intercourse among college women was revealed in a review of 30 studies conducted during the 1980s, with rates ranging from 37 percent[9] to 88 percent.[10] And a high level of participation by college women in premarital sexual intercourse remained evident in the 1990s, with the reported incidence ranging from 61 percent[11] to 78 percent.[12]

During this time, the age at first sexual intercourse among college students has converged for women and men and has continued to decline. The mean age reported in the mid-1980s was 17.7 years,[13] whereas by the mid-1990s it had dropped to 16.5 years.[14] With regard to number of sex partners, the reported mean number of lifetime partners for college women varies from 3.4[15] to 6.9 partners.[16] And a greater number of sex partners has been associated with a higher frequency of sexual intercourse,[17] as well as earlier age at first intercourse and liberal attitudes toward premarital sex and abortion.[18]

Risk-Related Sexual Practices

Contrary to popular opinion, becoming knowledgeable about sexual risks does not necessarily lead college women to implement behavioral changes.[19] For example, knowledge about AIDS has been found not to be correlated with condom use during sexual intercourse, less frequent sexual intercourse, or fewer sex partners. In fact, women in one study who claimed to have become more selective in choosing sex partners or to be engaging in sexual intercourse less often were as sexually active as those who claimed no changes in their sex lives.[20]

The reluctance to claim ownership of one's own sexual behavior and sexual guilt are known to result in noncontraceptive usage[21] or use of less effective contraceptive methods.[22] Condom usage by sex partners of college women, in general, continues to remain low, with 68 percent of sexually active college women reporting no condom usage by their sex partners during the past 12 months.[23] Carroll[20] suggests that one reason for little change in the initiation of "safer" sex practices by women may be that they have a low sense of self-efficacy and control.

Sexual Guilt

Guilt has been characterized as a generalized expectancy for self-punishment when failing to attain one's internalized standards.[24] A person's internal standards of proper sexual behavior result from two life experiences: prohibitions, or "should-not's," and idealized goals, or "ought-to's." Each of these factors is highly interrelated with a person's feelings of self-worth.

The Nature of Guilt

Most theorists agree that at least moderate degrees of guilt are part of normal development and, thus, crucial in the process of socialization. However, there are primary differences in viewpoints concerning the nature of guilt[25] and its effects.[26] Social-learning theorists, who view guilt feelings as a form of learned emotional arousal, suggest that the effects of guilt are relatively straightforward and specifiable. For example, research has found that inducing guilt in a person increases "helping" behavior.[27] Conversely, psychodynamic theorists argue that guilt feelings can be expressed in behaviors that may appear unrelated to the source of conflict. An example of such an outcome might be the development of agoraphobia as a result of sexual guilt.[28]

Guilt is viewed as both an emotion and a personality disposition.[29] As a personality dynamic, guilt is believed to be an affective-cognitive structure resulting from past guilt-related situations that influenced one's perceptions about sexual attitudes and behavior. And as an emotion, it is an affective-behavioral component, inhibiting or encouraging different types of sexual behavior.[30] Ample evidence exists that sexual guilt can inhibit future sexual arousal and lead to sexual dysfunction.[31] Not only is guilt implicated in inhibited sexual desire and other sexual dysfunctions but it is also involved in sexual acting out, as evidenced by affairs or promiscuity.[28] Guilt may also lead to sexual dissatisfaction. In a survey of college women, guilt was ranked as the most important reason why first sexual intercourse was not psychologically satisfying.[13]

Shame is an emotion often confused with guilt, but most of the psychological literature treats guilt and shame as two distinct entities. Accordingly, shame has been linked with depressed feelings, humiliation, and inferiority, while guilt is believed to manifest itself with obsessive and paranoid thinking, aggression, isolation, rationalization, and reaction formation.[32] So described, guilt elicits common feelings of blame when one's actions violate a code of conduct; shame relates more to personal identity and, thus, produces more painful feelings, such as defectiveness, dirtiness, or weakness.[33] People with shame-based feelings are more prone to avoid such memories than are those experiencing guilt, who may even wish to talk about their guilt feelings. Therefore, shame is assumed to more profoundly affect personality development, including one's sexual script.

Regret is another emotion closely aligned with guilt that has received little attention in the research literature. It has been defined as distress in recalling a past event and wishing that something had not happened. Landman[34] argues that regret is not pathological, but rather it serves many purposes. Regret warns, instructs, mobilizes, and promotes ethical behavior.

Sources of Sexual Guilt

Of the sources of sexual guilt, three are strongly reflected in the literature: religion, parents, and peers. Religious attitudes are influential in increasing levels of sexual guilt as suggested in numerous studies.[35] Therapists find that women with high levels of sexual guilt often have a history of parental or religious indoctrinations about sexuality. But it is difficult to delineate religion as the specific source when parents who convey unhealthy attitudes about sex to their children at very early ages are most likely to plant the seeds of such guilt feelings. For this reason, religion has been classified as an intervening variable.[36]

Herold and Goodwin[37] found that one of the best predictors of guilt at first sexual intercourse is low self-esteem. And parent-child relationships are recognized to be significant variables in the development of a child's self-esteem. Sexually active women who experienced guilt felt that they were violating standards of significant others, including their mother figure, father figure, and peers.[38]

Peers may also be sources of sexual guilt, contributing sexual pressures that ultimately lead to self-defeating guilt patterns. It is important to remember that sex partners, many of whom exert sexual pressures, are themselves usually peers. The literature reveals a dearth of research, however, concerning a much more subtle but, perhaps, pervasive source of influence: the media. With their unrealistic standards of beauty and behavior, the media promote unobtainable goals that may be highly defining in how women experience their sexuality.[35]

Finally, cultural norms may precipitate sexual guilt. Almost three decades ago, Christensen[39] postulated that premarital sexual attitudes and behavior and the consequences of those behaviors are related to cultural norms. These negative affective consequences often surface in the form of guilt. The influence of cultural norms on premarital sexual activity is reflected in the significantly greater acceptance of premarital sexual activity for an 18-year-old than for a 16-year-old.[40]

Effects of Sexual Guilt

Many authorities agree that learning about sex in America is learning about guilt.[41] Given the sexual double standard for women and men in our society, it is not surprising that women are more likely to report sexual guilt about first sexual intercourse than men, who are more likely to report pleasure.[14] Women also indicate feelings of fear, anxiety, and anxiousness more often than men.[42]

Research indicates that the quality of the physical aspect of first sexual intercourse affects the subsequent relationship with the partner. But the quality of sexual intercourse may be mediated by the different meanings that women and men assign to the experience. Sexual satisfaction is highly related to emotional closeness for women, whereas for men, sexual satisfaction is symbolic of future sexual rewards.[43] These divergent views may explain why only 7 percent of college women reported experiencing an orgasm during first sexual intercourse.[14] Unless a woman experiences an orgasm at least 50 percent of the time during sexual intercourse, she would be classified by many sex therapists as having secondary sexual dysfunction.[44] Given this criterion, along with the writings contained in many popular so-called women's magazines, it should not be surprising that many women experience guilt feelings because they are unable to experience an orgasm during sexual intercourse.

Physiological factors do contribute to variations in the orgasmic response for women during sexual intercourse, including type and length of stimulation provided before ejaculation by their male partner.[45] However, the importance of relationship factors as determinants of women's sexual functioning have been strongly supported in the research literature[46] even though behavioral factors—such as age at first sexual intercourse, number of lifetime sex partners, and frequency of sexual intercourse—have been found to be unrelated to orgasmic consistency during sexual intercourse.[47]

Women with high sex guilt, such as guilt over first sexual intercourse, are more likely to behave sexually in what has been termed a mechanical orgasm-oriented manner.[3] For such persons, guilt feelings are likely to be associated with absence of orgasm during sexual intercourse. Among college women, 60 percent indicated feeling guilty if no orgasm occurred during sexual intercourse. Those reporting guilt feelings about first sexual intercourse were also more likely to report guilt associated with absence of orgasm during current sexual intercourse.[41]

Although it is commonly recognized by therapists and psychiatrists that emotional states such as guilt affect sexual desire and sexual satisfaction, few studies have directly addressed the issue. And little research has focused on the feelings that women experience in the initiation of first sexual intercourse.[42] Further, even less research exists regarding the influence of guilt about first intercourse on later sexual satisfaction. Therefore, the purposes of this investigation were to identify the variables correlated with feeling guilty about first sexual intercourse. These variables included family background, risk-taking sexual behaviors, and sexual adjustment/satisfaction.

THE CURRENT STUDY

Method

An anonymous questionnaire was administered to volunteer respondents enrolled in select lower and upper division courses in the Schools of Arts and Sciences, Business, and Nursing at a Midwestern residential state university. Given the nature of this investigation, the data analyses were limited to 851 never-married women. In the interest of creating a more homogeneous sample, those who indicated their sexual orientation to be bisexual or lesbian or who failed to respond to the inquiry about sexual orientation were omitted from the data analyses. The final subsample of 571 never-married women included 23.3 percent freshmen, 25.6 percent sophomores, 26.3 percent juniors, and 24.9 percent seniors.

Results

Sexual History

The initial data analyses concerning guilt feelings associated with first sexual intercourse revealed that 20.1 percent of the women reported "frequently" having guilt feelings, 18.4 percent "occasionally," 23.5 percent "seldom," and 38.0 percent "never." For ease of reporting the data analyses, four respondent group categories were subsequently established: *F Group* = frequently have guilt feelings; *O Group* = occasionally have guilt feelings; *S Group* = seldom have guilt feelings; and *N Group* = never have guilt feelings.

Although a review of the sexual histories of these women reveals several significant differences between respondent groups, there are also numerous similarities. Before age 14, about two-thirds of all respondents had engaged in one or more petting activities with members of the opposite sex. However, F Group women were more likely than women from the other groups to have had their genitals caressed through their clothing. These women were also more likely to have reciprocated by touching their partner's clothed and unclothed genitals. There were no significant differences between respondent groups for the other petting activity variables. After age 14, F Group women were less likely to have engaged in petting than the other women. And, it should be noted that there were no significant differences between respondent groups with regard to age, or turning to orgasmic experience: ever experienced orgasm; age at first orgasm; orgasm via masturbation, petting, or sexual intercourse; age at first orgasm via sexual intercourse; or frequency of orgasm via sexual intercourse.

In terms of lifetime-partner relationship status, F Group women were more likely to have had sexual intercourse with occasional dating partners and casual acquaintances than O Group, S Group, or N Group women. No significant differences were reported for the other sex partner categories: steady dating partner, committed love relationship partner, friend, or person just met. And F Group women also reported having engaged in sexual intercourse with more different sex partners than all other women.

Circumstances/First Intercourse

An examination of the circumstances surrounding first intercourse revealed a number of significant differences between respondent groups. F Group women, in comparison to the others, were more likely to have had their first sexual intercourse experience with an occasional dating partner, friend, or person just met. In contrast, N Group and S Group women were more likely than O Group or F Group women to have had their first sexual intercourse with a steady dating partner or a committed relationship partner. Furthermore, N Group women were more likely to have given "verbal consent" for their first intercourse experience, whereas F Group, O Group, and S Group women more often gave "implied" consent. These circumstances surrounding first sexual intercourse appear to be related, in part, to the role that alcohol or other mind-altering substances may have played in the decision-making process. F Group women were more likely than the others to have been under the influence of alcohol or some other mind-altering substance at the time of first sexual intercourse. In fact, F Group women were more than twice as likely as N Group women to have been alcohol or substance impaired at first sexual intercourse. Although F Group women had their first sexual intercourse experience at a younger age ($M = 16.7$ years) than N Group ($M = 17.6$ years), S Group ($M = 17.5$ years), or O Group ($M = 17.1$ years) women, no significant differences were found between respondent groups concerning mean age of first sexual intercourse partner. Finally, more N Group women used a contraceptive at first sexual intercourse than women in the other groups.

Family Background

Concerning the family background of these college women, F Group women were more likely to have grown up having uncommunicative mother and father figures than in the other groups. They also had an overly strict father figure in comparison to the other respondents. Finally, F Group women were less likely than all other women to have grown up in a home where they observed their mother and father figures displaying affection toward each other. The perceived degree of religiosity of these college women was also measured using a quasi-Likert scale variable (*more* religious, *same*, or *less* religious in comparison to other members of your religious denomination). N Group women considered themselves to be less religious than the other groups of women.

Sexual Adjustment and Sexual Satisfaction

Given the dearth of research about the role of guilt in sexual adjustment and sexual satisfaction, it is important to examine the relationship between these two variables and guilt about first sexual intercourse. A review of the findings concerning physiological and psychological satisfaction with first sexual intercourse identified further significant differences between respondent groups. N Group women were more likely than all other women to have experienced both physiological and psychological satisfaction with their first sexual intercourse experience.

With regard to comfortableness with their sexuality, a variable used to help assess sexual adjustment, F Group women reported less comfort than all other women. Further, group differences on sexual adjustment approached statistical significance, with F Group women being less likely than the other women to report sexual adjustment. Significant differences were identified between respondent groups with regard to current psychological sexual satisfaction, with F Group women being less likely to report current psychological sexual satisfaction. However, no significant differences were found between respondent groups for the variable, "current sexual satisfaction."

Not surprisingly, F Group women were more likely than all others to report guilt about engaging in petting and about their current sexual intercourse episodes. They were also more likely than the other respondent groups to indicate feeling guilty if they did not experience an orgasm during sexual intercourse.

Discussion

The debate continues concerning the role of emotion in human behavior. The continuum ranges from the nineteenth-century James-Lange position[48] suggesting that emotional states result from behavior to that of theorists, such as Tomkins,[49] who believe emotions are the primary motivational system. After a century of study, the question still remains: Is the emotion of guilt a by-product of behavior, or does guilt play a role in determining behavior? This research certainly did not purport to answer such queries or even to explore the issues fully. It does, however, shed light on the substantial relationships between numerous variables and the emotion of guilt concerning first sexual intercourse.

Although other studies have found relationships between guilt and specific sexual attitudes and behaviors,[41,50] this study revealed a wide array of such relationships. In fact, the guilt-prone character portrayed by F Group women indicates that they were substantially different from N Group women in sexual attitudes and behavior. The statistical portrait that emerged from those more prone to guilt depicted a sexual history, family background, and subsequent sexual adjustment and satisfaction pattern that was far less than health promoting.

It will be remembered that F Group women not only experienced sexual intercourse at younger ages but also were twice as likely to be under the influence of alcohol or some other mind-altering substance at the time of their first intercourse. This finding is of particular interest, given that the mean age at first sexual intercourse for these women was considerably lower than the legal age for consumption of alcoholic beverages. These data substantiate the findings of Darling, Davidson, and Passarello[13] that alcohol may offer youth an enabling script that allows them to avoid guilt about sexual experience. Behavior precipitated by mind-altering substances may have contributed to both initiating sexual intercourse at younger ages and the less healthy response of implied consent for first intercourse.

The fact that first sexual intercourse for F Group women was more likely to occur with an "occasional dating partner" or a "person just met" was not an isolated event. This behavior among F Group women surfaced as a pattern, repeated in subsequent sexual experiences. Therefore, it was not surprising that they had greater numbers of lifetime sex partners than the other women. This is consonant with Mosher's finding[28] that guilt is implicated in sexual acting out as evidenced by promiscuity. And sexual involvement with an occasional dating partner or a person just met is a potentially guilt-inducing behavior in a society that equates sex and love.

Finally, that the greater number of sex partners and earlier age at first sexual intercourse were associated for F Group women corroborates the earlier data from Tanfer and Schoorl.[18] This study also supports the findings of Murray, Harvey, and Beckman,[21] who claim that sexual guilt and lack of contraceptive usage are related. From the weight of the composite findings revealed in this research, it could logically be argued that the guilt-prone F Group women lacked a strong sense of self-efficacy. Therefore, they may have been unduly influenced by their partner's decisions related to condom usage, as suggested by Carroll.[20]

Given the continued debate about the role of family values in the sexual decision-making process of American adolescents, the findings concerning the role of family variables are noteworthy. Parental influence can perhaps best be understood by the juxtaposition of the backgrounds of N Group women, who never felt guilty, and F Group women, who frequently did so. Consider the fact that N Group women were most likely to be from homes with characteristics that are reflective of functional families: communicative mother and father figures who display affection toward each other and father figures who are not too strict. Now contrast these findings with the exact opposite behaviors in the homes of F Group women: uncommunicative parents who did not exchange affection and very strict fathers.

The fact that N Group women were more comfortable with their sexuality was evidenced by an array of sexual behaviors that were health promoting. For example, they were older at first sexual intercourse and were more likely to have used a contraceptive. One of the most telling events occurred when they gave verbal consent for first sexual intercourse. This more mature, reasoned choice implies that they perceived themselves as having a choice and, therefore, felt empowered. Thus, it was only logical that these women experienced more physiological and psychological satisfaction at first intercourse. It was puzzling that they rated their current sexual life as more psychologically but not more physiologically satisfying. One could speculate that these women, who felt comfortable with their sexuality, also possessed an apparent self-efficacy that led to greater physiological expectations for sexual intercourse.

The guilt-prone F Group women, who lacked psychological sexual satisfaction and comfort with their sexuality, expressed the most guilt about masturbation, petting, current sexual intercourse, and absence of orgasm during sexual intercourse. These are the same women who had sexual intercourse at a young age, with an occasional dating partner or someone they had just met, and while under the influence of alcohol. Their self-defeating sexual behaviors may be related to two factors: young age at first sexual intercourse and a less functional family life. In regard to age at first sexual intercourse, the F Group women, who experienced sexual intercourse earlier than their peers, were in violation of the social norms—a circumstance that triggered negative affective consequences in the form of guilt.

Since religion is viewed as an important source of family values, it is also important to note its influence on sexual guilt. Greater levels of sexual guilt were correlated with a higher degree of religiosity. However, the weight of evidence herein concerning family background variables supports the contention of Billy, Brewster, and Grady[36] that religion itself is only an intervening variable.

Conclusion

The negative consequences of guilt in this study clearly appear to be pervasive and highly interrelated with unhealthy sexual scripts. The question of why there is a wide disparity of sexual behavior between groups who did and did not feel guilty about first sexual intercourse is perhaps less clear. In fact, this study, like most studies, raises more questions than answers. It does, however, suggest several interesting possibilities.

First one may ask, "Is guilt in this context desirable or undesirable?" Accepting the premise that at least a moderate degree of guilt is part of normal development and crucial to the process of socialization, one may ask, "Who were really the healthy players?" Are those who never felt guilt really the least healthy from a developmental point of view? Although this concept was interesting, it proved to be erroneous when the subsequent sexual patterns of N Group women were identified as more health promoting than those who did feel guilty.

A second question pertains to the sources of such guilt. Are sociological or psychological factors at work, or both? If sociological factors are involved, perhaps the guilt results from a perceptual dichotomy. First sexual intercourse is a societal marker in personal development. It is even a normative event in the eyes of most peers and the media, who encourage sexual participation. But it is a nonnormative marker in the eyes of most parents and religious denominations, who discourage premarital sexual intercourse. The emotional tug-of-war created by such opposing positions is a potential explanation for the evolving guilt. This dilemma may be especially true for young women who experience sexual intercourse at younger ages and, at the time, possess less well-developed self-efficacy or decision-making skills.

Psychological factors are implicated when sexual guilt is considered a personality disposition. Since personality dynamics are inherent in all sexual decisions, one could speculate about the differences in a guilt- or shame-prone personality. Al-though this study made no attempt to differentiate between guilt and shame as separate entities, some authorities believe the difference is significant.[33] Others maintain that either a guilt or shame-based persona greatly increases the odds that sexual behaviors will be expressed in less healthy ways. The degrees of guilt expressed by the respondents in this study could lend support to Kaufman's[25] thesis that guilt and shame are variants of one and the same affect or feeling. Thus, guilt as the internalized expression of shame was possibly generated by the blame and contempt activated by self-disappointment from having violated one's cherished values.

Some may argue that guilt as a personality disposition is an inherited trait. The authors would tend to agree only if one accepts the fact that one inherits not only one's genes but one's parents as well. If the overwhelming majority of sexual problems leading to guilt are, indeed, rooted in psychological or attitudinal determinants, early experiences would appear to be somewhat defining of later personality traits. Thus, parents must necessarily be considered the primary agents of change.

Finally, the possibility exists that issues raised in this study and in related research cannot be fully explored until more basic concepts of semantics are clarified. For example, does an emotional continuum exist that moves from regret to guilt and to shame? Do these emotions differ by degree or by their very nature? Could the women in this study who indicated the most guilt actually have reflected other emotions, such as shame and regret? If shame-based feelings precipitated the subsequent psychological and physiological risk-related sexual behaviors of these respondents, perhaps unhealthy personality predispositions could be postulated. Conversely, if the feelings of these women represented the other end of a hypothetical emotion continuum, this condition more simply could be labeled regret. In such an event, regret could serve as a transformative power,[34] moving the person toward more healthy choices.

Even when professional directions are indicated, more than mere movement is required to effect change. If making decisions that end without guilt or regret requires self-knowledge and self-esteem, the role of mental health professionals in promoting sexual satisfaction and adjustment may be substantially different from what was previously assumed. If self-knowledge and self-esteem are the primary variables in healthy sexual decisions and if they are components of the persona, rooted in life's earliest experiences, the role of parents becomes more focused. Professionals then must acknowledge and educate parents for their seminal role in the formative years of their children's personality development. These findings also confirm that professionals must be in touch with the needs of their student or clients for inner resources as well as cognitive information such as safer-sex techniques and decision-making skills.

This investigation has substantiated that a healthy sexual script, precluding disabling emotions—whether guilt, shame, or regret—is the basis for health-promoting sexual attitudes and behaviors. Although certain factors may augur sexual satisfaction and sexual adjustment, unfortunately there are no prescriptives for achieving such a panacea.

References

1. Resneck-Sannes H.: Shame, sexuality, and vulnerability. *Women Ther 11(2)*:111–125, 1991.

2. Davidson J.K. Sr., Moore N.B.: Guilt and lack of orgasm during sexual intercourse: Myth versus reality among college women. *J Sex Educ Ther 20*:153–174, 1994.

3. Kaplan H.S.: *The New Sex Therapy: Active Treatment of Sexual Dysfunctions*. New York, Brunner/Mazel, 1974.

4. Davidson J.K. Sr., Moore N.B.: *Marriage and Family: Change and Continuity*. Boston, Allyn & Bacon, 1996.

5. Talmadge W.C.: Introduction to sexuality. In L. L'Abate (ed.), *The Handbook of Family Psychology and Therapy*, vol. 1. Homewood, IL, Dorsey, 1985.

6. Engel J.W., Saracino M., Bergen M.B.: Sexuality education. In M.E. Arcus, J.D. Schvaneveldt, J.J. Moss (eds.), *Handbook of Family Life Education*, vol. 2: *The Practice of Family Life Education*. Thousand Oaks, CA, Sage, 1993.)

7. Cairns K.: The greening of sexuality and intimacy. *Sieccan J 25(2)*:1–10, 1990.

8. Valentich M.: Talking sex: Implications for practice in the 1990s. *Sieccan J 5(4)*:3–11, 1990.

9. Ishii-Kuntz M.: Acquired immune deficiency syndrome and sexual behavior in a college student sample. *Soc Social Res 73*:13–18, 1988.

10. Murstein B.I., Chapin M.J., Heard K.V., Vyse S.A.: Sexual behavior, drugs, and relationship patterns on a college campus over thirteen years. *Adolescence 24(93)*:125–139, 1989.

11. Pepe M.V., Sanders D.W., Symons C.W.: Sexual behaviors of university freshmen and the implications for sexuality educators. *J Sex Educ Ther 19*:20–30, 1993.

12. Reinholtz R.K., Muehlenhard C.L.: Genital perceptions and sexual activity in a college population. *J Sex Res 32*:155–166, 1995.

13. Darling C.A., Davidson J.K. Sr., Passarello L.C.: The mystique of first intercourse among college youth: The role of partners, contraceptive practices, and psychological reactions. *J Youth Adol 21*:97–117, 1992.

14. Sprecher S., Barbee A., Schwartz P.: "Was it good for you too?": Gender differences in first sexual intercourse experiences. *J Sex Res 32*:3–15, 1995.

15. Leitenberg H., Detzer M.J., Srebnik D.: Gender differences in masturbation and the relationship of masturbation experience in preadolescence and/or early adolescence to sexual behavior and sexual adjustment in young adulthood. *Arch Sex Behav 22*:87–98, 1993.

16. Weinberg M.S., Lottes I.L., Shaver F.M.: Swedish or American heterosexual college youth: Who is more permissive? *Arch Sex Behav 24*:409–437, 1995.

17. Tanfer K., Cubbins L.A.: Coital frequency among single women: Normative constraints and situational opportunities. *J Sex Res 29*:221–250, 1992.

18. Tanfer K., Schoorl J.J.: Premarital sexual careers and partner change. *Arch Sex Behav 21*:45–68, 1992.

19. Trocki K.F.: Patterns of sexuality and risk sexuality in the general population of a California county. *J Sex Res 29*:85–94, 1992.

20. Carroll L.: Gender, knowledge about AIDs, reported behavioral change, and the sexual behavior of college students. *J Am Coll Health* 40:5–12, 1991.

21. Murray J., Harvey S.M., Beckman L.J.: The importance of contraceptive attributes of college women. *J Appl Psychol* 19:1327–1350, 1989.

22. Strassberg D.L., Mahoney J.M.: Correlates of the contraceptive behavior of adolescents/young adults. *J Sex Res* 25:531–536, 1988.

23. Gray L.A., Saracino M.: College students' attitudes, beliefs, and behaviors about AIDS: Implications for family life educators. *Fam Relat* 40:258–263, 1991.

24. Wyatt G.E., Dunn K.M.: Examining predictors of sex guilt in multiethnic samples of women. *Arch Sex Behav* 20:471–485, 1991.

25. Kaufman G.: *Shame: The Power of Caring* (3rd ed, rev). Rochester, VT, Schenkman, 1992.

26. Lewis M.: Self-conscious emotions: Embarrassment, pride, shame, and guilt. In M. Lewis, J.M. Haviland (eds.), *Handbook of Emotions*. New York, Guilford, 1993.

27. Rawlings E.: Reactive guilt and anticipatory guilt in altruistic behavior. In J. Macauley, L. Berkowitz (eds.), *Altruism and Helping Behavior: Social Psychological Studies of Some Antecedents and Consequences*. New York, Academic, 1970.

28. Mosher D.L.: Guilt. In R.H. Woody (ed.), *The Encyclopedia of Clinical Assessment*, vol 1. San Francisco, Jossey-Bass, 1980.

29. Mosher D.L.: Sex guilt and sex myth in college men and women. *J Sex Res* 15:224–234, 1979.

30. Cado S., Leitenberg H.: Guilt reactions to sexual fantasies during intercourse. *Arch Sex Behav* 19:49–63, 1990.

31. Morokoff P.J.: Effects of sex guilt, repression, sexual arousability, and sexual experience on female sexual arousal during erotica and fantasy. *J Pers Soc Psychol* 49:177–187, 1985.

32. Lewis J.: *Shame and Guilt in Neurosis*. New York, International Universities, 1971.

33. Friedin B.: Survivor shame. *Contemp Sexual* 28 (March):1–4, 1994.

34. Landman J.: *The Persistence of Possible*. New York: Oxford University, 1994.

35. Daniluk J.C.: The meaning and experience of female sexuality: A phenomenological analysis. *Psych Women Q* 17:53–69, 1993.

36. Billy J.O.G., Brewster K.L., Grady W.R.: Contextual effects on the sexual behavior of adolescent women. *J Marr Fam* 56:387–404, 1995.

37. Herold E.S., Goodwin M.S.: Premarital sexual guilt. *Can J Behav Sci* 13:66–75, 1981.

38. Knox D., Walters L.H., Walters J.: Sexual guilt among college students. *Coll Stud J* 25:432–433, 1991.

39. Christensen H.T.: Normative theory derived from cross-cultural family research. *J Marr Fam* 31:209–222, 1969.

40. Sprecher S.: Premarital sexual standards for different categories of individuals. *J Sex Res* 26:232–248, 1989.

41. Darling C.A., Davidson J.K. Sr.: Guilt: A factor in sexual satisfaction. *Soc Inquiry* 57:251–271, 1987.

42. Schwartz I.M.: Affective reactions of American and Swedish women to their first premarital coitus: A cross-cultural comparison. *J Sex Res* 30:18–26, 1993.

43. Cate R.M., Long E., Angera J.J., Draper K.K.: Sexual intercourse and relationship development. *Fam Relat* 42:158–164, 1993.

44. Milan R.J., Kilmann P.R., Boland J.P.: Treatment outcome of secondary orgasmic dysfunction: A two- to six-year follow-up. *Arch Sex Behav* 17:463–480, 1988.

45. LoPiccolo J., Stock W.E.: Treatment of sexual dysfunction. *J Consult Clin Psychol* 54:158–167, 1986.

46. Rosen R.C., Taylor J.F., Leiblum S.R., Bachmann G.A.: Prevalence of sexual dysfunction in women: Results of a survey study of 329 women in an outpatient gynecological clinic. *J Sex Marital Ther* 19:171–188, 1993.

47. Raboch J., Raboch J.: Infrequent orgasms in women. *J Sex Marital Ther* 18:114–120, 1992.

48. James W.: What is emotion? *Mind* 9:188–205, 1884.

49. Tomkins S.S.: Affect as the primary motivational system. In M.B. Arnold (ed.), *Feelings and Emotions*. New York, Academic, 1970.

50. Koch P.B.: The relationship of first intercourse to later sexual functioning of adolescents. *J Adolesc Res* 3:345–362, 1988.

Adapted from Nelwyn B. Moore, & J. Kenneth Davidson, Sr., "Guilt About First Intercourse: An Antecedent of Sexual Dissatisfaction Among College Women." *Journal of Sex & Marital Therapy*, 23, 29–46. Copyright © 1997. Reprinted by permission. ✦

Chapter 13
Alcohol, Religious Beliefs, and Risky Sexual Behavior in College Students

Ronald L. Poulson
Marion A. Eppler
Tammy N. Satterwhite
Karl L. Wuensch
Lessie A. Bass

Alcohol consumption on college campuses is a multifaceted problem. Binge-drinking related deaths and alcohol-related date rape are likely to grab news headlines while a much more pervasive problem with alcohol lies hidden in the back—reports that alcohol consumption leads to sexual risk-taking. Typical sexual behaviors of college students place them at an already inordinate risk for contracting life-threatening sexually transmitted diseases (STDs). Add alcohol to this equation and the game can be deadly.

Are the odds in this game of Russian Roulette improved with the addition of a third factor, religious beliefs? Are differential effects between women and men concerning alcohol use, sexual risk-taking, and strength of religious beliefs the result of innate or societal factors? Such questions are raised by the researchers in a survey conducted in what the authors describe as a public university in the Bible Belt South. While there are few surprises about the relationship between alcohol consumption and sexual risk taking, the ad-
dition of a third variable, religious values, does promise a more interesting study.

Although a strong correlation between college students' alcohol consumption and risky sexual behavior has been reported in some studies,[1] other research findings do not agree that there is such a relationship.[2-3] According to some researchers,[4-6] these conflicting reports may be related to varying cultural and religious orientations associated with different regions of the country.

First, we wanted to estimate the incidence of risky sexual behavior at a large university in a geographic region that has been largely ignored in previous research, namely the predominantly rural, conservative agricultural area in the southeastern United States commonly referred to as the Bible Belt. Our second aim was to examine how both drinking patterns and strength of religious convictions are related to risky sexual behavior.

The typical sexual behavior of many college students places them at risk for contracting serious sexually transmitted diseases (STDs).[7-9] Current estimates are that one in every four new cases of HIV infection occurs in people under the age of 25 years,[10] the age group of a major percentage of undergraduate college students. Moreover, several studies[9,11-12] have reported that high numbers of students engage in risky sexual behaviors, such as unprotected intercourse or inconsistent use of condoms.

Research findings clearly indicate that 75 percent or more of college students are sexually active. In a national survey, Douglas et al.[8] found that 86.1 percent of college students reported that they had engaged in sexual intercourse and that 34.5 percent of the respondents in their study had had six or more sexual partners during their lifetimes. A primary concern is that fewer than 25 percent of the students who are sexually active report consistently using condoms in every sexual encounter.[8] To further compound the risks associated with unsafe sexual practices, college students with multiple partners were significantly less consistent in overall condom use, particularly when alcohol was involved, according to Desiderato and Crawford.[7]

Alcohol Consumption

Alcohol consumption is one major factor that has been repeatedly linked to unsafe sexual behavior. In a national sample of more than 17,000 college students, Wechsler et al.[13] reported that "binge" drinkers were 7 to 10 times more likely than "nonbinge" drinkers to engage in unplanned and unprotected sexual activity. Desiderato and Crawford[7] found alcohol had preceded the last occurrence of sexual activity for a majority of the students (66 percent of the men and 53 percent of the women) and that both the frequency and quantity of alcohol consumption had a significant bearing on the number of sexual partners. When drinking alcohol preceded sexual activity, 41 percent of the students said that they either did not use condoms at all or were much less likely to do so.[7]

Not all researchers agree that alcohol is a determining factor in the incidence of unsafe sexual practices. Temple and Leigh[3] found no significant relationship between alcohol consumption and sexual intercourse without a condom for respondents' most recent sexual encounter or their most recent encounters with new sexual partners. Leigh[14] concluded that risky sexual behavior may be more a function of general risk taking than the simple consequence of the disinhibiting effects of alcohol. One important consideration is that, in the studies cited earlier, older adult samples were used; in other studies, higher rates of unprotected sex associated with alcohol use in adolescent and college-aged samples were found.

More recently, MacDonald and colleagues[15] offered a controlled series of studies using a variety of methods (correlational and experimental, laboratory and field studies) focusing on college students. Their findings suggest that alcoholic intoxication does increase the probability of engaging in risky sexual activity, such as sex without using a condom.

Another possible explanation for the conflicting reports may be an intervening variable, such as how liberal or conservative the attitudes are in a particular geographic region. Leigh's studies[16-17] were conducted in San Francisco, where participants' views regarding alcohol use and sexual behavior may be more liberal than the views of students in the rural southeastern United States. In sum, liberal attitudes may very well be related to greater risk-taking behavior.

Religious Beliefs

Religious affiliation and the strength of religious convictions may contribute to a person's decisions about alcohol consumption. College students who reported that participating in religious activity was "not at all important" to them had a significantly higher likelihood of binge drinking than students for whom religion was somewhat important in their lives.[6] Donahue and Benson[18] found that stronger religious values were correlated with lower rates of drug and alcohol use and with a lower incidence of premarital sexual intercourse.

Hawks and Bahr[19] compared the drinking patterns of respondents belonging to abstinence-oriented religious groups, such as the Church of Jesus Christ of Latter-Day Saints (Mormons), with the drinking patterns of those belonging to less-restrictive religious groups and those with no religious affiliation. The Mormon respondents reported far less alcohol use than the other two groups. More specifically, only 31 percent of the Mormon group reported some alcohol use during the most recent 30-day period, compared with 63 percent of the respondents from other religious groups and 68 percent of the nonaffiliated group.

Carlucci et al.[5] reported similar findings when they compared Protestants and Jews, who are more likely to advocate abstinence, with Catholics, who tend to hold a more permissive attitude toward alcohol consumption. These studies[5,9] indicated that strong religious messages about alcohol abstinence can have a significant impact on personal rates of alcohol consumption.

THE CURRENT STUDY

We drew a convenience sample of 210 participants from the general student population at a large university in a rural region of the southeastern United States. The participants' characteristics were generally consistent with relevant demographic characteristics on this particular campus. For example, 61 percent (*n* = 129) of the respondents were women, and 39 percent (*n* = 79) were men. The ethnic status of respondents represented was 9 percent African American, 86 percent European American, and 4 percent other categories. Respondents in this study ranged in age from 18 to 36 years, with a mean age of 21 years.

Results

The vast majority of respondents (84 percent) reported having engaged in sexual intercourse. One-third of the entire sample reported a frequency of one to three times per week, and one-quarter reported a frequency of one to two times per month. Only 27 percent of the respondents reported they consistently used condoms, whereas more than one-half reported their condom use was inconsistent.

This high rate of unprotected sex, along with the fact that almost half of the respondents reported having engaged in sexual intercourse with multiple partners during the past year, indicated that many students were placing themselves at a significant risk for contracting STDs, including HIV.

Although virtually all students reported using precautionary methods to prevent pregnancy, many tended to use mostly unreliable methods or methods that do not provide any protection from STDs. It appeared that participants were more concerned with preventing pregnancy than with protecting themselves from STDs. Thus, whereas most students' intentions were good, almost half stated that they did not use protective methods because they were in love and trusted their partners.

Alcohol consumption was also quite high for this sample of students. When asked how often they had been intoxicated in the past month, 23 percent reported being intoxicated one or two times, 17 percent reported three to four times, 13 percent reported a frequency of five to six times, and 22 percent reported a frequency of seven to eight times. One-third (33 percent) reported having consumed so much alcohol that they passed out at least once during the past month.

Seventy-eight percent of the respondents reported that they had made one or more decisions while drinking that they later regretted. With regard to sexual activity, more than one third of our sample reported having used alcohol to enhance their sexual experiences, and 68 percent of the respondents reported that alcohol had at some time had a negative effect on their sexual behavior.

The strength and nature of a person's religious beliefs may also play a major role in decisions about sexual activity. We found that 60 percent of our respondents believed in attending church or attended church on a regular basis, 78 percent believed that God operated in their daily lives, and 80 percent believed that they would go to heaven when they died. Most of our respondents (66 percent) did not feel that premarital sex was a sin. Most respondents (77 percent) also did not believe that alcohol consumption was a sin.

To examine more closely the interrelationships among these three variables, we created composite variables. For the risky sex composite variable, we combined three items representing sexual behaviors that place students at risk for contracting STDs, including HIV: (a) how many sexual partners they have had in the past year; (b) specific activities, such as giving and receiving oral sex; (c) and exploring less common forms of sexual activity, such as group sex. For the alcohol consumption composite variable, we combined the following items: frequency and amount of alcohol consumption, frequency of intoxication, trouble with grades or police related to alcohol use, positive and negative effects of alcohol on sexual behavior, frequency of bad decisions made while under the influence of alcohol, frequency of blackouts or actually passing out, how often the student felt a need to get drunk, and how often he or she had been a passenger in a car driven by someone under the influence of alcohol.

For the strength of religious beliefs composite variable, we combined two items—how strongly the participant believed in God and whether the participant believed in attending church on a regular basis. Risky sexual behavior was positively correlated with alcohol consumption but not with religious beliefs. However, alcohol consumption was negatively correlated with religious beliefs.

The men had significantly higher rates of alcohol consumption than the women. The men also had higher rates of risky sexual behavior than the women. Men and women did not, however, differ significantly in their overall frequency of sexual activity. We also found no noteworthy differences for strength of religious beliefs for men and for women.

For the men in this sample, only one correlation was significant: Alcohol consumption was correlated with risky sexual behavior. Strength of religious convictions was unrelated to alcohol consumption and religious beliefs, and to risky sexual behavior and religious beliefs.

The pattern of correlations was quite different for women; all three correlations were significant. Alcohol consumption was positively correlated with risky sexual behavior. Strength of religious beliefs was negatively correlated with both alcohol consumption and risky sexual behavior.

Discussion

We examined the relations among alcohol consumption, strength of religious convictions, and risky sexual behavior in students at a large university in a relatively conservative, rural region of the United States. Our findings supported recent research documenting the high incidence of risky sexual behavior in college students. The number of students who were sexually active in our sample was comparable to findings in previous reports.[8-9] The proportion of students reporting consistent use of condoms was also quite similar. Many of our participants (48 percent) were engaging in sexual intercourse with multiple partners.

Our findings were consistent with reports from previous research[13,17,20] that alcohol use is a common practice on college campuses. Many of the students were using alcohol to the point of intoxication on a regular basis (one third of our respondents reported being intoxicated more than five times in the past month). Excessive use of alcohol is clearly linked to impaired judgment. More than three quarters of our respondents reported they had made decisions while under the influence of alcohol that they later regretted, and two-thirds reported that alcohol had at some time had a negative impact on their sexual behavior.

In particular, 70 percent of our respondents reported inconsistent use of condoms while under the influence of alcohol. This high rate of inconsistent condom use may have been attributable, in part, to the fact that almost half of our respondents reported they had only one sexual partner, perhaps making them feel less vulnerable to the risks associated with unprotected sex; 43 percent of the respondents reported that they did not use protection because they were in love and trusted their partners. We should underscore that existing research findings suggest that many college students may not be faithful in their dating relationships.

Alcohol consumption was strongly related to risky sexual behavior for both women and men in our study. Men had higher rates of alcohol consumption and higher rates of risky sexual behavior than women did, even though the overall rates of men's and women's sexual activity did not differ. Women with stronger religious convictions tended to consume less alcohol and were less likely to engage in risky sexual behavior, which was not true for men.

The observed gender differences may be attributable to broader societal attitudes regarding the use of alcohol. More specifically, alcohol consumption to the point of intoxication may be viewed as permissible for men but inappropriate for women. These attitudes may be different in geographic regions where people have more or less conservative values, because conservative values often include different expectations for men's and women's behavior. Thus, a critical question stemming from our study is whether religious sanctions against the use of alcohol and premarital sex influence women and men differently.

Although our findings in this study are consistent with previous research and provide insights regarding the interrelationships among three important variables, the methods we used prevent these findings from being generalizable to other students on this campus or on other campuses. The second methodological concern is that our data were based on self-reports. In such reports, respondents may desire to present themselves in a more favorable light or engage in what has commonly been termed *social desirability*. Researchers[21] suggest that if report bias does occur, it is more likely to result from underreporting, rather than overreporting, the frequency of problematic behavior.

Our preliminary data pointed to the possibility that many of our participants believed in a form of religion that is inconsistent with that taught in Christian churches in the Bible Belt. Our conversations with local clergy and religious leaders, for example, clearly suggested that premarital sex is a sin. Yet three quarters of our participants stated that it "should not be" and "is not" a sin.

Furthermore, drinking to excess was not considered a sin by many of our participants. In light of the reasonable percentage of participants who stated that they attended church on a regular basis, these findings appear quite intriguing. Perhaps the local clergy may want to address how students appear to go about reducing possible cognitive dissonance by modifying their thoughts rather than their behaviors.

This may be particularly true for many of our male participants, whose behaviors and religious beliefs appeared to be unrelated. All too often, men are told that having sex implies "manhood" or being a "real" man. Such attitudes may lead men to believe that they are invulnerable to HIV and other STDs. Indeed, parents, educators, and administrators may want to direct even more safer-sex campaigns toward men and their behaviors.

The high incidence of unsafe sexual practices is placing college students at risk for contracting STDs, including HIV. Our preliminary findings highlight the need for more detailed examinations of the interrelationship among alcohol consumption, religious beliefs, and risky sexual behavior among students who attend universities in the Bible Belt. We could then compare behaviors in this [region] and other regions of the country to see whether or not there is a link between religious value systems and the rates of alcohol consumption and safer sex practices. These kinds of studies could provide crucial data for educating college students about the consequences of their behaviors.

References

1. Robertson J., Plant M. Alcohol, sex and risks of HIV infection. *Alcohol Dependence*. 1988;22:75–78.

2. Doll L. Alcohol use as a cofactor for disease and high-risk behavior. Presented at the NIAAA Alcohol and AIDS Network Conference. Tucson, AZ; 1989.

3. Temple M.T., Leigh B.C. Alcohol consumption and unsafe sexual behavior in discrete events. *J Sex Research*. 1992;29:207–219.

4. Brannock J.C., Schandler S.L., Oncley P.R. Cross-cultural and cognitive factors examined in groups of adolescent drinkers. *J Drug Issues*. 1990;20:427–442.

5. Carlucci K., Genova J., Rubackin F., Rubackin R., Kayson W.A. Effects of sex, religion, and amount of alcohol consumption of self-reported drinking-related problem behaviors. *Psychol Rep*. 1993;72:983–987.

6. Wechsler H., Davenport A., Dowdall G., Moeykens B., Castillo S. Health and behavioral consequences of binge drinking in college. *JAMA*. 1994;272:1672–1677.

7. Desiderato L.L., Crawford H.J. Risky sexual behavior in college students: Relationships between number of sexual partners, disclosure of previous risky behavior, and alcohol use. *J Youth and Adolescence*. 1995;24:55–68.

8. Douglas K.A., Collins J.L., Warren C., et al. Results from the 1995 National College Health Risk Survey. *J Am Coll Health*. 1997;46:55–66.

9. Tewksbury R., Whittier N. Safer sex practices in samples drawn from nightclub, campus, and gay bars. *Sociology and Social Research*. 1992;76:185–189.

10. Centers for Disease Control. *AIDS Prevention Guide: The Facts About HIV Infection and Aids*. Atlanta, GA: U.S. Dept of Health and Human Services; 1994.

11. Bishop P.D., Lipsitz A. Sexual behavior among college students in the AIDS era: A comparative study. *J Psychology and Human Sexuality*. 1991;4:135–148.

12. Whitley B.E. College student contraception use: A multivariate analysis. *J Sex Research*. 1990;27:305–313.

13. Wechsler H., Isaac N. "Binge" drinkers at Massachusetts colleges. *JAMA*. 1992;267 (21):2929–2931.

14. Leigh B.C. The relationship of substance use during sex to high-risk sexual behavior. *J Sex Research*. 1990b;27:199–213.

15. MacDonald T.K., Zanna M.P., Fong G.T. Why common sense goes out the window: Effects of alcohol on intentions to use condoms. *Personality and Social Psychol Bull*. 1996;22:763–775.

16. Leigh B.C. The relationship of sex-related alcohol expectancies to alcohol consumption and sexual behavior. *Br J Addict*. 1990a; 85:919–928.

17. Leigh B.C. "Venus gets in my thinking": Drinking and female sexuality in the age of AIDS. *J Substance Abuse*. 1990c;2:129–145.

18. Donahue M.J., Benson P.L. Religion and the well-being of adolescents. *J Social Issues*. 1995;51:145–160.

19. Hawks R.D., Bahr S.H. Religion and drug use. *J. Drug Educ*. 1992;22:1–8.

20. Lo C.C., Globetti G. A partial analysis of the campus influence on drinking behavior: Students who enter college as nondrinkers. *J Drug Issues*. 1993;23:715–725.

21. Midanik L.T. Perspectives on the validity of self-reported alcohol use. *Br J Addict*. 1989;84:1419–1423.

Adapted from Ronald L. Poulson, Marion A. Eppler, Tammy N. Satterwhite, Karl L. Wuensch, & Lessie A. Bass, "Alcohol Consumption, Strength of Religious Beliefs, and Risky Sexual Behavior in College Students." *Journal of American College Health*, 46, 227–232. Copyright © 1998, by Heldref Publications, 1319 Eighteenth St., NW, Washington, DC 20036-1802. Reprinted with permission of the Helen Dwight Reid Educational Foundation. ✦

Chapter 14

Marital Style and Its Effects on Sexual Desire and Functioning

Barry W. McCarthy

In the Woody Allen movie Annie Hall, *an interesting scenario evolves in two scenes set in a marriage therapist's office. In the first scene, the therapist is inquiring of the wife, "How frequently do you two have sex?" to which she replies, "All the time, maybe twice a week." In the second scene, when the same question is posed to the husband, he answers, "Hardly ever, maybe twice a week." After reading the following article based on Gottman's four marital styles, put on a therapist's hat and classify the Woody Allen characters. Are they a complementary couple or a conflict-minimizing couple? If engaging in the stereotypical struggle in which the woman argues for closeness and affection and the man for intercourse frequency, it would probably be a conflict-minimizing marriage. If they are a couple who play very traditional roles in sex, then the complementary style is a better guess.*

McCarthy argues that when sex in marriage is good, it is a 15 percent to 20 percent factor in a positive marital bond. And, when sex is problematic, it is a 50 percent to 75 percent negative factor, draining the marriage of intimacy. This article is guaranteed to intrigue with its sweeping, and at times perhaps controversial statements about the importance of sexuality in marriage.

Research in the marriage therapy field has yielded extremely impressive results in the last decade. This is in contrast to the stagnation in the sex therapy field, especially in terms of outcome research. The lay public work of Gottman (1994), and Markman, Stanley, and Blumberg (1994) are particularly impressive. Interestingly, these authors give very little attention to the sexual dimensions of marriage, which is consistent with trends in marital research and therapy. Other therapists (Schnarch, 1991; Kaplan, 1995; and LoPiccolo, 1992) have explored the integration of marital and sexual therapy. This [chapter] explores the relationship between marital styles and sexual functioning, with a special focus on desire issues.

Rather than only one viable marital style, empirical research has identified at least four potentially viable marital styles (Gottman, 1993). By order of frequency they are:

1. Complementary couples—The most common marital style, involves respect for each spouse's contribution, each person has power in certain domains, moderate amounts of intimacy.

2. Conflict-minimizing couples—This is the most stable marital style, marriage is organized along culturally dictated gender roles, avoidance of strong emotional expression, especially anger, limited intimacy, and emphasis on child, family and religious values.

3. Best-friend couples—This style is characterized by highest degree of intimacy and sharing, equitably assigning roles and responsibilities, and a strong commitment to a vital marriage. This marital style runs the risk of disappointment and alienation if expectations are not met, resulting in inhibited sexual desire and marital dissolution.

4. Emotionally-expressive couples—This is the most volatile and unstable marital style, but the most engaging, erotic, and fun. Intimacy is like an accordion, sometimes very close, other

times quite distant. Emotion is strongly felt and expressed—joy, anger, and eroticism.

Of course, there are not "pure" styles. A prime couple task during the first two years of marriage is to adopt a comfortable, functional marital style (McCarthy, 1998). A chief issue is to find a mutually comfortable level of intimacy.

How important is sexuality in marriage? McCarthy and McCarthy (1998) postulate that when sex is good, it is a positive, integral factor in the marital bond, but not dominant (15–20 percent). The functions of marital sex are a shared pleasure, a means to deepen and reinforce intimacy, and a tension reducer to deal with the stresses of life and marriage. Sexuality energizes the marital bond and reinforces feelings of specialness. Dysfunctional sex or a non-sexual relationship plays an inordinately powerful role, 50–75 percent, draining the marriage of intimacy and good feelings. Paradoxically, problematic sex plays a more powerful negative role than vital sex plays a positive role in marriage.

Sexual functioning is divided into four components—desire, arousal, orgasm, and satisfaction. The original focus of sex therapy was arousal and orgasm. It is now understood that desire and satisfaction are the core dimensions in marital sexuality. Inhibited sexual desire or discrepancies in sexual desire are the major problems which bring couples to sex therapy. Problems involving sexual desire affect approximately one-third of couples and over 50 percent of those in sex therapy (Rosen and Leiblum, 1995). Key concepts for desire are sexual anticipation and feeling deserving of sexual pleasure. Having a variety of ways to connect—emotionally, affectionally, sensually, and erotically—is valuable. Developing individual and couple bridges for sexual desire is crucial for maintaining vital marital sexuality (McCarthy, 1995). Even more than a specific dysfunction, a non-sexual relationship is a major drain on the marital bond. If you define a non-sexual marriage as being sexual less than ten times a year, one in five married couples have a non-sex-

ual relationship (Michael, Gagnon, Laumann, and Kolata, 1994).

Sexual Strengths and Vulnerabilities of Each Marital Style

What degree of intimacy facilitates sexual desire and functioning? Contrary to cultural and media myths, increasing intimacy is not the answer for couples. The therapeutic focus is finding a mutually comfortable and agreeable level of intimacy, one which facilitates sexual desire (Lobitz and Lobitz, 1996).

Complementary Couples

Complementary (also called validating or supportive) couples have moderate degrees of intimacy, maintaining a balance between autonomy and coupleness. They reinforce each other's competency, validate the spouse's worth, experience an intimate connection and value the marital bond. This promotes sexual desire and functioning. However, complementary couples can fall into the trap of routine, mechanical sex. Sex becomes a low priority, occurring late at night after all the important things in life like putting the children to sleep, paying bills, walking the dog, and watching Jay Leno are completed. Sex might be functional, but it is low quality. The couple wistfully looks back on the romantic love/passionate sex of the premarital years. Couple sexuality cannot rest on its laurels—couple time and valuing intimate sexuality are crucial. The core intervention for complementary couples is to either make sexual initiation a shared domain or one spouse claims it as his/her domain. Ideally, each spouse would be comfortable initiating, each spouse could say no or preferably offer an alternative, there would be individual and couple bridges to sexual desire, and both spouses would value affection, pleasuring and eroticism.

In complementary marriages, one spouse, traditionally the male, makes sexuality his domain. Sexuality being one spouse's domain prevents sex from being treated with benign neglect or avoided. It's unusual for complementary marriages to degenerate into a non-sexual relationship. The danger is the male overemphasizes intercourse at the expense of intimacy, affection, and pleasuring so the woman's anticipation and satisfaction is lowered. The other danger, especially with the aging of the person and the marriage, is the male's performance/intercourse orientation subverts sexuality. Males over forty are vulnerable to the cycle of anticipatory anxiety, tense and dysfunctional sex, and avoidance. The sexual relationship becomes a source of embarrassment and withers. Revitalizing sexual desire is a couple task. The key is establishing a broad based, flexible, intimate, interactive couple style (McCarthy, 1997). That's easier to do if the woman has her own sexual voice. When both people value intimacy, pleasuring, and eroticism, the couple are inoculated against sexual dysfunction.

Conflict-Minimizing Couples

Conflict-minimizing (also called conflict avoiding or traditional) marriages are the most stable marital style. The rules of the marriage are easily understood and implemented. These marriages are organized around traditional male-female roles. The emphasis is stability, family, and religion. Strong emotional expression is discouraged, including sexual expression. Sexual conflicts are minimized and dealt with by avoidance of both the conflict and sex.

Typically, it's the husband who initiates sex and establishes the sexual style. The sexual scenario emphasizes intercourse, with foreplay to get the woman ready for intercourse. The expectation is her orgasmic pattern should mimic his, a single orgasm during intercourse. Sex is his domain, not hers. Intimacy and expression of feelings is her domain. What is unacceptable are intense feelings, especially anger. Demands and threats are unacceptable. These couples value security over intimacy and family over coupleness.

The danger in this marital style is sex settles into a predictable, mechanical routine. Sexuality is undervalued, becoming marginal and mechanical. The double standard sexual scenario makes them vulnerable to

sexual dysfunction and inhibited desire as the male ages and no longer has easy, automatic functioning. When couples stop having sex, whether at 40 or 60, it is the man's unilateral non-verbal decision. He is too frustrated or embarrassed by sexual problems, and decides sex isn't worth the effort. The couple has not been intimate friends, so it is hard to make the transition to intimate, interactive sex.

Best-Friend Couples

The marital style that most values intimacy is the best-friend (also called close or intimate) couple. This is the cultural ideal of marriage—the more intimacy the better. These couples are characterized by high degrees of acceptance, intimacy, satisfaction, and security. Sex is a positive, integral, vital element. Sexuality energizes the marital bond and makes it special. They have a strong bond of respect, trust, and intimacy. These couples value touching both inside and outside the bedroom and enjoy pleasuring and eroticism. They develop a sexual style that is flexible and responsive to the feelings and preferences of both partners.

What are the potential pitfalls of the best-friend marital style? Unfortunately, for most couples this is not a viable model. Best-friend couples have a high divorce rate, based on unmet expectations, anger, and alienation. Marriage cannot live up to the "love means never having to say you're sorry" promise. These couples lack conflict resolution skills and are bitter over thwarted expectations and hopes. They sacrifice autonomy and individuality for the sake of coupleness. The trap for best-friend couples is sacrificing autonomy and then being resentful and blaming.

The biggest sexual trap is inhibited desire. Intimacy and couple time are prime bridges to sexual desire, but too much intimacy stifles erotic feelings. The couple needs to have a mutually comfortable level of intimacy which promotes connection and sexual desire.

Best-friend couples are not assertive in dealing with sexual dysfunction or dissatisfaction. When there's a sexual problem, love is not enough. It is beneficial and necessary to develop sexual comfort and skill, especially making sexual requests. Positive feelings and closeness are helpful, but not enough to overcome dysfunctions such as early ejaculation or vaginismus. When one person develops a secondary dysfunction, erection or female non-orgasmic response, the spouse alternates between blaming self and blaming the partner. The therapeutic stance is to institute a one-two combination of taking personal responsibility for change and working as an intimate team. Best-friend couples often become stuck in a cycle of avoidance, not wanting to push the spouse, waiting for the spouse to initiate. Avoidance further drains the intimate bond.

Emotionally-Expressive Couples

Emotionally-expressive (also called volatile or explosive) couples have the highest intensity of feelings, both loving and angry. Intimacy is like an accordion—sometimes very close, other times alienated. When these marriages work they are exciting and vibrant. Sexually they are passionate and fun. Unfortunately, this is the most unstable marital style, most likely to result in divorce. Emotionally-expressive couples often have physical abuse incidents. A particularly unhealthy pattern is to use sex to make up after an abusive incident. Physical or emotional fights serve as foreplay for sex, a poisonous pattern.

Emotionally-expressive couples who thrive maintain awareness of personal boundaries. They express conflict, anger, and disappointment, but do not cross the line into personal put-downs, contempt, and loss of respect. These couples value intimacy and vibrancy while not being afraid of conflict or anger. Sex is likely to be spontaneous, playful, adventuresome, and energizing.

If one or both spouses develop a sexual dysfunction it is hard to adopt a stepwise, cognitive-behavioral sexual exercise approach. If the dysfunction is not quickly resolved, they easily become demoralized, bitter, and can't tolerate the sexual hiatus.

Problematic sex results in affairs and marital dissolution.

Couple Style and Sexuality

Couples with incompatible needs are likely to have a "fatally flawed" marriage. The wife who wants an emotionally-expressive marriage while the husband wants a conflict-minimizing style are vulnerable. On the other hand, a wife who prefers a complementary couple style while the husband prefers a best-friend marriage are likely to negotiate a mutually satisfying degree of connection and intimacy.

The two sexual issues most important to resolve are the amount of intimacy and the importance of sexuality. Intimacy includes sexuality but is much more than sexuality (Schaefer and Olson, 1981). One spouse desiring high levels of intimacy while the other wants a high level of autonomy with the major connection being sex are likely to develop inhibited sexual desire. The traditional pattern is the woman wants more intimacy, affection, and sensuality. The man withdraws emotionally and sees intercourse as the best way to reconnect. They engage in the stereotypic Ann Landers struggle with the woman arguing for closeness and affection while the man argues for intercourse frequency. For vital sexual functioning, the couple needs to break from rigid sex roles (this is hardest for conflict-minimizing couples). Each spouse would value intimacy, affection, pleasuring, eroticism, and intercourse. Each would be comfortable initiating, saying no, and offering an alternative sensual or erotic scenario.

Each marital style has strengths and vulnerabilities. The marital style least influenced by sexual issues is the conflict-minimizing couple. Sexual expectations are low and sex is not highly valued. What is most disruptive is an extra-marital affair, especially the wife's. Marital rules are very important for conflict-minimizing couples. They are more likely to emphasize rebuilding trust than rebuilding sexual vitality. Another vulnerability is an infertility problem. Having children is normal, so infertility is unexpected and unacceptable. The medical assessment procedures and intercourse on a rigorous schedule has a high probability of causing erectile dysfunction and/or inhibited sexual desire for one or both spouses.

Inhibited sexual desire and a non-sexual marriage are the death knell for best-friend marriages, and even more so for emotionally-expressive couples. Bad sex is better than no sex, especially when the lack of intercourse generalizes to avoidance of affection and sensuality. The best-friend couple feels betrayed and personally rejected. Lack of physical connection—whether affectionate, sensual, or sexual—is a major drain on the marital bond. The closeness and sharing which typifies the best-friend marriage is devastated by a non-sexual relationship.

The issues are different for an emotionally-expressive couple. Sexuality has been one of their joys and energizers. Rather than feeling support and gradually regaining sexual confidence, the couple explode in a torrent of accusations, anger, and tears. There is a great deal of heat and drama, too much for a traditional sex therapy program to contain. Interestingly, emotionally-expressive couples find it easier to recover from an affair than other couples. The best-friend marriage finds it very difficult to recover from an extra-marital affair, especially a comparison affair. Even more than sex are feelings of personal betrayal. These couples spend so much time and energy on trust and intimacy issues that they find it difficult to revitalize sexual desire and view the spouse as an erotic partner.

Complementary couples find sexuality the easiest fit with their marital style. The woman's domain is affection and intimacy while the man's domain is sexual initiation and intercourse. Both people value their contribution, including flexibility in roles. The man values intimacy and does initiate affectionate touching. The woman values eroticism and orgasm, and initiates sexual encounters. Sexuality is broad based and flexible, reinforcing desire and functioning.

A vibrant sexual relationship is most important for emotionally-expressive couples and least important for conflict-minimizing couples. Without a vital sexual life, emotionally-expressive couples question the value of the marriage. More than any other couple style, sexuality plays a dominant role for emotionally-expressive couples. Happiness and excitement can be expressed in a multitude of ways, but when not expressed sexually this void is starkly apparent. Conflict-minimizing couples deny the impact of sexual problems; this is especially true of the traditional wife. Even if the sex is unfulfilling she makes herself available. Unless the sexual problem interferes with fertility, the traditional wife does not complain about unfulfilled sexual needs. With the birth of children and the aging of the marriage, the importance of sex is further downplayed.

Complementary couples and best-friend marriages find it easiest to accept the guideline of sexuality being 15–20 percent. A satisfying sexual relationship energizes and makes special the marital bond. Couples adopt a broad-based, flexible approach to affectionate, sensual, erotic, and intercourse expression. Having a variety of ways and levels to emotionally and physically connect promotes intimacy. Having his, her, and our bridges to sexual desire ensures a vital sexual relationship. Sexuality can fulfill a multitude of functions and be expressed in a multitude of ways. Touching can be initiated by the woman or man, and occur inside or outside the bedroom. Touching is worthwhile whether or not it culminates in intercourse. These couples respond to the intimacy, nondemand pleasuring, eroticism prescription for maintaining satisfying marital sexuality.

Complementary couples are less emotionally vulnerable and less likely to overreact to a sexual problem than best-friend couples. Best-friend couples have a greater struggle with issues of autonomy and personal boundaries. If one spouse develops a sexual dysfunction, the partner feels responsible or guilty. Complementary couples emphasize individuation and maintain a sexual relationship. For example, if he develops an erection problem she is empathic and supportive, but doesn't blame herself or reduce her sexual interest. This is helpful since her desire and responsivity is a positive resource for marital sex. This facilitates regaining sexual comfort and confidence. The most powerful aphrodisiac is an involved, aroused partner. The wife in the best-friend couple overreacts and is demoralized by erectile dysfunction. Her desire and arousal are lessened. Both become passive spectators on the state of his penis. Self-consciousness, tentativeness, and second-guessing interfere with erotic flow. Each person is responsible for his/her desire, arousal, and orgasm. From this base, they work as an intimate team to revitalize sexual desire and functioning.

Closing Thoughts

This [work] is a heuristic attempt to integrate findings from marital theory and therapy with concepts of sexual desire, function and dysfunction. The couple's marital style—complementary, conflict-minimizing, best-friend, emotionally-expressive—has important implications for sexuality. A crucial concept is when sexuality functions well, it's a positive, integral component in the marriage, contributing 15–20 percent. The functions of sexuality are a shared pleasure, a means to deepen and reinforce intimacy, and a tension reducer to lessen the stresses of life and marriage. Sexuality energizes and makes special the marital bond. However, when sexuality is dysfunctional or non-existent it plays an inordinately powerful role, 50–75 percent, robbing the marriage of intimacy and vitality. Especially for best-friend and emotionally-expressive couples, sexual problems destroy marital viability.

Each marital style entails sexual strengths and vulnerabilities. This is reflected both in the degree of intimacy and the importance of sex in the relationship. There is a need for empirical and clinical exploration of the reciprocal effects of marital style with sexual desire and functioning.

References

Gottman, J. (1993). The roles of conflict engagement, escalation, and avoidance in marital interaction: A longitudinal view of five types of couples. *Journal of Consulting and Clinical Psychology, 61,* 6–15.

Gottman, J. (1994). *Why Marriages Succeed or Fail.* New York: Simon and Schuster.

Kaplan, H. (1995). *The Sexual Desire Disorders.* New York: Brunner/Mazel.

Lobitz, W. & Lobitz, G. (1996). Resolving the sexual intimacy paradox: A developmental model for the treatment of sexual desire disorders. *Journal of Sex and Marital Therapy, 22,* 71–84.

LoPiccolo, J. (1992). Postmodern sex therapy for erectile failure. In R. Rosen & S. Leiblum (Eds.). *Erectile Disorders: Assessment and Treatment* (pp. 171–197). New York: Guilford.

Markman, H., Stanley, S., & Blumberg, S. (1994). *Fighting for Your Marriage.* San Francisco: Jossey Bass.

McCarthy, B. (1995). Bridges to sexual desire. *Journal of Sex Education and Therapy, 21,* 132–141.

McCarthy, B. (1997). Strategies and techniques for revitalizing a non-sexual marriage. *Journal of Sex and Marital Therapy, 23,* 231–240.

McCarthy, B. (1998). Sex in the first two years of marriage. *Journal of Family Psychology.*

McCarthy, B. & McCarthy, E. (1998). *Couple Sexual Awareness, 9(4),* 4–11. New York: Carroll and Graf.

Michael, R., Gagnon, J., Laumann, F., & Kolata, G. (1994). *Sex in America.* Boston: Little, Brown.

Rosen, R. & Leiblum, S. (Eds.) (1995). Hypoactive sexual desire. *Psychiatric Clinics of North America, 18,* 107–121.

Schaefer, M. & Olson, D. (1981). Assessing intimacy. *Journal of Marital and Family Therapy, 7,* 47–60.

Schnarch, D. (1991). *Constructing the Sexual Crucible.* New York: Norton.

Chapter 15
Sexuality During Pregnancy and the Year Postpartum

Janet Shibley Hyde
John D. DeLamater
E. Ashby Plant
Janis M. Byrd

Despite a decrease in libido, most pregnant wives desire emotional closeness expressed through physical contact with their husbands. Depending on the medical condition of a woman and her individual comfort levels, sexual intercourse can continue during pregnancy. Although frequency of sexual intercourse may remain at the same level throughout pregnancy, it decreases substantially for most women during the third trimester. The most often reported reason for this decrease is physical discomfort, which develops as the uterus enlarges due to fetal growth. Other forms of sexual activity, such as mutual genital stimulation or solitary masturbation, may be preferred during the third trimester.

Research does indicate the need for some caution in sexual activity during the pregnancy. For example, it is extremely important that air not be blown into the vagina during cunnilingus, because fetal and maternal deaths caused by air embolisms (bubbles) could result from this practice. Others suggest a possible link between experiencing an orgasm via either sexual intercourse or masturbation during the last month of the third trimester and premature rupture of the amnion followed by initiation of labor.

Not only is sexuality a potential problem in pregnancy, but in the year following the birth of the baby, the postpartum year, a young couple will be called upon also to make numerous adjustments in their lives, some of which can affect their sexual relationship. This research will fill in the blanks for students who have questions about sexual activity during pregnancy and the year beyond. It adds to the storehouse of knowledge necessary for navigating these major life transitions successfully.

Pregnancy, childbirth, and the postpartum period represent a major life transition. Moreover, it usually has a substantial impact on the sexual adjustment and behavior of mothers and fathers. Yet there are remarkably little empirical data about sexuality during pregnancy and following childbirth. We report data on the largest sample of couples who have been studied on this topic.

Sexuality During Pregnancy

Researchers studying sexuality during pregnancy have reported a decrease in sexual desire and coital frequency from the first to the third trimester (Alder, 1989). Masters and Johnson (1966), reported "a marked increase in eroticism and sexual performance" (p. 158) in the second trimester, but this finding has not been replicated. Other researchers have reported either no change in sexual activity from the first to the second trimester, or a slight decline. Most investigators, including Masters and Johnson (1966), reported a marked decline in frequency of coitus from the second to the third trimesters. Call, Sprecher, and Schwartz (1995) recently studied frequency of marital intercourse, using data from the National Survey of Families and Households, and reported that pregnancy is associated with a significant decrease in monthly frequency of intercourse.

A variety of reasons have been suggested for this decline in sexual desire and frequency of intercourse during pregnancy. Reports of decreased desire early in pregnancy are related to the woman's fears about the pregnancy; at the third trimester

[they] are related to the woman's fears about the health of the child at birth and to both mothers' and fathers' fears that the fetus might be harmed by intercourse or orgasm (Bogren, 1991). However, according to the authoritative *Williams Obstetrics*, "it has been generally accepted that in healthy pregnant women, sexual intercourse usually does no harm before the last four weeks or so of pregnancy" (Cunningham, MacDonald, Leveno, Gant, & Gilstrap, 1993, p. 263). Other reasons that have been cited include physical discomfort associated with intercourse, particularly in the man-on-top position, and loss of interest in sex. Also, some women report feeling less physically attractive and sexually desirable as pregnancy progresses.

Sexuality Following Childbirth

There is less agreement in the findings of research on the resumption of sexual activity following childbirth (Reamy & White, 1987). Most researchers have collected data 4 to 12 weeks following delivery. Grudzinskas and Atkinson (1984) interviewed women at 5–7 weeks postpartum; they report that only 50 percent had resumed intercourse.

Kumar, Brant, and Robson (1981) reported results from the most intensive longitudinal study carried out to date. They recruited 147 women who were in the first 14 weeks of pregnancy. The women were interviewed at about 12, 24, and 36 weeks during the pregnancy [and] at about 1, 12, 26, and 52 weeks after delivery. During the pregnancy, frequency of intercourse declined slightly from 12 to 24 weeks, and more substantially from 24 to 36 weeks. In contrast, reported sexual pleasure increased from 12 to 24 weeks and then declined. Ninety-five percent of the women had resumed intercourse by the twelfth week following delivery, but coitus was less frequent at one year postpartum than it was prior to the pregnancy. Reported level of enjoyment at 12 weeks postpartum was similar to levels reported at the twelfth week of pregnancy.

Numerous reasons have been suggested for delaying resumption of vaginal intercourse after childbirth (Reamy & White, 1987). The principal ones are pain and tenderness (dyspareunia) related to the episiotomy, vaginal bleeding/discharge, fatigue, and discomfort related to inadequate lubrication of the vagina (which is due to low levels of estrogen in the postpartum period). According to *Williams Obstetrics*, "coitus should not be resumed prior to 2 weeks postpartum" in order to reduce the risk of hemorrhage, infection, and pain. Beyond two weeks, "coitus may be resumed based upon the patient's desire and comfort" (Cunningham et al., 1993, p. 470).

A few researchers have reported that women who breastfeed are less likely to resume intercourse by a specific time compared with women who bottle feed. Alder and Bancroft (1988) found that breastfeeding women were less likely to have resumed intercourse 3 months postpartum, and they reported less sexual interest and enjoyment than before the pregnancy. By six months the differences between breastfeeding and nonbreastfeeding women had disappeared. Forster and colleagues (Forster, Abraham, Taylor, & Llewellyn-Jones, 1994) studied women before and after weaning; after weaning they reported an increase in frequency of intercourse. In another study, Alder (1989) found no relationship between breastfeeding and resumption of intercourse.

Most studies of the interrelations of pregnancy, childbirth, and sexuality suffer from methodological problems. The studies are based on nonrandom convenience samples. The samples are often small. Some studies have been based on retrospective reports about sexual behavior during pregnancy or about resumption of sexual activity after childbirth. Most studies have been focused on a limited set of outcome measures, usually sexual intercourse. There has been little consistency across studies in the variables measured or the definition of key variables, such as breastfeeding. These problems make it very difficult to reconcile the conflicting results.

THE CURRENT STUDY

The purposes of the current study were as follows: (a) to provide descriptive data on the sexual behaviors (intercourse, masturbation, fellatio, and cunnilingus) and sexual satisfaction of both mothers and fathers at 4 time points from pregnancy through 12 months postpartum; (b) to compare the sexuality of women who deliver vaginally with those who deliver by cesarean; (c) to compare the sexuality of women who breastfeed with those who do not; and (d) to provide data relevant to the methodological issue of the accuracy of self-reports of sexual behavior by comparing husbands' and wives' reports.

Method

The sample consisted of 570 pregnant women and 550 husbands/partners of the women (all partners were men) who were recruited for participation in the Wisconsin Maternity Leave and Health (WMLH) Project. Attempts were made to recruit as diverse a sample as possible.

The average age of the mothers in the sample at the beginning of the study was 29 years, ranging between 20 and 43 years; 95 percent of the mothers were married to the father. Regarding ethnic heritage, 93 percent of the mothers were White (not of Hispanic origin); 2.6 percent were Black (not of Hispanic origin); 1.8 percent were Hispanic; 1.9 percent were Native American; and 0. 7 percent were Asian. In regard to educational level, 1.8 percent had achieved less than a high school education; 15.4 percent graduated from high school or had a GED; 9.6 percent received some technical training beyond high school; 19.8 percent had some college; 34.9 percent had earned a college degree; 7.5 percent received some education beyond the college degree; and 10.9 percent had completed a master's, doctoral, or professional degree. At the beginning of the study, the average age of the fathers was 32 years (range 20 to 56). In regard to ethnicity, 92.9 percent of the fathers were White,

4 percent were Black, 1.1 percent were Hispanic, 0.9 percent were Native American, 0. 7 percent were Asian, and 0.4 percent were "other."

At the time of the first interview, 81.5 percent of the women were employed. Of those women who were, employed and whose husbands also participated, 97.5 percent had husbands who were employed at Time 1. For 38 percent of the women, this was their first child; for 37 percent, the second; for 19 percent, the third; for 3 percent, the fourth; and for 3 percent, the fifth or later.

A one-page, author-designed questionnaire was administered during the mother's face-to-face interview and was part of father's mail-out questionnaire. All questions (except frequency of masturbation) were asked of both mothers and fathers, at all four waves of data collection. In addition, at Time 4, mothers were asked how long after the birth they had resumed sexual intercourse.

Mothers were interviewed in their homes by a female interviewer: (a) during second trimester of pregnancy (Time 1), (b) 1 month after the birth (Time 2), (c) 4 months after the birth (Time 3), and (d) 12 months after the birth (Time 4). In addition, mothers completed mail-out questionnaires on their own in advance of the interview and returned them to the interviewer.

Fathers were interviewed by telephone on each of the same four occasions, as soon after the mother's interview as possible but always within two weeks of the mother's interview. Fathers also completed a mail-out questionnaire on each occasion, which was returned to the mother's interviewer at the time of her home interview or mailed back.

One page of questions about sexual behavior was part of the mothers' home interview. About halfway through the interview, the page was handed to the woman, who filled it out in privacy, placed it in a sealed envelope, and returned it to the interviewer. For fathers, the page of questions about sexual behavior was included in the mail-out questionnaire.

Results

Descriptive Data on Sexual Behaviors, Pregnancy to 12 Months Postpartum

The percentage who engage in intercourse in any month was around 90 percent, except at Time 2, 1 month postpartum, when the majority of couples had not yet resumed intercourse. The frequency of intercourse was estimated somewhat higher by women than by men, and was about 5 times per month during pregnancy and at 4 months and 12 months postpartum; it was strikingly low, as expected, at 1 month postpartum. The percentage of men who masturbate in a month held relatively constant at around 44 percent at each time. The percentage for women was significantly lower and was especially low one month postpartum. The question on frequency of masturbation was asked only at Time 4: the frequency was considerably higher for men than for women. The incidence of fellatio showed close agreement in mothers and fathers' reports and was fairly constant at around 45 percent, except that it dropped to around 33 percent at 1 month postpartum. The incidence of cunnilingus was around 45 percent at Time 3 and Time 4, but was slightly lower at Time 1, during pregnancy, and was especially low, around 7 percent, at 1 month postpartum. Although there was a slight dip in satisfaction with the sexual relationship at one month postpartum, both men and women, on the average, were moderately satisfied with their sexual relationship at all waves.

The question regarding decreased sexual desire was administered to women only. The results indicate that the women experienced decreased sexual desire fairly frequently both during the middle trimester of pregnancy and at one month postpartum. Reports of decreased sexual desire declined at 4 months postpartum and were still less frequent by 12 months postpartum, when 56 percent of the women reported that currently they never experienced decreased sexual desire.

At Time 4, we asked the women a retrospective question, "How long after your baby's birth was it before you started having intercourse again?" The mean was 7.33 weeks, but there was wide variability; 19 percent of the couples had resumed intercourse within the first month after birth.

Breastfeeding and Sexual Patterns

At Time 2, one month after birth, a comparison of women who were currently breastfeeding (BF, 68 percent of sample) with those who were not (NBF, 32 percent of sample) revealed several differences. NBF women were significantly more likely to have resumed intercourse (28.7 percent) than BF women (14.9 percent). BF women reported more frequent lack of sexual desire than NBF women. There was no difference for incidence of masturbation: 11.4 percent BF women had, and 10.9 percent of NBF women had. Neither was the difference significant for performing fellatio; 32.5 percent of BF women had, compared with 39.9 percent of NBF women; [and] in having experienced cunnilingus (6.8 percent and 10.4 percent for BF and NBF groups, respectively).

For ratings of sexual satisfaction, there were no significant differences between the two groups of women. However, husbands of NBF women were significantly more satisfied than husbands of BF women. There were no differences between BF and NBF women in their ratings of how physically affectionate their husbands were. However, husbands of NBF women rated their wives as more physically affectionate than did husbands of BF women. NBF women rated their sexual relationship as significantly more rewarding than BF women did. Consistent with the ratings by wives, husbands of NBF women rated their sexual relationship as significantly more rewarding than did husbands of BF women. At 4 months postpartum, BF women were still less likely than NBF women to have resumed intercourse; 84.5 percent of BF women and 94.9 percent of NBF women had resumed. BF women reported more frequent lack of sexual desire than NBF women.

For subjective ratings of satisfaction, the results were much like those for Time 2. Both NBF women and their husbands gave higher ratings on the subjective satisfaction measures. There were no differences between BF and NBF women in sexual satisfaction. In contrast, husbands of BF women gave significantly lower ratings of sexual satisfaction than husbands of NBF women. NBF women gave significantly higher ratings than BF women did to the physical affection in the relationship, and husbands showed the same pattern. NBF women rated their sexual relationship as significantly more rewarding than BF women did, and the same pattern was found for the husbands. At 12 months postpartum, when the couple had resumed intercourse, women who breastfed resumed intercourse, on the average, about a week later than those who did not.

In summary, nonbreastfeeding women were more likely to have resumed intercourse by one month postpartum, although there were no differences between BF and NBF women for other behaviors. On several measures of satisfaction, both NBF women and their husbands gave higher ratings than BF women and their husbands. This pattern occurred at one month postpartum and still was present four months postpartum. By 12 months postpartum, this pattern had disappeared, and there were no differences between the two groups.

Vaginal vs. Cesarean Delivery Sexual Patterns

We compared women who had a vaginal delivery (83 percent of sample) and women who had a cesarean delivery (17 percent of sample) on a number of variables at Time 2, one month after delivery. Surprisingly, women with cesareans were significantly more likely to have resumed intercourse (27 percent) than women who delivered vaginally (18 percent). On most other variables, however, there were no significant differences between the two groups. There were no significant differences for mothers in the percentage who had masturbated, engaged in fellatio, engaged in cunnilingus, or engaged in petting.

Parity

The parity variable was coded into three categories: first-born child, second-born child, and third or later born. At Time 2, there was a significant association between parity and whether the woman was currently breastfeeding. Women with a third or later born child were more likely to breastfeed (77.0 percent) than were mothers with a first born (67.6 percent) or a second born (63.1 percent).

At Time 2, there was no significant association between parity and whether the couple had resumed intercourse. There were no differences among the three parity groups on women's ratings of overall sexual satisfaction, nor on ratings of how rewarding the sexual relationship was. However, there was a significant difference for ratings of how physically affectionate the husband/partner was. Mothers of first borns gave significantly higher ratings of physical affection than did mothers of second borns and mothers of third or later borns. This same pattern appeared in the four months postpartum data. Again, the difference among groups was for the physical affection variable, mothers of first borns gave the highest ratings of physical affection to their husbands, compared with mothers of second children and third or later children.

The results indicate a high degree of agreement between the two different respondents reporting on the same events. Percentage agreements generally were around 90 percent. On the quantitative item, the number of times the couple have had intercourse in the last month, the correlation was somewhat lower, particularly at Time 3 and Time 4, when the frequency of intercourse was higher.

Discussion

We have reported data on sexual patterns during pregnancy and the year postpartum for a large sample, not recruited specifically for sex research, and the data set includes reports from both husbands and wives. The results indicate that sexual patterns were remarkably constant at the fifth month of pregnancy, 4 months postpartum, and 12 months postpartum, but that sexual expression was considerably reduced at 1 month postpartum, when the majority of couples have not resumed sexual intercourse. On the average, couples resumed intercourse around seven weeks postpartum. There were significant differences between breastfeeding and nonbreastfeeding women, both at one month and four months postpartum; breastfeeding women generally showed less sexual activity and less sexual satisfaction. Comparisons of women who had delivered vaginally with those who had delivered by cesarean indicated surprisingly few differences, with the exception that women with cesareans were significantly more likely to have resumed intercourse at one month postpartum. There were few differences in reported sexual behavior satisfaction as a function of parity. Finally, there was a high degree of agreement between husbands' and wives' reports.

Breastfeeding and Sexuality

At one month postpartum, the sexual relationship was more positive for nonbreastfeeding couples than breastfeeding couples, although husbands seemed to be more sensitive to the differences than wives. This contrasts with the assertions of Masters and Johnson (1966), who reported that sexual responsiveness returns sooner after childbirth among women who breastfeed than among those who don't. Our results, however, are consistent with those of Alder & Bancroft (1988).

There are three possible explanations for lesser sexual activity and sexual satisfaction among breastfeeding couples, compared with nonbreastfeeding couples. The first is biological. Estrogen production is suppressed during the period of lactation (Cunningham et al., 1993). Because estrogen functions to maintain the lining of the vagina, decreased levels of estrogen result in decreased vaginal lubrication, making intercourse uncomfortable. Much of the difficulty can be overcome with the use of lubricants. In addition, prolactin levels are substantially and chronically elevated by breastfeeding (Stern, Konner, Herman, & Reichlin, 1986). Evidence indicates that elevated prolactin levels are associated with decreased sexual interest (Stern & Leiblum, 1986). Moreover, Alder, Cook, Davidson, West, and Bancroft (1986) found that testosterone levels were significantly lower in breastfeeding women compared with bottle-feeding women and that testosterone levels were lower in breastfeeding women who reported reduced sexual interest compared with breastfeeding women who did not report decreased sexual interest. There is increasing evidence that androgens are related to sexual desire in women (Sherwin, 1991). Therefore, it appears that elevated levels of prolactin, decreased levels of testosterone, or both, may contribute to reduced sexual desire among breastfeeding women.

The second possible explanation involves psychological factors. Masters and Johnson (1966) reported that breastfeeding is erotically satisfying to some women, and in some cases stimulates women to orgasm. One possibility is that breastfeeding mothers derive erotic satisfaction, or at least have their needs for intimate touching met, by breastfeeding, and therefore show less interest in sexual expression with their husband. Husbands, in contrast, do not receive this satisfaction from the baby and continue to seek sexual intimacy with their wives, who are less interested than usual, leading husbands of BF women to report less sexual satisfaction than husbands of NBF women, whereas there are no differences in satisfaction between BF and NBF women.

A third possibility is that BF women are more fatigued because they must do all the feeding and therefore, for example, cannot share nighttime feedings. It may be, of course, that all three factors exert an influence. We do not mean to imply that these findings are an argument against breastfeeding, which is known to have substantial health benefits to infants (Newman, 1995). We do believe that couples will benefit from being informed about the sexual effects of breastfeeding so that (a) they understand the source of the problem and do not conclude that it indicates that there is a problem in their relationship and (b) they can take appropriate measures, such as the use of vaginal lubricants, to deal with the effects.

Vaginal vs. Cesarean Deliveries

It might be expected that, because cesarean deliveries involve major surgery, women who delivered by cesarean section would show less sexual activity at one month postpartum, compared with women who delivered vaginally. Our findings, however, did not support this belief. There were no significant differences between the two groups of women on a variety of variables. The one exception was that women with cesareans were actually more likely to have resumed intercourse at one-month postpartum then women who delivered vaginally.

Why is there a general pattern of no differences between the two groups? It may be that incisions from cesareans heal about as quickly as episiotomies, so that the groups are more equal than it might appear in regard to healing.

Total Sexual Outlet

These data provide no support—at least during the postpartum period—for Kinsey's concept of total sexual outlet (Kinsey, Pomeroy, Martin, & Gebhard, 1953) and the notion that if one form of sexual expression is not available, others will be substituted. The relevant data are from one month postpartum. The majority of women did not engage in intercourse at this time; according to the concept of total sexual outlet, they might well turn to masturbation as a substitute. Yet the incidence of masturbation was lower, not higher, for women at Time 2 compared with the other three times. One might argue, however, that masturbation, like intercourse, is uncomfortable if there has been an episiotomy, for example. The data for the fathers address this objection. Although the majority of them were not engaging in intercourse at Time 2 (although it must be noted that we did not inquire about extramarital sex), the incidence of masturbation was the same for men at Time 2 as it was at the other three time points. That is, there is apparently no increase in masturbation to compensate for reduced sexual expression in intercourse.

Conclusion

These data yielded a number of important findings. First, the incidence of sexual intercourse, fellatio, and cunnilingus is very similar in the fifth month of pregnancy and at 4 and 12 months postpartum. The mean frequency of coitus per month is also similar at these three times. This pattern is evident in both the reports of women and their husbands/partners. According to our results, the major change in sexual activity associated with childbirth is a reduced incidence of sexual expression at one month postpartum. Second, mean ratings of satisfaction with the sexual relationship in the fifth month of pregnancy indicate that both women and men are moderately satisfied. Satisfaction was lower at 1 month postpartum and gradually increased from 1 month to 12 months. Thus, many couples can expect a decline in sexual satisfaction at childbirth and slow recovery during the following year. Third, breastfeeding was significantly related to a couple's sexual expression. Women who breastfed resumed coitus one week later, on the average, compared with women who did not breastfeed. Breastfeeding was also associated with reduced sexual satisfaction for both women and their partners at one and four months postpartum.

These results are based on the largest sample of women ever studied in regard to sexuality during pregnancy and the year postpartum. The longitudinal design yielded responses to the same questions by the same people at four points in time. The data collected from the husbands/partners showed the same pattern of results. There was a high degree of agreement between the reports of the women and their partners. For these reasons, one can have considerable confidence in the validity of the results.

References

Alder, E. M. (1989). Sexual behaviour in pregnancy, after childbirth and during breast-feeding. *Balliere's Clinical Obstetrics and Gynaecology, 3*, 805–821.

Alder, E. M., & Bancroft, J. (1988). The relationship between breastfeeding persistence, sexuality and mood in postpartum women. *Psychological Medicine, 18*, 389–396.

Alder, E. M., Cook, A., Davidson, D., West, C., & Bancroft, J. (1986). Hormones, mood and sexuality in lactating women. *British Journal of Psychiatry, 148*, 74–79.

Barnett, R. C., & Marshall, N. L. (1989). *Preliminary Manual for the Role Quality Scales*. Wellesley, MA: Wellesley Center for Research on Women.

Bogren, L. (1991). Changes in sexuality in women and men during pregnancy. *Archives of Sexual Behavior, 20*, 35–45.

Call, V., Sprecher, S., & Schwartz, P. (1995). The incidence and frequency of marital sex in a national sample. *Journal of Marriage and the Family, 57*, 639–652.

Cohen, J. (1961). A coefficient of agreement for nominal scales. *Educational and Psychological Measurement, 20*, 37–46.

Cunningham, F. G., MacDonald, P. C., Leveno, K. J., Gant, N. F., & Gilstrap, III, L. C. (1993). *Williams Obstetrics* (19th ed.). Norwalk, CT: Appleton and Lange.

Forster, C., Abraham, S., Taylor, A., & Llewellyn-Jones, D. (1994). Psychological and sexual changes after the cessation of breast-feeding. *Obstetrics Gynecology, 84*, 872–876.

Grudzinskas, J. G., & Atkinson, L. (1984). Sexual function during the puerperium. *Archives of Sexual Behavior, 13*, 85–91.

Kinsey, A. C., Pomeroy, W. B., Martin, C. E., & Gebhard, P. H. (1953). *Sexual Behavior in the Human Female*. Philadelphia: Saunders.

Kumar, R., Brant, H. A., & Robson, K. M. (1981). Childbearing and maternal sexuality: A prospective survey of 119 Primiparae. *Journal of Psychosomatic Research, 25*, 373–383.

Masters, W. H., & Johnson, V. E. (1966). *Human Sexual Response*. Boston: Little Brown.

Newman, J. (1995, December). How breastmilk protects newborns. *Scientific American*, 76–79.

Reamy, K. J., & White, S. E. (1987). Sexuality in the puerperium: A review. *Archives of Sexual Behavior, 16*, 165–186.

Sherwin, B. B. (1991). The psychoendocrinology of aging and female sexuality. *Annual Review of Sex Research, 2*, 181–198.

Stern, J. M., Konner, M., Herman, T. N., & Reichlin, S. (1986). Nursing Behavior, prolactin and postpartum amenorrhoea during prolonged lactation in American and !Kung mothers. *Clinical Endocrinology, 25*, 247–258.

Stern, J. M., & Leiblum, S. R. (1986). Postpartum sexual behavior of American women as a function of the absence or frequency of breastfeeding: A preliminary communication. In J. G. Else and P. C. Lee (Eds.), *Primate Ontogeny, Cognition, and Social Behavior* (pp. 319–328). Cambridge, England: Cambridge University Press.

Chapter 16
Sexual Infidelity Among Married and Cohabiting Americans

Judith Treas
Deirdre Giesen

Tabloids herald extramarital sexual relationships of the famous and infamous. From Prince Charles to President Clinton, to the "woman or man on the street," no detail is too personal or too private to escape scrutiny. Sexual infidelity, it seems, captures the imagination of all America. Although the topic is a favorite pastime for the public, there is a dearth of empirical data about extramarital affairs. Treas and Giesen take a small step in correcting this imbalance.

If, as claimed by researchers, 90 percent of the general public believe that it is "always wrong" or "almost always wrong" to engage in extramarital sex, how do such beliefs translate into behavior? This is a fair but complex question in a society in which the percentage of women who have participated in extramarital affairs ranges from 15 percent to 29 percent and for men, 25 percent to 44 percent. Somehow the numbers confirming beliefs and behaviors don't compute.

Are psychological or sociological factors more influential in affecting the likelihood of extramarital affairs? And what is the role of permissive sexual values in infidelity? Reading the following article may help provide answers, but again, it may raise more questions than answers about this important topic.

Americans disapprove of sexual infidelity. More than 90 percent of the general public say it is "always" or "almost always" wrong for a married person to have sex with someone besides the marriage partner (Smith, 1994). About half the states in the U.S. retain laws against adultery that, although they are rarely enforced, would deny married persons who have extramarital sex the right to vote, serve alcohol, practice law, adopt children, or raise their own children (Constitutional barriers, 1992). American couples, whether married or cohabiting, agree that it is important to be monogamous (Greeley, 1991).

Couples' agreements about sexual exclusivity are a contractual condition of their unions. As with all contracts, bargains are sometimes broken. Although sexual fidelity is the dominant practice, recent surveys show that between 1.5 and 3.6 percent of married persons had a secondary sex partner in the past year (Choi, Catania, & Dolcini, 1994; Leigh, Temple, & Trocki, 1993). This article asks why some people are sexually exclusive while others have sex with someone besides their mate.

Previous Research

Research on sexual infidelity has focused on three domains—the personal values of the individual, the opportunities for extramarital sex, and the couple's relationship.

Permissive sexual values are associated with extramarital sex. Among Americans who believe extramarital relations are "not at all wrong," 76 percent report having had extramarital sex compared to only 10 percent of those who think extramarital sex is "always wrong" (Smith, 1994). Being male, African-American, and well educated are all associated with permissive sexual values (Smith, 1994). So is living in a big city. Extramarital permissiveness is linked to liberal political and religious ideologies (Smith, 1994). It is also related to gender egalitarianism and premarital permissiveness (Reiss, Anderson, & Sponaugle, 1980).

Opportunities, namely potential partners and circumstances assuring secrecy, facilitate extramarital sex. Some Americans admit they would have extramarital sex if their mate would not find out (Greeley, 1991). Couples who lead separate lives have more opportunities and are more likely to have secondary sex partners (Blumstein & Schwartz, 1983). Married people who perceive alternative partners to be available are more likely to have had extramarital sex (Maykovich, 1976). Of course, those predisposed to extramarital sex might be more likely to recognize opportunities that arise.

Dissatisfaction with the marital relationship itself is associated with extramarital sex (Brown, 1991; Vaughn, 1986). Those who engage in adultery are less likely to report happy marriages (Greeley, 1991). Infidelity has been linked to men's sexual dissatisfaction (Maykovich, 1976) and to women's perception of inequity in the marriage (Prins, Buunk, & Van Yperen, 1983). However, other studies fail to find a significant association for marital happiness (Maykovich, 1976), marital adjustment (Johnson, 1970), seeing a mate as less affectionate (Edwards & Booth, 1976), or, for Whites, quality of marital sex (Choi et al., 1994). National surveys identify demographic risk factors for multiple sex partners. Education is positively related not only to permissive sexual values, but also to sexual infidelity (Leigh et al., 1993). Being African-American is associated with greater likelihood of multiple sexual relationships than being White (Smith, 1991). Men engage in more extramarital sex than women (Smith, 1991), perhaps because of male-female differences in reproductive strategies (Lancaster, 1994), the gendered nature of learned sexual scripts (Gagnon & Simon, 1973), or a double standard that judges men's sexual permissiveness less harshly than women's. The number of sex partners declines with age (Dolcini et al., 1993; Smith, 1991), which might reflect biological effects of aging (Edwards & Booth, 1994) or recent cohorts' more permissive sexual values (Smith, 1994). Compared to married couples, cohabitors are not as sex-

ually exclusive (Forste & Tanfer, 1996)—consistent with their less conventional values (Clarkberg, Stolzenberg, & Waite, 1995), with the lower levels of commitment in cohabiting unions (Bumpass, Sweet, & Cherlin, 1991), and with differences in the sorts of partners chosen for cohabitation as opposed to marriage (Forste & Tanfer, 1996).

Conceptual Framework

Everyday accounts of extramarital sex often stress irrational causes like alcohol-impaired judgment or sexual addiction (Giddens, 1992). Although cultural scripts focus on romance and passion, people contemplating infidelity describe considered decisions. The self-conscious evaluation of extramarital options has been called "thinking" (Atwater, 1982) or "the debate" (Lawson, 1988). A wife reports making "a quick sort of negative and positive checklist" (Lawson, pp. 134–136). A husband confides, "(I)t's a question you have to ask yourself before. . . . 'Why am I doing this? What will I get out of it? How does this affect the status quo?'" (Lawson, p. 147).

Given social norms and strong dyadic expectations for sexual exclusivity, sexual infidelity demands calculated behavior. Theorizing about sex in terms of anticipated costs and gains yields useful insights, as Reiss and Miller (1979) suggested when hypothesizing a "reward-cost balance" for premarital permissiveness. A decision-making framework also serves to integrate piecemeal results of prior studies on extramarital sex.

Tastes and Values

A review of clinical and research studies identifies 31 reasons for extramarital relations; most, falling under the categories of sex, emotional intimacy, love, and ego bolstering, pertain to personal gratification (Glass & Wright, 1992). Some people's tastes and values increase the likelihood that they will engage in extramarital sex. People highly interested in sex might eschew sexual exclusivity because they anticipate greater pleasure from extramarital relations. On the other hand, nonpermissive values are known to be negatively associated with sexual infidelity, perhaps because people who hold these values anticipate discomfort reconciling dissonant beliefs and behavior (Lawson, 1988).

Hypothesis 1a: Greater interest in sex is associated with a greater likelihood of infidelity.

Hypothesis 1b: Nonpermissive sexual values are associated with a lower likelihood of infidelity.

Opportunities

People with fewer opportunities for undetected sex must go to greater lengths to have extramarital sex. Individual endowments and learned skills affect how many sexual opportunities come one's way. People with more sexual relationships in the past are more likely to have a secondary sex partner (Bozon, 1996). The sexually experienced might be more attractive; or they might have a "learned advantage" if they are more efficient than novices at recognizing sexual opportunities, recruiting sex partners, and managing sexual encounters.

H2a. Having had more sexual partners previously is associated with a greater likelihood of infidelity.

Social context also determines opportunities. As a place to socialize outside the company of a mate, the workplace offers access to potential partners (Lawson, 1988). Some work presents greater opportunities than other work. For instance, people whose jobs require overnight travel are more likely to have multiple sex partners (Wellings, Field, Johnson, & Wadsworth, 1994). Compared to small towns, big cities offer more opportunities for undetected sex—more potential partners, greater anonymity, and more permissive sexual values (Smith, 1994). In fact, big city residents do average more sex partners (Smith, 1991).

H2b. A job requiring personal contact with potential sex partners is associated with greater likelihood of infidelity.

H2c. Big city residence is associated with greater likelihood of infidelity.

Social networks composed of people who are apt to disapprove of adultery discourage extramarital relations, if only because one must go to greater lengths to keep sexual infidelity secret. Interestingly, married couples who became nonmonogamous "swingers" were insulated from social networks monitoring behavior and imposing costs on nonconformists: Swingers knew fewer neighbors, visited relatives less often, and joined fewer religious groups (Gilmartin, 1974).

H2d. When partners enjoy one another's kinship and friendship networks, the likelihood of infidelity is lower.

H2e. Controlling for sexual values, attending religious services more frequently is associated with lower likelihood of infidelity.

Primary Relationship

Because partners expect fidelity, potential costs to the primary relationship loom large in the face of infidelity. A mate who learns of a partner's infidelity might respond with emotionally draining recriminations, tit-for-tat infidelities, physical abuse, the withholding of couple services (e.g., sex, companionship, monetary support), and even divorce (Pittman, 1989).

Marital quality mediates costs. If a marriage is judged to be unrewarding, one has less to lose from extramarital sex. One can afford to be indifferent, both to costs to the marital relation and to sanctions a mate might offer. An extreme example is the "out-the-door" affair where one partner pursues an extramarital relationship to force a mate to end an unhappy marriage (Brown, 1991). Like subjective marital dissatisfaction, mates' social dissimilarity or heterogamy might prompt infidelity because social differences imply lower marital returns as a result of fewer stabilizing commonalities in the relationship (Lehrer & Chiswick, 1993).

H3a. Greater dissatisfaction with the union is associated with greater likelihood of infidelity.

H3b. Greater disparity in partners' social characteristics is associated with greater likelihood of infidelity.

People get locked into a union, however unfulfilling, by investments that they cannot recoup outside the relationship. Married people have more invested in their unions than do cohabitors. Besides a public commitment, the married are more likely to have children and to own a home jointly. They face higher exit costs should the relationship end. Because cohabitors risk less by an affair, it is not surprising that cohabitors are more likely to have secondary sex partners (Dolcini et al., 1993).

H3c. Cohabiting is associated with a greater likelihood of infidelity.

The likelihood of ever having been unfaithful increases with the duration of the union due to longer exposure to the risk of infidelity. At any given time, however, the likelihood of infidelity might vary with union duration. There are two competing arguments. If couples who have been together longer have made more stabilizing investments in their relationship, what they stand to lose will discourage infidelity. Yet, declines in coital frequency (Wellings et al., 1994) suggest that some marital benefits wane with time. If benefits jeopardized by infidelity decline over time, the likelihood of infidelity will increase at longer union durations.

H3d. (investment hypothesis) Longer union duration is associated with lower likelihood of infidelity at a given time.

H3e. (habituation hypothesis) Longer duration is associated with greater likelihood of infidelity at a given time.

Integrating prior findings on sexual infidelity, a decision-making framework generates hypotheses to be tested with superior survey data now available. We estimate a multivariate model of sexual infidelity incorporating personal tastes and values, the sexual opportunity structure, and features of the primary (i.e., marital or cohabiting) relationship. We control for demographic "risk factors" that might confound the associations among variables and consider whether factors informing sexual decision making can account for the effects of gender, race, age, and education.

THE CURRENT STUDY
Method

The 1992 National Health and Social Life Survey (NHSLS) is a national probability sample of 3,432 English-speaking Americans ages 18–59 who were interviewed about sexual attitudes and behavior (Laumann, Gagnon, Michael, & Michaels, 1994, pp. 42–73). In a face-to-face survey, interviewers asked about social background, health, fertility, sexual activities, attitudes, and fantasies. After answering demographic questions at the start of the interview, respondents filled out a short, self-administered questionnaire inquiring, among other things, whether they had ever had extramarital sex and whether they had had sex with someone besides their regular partner in the last 12 months. Interviewers then collected detailed marital, cohabitation, and sexual histories. Data quality is a concern with sensitive matters like extramarital sex. NHSLS self-reports of extramarital sex are consistent with those from the General Social Survey (Laumann et al., 1994).

On a self-administered questionnaire to be sealed in a "privacy" envelope, respondents marked whether they had ever had sex with someone other than their husband or wife while they were married. This self-recorded item was less vulnerable to social desirability bias than a person-to-person interview. Extramarital sex was reported by 15.5 percent of the 1,717 respondents in this category. Interviewer-collected data on the timing of sexual relationships showed 4.7 percent of the 2,010 respondents cohabiting and/or married in the past year had been unfaithful to their primary partner during this time.

Results

Expectations for Sexually Exclusive Unions

NHSLS respondents, whether married or cohabiting, held similarly high expectations for sexual exclusivity. Respondents who had had sex with a primary partner at least 10 times over the past year were asked about expectations for sexual fidelity. Nearly 99 percent of married persons expected their spouse to have sex only in marriage, and 99 percent assumed their partner expected sexual exclusivity of them. We found less than 1 percent of heterosexuals, married or cohabiting, reported that a partner had changed expectations for fidelity during the relationship.

Although cohabitors held less conventional gender and family values (Clarkberg et al., 1995), cohabiting heterosexuals were only slightly less likely (94 percent versus 99 percent) to expect sexual exclusivity than married persons who had never lived together. Once married, those who had once lived together held expectations that were not significantly different from the expectations of other married people.

Were respondents sexually exclusive? People who married without first cohabiting were no more faithful than either married persons who cohabited together or current cohabitors. Nor were current cohabitors and previously cohabiting marrieds statistically different from one another. Of course, cumulative incidence was affected by union duration, and cohabiting persons were apt to have had less time "at risk."

Cumulative Incidence of Extramarital Sex

If concerns about social acceptability deter people from admitting sexual infidelity, the self-administered questionnaire offered better data than the person-to-person interview. Tastes and values demonstrated the hypothesized relationships: Greater interest in sex was positively associated with the likelihood of infidelity, while nonpermissive sexual values were negatively associated. Thinking about sex daily instead of just a few times a week meant a 22 percent increase in the odds of ever having had extramarital sex.

The hypothesized link between infidelity and opportunities for undetected sex received mixed support. For once-married persons in central cities, compared to other communities the odds of extramarital sex were 39 percent higher. Partners' shared networks showed the predicted negative association: All things being equal, enjoying time spent with a mate's family lowered the odds of extramarital sex by 24 percent. Prior sexual experience, attendance at religious services, and workplace opportunities for extramarital sex were statistically insignificant.

As for the couple's relationship, no statistically significant association was found for any measures of social dissimilarity. However, living together before marriage raised the odds of marital infidelity by 39 percent even controlling for sexual values and frequency of attendance at religious services—variables that distinguish married couples who first cohabited from the more conventional married couples who did not.

Gender and race were statistically significant. All things considered, being male increased the odds of having engaged in extramarital sex by 79 percent. Being African-American [also] raised them by 106 percent even though education controlled for racial differences in socioeconomic status. Education showed a weak negative association. Both frankness and marital duration (i.e., exposure time) showed the expected positive relationships.

Cumulative Incidence for Married and Cohabiting Persons

Both cohabitors and married people expect sexual exclusivity. The gender's effect was markedly reduced when we added other variables hypothesized to affect sexual decision-making but [less] when sexual interest and nonpermissive values were considered. Analyses demonstrated that controlling for permissiveness eliminated most gender differences in infidelity: Because men's sexual values are more permissive, men faced fewer impediments to infidelity. By contrast, variables influencing decision-making did not much diminish the effect of being African-American.

Those with strong interest in sex—those apt to gain most from sexual encounters—were significantly more likely to have been unfaithful. Those facing stiffer personal costs—for example, those with nonpermissive values—were significantly less likely to engage in infidelity.

Early sexual experience and central city residence were positively associated with the likelihood of having ever been unfaithful. Sharing a mate's social network was negatively associated with infidelity. All things considered, befriending a partner's family was associated with a 26 percent decrease in the odds of sexual infidelity. Workplace sexual opportunities and religious service attendance were not statistically significant. Relationship measures of heterogamy were statistically insignificant, too. Cohabitation fell short of statistical significance at the .05 level.

Prevalence of Infidelity for Married and Cohabiting Persons

Sexual interest might prompt infidelity, but infidelity might stimulate interest in sex, leading to frequent erotic thoughts. Although permissive values no doubt encourage adultery, adulterers might rationalize their behavior by adopting permissive views. Results for short-term infidelity largely paralleled those from earlier analyses. Personal tastes and values were significantly associated with the likelihood of infidelity. With the exception of central city residence, so were measures of sexual opportunities. Even workplace opportunity, which was not statistically significant in earlier analyses, showed the hypothesized positive relationship for the previous 12 months. This suggests that characteristics of the job mattered, but the current job's social interactions did not adequately capture previous work conditions influencing past sexual behavior. Although previous cohabitation increased the odds of infidelity, other features of the relationship did not prove statistically significant. Union duration was not significant either, implying that the passage of time had no effect on the marital gains that would be jeopardized by sexual infidelity. Gender's effect—reduced when other factors were controlled—was not statistically significant for the previous 12

months. Race continued to be strongly significant, however.

Sexual opportunity measures—early sexual experience, workplace opportunity, central city residence—were all statistically significant. Heterogamy in education and age showed no hypothesized effects, but dissimilar religions raised the likelihood of sexual infidelity, suggesting that excluded variables like sexual values and religious service attendance accounted for the religious heterogamy effect. Gender and race were statistically significant. Youngest ages were associated with greater infidelity; all things being equal, the odds of infidelity were twice as high for those ages 18–30 as for those over 50.

Tastes and values were statistically significant. When "cosmopolitan" values were incorporated, the effect of central city residence ceased to be statistically significant. Other measures of sexual opportunity—whether clearly prior or less remote in time—showed the predicted associations. The odds of a recent infidelity were more than twice as high for cohabitors than for married persons. Although cohabitation increased the likelihood significantly, we did not find the predicted association between partners' social dissimilarity and sexual infidelity. Subjective dissatisfaction, however, *was* positively and significantly associated with the likelihood of infidelity in the preceding 12 months. Most people reported high satisfaction with both the emotional and physical aspects of their union.

Subjective perception of the relationship was more closely associated with infidelity than objective heterogamy measures, which—although stable and causally prior to infidelity—did not demonstrate uniform effects on sexual behavior. Whether subjective dissatisfaction prompted infidelity or vice versa, any effect might be relatively short-term, especially if unhappy partners either reconciled or separated after an infidelity. If subjective evaluations of the match were not very stable, this might explain why prior studies did not always find current marital evaluations to be significantly associated with cumulative incidence of infidelity over the course of a union.

Discussion

Although previous research has reported personal values, sexual opportunities, and the marital relationship as determinants of extramarital sex, these studies have been largely piecemeal and based on small samples of limited generalizability. To the best of our knowledge, our research is the first to include measures of all three sets of determinants in multivariate analyses based on a large, representative sample of the U.S. population. The analyses show that values, opportunities, and the marital relationship are associated with sexual infidelity, even when other factors and demographic risk variables are controlled.

As we predicted, people who were more interested in sex were more likely to have multiple partners. As we hypothesized, people with nonpermissive values were less likely to engage in sexual infidelity. Considering sexual opportunities, we found evidence that prior sexual experiences were positively associated with infidelity. The behavioral constraints posed by overlap of mates' social networks reduced the likelihood of infidelity. In the short run, so did involvement in a religious community: Those who often attended religious services were less likely to have had multiple sex partners in the previous year, even when sexual values associated with religiosity were controlled. Sexual opportunities of the workplace also increased the likelihood of infidelity during the last 12 months. At least in the short run, however, any effect of city residence was substantially reduced when "cosmopolitan" sexual values and tastes were controlled.

The nature of the primary relationship proved important. We found cohabitors more likely than married people to engage in infidelity, even when we controlled for permissiveness of personal values regarding extramarital sex. This finding suggests that cohabitors' lower investments in their unions, not their less conventional values, accounted for their greater risk of infidel-ity. Cohabitors who went on to marry were no less likely to demand sexual exclusivity than people who married without having lived together. Neither the habituation nor the investment hypothesis about the effects of union duration was empirically supported.

As for measures of marital quality, partners' social dissimilarity was statistically insignificant, but subjective dissatisfaction with a union was associated with greater likelihood of recent infidelity. Prior studies yielded inconsistent results on whether poor relationships led to extramarital sex. Current relationship quality might not demonstrate an association with cumulative incidence—that is, having ever been unfaithful: Relationship problems were apt to be short-term if couples either reconciled or divorced soon after an infidelity.

Although epidemiological research consistently reports men to be at higher risk of infidelity than women, studies have not usually included indicators of sexual values and tastes. When we controlled for interest in sex and permissiveness of sexual values, we found that the main effects of gender were markedly reduced or even eliminated. Consistent with prior research, we found that being African-American was positively associated with multiple sex partners, even when educational attainment (an indicator of socioeconomic status) and other variables were controlled. The persistence of this effect points to the need for further research to clarify the role of race. Because we found the sexual opportunity structure to be important in understanding sexual behavior, racial differences in the sex ratio might influence the likelihood of having multiple partners.

We argue for thinking about sexual infidelity as the product of rational decision-making. Assuming sexual behavior is subject to rational calculation, we derived a series of testable hypotheses. NHSLS measures did not permit us to examine intrapsychic, cognitive processes or to compare directly preferences for alternative courses of behavior. To the extent that preferences are revealed in behavior, however, we can evaluate our approach by asking whether empirical results are consistent with predictions. Indeed, they are largely consistent even given different operationalizations of sexual infidelity.

Previous research reported that sexual infidelity is associated with values, opportunities for secret sex, the quality of the primary relationship, and sociodemographic risk factors. Integrating these piecemeal findings into a unified model revealed some well-documented relationships to be spurious. Our multivariate model also clarified the mechanisms by which variables might influence infidelity. For example, differences in tastes and values largely accounted for the effects of city residence and male gender. Controlling for sexual values, however, did not eliminate the significant association between infidelity and cohabitation, a result that pointed to commitment mechanisms as likely influences on sexual behavior. Nor could sexual values account for the negative association of churchgoing and recent infidelity. The multivariate analysis suggested that religiosity constrained sexual behavior not only through internalized moral beliefs, but also via supportive social networks. The integrated model pointed to one clear result: Being subject to preferences, constraints, and opportunities, sexual behavior is social behavior.

References

Atwater, L. (1982). *The Extramarital Connection: Sex, Intimacy, and Identity*. New York: Irvington.

Blumstein, P., & Schwartz, P. (1983). *American Couples*. New York: Morrow.

Bozon, M. (1996). Reaching adult sexuality: First intercourse and its implications. In M. Bozon & H. Letridon (Eds.), *Sexuality and the Social Sciences* (pp. 143–175). Aldershot, England: Dartmouth.

Brown, E. M. (1991). *Patterns of Infidelity and Their Treatment*. New York: Brunner-Mazel.

Bumpass, L. L., Sweet, J. A., & Cherlin, A. (1991). The role of cohabitation in declining rates of marriage. *Journal of Marriage and the Family, 53*, 913–927.

Choi, K.-H., Catania, J. A., & Dolcini, M. M. (1994). Extramarital sex and HIV risk behavior among American adults: Results from the National AIDS Behavioral Survey. *American Journal of Public Health, 84*, 2003–2007.

Clarkberg, M., Stolzenberg, R. M., & Waite, L. J. (1995). Attitudes, values, and entrance into cohabitational versus marital unions. *Social Forces, 51*, 609–633.

Constitutional barriers to civil and criminal restrictions on pre- and extramarital sex. (1993). *Harvard Law Review, 104*, 1660–1680.

Dolcini, M. M., Catania, J. A., Coates, T. J., Stall, R., Hudes, E. S., Gagnon, J. H., & Pollack, L. M. (1993). Demographic characteristics of heterosexuals with multiple partners: The National AIDS Behavior Surveys. *Family Planning Perspectives, 25*, 208–214.

Edwards, J. N., & Booth, A. (1976). Sexual behavior in and out of marriage: An assessment of correlates. *Journal of Marriage and the Family, 38*, 73–83.

Edwards, J. N., & Booth, A. (1994). Sexuality, marriage, and well-being: The middle years. In A. S. Rossi (Ed.), *Sexuality Across the Life Course* (pp. 233–299). Chicago: University of Chicago Press.

Forste, R., & Tanfer, K. (1996). Sexual exclusivity among dating, cohabiting, and married women. *Journal of Marriage and the Family, 58*, 33–47.

Gagnon, J., & Simon, W. (1973). *Sexual Conduct: The Social Sources of Human Sexuality*. Chicago: Aldine.

Giddens, A. (1992). *The Transformation of Intimacy: Sexuality, Love and Eroticism in Modern Societies*. Cambridge, England: Polity Press.

Gilmartin, B. G. (1974). Sexual deviance and social networks: A study of social, family, and marital interaction patterns among comarital sex participants. In J. R. Smith & L. G. Smith (Eds.), *Beyond Monogamy* (pp. 291–323). Baltimore, MD: Johns Hopkins University Press.

Glass, S. P., & Wright, T. L. (1992). Justifications for extramarital relationships: The association between attitudes, behaviors and gender. *The Journal of Sex Research, 29*, 361–387.

Greeley, A. M. (1991). *Faithful Attraction*. New York: A Tom Doherty Associates Book.

Johnson, R. E. (1970). Some correlates of extramarital coitus. *Journal of Marriage and the Family, 32*, 449–456.

Lancaster, J. (1994). Human sexuality, life histories, and evolutionary ecology. In A. S.

Rossi (Ed.), *Sexuality Across the Life Course* (pp. 39–62). Chicago: University of Chicago Press.

Laumann, E. O., Gagnon, J. H., Michael, R. T. & Michaels, S. (1994). *The Social Organization of Sexuality*. Chicago: University of Chicago Press.

Lawson, A. (1988). *Adultery: An Analysis of Love and Betrayal*. New York: Basic Books.

Lehrer, E. L., & Chiswick, C. U. (1993). Religion as a determinant of marital instability. *Demography, 30*, 385–404.

Leigh, B. C., Temple, M. T., & Trocki, K. F. (1993). The sexual behavior of U.S. adults: Results from a national survey. *American Journal of Public Health, 83*, 1400–1408.

Maykovich, M. K. (1976). Attitudes versus behavior in extramarital sexual relations. *Journal of Marriage and the Family, 38*, 693–699.

Pittman, F. (1989). *Private Lives: Infidelity and the Betrayal of Intimacy*. New York: W. W. Norton.

Prins, K. S., Buunk, B. P., & Van Yperen, N. W. (1983). Equity, normative disapproval, and extramarital relations. *Journal of Social and Personal Relationships, 10*, 39–53.

Reiss, I. L., Anderson, R. E., & Sponaugle, G. C. (1980). A multivariate model of the determinants of extramarital sexual permissiveness. *Journal of Marriage and the Family, 42*, 395–411.

Reiss, I. L., & Miller, B. C. (1979). Heterosexual permissiveness: A theoretical analysis. In W. R. Burr, R. Hill, F. I. Nye, & I. L. Reiss (Eds.), *Contemporary Theories About the Family* (Vol. 1, pp. 57–100). New York: Free Press.

Siegel, M. J. (1992). For better or worse: Adultery, crime and the Constitution. *Journal of Family Law, 30*, 45–95.

Smith, T. W. (1991). Adult sexual behavior in 1989: Numbers of partners, frequency of intercourse and risk of AIDS. *Family Planning Perspectives, 23*, 102–107.

Smith, T. W. (1994). Attitudes toward sexual permissiveness: Trends, correlates, and behavioral connections. In A. S. Rossi (Ed.), *Sexuality Across the Life Course* (pp. 63–97). Chicago: University of Chicago Press.

Vaughn, D. (1986). *Uncoupling*. Oxford, England: Oxford University Press.

Wellings, K., Field, J., Johnson, A., & Wadsworth, J. (1994). *Sexual Behavior in Britain*. London: Penguin Books.

Part IV

Sexuality and the Life Cycle: Middle and Later Adulthood

The woman of 60, flying to her winter home in Florida, detailed a somewhat convoluted saga to her seatmate. Her latest boyfriend, a 70-year-old businessman, had recently acquired a mark of distinction from his peers when sued by a young female employee for sexual harassment. Although neither the woman nor the jury faulted her boyfriend, it troubled her mother, age 85, whose 91-year-old fifth husband had read about it in a professional business journal he received in his office (Clendinen, 2000). Such copy may seem to set the stage for an off-Broadway play, but this actually occurred, epitomizing "third-stage adulthood"—the fastest growing demographic category in America.

A recent Harris poll found that almost one-half of persons ages 65 to 69 consider themselves as middle-aged, as do one-third of those in their 70s. Elliot Jacques, a psychologist who began to write about midlife crisis when he was age 38, now at age 83 has proposed the name "third-stage adulthood" for ages 62 to 85. According to Jacques, the first stage is from ages 18 to 40 and the second stage, ages 40 to 62. It was not until the second half of the twentieth century that changing demographics, resulting from the "graying of America," spawned the fertile field of geriatrics to care for America's fastest growing population, the elderly. In this process, a face was finally placed on sexuality throughout a lengthening life span.

Sex therapists and sexuality educators with a life-span perspective have responded to the need to expand their services to encompass new markets. Sexuality researchers have also expanded their parameters beyond the issues of the early adolescent and the young adult years, as reflected in the selections in this unit that showcase sexuality in the middle and later years. Regardless of the market or issues, a firm understanding of life-span sexuality development can contribute to personal happiness or professional success. This knowledge is especially important for today's aspiring sexuality professionals, who will work with myriad populations in search of individual and family stability.

Helping couples decode the language of their sexuality in "Passionate Marriage," Schnarch addresses what he calls the vortex of the emotional struggle in marriage, in which to grow up, each must hold on to self in the context of the other. This seasoned therapist is a founder of the Sexual Crucible Approach that conceptually integrates individual sexual and marital therapies. The article is included here not only for those few who would be sex therapists. It is included for all because it illustrates that sexual-marital therapy is an excellent context for gratifying personal growth and relationship development. This selection is a timely feature about the middle adult years, one of the foci of this unit. When marriages end at this juncture in life, they usually do so because of having been "neglected to death." As such malaise is addressed, nearly always, sexuality is raised as an issue.

Those whose interest is piqued by the article are referred to Schnarch's (1991) breakthrough book, *Constructing the Sexual Crucible: An Integration of Sexual and Marital Therapy*. He engages in highly explicit discussion of what goes on in bed in presenting the reality of our struggles with sex. The time spent reading this selection will yield rich dividends.

Although perimenopause has been around as an accepted medical phenomenon since it was recognized by the American medical establishment in the 1970s, many physicians are still unfamiliar with this medical condition. Because it still is not a part of most medical school curricula, some physicians even dismiss a woman's perimenopause symptoms as imaginary. When perimenopause begins as much as a decade before menopause, it presents as a wild hormone ride of ups and downs. If uninformed about this aspect of their bodies, many women may believe their symptoms are indications of a serious, life-threatening illness. Just as premenstrual syndrome (PMS) took many years to be established as a medically accepted condition, recognition of perimenopause may face an uphill battle. Inclusion of Begley's article in this mid-life section can furnish valuable ammunition for such a challenge.

The review of aging and sexuality by Kingsberg is a useful addition to this unit on later adulthood. Although the article's primary emphasis concerns the psychological aspects of aging on sexuality, it contains a wealth of information on related sociological and physiological factors. For example, the author pays particular atten-

tion to the impact on sexuality of various roles played by these people often referred to as the sandwich generation. And, the concise explanation of the three components of desire and the term *sexual equilibrium*, as applied to the aging process, offers valuable physiological insights into this specific subject. Even though this offering overviews the major sexual problems attributable to the aging process, its most valuable contribution may be the excellent development of the idea that sexual intimacy later in life is very much a reality that may assume many different faces.

Nobel laureate Gary Becker suggested that the physical extension of life may be the greatest single achievement of the twentieth century, and this reality could prove to be the greatest single influence on the current century. That is the good news. The bad news is that redefinitions do not come easily. Even with all of the excitement about the map of the human genomes, the work of recrafting the language of longevity is just beginning (Clendinen, 2000). Wright's research is a small but significant step in this direction, adding to the sparse data about the effects of Alzheimer's disease on affection and sexuality among married couples. Contrasting normal aging from pathological deviations and framing them within a human development perspective, this study draws some surprising conclusions. Although more data are certainly needed due to the very small sample, the work's value is enhanced by its longitudinal design. This effort expands our thinking about an important personal and social issue.

References

Clendinen, D. (2000, July 14). "Third-Stage Adulthood Is Fast-Growing Demographics." *New York Times*, p. 15A.

Schnarch, D. (1991). *Constructing the Sexual Crucible: An Integration of Sexual and Marital Therapy*. New York: Norton. ✦

Chapter 17
Passionate Marriage

David M. Schnarch

Individuals for whom orgasm is the ultimate in sexual functioning may find David Schnarch's article simply boring. His counter-belief that sexual potential extends far beyond the physical point of release is skillfully woven into the case of Betty and Donald, an actual married couple with real-life issues. Challenging the common foci of many sex therapists, i.e., sexual technique, reversal of sexual symptoms, or the pursuit of intimacy for intimacy's sake, Schnarch proposes another theory. From his perspective, it is within what he calls the "sexual crucible" that unresolved individual and relationship problems surface to reveal themselves in common dysfunctional sexual styles.

One does not have to be an aspiring sex therapist to be enlightened and liberated by this important work. Of the many insights to be gained, two points are especially helpful for young persons just embarking on their personal odysseys. The first is the distinction between a person's genital prime, the peak years of physical reproductive maturity, and one's sexual prime, the human capacity for adult eroticism and emotional connection. The potential for sex to be even better in the sexual prime that occurs with age than in the genital prime of youth has to be an intriguing concept for all mortals because aging is seldom an option. The second point, concerning the author's thesis that mutual completion of the sexual response cycle is not the same thing as intimacy, is well-supported. Although this assertion may be assumed to be self-evident, the number of failed marriages among Americans perhaps belies this assumption. This is a definitely not-to-be-missed offering.

Betty, a designer in a high-powered advertising firm, and Donald, a college professor bucking for tenure, had been married for 15 years. They spent the first 10 minutes in my office invoking the standard litany of our times as an explanation for their lousy sex life—they were both just too busy. Not that this focus precluded blaming each other for their difficulties. "Betty gets home from work so late that we barely see each other anymore, let alone have sex," said Donald resentfully. "We're collaborators in child raising and mortgage paying, but we're hardly lovers anymore. I've taken over a lot of the household chores, but she often doesn't get home until 9 p.m.—and most nights, she says she's just 'too tired' for sex." Betty sighed in exasperation. "Sometimes I think Donald wants me to leap from the front door to the bedroom and take care of him," she said. "But I'm being swallowed up by a sea of obligations—my boss, the kids, the house, the dog, Donald, everybody wants a big chunk of me. Right now, I feel there's nothing left of me for *me*, let alone for *him*. He just doesn't get it that I need more time for myself before I'm interested in sex." I asked them to be specific about how the stress from their very demanding lives revealed itself in bed—exactly what happened, and in what order, when they had sex. Several moments of awkward silence and a number of false starts ensued before another, much more intimate, level of their marital landscape revealed itself.

Betty looked hard at Donald, then at me. "The fact of the matter is, he doesn't even know how to kiss me!" she said grimly.

"How would you know? It's been so long since you *let* me kiss you!" hissed Donald.

When I asked them to describe their foreplay, Betty looked embarrassed and Donald sounded frustrated. "During sex, she turns her face to the side and I end up kissing her cheek. She won't kiss me on the mouth. I think she just wants to get sex over with as fast as possible. Not that we have much sex." Betty shook her head in distaste. "He always just rams his tongue halfway down my throat—I feel like I can't breathe. Besides, why would I want to kiss him, when I can't even talk to him! We don't communicate at all."

Over the years, I've worked with many couples who complain bitterly that the other kisses—or touches, fondles, caresses, strokes—the "wrong" way. I used to take these complaints at face value, trying to help the couple solve their problems through various forms of marital bargaining and forbearance—listen empathetically, give a little to get a little, do something for me and I'll do something for you—teach them the finer points of sexual technique and send them home with detailed prescriptions (which they usually didn't follow) until I realized that their sexual dissatisfactions did not stem from ignorance, ineptitude or a "failure to communicate." On the contrary, "communicating" is exactly what Donald and Betty were already doing very well, only neither much liked the "message" the other was sending. The way this couple kissed each other, indeed their "vocabulary" of foreplay, constituted a very rich and purposeful dialogue, replete with symbolic meanings. Through this finely nuanced, but unmistakable language, both partners expressed their feelings about themselves and each other and negotiated what the entire sexual encounter would be like—the degree and quality of eroticism, connection and intimacy, or their virtual absence.

Donald and Betty had tried marital therapy before, but their therapist had taken the usual approach of dealing with each complaint individually—job demands, parenting responsibilities, housework division and sexual difficulties—as if they were all separate but equal situational problems. Typically, the clinician had tried to help Donald and Betty resolve their difficulties through a skill-building course on compromise, setting priorities, time management and "mirroring" each other for mutual validation, acceptance and, of course, better communication. The net result of all this work was that they felt even worse than before, even more incompetent, inadequate and neurotic, when sex didn't improve.

Knowing that Betty and Donald were most certainly communicating something via their gridlocked sexual styles, I asked them, "Even if you are not talking, what do you think you might actually be 'saying' to each other when you kiss?" After a minute, Donald said resentfully, "She's telling me I'm inadequate, that I'm not a good lover, I can't make her happy and she doesn't want me anyway." Betty defensively countered, "He's saying he wants me to do everything exactly his way and if I don't just cave in, he'll go ahead and do what he likes, whether I like it or not!" I asked her why she was willing to have intercourse at all if she didn't even want to kiss him. "Because he is such a sullen pain in the ass if I don't have sex," Betty replied without hesitation. "Besides, I like having orgasms."

Donald and Betty perfectly illustrated the almost universal, but widely unrecognized, reality that sex does not merely constitute a "part" of a relationship, but literally and metaphorically embodies the depth and quality of the couple's entire emotional connection. We think of foreplay as a way couples establish connection, but more often it's a means of establishing disconnection. Betty was a living rebuttal of the common gender stereotype that all women always want more foreplay; she cut it short so they could get sex done with as quickly as possible—and Donald understood. Donald returned the compliment by "telling" Betty he knew she didn't like him much, but he was going to get something out of her anyway—with or without her presence, so to speak.

Clearly, foreplay for this couple was not simply a mechanical technique for arousal, amenable to the engineering, skill-building approach still dictated by popular sex manuals. Nor were they likely to improve sex just by being more "open" with each other, "asking for what they wanted"—another popular remedy in self-help guides and among marital therapists—as if they weren't already "telling" each other what each did and did not want, and what each was or was not willing to give. Instead of trying to spackle over these normal and typical "dysfunctional" sexual patterns with a heavy coat of how-to lessons, I have learned that it makes much more sense to help the couple analyze their behavior, to look for the meaning of what they were already doing before they focused on changing the mechanics.

Rather than "work on their relationship" as if it were some sort of hobby or homebuilding project, Betty and Donald, like every other couple I have seen, needed to understand that what they did in bed was a remarkably salient and authentic expression of themselves and their feeling for each other. The nuances of their kissing style may have seemed trivial compared to the screaming fights they had about money or long days of injured silence, but in fact was an open window into their deepest human experience—who they were as people, what they really felt about each other, how much intimacy they were willing to risk with each other and how much growing up they still had to do.

As in any elaborate and nuanced language, the small details of sex carry a wealth of meaning, so while Donald and Betty were surprised that I focused on a "little thing" like kissing, rather than the main event—frequency of intercourse, for example—they were startled to find how truly revealing it was, about their personal histories as well as their marriage. I told Betty I thought she had probably come from an intrusive and dominating family that never dealt openly or successfully with anxiety and conflict. "So now, you have a hard time using your mouth to tell Donald not to be so overbearing, rather than turning it away to keep him from getting inside it. You've become very good at taking evasive action to avoid being overwhelmed," I said. "You're right about my family," Betty said softly, "we kids didn't have any privacy or freedom in my family, and we were never allowed to complain openly about anything—just do what we were told, and keep our mouths shut."

On the other hand, I said, I imagined Donald had never felt worthwhile in his family's eyes. He had spent a lot of time trying to please his parents without knowing what he was supposed to do, but he got so little response that he never learned how to read other people's cues—he just forged blindly ahead, trying to force his way into people's good graces and prove himself without waiting to see how he was coming across. "Come back here and give me a chance to prove myself!" his behavior screamed. "Are you so used to being out of contact with the people you love that you can successfully ignore how out of sync you are with them?" I asked. To Donald's credit, he didn't dodge the question, though he seemed dazed by the speed with which we'd zoomed in on such a core issue.

Nevertheless, Donald and Betty discovered that their discomfort in describing, in exact detail, what was done by whom, when, how and where, was outweighed by their fascination at what they were finding out about themselves—far more than was remotely possible from a seminar on sex skills. Betty, for example, had suggested that once kissing had stopped and intercourse had started, her sexual life was just fine—after all, she had orgasms and she "liked" them. But when I asked her to describe her experience of rear-entry intercourse—a common practice with this couple—she did not make it sound like a richly sensual, erotic or even particularly pleasant encounter. During the act, she positioned herself on elbows and knees, her torso held tense and rigidly parallel to the mattress while she protectively braced her body for a painful battering. Instead of moving into each thrust from Donald, she kept moving away from him, as if trying to escape. He, on the other hand, clasped her hips and kept trying to pull her to him, but never got a feeling of solid physical or emotional connection.

In spite of the fact that both were able to reach orgasm—widely considered the only significant measurement of successful sex—Betty and Donald's minute-by-minute description of what they did made it obvious that a lot more was happening than a technically proficient sex act. I told Betty I was glad she had told me these details, which all suggested that she thought it was pretty hopeless trying to work out conflicts with people she loved. "I suspect you've gotten used to swallowing your disappointment and sadness without telling anybody, and just getting along by yourself as best you can," I said. "It sounds very lonely." At that point, much to Donald's shock, Betty burst into tears. I said to Donald that he still seemed resigned to chase after people he loved to get them to love and accept him. "I guess you just don't believe they could possibly love you without being pressured into it. In fact, I think both of you use sex to confirm the negative beliefs you already have about yourselves."

For several seconds Donald looked at his lap, while Betty quietly cried in the next chair. "I suppose we must be pretty screwed up, huh?" Betty snuffled. "Nope," I said. "Much of what's going on between you is not only understandable, it's predictable, normal and even healthy—although it doesn't look or feel that way right now." They were describing the inevitable struggle involved in seeking individual growth and self-development within the context of marriage.

Betty said she used to enjoy sex until she became overinvolved with her job, but I suggested that the case was more likely the reverse—that the demands of her job gave her a needed emotional distance from Donald. Her conscious desire to "escape" from Donald stemmed from emotional fusion with him—she found herself invaded by his worries, his anxieties, his insecurities and his needs as if she had contracted a virus from him. "You may feel that you don't have enough inside you to satisfy his needs and still remain a separate, whole person yourself," I said. "Your work is a way of keeping some 'self' *for* yourself, to prevent being absorbed by him. That's the same reason you turn your head away when he tries to kiss you."

I suggested that Donald's problem was a complementary version of the same thing: in order to forestall the conviction that he had no worthwhile self at all, he felt he had to pressure Betty, or anybody he loved, to demonstrate they loved him—over and over. Donald, of course, did not see that he was as important to Betty as she was to him, but their mutual need for each other was really a function of two fragile and insecure selves shoring each other up.

Like most of us, neither Betty nor Donald was very mature when they married; neither had really learned the grown-up ability to soothe their own emotional anxieties or find their own internal equilibrium during the inevitable conflicts and contretemps of marriage. And, like most couples after a few years of marriage, they made up for their own insecurities by demanding that the other provide constant, unconditional acceptance, empathy, reciprocity and validation to help them each sustain a desired self-image. "I'm okay if, but only if, you think I'm okay," they said, in effect, to each other, and worked doubly hard both to please and be pleased, hide and adapt, shuffle and dance, smile and agree. The more time passes, the more frightened either partner is of letting the other know who he or she *really* is.

This joint back-patting compact works for a while to keep each partner feeling secure, but eventually the game becomes too exhausting to play. Gradually, partners become less inclined to please each other, more resentful of the cost of continually selling themselves out for ersatz peace and tranquillity, less willing to put out or give in. The ensuing "symptoms"—low sexual desire, sexual boredom, control battles, heavy silences—often take on the coloring of a deathly struggle for selfhood, fought on the implicit assumption that there is only room for one whole self in the marriage. "It's going to be my way or no way, my self or no self!" partners say in effect, in bed and out—leading to a kind of classic standoff.

Far from being signs of a deeply "pathological" marital breakdown, however, as Donald and Betty were convinced, this stalemate is a normal and inevitable process of growth built into every marriage, as well as a golden opportunity. Like grains of sand inexorably funneling toward the "narrows" of an hourglass, marriage predictably forces couples into a vortex of emotional struggle, where each dares to hold onto himself or herself in the context of each other, in order to grow up. At the narrowest, most constricting part of the funnel—where alienation, stagnation, infidelity, separation and divorce typically occur—couples can begin not only to find their individual selves, but in the process acquire a far greater capacity for love, passion and intimacy with each other than they ever thought possible.

At this excruciating point in a marriage, every couple has four options: each partner can try to control the other (Donald's initial ploy, which did not succeed), accommodate even more (Betty had done so to the limits of her tolerance), withdraw physically or emotionally (Betty's job helped her to do this) or learn to soothe his or her own anxiety and not get hijacked by the anxiety of the other. In other words, they could work on growing up, using their marriage as a kind of differentiation fitness center par excellence.

Differentiation is a lifelong process by which we become more uniquely ourselves by maintaining ourselves in relationship with those we love. It allows us to have our cake and eat it too, to experience fully our biologically based drives for both emotional connection and individual self-direction. The more differentiated we are—the stronger our sense of self-definition and the better we can hold ourselves together during conflicts with our partners—the more intimacy we can tolerate with someone we love without fear of losing our sense of who we are as separate beings. This uniquely human balancing act is summed up in the striking paradox of our species, that we are famously willing both to die for others, and to die rather than be controlled by others.

Of all the many schools of hard experience life has to offer, perhaps none but marriage is so perfectly calibrated to help us differentiate—if we can steel ourselves to take advantage of its rigorous lessons, and not be prematurely defeated by what feels at first like abject failure. Furthermore, a couple's sexual struggle—what I call the sexual crucible—is the most powerful route both to individual maturity and the capacity for intimate relationship, because it evokes people's deepest vulnerabilities and fears, and also taps into their potential for profound love, passion, even spiritual transcendence.

In the typically constricted sexuality of the mid-marriage blues, Betty and Donald's sexual repertoire consisted of "leftovers"—whatever was left over after eliminating every practice that made one or the other nervous or uncomfortable. The less differentiated a couple, the less they can tolerate the anxiety of possibly "offending" one another, the more anxiety they experience during sex and the more inhibited, rigid and inflexible their sexual style becomes: people have sex only up to the limits of their sexual and emotional development. Unsurprisingly, Donald and Betty's sexual routine had become as predictable, repetitious, unadventurous and boring as a weekly hamburger at McDonald's. This is why the standard advice to improve sex by negotiating and compromising is doomed to failure—most normally anxious couples have already long since negotiated and compromised themselves out of any excitement, variety or sexual passion, anyway.

And yet, it would have been pointless and counterproductive to march Donald and Betty through a variety of new sexual techniques. Using sex as a vehicle for personal and relational growth is not the same as just doing something new that raises anxieties. Rather, it depends on maintaining a high level of personal connection with someone known and loved during sex—allowing ourselves to really see and be seen by our partners, feel and be felt, know and be known by them. Most couples have spent years trying not to truly reveal themselves to each other in order to maintain the illusion of complete togetherness, thus effectively smothering any true emotional connection, with predictably disastrous effects on sex.

Donald and Betty were so obsessed with sexual behavior, so caught up in their anxieties about who was doing or failing to do what to whom in bed, that they were not really emotionally or even physically aware of each other when they touched. Like people "air kissing" on social occasions, they were going through the motions while keeping a kind of emotional *cordon sanitaire* between them. Their sex was more like the parallel play of young children than an adult interaction—except that they each watched the other's "play" with resentment and hurt feelings. Betty complained that Donald touched her too roughly—"He's crude and selfish!" she said, "and just uses me to please himself." Her complaint undercut Donald's sense of self, and he defensively accused her of being a demanding bitch, never satisfied and fundamentally unpleasable—thereby undermining her sense of self.

In order to help them each find a self and each other, I had to redirect their gaze away from their obsession with mutually disappointing sexual behavior, and encourage them to "follow the connection"—rediscover or establish some vital physical and emotional link as a first building block to greater intimacy. To consciously "follow the connection," however, requires the full presence and consent of both partners, each purposely slowing down and giving full attention to the other, feeling and experiencing the other's reality.

The next session, Donald reported that he now understood why Betty felt he was too "rough"; he said the experience made him realize that he usually touched her with about as much care and sensitivity as if he was scouring a frying pan! But slowing down to really become conscious of what he was doing made him experience a sudden jolt of emotional connection with Betty. This awareness was an unnerving sensation for someone who had spent his life performing for other people (including his wife) rather than actually being *with* them.

Betty, too, was shaken by the jarring reality of their connection. She hadn't liked being touched roughly, but the concentration and attention in Donald's hands as he really felt and got to know her body was deeply disturbing; she found herself suddenly and unexpectedly sobbing with grief and deprivation for the warmth and love she'd missed as a child, and that she had both craved and feared in her marriage. Later that night, they had the best sex they had experienced in a very long time.

Buoyed by this first success, more hopeful about their future together, they both wanted to know how they could enhance this new and still tentative sense of connection. I suggested they try something called "hugging till relaxed," a powerful method for increasing intimacy that harnesses the language and dynamics of sex without requiring either nudity or sexual contact. Hugging, one of the most ordinary, least threatening gestures of affection and closeness, is also one of the most telling. When they hugged, Betty complained that Donald always leaned on her—making her stagger backward—while Donald accused Betty of pulling away from him, letting go "too soon," and leaving him "hugging air."

I suggested that Betty and Donald each stand firmly on their own two feet, loosely put their arms around each other, focus on their own individual experience and concentrate on quieting themselves down while in the embrace—neither clutching nor pulling away from or leaning on each other. Once both partners can learn to soothe themselves and maintain their individual equilibrium, shifting their own positions when necessary for comfort, they get a brief, physical experience of intimate connection without fusion, a sense of stability and security without overdependency.

While practicing hugging until relaxed with Donald, Betty found that as she learned to quiet her own anxiety, she could allow herself to be held longer by Donald without feeling claustrophobic. Just relaxing in the hug also made her realize that she normally carried chronic anxiety like a kind of body armor. As Betty calmed down and began to melt peacefully into the hug, not pulling away from fear that Donald would, literally, invade her space, he noticed his own impulse to break it off before she wanted to. When they each could settle down in the hug, they discovered that together they eventually would enter a space of great peace and tranquillity, deeply connected and in touch with each other but secure in their self.

Soon, they could experience some of the same kind of deep peace during sex, which not only eliminated much of the anxiety, resentment and disappointment they had felt before, but vastly increased the eroticism of the encounter. Now that they knew what they were looking for, they could tell when it was absent. Later, in my office, while Betty gently stroked his arm, Donald teared up as he told me about the new sense of quiet but electric connection he felt with her. "I just had no idea what we were missing; she seemed so precious to me that it almost hurt to touch her," he said, his voice thick with emotion.

This leap in personal development didn't simply occur through behavioral desensitization. Sometimes, Betty and Donald got more anxious as their unresolved issues surfaced in their physical embrace. At times, when Betty dared to shift to a more comfortable position, Donald felt she was squirming to avoid him. It was my job to help them see how this reflected the same emotional dynamics present in other aspects of their marriage. Betty was attempting to "hold onto herself" while remaining close to someone she loved, and likewise, Donald was refusing to chase after a loved one to get himself accepted. Insight alone didn't help much; a lot of self-soothing was required. Ultimately, they stopped taking each other's experience and reaction as a reflection on themselves and recognized that two separate realities existed even during their most profound physical union.

Building on their new stockpiles of courage earned in these experiments with each other, I suggested that Donald and Betty consider eyes-open sex, the thought of which leaves many couples aghast. Indeed, Donald's first response to the suggestion was that if he and Betty tried opening their eyes during sex, they wouldn't need birth control because the very thought made him so anxious he could feel his testicles retreating up into his windpipe! But eyes-open sex is a powerful way of revealing the chasm between sensation-focused sex and real intimacy. Most couples close their eyes in order to better tune out their partners so that they can concentrate on their physical feelings; it is a shocking revelation that to reach orgasm—supposedly the most intimate human act—most people cannot tolerate too much intimacy with their part-

ners, so they block the emotional connection and concentrate on body parts.

Eyes-open sex is not simply a matter of two pairs of eyeballs staring at each other, but a way to intensify the mutual awareness and connection begun during foreplay; to really "see" and "be seen" is an extension of feeling and being felt when touching one another. But if allowing oneself to be known by touch is threatening, actually being seen can be positively terrifying. Bravely pursuing eyes-open sex in spite of these misgivings helps couples not only learn to tolerate more intimacy, it increases differentiation—it requires a degree of inner calm and independent selfhood to let somebody see what's inside your head without freaking out.

But the experience was also exhilarating. As Donald and Betty progressed from shy, little, peekaboo glimpses into each other's faces to long, warm gazes and soft smiles, each found their encounters more deeply moving. Betty slowly realized that whereas before she had wanted to escape from Donald, now she yearned to see all of him, and for him to see all of her. "I felt so vulnerable, as if he could see all my inadequacies, but the way he looked at me and smiled made all that unimportant." Donald gradually relinquished the self-image of a needy loser; he no longer needed to pursue Betty for reassurance and found, to his delight, that she wanted him—a breathtaking experience. "Her eyes are so big and deep, I feel I could dive into them," he said in wonder.

Both began to experience an increasing sense of self-acceptance and personal security. "We're having better sex now than we've ever had in our lives," Betty reported, "And I thought we were getting to be too old and far too married for exciting sex." Donald agreed. Betty and Donald, like society at large, were confusing genital prime—the peak years of physical reproductive maturity—with sexual prime—the specifically human capacity for adult eroticism and emotional connection. "Are you better in bed or worse now than you were as an adolescent?" I asked them. "Most people definitely get better as they get older, at least potentially. No 17-year-old boy is sufficiently mature to be capable of profound intimacy—he's too preoccupied with proving his manhood; and a young woman is too worried about being 'used' or too hung up about romance and reputation to really experience her own eroticism. Most 50-year-olds, on the other hand, have a much better developed sense of who they are, and more inner resources to bring to sex. You could say that cellulite and sexual potential are highly correlated."

As far as issues of gender equality are concerned, both men and women become more similar as they age and approach their sexual potential. Men are not as frightened of letting their partners take the lead in making love to them, and they develop far greater capacity and appreciation for emotional connection and tenderness than they had as young men. Women, on the other hand, become more comfortable with their own sexuality, more likely to enjoy sex for its own sake and less inclined to apologize for their eroticism or hide behind the ingenue's mask of modesty. As they age, women feel less obligated to protect their mate's sexual self-esteem at the cost of their own sexual pleasure.

Once a couple's sexual potential has been tapped, partners are no longer afraid to let their fantasies run free with each other. Donald, for example, let Betty know that he dreamed of her tying him up and "ravishing" him sexually—so one day, she bought four long, silk scarves and that night, wearing three-inch high heels and a little black lace, she trussed him to the bed and gave him what he asked for, astounding him and surprising herself with her own dramatic flair. Betty had always secretly cherished a fantasy of being a dangerous, sexually powerful femme fatale, but Donald's clingy neediness had dampened her enthusiasm for trying out the dream—also she had been afraid it would make him even more demanding. But now, knowing he was capable of being himself regardless of what she did or did not do, Betty felt much more comfortable expressing her own sense of erotic play.

The Sexual Crucible Approach encourages people to make use of the opportunity offered by marriage to become more married and better married, by becoming more grown-up and better at staking out their own selfhood. But the lessons learned by Betty and Donald, or any couple, extend far beyond sex. The same emotional development that makes for more mature and passionate sexuality also helps couples negotiate the other potential shoals of marriage—money issues, childrearing questions, career decisions—because differentiation is not confined to sex. In every trouble spot, each partner has the same four options: dominate, submit, withdraw or differentiate. Differentiation does not guarantee that spouses can always have things their own individual way and an unfailingly harmonious marriage besides. Marriage is full of hard, unpleasant choices, including the choice between safety, security and sexual boredom, on the one hand, and challenge, anxiety and sexual passion, on the other.

But spouses who have learned to stand on their own two feet within marriage are not as likely to force their own choices on the other or give in or give up entirely just to keep their anxiety in check and shore up their own frail sense of self. Learning to soothe ourselves in the middle of a fight with a spouse over, say, the choice of schools for our child or a decision to move, not only helps keep the discussion more rational, but makes us more capable of mutuality, of hearing our partner, of putting his or her agenda on a par with our own. The fight stops being, for example, a struggle between your personal needs and your spouse's personal needs, often regarded by each as my "good idea" and her/his "selfishness," but which is really often my fragile, undeveloped self versus his/her equally fragile, undeveloped self. Instead, we can begin to see that the struggle is inside each of us individually, between wanting what we want for ourselves personally, and wanting for our beloved partner what he or she wants for himself or herself. Becoming more differentiated is possibly the most loving thing you can do in your lifetime—for those you love as well as yourself. Someone once said that if you're going to "give yourself" to your partner like a bouquet of flowers, you should at least first arrange the gift!

There is no way this process can be foreshortened into a technical quick-fix, no matter how infatuated our culture is with speed, efficiency and cost containment. Courage, commitment, a willingness to forgo obvious "solutions," tolerating the anxiety of living without a clear, prewritten script, as well as the patience to take the time to grow up are all necessary conditions, not only for a good marriage, but for a good life. At the same time, reducing all marital problems to the fallout from our miserable childhoods or to gender differences not only badly underestimates our own ability to develop far beyond the limitations of our circumstances, but misjudges the inherent power of emotionally committed relationships to bring us (drag us, actually, often kicking and screaming) more deeply and fully into our own being. Marriage is a magnificent system, not only for humanizing us, maturing us and teaching us how to love, but also perhaps for bringing us closer to what is divine in our natures.

Adapted from David M. Schnarch, "Passionate Marriage." *Family Therapy Networker*, (September/October) pp. 42, 44–49. Copyright © 1997, *Family Therapy Networker*. Reprinted by permission. ✦

Chapter 18
Understanding Perimenopause

Sharon L. Begley

It can masquerade as insomnia, moodiness, forgetfulness, or depression, but physicians now understand that in the years before menopause, women ride a hormonal roller coaster. The grab bag of symptoms that it brings has a single underlying, yet treatable, cause. Women who discover this little known phenomenon, perimenopause, can become active agents in combating its effects.

Students, especially women, will appreciate the clearly and concisely described function of estrogen and the role of FSH in estrogen production. This somewhat newly designated, age-related condition may apply to many mothers of college students who are yet unaware of its existence but very much aware of its symptoms. As in so many other areas of life, forewarned is forearmed. Knowledge of perimenopause is a powerful tool to help women assume management of their own health-related issues. Knowledge, then, truly becomes power.

For a professional party planner like Bonnie Leopold, irritability is about as welcome as gate crashers. But there it was: Leopold, 48, of Manhattan Beach, California, started feeling nonstop grouchy and snappish. She also got hot flashes so often that she didn't dare leave the house without her portable fan. And when she had two menstrual periods in one month, she was convinced she had ovarian cancer. Susan Santacaterina, 46, didn't think she had a fatal disease, but after suffering for months from insomnia and headaches before every period, she had an MRI scan of her brain

anyway. Donna Lambert, 47, sums up her situation like this: "I feel like I'm brain-dead." [Lambert], who lives in Charlottesville, Va., walks into rooms and wonders why she is there; once able to memorize a two-page grocery list, she now can't go shopping without one.

The three women's disparate symptoms would seem to suggest they've got totally different illnesses. But, in fact, they're all on the same wild hormonal roller-coaster ride, and it's called perimenopause.

If you like the prospect of menopause, you'll love perimenopause. Literally "around menopause," perimenopause begins when hormone-related changes kick in, as long as 10 years before menopause. Menopause itself begins 12 months after a woman's final period, and in the United States comes at an average age of 52. If you define perimenopause as lasting 10 years, then more than 20 million American women are now going through it. Perimenopause promises many of the same hot flashes, concentration gaps, mood swings, sleep troubles and migraines associated with menopause, as well as irritability and memory loss, with an added sweetener: the symptoms come earlier and last longer. As early as 35 but almost certainly in your 40s, your hormones start to betray you. Estrogens, progesterone and other reproductive hormones no longer work together with the precise timing of a Rolex, but instead act like "a Swiss watch that's gotten rusty," says Dr. Wulf Utian, Executive Director of the North American Menopause Society. That is a radically new understanding of perimenopause. Despite claims that its symptoms reflect plunging levels of estrogen, and that women should seek relief through estrogen replacement, perimenopause is marked by hormones riding a roller coaster. Breast surgeon Susan Love, in her "Dr. Susan Love's Hormone Book," calls it "the mirror image of puberty," and that has important implications for treatment.

There is no typical perimenopause, just as there is no typical puberty. But in general perimenopause brings, first and most obviously, wacky menstrual periods: more often, less often, heavier or lighter. It can also worsen PMS, cause night sweats, diminish libido and cause skin, hair and vaginal walls to thin and dry out. Each of these reflects changes in the river of hormones coursing through a woman's body. The better a woman understands these changes, the better care she is likely to get from her doctor, for although perimenopause has been recognized by the American medical establishment since the 1970s, many doctors had not heard of it before the 1990s. It still isn't part of most med-school curricula, and there are still physicians who dismiss a woman's perimenopause symptoms as all in her head. Here's what really happens:

- Follicle-stimulating hormone (FSH) is secreted by the brain's pituitary gland. True to its name, FSH stimulates eggs to mature. Older ovaries have gotten a little deaf to these signals, so the brain has to pump up the volume: it emits more FSH in order to get some response from the ovaries. "FSH gets cranked up as the pituitary tries to drive the poor ovary to make estrogen," explains Mary Jane Minkin, an OB-GYN at Yale University School of Medicine. FSH also, indirectly, dilates blood vessels that lie just beneath the skin. Dilating a blood vessel can produce a feeling of warmth and may be a cause of hot flashes and night sweats. An FSH level above 30 (in units called milli-international units per milliliter), as measured in a blood test on any of the first six days of a woman's period, is the most reliable indication that she is in perimenopause. But it's not foolproof. If the test is done in a month when the woman has a normal period, her FSH may look normal. That's why the test should be repeated the following menstrual cycle, but at $200 a pop, that gets a little pricey.
- Progesterone is secreted from empty egg follicles (little sacs within the ovaries that contain one ovum apiece). To become empty, the follicle obviously has to release its ovum; that's ovulation. But if no egg ripens, no ovulation

occurs, and no progesterone is released. It's progesterone that both stabilizes the uterine lining and signals when to slough it off. Without progesterone, a perimenopausal woman can therefore miss periods. "Some women are skipping periods all over the place," says Minkin, while others have "screwy bleeding." Progesterone also affects moods: it binds to the same sites in the brain as does a neurochemical, called GABA, that tamps down anxiety. The precipitous drop in progesterone after a woman gives birth may trigger postpartum depression; its gradual falloff during the second half of a woman's monthly cycle may usher in the PMS blues. How much progesterone levels dip during perimenopause, and what effect that has, varies from one woman to the next and from one month to the next. But the otherwise inexplicable weepiness during one's 40s might reflect diminished progesterone.

- Levels of estrogen rocket up tenfold— as in 1,000 percent—during puberty. They plateau between the ages of 25 and 40 or so. It's downhill from there, as estrogen levels fall by that same tenfold amount, to one tenth their peak, once a woman has passed through menopause. As for what happens between the plateau and the valley—during perimenopause—researchers are scrambling for answers. Despite the drumbeat of stories about how perimenopause is marked by a relentless fall in estrogen levels, one thing estrogen levels do not do is decline gradually, like a skier down a bunny slope. Most researchers believe instead that estrogen fluctuates wildly during perimenopause. A 1996 study led by researchers at the University of Washington found that all 16 women 40 to 45 whom they studied had overall estrogen levels comparable to the 12 twentysomethings in the group. But during the first few days of their monthly cycle, the older women experienced a rise in estrogen to a level higher than in the younger women. So while estrogen levels may decline overall after 40, they decline like a skier on a slope studded with moguls—from towering bump to towering bump. "The best way to think about it," says endocrinologist Richard Santen of the University of Virginia, "is up, down, up, down, stop."

A typical woman might have very low estrogen at the beginning of her menstrual cycle. That could give her hot flashes for two weeks, explains Susan Love. Although as many as 70 percent of women in their 40s experience irregular menstrual periods, only 30 percent suffered hot flashes in the three years before menopause, a 1991 study found. Low estrogen will also goad the pituitary to churn out more FSH. That, in turn, will stimulate the ovaries to produce twice as much estrogen as normal, ushering in the PMS-like symptoms of high estrogen-low progesterone.

What can women do to alleviate the symptoms of perimenopause? Some things are easy calls. It makes sense to avoid alcohol and spicy foods to minimize hot flashes, and to swear off caffeine (especially after midday) to sleep better. Weight-bearing exercise (that includes walking) stimulates the production of new bone, which is a good way to enter menopause itself. But after these no-brainers, the treatment advice depends on what a woman's hormones are up to (or down to).

Say a woman has erratic estrogen levels. The surest sign of such a hormonal roller coaster is weird menstrual cycles, but also mood swings like those of PMS. More doctors are therefore recommending birth control pills, which even out hormone levels. Alesse, Lo-estrin and Mircette are called low dose, but in fact they contain enough estrogen to suppress ovulation.

This wallop of estrogen "will basically shut down the ovaries," says Dr. Brian Walsh of Brigham and Women's Hospital in Boston, so they no longer secrete estrogen. Hormone levels, now set completely by the medication, settle down. (A woman who smokes or has high blood pressure should not take the pill, however, because it can raise her risk of fatal blood clots. And all women need to consult their doctor about the best way to alleviate the symptoms of perimenopause.)

If a perimenopausal woman is suffering from a dearth of estrogen, she needs different treatment. Estrogen stimulates production of the brain chemical serotonin, which, among other jobs, regulates sleep and emotion. Less estrogen can bring insomnia and mood swings. In addition, estrogen can twiddle the body's thermostat, the hypothalamus, which sits deep inside the brain. "When estrogen declines," says Walsh, "it causes the temperature center to become unstable." That can trigger hot flashes. Chronically low estrogen can also impair verbal memory. How bad can the memory loss be? Novelist Anna Quindlen, 46, wrote in 1997 about waking up in the middle of the night and "forgetting the names of my children." The reason, new research shows, is that estrogen stimulates neurons to sprout new branches, helps generate new synapses and triggers production of substances that promote neuronal growth—all of which weave brain neurons into networks that learn and remember. To kick estrogen levels back up, hormone-replacement therapy might seem an obvious choice. Bonnie Leopold swears by the Vivelle estrogen patch on her backside. A two-inch clear oval that resembles a nicotine patch, it slowly releases the form of estrogen; she credits it with wiping away her irritability. But many doctors are wary about putting premenopausal women on HRT; such use is not approved by the Food and Drug Administration. An authoritative 16-year study of some 40,000 nurses found, in June 1997, a 43 percent higher risk for fatal breast cancer among postmenopausal women who took HRT for 10 years or more. Other studies have shown a risk even at five to seven years, says Dr. Nananda Col of New England Medical Center in Boston. That makes starting HRT at, say, 42 a potentially dicey proposition. Women who reject HRT often turn to "natural hormone replacement." Supplements like black cohosh [root] promise to deliver phytoestrogens (from plants) and relieve perimenopausal symptoms. But this market is so underregulated that you can't be sure what's in any of these pills; few have been thoroughly studied. They probably won't cause any harm, but a surer bet is to obtain phytoestrogens from foods like soy (as tofu, soy milk, tempeh, miso) and flaxseed oil. How much do you have to eat? In one study a daily regimen of six tablespoons of soy flour reduced hot flashes, sleep disturbances, depression and loss of libido. The 1998 book *Estrogen: The Natural Way* contains more than 250 phytoestrogen-packed recipes for, among other delicacies, orange-apricot bars, noodles with creamy sesame sauce and mackerel-and-onion quiche.

Although some women's health activists complain that doctors are "pathologizing" a normal stage of life, there are two sound medical reasons for acknowledging perimenopause. The first is that if a woman doesn't understand that waking up every night at 3 has the same underlying cause as the worst PMS she's ever suffered, and that her insomnia is in turn related to irregular periods and mood swings and an inability to remember where she was in a conversation before the phone rang, she may wind up with a fistful of symptom-by-symptom prescriptions. She'll get sleeping aids, tranquilizers, antidepressants and appointments with therapists, but not treatment for the underlying hormonal swings. Worse, if doctors don't recognize that hormonal upheavals kick in long before menopause, they may dismiss women's perimenopausal complaints as imaginary. "It used to be thought that women didn't really have symptoms until their final period," says Walsh. "But in reality, hot flashes are worst about three or four years before that. If you wait for her final period before you listen to her concerns and treat her, you'll miss most of the misery."

The second reason to recognize perimenopause is to treat it as a wake-up call. You are approaching the next stage of your life, but you've got advance warning. So heed it: give up cigarettes, eat right, exercise, reduce. That way, when you go through menopause itself you will be in the best shape you can. In the meantime, just knowing that your crazy symptoms have a name and a cause might be relief enough.

Adapted from Sharon L. Begley, "Understanding Perimenopause." *Newsweek* Special Issue, Spring/Summer, pp. 31–34. Copyright © 1999, Newsweek, Inc. All rights reserved. Reprinted by permission. ✦

Chapter 19
The Psychological Impact of Aging on Sexuality and Relationships

Sheryl A. Kingsberg

Myths concerning the "nonsexual senior" abound, with perhaps the greatest being that sexual activity is not prevalent among the elderly. In reality, sexual needs do not change abruptly with age, and, in fact, the potential for sexual expression continues until death. Although sexual vigor is not necessarily age-related, age does appear to have its effects on both women and men as physiological changes occur in the later years. Touching, caressing, masturbation, and sexual intercourse are all forms of sexual activity preferred by these later-age seniors.

Despite the explosion of knowledge about sexuality, most physicians receive little, if any, sexuality education in medical school, especially that which pertains to the elderly. Similarly, nursing home staffs are only moderately knowledgeable about sexuality in older persons and often, as a result, highly restrictive and judgmental in their attitudes and rules about elderly sexuality. What are the sources of such repression of sexual fulfillment for the elderly? Certainly the lack of knowledge is a factor, but the negative reaction of health professionals may also be a manifestation of their own fears of aging, or simply, nonacceptance of their own sexuality.

Aging and Change

Even if our physical bodies did not age, the passage of time alone results in experiences, learning, and maturity that change who we are—our identity, values, attitudes, and goals. Some of these changes are obvious or abrupt, whereas others occur so gradually that we hardly realize what is happening until we look back much later. However, the physical aging process is not to be minimized, and the interaction of time and aging is incredibly powerful, causing tremendous alterations in people and their lives. This is particularly evident in emotional and sexual relationships.

The psychological and physiological impact of aging on sexuality and relationships is a particularly timely topic for a number of reasons. First, the most obvious reason is the "*Viagratization*" of America. Whether or not *Viagra* ultimately lives up to its initial promise to be the sexual salvation for aging men, its arrival into our culture has renewed attention in the topic of sexuality in older people. Sex in aging Americans was the cover story of most magazines and newspapers at some point in 1998.

Second is the fact that the baby boomers have arrived at middle age, a trend popularly termed "the graying of America." In the next two decades, approximately 40 million women will experience menopause. Women can now expect to live an average of 82 years, which means that women will now live one third of their lives postmenopausally.[1]

Third, the baby boomer generation has never been known for passively accepting models for living handed down from prior generations. It is already evident that the women of this generation are negotiating midlife and menopause in different ways from their mothers and grandmothers. Cultural stereotypes of the middle-aged woman as gray-haired, frail, and asexual have given way to images of strong, active, and sexual women. The image of the typical middle-aged woman is now career-oriented, successful, vibrant, and sexual.

Finally, most central to the topic, interest and research on postmenopausal sexuality have finally begun receiving the kind of attention that has resulted in better understanding and success in treating sexual problems. Postmenopausal sexuality cannot truly be understood by studying it in a vacuum. That is, one must understand the context of the relationship in which it occurs and the significant issues affecting a person's life.

Relationships

The stereotype of a relationship in midlife remains one of a long-term partnership (e.g., 20 years or more of marriage), although a person's age provides no reliable predictor of where he or she is in a relationship. Many women and men in midlife and beyond remain in a long-term marriage or relationship that began in their 20s. Others, however, are divorced or widowed by this time and may be alone, dating, or in a new longterm relationship, in second or even third marriages, raising a new family, or enjoying the relative tranquillity of an empty nest. Some care for grandchildren, and others care for aging parents who have moved in or are close by.

Each variant of a relationship as just delineated carries advantages and disadvantages for enhancing its quality. For those couples who have been together a long time, years of emotional intimacy, communication, and partnership often provide the foundation for the most satisfying of relationships.[2] However, the paradox exists that an increase in intimacy may not lead to an increase in sexual desire. The mystery, novelty, and risk that promote passion in new relationships are missing from these relationships.[3] In addition, couples in longer-term relationships may grow psychologically fused and dependent, resulting in a loss of desire for each other.

At the other extreme are couples who grow complacent and bored because they are too emotionally distant. They may take their emotional and sexual relationship for granted and become lazy and inattentive in their sexual activities. External factors, such as the needs of aging parents or grandchildren, may draw emotional energy away from a couple.

The need for an emotionally intimate connection is still strong no matter what age and, if not met within the primary relationship, can result in extrarelationship affairs that exacerbate the problems of poor communication, distance, and lack of intimacy. The healthiest relationship is one in which a couple is close but have autonomous and differentiated identities.[3] Even so, according to Levine,[2] the sexual developmental task of older couples is to "keep the pleasure going."

Couples who are in new relationships are more likely to put more energy into and have more interest in building a strong intimate relationship and can rely on the passion of a new relationship to keep sex exciting. However, those who are in new relationships with new children carry the same risk as younger couples with young children—no time, no privacy, and no energy. These couples need to work hard to reestablish the couple as separate from the family. The same is true for sandwich generation couples who are also caring for ailing elderly parents.

Thus, aging is not only a physical transition but a psychological one as well. As our bodies age, our mind and personality age and change too. For most of us, this equates to personal growth and maturation, and maturity provides a different set of priorities and goals. What one thought was critical in one's 20s may seem quite trivial in one's 50s. This change in perspective can have a tremendous impact on how we perceive our primary relationships and our needs and goals, both emotionally and sexually. Nowhere are these changes as apparent as in the approach to midlife career choices.

Regardless of where one is in a job/career/education, quality of life is improved by satisfaction with one's work, which enhances self-esteem and feelings of worth. Satisfaction is an individual perception. For example, some people consider intellectual stimulation to be a priority, some make financial success a priority, and others prefer improving the well-being of others. The same holds true for an avocation, particularly if one does not hold a paying job or does not find one's paying job to be satisfying.

Middle-aged women whose primary role was homemaker may need to consider looking for new challenges outside the home as their role within the home changes as children grow. In addition, a sense of identity is affected by where one is in the job cycle. Many middle-aged people may begin to feel the effects of aging in the form of age discrimination, which will have a powerfully negative effect on identity and self-esteem. Others approaching retirement may begin to feel old and useless while some are planning for next careers or ignoring the concept of retirement altogether.

The Impact of Aging on Sexuality

As the focus narrows to specifically address sexuality, it is important to review the most relevant concepts in the sexuality literature. First is the concept of sexual desire. Desire is a term that reflects the interaction of three separate but related components: drive, expectations/beliefs/values, and motivation.[4] Drive is the biological component of desire. It is the result of neuroendocrine mechanisms and is experienced as spontaneous, endogenous sexual interest. Drive is typically manifested by genital tingling, sexual thoughts or fantasies, increased erotic interest in others nearby, and seeking out sexual activity. Although we do not fully understand the exact neuroendocrine mechanisms that are responsible for drive, we do know that testosterone is necessary in both men and women. It is also known that drive declines in both men and women with age.[4] The second component of sexual desire is a cognitive component. This reflects a person's expectancies, beliefs, and values that affect interest toward or away from behaving sexually. The third component of desire is the psychological motivation, which is the emotional or interpersonal component and is characterized by the willingness (or lack of willingness) of a person to behave sexually with a given partner. This is the most complex and often the strongest component of desire.[4]

The second concept essential to the understanding of sexuality is the sexual equilibrium. According to Levine,[4] the sexual equilibrium is a balance of sexual capacities between two people and their perceptions of those capacities. The equilibrium is either comfortable or uncomfortable. The components involved in the equilibrium are the capacity for desire, arousal, and orgasm. Physical and psychological changes that occur as couples age can easily disturb their equilibrium and result in a variety of sexual problems.[4]

McCarthy,[5] citing the data from the Sex in America Survey,[6] considers nonsexual relationships to be a significant mental health problem. Using an arbitrary definition of nonsexual to mean a couple has sexual relations less than 10 times per year, McCarthy estimates that 20 percent of married couples and 40 percent of unmarried couples who have been together longer than 2 years meet this criterion.[5] Keep in mind, nonsexual relationships are only a problem and only reach the attention of mental health professionals and physicians when there is dissatisfaction with this in one or both partners, or sexual disequilibrium. Because it is so easy and common for any sexual relationship, regardless of age, to fade away, and fairly rapidly at that, given the psychological and physical factors that impact sexual functioning with aging, older couples are at even greater risk to become nonsexual. They must put considerable effort into keeping their sexual relationship alive and healthy despite the odds.

Body Image and Identity

Regardless of the nature of the relationship, it will be affected by the aging process. Women's sense of identity and sensuality change as it relates to their beliefs about aging. For example, age-related physiological alterations with resulting changes in body image may influence sexual interest. Women who perceive the physical signs of aging (e.g., graying hair, wrinkles) as unattractive will develop a poor body image, particularly if they associate these changes with loss of femininity.[7]

The corresponding loss of reproductive capacity at menopause may also negatively affect the body image and sexual identity of some women. This effect is noted even in younger women undergoing hysterectomies. They may believe that the loss of their uterus or their capacity to reproduce interferes with sexual activity and orgasm, exerting a subsequent negative impact on their sense of femininity. The result is often a significant decrease in sexual desire, as sexual activity requires some emphasis on the body, which is anxiety producing and depressing for these women. On the other hand, a hysterectomy may improve sexual desire and body image because of the resulting relief from pain, embarrassing and troubling heavy bleeding, and fear of pregnancy.[7] In the same way, many women find the effects of menopause liberating, as they are released from birth control worries and no longer have to deal with menstruation.

Our society's image of a menopausal woman is evolving into someone who is more youthful, energetic, and sexy. As a result, however, there is more pressure for women to continue to try to meet the impossible ideal of beauty that was foisted on them at puberty. Some women may feel the expectation to look 30 when they are 50 and become distressed when their bodies change despite all efforts to the contrary. Alternatively, middle-aged women who perceive the aging process as a positive reflection of their maturity and self-confidence may experience an enhancement in their sense of desirability and sexual desire.[8]

Male Sexual Dysfunction

The stereotype of the menopausal woman as asexual persists, although we know this to be a myth. In many older heterosexual couples who cease being sexual, it is the man whose interest declines usually because of his experiencing erectile dysfunction.[9] Erectile dysfunction is a major source of poor body image and resulting low desire for men. Ironically, changes in male sexual functioning with age have largely been ignored by the media until recently. With all the publicity surrounding Viagra, it has become more acceptable to discuss the subject of male erectile dysfunction. The Massachusetts Male Aging Study[10] reports that erectile dysfunction occurs in 57 percent of men aged 60 and 67 percent of men by the time they reach 70 years of age. It is, therefore, reasonable to hypothesize that a significant amount of abstinent postmenopausal women are so because of their male partner's erectile difficulties, or his decline in drive.

Prevention and Treatment of Sexual Dysfunction

Although erectile dysfunction is a major problem for older men, excellent treatment, both psychological and medical, is available. A problem to recognize is that now this causes another shift in the sexual equilibrium. For heterosexual couples, as women first adjusted to the sexual equilibrium of abstinence because of their partner's dysfunction, now they must once again accommodate to another change in equilibrium. This created a challenge. Not only do older people require a longer adjustment period to make the necessary accompanying cognitive shift, but older women definitely need time for their bodies to readjust to a partnered sexual life. Unfortunately, if the couple has not had intercourse for a long time, her aging vagina has likely narrowed and atrophied some and will not immediately accommodate a penis without risking pain or injury. This may lead to a secondary female sexual dysfunction of dyspareunia or vaginismus.

Postmenopausal women who have been sexually abstinent a long time must begin slowly by stretching and exercising their vaginas. They need to start by penetration with a finger or dilator and gradually stretch the vagina to accommodate a penis. They cannot return to sexual functioning instantaneously if sexual functioning for them has always meant intercourse. Water-based lubricants are extremely useful in providing much needed vaginal lubrication. In addition, estrogen replacement may help retard genital atrophy, and some of these women may now benefit from testosterone replacement. Some women may have experienced a hormone-related loss of some or all of their sexual drive postmenopausally, but given their nonsexual relationship because of their partners' erectile or desire problems, there was no need or interest in regaining drive. With their partners' renewed interest and ability, testosterone replacement may help recalibrate the sexual equilibrium by improving drive in these women.

Thus, older couples may need to redefine what normal sexual activity entails. Heterosexual couples may no longer rely on intercourse as their main sexual event. If a man has some erectile problems or a woman has some vaginal atrophy or dyspareunia or both are experiencing problems, intercourse may not be possible or may not be as enjoyable as other activities.

Physicians and mental health professionals can be extremely helpful in giving permission and encouraging older couples to change their sexual activities as well as providing simple education. For example, many couples are ignorant of the fact that despite erectile dysfunction, men are still able to experience desire, arousal and orgasm. Despite our sexually enlightened culture, many older couples still hold onto fairly restrictive and conservative views of what is appropriate and normal. It may be difficult, though very satisfying for older couples to move away from the standard missionary position and intercourse toward different positions and ways of stimulation (e.g. increased use of oral sex, manual stimulation, sexual aids, and sensual nongenital activities like bathing together, massage, or erotic movies/literature).

Change does not have to be extreme for couples to notice significant improvement in sexual fulfillment. It may imply something as simple (but often not considered), as making love in the morning when older people have more energy instead of late in the evening when there is a greater likelihood of fatigue. Furthermore, older couples need to learn to communicate better both in and out of the bedroom. As their sexual repertoire requires some adjustment or change, the couple needs to effec-tively communicate to accomplish this smoothly. In addition, communication itself can be seductive, enticing, and sexual. Effective communication in everyday life is also important for the quality of the overall relationship, which is also critical to the couple's sexual life, and vice versa.

Health Changes and the Impact on Sexuality and Relationships

Not only does the aging body experience problems with sexual functioning, but the likelihood of developing other health problems increases in older age, with a subsequent impact on relationships and sexuality. The equilibrium of the emotional component of a relationship also changes when one or both partners in a couple become ill or develop chronic health problems. One partner may end up as the nurse or full-time caregiver to the other. Even excluding the physical problems, the imbalance of these roles would likely result in sexual problems, with one or both partners losing desire.

One of the most significant health changes that occurs in older age is the fact that women typically outlive men by several years. Thus, the population of the oldest old heterosexual women will not have available male partners. The result may be that some women who would otherwise remain sexually active well into their 80s, 90s, and beyond are forced into abstinence because they have no access to partners. However, some women may continue sexual activity in the form of masturbation, some may find younger men, and still others may explore being sexual with other women.

Conclusions

Although many of us fear aging and anticipate a narrowing of physical abilities and range of enjoyable experiences, quality of life, particularly in the relationship and sexual domains, need not be diminished. Cognitive flexibility and adjusting to the changes that accompany age instead of fighting against the inevitable permit the likelihood of continued emotional and sexual satisfaction—if not enhancement. As we continue to understand the physiological and psychological changes that occur with age in women and men that affect their sexual functioning, we are developing increasingly effective and safe treatments, both medical and nonmedical, for these sexual problems.

References

1. Cope E. Physical changes associated with the menopause. In: Campbell S., ed. *The Management of the Menopausal Years*. Baltimore, MD: University Park Press, 1976: Chapter 4.

2. Levine S. Psychological intimacy. *J Sex Marital Ther* 1991;17:259.

3. Lobitz W.C., Lobitz G.K. Resolving the sexual intimacy paradox: A developmental model for the treatment of sexual desire disorders. *J Sex Marital Ther* 1996;22:71.

4. Levine S. *Sexual Life*. New York: Plenum Press, 1992.

5. McCarthy B. Strategies and techniques for revitalizing a nonsexual marriage. *J Sex Marital Ther* 1997;23:231.

6. Michael R.T., Gagnon J.K., Laumann F.O., Kolata G. *Sex in America*. Boston, MA: Little, Brown, 1994.

7. Leiblum S.R. The midlife and beyond. Presented at the 24th Annual Postgraduate Course of the American Fertility Society, Orlando, FL, October 1991.

8. Kingsberg S.A. Postmenopausal sexual functioning: A case study. *Int J Fertil Womens Med* 1998;43:122.

9. Laumann E.O., Paik A., Rosen R.C. Sexual dysfunction in the United States. *JAMA* 1999;281:537.

10. Feldman H.A., Goldstein I., Hatzichristou D.G., Krane R.J., McKinlay J.B. Impotence and its medical and psychosocial correlates: Results of the Massachusetts Male Aging Study. *J Urol* 1994;151:54

Chapter 20
Affection and Sexuality in the Presence of Alzheimer's Disease

Lore K. Wright

*Variations in sexual capacity and perfor-
mance among the elderly are greater than
among persons in the young or middle years.
Add to this already imbalanced equation the
disease of Alzheimer's and the scale of sexual
satisfaction is bound to tip. Or is it?*

*The interesting findings in the Wright
study will raise questions in the minds of the
readers of previous articles in this anthology.
For example, because men tend to underreport the frequency of sexual contact and
women to overreport it, why was this issue
not raised in interpreting the findings in this
study? Also, could the reported increase in
sexual desire for some be the result of Alzheimer's disease or could it perhaps be related to
medication? L-Dopa reportedly does enhance
sexual desire in Parkinson's disease patients.
In spite of limited sample size, this research
makes a significant contribution to a pressing problem about which we have very limited empirical data.*

Affection and sexual intimacy in adult relationships are physical expressions of affirmation and caring between two people.
It is generally accepted that in community
residing older adults, expression of affection increases with age (1,2), interest in sexuality remains high (3), but frequency of
sexual intercourse declines (3). These findings are mostly based on cross-sections
data; they were challenged to some extent
by George and Weiler (4), who found that
over a period of six years, sexual activity remained stable for three adult cohorts (ages
46–55, 56–65, and 66–71).

Various physical ailments are known to
adversely impact a couple's intimate relationship, and conditions such as cardiovascular disease, cancer, arthritis, diabetes, as
well as the adverse effects on sexuality from
medications, surgery, and radiation treatment have been researched extensively (5).
However, the presence of cognitive impairment and its impact on affection and sexuality have been the focus of only a few investigations. Yet it is cognitive ability,
perhaps more so than physical health,
which sustains the quality of affectional expressions between partners, and cognitive
ability is necessary to perform sexual activities in a manner which shows awareness of
the partner's feelings and needs (6).

Progressive loss of cognitive ability is the
cardinal feature of Alzheimer's disease
(AD), an illness that affects over four million Americans, typically after age 65. The
illness is characterized by initial forgetfulness which progresses to loss of independent social functioning, followed by
loss of physical abilities to a stage of total
dependence on a caregiver (7). This decline
typically occurs over the course of eight to
12 years.

Duffy (6) provided rich data on how Alzheimer's disease affects intimate relationships. Of husband and wife caregivers,
close to 80 percent perceived a change in
their emotional relationship to the AD
spouse, characterizing the relationship in
non-sexual terms as the illness progressed;
a similar percentage experienced a change
in sexual intimacy with a gradual decline in
interest most commonly reported (9).
Hypersexual interest displayed by a few
male afflicted spouses caused wife caregivers to have feelings ranging from mild ir-
ritation to strong aversion; male caregivers,
however, did not report such sentiments to
an afflicted wife's increased receptiveness

184

to sexual overtures (6). Wright (8) reported similar findings for sexual activities of AD couples, but, based on cross-sectional data, found that expression of affection was not significantly different for AD couples and healthy couples. Davies, Zeiss, and Tinklenberg (9) distinguished between sexual problems within the marital relationship and inappropriate sexual behavior in social situations. Their research showed that 53 percent of men reported erectile failure since the onset of AD symptoms, but inappropriate sexual behavior such as exposing or masturbation in public was rare (10). Taken together, these findings provide important insights into a sensitive topic, but fail to provide a long-range perspective of affection and sexuality which contrasts normal aging and illness.

THE CURRENT STUDY

The purpose of this study was to investigate longitudinal trends of marital intimacy in the presence of a dementing illness, AD, versus healthy aging. The study sought answers to the following questions: 1) Are affectional interactions different for AD couples compared to healthy couples, and do affectional interactions change over time? 2) Is sexual intimacy different for AD couples compared to healthy couples, and does it change over time? 3) Are affection and sexual expression related to the afflicted spouse's longitudinal outcome variables?

Method

The sample consisted of two groups of community-residing couples, an "AD group" and a comparison group or "well group" recruited from 10 agencies in two southeastern states. The AD group comprised 30 couples each: an AD afflicted spouse and the other spouse functioned as the primary caregiver. There were 24 male and 6 female afflicted spouses; all were in the early to middle phases of the illness. The comparison group comprised 17 couples without cognitive impairment in either spouse, but several spouses had com-

mon medical problems such as arthritis, hypertension, and heart disease. The two groups were similar in age, years of education, and monthly income. However, mean length of marriage was 38 years for the AD group and 45 years for the comparison group. The difference was due to greater numbers of second and third marriages in the AD group.

Affection was measured with the Dyadic Adjustment Rating Scale (11). In addition to the original item, "kissing the spouse," five new items were added; these were "touching the spouse lovingly," "caressing the spouse," "holding hands," "putting an arm around the spouse," and "sleeping in the same bed." Sexual intimacy data were based on two measures, frequency of and agreement over sexual intimacy. Frequency of current sexual intimacy per month was ascertained through direct questioning. Agreement over sexual expression was assessed with the Dyadic Adjustment Rating Scale (10) which questioned the degree to which spouses agreed over sexual relations.

Retrospective (time 1) data were conceptualized as the time prior to onset of memory problems in the AD spouse, and for the comparison group as the time prior to a spouse's retirement. These data were obtained from caregivers and well spouses. Concurrent (time 2) data were conceptualized as "now," i.e., thinking about the past few weeks. These data were obtained from all spouses including the afflicted, but spouses were interviewed in separate rooms. Follow-up (time 3) data were obtained from caregivers and well spouses two years after the home interview, with a response rate of 98 percent.

First, congruence between answers from each husband-wife dyad was tested. This showed that answers given by husbands-wives from both groups were very similar for frequency of affection. Answers for frequency and agreement over sexual relations were also nearly identical for husbands-wives of the well group. Answers from AD group couples differed significantly, with afflicted spouses reporting higher agreement than caregivers. In addition, approximately one-fourth of AD afflicted spouses reported more frequent sexual contacts per month than the respective caregiver spouse. Because answers from afflicted spouses were considered less reliable, comparisons between the AD and well groups were made as follows: Only caregiver spouses' answers were used to represent the AD group; to represent the comparison group, answers from only one spouse per well couple were used.

Results

Affection

Perception of past affection (time 1) was very similar for both groups of couples for the AD group and for the well group. At the time of the home interview (time 2), affectional of expression had declined significantly for the AD group, but differences between the AD and well group remained insignificant. Two years later (time 3), outcomes for afflicted spouses had to be considered. Only 43 percent of couples in the AD group still lived at home together, 27 percent of the afflicted spouses were in a nursing home, and 30 percent were deceased. Among well couples, only one spouse had died, and no spouse had been placed into a nursing home. Information on time 3 affection was obtained from all intact well couples and from AD caregivers who either continued to be in-home caregivers or had placed the spouse into a nursing home.

Past (time 1) affection was similar for continued in-home caregivers, nursing home placement caregivers, and well spouses, but was lower for caregivers whose spouses had died by time 3. At the time of the home interview (time 2), affection was rated markedly lower by those caregivers who subsequently became widowed and also by caregivers who subsequently placed the spouse into a nursing home. However, those who would continue in-home caregiving and the well spouses remained at similar levels of affection as observed for time 1. Another interesting effect can be noted for time 3 in that the nursing home placement caregivers increased significantly in their rating of affection, while well spouses and in-home caregivers remained fairly stable.

Sexual Intimacy

Only 27 percent of AD couples were sexually active at time 2 (about 5 years after the onset of AD) in contrast to 82 percent of well couples. Mean sexual contacts per month were 8.0 for AD couples and 3.8 for well couples. Range of sexual contacts was 1 to 14 (or more) times per month for AD couples and <1 to 10 times per month for well couples.

Demand for frequent sexual contacts by AD spouses was reported by 14 percent of caregivers when the entire group was counted, but this translated to 50 percent when only the still sexually active couples were considered. Caregivers' reaction to hypersexuality ranged from acceptance to strong aversion. Of the intact AD couples, only 19 percent were reported to be still sexually active. Mean number of sexual contacts at time 3 was 3.75 per month for the AD group. Among intact well couples, 62.5 percent were still sexually active. Their mean number of sexual contacts per month was 5.2. The difference between the two groups was not significant.

An intriguing question is whether sexual activity at time 2 is related to outcomes of afflicted spouses at time 3, i.e., still at home, nursing home, or deceased. Of the 73 percent AD couples who had not been sexually active at time 2, only 32 percent still lived together at time 3, and nursing home placement and death had resulted at similar frequencies. However, of the 27 percent AD couples who were sexually active at time 2, 75 percent were still living together at home two years later (time 3).

For AD couples, about five years into the illness (time 2), sexual activity was significantly related to the caregivers' better physical health and lower depressed moods but not to the afflicted spouses' mental status. There were no significant relationships between these variables and AD couples' sexual activity two years later (time 3). For well couples, sexual activity at time 2 was significantly related to better physical health and being younger. At time 3, only better physical health was related to sexual activity.

In addition to frequency of sexual intimacy, agreement over sexual relations was evaluated longitudinally. There was no significant difference between the groups' past perception of agreement. By time 2, the home interview, caregivers rated agreement over sexual issues lower than well spouses but this difference was not statistically significant. Taking outcomes for afflicted spouses into consideration, agreement for the still at home and the nursing home placement groups bounced back from a lower level at time 2 to similar levels as those reported by well spouses at time 3.

Discussion

This study began by asking whether, compared to normal aging, affection and sexual intimacy are different and change over time when a spouse has AD. The data support that yes, the illness leads to differences between the two groups of couples, and there is change over time.

The fact that ratings of past affection and past agreement over sexual relations were very similar for the two groups lends support to the validity of the findings, despite the limitations inherent in generalizing from a small sample size. Most likely these couples were not different in their affectionate and sexual relationships when all were well, but it was illness, i.e., AD, which brought about significant changes: affection declined significantly, fewer AD than well couples were sexually active (27 percent versus 82 percent), and frequency of sex per month was significantly higher for the AD group (Mean of 8.0 versus 3.8). Poor physical health and depression in caregivers was related to less frequent sexual contacts. This supports findings from other studies documenting that physical and emotional health of both partners influence the sexual relationship (4).

Approximately five years after the onset of AD, demands for frequent sexual contacts occurred by a small percentage of AD afflicted spouses, and their behavior was distressing to caregiver spouses. However, two years later, which amounts to seven years since the onset of AD, this higher frequency of sexual relations had declined for all but one couple. Agreement over sexual relations was rated lowest by caregiver spouses at time 2, but was again similar to that reported by the well group at time 3, when for the AD group the problem had abated for all but one couple.

When examining the pattern for well group couples, affection shows stability over time. The stable pattern of affection could be attributed to the relatively short time frame examined (seven years in total) and to the measure of affection used in this study. Behavioral indicators such as kissing, caressing, and putting an arm around the spouse do not necessarily capture the emotional bond between spouses. Feelings of trust, being comfortable with each other, and helping each other are other indicators of affection which may increase with age, and which could be assessed in future studies.

The percent of well couples who remained sexually active did decline over time (from 82 percent to 62.5 percent). This is consistent with most other studies (3,5), and is further supported by the negative correlation between age and frequency of sex per month found in this study for time 2 and also by the positive correlation with physical health and frequency of sexual intimacy at time 2 and time 3. But in addition to an overall decline, some stability over time was found which is consistent with findings by George and Weiler (4). In this study, several well couples with high sexual activity at time 2 remained high, i.e., actually reported an increase at time 3.

Intriguing are the findings for affection and sexual relations when outcomes of still being together at home, the afflicted spouse having been placed into a nursing home, or the afflicted spouse having died are taken into consideration. Normal aging is clearly different compared to the life of couples with AD. Despite the fact that well group couples had a variety of physical illnesses such as heart disease, arthritis, and hypertension, only one spouse had died over a two-year period, and no spouse had been institutionalized. Yet in the AD group, 30 percent of afflicted spouses had died, and 27 percent were in a nursing home. From a human developmental perspective, this loss demonstrates what Riegel (12) termed pathological deviations from normal development or the "catastrophic" impact of disease for over half of the couples. AD robbed 30 percent of couples of any further interactions and, one would anticipate, severely limited interactions for another 27 percent of couples due to the nursing home placement of the afflicted spouse.

It should be remembered that at the time of home interview (time 2), neither caregivers nor the researcher knew what the outcomes would be at time 3, and the reports of affection given at time 2 can be considered genuine reflections of spousal interactions at that time. Affection was rated significantly lower by those caregivers who subsequently became widowed and by those who subsequently placed the spouse into a nursing home. So the question arises whether caregivers had "given up" on the ill spouses, and whether this lack of interaction between spouses contributed to the afflicted spouses' death or their institutionalization.

It is, therefore, surprising to see that frequency of affection increased dramatically at time 3 for the nursing home placement group. Possibly, the stress of in-home caregiving had been alleviated, and positive feelings for the ill spouse could re-emerge. King et al. (13) have reported that spouses visit the nursing home almost daily and want to be involved in the care of their mate. The increase in affection after nursing home placement noted in this study may reflect this. Caregivers may indeed be re-experiencing positive feelings toward their mate, intertwined perhaps with some feelings of guilt for earlier inattention. Another interesting observation is that a much higher percentage of afflicted spouses who were sexually active at time 2 had remained at home by time 3. But the numbers on which these percentages are based are too small to speculate on their meaning.

Findings from this longitudinal study have several implications. The middle phase of AD seems to be the most problematic for sexual intimacy. Health professionals need to ask about the sensitive issue of sexual relations when interacting with caregivers and afflicted spouses. The use of prescription tranquilizers is debatable, but caregivers can be supported in their need to limit sexual relations. Distraction techniques and environmental manipulation (e.g., separate bedrooms) can be taught.

A professional who observes affectional gestures by a caregiver can provide positive reinforcement by commenting that such expressions are likely to contribute to the afflicted spouses' comfort. But professionals should not use findings from this study as a "threat" by telling caregivers that absence of affection may contribute to nursing home placement or early death.

Nursing home staff need to be especially sensitive to the needs of spouses who have relinquished the caregiver role. Visiting the afflicted spouse, kissing, hugging, and caressing are expressions of the bond between two people, no matter how difficult the years prior to nursing home placement may have been. When memory has been lost, expressions of affection are all that is left to form a bridge to the past. Connecting to that past in a positive way may be important for the caregiver's continued and future development.

References

1. Reedy M.N., Birren J.E., Schaie K.W.: Age and sex differences in satisfying love relationships across the adult life span. In *Readings in Adult Development and Aging*, K. Schaie, J. Geiwitz (eds). Boston, Little, Brown and Company, 1982, pp 158–160.

2. Wright L.K.: *Alzheimer's Disease and Marriage*. Newbury Park, Sage, 1993.

3. Brecher E.M.: *Love, Sex, and Aging*. Boston, Little, Brown and Company, 1984.

4. George L.K., Weiler S.J.: Sexuality in middle and late life. *Arch Gen Psychiatry*, 38:919–923, 1981.

5. Wright L.K.: Sexual dysfunction in the elderly. Forthcoming in Meridean L. Mass (ed.), *Nursing Diagnoses and Interventions*

for the Elderly (second edition). Newbury Park, Sage.

6. Duffy L.M.: Sexual behavior and marital intimacy in Alzheimer's couples: A family theory perspective. *Sexuality & Disability,* 13(3):239–254, 1995.

7. Reisberg B.: Dementia: A systematic approach to identifying reversible causes. *Geriatrics,* 41(4):30–46, 1986.

8. Wright L.K.: The impact of Alzheimer's disease on the marital relationship. *Gerontologist,* 31(2):224–237, 1991.

9. Davies H.D., Zeiss A., and Tinklenberg J.R.: 'Til death do us part: Intimacy and sexuality in the marriages of Alzheimer's patients. *Journal of Psychosocial Nursing,* 30(11):5–10, 1992.

10. Zeiss A.M., Davies H.D., Wood M., Tinklenberg J.R.: The incidence and correlates of erectile problems in patients with Alzheimer's disease. *Archives of Sexual Behavior,* 19(4):325–331, 1990.

11. Spanier G.B. and Thompson L.: A confirmatory analysis of the Dyad Adjustment Scale. *Journal Marriage and the Family,* 38:731–741, 1982.

12. Riegal, K.F.: Foundation of dialectal psychology. New York, Academic Press, 1979.

13. King S., Collins C., Given B., and Vredevoogd J.: Institutionalization of an elderly family member: Reactions of spouse and nonspouse caregivers. *Archives of Psychiatric Nursing,* 5(6):323–330, 1991.

Part V

Physiology, Sexual Desire, and Sexual Response

Although American society has always had a great fascination with sexuality, this has long been a conversational taboo, especially in mixed-sex groups. However, the flurry of media attention around the Clinton-Lewinsky scandal bestowed a certain legitimacy upon this controversial topic. In fact, sex became the subject of dinner-table conversation for many American families faced with answering questions from their young children about the news of the day. The debacle even sent sexologists and sex therapists scrambling to justify or denigrate newly suggested definitions of "sexual relations" that would exclude oral sex. One of the inescapable questions after reading the Lapham article, which explores sex, Americans, scandal, and morality, is, "How much have things really changed since the early twentieth century"? If Will and Ariel Durant accurately assessed the garden of tabloid delight of their own day in the opening quote for this selection, the answer is, "Not much."

During the human life cycle, as puberty progresses and sex hormones flood the body, the biological basis of an individual's sex-role development becomes more focused on issues of sexuality, and the self as well as others are increasingly viewed as sexual beings. At this time, heterosexual relationships become the focus for most ado-

lescents as they make personal decisions about the use of sexuality by choosing from the range of possible expressions: masturbation, petting, and sexual intercourse. Although masturbation is the most common type of sexual activity for teenagers, it is still considered by some societal members to be harmful, sinful, or mentally unhealthy. However, it is increasingly viewed by professionals, such as sexologists and sex therapists, as rehearsal for mature sexual involvement. They contend that just as adolescents are constantly testing their bodies in sports or other activities, they also need to find out how their bodies perform sexually. Self-stimulation is viewed as a safe way to accomplish this goal because it does not involve another person. Davidson and Moore provide an empirical view of masturbation as reflected in the sexual attitudes and behaviors of college women that suggest that older is not necessarily wiser when it comes to a subject that is still suspect among many American adults.

The Wiederman replication of the earlier Darling and Davidson (1986) study about women pretending orgasm during sexual intercourse is a topic that apparently remains fascinating to college women who are sexually active, because more than one-half of them do "pretend." But questions about this practice abound. Is this subterfuge because women fall prey to their partners asking, "Did you come"? Or, is it in response to the myths espoused in some women's magazines declaring that all able-bodied women should experience an orgasm 100 percent of the time? Seemingly, neither the earlier study a decade ago, using post-college-age women, nor the present one using college women discovered the answers to these difficult "why" questions. Although a major reason given by married women for pretending orgasm is "to get it over with," one would assume that this reason would not be as applicable to unmarried college women. Or would it? A perusal of the Wiederman study may prove this and other commonly held assumptions to be terminally flawed. Speculations aside, this selection will provoke a lively exchange among students.

In Regan's review of rhythms of female sexual desire, the focus is on the female sex hormones and on hormonally mediated life events. In summarizing the empirical research, the relationship between the menstrual cycle and sexual desire is specifically explored. An intriguing question that goes unanswered is the degree to which physiological sexual desire in women is influenced by psychological factors and cultural norms. For example, does abstinence from sexual activity during the menstrual period for cultural reasons result in an increase in sexual desire in the days immediately following the conclusion of menses? Or, is the elevation of desire a result of the rising levels of estrogen? A major contribution of this selection is the lucid explanation offered of the various methods for determining cycle phases and the confusion in the research caused by the lack of agreement about the appropriate labels given to each menstrual phase. Although focusing primarily on biological factors, interesting psychological and sociological questions are posed.

When levels of sexual satisfaction and sexual drive in women with spinal cord (SCI) injuries, were examined by Black, Sipski, and Strauss, an important step was made for SCI women. Especially so because their study was the first to compare the sexual functioning of SCI women with those who are able-bodied. However, the fact that all of the subjects were members of the National Spinal Cord Injury Association, with a membership of only 346 women, can raise questions concerning the representativeness of the sample. Such women are assumed to be much more educated about the impact of spinal cord injury on sexuality. Also problematic, the procedure for selecting the comparison group was not random. In spite of these methodological issues, the research does furnish a glimpse into a neglected area of sexuality.

Reference

Darling, C. A., & Davidson, J. K., Sr. (1986). Enhancing relationships: Understanding the feminine mystique of pretending orgasm. *Journal of Sex & Marital Therapy, 12,* 182–196. ✦

Chapter 21
In the Garden of Tabloid Delight: Notes on Sex, Americans, Scandal, and Morality

Lewis H. Lapham

Master of metaphor, Lapham attains the very essence of "tabloid delight" with musings from his notes on sex, Americans, scandal, and morality—an irony that is hopefully not lost on the reader. Although the litany of sexual scandals in the summer of 1997 fostered both pious "op-ed page sermonettes" and "ribald commentary" in the media, most Americans barely acknowledged the blip on their screens of conscience. The flash of media attention did, however, legitimize talking about sexuality in a society that has always had a great fascination with sex but a conversational taboo against it.

The fact that a commercial presentation of sexuality as a commodity allows consumers to select from a smorgasbord of options seems to offer the best in the world of choice and exchange. Nevertheless, Lapham believes the resulting contradictions lead to confusion about what is moral and what is virtue, existential questions for which there are no societally-sanctioned answers. The author raises issues that are germane not only for a mooringless society, but also for individuals who operate without the strength of a moral order, risking their chance for love or meaning in life. Citing the failure of the nation's moral guidebook to adapt to political, eco-
nomic, social, and technological changes of the last century, Lapham urges a reassessment of both our sexual behavior and the rules by which we play.

> *Caught in the relaxing interval between one moral code and the next, an unmoored generation surrenders itself to luxury, corruption, and a restless disorder of family and morals.*

> —Will and Ariel Durant

The news media in May of 1997 bloomed with so exuberant a profusion of sexual scandal that by the first week of summer it was hard to tell the difference between the front-page political reporting and the classified advertising placed by men seeking women and women seeking men. Every day for thirty days some sort of new or rare flowering appeared in the garden of tabloid delight, prompting the headline writers to dance joyously around the maypoles of 72-point type, singing their songs of spring with lyrics supplied by a grand jury or the police. Some of the stories were better than others, and although not all of them resulted in invitations to talk to Oprah, even a brief summary of the leading attractions fairly describes the gifts of the season's abundance.

May 2—Eddie Murphy, noted comedian and screen actor, found by sheriff's deputies, at 4:45 a.m. on Santa Monica Boulevard in West Hollywood, in the company of a transvestite prostitute.

May 10—Congressman Joseph P. Kennedy declines to explain how it came to pass that his younger brother Michael, thirty-nine, embarked upon a love affair with the fourteen-year-old girl employed as the baby-sitter to his infant son.

May 22—Frank Gifford, a famous television sportscaster, reported to have been photographed in a New York hotel room, parading around on a bed with a woman not his wife.

May 22—Lieutenant Kelly Flinn, "the perfect picture girl" of the United States Air Force and the first woman to command a B-52 bomber, drummed out of the service for committing adultery with a civilian soccer coach.

May 27—The Supreme Court directs the President of the United States to answer questions about the administration of his penis, all nine justices concurring in the opinion that the discussion cannot be postponed for reasons of state.

May 30—Staff Sergeant Vernell Robinson Jr. expelled from the United States Army and sentenced to six months in prison for forcing sodomy on five female recruits.

June 1—Robert S. Bennett, the Washington lawyer defending President Clinton against the charges brought by Paula Corbin Jones (attempted sodomy, violation of civil rights), informs two television networks that he intends to entertain the court with tales of the plaintiff's lurid past.

June 2—Major General John E. Longhouser announces his retirement from the Army and resigns his command of the Aberdeen Proving Ground (the scene of the crimes committed by Sergeant Robinson) because an anonymous tipster telephoned headquarters to report that five years ago, while briefly separated from his wife, the general had formed a liaison with a female civilian.

June 3—Concerned Women for America characterizes Lawyer Bennett's legal tactics as those "normally used by a rapist's attorney" and reminds him that two years ago President Clinton signed a law excusing sexually abused women from questions about their prior conduct.

June 4 (late morning)—Lawyer Bennett disavows his proposed line of questioning. "I'm not a fool. It's my intention to take the high ground. . . . Her sex life is of no particular concern to me."

June 4 (early afternoon)—Secretary of Defense William S. Cohen recommends the appointment of Air Force General Joseph Ralston as the next Chairman of the Joint Chiefs of Staff, despite the General's confession that fourteen years ago (while separated from his wife) he carried on a love affair with a woman in the CIA. Secretary Cohen says that the time has come "to draw a line" against "the frenzy" of allegations spreading panic among military officers in all grades and ranks: "We need to come back to a rule of reason instead of a rule of thumb."

June 6—The major news media, allied with indignant voices in both Houses of Congress, overrule Secretary Cohen's call for reason. If bomber pilot Flinn must wear the scarlet letter, how then does fighter pilot Ralston escape the same marking?

June 7—Congressman Kennedy informs 2,000 cheering delegates to the Democratic State Convention in Salem, Massachusetts, that he is "so very sorry, so very, very sorry" for any damage that his brother might have done to the baby-sitter or the baby-sitter's family.

June 9—General Ralston withdraws his name from consideration as Chairman of the Joint Chiefs of Staff.

The news offered so many occasions for pious or ribald commentary that any chance of agreement about what any of it meant was lost in a vast din of clucking and sniggering. The upscale newspapers published prim, op-ed-page sermonettes (about the country misplacing the hope chest filled with old family values); downmarket talk-radio hosts told prurient jokes (about Paula's mouth, or Marv's toupee, or Bill's mole); the television anchorpersons were merely happy to be told that a lot of important people (many of them grownups and some of them celebrities) had been seen loitering (well past their bedtimes) on Love Street.

Although a few of the country's more high-minded commentators attempted professions of shock and alarm, the sentiments didn't draw much of a crowd. Most Americans know by now that the country's moral guidebooks (government-inspected, church-approved) fail to account for the political, economic, social, and technological changes that over the last 100 years have reconfigured not only the relation between the sexes but also the Christian definitions of right and wrong. The old guidebooks were written for nineteenth-century travelers apt to fall afoul of Satan in a San Francisco bordello, and either they require extensive revision or we need to adjust our present behavior. For the time being, the words don't match the deeds, and the ensuing confusion inflates the currencies of scandal. But because not enough people can agree to common terms of discourse, whether to begin with A for Abortion or with C for Clone, whether to proceed with reference to the Bible or to the Kinsey Report, we avoid the arguments by classifying human sexuality as a consumer product—a commodity, like cereal or furniture polish, packaged under as many brands and in as many forms (powdered or freeze-dried) as can be crowded onto the shelves in the supermarkets of desire. The commercial presentations allow us to have it both ways from the end and all ways from the middle—to meet the demand for hard-line feminist theory and the *Victoria's Secret* catalogue, for Robert Bork's sermons and Tony Kushner's plays, for breast or penile implants and software programs blocking out displays of nudity on the Internet, for as many different kinds of marriage (homosexual, heterosexual, open, closed, Christian, pagan, alternative, frankly perverse) as can meet with the approval of a landlord. The contradictions show up in every quarter of the society—posted on billboards and flashing on neon signs, available twenty-four hours a day on both the Playboy and the Disney channels, in the fashion photographs selling Donna Karan's dresses and Giorgio Armani's suits, in David Letterman's jokes and Senator Strom Thurmond's speeches, in the mirrors behind a hotel bar or on the walls of a health club, in the leaflets and lectures distributed (sometimes with condoms) to grammar school students, in newspaper ads hawking big-city prostitutes with the same adjectives that greengrocers assign to the grapefruit and the plums.

As might be expected of people engulfed in a haze of quasi-pornographic images, the subsequent confusion raises questions to which nobody has any good answers but which in the meantime provide the topics for the best-selling books of ethical self-help. What is moral, and where is virtue? Who is a man and who is a woman, and how do I know the difference? Is marriage forever, or is it another one of those institutions (like the churches and the schools) wrecked on the reefs of progress? Do the doors of the future open only to people who observe the rules and watch their diets, or must we, as true Americans and therefore rebellious at birth, knock down the walls of social convention? Suppose for a moment that we wish to obey the rules: What do they mean and where are they written?

During the daylight hours such questions take the form of political disputes—about a woman's due or a man's debt, about the reasons why a gay and lesbian alliance is marching in Beverly Hills, about the academic poetess who didn't receive tenure, or the diaspora of Real American Men (hard-drinking and unshaven) tracking the spoor of William Faulkner's bear in a Mississippi forest. Like CNN or Batman, the questions never sleep, and late at night they turn inward and existential—am I inside the television set with Marv and Paula and Kathie Lee, or am I out here in the middle of nowhere with the wrong nail polish and last season's beer? Is the search for the perfect orgasm like the search for the perfect apartment—always lost and never found? If I highlight my hair and redistribute the weight of my stomach, will I live happily ever after in the land of Calvin Klein?

Maybe the questions need never be answered, but when and if we get around to doing so, we at least should admit that the events of the last fifty years can't be ignored or reversed. It's no good demanding (as do quite a few of our prophets on the Christian and neoconservative right) that the changes be sent back for credit to Bloomingdale's or L. L. Bean, or that somehow it still might be possible to bring back the summer of 1947. Most of the changes probably have been for the better rather than the worse. It's true that freedom doesn't come without its costs, but how many people willingly would return to a society that insisted upon the rigid suppressions of human sexuality dictated by a frightened aunt or a village scold? In 1947 a Hollywood movie couldn't be released to the public without the prior consent of the Hayes office, a bureau of censors loyal to the rules of decorum in effect at a New England school for girls. Husbands and wives couldn't be seen occupying the same bed, and children were brought into the world by storks. Under the threat of boycott by the Catholic Archdiocese of New York, Leo Durocher, the manager of the Brooklyn Dodgers, was suspended from the team during the 1947 season because he was conducting a love affair with Laraine Day, an actress to whom he was not married. The booksellers in Boston banned the sale of novels found guilty of sentences that described either the hero or heroine in states of wanton undress. Young men at college in 1947 hadn't been introduced to television, much less to Robert Mapplethorpe or Helmut Newton; genetics was a subject that had to do mostly with mice, a woman's place was in the home, and sex was something that happened in France.

Looking back on the transformations that have occurred within the span of my own lifetime, I remember that during the decade of the 1960s, in the early stages of what later became known as the sexual revolution, the photographs in Hugh Hefner's *Playboy* magazine opened a window in what I suddenly saw as a prison wall made of sermons in Protestant stone. I lose track of chronological sequence, but the rules seemed to change every year with the new fall clothes—first the forwardness of young women relieved of their inhibitions by the birth control pill, then the grievances (some of them surprising, most of them just) revealed in the commotion of the feminist movement, eventually the enlarged and public assertions of the gay and lesbian points of view, lastly the news that women no longer require men to perform the functions of husband and father. These days a woman of almost any age can choose to bear and raise a child under circumstances matched to her own history and understanding of the world—with a husband, with a man not her husband, from a zygote supplied by a sperm bank, by a fertilized egg borrowed from her daughter or mother, by adoption with a gay man, by adoption with a lesbian companion, by adoption with herself as the sole parent.

Nor have the changes been confined to what Pat Robertson likes to imagine as the red-light districts of Los Angeles and New York, as if the appetite for sexual fantasy presupposed a jaded, metropolitan taste. When the news of adultery usurped the headlines in late May, the *New York Times* dispatched a reporter to search the country for pockets of Christian rebuke. Generals were falling like ninepins into the gutters of lust, and the editors assumed that west of the Hudson somebody cared. The reporter, Carey Goldberg, returned with the news that not many did. A woman in Greenville, South Carolina, speaking on behalf of a clear majority, observed that although adultery wasn't legal in her state, "In this day and time, it's going on everywhere, and I mean everywhere." Were the authorities to enforce the law, she said, "everybody'd be in jail."

Among the guests who entertain Ricki Lake's afternoon television audiences with tales of their cross-dressing and cosmetic surgery, most of the people onstage come from places like Des Moines, Iowa, or Grand Rapids, Michigan. To meet the demand of the nation's video stores (most of them located in suburban shopping malls) the pornographic film industry last year provided 7,852 new releases (as opposed to the 471 supplied by Hollywood), and under the tolerant auspices of the World Wide Web, any child of nine sitting at a computer in Medford, Oregon, or Opa-Locka, Florida, can explore the landscape of sexual deviance first mapped by the Marquis de Sade.

About the perils of the voyage to paradise, the old moral guidebooks were not wrong. What at first glance looks like a ticket to the islands of bliss often proves more nearly to resemble a reserved seat in one of the eight dress circles of Dante's *Inferno*. I think of the numbers of people I've known over the last twenty or thirty years who sacrificed themselves on the altars of the imaginary self—marooned in a desolate marriage, so paralyzed by so many sexual options that nothing ever came of their talent and ambition, dead of AIDS at the age of thirty-one. The glittering invitations to everlasting orgy that decorate the drugstores and the movie screens are meant to be understood not as representations of reality but as symbols and allegories. Any customer so foolish as to mistake the commercial intent has failed to read properly the instructions on the label. One is supposed to look, not touch; to abandon oneself to one's desire not in a cocktail lounge but in a nearby mall.

The credit-card statements don't show the arithmetic of human suffering and unhappiness. It might well be true that if South Carolina enforced the laws against adultery, everybody would be in jail, but it is also true that sexual promiscuity and infidelity cause more misery (for the featured players as well as for the children in the supporting cast) than ever gets explained in the program notes. Over the years I've listened to a good many stories of bewilderment and loss, but none sadder than the one that appeared in the New York tabloids on June 9 about the eighteen-year-old girl, a student at the Lacey Township School in Ocean County, New Jersey, to whom a son was born at her graduation prom. During a break in the music, she left the ballroom, gave birth to the baby in a bathroom stall, wrapped it in paper towels, discarded it in a wastebasket, washed her hands, smoothed her evening dress, and returned for the next dance. From the perspective of the consumer market, the girl's actions make perfect sense. Sex is merchandising, and the product of desire, like Kleenex, is disposable. In the garden of tabloid delight, there is always a clean towel and another song.[1]

Like the high-speed computers that collate restaurant checks with telephone bills and drugstore receipts, the market can't tell the difference between adultery and a program of aerobic exercise; it doesn't know or care who said what to whom or whether the whip was meant to be used on a horse from Kentucky or a gentleman from Toledo.

Human beings who tailor themselves to the measures of the market float like numbers across the surface of the computer screen. Without the strength and frame of a moral order—some code or rule or custom that provides them with a way and a place to stand against the flood of their own incoherent desire—they too often lose the chance for love or meaning in their lives, unable or unwilling to locate the character of their own minds or build the shelters of their own happiness.

The loss of identity is good for business. The conditions of weightlessness not only set up the demand for ballast—heavier gold jewelry, more golf clubs, bigger cigars—but also encourage the free exchange of sexual identities, which, like the liquidity of cash, preserves the illusion of infinite options and holds out the ceaselessly renewable prospect of buying into a better deal. The pilgrims in search of a more attractive or plausible face can try on the 1,001 masks to which Freud gave the name of polymorphous perverse and to which the trendier fashion designers now affix the labels of androgynous chic. The structures of gender present themselves as so much troublesome baggage impeding the migration into F. Scott Fitzgerald's "orgiastic future." Let human sexuality be understood as a substance as pliable as modeling clay, and maybe it becomes an asset, easily worked into the shape of a stock-market deal, a music video, a celebrity crime.

Transferred to what was once known as the public square, the descent into narcissism makes of politics a trivial pursuit. A society adjusted to the specifications of the tabloid press draws no invidious distinctions between the foreign and domestic policies of the President's penis and the threat of nuclear annihilation. Both stories guarantee record sales at the newsstands. On the day after the Supreme Court certified Paula's complaint about Bill (which also happened to be the day on which Boris Yeltsin announced at the NATO conference in Paris that Russia no longer would target its missiles on New York and Washington) the newspapers assigned the bigger headlines to the targeting error that either did or did not take place six years ago in an upstairs room of the Excelsior Hotel in Little Rock, Arkansas.

The distribution of news value should have come as no surprise. The voters last November saw in Clinton's narcissism a reflection of their own self-preoccupations, and although well aware of his appetites for hard women and soft money, they were happy to send him to Washington as a representative of their collective moral confusion—a man no better than the other men that one was likely to meet at a sales conference or in a topless bar, always smiling and polite but in it for the money, in his own way as much of a hustler as Paula, as lost as most everybody else in the maze of amorphous sexuality. One day he appears in his masculine character (speaking sternly to the Serbs or the Albanians, making the strong, decisive, executive movements expected of a successful American businessman); the next day he shows up smiling like a debutante, pouring sentiment and sympathy into the teacups of the White House press corps, bravely holding back the tears that he otherwise would shed for a flood victim, a welfare mother, or a sick dog. Who but the old fools at the Pentagon could expect such a man to keep his penis in his pants or his fingers out of the Boston cream pie? The poor fellow is always so desperately needy, so insatiably eager for approval and affection, that it's a wonder he hasn't yet sold the Lincoln Memorial to a Korean amusement park.

A President so obviously unable or unwilling to tell the difference between right and wrong (much less, God forbid, to stand on or for anything other than the platform of his own need) clearly cannot ask anybody to grow up. He presents a role model not unlike that of Peter Pan (albeit an increasingly stout Peter Pan) and so excuses the rest of the class from the tedium of moral homework. With such a President, why bother to aspire to an adult code of ethics? We need not seek our own best selves, and in the meantime we inoculate ourselves against the viruses of age and idealism, which, as the advertising agencies well know depress sales and sour the feasts of consumption.

Sex in the United States is no laughing matter, and although the commercial synthetics tend to leech the life out of the enterprise—the chance of meaning and the hope of intimacy as well as humor and eroticism—I take it for granted that the promises of eternal youth and everlasting orgy will continue to be more widely available and more innovatively sold. I'm glad that I'm not twenty years old, my name, address, and DNA stored in a data bank available to any mail-order operation. I expect that it probably would take me another twenty years to solve the riddle of my own identity, which is, of course, the point. If I knew who I was, why would I keep buying new brands of aftershave lotion, and how then would I add to the sum of the gross domestic product?

Given the sophistication of our current marketing techniques and the boundless resource of human curiosity and desire, the media undoubtedly will continue to post their scarlet letters and deliver their bouquets of scandal. The demand for gaudier sensations, for more telephone sex and brighter lip gloss, presumably will foster competing markets in small-time puritanism. Absent a unified field of moral law that commands a sufficiently large number of people to obedience and belief, with what else do we fill in the blanks except a lot of little rules—rules about how to address persons of differing colors or sexual orientation, about when to wear fur and when not to eat grapes, about what to read or where to smoke?

Although I can imagine books of rules as extensive as encyclopedias, I can't imagine them quieting the rage of the market. If I can lust after the girls on 300 pornographic cable channels, why can't I order one from a shopping network? If the editors of the *Globe* can pay an airline stewardess $75,000 to pose with Frank Gifford for the video camera in the Regency Hotel, what will they bid for the sight of a fireman in bed with Barbara Walters?

For the time being, and not yet having discovered a system of moral value that corresponds to the workings of big-time, postindustrial capitalism, where else can we live except in the garden of tabloid delight with Marv and Bill and Paula and Batman? Unless we wish to say that what is moral is what an insurance company will pay for (which, in our present circumstances, comes fairly close to the truth), what other arrangement meets the presumption—accepted as revered truth on both the liberal and conservative sides of the bed—that ethics and politics constitute increasingly marginal subsections of economics? If the lights must never go out and the music must always play, how do we even begin to talk about the discovery or construction of such a thing as a new moral order? Who has time for so slow a conversation? Who could hear what was being said?

Note

1. Babies dropped into garbage cans sometimes survive, but the one who died at the prom reminded me of another newspaper story I had read several weeks earlier about the Lacey Township School. The administrators apparently were worried about rumors of sexual malfeasance on the part of faculty or staff, and so they had ordered all adult personnel to approach the students with extreme caution. No touching, no hugs, no possibly suspicious pats on the shoulder, and when face to face with a student at a distance of less than three feet, the teachers and custodians were to raise both arms above their heads in a gesture of surrender. Both incidents (the one brutal, the other absurd) exemplify the character of what Will and Ariel Durant described as an "unmoored generation" drifting between one moral order and the next.

Chapter 22
Masturbation and Premarital Sexual Intercourse: Choices for Sexual Fulfillment

J. Kenneth Davidson, Sr.
Nelwyn B. Moore

In spite of former dire predictions that self-stimulation would result in numerous maladies, gynecologists, urologists, and sex therapists today agree that masturbation can provide a harmless outlet for sexual needs, especially among persons who lack other means of sexual expression. As this selection addresses the topic of masturbation and college women, it becomes apparent that, though times have changed considerably in our modern world, the subject is still taboo. This archaic position was noted in 1994 when President Clinton called for the resignation of Surgeon-General Joycelyn Elders following a furor over her using the "M" word publicly when referring to masturbation as a needed component in public-school sexuality education curricula.

But the research reported here about one aspect of sexuality does more than just reveal the sexual attitudes and behaviors of today's college women. It portends the sexual attitudes and behaviors of generations yet to come: Among these college women are many who will one day fulfill roles as parents and, as such, they will be their child's most influential sexuality educator. Is it indeed a truism that parents do unto their children what was done unto them? In terms of sexuality, it probably is, unless, of course, something in-

tervenes. Hopefully, sexuality education is that variable that can make a significant difference in future lives.

Historically, societal attitudes about sexuality have been dominated by a religious philosophy that relegated sex to a highly suspect category. Accordingly, sexual desires were to be restrained to prevent persons from engaging in various forms of sexual activity merely for the sake of experiencing sexual pleasure. Thus, many individuals were taught a type of sexual dualism: the soul is good, the body is evil.[1] Based on this teaching, masturbation was especially suspect. It has been variously characterized as "self-abuse," "defilement of the flesh," and/or "self-pollution."[2] And some religious leaders still refer to masturbation as an "unnatural" act because it has no reproductive goal.[3] As a consequence, religious orthodoxy has been found to be associated with impaired sexual functioning, including guilt, inhibition, and low levels of sexual interest, activity, and responsiveness.[4] This is especially true for women, who, within traditional contexts, have been viewed as the guardians of religion and morality in both the family and the community.[5] Given all of these factors, it is not surprising that many college women today feel uncomfortable with masturbation as a sexual outlet.

During the 19th century, Victorian-era women were viewed as being essentially devoid of sexual feelings. This legacy so dominated female sexual attitudes and behaviors that, until the second half of the 20th century, most women concealed their sexual desires for fear of being considered deviant.[6] However, the feminist movement that began in the 1960s promoted the claims of women as sexual beings in their own right, no longer having to subordinate their sexual desires to those of men. By the late 1970s, sex manuals were proclaiming the concept of female sexual autonomy, whereby women were to be viewed as sexually self-sufficient and in control of their own sexuality.[7] Thus, the experience of orgasm came to be perceived as a woman's right. By empowering women to claim that right, women's sexuality was elevated to the same status as that of men.[8] Accordingly, greater knowledge of their own sexuality places women in control of their sexual needs, freeing them from dependency on men for sexual gratification.

While masturbation has come to be viewed as an appropriate sexual outlet for women, the practice itself is the one form of sexual behavior that has been most harshly treated throughout the centuries. This is true for society, in general, as well as for religion and the field of medicine. Samuel Tissot, a Swiss-Catholic neurologist and Vatican adviser, published *Onania* in 1758, linking masturbation to insanity. His work served to reinforce the Judeo-Christian belief that masturbation was a sin and furnished a pseudoscientific basis for the traditional hostility toward sexual pleasure. Subsequently, over 800 medical books and articles were published denouncing masturbation as an undesirable practice.[1]

Although it is the most often practiced form of sexual activity, the subject of masturbation is rarely mentioned in professional journals except those associated with the women's movement.[1] And researchers are not alone in their neglect of the topic. Educators also have been remiss, as was illustrated by a survey of teachers that found masturbation to be the topic least likely to be considered in sex education classes.[9] Furthermore, parents seldom discuss masturbation with their daughters. Gagnon[10] found that only 14 percent of mothers and 7 percent of fathers had discussed masturbation with their preteen daughters. In fact, just 35 percent of mothers and 36 percent of fathers indicated they wanted their daughters to have positive views of masturbation during adolescence.

Masturbation

Historically, masturbation has been viewed as causing myriad ills, ranging from frigidity to severe mental disorders. As late as 1975, 16 percent of medical students and medical residents at one university still believed that certain conditions of mental and emotional instability were caused by masturbation.[11] And Gagnon[12] has observed, "People who masturbate in adulthood when there are appropriate sexual partners around, seem to us to be withdrawing from social responsibility" (p. 153). Whether intentional or not, the total effect of Western traditions made masturbation a highly censored and punishable behavior. Unfortunately, this negative perception of masturbation remains today because of the failure of medical, religious, and educational institutions to accept a share of the awesome responsibility for the fact that "their respective theories of masturbation [have] . . . caused untold human suffering and damage"[1] (p. 300).

Beginning in the 1960s, women were urged to explore their own sexuality in intimate physical contact for pleasure, whether with another person or alone. Gradually, the beneficial aspects of masturbation took on special meaning for many women. It was even found to help alleviate menstrual cramps.[13] Today, in addition to serving as a means of sexual self-expression, it is frequently promoted as a form of sex therapy for those who are unable to experience orgasm through sexual intercourse. Through masturbation, women can develop cognitive awareness of the kinds of stimulation that provide the most pleasure and, thus, increase their levels of comfort with their own bodies and sexual responses.[14]

Among both college and postcollege women, the incidence of masturbation has continued to increase. During the 1980s, the reported percentages among college women ranged from 46 percent[15] to 69 percent,[16] and in the 1990s, 45 percent[17] to 78 percent.[18] Postcollege-age women also became more accepting of masturbation as they received psychological permission, instruction, and support in learning about their own bodies. In fact, in self-reports of masturbation, a majority of postcollege-age, college-educated women indicated this practice as a sexual outlet.[19] However, not all women feel comfortable with masturbation. Among college women, 30 percent reported "shame" as the major reason for not engaging in masturbation.[20] Other research indicates that only 50 percent of college women believe that masturbation is a "healthy practice."[21] And those who do engage in masturbation do so much less frequently than men.[22] The reported masturbation frequency for college women was 3.3 times per month in comparison to 4.8 times per month for college men.[21]

In general, women are more likely to report guilt feelings about their masturbatory activity than men.[23] Further, substantial evidence suggests that such guilt feelings may interfere with the physiological and/or psychological sexual satisfaction derived from masturbation.[24] In fact, the presence of masturbatory guilt has various implications for female sexuality. Such guilt feelings have been found to inhibit the use of the diaphragm as a contraceptive technique, supposedly because of the necessity to handle the genitals during insertion.[25] Women with high levels of masturbatory guilt experience more emotional trauma after contracting a sexually transmitted disease (STD). They also exhibit greater fear about telling their sex partner about being infectious than women with low masturbatory guilt.[26]

Partner-Related Sexual Practices

A review of 30 studies of college women conducted during the 1980s revealed a range of premarital coital rates from 37 percent[27] to 88 percent.[28] Interestingly, data from two longitudinal studies involving college women during the 1980s suggest that the advent of AIDS has had little effect on the incidence of premarital sexual intercourse. For example, Bishop and Lipsitz[29] determined that by 1982 only 58 percent of their female college respondents had experienced sexual intercourse, but by 1988 that percentage had increased to 74 percent. Other surveys at a large university health service found that, in 1986, 87 percent of women reported having engaged in sexual intercourse, a percentage that remained relatively constant through 1989, when it was 86 percent.[30] The reported incidence of premarital sexual intercourse for college women ranges from 72 percent[21] to 85 percent.[31]

The mean number of lifetime sex partners for college women ranges from 4.0[32] to 6.7 partners.[33] As might be anticipated, a higher frequency of sexual intercourse among college women has been associated with a greater number of sex partners.[34] Earlier age at first intercourse and liberal attitudes toward premarital sex and abortion are other factors linked to higher numbers of sex partners, as indicated by almost one-half (43 percent) of the college women in one study who reported 4 or more lifetime sex partners.[35]

Engaging in oral-genital sex has become a prevalent sexual practice among college women. The reported range for cunnilingus varies from 68 percent[30] to 72 percent,[21] while the range for fellatio varies from 73 percent[21] to 86 percent.[30] Participation in anal intercourse has also become an alternative sexual practice for some college women (18 percent[21] to 20 percent[36]).

'Safer Sex' and Risk-Related Sexual Practices

In spite of the campaigns for "safer sex" to limit the number and choice of sex partners, use condoms, and avoid high-risk behaviors, risk-taking sexual practices among college women today have changed very little. Apparently, knowledge about AIDS is not associated with increased condom use during sexual intercourse, less frequent sexual intercourse, or fewer sex partners. Those women who claimed to have become more selective in their choice of sex partners or engaged in sexual intercourse less frequently due to concerns about AIDS were found to be as sexually active as those who claimed no change in behavior.[37]

Recently documented high-risk behaviors include alcohol use, failure to use condoms, and failure to seek medical services. Among sexually active college women, 69 percent were found to have engaged in sexual intercourse while intoxicated.[38] Further, college women report that regular condom usage by their partner ranges from only 15 percent[39] to 46 percent.[30] Finally, college women are three times more likely than college men to have been treated for an STD.[32] This circumstance may reflect two facts: Women are generally more likely than men to seek medical care and men are more likely to be asymptomatic when infected with an STD.

THE CURRENT STUDY

Masturbation as a means of sexual self-expression has tremendous potential as an option to provide physiological sexual fulfillment, while avoiding high-risk sexual encounters. However, there is a paucity of research revealing reasons why this safe-sex practice is not more widely implemented. Therefore, the purpose of this investigation was to examine the differences, if any, between those college women who have engaged in masturbation only, both masturbation and sexual intercourse, and sexual intercourse only.

Methodology

This investigation is part of a larger research project conducted to assess whether or not any significant changes in the sexual attitudes and behaviors of college students had occurred as a consequence of increasing AIDS awareness. In order to produce a representative sample, an anonymous questionnaire was administered during regular university classes to volunteer respondents enrolled in select lower division and upper division courses in the Schools of Arts and Sciences, Business, and Nursing.

The initial sample consisted of 942 women and 509 men who were enrolled as undergraduate students at a Midwestern residential state university. Since the investigators were specifically interested in the role of masturbation as a safe-sex behavior compared to premarital sexual intercourse, only the never-married women (851) were included in this study. Of the women in this preliminary subsample (N = 777), 54.1 percent had engaged in masturbation and 72.8 percent had experienced sexual inter-

course. Given the focus of this particular investigation, the use of masturbation as an alternative source of sexual fulfillment, respondents who reported neither masturbation nor sexual intercourse were declared as missing values. Of the final subsample of 676 never-married women, 16.3 percent had participated in masturbation only, 45.9 percent in both masturbation and sexual intercourse, and 37.9 percent in sexual intercourse only. Data on class standing for the subsample indicated that 25.0 percent were freshmen, 25.9 percent sophomores, 25.0 percent juniors, and 24.1 percent seniors. For purposes of clarity and brevity, the data will hereafter be reported by MO Group (Masturbation Only), MSI Group (Masturbation and Sexual Intercourse), and SIO Group (Sexual Intercourse Only). It should be observed that a significant age difference existed between these groups: MO Group, 19.8 years; MSI Group, 20.5 years; and SIO Group, 19.9 years.

Results

Family Background

In the examination of family background factors, MSI Group women, when compared with MO and SIO Group women, had the least positive feelings toward their mother and father figures while growing up. Further, MSI Group women were more likely to have had uncommunicative mother and father figures and to report their parental figures as having a lower quality marriage. MO Group women had the most positive feelings toward both mother and father figures while growing up, but SIO Group women rated the quality of their parental figures' marriage the highest.

The role of religion in the lives of these women was also analyzed as a family background factor. Among MO Group women, 26.2 percent believed themselves to be "more religious" in comparison to others in their denomination, in contrast to only 17.7 percent of MSI Group and 11.0 percent of SIO Group women. Supporting this religious difference, the mean number of times per year for attendance at religious services was 32.3 times for the MO Group, 23.8

times for the MSI Group, and 23.3 times for the SIO Group.

In terms of childhood sex education, there were no significant differences found regarding source of first sex information or first contraceptive information (parents, peers, or teachers). However, MSI Group women did receive their first sex information at a slightly earlier age in comparison to the MO Group women and the SIO Group women.

Sexual Attitudes

MO Group women, in comparison to MSI and SIO Group women, were more likely to believe that no sexual intercourse should occur without love. MO Group women also were more likely to want to marry a virgin or to marry someone who had experienced sexual intercourse only with them. These same MO Group women were least likely to approve of cohabitation, oral-genital sex, and abortion during the first trimester. And SIO Group women were more likely than either MO or MSI Group women to disapprove of same-sex anal intercourse, even if wearing a condom.

Concerning their reasons for abstaining from masturbation, the most important reason, in order of mention, was "Improper Use of Time," 54.0 percent; "Abnormal Behavior," 22.3 percent; "Didn't Want To," 12.5 percent; "Social-Peer Disapproval," 5.8 percent; and "Against Religious Teachings," 2.7 percent. And the second most important reason, in order of mention, was "Abnormal Behavior," "Against Personal Values," "Peer-Social Disapproval," "Against Religious Teachings," and "Parental Disapproval."

Dimensions of Sexual Behavior

Petting activities. A review of participation in various petting activities with the opposite sex since age 14, ranging from having clothed breasts fondled to giving and receiving oral-genital stimulation, revealed significantly greater involvement by MSI Group women in all petting activities. It is of interest to note that 95.5 percent of MSI Group women had received oral-genital stimulation in contrast to 91.4 percent of SIO Group and only 48.1 percent of MO Group women. Further, 90.6 percent of MSI Group women had given oral-genital stimulation in comparison to 86.3 percent of SIO Group and just 37.0 percent of MO Group women.

First sexual intercourse. An analysis of the circumstances surrounding first sexual intercourse found no significant differences between MSI and SIO Group women in terms of having voluntarily consented to sexual intercourse, being under the influence of alcohol and/or a mind-altering substance at the time, age at first sexual intercourse, age of first sex partner, and physiological and psychological sexual satisfaction with first sexual intercourse. However, SIO Group women and/or their partners were more likely to have used a contraceptive at first sexual intercourse than MSI Group women and/or their partners.

General sexual history. Regarding orgasmic experience, 89.4 percent of MSI Group women had experienced orgasm as compared to 84.4 percent of SIO Group and 74.3 percent of MO Group women. However, MO Group women reported the youngest mean age for experiencing their first orgasm, 15.1 years. This circumstance is partially explained by the fact that MO Group women began masturbating at a somewhat earlier age than MSI Group women. But MSI Group women actually experienced orgasm via masturbation more frequently than MO Group women. Although SIO Group and MSI Group women reported engaging in petting three times more often than MO Group women, there were no significant group differences for experiencing orgasm via petting.

No group differences were found between MSI and SIO Group women for mean number of times per year for sexual intercourse. However, significant differences were found with regard to mean number of lifetime sex partners: 3.6 partners for the SIO Group and 5.7 partners for the MSI Group. Further, analyses of the interpersonal relationship with lifetime sex partners revealed that MSI Group women were more likely than SIO Group women to have experienced premarital sexual intercourse with an occasional dating partner, a person just met, and a casual acquaintance.

Risk-Related Sexual Behaviors

Previously reported findings suggest that many of these young women were at risk of becoming premaritally pregnant. As will be recalled, MSI Group women and/or their partners were less likely to use a contraceptive at first sexual intercourse than SIO Group women. This difference, however, gradually disappeared as both groups became older and more sexually experienced. When asked about their most recent episode of sexual intercourse, 82.2 percent of MSI Group and 82.6 percent of SIO Group women indicated that a contraceptive had been used either by themselves or by their partner. With regard to the question of unintended pregnancy, 10.5 percent of SIO Group and 13.7 percent of MSI Group women reported having ever been pregnant. Of those who had been pregnant, no significant differences were identified for mean age at first pregnancy, number of times ever pregnant, or induced abortion.

A review of risk-related sexual practices found that a greater percentage of MSI Group than SIO Group women reported that their most recent sexual intercourse experience was unplanned. Although over one-third of MO Group women had given oral-genital stimulation, they were unlikely to have ever used a condom when giving oral-genital stimulation. But, for that matter, despite the finding that most had given oral-genital stimulation to the opposite sex, only about one-third of MSI Group and SIO Group women indicated their partner had used a condom during oral-genital sex. Finally, there were no differences between MSI Group women and SIO Group women with regard to frequency of condom use in conjunction with oral contraceptive use.

On the issue of STDs, respondents were asked what effects the increasing awareness about AIDS had had on their current sexual activity patterns. SIO Group women were more likely to indicate "No Effect" on their current sexual activity pattern in comparison to MSI Group women who reported "Less Sexual Activity" and "More Selective of Sex Partners." This finding is of particular interest, since there were no significant differences between MSI Group and SIO Group women regarding the mean number of sexual intercourse partners during the past year. Although MSI Group women had a greater number of lifetime sex partners, they were twice as likely as SIO Group women to underreport their total number of lifetime partners if they discussed the issue with their most recent sex partner. But it should be noted that almost one-third of both groups had never discussed the matter with their most recent sex partner.

MSI Group women were more likely than either MO Group or SIO Group women to believe that they would contract an STD in the future. Of those with sexual intercourse experience, MSI Group women, who had more lifetime partners, were more than twice as likely as SIO Group women to have already been diagnosed as having an STD.

Sexual Adjustment and Sexual Satisfaction

In terms of overall sexual adjustment, MSI Group women perceived themselves as better sexually adjusted than either MO Group or SIO Group women. However, SIO Group women reported a greater degree of comfort with their sexuality, [while] MO Group women felt more guilty about engaging in masturbation than MSI Group women. Data regarding potential embarrassment over telling a close female friend about engaging in masturbation revealed that a large majority of all women would be embarrassed over such a revelation: MO Group, 90.9 percent; MSI Group, 86.4 percent; and SIO Group, 89.6 percent.

Further, differences were identified regarding guilt feelings toward petting. MO Group women more frequently experienced guilt feelings associated with petting than either MSI Group or SIO Group women. Women in the SIO Group were much more likely to indicate feeling guilty if they did not experience an orgasm during petting or sexual intercourse. Finally, substantial group differences existed regarding physiological and psychological sexual satisfaction. MO Group women reported the lowest and MSI Group women the highest levels of both physiological and psychological sexual satisfaction.

Discussion

Young women [today] face special challenges as they make choices for sexual fulfillment. The physiological and psychological safety dimensions that must be considered are within the context of vastly changing social conditions and values. Family background, religion, sexuality education, and sexual attitudes all appear to be important variables influencing choices in sexual behavior.

The nature of the family emotional bond has been found to influence the at-risk potential for a too early pregnancy, specifically among teens.[40] Pregnant teens are significantly more likely to come from homes that lack family adaptability.[41] Although the women in this study were chronologically older than teens, age in years does little to assure developmental maturity. It is plausible that college-age women who are developmentally immature may engage in risk-taking behavior as a means of gaining the intimacy they missed in uncommunicative, nonaffirming families. MSI Group women who perceived their family life as least satisfactory were less likely to have used a contraceptive at first sexual intercourse and more likely to have subsequently engaged in risk-related sexual behaviors such as casual sex. Consequently, the fact that MSI Group women, who had more lifetime partners, were more than twice as likely as SIO Group women to have been diagnosed with an STD and significantly more likely to have been pregnant was not unexpected. However, age and life experience are suspected as mitigating factors, since MSI Group women were significantly older and more experienced than the others.

The fact that older MSI Group women were more likely to have planned their most recent sexual intercourse experience and to

have used a condom during oral-genital sex suggests modest progress. With age, these women demonstrated a more deliberate and responsible approach to meeting their sexual needs. Such interpretation is supported by evidence indicating that the sexual behavior patterns of MSI Group women have been somewhat more influenced, albeit limited, by AIDS awareness than those of SIO Group women. It is puzzling then that MSI Group women evidenced spontaneous, "swept-away" sexual reactions by choosing occasional dates, casual acquaintances, or persons just met as sex partners, clearly positioning them in the highest risk category. Because of the interdependence of many factors, further investigation may reveal the developmental hypothesis employed in the interpretation of these data to be oversimplistic.

Overall, the findings concerning the effect of AIDS awareness on sexual activity patterns were not very promising. The percentages indicating that AIDS awareness had had no effect on their sexual activity patterns were virtually unchanged from those in an earlier study by Carroll.[42] The fact that the women in this study indicated little change in high-risk sexual practices may substantiate later findings of gender-based differences in response to AIDS.[37] Carroll contends that because women feel less of a sense of self-efficacy and control than do men, they are less likely to implement desired changes in sexual relationships.[42]

These findings suggest that the influence of religion in the sexual lives of college women is a complex phenomenon. SIO Group women indicated their major reasons for not participating in masturbation were "improper use of time," "abnormal behavior," and "against personal values." It can be argued that these reasons may have a religious basis, at least in part. And yet these same women reported the lowest degree of religiosity of the three groups. SIO Group women not only perceived themselves as less religious but also indicated a lower frequency of attendance at religious services than MO Group women. MSI Group and SIO Group women had essentially the same level of attendance at religious services. However, the variable "attendance at religious services" has been questioned as an accurate indicator of whether or not college students, in fact, subscribe to the social-sexual norms advocated by their religious denomination. College students who attend religious services weekly but believe premarital sexual intercourse to be acceptable if strong affection exists are as likely to report a high frequency of sexual intercourse as inconsistent church attendees.[43]

Not only were MO Group women more religious, but they expressed more positive feelings for their mother and father figures and significantly more conservative sexual attitudes. The influence of religion and family closeness on value formation may help explain why MO Group women had refrained from sexual intercourse. These women apparently held values that sexual intercourse and love should go together. They expressed the opinion that one should marry a virgin or at least a person who had experienced sexual intercourse only with their future marital partner. Thus, it was not unexpected that MO Group women were least likely to approve of cohabitation, oral-genital sex, and abortion in the first trimester. It was, however, puzzling why these women, who began masturbating earlier than those in the MSI Group, expressed more guilt about masturbation. Possible explanations may relate to developmental factors, since MO Group women were significantly younger than MSI Group women. Zabin[44] postulated that three age-related influences exert pressure of relative strengths on sexual initiation: the biological influence, based on hormone level [source of sexual motivation/libido]; the social influence, based on the normative age for beginning sexual intercourse; and the interaction of the biological and the social influences, leading to self-perceived appropriate behavioral choices.

One interpretation of these findings is that these religiously oriented MO Group women, with positive feelings toward both parental figures, possessed a higher self-efficacy. And, therefore, these women re-

sponsibly chose to abstain from sexual intercourse, using masturbation to satisfy their sexual needs. However, this may be an oversimplistic explanation, ignoring the interdependence of the many factors involved. The fact that MO Group women, the safest-sex group, were more likely to have had a college course containing sex education is promising. However MSI Group women, who engaged in the most risk-related behaviors, received their sex education earliest. This circumstance raises issues not only of timing but also of the efficacy of current sex education programs. Studies of sexual decision-making have long noted that simply providing educational information about sexuality is inadequate for pregnancy prevention.[44] Educators and counselors must attend to the voices in research that are determining more salient variables. For example, if, as advanced by some researchers, formal operational thinking is a key variable in making healthy choices for sexual fulfillment, the entire issue of timing in sex education must be reevaluated.[45] However, it should be noted that this study did not attempt to determine the quality and/or quantity of the sex education of respondents, both of which could have greatly affected outcomes.

Conclusion

Since masturbation is suggested as a means for women to engage in personal body exploration and as a preferred "safe-sex outlet," these data have substantial implications. The fact that, for many, masturbation continues to be a guilt-ridden sexual outlet is problematic for the mental and physical health of women. The taboos associated with masturbation relate to the perception that this form of sexual activity is abnormal. These data support other findings that indicate many college women have never engaged in masturbation because they believe it to be an improper use of time, abnormal behavior, and/or contrary to their personal values. Yet, as corroborated by these findings, many of these same women choose to have unprotected sexual intercourse and multiple sex partners. Still others engage in masturbation but report experiencing guilt feelings regarding the practice. Therefore, it is of crucial importance that the negative connotations related to masturbation and its attendant impact on sexual satisfaction and adjustment be further addressed in the research.

Several findings in this study also pose unanswered questions. Why were MO Group women, who were least likely to experience an orgasm during masturbation and had less experience with various opposite-sex petting behaviors, more likely to feel guilty about masturbation and petting? And, even more puzzling, why were they least likely to report physiological and psychological sexual satisfaction as well as comfort with their own sexuality? Perhaps the most confounding question to surface is why the greatest behavioral risk-takers, MSI Group women, rated their sexual adjustment and physiological and psychological sexual satisfaction higher? This phenomenon, indicated by those who had experienced more casual sexual relations, may substantiate the changing mores theory postulated by Cobliner.[47]

That we have moved to a more depersonalized approach to sex is logical to conclude from a perusal of the current professional and scientific writings on sexuality that are largely concerned with physical rather than emotional aspects. Psychiatrists link the current premeditated restraint of affect in sexual relations to sexual apathy and psychiatric disturbances such as depersonalization and derealization.[47] Perhaps, as admonished by Simon et al.,[46] researchers do need to replace social bookkeeping (counting virgins) with methodologies that would lead to an understanding of the social/psychological process influencing sexual behavior. One could question whether or not prevailing college-age mores are nonadaptive on both individual and interpersonal levels. In making choices for sexual fulfillment, there appear to be not only missing answers but also unformulated questions. What is certain, however, in the midst of the "safe-sex" mania, is that professionals must be invested in not only physiological but psychological safety. To do less is to face grave personal and social consequences.

References

1. Patton MS: Twentieth-century attitudes toward masturbation. *J Rel Health* 25:291–301, 1986.

2. Masters WH, Johnson VE, Kolodny RC: *Human sexuality* (3rd ed). Glenview, IL, Scott Foresman, 1988.

3. Patton MS: Masturbation from Judaism to Victorianism. *J Rel Health* 24:133–146, 1985.

4. Purcell SL: An empirical study of the relationship between religious orthodoxy (defined as religious rigidity and religious closed-mindedness) and marital sexual functioning (Doctoral dissertation, Andrews University, 1984). *Dis Abst Int* 45:1695A, 1984.

5. Bahr H, Chadwick B: Religion and family in Middletown, U.S.A. *J Marr Fam* 47:407–414, 1985.

6. Allgeier ER, Allgeier AR: *Sexual interactions* (3rd ed). Lexington, MA, Heath, 1991.

7. Weinberg MS, Swensson RG, Hammersmith SK: Sexual autonomy and the status of women: Models of female sexuality in U.S. sex manuals from 1950 to 1980. *Soc Prob* 30:312–323, 1983.

8. Williams JH: *Psychology of women: Behavior in a biosocial context* (3rd ed). New York, Norton, 1987.

9. Schultz JB, Boyd JR: Sexuality attitudes of secondary teachers. *Fam Rel* 33:537–541, 1984.

10. Gagnon JH: Attitudes and responses of parents to pre-adolescent masturbation. *Arch Sex Behav* 14:451–466, 1985.

11. Miller WR, Lief HI: Masturbatory attitudes, knowledge, and experience: Data from the sex knowledge and attitude test (SKAT). *Arch Sex Behav* 5:447–467, 1976.

12. Gagnon JH: *Human sexualities*. Glenview, IL, Scott Foresman, 1977.

13. Stewart FH, Guest FJ, Stewart GK, Hatcher RA: *My body, my health: The concerned woman's guide to gynecology*. New York, Wiley, 1979.

14. Lips HM: *Sex and gender: An introduction*. Mountain View, CA, Mayfield, 1988.

15. Davidson JK, Sr: Autoeroticism, sexual satisfaction, and sexual adjustment among university females: Past and current patterns. *Deviant Behav 5*:121–140, 1984.

16. Pelletier LA, Herold ES: The relationship of age, sex guilt, and sexual experience with female sexual fantasies. *J Sex Res 24*:250–256, 1988.

17. Leitenberg H, Detzer MJ, Srebnik D: Gender differences in masturbation and the relationship of masturbation experience in preadolescence and/or early adolescence to sexual behavior and sexual adjustment in young adulthood. *Arch Sex Behav 22*:87–98, 1993.

18. Bancroft J, Sherwin BB, Alexander GM, Davidson DW, Walker A: Oral contraceptives, androgens, and the sexuality of young women: I. A comparison of sexual experience, sexual attitudes, and gender role in oral contraceptive users and nonusers. *Arch Sex Behav 20*:105–120, 1991.

19. Davidson JK, Sr, Darling CA: Masturbatory guilt and sexual responsiveness among adult women: Sexual satisfaction revisited. *J Sex Marital Ther 19*:289–300, 1993.

20. Atwood JD, Gagnon JH: Masturbatory behavior in college youth. *J Sex Ed Ther 13*:35–42, 1987.

21. Weis DL, Rabinowitz B, Ruckstruhl MF: Individual changes in sexual attitudes and behavior within college-level human sexuality courses. *J Sex Res 29*:43–59, 1992.

22. Jones JC, Barlow DH: Self-reported frequency of sexual urges, fantasies, and masturbatory fantasies in heterosexual males and females. *Arch Sex Behav 19*:269–279, 1990.

23. Davidson JK, Sr, Darling CA: The impact of college-level sex education on sexual knowledge, attitudes, and practices: The knowledge/sexual experimentation myth revisited. *Deviant Behav 7*:13–30, 1986.

24. Davidson JK, Sr, Darling CA: Self-perceived differences in the female orgasmic response. *Fam Pract Res J 8*:75–84, 1989.

25. Gerrard M: Sex, sex guilt, and contraceptive use revisited: The 1980s. *J Pers Soc Psychol 52*:975–980, 1987.

26. Houck EL, Abramson PR: Masturbatory guilt and the psychological consequences of sexually transmitted diseases among women. *J Res Pers 20*:267–275, 1986.

27. Ishii-Kuntz M: Acquired immune deficiency syndrome and sexual behavior in a college student sample. *Soc Social Res 73*:13–18, 1988.

28. Murstein BI, Chapin MJ, Heard KV, Vyse SA: Sexual behavior, drugs, and relationship patterns on a college campus over thirteen years. *Adolescence 24*(93):125–139, 1989.

29. Bishop P, Lipsitz A: Sexual behavior among college students in the AIDS era: A comparative study. *J Psych Hum Sex 3*(2):35–52, 1990.

30. DeBuono BA, Zinner SH, Daamen M, McCormack WM: Sexual behavior of college women in 1975, 1986, and 1989. *N Engl J Med 322*:821–825, 1990.

31. Hale RW, Char DFB, Nagy K, Stockert N: Seventeen-year review of sexual and contraceptive behavior on a college campus. *Am J Obstet Gynecol 168*:1833–1838, 1993.

32. Cochran SD, Peplau LA: Sexual risk reduction behaviors among young heterosexual adults. *Soc Sci Med 33*:25–36, 1991.

33. Walsh A: Self-esteem and sexual behavior: Exploring gender differences. *Sex Roles 25*:441–450, 1991.

34. Tanfer K, Cubbins LA: Coital frequency among single women: Normative constraints and situational opportunities. *J Sex Res 29*:221–250, 1992.

35. Tanfer K, Schoorl JJ: Premarital sexual careers and partner change. *Arch Sex Behav 21*:45–68, 1992.

36. Trocki KF: Patterns of sexuality and risk sexuality in the general population of a California county. *J Sex Res 29*:85–94, 1992.

37. Carroll L: Gender, knowledge about AIDS, reported behavioral change, and the sexual behavior of college students. *J Am Coll Health Assoc 40*:5–12, 1991.

38. Butcher AH, Manning DT, O'Neal EC: HIV-related sexual behaviors of college students. *J Am Coll Health Assoc 40*:115–118, 1991.

39. Pepe MV, Sanders DW, Symons CW: Sexual behaviors of university freshmen and the implications for sexuality educators. *J Sex Educ Ther 19*:20–30, 1993.

40. Hart B, Hilton I: Dimensions of personality organization as predictors of teenage pregnancy risk. *J Pers Assess 52*:116–132, 1988.

41. Romig CA, Bakken L: Teens at risk for pregnancy: The role of ego development and family processes. *J Adolesc 13*:195–199, 1990.

42. Carroll L: Concern with AIDS and the sexual behavior of college students. *J Marr Fam 50*:405–411, 1988.

43. Jensen L, Newell RJ, Holman T: Sexual behavior, church attendance, and permissive beliefs among unmarried young men and women. *J Sci Study Rel 29*:113–117, 1990.

44. Zabin LS: Adolescent pregnancy: The clinician's role in intervention. *J Gen Inter Med 5*(5 Suppl.):S81–S88, 1990.

45. Gordon DE: Formal operational thinking: The role of cognitive-developmental processes in adolescent decision-making about pregnancy and contraception. *Am J Orthopsychiatry 60*:345–356, 1990.

46. Simon W, Berger AS, Gagnon JH: Beyond anxiety and fantasy: The coital experiences of college youth. *J Youth Adolesc 1*:203–222, 1972.

47. Cobliner WG: The exclusion of intimacy in the sexuality of the contemporary college-age population. *Adolescence 23*(89):99–113, 1988.

Chapter 23
Pretending Orgasm During Sexual Intercourse

Michael W. Wiederman

During the past two decades, the traditional view that women are less sexual than men has largely disappeared, and the sexual needs of women have been increasingly recognized and accepted. Therefore, today a woman who perceives herself as sexually unresponsive may become embarrassed or experience other stressful emotions, such as guilt.

Although the vast majority of men usually experience orgasm with every episode of sexual intercourse, this research suggests that this is not true for many women. The reported percentage of women who always or almost always experience orgasm during sexual intercourse is about one-half. But, because most men consider a woman's orgasm as symbolic of their prowess as lovers, many women feel pressured to have an orgasm during sexual intercourse. Thus, it is known that a majority of women at least occasionally pretend to experience an orgasm. This not-to-be-missed selection will furnish an interesting perspective on a topic assumed to be of considerable interest, if one believes the hype in popular women's magazines.

To the extent that women are expected to be sexually responsive to their partners, women may experience some degree of pressure to experience an orgasm during sexual intercourse. In response to such pressure, some women may pretend, or "fake," an orgasm during coitus. Indeed, popular films (e.g., *When Harry Met Sally*)

and television programs (e.g., *Seinfeld*) have tackled the issue of women pretending orgasms during sexual intercourse. In contrast, it is surprising how little empirical research has been conducted on the phenomenon.

In the only study focused on the topic, Darling and Davidson[1] explored the prevalence and correlates of pretending orgasm in a large sample of professional nurses. In their sample, 58 percent of the women reported ever having pretended orgasm during sexual intercourse. In comparing "pretenders" to "nonpretenders," Darling and Davidson found that the pretenders were more likely to have masturbated and explored a variety of techniques for achieving orgasm (e.g., use of vibrators, erotic literature, fantasy). Also, relative to the nonpretenders, pretenders were slightly older, had started having sexual intercourse at a younger age, and had greater number of lifetime intercourse partners.

The results from Darling and Davidson's survey are interesting. However, many questions remain. Pretending orgasm appears to be related to greater sexual experience, but why? Is pretending orgasm related to more liberal sexual attitudes? To sexual esteem? If pretending orgasm is related to increased numbers of sexual partners, unrelated to sexually permissive attitudes, and related to decreased sexual esteem, pretending orgasm may be one way some women attempt to compensate for feeling less than adequate as a sexual partner. Such women may have had more partners not because of permissive attitudes or high sexual esteem but, rather, in an attempt to find male acceptance.

Similarly, is pretending orgasm related to physical attractiveness or, at least, self-perception of attractiveness? Women's physical attractiveness is more highly related to their sexual desirability than is men's physical attractiveness.[2] Correspondingly, women with negative body image appear to have less sexual experience.[3] It would stand to reason that women who were less attractive, or believed themselves to be, might attempt to compensate through being more sexually responsive, even to the point of pretending orgasm during coitus.

Is pretending orgasm related to more general self-monitoring propensities? Self-monitoring refers to the degree to which the individual tends to regulate self-presentation for the sake of desired public appearance.[4] Highly self-monitoring persons are said to exhibit greater responsiveness to social and interpersonal cues of situationally appropriate performance, whereas the expressive behavior of less self-monitoring persons is said to more closely reflect enduring and momentary inner states, including the person's attitudes, traits, and feelings.[5] Self-monitoring has been shown to be positively related to sexual experience,[6] and it would stand to reason that highly self-monitoring people would be more likely to pretend orgasm. That is, women who typically monitor their own expressive behavior in social situations might be expected to be more likely to "act" when in a sexual situation with a partner.

The objective of the current study was to investigate potential relationships between having pretended orgasm and sexual experience, sexual attitudes and sexual esteem, actual and self-perceived physical attractiveness, and self-monitoring. I decided to attempt to replicate Darling and Davidson's findings[1] regarding greater number of sex partners among women who pretended orgasm because they did not trim statistical outliers before conducting their analyses. That is, in their study, the range in number of lifetime intercourse partners appeared larger for the pretenders (range: 1–75) than for the nonpretenders (range: 1–35). So, the apparent difference between the mean number of sex partners in each group may have been due to a few statistical outliers among the pretenders.[7] Also, in their study, pretenders were older and had started having sexual intercourse at a younger age than nonpretenders. The apparent group differences in lifetime number of sex partners could have been due to the pretenders simply having been sexually active longer. I also chose a younger sample than that employed by Darling and Davidson[1] so as to

explore the phenomenon during courtship. The mean age of the women in their sample was approximately 30 years, the mean age at which these women first experienced sexual intercourse was approximately 20 years, and a large proportion of the women were (or had been) married.

THE CURRENT STUDY

Method

Sample

Initial research participants were 232 women recruited from introductory psychology classes at a midsize Midwestern state university who received research credit toward partial completion of their psychology course. To ensure a rather homogeneous sample with regard to age, women ages 29 and older were excluded from further analysis. However, 24.4 percent of these women reported not having had sexual intercourse. Therefore, the final sample consisted of 161 young women who reported having experienced coitus, and nearly all (94.4 percent) of the women were between the ages of 18 and 22 years. The large majority of these participants (88.8 percent) were white, 8.7 percent were black, and the remaining 2.5 percent were Latino.

Measures

Respondents were asked whether they had ever experienced "sexual intercourse with a male (penis in vagina)," the age at which they had first experienced sexual intercourse, and the number of different males with whom they had ever experienced sexual intercourse. Additionally, respondents were asked whether they had ever experienced oral stimulation of their genitals by a male, and if so, with how many different males. Lastly, respondents were asked whether they had ever orally stimulated a male's genitals, and if so, with how many different males. Respondents also were asked to indicate "true" or "false" in response to the statement, "I have, at one time or another, pretended to have an orgasm during sexual intercourse."

Sexual Attitudes

Respondents completed the brief form of the Sexual Opinion Survey (SOS)[8] as a measure of their affective orientation toward erotic stimuli. Specifically, respondents indicated their degree of agreement or disagreement with each of five statements using a seven-point scale (ranging from 1, "Strongly agree," to 7, "Strongly disagree").

Sexual esteem, or the tendency to evaluate oneself positively as a sexual partner, was measured with the short form[9] of the sexual esteem scale from Snell and Papini's Sexuality Scale.[10] Respondents indicated their degree of agreement or disagreement with each of the five statements using a five-point scale (ranging from 1, "Strongly disagree," to 5, "Strongly agree"). Respondents were asked to rate the overall attractiveness of their face and their body separately, using a seven-point scale for each rating (ranging from 1, "Well below average," to 4, "Average," and 7, "Well above average"). As a measure of actual facial attractiveness (as opposed to self-reported facial attractiveness), research participants were unobtrusively and independently rated by a male and female research assistant using a seven-point scale (ranging from 1, "Not attractive," to 4, "Average attractiveness," and 7, "Very attractive"). Participants completed the 18-item revised Self-Monitoring Scale[8] by indicating whether each of the items was "true" or "false." Higher scores indicate a greater tendency to engage in self-monitoring of expressive behavior. Briggs and Cheek[11] demonstrated that the Self-Monitoring Scale is composed of two distinct factors, one having to do with "other-directedness" (five items) and one having to do with "public performing" (eight items).

Results

Of the 161 women, 55.9 percent reported having pretended orgasm during sexual intercourse. Relative to nonpretenders, women who reported having pretended orgasm during coitus were slightly older, had more liberal sexual attitudes, had higher sexual esteem, had started having coitus at a younger age, and perceived themselves to be more facially attractive. Surprisingly, there were no group differences in experimenter-rated facial attractiveness, self-perceived body attractiveness, or self-monitoring. Still, pretenders reported greater numbers of sexual intercourse and oral sex partners relative to nonpretenders.

Both age and age at first coitus were significant predictors. And, [number of] fellatio partners and age at first intercourse were marginally significant. Age was not a significant predictor nor was self-rated facial attractiveness. However, SOS scores and sexual esteem scores were significant predictors, even after controlling for age and self-rated facial attractiveness.

Discussion

In the current sample of young adult women who had experienced sexual intercourse, more than one-half reported having pretended orgasm during coitus. The rate of 55 percent reporting having pretended orgasm was very similar to the 58 percent rate in Darling and Davidson's sample,[1] even though those authors surveyed women who were 10 years older on average than were the women in the current sample. In attempting to understand the nature of this phenomenon, it is important to note the variables that were expected to be related but were not. For example, I expected women who were more highly self-monitoring of their expressive behavior in social situations to be more likely to have pretended orgasm. However, pretenders and nonpretenders did not differ in their self-monitoring scores.

Pretenders and nonpretenders also did not differ in self-rated body attractiveness or in experimenter-rated facial attractiveness. However, pretenders rated their own facial attractiveness higher than the self-ratings of nonpretenders, [but] this relationship disappeared after controlling for other variables on which pretenders and nonpretenders differed.

As with Darling and Davidson,[1] pretenders in the current study reported having greater numbers of lifetime intercourse as well as cunnilingus partners relative to nonpretenders. However, this difference apparently was due to the pretenders' being older and having had sexual intercourse at a younger age. In other words, pretenders and nonpretenders did not differ in their mean number of intercourse and cunnilingus partners per unit of time during their sexual careers after statistically controlling for current age and age at first sexual intercourse.

With regard to fellatio partners, however, pretenders had marginally more lifetime partners than nonpretenders, even after controlling for current age and age at first intercourse. This finding suggests that young women who pretend orgasm may be more focused on their partners' satisfaction, or more invested in appeasing their sexual partners, than young women who do not pretend orgasm during sexual intercourse. This speculation fits with Darling and Davidson's finding[1] that, to an open-ended question regarding personal feelings about faking orgasm, the most frequent response was "feel guilty, but it is important that I satisfy my partner" (p. 192).

The only unique predictor of having pretended orgasm during coitus was sexual esteem scores. Young women who reported having pretended orgasm had higher sexual esteem scores than women who denied ever having pretended orgasm. The items that constitute the sexual esteem scale refer generically to rating oneself "high" as a sex partner or being "confident" as a sex partner. The results of the current study raise interesting questions regarding the nature of sexual esteem for young women. It may be that, for women, being a "good" sexual partner is defined as being responsive to one's partner. If that is the case, women who can "put on an act" during sexual intercourse apparently view themselves as "good" sexual partners. Another possibility is that women who are confident as sex partners are simply more comfortable pretending orgasm should the situation, in their judgment, call for it.

A third explanation for the unique relationship between women's sexual esteem and having pretended orgasm has to do with orgasm consistency. Darling and Davidson[1] found that pretenders in their study had experienced orgasm in response to a greater number of different forms of stimulation than had nonpretenders. Also, pretenders were more likely than nonpretenders to experience guilt if they did not experience an orgasm during sexual intercourse. It may be that pretenders in the current study experience higher sexual esteem because they generally are more sexually responsive (have orgasms more consistently) than nonpretenders. If this were the case, pretenders might be holding themselves to a higher standard of sexual performance and engaging in pretended orgasm to compensate for perceived deficits in sexual responsiveness. Unfortunately, in the current study, respondents did not report on orgasm consistency or self-expectations regarding sexual responsiveness.

The results of the current study, coupled with those of Darling and Davidson,[1] indicate that pretending orgasm during sexual intercourse is a fairly widespread phenomenon among women and is related to their self-view as a sexual partner. Further investigation is needed to elucidate how pretending orgasm is related to women's attributions and sexual interactions with partners. For example, how is pretending orgasm related to sexual communication, sexual satisfaction, and expectations within the dyad? How do women communicate a pretend orgasm, and what effect, if any, does pretending have on women's sexual partners? Do their partners perceive or suspect a faked orgasm? What cues do partners use to make such a judgment? Do women who pretend orgasm to please a partner differ from those who pretend in order to enhance their own sexual appeal or to end an unsatisfying sexual interaction? All these questions await further research.

References

1. Darling CA, Davidson JK: Enhancing relationships: Understanding the feminine mystique of pretending orgasm. *J Sex Marital Ther 12*:182–196, 1986.

2. Gangestad SW: Sexual selection and physical attractiveness: Implications for mating dynamics. *Hum Nature* 4:205–235, 1993.

3. Faith MS, Schare ML: The role of body image in sexually avoidant behavior. *Arch Sexual Behavior* 22:345–356, 1993.

4. Snyder M: *Public appearance/private realities: The psychology of self-monitoring.* New York, Freeman, 1987.

5. Snyder M, Gangestad S: On the nature of self-monitoring: Matters of assessment, matters of validity. *J Pers Soc Psychol* 51:125–139, 1986.

6. Snyder M, Simpson JA, Gangestad S: Personality and sexual relations. *J Pers Soc Psychol 51*:181–190, 1986.

7. Tabachnick BG, Fidell LS: *Using multivariate statistics* (3rd ed). New York, HarperCollins, 1996.

8. Fisher WA, Byrne D, White LA, Kelly K: Erotophobia-erotophilia as a dimension of personality. *J Sex Res 25*:123–151, 1988.

9. Wiederman MW, Allgeier ER: The measurement of sexual esteem: Investigation of Snell and Papini's (1989) Sexuality Scale. *J Res Pers* 27:88–102, 1993.

10. Snell WE, Papini DR: The sexuality scale: An instrument to measure sexual-esteem, sexual-depression, and sexual-preoccupation. *J Sex Res* 26:256–263, 1989.

11. Briggs SR, Cheek JM: On the nature of self-monitoring: Problems with assessment, problems with validity. *J Pers Soc Psychol* 54:663–678, 1988.

Chapter 24
Menstrual Cycle Phases and Female Sexual Desire

Pamela C. Regan

According to therapists, hypoactive or inhibited sexual desire is a sexual dysfunction among women characterized by little or no interest in initiating or encouraging sexual activity. Although the primary causes of inhibited desire can be psychological, such as power struggles or intimacy issues, they can also be biological, as evidenced in those coping with depression, alcoholism, substance abuse, or hormone imbalance. But, even for women with normal levels of sexual desire, the emotional state is a very important factor in whether she will experience pleasure and sexual arousal during sexual activity, or whether she wants to engage in it at all. For example, if a situation is pleasant, her sexual desire will more than likely be elevated.

Conventional wisdom has held that women experience peaks and valleys of desire associated with fluctuations of hormone levels during their menstrual cycle, but researchers do not agree about the pattern. This literature review does not establish definitive patterns or end the controversy about the rhythms of sexual desire. It does, however, raise thought-provoking questions for students about the relationships between sexuality and physiological, psychological, and sociological factors. For example, some women experience peaks of physiological sexual desire during their menses, yet cultural taboos can inhibit sexual activity at this time. This offering may be especially affirm-ing for women who have long been aware of their own rhythms of desire, and yet surprised by the dearth of empirical evidence to support their reality.

Introduction

Sexual desire is associated with several significant individual and interpersonal human life events. For example, feelings of desire or sexual attraction may prompt individuals to seek and engage in sexual intercourse; such feelings, therefore, have implications for reproduction and species survival (Buss & Schmitt, 1993). Sexual desire also appears intricately linked to relationship adjustment and quality. A growing body of clinical evidence suggests that relationships in which one or both partners experience low sexual desire are often characterized by conflict, power struggles, anger, and hostility (Leiblum & Rosen, 1988). Consequently, a number of theoretical and empirical attempts have been made to delineate and explore the correlates and presumed causal antecedents of sexual desire. Although some researchers have examined external causes located in the physical or social environment (e.g., physically attractive others, erotic or pornographic media), the majority have focused on causes located within the individual. A variety of intraindividual factors have been examined, including age, gender, personality, mood, and hormonal or biological processes. Of these presumed causes of sexual desire, the latter have received the lion's share of empirical attention. Certainly human sexual response is less biologically determined and more volitional than any reference to "raging hormones" would have us believe. Nonetheless, many young adults believe that biological and hormonal processes cause female (and male) sexual desire (Regan & Berscheid, 1995), and research strongly indicates that endogenous hormones contribute at least partially to the timing and magnitude of this particular aspect of sexuality.

Overview

One method of examining the relation between the sex hormones (e.g., androgens, estrogens, progesterone) and sexual desire involves investigating life events and changes that are hormonally mediated. The majority of major, hormonally mediated life events are exclusively female (e.g., pregnancy, menstruation). Women experience greater variations in circulating hormone levels during their lifetimes than do most men and, for this reason, women make ideal participants for researchers interested in the relationship between hormones and sexual desire.

Definition and Operationalization of Sexual Desire

Sexual desire is commonly defined as a subjective, psychological experience or state that can be understood broadly as an interest in sexual objects or activities, or as a wish, need, or drive to seek out sexual objects or to engage in sexual activities (Bancroft, 1988; Regan & Berscheid, 1996). This experience is presumed to be distinct from both sexual arousal and sexual activity. *Sexual arousal* consists of two basic components. The first is termed physiological-genital sexual arousal, and is defined as a state of activation of a complex system of reflexes that involve the sex organs and the nervous system (Masters, Johnson, & Kolodny, 1994). Indicants of physiological-genital arousal include, for men, penile tumescence and, for women, vaginal blood volume or temperature. The second component of sexual arousal, subjective sexual arousal, is defined as the subjective awareness that one is genitally and physiologically aroused (Green & Mosher, 1985). Subjective sexual arousal is typically assessed via perceptions of genital or physiological changes that occur during exposure to sexual stimuli (e.g., increased heart rate and/or perspiration, awareness of such genital sensations as penile erection or vaginal lubrication). *Sexual activity* is commonly defined as any overt behavioural response involving the external sex organs, including autoerotic (e.g., masturbation) and interpersonal (e.g., "petting," oral manipulation of genitalia, intercourse) activities.

Sexual desire undoubtedly is closely associated with physiological/genital and subjective sexual arousal, and desire often precedes sexual activity. However, although desire, arousal, and activity may co-occur, the latter do not themselves constitute adequate indicants of sexual desire. That is, the occurrence of sexual activity does not necessarily imply a desire for such activity, nor does the absence of sexual activity necessarily reflect a lack of desire. For example, young adults often report having engaged in sex without desire (Beck, Bozman, & Qualtrough, 1991), and relationship partners may abstain from intercourse during times of menstruation or pregnancy due more to cultural proscriptions than to personal inclination (Kenny, 1973). Thus, it is important to maintain both a theoretical and empirical distinction among these three aspects of human sexuality. In sum:

> Sexual desire is a subjective sexual experience that is sometimes but not always accompanied by physiological (e.g., increased heart rate, perspiration) or genital (e.g., erection, vaginal lubrication) sexual arousal, subjective sexual arousal (awareness of physiological and/or genital arousal), and such sexual behaviors as masturbation, "making out" or "petting," and intercourse. Sexual desire can be understood broadly as an interest in sexual objects or activities, or as a wish, longing, or craving to seek out sexual objects or to engage in sexual activities. (Regan & Berscheid, 1995, p. 349)

A variety of operationalizations for sexual desire are utilized in the literature. The majority of researchers directly ask their participants about sexual desire or sexual interest (frequency, level, degree, or amount). Others employ such motivationally oriented euphemisms as sexual motivation, sex drive, sexual urge, sexual craving, and sexual appetite. Still others refer to the Freudian motivational concept of *libido*, explicitly defined as erotic or sexual desire or interest (Benedek & Rubenstein, 1939).

Other researchers attempting to measure sexual desire have operationalized the concept in terms of cognitive events (e.g., sexual wishes, thoughts, fantasies) not associated with any overt sexual activity, under the assumption that these phenomena represent motivational aspects of sexual experience and therefore may serve as indirect measures of sexual desire (Sherwin, 1985). The fact that women who seek treatment for low sexual desire also fantasize less during sexual activity and general daydreaming than normal controls lends support to this assumption (Nutter & Condron, 1983). A final operational category includes such psychological events as sexual feelings not associated with overt sexual activity and not meant to include genital sensations, and sexual attraction or an attraction to another individual that is explicitly based on sexual feelings.

The Menstrual Cycle: Measurement Techniques and Phases

There are four major sex hormones associated with the menstrual cycle. These hormones are produced by the ovaries and by several of the various glands that comprise the endocrine system (e.g., the adrenal glands and the pituitary gland). In women, androgens (masculinizing hormones) are primarily synthesized in the adrenal cortex (the outer section of the adrenal glands) and to a lesser extent in the ovaries. The feminizing hormones known as estrogens are largely secreted by the ovaries, with lesser amounts manufactured in the adrenal cortex and peripheral tissues, e.g., fat, muscle, kidney, liver, hypothalamus (Fotherby, 1984). The primary naturally occurring estrogenic hormone is estradiol. The sex hormone progesterone is primarily produced by the ovaries (and, during pregnancy, the placenta), with lesser amounts manufactured in the adrenal cortex. Prolactin is produced by the pituitary gland.

Most women menstruate, and therefore experience rhythmic fluctuations in these hormones. The majority of researchers, recognizing the relative invariability of this monthly hormonal secretory pattern, have related measures of sexual desire to temporal phases of the menstrual cycle (as opposed to actual circulating levels of specific hormones). Several nonhormonally derived "menstrual marker" techniques have been utilized to both estimate the timing of ovulation and to divide the cycle into its various discrete phases. These include the "reverse cycle technique" in which the 14th day counting backward from the succeeding menstruation is defined as the time of ovulation, with the record stopping at the 28th day (Alexander, Sherwin, & Bancroft, 1990); the "forward cycle technique" in which the days of the cycle are numbered forward from the beginning of the preceding menstruation and the record is stopped at 28 days, with the 14th day again serving as the best estimate of ovulation (Udry & Morris, 1977); the "standardized cycle technique" in which the events of the entire cycle are expanded or reduced to fit a 28-day cycle according to a mathematical formula (Udry & Morris, 1977); and the "basal body temperature (BBT) technique," in which ovulation is identified by a specific BBT in the cycle, closely followed by a sudden BBT rise (Stanislaw & Rice, 1988; Wade & Cirese, 1991).

Other researchers, criticizing such techniques as methodologically imprecise and interpretatively ambiguous (Persky et al., 1978), rely instead upon such hormonally derived methods as the "luteinizing hormone (LH) technique" in which the concentrations of LH in a woman's plasma or urine are monitored, an identifiable LH surge serves as an indication of impending ovulation, and the remaining days of the cycle are numbered positively (after ovulation) and negatively (before ovulation) around that point (Silber, 1994; Udry & Morris, 1977). A similar technique involves monitoring levels of plasma progesterone as a means of assessing luteal function; high levels are regarded as evidence of ovulation (Alexander et al., 1990). The "vaginal smear technique" is used less frequently than the former methods, and involves analyzing cells obtained from vaginal smears for the presence or absence of various sex hormones, and then inferring a particular menstrual phase (Benedek & Rubenstein, 1939).

Researchers utilize any or all of these methods to divide the menstrual cycle into its various phases; no standard method of cycle phase derivation has been accepted. In addition, there is little general agreement about the appropriate label to be given to each phase. The possible variations in phase number and terminology are endless and, as Steklis and Whiteman (1989) observe, can result in the same data yielding radically different conclusions about the exact timing of peaks and troughs of sexual desire. Fortunately, most researchers note the precise days on which sexual desire or other sexual events occurred, and thus it is often possible to compare results across various studies by focusing on the date of occurrence of an event rather than on the researcher's interpretation of the phase of occurrence. I have chosen to present the results of the studies reviewed below in accordance with the typical 28-day, seven-phase cycle profile. Thus, when a researcher indicated that the greatest amount of sexual desire was experienced on the 8th day of a 28-day cycle, I concluded that desire peaked in the mid-follicular phase (as defined below), even if the researcher defined the eighth day as failing within the "postmenstrual" or even the "preovulatory" phase.

One complete menstrual cycle generally ranges from 21 to 35 days in length, although the majority of women menstruate at approximately 28-day intervals (Wade & Cirese, 1991). Ovulation typically occurs on the 14th day of the cycle. For descriptive purposes, the cycle [is] composed of seven somewhat overlapping yet distinct phases, each characterized by a different hormonal milieu, and each derived from the corresponding ovarian state.

The *follicular phase* consists of the first 14 days of the menstrual cycle. During this half of the cycle, the ovarian follicle develops and matures under the influence of follicle stimulating hormone (FSH), lutein-

izing hormone (LH), and possibly prolactin. The *early follicular phase* encompasses the onset through the cessation of menstrual bleeding, and is characterized by low levels of estrogen (primarily estradiol), progesterone, and androgen (e.g., testosterone, androstenedione). Near the end of this phase, the low levels of ovarian estrogens begin to rise. The *mid-follicular phase* (also called the postmenstrual phase) follows and extends from the end of menstruation to approximately 2 to 3 days prior to the midcycle estradiol peak. During this period, progesterone remains low, estradiol continues to rise, and androstenedione and testosterone begin a gradual ascent. The *late follicular phase* is an approximately 4-day period prior to ovulation that is centered around a sharp mid-cycle estradiol peak, which rapidly declines as ovulation approaches. The level of progesterone, although still lower than that of estradiol, begins to rise during this phase, and testosterone and androstenedione levels reach their respective peaks.

At mid-cycle, a surge of LH secretion is responsible for ovulation, the process whereby the mature follicle in the ovary ruptures and releases the ovum. Ovulation begins roughly 18–24 hours after the LH surge and extends for approximately 60 hours. During this brief phase, estrogen values continue to decline, progesterone continues to slowly rise or stabilizes briefly, and androgen levels remain comparable to their late follicular values.

The *luteal phase*, like the follicular phase, also lasts approximately 14 days. After ovulation, the developed egg leaves the ovary and the ruptured follicle undergoes luteinization and becomes a progesterone secreting structure known as the *corpus luteum*. After 10 to 12 days of secretion, the corpus luteum involutes, the plasma concentrations of estrogens and progesterone decrease, menses occurs, and the cycle begins again. Specifically, during the *early luteal period* the estrogen level begins another gradual increase, the progesterone level starts on a more rapid upward climb, and androgen levels enter a progressive decline from their late follicular peaks. The progesterone level peaks during the following *mid-luteal phase*, mimicked by a second, more modest peak in estrogen. Androgen levels, however, continue to decline. The *late luteal phase* (or premenstrual phase) is characterized by progressive declines in estrogen, progesterone, and androgen levels as the cycle begins again with the occurrence of menstrual bleeding.

Do Women Experience Reliable Rhythms or Peaks in Sexual Desire?

The association between sexual desire and the rhythmic hormonal events experienced by women is of great interest to theorists from a number of disciplines. For example, evolutionary psychologists argue that sexual desire may be a basic biological mechanism designed to increase the likelihood of conception and the propagation of the species (Buss, 1994). According to this framework, a woman's sexual activity and her desire to engage in such activity therefore should peak at the time of maximum fecundity (i.e., ovulation or that hormonally-mediated phase of the menstrual cycle in which coitus is most likely to result in conception). Certainly, research in comparative psychology has demonstrated that the female members of many mammalian species experience rhythmic hormonal changes that have relatively clear effects upon various aspects of sexuality. Female lower mammals are most likely to evidence an interest in sexual activity and to accept the sexual overtures of males during estrus, or the time corresponding to ovulation (Baum et al., 1977; Beach, 1976). In addition, although in many non-human primates sexual activity or behavior seems less confined to one particular phase of the estrus cycle than in lower mammals (Kendrick & Dixson, 1983), a number of laboratory and naturalistic studies have demonstrated mid-cycle peaks in female sexual proceptivity, receptivity, and attractivity (Beach, 1976; Kendrick & Dixson, 1983; Nadler, 1982).

Some researchers have noted an association in human females, similar to those observed in females of other mammalian species, between the ovulatory portion of the menstrual cycle and increased sexual desire. Recall that the ovulatory phase generally occurs fourteen days after the onset of the menses, follows a sudden surge in LH secretion, and is characterized by declining estrogen levels, rising progesterone levels, and relatively high amounts of the androgenic hormones. Specifically, a number of women have prospectively reported a significant increase or peak in sexual desire, feelings, fantasies, dreams, and free associations during this phase of the cycle (Adams et al., 1978; Harvey, 1987; Stanislaw & Rice, 1988). Although the techniques employed in many of these studies to estimate the timing of ovulation are diverse, the similarity in the above pattern of results is certainly worthy of note. In addition, at least one early study involving retrospective reports of sexual function has corroborated these findings. Cavanagh (1969) interviewed women who were currently using the rhythm method of contraception (which involves employing a mathematical formula to estimate fertile and non-fertile cycle phases); the majority indicated that their sexual desire was greatest at the time of ovulation.

This pattern is not universal, however. Other researchers have discovered that sexual desire for some women may in fact be lower during the ovulatory phase than other portions of the cycle. For example, several prospective studies have revealed an association between the mid-follicular phase and peaks in sexual feelings, thoughts, and fantasies (Bancroft et al., 1983; Matteo & Rissman, 1984), and sexual interest and desire (Laessle et al., 1990; Walker & Bancroft, 1990). In fact, even when different methods were employed to estimate the time of ovulation and standardize menstrual cycles of disparate length into one general pattern, Udry and Morris (1977) discovered that the desire for intercourse as reported in daily diaries tended to peak approximately 5–6 days prior to ovulation, during the mid-follicular phase. Similar results have been reported in retrospective studies; women in

Warner and Bancroft's (1988) survey retrospectively reported experiencing mid-follicular highs in sexual interest. In direct opposition to the results noted above, then, these results indicate that desire, at least for some women, is more likely to peak during the first postmenstrual week.

Peaks in sexual desire also have been observed to occur during the late luteal period, commonly referred to as the premenstrual period. Davis' (1926) sample retrospectively reported that their highest level of desire occurred on the 27th or 28th day of the cycle, just prior to menstruation, and more recently Stewart's (1989) sample recalled an increase in sexual interest during this period. Similarly, 42 percent of the women in Chaturvedi and Chandra's (1990) study reported premenstrual increases in sexual desire, with 29 percent experiencing marked increases.

The studies cited above all found a single peak in desire reported by women who experienced only one noticeable heightening or intensification of sexual feelings during the course of each menstrual cycle. Some women, however, experience more than one peak in sexual interest. Interestingly, the majority of those who report two reliable peaks in sexual desire each month also tend to do so during the ovulatory, mid-follicular, or late luteal phases, thus providing additional support for the hypothesis that all three of these phases are likely to be associated with peaks in desire and interest. For example, higher levels of sexual desire (Alexander et al., 1990) and sexual interest (Silber, 1994) have been prospectively reported by non-pill using women during the postmenstrual (mid-follicular) and ovulatory phases. In addition, the majority of the 89 women in an early study conducted by Davis (1926) who experienced two periods of heightened sexual desire each month retrospectively reported that these occurred on days 5–8 of the cycle, during the mid-follicular phase, and also on cycle days 26–28, or the late luteal phase. Forty-four percent of Tinklepaugh's (1933) sample experienced a similar bimodal rhythm of sexual desire, prospectively reporting immediate pre- and post-

menstrual peaks and McCance et al.'s (1937) analysis of daily log data revealed that women experienced a primary peak in sexual feeling on cycle day 8, as well as a secondary, lesser peak on the 26th cycle day. Similar results are reported by Hart (1960), who assessed "Interest in having intercourse," and by Ferrero and LaPietra (1971), who measured "libido."

Thus, it appears that sexual desire, in general, reaches its peak intensity or greatest frequency during the mid-follicular phase, characterized by low androgen and progesterone levels and rapidly rising estrogen levels; and/or at or around ovulation, a time of relatively high androgen levels, rising progesterone levels, and rapidly descending estrogen levels; and/or during the late luteal phase, associated with low androgen levels and rapidly falling progesterone and estrogen levels.

However, while some agreement appears to exist as to the timing of such peaks in sexual desire, the assumption that such peaks occur in all women is unwarranted. Desire may peak once or twice in any given menstrual cycle, but it may also occur fairly consistently throughout the course of the entire cycle and thus fail to reach a noticeable peak. For example, approximately 34.4 percent of Ferrero and LaPietra's (1971) sample and 29.5 percent of Davis' (1926) sample failed to observe or report any periodicity of sexual desire or feelings. For these women, desire may be high or low or even moderate; whatever the case, this aspect of sexual experience appears to progress along on a relatively even keel, untouched by soaring highs or precipitous lows.

Conclusion

In sum, sexual desire does appear to increase during certain menstrual cycle phases for some women. Specifically, the subset of women who experience one single peak in desire tend to do so at ovulation or during the weeks immediately prior to or subsequent to menstruation. Those women who experience more than one peak in desire also tend to do so during two of the aforementioned phases (i.e., ovulation, mid-follicular, late luteal). Other women, however, do not report reliable peaks or fluctuations in their feelings of sexual interest and desire. Consequently, no single rhythmic pattern emerges that can be said to definitively characterize the sexual experience of the human female. It is possible that such a pattern does not exist; that is, the human female simply may not be as influenced by cyclic, hormonal fluctuations as are her primate cousins. Alternately, such a pattern may exist but be obscured by the various methodological difficulties that plague menstrual cycle research. For example, if one researcher's premenstrual phase is another's postovulatory phase, and yet still another's mid- or late luteal phase, and if all three researchers report peaks in desire during their respective phases, unwary readers of this literature may conclude that the data are contradictory—that sexual desire reached its maximum height in three separate phases—when, in fact, it peaked in but one phase. Continued advances in the arena of hormonal assay will allow researchers to more precisely define the type and amount of hormones actively present when various sexual experiences occur.

Data collection procedures also pose methodological dangers for researchers who venture into this arena. Many researchers rely upon retrospective, as opposed to prospective, data collection procedures. In the typical retrospective questionnaire study, however, women must remember instances of desire that may or may not have been experienced at certain times throughout one or more cycles; this is a relatively difficult task that requires cognitive effort and excellent recall ability (Bradburn, Rips, & Shevell, 1987). In addition, desire experienced postmenstrually one month may become confused with desire experienced premenstrually the following month; memories may be biased by beliefs about sexuality and the menstrual cycle and the menstrual flow itself may serve as a convenient marker during the cycle such that events that occur near or during menstruation are recalled more easily, even though they may not actually occur with greater frequency or consistency.

In addition, the fact that alternative explanations exist for many of the changes in desire attributed to the hormonal fluctuations of the menstrual cycle adds to the difficulty in interpreting the research in this area. Specifically, menstruation not only involves oftentimes drastic alterations in the existing hormonal milieu of the human female, but also invokes a variety of cultural and societal stereotypes and expectations whose very presence renders it difficult to pinpoint uniquely hormonal effects upon sexual experience. For example, many women view the menstrual flow itself as a negative event, and both men and women subscribe to the belief that women experience cycle-related changes in aspects of physical and psychological function (Brooks-Gunn & Ruble, 1986). Thus, it is difficult to know whether fluctuations in sexual desire seen during the cycle are primarily due to a specific hormonal configuration present at a particular time or, rather, reflect a woman's psychological response to a given period in the menstrual cycle. For example, a woman may be less likely to report and perhaps even to experience sexual desire during the premenstrual phase in a culture that has taught her to associate that time of the cycle with physical and emotional debilitation.

These limitations notwithstanding, it is certainly important to recognize and to explore the contribution made by the sex hormones to the experience of sexual desire. It is also important, however, to pursue nonhormonal factors as we attempt to conceptualize and understand the causal antecedents, correlates, manifestations, and consequences of this human sexual experience.

References

Adams, D. B., Gold, A. R., & Burt, A. D. (1978). Rise in female-initiated sexual activity at ovulation and its suppression by oral contraceptives. *New England Journal of Medicine, 299*, 1145–1150.

Alexander, G. M., Sherwin, B. B., Bancroft, J., & Davidson, D. W. (1990). Testosterone and sexual behavior in oral contraceptive users and nonusers: A prospective study. *Hormones and Behavior, 24,* 388–402.

Bancroft, J. (1988). Sexual desire and the brain. *Sexual and Marital Therapy, 3,* 11–27.

Bancroft, J., Sanders, D., Davidson, D., & Warner, P. (1983). Mood, sexuality, hormones, and the menstrual cycle. III. Sexuality and the role of androgens. *Psychosomatic Medicine, 45,* 509–516.

Baum, M. J., Everitt, B. J., Herbert, J., & Keverne, E. B. (1977). Hormonal basis of proceptivity and receptivity in female primates. *Archives of Sexual Behavior, 6,* 173–192.

Beach, F. A. (1976). Sexual artractivity, proceptivity, and receptivity in female mammals. *Hormones and Behavior, 7,* 105–138.

Beck, J. G., Bozman, A. W., & Qualtrough, T. (1991). The experience of sexual desire: Psychological correlates in a college sample. *Journal of Sex Research, 28,* 443–456.

Benedek, T., & Rubenstein, B. B. (1939). The correlations between ovarian activity and psychodynamic processes. II. The menstrual phase. *Psychosomatic Medicine, 1,* 461–485.

Bradburn, N. M., Rips, L. J., & Shevell, S. K. (1987). Answering autobiographical questions: The impact of memory and inference on surveys. *Science, 236,* 157–161.

Brooks, R. V. (1984). Androgens: Physiology and pathology. In H. L. J. Makin (Ed.), *Biochemistry of steroid hormones* (2nd ed., pp. 565–594). Oxford: Blackwell Scientific Publications.

Brooks-Gunn, J., & Ruble, D. N. (1986). Men's and women's attitudes and beliefs about the menstrual cycle. *Sex Roles, 14,* 287–299.

Buss, D. M. (1994). *The evolution of desire.* New York: Basic Books.

Buss, D. M., & Schmitt, D. P. (1993). Sexual strategies theory: An evolutionary perspective on human mating. *Psychological Review, 100,* 204–232.

Cavanagh, J. R. (1969). Rhythm of sexual desire in women. *Medical Aspects of Human Sexuality, 3,* 29–39.

Chaturvedi, S. K., & Chandra, P. S. (1990). Stress-protective functions of positive experiences during the premenstrual period. *Stress Medicine, 6,* 53–55.

Davis, K. B. (1926). Periodicity of sex desire. Part I. Unmarried women, college graduates. *American Journal of Obstetrics and Gynecology, 12,* 824–838.

Ferrero, G., & LaPietra, O. (1971). Libido fluctuations during the menstrual cycle. *Panminerva Medica, 13,* 407–409.

Fotherby, K. (1984). Biosynthesis of the oestrogens. In H. L. J. Makin (Ed.), *Biochemistry of steroid hormones* (2nd ed., pp. 207–229). Oxford: Blackwell Scientific Publications.

Green, S. E., & Mosher, D. L. (1985). A causal model of sexual arousal to erotic fantasies. *Journal of Sex Research, 21,* 1–23.

Hart, R. D. (1960). Monthly rhythm of libido in married women. *British Medical Journal, 1,* 1023–1024.

Harvey, S. M. (1987). Female sexual behavior: Fluctuations during the menstrual cycle. *Journal of Psychosomatic Research, 31,* 101–110.

Kendrick, K. M., & Dixson, A. F. (1983). The effect of the ovarian cycle on the sexual behaviour of the common marmoset (Callithrix jacchus). *Physiology & Behavior, 30,* 735–742.

Kenny, J. A. (1973). Sexuality of pregnant and breastfeeding women. *Archives of Sexual Behavior, 2,* 215–229.

Laessle, R. G., Tuschl, R. J., Schweiger, U., & Pirke, K. M. (1990). Mood changes and physical complaints during the normal menstrual cycle in healthy young women. *Psychoneuroendocrinology, 15,* 131–138.

Leiblum, S. R., & Rosen, R. C. (1988). Introduction: Changing perspectives on sexual desire. In S. R. Leiblum & R. C. Rosen (Eds.), *Sexual desire disorders* (pp. 1–17). New York: Guilford Press.

Masters, W. H., Johnson, V. E., & Kolodny, R. C. (1994). *Heterosexuality.* New York: HarperCollins.

Masters, W. H., Johnson, V. E., & Kolodny, R. C. (1995). *Human sexuality* (5th ed.). New York: HarperCollins.

Matteo, S., & Rissman, E. (1984). Increased sexual activity during the midcycle portion of the human menstrual cycle. *Hormones and Behavior, 18,* 249–255.

McCance, R. A., Luff, M. C., & Widdowson, E. E. (1937). Physical and emotional periodicity in women. *Journal of Hygiene, 37,* 571–611.

Nadler, R. D. (1982). Laboratory research on sexual behavior and reproduction of gorillas and orangutans. *American Journal of Primatology Supplement, 1,* 57–66.

Nutter, D. E., & Condron, M. K. (1983). Sexual fantasy and activity patterns of females with inhibited sexual desire versus normal controls. *Journal of Sex & Marital Therapy, 9,* 276–282.

Pennington, G. W., Naik, S., & Bevan, B. R. (1981). The pituitary gland. In G. W. Pennington & S. Naik (Eds.), *Hormone analysis: Methodology and clinical interpretation* (Vol. 1, pp. 119–156). Boca Raton, FL: CRC Press, Inc.

Persky, H., Charney, N., Lief, H. I., O'Brien, C. P., Miller, W. R., & Strauss, D. (1978). The relationship of plasma estradiol level to sexual behavior in young women. *Psychosomatic Medicine, 40,* 523–535.

Regan, P. C., & Berscheid, E. (1995). Gender differences in beliefs about the causes of male and female sexual desire. *Personal Relationships, 2,* 345–358.

Regan, P. C., & Berscheid, E. (1996). Beliefs about the state, goals, and objects of sexual desire. *Journal of Sex & Marital Therapy, 22,* 110–120.

Sherwin, B. B. (1985). Changes in sexual behavior as a function of plasma sex steroid levels in post-menopausal women. *Maturitas, 7,* 225–233.

Silber, M. (1994). Menstrual cycle and work schedule: Effects on women's sexuality. *Archives of Sexual Behavior, 23,* 397–404.

Stanislaw, H., & Rice, F. J. (1988). Correlation between sexual desire and menstrual cycle characteristics. *Archives of Sexual Behavior, 17,* 499–508.

Steklis, H. D., & Whiteman, C. H. (1989). Loss of estrus in human evolution: Too many answers, too few questions. *Ethology and Sociobiology, 10,* 417–434.

Stewart, D. E. (1989). Positive changes in the premenstrual period. *Acta Psychiatrica Scandinavia, 79,* 400–405.

Tinklepaugh, O. L. (1933). The nature of periods of sex desire in women and their relation to ovulation. *American Journal of Obstetrics and Gynecology, 26,* 335–345.

Udry, J. R., & Morris, N. M. (1977). The distribution of events in the human menstrual cycle. *Journal of Reproduction and Fertility, 51,* 419–425.

Wade, C., & Cirese, S. (1991). *Human sexuality* (2nd ed.). San Diego: Harcourt Brace Jovanovich, Publishers.

Walker, A., & Bancroft, J. (1990). Relationship between premenstrual symptoms and oral contraceptive use: A controlled study. *Psychosomatic Medicine, 52,* 86–96.

Warner, P., & Bancroft, J. (1988). Mood, sexuality, oral contraceptives and the menstrual cycle. *Journal of Psychosomatic Research, 32,* 417–427.

Chapter 25
Sexual Satisfaction and Sexual Drive in Spinal Cord Injured Women

Kimberly Black
Marca L. Sipski
Susanne S. Strauss

The recognition that Christopher Reeves has brought to issues surrounding spinal cord (SC) injury is noteworthy. His willingness to openly share his recovery process has raised public awareness and sensitivity about the need for SC injury research. Not much awareness exists, however, concerning the effects of spinal cord injury on a person's sexual functioning. This is especially true for SC injured women. The little research that has been conducted on this population focuses mainly on pregnancy and childbirth issues. After reading this selection, students should be better able to formulate questions for continued research on the psychological aspects of sexuality and sexual functioning after SC injuries. Perhaps at least one reader will be challenged to undertake such an ambitious project as a future professional.

Introduction

Women with spinal cord injuries (SCI) have been underrepresented in research that examined sexual functioning of individuals with SCI. Most of the previous research available on women with spinal cord injuries and sexual functioning focused primarily on pregnancy and childbirth.[1-2] Recently, studies have begun to measure and compare sexual functioning in women pre-SCI to that of post-SCI.[3-4] However, this method is subject to the limitations of retrospective studies and does not take into account the percentage of subjects with sexual dysfunction that occurs in the able-bodied (AB) population. No studies comparing the sexuality and sexual functioning of SCI women with that of AB women were identified.

Women with SCI continue to engage in sexual activities. White et al.[5] studied the sexual activities of 40 SCI women and reported that 80 percent of the women had had a sexual relationship (emotional, physical, or both) since the time of injury, and 65 percent had had a physical relationship within the previous year. Having had a physical relationship since injury was significantly related to age at onset and years since injury. Women who had been involved in a physical relationship since injury were younger at the onset of injury and had been injured for a longer time than those who had not had such a relationship.

Sexual intercourse is one activity many SCI women continue to engage in. White et al.[5] reported that 72 percent of women had had sexual intercourse since their injury and 58 percent had had intercourse within the previous 12 months. Having had intercourse since their injury was correlated with age at onset; women who had had intercourse since injury were younger at the onset of injury. Sipski and Alexander[6] noted that although intercourse had been the favored activity pre-injury, kissing, hugging, and touching were the favored activities post-injury. After injury, 76 percent of the women engaged in both kissing and hugging, 68 percent in penis-vagina intercourse, 68 percent in touching, 56 percent in oral sex, 40 percent in manual stimulation, 24 percent in vibratory stimulation, and 12 percent in anal intercourse.

Although sexual activity continues post-injury, the frequency of sexual activity decreases. Sipski and Alexander[6] assessed sexual functioning pre- and post-injury in

25 SCI women, 64 percent of the women had engaged in a sexual activity at least one time per week pre-injury and only 48 percent had engaged in a sexual activity at least one time per week post-injury.

Charlifue et al.[4] surveyed 231 SCI women and found that prior to injury, 76 percent of the women reported having had sexual contact at least once a week; after injury, only 52 percent reported having had sexual contact at least once a week (with 34 percent having sexual contact less than once per month). Factors interfering with sexual activity included spasticity, lack of spontaneity, motion limitations, catheter interference, inadequate vaginal lubrication, and autonomic hyperreflexia. Zwerner,[7] reporting on the frequency of sexual activity in SCI females, found that just under half had a decrease in frequency post-injury, approximately 37 percent had no change, and 15 percent had an increase. Women with very high (daily) or very low (less than once a month) pre-injury sexual activity had less change in frequency than women with moderate (two to three times a week) sexual activity pre-injury. Age and marital status were thought to have influenced the frequency of sexual activity in these women.

Level of sexual satisfaction has also been found to decrease following SCI. In Sipski and Alexander's study,[6] 72 percent of the women felt sexually satisfied or very satisfied prior to injury, whereas only 48 percent of the women felt satisfied post-injury. Charlifue et al.[4] also noted that 69 percent of the women in their study expressed satisfaction with their post-injury sexual experiences.

Whereas the earlier studies began to examine the impact of SCI on sexuality, none of them compared the SCI population with the general population. However, Sipski et al.[8] conducted a laboratory-based assessment of the characteristics and physiological sexual responses during orgasm in 25 SCI women and compared their responses with those of 9 AB women. AB women reported greater levels of sexual satisfaction than did SCI women; however, SCI women had a more integrated gender role defini-

tion. Further, subjects who achieved orgasm had a higher sex drive and were significantly more educated about sexual functioning.

The Current Study

In the present study comparing SCI subjects with an AB comparison group, the DSFI was used to measure differences in sexuality and sexual functioning in 10 areas: information, experience, drive, attitude, psychological symptoms, affect, gender role definition, fantasy, body image, and sexual satisfaction.

Methods

Subjects included 84 women with SCI and 37 able-bodied (AB) women. Ages ranged from 18 to 61 years with a median age of 37 for SCI women and 32 for AB women. Most of the women were single and never married (40.5 percent of SCI and 41.7 percent of AB); however, the next largest group reported being currently married (27.0 percent and 35.7 percent, respectively). Number of children ranged from 0 to 5, with the majority of women having 0 children (75.7 percent and 57.1 percent). Education ranged from completing some high school to earning a graduate degree. The two largest categories of SCI women were those describing their highest level of education as four years of college (24.7 percent) or a graduate degree (23.5 percent). The two largest categories of AB women were those reporting some college (18.8 percent) or a graduate degree (18.8 percent). Annual incomes ranged from less than $10,000 to more than $40,000, with means of $27,000 for SCI women and $25,000 for AB women.

The largest group of SCI women reported injury in the thoracic region (38.6 percent) and the next largest group reported injury in the cervical region (32.5 percent). Of those who responded, 52 percent reported complete lesions and 48 percent reported incomplete lesions.

Subjects were recruited from a national list produced by the National Spinal Cord Injury Association (NSCIA). Return-addressed, stamped postcards requesting voluntary participation were mailed [and] one hundred twenty-six women returned the postcards, for a response rate of 36 percent. Two questionnaires were mailed to the respondents: one for each SCI woman and one for the SCI woman to give to an able-bodied friend. Eighty-four questionnaires were returned by SCI women and 37 were returned by AB women.

We used the DSFI,[9] a multidimensional test designed to measure current level of sexual functioning. It consists of 10 subsets: *Information* measures the subject's general knowledge regarding sexual functioning. *Experience* measures the variety of sexual behaviors that the subject has experienced. *Drive* assesses the person's level of interest in sex as determined by the frequency of various sexual activities. *Attitude* measures attitudes toward sexual activities and relationships. *Psychological symptoms* measure distress arising from psychological symptoms. *Affect* measures the subject's mood status. *Gender role definition* measures the balance between the subject's masculine and feminine characteristics. *Fantasy* assesses the number of different sexual fantasies acknowledged by the subject. *Body image* assesses the subject's satisfaction with her own body. *Sexual satisfaction* measures the degree to which the subject is gratified by her sexual life.

Results

Scores on drive, sexual satisfaction, psychological symptoms, and affect all differed at a significant level between SCI and AB women. SCI women scored significantly lower than AB women on the drive subscale and significantly lower on the sexual satisfaction subscale. Thus, SCI women engaged in sexual activities less frequently and experienced lower levels of sexual satisfaction in their current relationships than did AB women. SCI women scored significantly higher on the psychological symptoms subscale than did AB women and significantly lower on the affect subscale. SCI women experienced higher levels of psychological distress and higher negative affect than did AB women.

Age was found to be significantly related to sexual satisfaction among both SCI and AB women, but in opposite directions. The older the SCI women, the lower the score on the sexual satisfaction subscale. In contrast, the older the able-bodied women, the higher the score on the sexual satisfaction subscale. Women who were older at the time of injury indicated less sexual satisfaction in their current relationships by scoring significantly lower on the sexual satisfaction subscale. These women expressed more liberal attitudes about sexuality, had a more integrated gender role definition, and had more fantasies than did women whose injuries were of shorter duration. However, no significant associations were found with level of injury or severity of lesion.

Among SCI women, significant findings were also reported for income and education. The higher the income, the higher the score on the drive subscale. Educated SCI women experienced lower levels of psychological distress, felt more positive affect, and established a more integrated gender role definition. Lower levels of sexual satisfaction were [not found] among SCI women who were married.

Discussion

Married SCI women were no less sexually satisfied than AB women. Partner availability may influence levels of sexual satisfaction. Unmarried SCI women may have had more difficulty finding partners and thus achieving high levels of sexual satisfaction. Married SCI women may have found more security in their relationships, may have been more willing to experiment with different techniques, and may have found alternate ways of achieving sexual satisfaction. Similarly, Nosek et al.[10] found that women with disabilities who lived with a significant other reported greater sexual satisfaction and had a higher level of sexual activity.

Interpretation of the data poses certain challenges. In this study, responses were self-reported. Only perceptions of behavior were assessed, as opposed to actual behavior. Sexual functioning, sexual experiences, and sexual satisfaction are subject to response bias and subject uncertainty. There was also a relatively low response rate from both SCI and AB women. It is unclear whether women who were more adjusted and who felt more comfortable in answering questions on sexuality were more likely to respond.

In the present study, the procedure for selecting the comparison group was not random. The size of the comparison group in the present study [also] was less substantial than the SCI group, weakening the power of the analyses. Further, many of the women in the present sample were highly educated, single, and childless; therefore, the findings of this study may be most appropriately generalized to similar groups of women. However, Nosek et al.[10] also found that women with disabilities were more likely to be single and were much less likely to bear children than AB women. Similarly, the women in their study were well educated; 54 percent of women with disabilities and 42 percent of able-bodied women had college degrees.

The results of the present study indicate a need to continue addressing both the psychological and physiological aspects of female sexual functioning in SCI. Laboratory assessment can clarify the physiological aspects of sexual functioning. In the laboratory-based assessment of Sipski et al.,[8] 52 percent of SCI women were able to stimulate to orgasm. The ability to achieve orgasm in SCI women was not related to the degree or type of injury; no significant differences were found between any of the subject groups for heart rate and systolic and diastolic blood pressure during orgasm and no characteristics were identified that would have allowed prediction of which SCI women would be able to achieve orgasm. However, the ability to have an orgasm was related to the level of sexual knowledge and level of desire.

Further research is needed to identify possible predictors of orgasmic ability and the relationship of the predictors to sex drive and sexual satisfaction. Examination of the influence of both psychological and physiological factors on female sexual functioning is important in order to reach a more accurate diagnosis and identify treatment interventions that maximize sexual satisfaction in women with SCI.

References

1. Comarr A. Observations on menstruation and pregnancy among female spinal cord injury patients. *Paraplegia* 1996;3:263–72.

2. Ohry A, Peleg D, Goldman J, David A, Rozin R. Sexual function, pregnancy and delivery in spinal cord injured women. *Gyn Obstet Invest* 1978;9:281–291.

3. Kettl P, Zarefoss S, Jacoby K, et al. Female sexuality after spinal cord injury. *Sexual Disabil* 1991;9:287–95.

4. Charlifue SW, Gerhart KA, Mentor RR, Whiteneck GG, Manley MS. Sexual issues of women with spinal cord injuries. *Paraplegia* 1992;30:192–99.

5. White M, Rintala D, Hart KA, Fuhrer MJ. Sexual activities, concerns and interests of women with spinal cord injury living in the community. *Amer J Phys Med Rehabil* 1993;72:372–78.

6. Sipski ML, Alexander CJ. Sexual activities, response and satisfaction in women pre- and post-spinal cord injury. *Arch Phys Med Rehabil* 1993;74:1025–1029.

7. Zwerner J. Yes, we have trouble but nobody's listening: Sexual issues of women with spinal cord injury. *Sexual Disabil* 1982;5:158–71.

8. Sipski ML, Alexander CJ, Rosen RC. Orgasm in women with spinal cord injuries: A laboratory-based assessment. *Arch Phys Med Rehabil* 1995;76:1097–1102.

9. Derogatis L. Derogatis sexual functioning inventory. Baltimore; Clinical Psychometrics, 1975.

10. Nosek MA, Rintala DH, Young ME, et al. Sexual functioning among women with physical disabilities. *Arch Phys Med Rehabil* 1996;77:107–115.

Part VI

Birth Control and Sexually Transmitted Diseases

The vast majority of adults have engaged in sexual behavior that could potentially result in conception. We know this fact because only 2.8 percent of adults report never having had sex with a partner, and of those who have, 97 percent have had vaginal intercourse (Laumann, Gagnon, Michael, & Michaels, 1994). But, in "connecting the dots" of sex, contraception, and birth, a number of outcomes are possible, some of which are by choice and others by chance. Those variables subject to choice are fertility, sexual practices, and fertility control. Disconnecting these dots at any point can separate the act of sex from the consequence of having a baby (Laumann et al., 1994).

First, in order for a woman and man to produce a fertilized egg, they must both be fertile. Second, sexual practice affects the likelihood of conception because many sexual activities, such as oral sex, cannot result in conception. Third, many measures can be taken to reduce the likelihood that sexual intercourse will result in conception: contraception, timing of sexual intercourse during the menstrual cycle, and medical sterility. Finally, various factors can break down the connection between conception and birth. Some of these occur by chance, such as spontaneous abortion (i.e., miscarriage) and stillbirth, and some, by choice,

such as therapeutic abortion. In the two articles about abortion in Part VI, the subject of abortion by choice is raised.

RU-486 is hailed by leading contraceptive researchers as the only real discovery in birth control since the pill, and it is described by the Pope as the "Pill of Cain, the monster that cynically kills its brothers." With such confusing messages, readers of the Talbot selection initially are led down the science versus religion path in this controversy. But as the history of RU-486 unfolds, a number of related variables surface.

Most troubling to both factions in the abortion conflict is the issue of viability, an ever-present moral dilemma of gigantic proportions. Because viability is almost solely defined by evolving medical technology, it is a constantly moving target. And, for the majority of Americans, the concept of timing does make a difference in their opinion about abortion. For example, given the ability of a fetus at six months to survive outside of the womb, many persons are rethinking their positions on late-term abortions. Does, then, the fact that medical abortions can be accomplished so much earlier in pregnancy than most surgical abortions make them the more desirable of the two options? And does the fact that the use of RU-486 moves the setting to the privacy of a doctor's office, far from picket lines, diminish problems related to surgical abortion? These and other questions will be more easily answered by sexuality students after reading this selection. In fact, "The Little White Bombshell" is an excellent article to promote a lively class debate.

Much attention has been focused on the question of the physiological and psychological effects of abortion. At the present time, considerably more is known about the subsequent physiological health of women who have had abortions than about the psychological effects. In the late 1980s, the U.S. Surgeon General concluded that sufficient scientific evidence did not exist to condemn abortion as psychologically harmful (Carlson, 1989). Even so, there is concern about the issue of regret and about the long-term emotional effects of abortion. In fact, few, if any, longitudinal studies report data about long-term effects, as illustrated by their absence in the Adler et al. meta-analysis of the research literature. Nevertheless, this 1992 American Psychological Association-commissioned study is the most often cited source concerning the short-term psychological effects of abortion and one that sexuality students should not miss.

The sexual behavior patterns of individuals affect not only their chances for involvement in an unplanned pregnancy, but also their chances for contracting sexually transmitted diseases (STDs). The Centers for Disease Control (CDC) estimate that 15.5 million Americans become infected with STDs each year, two-thirds of whom are under age 25 (Kelly, 2001). Although the likelihood of STDs is affected by behavioral risk factors, among college students, knowledge about STDs does not appear to be associated with a reduction in risk-taking behavior. Large numbers of college students continue to report multiple sex partners, nonusage of condoms, and sexual intercourse undertaken with persons just met as well as sexual intercourse while under the influence of alcohol (Herold & McWhinney, 1993).

Medical evidence indicates that sexual activity that is anonymous, casual, with multiple partners, and/or with high-risk partners substantially increases the likelihood of contracting an STD. But, a body of evidence exists that shows consistent use of condoms greatly reduces this likelihood. However, consistent condom usage is affected by both psychological and interpersonal factors as well as those cultural in nature. For example, white men are more likely to indicate that condoms are embarrassing to buy and to discard, while African American men are more likely to report that condom usage reflects a caring attitude (Grady, Klepinger, Billy, & Tanfer, 1993). On the other hand, African American women are less likely to insist on the use of condoms than are white women (U. S. Bureau of the Census, 1998). The offering by Norris and Ford will certainly help confirm the interdependence of cultural factors and sexual behavior patterns.

The Tanfer and Aral survey of women who report having sexual intercourse during menstruation offers another important piece of the STD puzzle for readers. Although the prevalence of certain sexual and hygienic practices has been the subject of many research efforts, this 1995 study appears to be the first population-based estimate of the relationship between the practice of sexual intercourse during menstruation and STDs. The number of cultural and normative factors teased from the data regarding sexual practices may provoke more questions than answers among students. Nevertheless, the article is a "must read" for students who wish to assume their own advocacy in the STD arena.

The Burk et al. article, derived from their presentation at the International Human Papillomavirus (HPV) Workshop in Amsterdam in 1994, contributes significantly to the present knowledge about the HPV infection. With over three million cases of genital warts requiring treatment annually, HPV is the most common viral STD in the United States (Hyde & DeLamater, 2000). Like the genital herpes virus, it is a "gift" that keeps on giving. Not only can subsequent partners be affected, but it can be transmitted to a baby during vaginal delivery if the warts are on the cervix or in the vagina.

The strengths of this study are rigorous design and execution by a team of medical researchers who test the hypothesis that sexual behavior and partner characteristics are the major risk factors for HPV in young women. The analysis of the data yields valuable information for young persons in today's world. Because the association between sexual behavior and female HPV infection in previous studies has not been reported consistently in the literature, this selection is an important feature in this unit.

References

Carlson, M. (1989, April 24). A doctor prescribes hard truth. *Time*, pp. 82, 84.

Crooks, R., & Baur, K. (1999). *Our sexuality* (7th ed.). Pacific Grove, CA: Brooks/Cole.

Davidson, J. K., Sr., & Moore, N. B. (1996). *Marriage and family: Change and continuity.* Boston: Allyn & Bacon.

Grady, W. R., Klepinger, D. H., Billy, J. O. G., & Tanfer, K. (1993). Condom characteristics: The perceptions and preferences of men in the United States. *Family Planning Perspectives, 25,* 67–73.

Herold, E. S., & McWhinney, D. K. (1993). Gender differences in casual sex and AIDS prevention: A survey of dating bars. *The Journal of Sex Research, 30,* 36–42.

Hyde, J. S., & DeLamater, J. D. (2000). *Understanding human sexuality* (7th ed.). Boston: McGraw-Hill.

Kelly, G. F. (2001). *Sexuality today: The human perspective* (7th ed.). New York: McGraw-Hill.

Laumann, E. O., Gagnon, J. H., Michael, R. T., & Michaels, S. (1994). *The social organization of sexuality: Sexual practices in the United States.* Chicago: University of Chicago Press.

U.S. Bureau of the Census. (1998). No. 119. Contraceptive use by women, 15 to 44 years of age: 1985. In *Statistical abstracts of the United States, 1998* (118th ed., p. 90). Washington, DC: U.S. Government Printing Office. ✦

Chapter 26
Condom Use of Heterosexual African American and Hispanic Youth

Anne E. Norris
Kathleen Ford

In researching condom usage among African American and Hispanic youth, Norris and Ford focus on the male condom. By contrast, there is so far a dearth of empirical findings about the female condom, which has been available only since the early 1990s. Perhaps related to the lack of research is the limited interest in and use of the female condom to date. The fact that the majority of women and men report decreased sensation and pleasure while using it may be another contributing factor. In particular, it makes penile penetration more difficult and sometimes leads to soreness of the penis due to inadequate lubrication. However, some African American women have expressed strong support for the female condom because they believe its use allows them to practice "safer sex" without having to challenge the power of their male partners. After reading this article, consider the following: Because African American women strongly support use of the female condom, could its inclusion in the research paradigm have changed the study results significantly? If so, what would be the implications for future research? And, finally, how influential is the balance of female and male power in contraceptive choice and use?

Recent statistics on the incidence of sexually transmitted diseases (STDs), including HIV, continue to argue for condom use interventions for adolescents and young adults.[1] An understanding of the differences and similarities between adolescents who practice relative monogamy (a single, longer term monogamous relationship), serial monogamy (a series of shorter term, monogamous relationships), and nonmonogamy (involvement in concurrent relationships) is important to the design and targeting of condom use interventions because these groups may have different needs and concerns regarding condom use. For example, nonmonogamous youth may perceive their behavior as more risky and be more likely to use condoms. Such youth might benefit from interventions that stress how to use condoms effectively and for pleasure. In contrast, those that engage in relative or serial monogamy may believe that by doing so they have minimized their exposure to HIV and other STDs and do not need to use condoms.[2–3] These youth might need interventions that stress their vulnerability to infection and how to talk about condoms with a partner. However, relative and serial monogamous youth might in turn need different interventions to help them effectively talk with their partner given the different social contexts that may arise as a function of differences in relationship length.

This study has two purposes. First, it describes demographic characteristics, sexual history, perceived HIV susceptibility, and current sexual behavior, condom use, and alcohol and marijuana use of heterosexual, low-income African American and Hispanic youth categorized as relatively monogamous, serial monogamous, or nonmonogamous. Second, the study explore[s] what demographic and sexual history variables may differentiate between youth who practice relative monogamy, serial monogamy, or nonmonogamy.

In general, current research and theories offer competing hypotheses as to how relatively monogamous, serial monogamous, and nonmonogamous youth may differ in their perceived susceptibility to HIV, sexual behavior, and condom use. The perception of safety from harm believed to surround monogamous (both relative and serial) relationships[4] may lead to a reduced perceived susceptibility[5] to HIV infection and foster involvement in other risky sexual practices such as anal intercourse. Yep[6] found that perceived susceptibility to HIV was associated with college students' practice of monogamy. Findings from the National Health and Social Life Survey (NHSLS) suggest that anal sex may be more common for adults in relationships of greater than a month's duration and in cohabitational and marriage relationships.[7] Other research suggests that many individuals who practice relative or serial monogamy may not use condoms consistently. More than half of the participants in the National Survey of Adolescent Males [NSAM] who were between the ages of 17 and 22 years reported using condoms at first intercourse with a new partner, with condom use declining substantially with subsequent episodes of intercourse with this same partner.[8] Findings from national surveys of adults indicate that adult men and women involved in monogamous (relative and serial combined) relationships are less likely to use condoms than those involved in nonmonogamous relationships.[7,9] A study of patients at a university-based adolescent clinic found that sexually experienced adolescents believed condoms were used less frequently with steady partners and more frequently with one night stands.[10]

Alternatively, Zuckerman's theory of sensation seeking and related research predict that nonmonogamous youth should have a lower consistency of condom use and be more likely to use drugs and engage in anal sex than relatively and serial monogamous youth.[11] This theory holds that certain individuals ("sensation seekers") are chronically underaroused and consequently seek to improve their arousal levels through involvement in activities that are inherently physiologically arousing (e.g., anal sex) or arousing because of how they have come to be socially defined (e.g., sex with a partner

that you don't know well).[11] The social definitions associated with nonmonogamy, anal sex, etc. should make these sensation seekers more likely to engage in these behaviors and also more likely to perceive their susceptibility to HIV as high.

Clear predictions regarding demographic differences between these three groups are also difficult to make because the literature tends to cite statistics for persons with more than one partner in the past year, thereby lumping serial and nonmonogamous individuals together.[12] However, gender differences in sensation seeking would argue that nonmonogamous youth are more likely to be male.[11] In addition, data from the NHSLS indicate that men tend to have more partners than women and Hispanic adults have fewer sexual partners than African American or white adults.[7] Analyses of data from several national surveys indicate that younger individuals (age 18–24 years) are more likely to have multiple, serial partners than older individuals (age 25–59 years).[13]

THE CURRENT STUDY
Method

Sample

A probability sample was used: 724 African American and 711 Hispanic youth (ages 15 to 24 years) participated in a low-income area of Detroit. Data are based on the 73.2 percent of the total sample that could be categorized as being in a relatively monogamous, serial monogamous, or nonmonogamous heterosexual relationship during the year preceding the survey interview. Respondents were categorized as *Relatively Monogamous* if they reported having had only one married/lived with partner or only one partner that they knew well in the past year and they were monogamous in this relationship. Respondents were categorized as *Serial Monogamous* if they reported having had more than one married/lived with partner or partner that they knew well in the past year, they were monogamous in these relationships, and the dates for first and last sexual experiences within these relationships did not overlap. Respondents were categorized as *Nonmonogamous* if they reported having had more than one married/lived with partner or partner that they knew well in the past year, and reported that they were not monogamous in these relationships.

Survey Interview

A history of pregnancy was measured by asking a respondent if she had ever been pregnant or if he had ever made a woman pregnant. A history of a sexually transmitted disease was measured by asking if the respondent had ever been told by a doctor or a nurse that she or he had a disease that might have been caused by having sex.

Perceived susceptibility to HIV was measured in four ways. The first two measures were fairly standard: Respondents were asked in general how often they worry about getting AIDS and whether they worried about getting AIDS from a specific partner (e.g., married/lived with partner; well known, but not lived with partner; not well known partner). The third and fourth measures were indirect: Respondents were asked if they thought their partner had sex with other people or had any diseases that people get by having sex during their relationship.

Consistency of condom use was assessed for an average month of sexual activity in the year preceding the interview. Respondents were asked how much of the time during this average month did they or their partner put a condom on the penis.

Respondents were also asked about their reasons for use and nonuse of condoms. For purposes of the analyses reported here, reasons for using condoms were: STD prevention only; pregnancy prevention or both pregnancy and STD prevention; neither STD prevention nor pregnancy prevention.

Frequency of intercourse was measured by asking respondents how often in an average month during the year preceding the interview they had vaginal, anal, or oral intercourse with their partner. Drug use with the partner was measured by asking respondents if they had ever used alcohol or marijuana when they were with their partner in the year preceding the interview.

Procedure

Sixty interviewers were specially hired and trained for the study. They ranged in age from 20 to 60 years. All but two were African American or Hispanic. All lived in or near the area in which the study was conducted, but did not interview any respondents that they knew personally. Respondents were interviewed face-to-face at home or in a neutral setting (e.g., public library) if privacy could not be assured in the home. The interview was offered in English and Spanish, and 15 percent of the Hispanic respondents did the interview in Spanish.

Interviewers and respondents were matched regarding ethnicity to the extent possible. Female respondents were interviewed by female interviewers. Male respondents chose to be interviewed by either male or female interviewers.

Results

Demographic Characteristics

Results from these analyses suggest that relatively monogamous, serial monogamous, and nonmonogmous youth have different demographic characteristics. Monogamous youth were most likely to be female and Hispanic and to have been married. Serial monogamous youth were younger, and consistent with this, most likely to be currently attending school. Relatively monogamous, serial monogamous, and nonmonogamous youth did not differ according to employment status, parental level of education, religion, Hispanic origin, or level of acculturation after controlling for age, gender, and ethnicity.

Sexual history. Relatively monogamous youth initiated sexual intercourse later, and consistent with this, had the fewest number of lifetime sexual partners and were least likely to have ever been diagnosed with an STD. Nonmonogamous youth were least likely to have used a condom at first intercourse and most likely to have engaged in oral and anal sex . They were also less likely than relatively and serial monogamous youth to have experienced a pregnancy (or impregnated their partner)—perhaps because pregnancy could more likely be a goal in the latter types of relationships. Note that a high percentage reported ever using a condom in all three groups, but that relatively monogamous youth are somewhat less likely to have ever used a condom.

Perceived HIV Susceptibility

General worry about getting HIV was low, with nonmonogamous youth reporting slightly more worry than relatively and serial monogamous youth. A pattern emerged such that relatively monogamous youth seemed least likely to perceive themselves as susceptible, nonmonogamous youth, most likely, and serial monogamous youth falling about midway between these two groups.

Sexual behavior in year preceding interview. Nonmonogamous youth engaged in sexual intercourse slightly more often than relative and serial monogamous youth, had the greatest number of partners in the past year, and were most likely to have engaged in oral and anal sex. They were also least likely to have engaged in sex without a condom or other method of birth control.

Condom use in year preceding interview. The three groups did not differ significantly in terms of consistency of condom use. However, serial monogamous youth were most likely to have used a condom at last intercourse. In addition, relatively monogamous youth were least likely to both carry condoms and keep them at home and slightly less likely than the other two groups to have used a condom at least once in the year preceding the interview. In general, consistency of condom use did not vary as a function of perceived partner monogamy or likelihood that partner had an STD.

The three groups did differ in their reasons for using condoms. Relatively monogamous youth were less likely to report using condoms solely for STD prevention than serial or nonmonogamous youth. However, similar proportions in all three

groups (54.9 percent to 60.0 percent) reported using condoms for pregnancy or both pregnancy and STD prevention.

Drug use in year preceding interview. Group differences were noted for both alcohol and marijuana use. Nonmonogamous youth were most likely to have used these drugs with their partner during this time period.

Looking across the results for the sample subgroups and the sample as a whole, we find that age at first intercourse, experience with oral sex, and number of partners are the best predictors for discriminating between relatively monogamous youth and youth who are serial monogamous or nonmonogamous. Conversely, age and being in school are the best predictors for discriminating between serial monogamous youth and relatively monogamous and nonmonogamous youth. Note, some predictors fail to be significant in all subgroup analyses. For example, gender is not a significant predictor for African Americans, experience with pregnancy is not a significant predictor for females, having had an STD is not a significant predictor for Hispanics, and condom use at first intercourse is not a significant predictor for females or Hispanics.

Conclusion

Findings from this study suggest that there are distinct subgroups of youth who practice relative monogamy, serial monogamy, and nonmonogamy. Youth who practiced these partnership behaviors differed significantly in terms of demographic characteristics, sexual history, perceived susceptibility to HIV, and sexual behavior in the year preceding the interview. The findings argue that nonmonogamous youth may be sensation seekers[11]—individuals who engage in a variety of risky behaviors to increase their level of arousal. In this study, nonmonogamous youth were most likely to have engaged in oral and anal intercourse, used alcohol and marijuana with a partner, and believed that their partners were nonmonogamous and had an STD. However, the three groups did not differ in their consistency of condom use in the year preceding the time of interview. This suggests that failure to use condoms may not have been perceived as risky by nonmonogamous youth, and given the social context of risk definition,[14] potentially the other two groups of youth as well.

We found mixed support for the notion that relatively and serial monogamous youth engage in more risky behaviors perhaps as a function of the belief that monogamous relationships are safer than nonmonogamous ones. Anal sex was not more common in these relationships, and serial monogamous youth were as likely as nonmonogamous youth to carry condoms. However, relatively monogamous youth were least likely to worry about getting AIDS from their partner, least likely to keep condoms at home, least likely to report using condoms solely for STD prevention, and most likely to have engaged in unprotected intercourse.

The groups could be differentiated on the basis of age, current school attendance, age at first intercourse, experience with oral sex, and not surprisingly, number of lifetime partners. This supports targeting interventions toward youth who begin intercourse at an early age (i.e., youth who are not likely to be monogamous). Gender was also important for Hispanic, but not African American youth. This provides further support for the distinctiveness of the groups and argues for the importance of social and cultural influences on sexual behavior.

Four cautions are in order in interpreting these data. First, the age range (15–24 years) of the sample was broad for this developmental stage. We statistically controlled for age effects, but were not able to explore how sexual practices differed within particular age groups.

Second, the study sample did not contain any urban, low-income white youth or middle and upper income African American and Hispanic youth and was conducted in Detroit. Therefore, it is unclear how these findings would generalize to other population subgroups, and these findings may not generalize to low-income African American and Hispanic youth from other parts of the country.

Third, our measures for frequency of intercourse and consistency of condom use are imprecise, and this imprecision may have minimized differences between the groups for these two variables. Respondents estimated the frequency of these behaviors for an average month during the past year. Frequency of intercourse for adolescents may vary widely with respect to privacy opportunities and relationship status. It is also possible that consistency of condom use may vary as a function of perceived partner monogamy or likelihood that the partner has an STD, but we found no evidence of this in these data.

Fourth, the use of a 1-year period to study relative monogamy, serial monogamy, and nonmonogamy provides only a beginning appreciation of the potential differences between relatively monogamous, serial monogamous, and nonmonogamous individuals. For example, longitudinal data might show that there are four groups of individuals: *relatively or truly monogamous* (only 1 partner in 3 to 5 years), *slow serial monogamous* (i.e., a series of two to three monogamous relationships over the 3 to 5 years), *fast serial monogamous* (i.e., two to three monogamous relationships every year), and *nonmonogamous* (more than one partner concurrently). A longitudinal study would be extremely useful because it would allow detection of moderators and mediators of membership in these three groups, as well as risk behaviors in general.

Although some caution is in order, it is, nevertheless, important to consider what these findings imply: It may be wise to take an existing program that has known efficacy (e.g., one emphasizing condom negotiation skills and the pleasure aspects of condom use[15-16]) and adapt it slightly to meet the needs of a particular group. For example, programs targeting nonmonogamous youth might avoid any discussion of susceptibility and instead emphasize how to use condoms to increase sexual pleasure (e.g., discuss use of lubricants, implications for orgasm) and distribute condoms that are likely to encourage use for experi-

years production and distribution in this country hit snag after snag.

When the French manufacturer, Roussel-Uclaf, and its parent company, Hoechst A. G. of Germany, refused to sell RU-486 here, American feminists organized picket lines outside Hoechst plants in this country and flew delegations to Paris to lobby company officials. It didn't work. By then, the Pope himself had denounced RU-486 as the "pill of Cain—the monster that cynically kills its brothers," and Hoechst feared boycotts of its products in the United States, where it does more than $6 billion worth of business. Moreover, Hoechst had particular reason to be touchy. It was one of the corporations that emerged from the breakup of I.G. Farben, the German chemical company that manufactured the cyanide gas, Zyklon B for Nazi death camps, and Hoechst was sensitive to charges that it was again manufacturing what one right-to-life group called "a human pesticide." In 1988, in the face of opposition from anti-abortion groups and Catholic bishops, in France, Hoechst's subsidiary, Roussel, announced it would drop the drug entirely. Only after the French Health Minister declared RU-486 "the moral property of women" and ordered Roussel to bring it to market, did the company do so. In the United States, where abortion is a far more volatile issue, Hoechst seemed determined to stay out of the fray. "We've been petitioned, we've been yelled at and we've been telephoned by everybody," Edward Norton, the spokesman for Hoechst-Roussel Pharmaceuticals of New Jersey, said. "But our formal position hasn't changed in two years, and I don't expect it to change."

During the Reagan and Bush Administrations, the FDA classified RU-486 as a banned drug, effectively halting all Federal research on it, and pro-choicers decided they would resort to more unconventional means. In 1992, a pregnant 29-year-old social worker named Leona Benten tried to challenge the law by bringing her own personal stash of RU-486 into the country from England, only to see it confiscated by U.S. Customs. The Supreme Court heard Benten's appeal but upheld the confiscation just 16 days after she arrived at J.F.K. accompanied by the abortion-rights activist Lawrence Lader.

Next, Lader and his organization, Abortion Rights Mobilization (ARM), fixed on the daring idea of making the pill themselves, using published patents. In 1993, they rented part of a warehouse in a Westchester County suburb and, unbeknown to the landlord, set up what was in effect an underground drug lab, complete with plentiful dry ice, an oversize ventilation hood and a volunteer scientist who agreed to moonlight there only if he could be known to his new colleagues as Dr. X, for fear of reprisals from anti-abortion extremists. If outsiders questioned them, project members agreed to say they had been working on a new treatment for cancer, Lader recalls in his book, "A Private Matter: RU-486 and the Abortion Crisis." Even logistically, it was a complicated process; the synthesis of mifepristone involved 10 separate steps, and since the equipment Lader and his colleagues could afford wasn't really big enough for the task, each step had to be repeated many times. Yet by 1994 ARM had developed its own copy of the drug, and by 1997 Lader was announcing plans to offer mifepristone to as many as 10,000 women. ARM would donate the supply to clinics conducting research on it.

Still, the only real hope for a more reliable source of mifespristone, and for FDA approval, lay in persuading Hoechst to give up its patent on the drug or else start making it itself. Soon after Bill Clinton was elected in 1992, his Administration had begun exerting pressure on Roussel-Uclaf, and in 1994, the company, which stopped manufacturing the drug in 1997, donated the U.S. rights to the Population Council, a New York-based nonprofit organization that promotes reproductive health.

Now the day is at hand when RU-486 will at last be widely available—and we can see for ourselves whether a significant change in abortion technology really can transform the abortion debate. To talk to the doctors and nurses and patients who have been using this method over the last few years is to be persuaded that it may well reconfigure the politics and perception of abortion in this country more definitively than any piece of legislation has in the quarter century since *Roe v. Wade*. As Suzanne Poppema, a Seattle doctor who has participated in both of the major clinical trials of mifepristone in the United States, puts it, "This method is the best means we've had yet for defusing the abortion conflict."

Her optimism seems well founded. Not only are mifepristone abortions, by nature, more discreet than their surgical equivalents, but the practitioners who prescribe them will almost certainly constitute a larger and a more varied group than the dwindling corps of OB-GYNs willing to do surgical abortions. In 1998, when the Henry J. Kaiser Family Foundation polled family practitioners about their interest in using mifepristone once it was approved and available, 45 percent of doctors responding said they were "very" or "somewhat" likely to do so. Fifty-four percent of nurse-practitioners and physician assistants expressed interest in offering the drug. Yet only 3 percent of the physicians in the study and 2 percent of the practitioners and assistants had performed surgical abortions.

Similarly, in a 1996 survey of doctors who belong to the Society for Adolescent Medicine, 42 percent said they would prescribe legal medical abortion, though only 2 percent currently offered the surgical option. The potential for expanding the number of abortion providers in rural areas is perhaps even more dramatic. One study found that while less than 4 percent of all OB-GYNs, family practitioners and general surgeons practicing in rural Idaho performed abortions, 26 percent said they would definitely be interested in prescribing RU-486, and another 35 percent were uncertain.

"One of my real, and I think realistic, hopes for this method," says Carolyn Westhoff, an OB-GYN at Columbia University medical school who offers medical abortion as part of a clinical trial, "is that it will help get abortion back into the medical mainstream and out of this ghettoized place it's been in." And if that is indeed the scenario we're looking at—a scenario in which abortion is folded far more seamless into regular medical practice—then it has implications not only for women's experience of abortion but for the politics of abortion as well.

At the very least, it will present the right-to-life movement with new tactical challenges. If abortions are taking place in all kinds of medical settings, and at home, then abortion clinics can no longer be the potent symbols they have become over the last decade. Mifepristone is also an abortifacient that can be used very early in pregnancy—earlier, by as many as five weeks, than surgical abortions have typically been offered. Along with other new methods, including a less practical but already FDA-approved drug called methotrexate and a newly revived technique called manual vacuum aspiration, mifepristone pushes back the time at which women can get abortions—back as far as the point at which sophisticated new home-pregnancy tests can first tell them they are pregnant.

"The other question then," says Carole Joffe, a sociologist at the University of California at Davis who has been studying the probable response of doctors to mifepristone, is, "Will abortion become more socially acceptable in this country if these technologies help to make more and more abortions happen earlier and earlier?" Abortions in the earliest weeks of pregnancy are not only safer, cheaper and less emotionally wrenching for the women who undergo them; they are also more politically tenable.

A 1998 *New York Times/CBS News* poll showed that 61 percent of Americans favor legal abortion in the first trimester of pregnancy, but that support drops precipitously as pregnancy develops, down to 15 percent in the second trimester and a mere 7 percent in the third. "For most Americans, as opposed to most of the right-to-life movement," says Cory Richard, the vice president for public policy at the Alan Guttmacher Institute, the family-planning think tank, "an abortion at 3 weeks is a very different thing from an abortion at 23 weeks. Earlier is better, and prevention is better yet."

Not that, in the short term, these political changes will necessarily be evident. Some anti-abortion tactics will be easily adaptable to the new terrain. "We intend to target the distributors of this drug, just as we have doctors," says Jeff White, a spokesman for the radical anti-abortion group Operation Rescue West. "We'll do our investigations; we'll find out the names of company executives; we'll go to their neighborhoods." On the other hand, even White admits that doctors who offer mifepristone as one of a diverse range of services will be much more difficult to identify than those who do surgical abortion now. All of which calls to mind what Joffe calls "the only solution I see to being targeted by terrorists. It's what I think of as the King of Denmark model. If everyone in Denmark puts on a yellow star, how do you know who the Jews are? If all kinds of practitioners—OB-GYNs, nurse-midwives, family docs—are doing abortions, how do you single out your targets?"

Of course, until mifepristone is actually on the market, speculation about how it will change the world of abortion can only be that. And if the past is any indication, there may still be stumbling blocks. In 1996, the FDA declared mifepristone "approvable," meaning that it considered the drug safe and effective for American women and expected to grant a final O.K. when it could obtain further information about how the drug would be manufactured and labeled. Finding a U.S. manufacturer was up to the Population Council. But in an era when most big pharmaceutical companies are reluctant to develop new contraceptives, let alone new abortifacients, identifying a company that would actually make the pill on a large scale turned out be the hardest part of all. Lobbied vigorously by conservative investment funds, virtually all of the major U.S. pharmaceutical companies are said to have declined to either produce or distribute mifepristone.

Then, when the Population Council finally did find a distributor, a lawyer turned entrepreneur named Joseph Pike, it seemed to have compounded risky politics with sheer bad luck. Pike turned out to have been disbarred after pleading guilty to forgery, and the Council filed suit against him. When it turned to Danco and its group of investors assembled solely for the purpose of marketing mifepristone, Danco in turn picked a Hungarian company called Gedeon Richter to actually manufacture the pill. But in 1997, Gedeon Richter suddenly backed out of the deal.

Now Danco's spokeswoman, Heather O'Neill, says the company has found manufacturers—more than one—that it trusts, and plans for a 1999 release of the drug are proceeding on schedule. Danco's investors may be politically motivated in part, but they also hope to make money and believe, based on the drug's pattern of adoption in France, that they will. Yet the company is still extraordinarily skittish about publicity. I called Danco's New York offices for weeks before anyone phoned me back. O'Neill, a 28-year-old Harvard graduate who went on to the Kennedy School and whose real interest is women's health policy, not running interference for jumpy investors, is the only public voice of Danco. Most of the questions I ask her elicit nervous laughter and long pauses, followed by the most parsimonious of replies. She won't reveal the names or the locations of the manufacturer or even whether they are start-ups for this purpose or established companies, and she says that Danco will try to maintain this secrecy throughout the manufacturing process.

She does, however, say that Danco has finessed one potential complication by deciding to distribute mifepristone directly to doctors and clinics, rather than to pharmacists. "It won't be available through pharmacies," say O'Neill, "because it's a medical procedure and proper counseling is really important." But the more compelling reason, surely, is the likelihood that some individual pharmacists and even some drugstore chains would simply refuse to dispense it, as some of them have already refused to dispense Preven, the emergency contraception kit. Wal-Mart, one of the country's biggest pharmaceutical retailers, announced last fall, for instance, that it would not sell Preven, and a small but noisy group called Pharmacists for Life International has been pushing for state laws and professional "conscience clauses" protecting druggists who refuse to fill prescriptions for abortifacients and even birth-control pills.

Other hazards are still looming, though. Sources close to Danco say it's unlikely that any of the manufacturers will pull out at this point, if their anonymity is protected. But that's a big if. The FDA will know who and where the manufacturers are, because its agents will have to inspect the plants. And once a public agency has the information, keeping it out of the public's hands becomes a much dicier matter. "I can't think of any precedent for that kind of secrecy," says Lars Noah, a law professor at the University of Florida whose expertise is food and drug law. "I've never heard of a situation where, with the blessing of the FDA, you could keep the manufacturer of a drug secret. Then again, it's hard to think of any other pharmaceutical with the potential political impact this one has."

The FDA itself "doesn't have to make a big deal out of it," says Noah. "I'm sure they're sympathetic, and they don't have to publicize the names. The more important question is, Can the agency resist efforts by members of the public to find out where the facilities are? Anybody can request that information under F.O.I.A."—the Freedom of Information Act. There is an exemption to the act that covers confidential commercial information, and Danco might argue that revealing the names of manufacturers would harm commercial prospects. "But that's not the way that exemption has ever been interpreted in the past," Noah says. "And it's unlikely that any of the other exemptions would apply."

Moreover, even if the marketing of mifepristone comes off without a hitch, right-to-life legislators might well succeed in restricting access to it. "I've seen so many corners we were about to go around, that

while I'm optimistic, I'm also skeptical," says Felicia Stewart, the former director of reproductive health programs at the Kaiser Family Foundation and a longtime advocate of medical abortion. Eric Schaff, at the University of Rochester, who is supervising the current round of clinical trials for mifepristone in which about 4,000 women have participated, says he is convinced that the drug is safe and that administering it is a simple procedure that midwives or nurse-practitioners could do. "Given that, it's almost ludicrous to imagine the kind of regulations that we may see," he says. "But that doesn't mean we won't see them."

Last year, the House of Representatives voted 223 to 202 to bar the FDA from spending federal money on the testing or development of any drug that chemically induces abortion. The amendment has failed to find a sponsor in the Senate, but Tom Coburn, the Oklahoma congressman who introduced the amendment, reintroduced it last month (and it passed again). Other anti-abortion members might sponsor legislation that limits who can provide mifepristone or requires that misoprostol, the drug that is used in tandem with it and that induces contractions, be administered in a doctor's office or hospital. (This is the protocol required in France, and it will be the one recommended by Danco, but Schaff's trials have shown considerable success with at-home use and virtually all patients prefer it.) And opponents may still seek to circumvent the FDA's decision entirely, although approval is all but certain. "It's true that the approval process is very far along," admits Jim Sedlak, the director of public policy for the staunchly anti-abortion American Life League. "But we're not going to give up. We'll appeal to Congress to override the FDA."

Yet the truth is, none of this may matter quite as much as it seems because in some ways medical abortion is already a reality. Once the FDA issues final approval of mifepristone, and regardless of the protocol stipulated on the label, doctors may make use of the drug more or less as they like. Misoprostol, which is already approved for ulcer therapy, can also be used alone as an abortifacient, though it is more effective in combination with other drugs. Abortions induced by misoprostol in conjunction with a drug called methotrexate, which has been approved since 1954 as a treatment for cancer and other diseases but not as an abortifacient, are already available at no fewer than 75 facilities across the country. (The main strike against methotrexate is that it takes longer and is less predictable than mifepristone; a woman who takes it could miscarry as much as two weeks later.)

Besides, the clinical trials of mifepristone in the United States have helped generate interest in the drug that may prove hard to squelch, especially since women reported such high levels of satisfaction with it. In the Population Council trial, 88 percent of women who took mifepristone said they found the pill very or moderately satisfactory, while 96 percent said they would recommend it to friends or relatives. Even among women for whom the method failed—they ended up having to get vacuum aspirations—mifepristone proved surprisingly acceptable: 70 percent of them said they would try it again if they had to have an abortion.

Just as important, the promise of RU-486, and even the delays in bringing it here, have already helped shift the focus of many doctors and pro-choice activists alike to earlier abortion, pushing clinicians to reconsider the seven- or eight-week threshold at which many of them would do surgical abortions. Over the last few years, clinics across the country have begun employing manual vacuum aspiration earlier than they have traditionally performed abortions—in some places as early as four or even three weeks after a woman's last period. Combine this with the availability of emergency contraception—which can work up to 72 hours after unprotected intercourse, either to block ovulation, to thwart fertilization or to prevent a fertilized egg from implanting itself in the wall of the uterus—and you close the gap between the time a woman knows or suspects she is carrying an unwanted pregnancy and the time she can end it.

On the day I spend in Schaff's Rochester office, his first medical abortion patient is the college student who cares most of all about what the embryo looks like. The last is a 28-year-old secretary from a little upstate town who cares most of all about the privacy this method affords her. In the counselor's office, she sounds articulate and self-possessed and even cheerful. Her plaid flannel shirt is neatly pressed, and she wears tortoise-shell glasses and tiny diamond earrings. She has been reading about mifepristone on the Internet and anticipates much of what the counselor has to tell her. "I didn't want to go to a clinic and have to walk through a big line of protestors," she says, without hesitation, when I ask her why she didn't choose a surgical abortion. "I liked the idea of going to a hospital, of nobody knowing why I was going. My family and certain friends I've told know about this. I just don't think there's anyone else who needs to know."

Another of Schaff's patients, a 23-year-old waitress and part-time student who is the single mother of a 3-year-old, is in a much different mood. She cries off and on during her examination, and there are dark crescents of sleeplessness under her eyes. When Schaff asks her if she needs anything, she says, "How about a shot of Cuervo?" She has opted for a manual vacuum aspiration, a kind of surgical abortion in which doctors use a hand-held tube rather than a noisy machine to empty the contents of the uterus. It is faster than medical abortion—which appeals to this woman because, she says, "I just want to get it over with. I don't believe in this. I don't know how I'm going to live with myself. But I have to think of my son." It can also be done early, though, and because it does not require expensive specialized equipment, it can be performed in a variety of doctors' offices. Like the secretary, this woman, too, had wanted to avoid a clinic, threading through a phalanx of demonstrators, the whole chaotic scene.

When you consider how many women in the United States would be likely to choose medical over surgical abortion if they had the chance, the statistics from Europe can offer some sort of benchmark. Between 16 and 25 percent of abortions in France are RU-486-induced; in Sweden, the figure is about 17 percent, and in England, where coverage for abortions by the National Health Service has encountered administrative problems, it is about 6 percent.

But as a predictor of the drug's adoption here, those numbers probably aren't all that helpful, for the simple reason that in France, Sweden and Britain, abortion is not the bitterly divisive issue it is here. Avoiding a clinic because you fear violence or don't want to be harangued is not a motivation for seeking out non-surgical methods. Privacy isn't as much of a value unto itself. Being able to abort at home holds less appeal. In Scotland, says David Grimes, an OB-GYN and vice president of biomedical affairs at Family Health International, a family-planning think tank in Durham, N.C., researchers have found that "given the choice, women like taking the second dose in the clinic, waiting with other women, sort of bonding with other women in the same situation. U.S. women are very different. Privacy is very important to them."

When women who have tried RU-486 here are asked, in various studies, why they chose it, they often say that they wanted to avoid surgery or that they preferred a less invasive method that they regarded as more "natural," more like a spontaneous miscarriage. "The women who prefer it," says Suzanne Poppema, the Seattle doctor, "like the idea that instead of having instruments placed inside them and having something removed, they are working with their own bodies to expel the pregnancy."

But even these reasons can't entirely be disentangled from the conflict over abortion. The fear of surgical abortion is partly an artifact of polemics. The vague conviction that abortion is a dirty, dangerous business has been fed not only by the pro-life forces but also, inadvertently, by the pro-choice movement, which by telling over and over again the grim story of back-alley abortions, helps affix to the procedure itself a permanent aura of risk and disrepute. In fact, surgical abortion in the United States is safer than childbirth. Serious complications are rare, especially in the first trimester, when about 90 percent of all abortions are performed. "If you're instrumenting the uterus, there is some small risk of infection," says Elizabeth P. Newhall, a gynecologist in Portland, Oregon. "So to the extent that infection can compromise fertility, there is less risk with medical abortion than there is with surgical. The fact is, though, that both methods carry extremely low risks, so we're talking about the difference between microscopic and infinitesimal."

For all of these reasons, it is probably true that medical abortion will meet more needs in the United States than it does in France, say, and that we can probably expect more women to choose it here. The Feminist Majority Foundation has predicted that in the future 50 percent of abortions will be medical. This seems high, at least in the short term; plenty of women will always prefer a surgical procedure that can be done quickly and with a minimum of side effects, particularly if they work and have small children at home. But it may not be so far off, either. "Abortion in the U.S. is this degraded, shameful, violence-surrounded thing," says Carole Joffe. "It's not like that in Europe. So that makes our context for medical abortion unique."

What, though, about the other major appeal of the mifepristone method—the fact that it can be accomplished so much earlier in pregnancy than most surgical abortion is? For the majority of Americans, who have not shown themselves to be moral absolutists on this issue but who do, increasingly, want to draw moral distinctions about it, the timing of abortion does make a difference. Poll after poll confirms this. Indeed timing—which is to say the development of the embryo or fetus to be aborted, the closeness of its resemblance to a baby, the likelihood that it can experience pain and so on—carries more weight in their moral calculus than do a woman's stated motivations for seeking an abortion. In some ways, it always has, which is why, for instance, abortion in the early nineteenth century was illegal only after "quickening," the point, usually in the fifth month of pregnancy, when women can first feel fetal movement. This attitude toward abortion was based, writes Leslie J. Reagan in her history of abortion pre-Roe, "on an understanding of pregnancy and human development as a process rather than an absolute moment."

And there are good, even philosophically sound, reasons for this. "It is an almost universal conviction that abortion becomes steadily more problematic morally as a fetus develops toward infanthood," writes the legal scholar Ronald Dworkin, "as the difference between pregnancy and infancy becomes more a matter of the baby's location than of its development." If you accept Dworkin's general argument that fetal life is a rapidly progressing continuum and that the more babylike an aborted fetus, the greater the insult to the sanctity of human life, then even in the first trimester earlier abortion is more acceptable. So, for example, while 88 percent of abortions are performed in the first trimester, 34 percent of those now occur between 9 and 12 weeks, by which time the developing life is considered a fetus, not an embryo. If medical abortions—or even manual vacuum aspirations—become more common, then many of those abortions could happen in the three- to eight-week range instead.

Technological and cultural changes have made all of us a little more sentimental about the fetus in recent years, even as they have blurred long-standing notions of what constitutes fetal viability. Expectant mothers are now more and more likely to see ultrasound pictures of their babies-to-be and to catch sight of a touchingly banal gesture like a yawn. Meanwhile, the cumulative, if unintended, effect of aggressive campaigns against prenatal smoking and alcohol use has been to encourage pregnant women to think explicitly about the fetuses they are housing as beings with autonomous interests. And advances in the care of preemies have made it possible to deliver a viable baby as early as 24 weeks, confounding older assumptions about when, exactly, a developing baby could make it outside the hospitable womb. For all of these reasons, hostility toward abortion later in pregnancy seems to be growing, even among people who may be fundamentally in favor of a woman's right to choose.

If abortion does begin to happen earlier on average, then it may accelerate a shift in pro-life rhetoric toward the plight of the woman who terminates her pregnancy, allowing her at least to share the stage with the photogenic late-term fetus. In a sense, this subtle transformation is already under way. The latest wave of anti-abortion pamphlets and videos incorporates modish therapeutic language about "healing help" for women who have undergone abortions and dwells at length on the diagnosis prolifers call "post-abortion syndrome." Books like "Helping Women Recover From Abortion," described as "a step-by-step Biblical guide to restoration for those caught in the aftermath of an abortion," seem to promise women psychologically attuned solace, not a scarlet letter. And when it comes to mifepristone, anti-abortion activists have been stressing the medical (and psychological) risks they argue it poses for women at least as much as the threat to the unborn child. "Women are going to be facing a whole new category of dangers," says Randall K. O'Bannon, the director of education and research for the National Right to Life Committee. "Instead of facing the risk of a perforated uterus, they may face the risk of bleeding to death."

Other right-to-life activists cite the case of Nadine Walkowiak, a 31-year-old French woman, mother of 12 and a heavy smoker who died in 1991 of cardiovascular shock after getting mifepristone and a prostaglandin shot. (What they don't say is that of the approximately 500,000 women in Europe who have used a mifepristone-prostaglandin regimen, this is the only fatality. Nor do they say that the protocol has changed since then: the particular prostaglandin Walkowiak took is no longer used; misprostol is now given instead and in oral form; in France, any woman with a history of heart problems or hypertension comes under tighter scrutiny for RU-486.) In its list of "key facts" that ought to form the "core message" for the movement, the Life Issues Institute cites first the proposition that RU-486 "will injure, and possibly kill" women and next to last that it "will kill an unborn baby whose heart has started to beat."

It is also clear that many in the movement are placing a great deal of hope on a product-liability suit that would taint medical abortion. "Many of these products come on the market, and there are side effects," says Jim Sedlak of the American Life League. "And I would suspect that it would be the right of the American people to know who the manufacturers are so they can demand legal redress if something goes wrong."

In the meantime, anti-abortionists have also got themselves into something of a rhetorical tangle about whether RU-486 is actually an easier method that will make abortion more common or a harder one that will take more of an emotional toll on women. They started out with the argument that RU-486 trivialized abortion and that women were in danger of resorting to it casually as a means of birth control. But the evidence that it is "easier" or that it will raise the overall abortion rate isn't especially compelling. The availability of medical abortion in France, England and Sweden has not increased the number of abortions overall in those countries. In the United States, the incidence of abortion has been falling anyway for a variety of reasons, including a decline in unwanted pregnancies and the aging of the population, and this trend is unlikely to be reversed.

Besides, even women who prefer the method would be loath to call it easy. Medical abortion requires stamina, patience and tolerance for bleeding that will amount to more than a regular period and that may continue in diminished form for several weeks. It can cause nausea and diarrhea, and it always causes cramps—that's not even a side effect; it's the process itself. A couple of months later, when I talked to the college student I had met in Schaff's office, she said the cramps she had experienced with her mifepristone abortion were severe and had lasted for several hours, though Tylenol and her boyfriend's company had indeed helped, and she was still relieved not

to have had surgery. For the 28-year-old secretary, on the other hand, "there was very little pain. It was nothing compared to labor." After a few hours during which she made many trips to the bathroom, she spent the day playing with her young son and doing yard work, and by evening felt well enough to go out to dinner. Yet she was struck by the fact that this was a method "in which you really confront what you're doing. It was a little overwhelming to see. If you had any kind of doubts about having an abortion, I think it could be difficult. With the surgical method, you lie there and it's done."

And it is certainly true that all medical abortion involves a woman much more in the whole experience. "For those women who want to take a couple of days off and sort of be with their abortion," as Elizabeth Newhall puts it, "this gives them the opportunity. Some women really do." Which implies, of course, that some really don't. A patient I spoke to at Schaff's office, a friendly, tattooed, rocker-girl type, had come in fully expecting to get a mifepristone abortion. "My girlfriend did it and told me it worked out great," she said. "But I thought it was just take a pill and it's over. And from what they're saying today, it sounds like it's a lot more painful than surgical is. And slow, too. So I was like, no way."

Moreover, price won't be an incentive to try medical abortion: health policy analysts who have been following its progress say it will probably cost about the same as surgical abortion—an average of $350 or so— and some doctors say they may charge $75 to $100 more than that. Even if the pills themselves are priced fairly reasonably, medical abortion is labor-intensive for the practitioners who offer it. Women have to make at least two visits (one for the mifepristone, one for follow-up). And medical abortion, since it requires more of the patient, requires more counseling. Besides, any doctor who does it must have surgical back-up and probably an ultrasound machine, and those are expensive.

So lately, right-to-life activists have been contending that, as Wanda Franz, the president of the National Right to Life Committee, has put it: "Women who use mifepristone are exposing themselves to the emotional sharp edges of the event. Our concern is for the psychological well-being of these women." But this is a tricky argument, too, since it acknowledges that medical abortion is a process in which women are more aware, more complicit, more active—they may see the gestational sac, for example—and that they may nonetheless find acceptable.

In the end, placing too much hope for social change on any technological innovation is always risky. But if Americans do care as much as they say they do about making abortion happen earlier, then medical abortion is the best means yet for enacting that shift. The paradox of most of the legislative restrictions that have been passed over the last 20 years or so—mandatory waiting periods, the ban on Federal Medicaid financing for abortions and parental-consent, or notification laws—is that one of their prime effects has been to push abortions later into pregnancy. A year after Mississippi passed a law requiring a 24-hour waiting period and mandatory counseling, for example, the percentage of abortions performed after 12 weeks gestation increased 39 percent more than it did in the neighboring states of South Carolina or Georgia. The promise of medical abortion is quite the opposite.

There are those who worry, nonetheless, about the social costs of emphasizing early abortion and its virtues. "One real possibility in the move to earlier abortion," says Joffe, "would be to further polarize the world of abortion recipients, so that you have the good girls, who dutifully go out and get their E.P.T.'s the day their period is late, and then a much smaller group who, for one reason or another are going to come in late." There will "be a lot of pressure on the pro-choice movement to sort of make a deal: first-trimester abortions are O.K., but we'll trade away the rights to anything after that. The history of American political culture is the middle. People are sick and tired of this conflict and repulsed by the extremes, and I understand that. But I also fear for the group of women who may get left behind."

Could we live, though, with a few more restrictions on second-trimester abortions and a ban on third-trimester abortions? If more providers insured access to first-trimester abortions, if exceptions were made for serious health consequences for the mother—and if the restrictions were not disproportionately burdensome to poor women—probably so. "I don't know of any country in the world where second- and third-trimester abortions are not heavily regulated," says Marie Bass, a pro-choice political consultant in Washington who has worked for years to help bring RU-486 to this country. "A lot of pro-choice leaders believe you have to stand your ground against all restrictions, that there really is a slippery slope. I'm not so sure." In France, for example, abortion is legal only till 12 weeks, but it is not socially stigmatized before then, and just as important, it is state-financed and easily accessible.

When I spoke with Cory Richards of the Alan Guttmacher Institute, he outlined one of the more expansive and humane scenarios I'd heard. Maybe, he said, "societal attention to the availability of these new techniques could create a mandate for early pregnancy detection and intervention—a whole campaign. If you think you might be pregnant, find out early. If you want to carry it to term, get into prenatal care right away. If you don't, and you're going to terminate the pregnancy, do it early." It's an idea full of political promise—and maybe of moral promise, too.

Epilogue

On September 28, 2000, abortion rights supporters celebrated a long-sought victory with the Food and Drug Administration's (FDA) approval of RU-486. But, in many ways, this decision is not viewed as the final answer. According to Janet Benshoof, President of the Center for Reproductive Law and Policy, an advocacy organization representing abortion providers, "In general, if you're opening medical abortions to a wider range of doctors, they have no idea that this is a dungeon of criminal law, and once you do an abortion, the laws may apply even if it is just giving women a pill" (Kolata, 2000, p. 1). For example, many states require that abortion providers register and report every abortion. Some states have detailed requirements for the design of offices and clinics. Other states, like Alabama, North Carolina, and South Carolina require that the doctor examine the tissue from the abortion. In North Dakota, the remains must be cremated, incinerated, or buried. Dr. Stuart Schnider, who runs abortion clinics in Raleigh and Charlotte, North Carolina, said he is worried about the Fetal Remains Law. "We asked them to bring back whatever remains were passed, . . . and did the woman comply? Of course not." (Kolata, 2000, p. 11).

Dr. Mitchell Creinin, who runs an abortion clinic in Pittsburgh, has traveled across the country giving medical seminars to physicians considering the use of RU-486 in their practices. According to Dr. Creinin, after he tells them the number of office visits a woman must make, the counseling the physician must do, the back-up medical services that must be provided, and the state laws that must be followed, their eagerness to use RU-486 often diminishes. It appears that a battle may have been won, but the war still is at stake (Kolata, 2000).

Reference

Kolata, G. (2000, September 30). Doctors looking at abortion pill are often unaware of obstacles. *New York Times*, pp. 1, 11.

Chapter 28
Psychological Factors in Abortion

Nancy E. Adler
Henry P. David
Brenda N. Major
Susan H. Roth
Nancy Felipe Russo
Gail E. Wyatt

At the time of an abortion, many concerns may surface in a woman's mind. She may worry about disapproval by her family or friends, her partner's reaction, or not being able to have another child or to become a mother. A woman may also feel anger toward her sex partner for not using an effective contraceptive or toward her parents for providing inadequate information about contraception. Intense feelings ranging from guilt to relief, from being sad about aborting the fetus to being happy not to be pregnant—any of these common feelings can occur.

The findings reported in the Adler et al. article reveal that whatever the short-term psychological effects of abortion, they can best be understood in a framework of normal stress and coping reactions. Students may wish to consider a number of questions before reading this early 1990s research analysis. When is the period of greatest psychological stress for those having an abortion? What factors contribute to positive post-abortion psychological adjustment? What is the role of post-abortion counseling? Why is there no research reporting the psychological effects for men involved in pregnancy? Or why are so few studies reviewed about the long-term psychological effects of abortion? These are all important questions to be entertained by the nation's brightest young people, many of whom could be tomorrow's researchers and all of whom will be recipients of scientific findings.

The American Psychological Association (APA) has had a long history of involvement in relation to psychological factors associated with abortion. Public policy and other debates have increasingly included psychological issues, and findings from psychological research have been conveyed to policymakers. When APA, in 1989, appointed a panel of experts to examine relevant psychological considerations, it was recognized that differing moral, ethical, and religious perspectives impinge on how abortion is perceived. Our mission, however, was not to assess values but to consider the best available scientific evidence on psychological responses to abortion. In this article we summarize APA's involvement with abortion issues, examine the status of abortion in the United States, and report our conclusions about psychological responses of women after abortion.

APA Involvement in Abortion Issues

In 1969, the APA Council of Representatives adopted a resolution that identified termination of unwanted pregnancies as a mental health and child welfare issue, resolving that termination of pregnancy be considered a civil right of the pregnant woman, to be handled as other medical and surgical procedures in consultation with her physician. Since that initial resolution, APA and some of its divisions and members have conducted and disseminated research on abortion issues to fellow psychologists, policymakers, and the public. APA staff have prepared reports and met with government officials (Wilmoth, 1989) and arranged testimony by experts before Congress on abortion issues (Adler, 1989; David, 1989). In addition, APA has submitted amici curiae [friend of court briefs] in eight court cases on abortion issues. These cases involved a range of public policy issues, including preabortion counseling, parental notification, and waiting periods.

In 1980, in response to governmental attempts to suppress research on abortion, APA Council of Representatives passed a resolution supporting the right to conduct scientific research on abortion and reproductive health, stating that APA "affirms the right of qualified researchers to conduct appropriate research in all areas of fertility regulation" (Abeles, 1981, p. 581). In 1987, public debate began to focus on postabortion psychological responses. President Ronald Reagan directed his Surgeon General, C. Everett Koop, to develop a comprehensive report on the psychological and medical impact of abortion on women. Over the next 15 months, Koop and his staff met with a variety of groups and experts, including psychologists. APA representatives presented oral testimony to the Surgeon General's office on methodological issues in research on the psychological sequelae of abortion. APA Public Interest Directorate staff prepared a written report on those issues and delivered the testimony (Wilmoth, 1989).

In January, 1989, Koop and Otis Bowen, Secretary of Health and Human Services, met and decided that Koop would not issue a report. Instead, the Surgeon General sent a letter to President Reagan stating that "despite a diligent review . . . the scientific studies do not provide conclusive data on the health effects of abortion on women." The APA staff report was prominently included in the wave of publicity that followed. The APA, wishing to improve the accuracy of the debate, convened a panel of experts to review the best scientific studies of abortion outcome. On March 16, 1989, the Human Resources and Intergovernmental Relations Subcommittee of the Committee on Government Operations of the U.S. House of Representatives held hearings to investigate possible discrepancies between the Surgeon General's draft report and information made public. In those hearings, Nancy E. Adler testified on behalf of APA, and another panel member,

Henry P. David, testified on behalf of the American Public Health Association.

In August, 1989, the APA Council of Representatives, concerned about the distortions of the research findings in the press, passed its third abortion resolution. This resolution, which cited the work of the panel, initiated a public awareness effort to correct the record on the scientific findings of abortion research. The current article supplements our initial summary (Adler et al., 1990) and is designed to improve understanding in the psychological community about theoretical, methodological, and substantive findings on psychological responses following abortion.

History and Status of Abortion in the United States

Since the 1973 Supreme Court decision *Roe v. Wade* (1973), abortion has been a legal, albeit controversial, surgical procedure in all states of the United States. That landmark ruling set out the circumstances under which an abortion may be legally regulated. In essence, in *Roe v. Wade* (1973) the Court ruled that the abortion decision was protected by the right of privacy but that the state has legitimate interests in protecting both the pregnant woman's health and potential human life—interests that grow and reach a compelling point at later stages of gestation. In the first trimester, when abortion is safer than normal childbirth, the abortion decision is protected by the right of privacy and rests with a woman and her physician. Later in pregnancy, however, the state "may regulate the abortion procedure in ways that are reasonably related to the preservation and protection of maternal health" (*Roe v. Wade*, p. 732). In the third trimester, the viability of the fetus permits the state to exercise its interest in protecting potential life, and regulation and prohibition of abortion is thus permitted except where abortion is necessary to preserve the life or health of the woman.

In weighing the health risks of unwanted pregnancy and its alternatives, the Supreme Court identified mental health and child welfare issues as important to its consideration, creating a critical role for psychological research in challenges to the court's opinion. After the 1973 decision, organized opposition to abortion became a national movement (Packwood, 1986). Some supporters of this movement have asserted that the abortion experience produces widespread and severe negative mental health effects among women who have undergone the procedure (Speckhard, 1987).

Abortion Practices Before 1973

Determining numbers of abortions in the United States before 1973 is difficult because the vast majority were clandestine procedures. Estimates range from a low of 200,000 to a high of 1,200,000 per year (Tietze & Henshaw, 1986). The consequences of illegal abortions were clear in relation to maternal mortality, however. In 1965, an estimated 20 percent of all deaths related to pregnancy and childbirth were attributable to illegal abortion (Alan Guttmacher Institute, 1982).

Under some state laws existing before the 1973 *Roe v. Wade* decision, psychological issues provided a basis for access to legal abortion. As described by Schwartz (1986), physicians, under increasing pressure from upper and middle class patients to perform safe abortions, turned to psychiatrists to certify the need for the procedure. Hospitals established rules that permitted abortion if a woman could provide a letter from one or two psychiatrists certifying that it was needed to prevent suicide. Abortions for psychiatric reasons increased from 10 percent of procedures in 1943 to 80 percent in 1963; about 8,000 such "therapeutic abortions" were performed each year from 1963 to 1965 (Schwartz, 1986). In 1970 more than 98 percent of the legal therapeutic abortions performed in the state of California were for mental health reasons (Niswander & Porto, 1986).

Abortion Practices After 1973

After 1973, the number of clandestine abortions in the United States dropped sharply, and the number of legal abortions rose steadily, from nearly 800,000 in 1973 to more than 1.5 million in 1980. Between 1.5 and 1.6 million abortions have been performed annually for the past decade—about 3 out of 10 pregnancies. The number of abortions reflects the actual abortion rate and the number of women of reproductive age, both of which have increased since 1973. In 1987 the U.S. abortion rate was 27 per 1,000 women aged 15–44 years (Henshaw, Koonin, & Smith, 1991). An estimated 21 percent of American women of childbearing age have experienced this procedure (Tietze, Forrest, & Henshaw, 1988).

After *Roe v. Wade*, several aspects of the abortion context changed. The proportion of legal abortions performed in hospitals dropped from 52 percent in 1973 to 13 percent in 1985 (four-fifths of them outpatient procedures). The proportion of abortions performed in nonhospital clinics rose from 46 percent to 83 percent, while the proportion in doctors' offices stayed low—2 percent compared with 4 percent (Henshaw, Forrest, & Van Vort, 1987). The geographic locale of abortions also changed. The proportion of women obtaining abortions outside their city of residence decreased markedly from about 40 percent in 1972 to about 6 percent in 1982 (Tietze et al., 1988). Finally, the time of gestation at which abortion was typically performed has dropped; since 1973 the proportion of legal abortions performed at eight weeks or less has increased from 38 percent to nearly 50 percent.

Demographic Characteristics of U.S. Abortion Patients

Data on the characteristics of abortion patients are derived mainly from national surveys of providers conducted by the Alan Guttmacher Institute (AGI), and reports to the Centers for Disease Control Abortion Surveillance Unit. The summary is based on 1987 data from the AGI surveys (Henshaw et al., 1991), unless otherwise noted, and presents proportions and relative rates of abortion for women varying on key demographic characteristics. Although we discuss each variable separately, these should be read with an understanding that demographic variables are intercorrelated, making it difficult to attribute differences in abortion rates to any given variable. Compared with older women, younger women are more likely to be unmarried and nulliparous. Similarly, ethnicity is confounded with socioeconomic and marital status.

Age. The majority of women seeking abortion are young. The modal age of abortion patients is 20–24 years, and almost 60 percent are less than 25 years old; 12 percent are minors, aged 17 years or less. Abortion rates are highest among women 18–19 years of age and begin to drop after age 19, reaching a low among women 40 and over.

Race and ethnicity. Statistics on abortion are grouped by race (White vs. non-White), or ethnicity (Hispanic vs. non-Hispanic). Based on total numbers nearly 69 percent of women obtaining abortions in 1987 were White (and of these 13 percent were Hispanic), and 31 percent were non-White. Abortion rates, which are based on the numbers of abortions within each population, show that rates are higher for non-Whites than for Whites and for Hispanics compared with non-Hispanics.

Marital status. Most abortion patients are not married; 63 percent have never been married. Estimates of age-adjusted abortion rates among women who are separated, divorced, or widowed are approximately four to five times the rate of women married and living with their husbands. Women cohabiting with men had abortion rates estimated to be five times greater than the overall abortion rate and nine times greater than that of married women (Henshaw, 1987).

Parity. Abortion is used both to postpone births and to limit them. Over half of women having abortions have had no previous births. Nearly 70 percent of women having abortions say they intend to bear children in the future.

Abortion procedure and gestational age. The safest procedures for abortion are "instrumental evacuation" (e.g., vacuum curettage, surgical curettage, and dilation and evacuation); the vast majority (97 percent) of procedures done are of this type.

Approximately 3 percent of procedures are medical induction of labor to expel the fetus, and about 0.1 percent are uterine surgery—hysterotomy and hysterectomy (Tietze & Henshaw, 1986). The procedure used is largely a function of the length of gestation, with instrumental evacuation being the method of choice up to 16 weeks of pregnancy (Tietze & Henshaw, 1986). The median gestation period for all women having abortions is 9.2 weeks (Kochanek, 1990); more than 90 percent of all abortions are performed at less than 13 weeks gestation (Tietze & Henshaw, 1986).

A number of factors can contribute to delay in obtaining an abortion. Failure to suspect pregnancy and difficulty in making arrangements to have an abortion are most frequently cited as reasons for delay (Torres & Forrest, 1988). The health care system and the woman's financial state have been implicated in delay in other studies (Henshaw & Wallisch, 1984). Finally, approximately 1,500–3,750 second-trimester abortions are performed each year as a result of a detected defect in the fetus from diagnostic testing (Grimes, 1984). Bracken and Kasl (1975) found that, compared with women having first-trimester abortions, those delaying until the second trimester generally are younger and more likely to be unmarried, Black, nulliparous, in a relatively unstable relationship, Protestant rather than Catholic, and to have a lower level of education and socioeconomic status.

Postabortion Emotional Responses: The Research Literature

Theoretical Frameworks

Much of the research on abortion has been descriptive rather than theory based, but two broad types of theoretical perspectives underlie the research. One perspective, deriving from clinical experience and theories, focuses on psychopathological responses following abortion. This perspective, drawing heavily from psychoanalytic theory, characterized earlier work on abortion. The second perspective, characterizing more recent work, is that of stress and coping. From this perspective, unwanted pregnancy and abortion are seen as potentially stressful life events, events that pose challenges and difficulties to the individual but do not necessarily lead to psychopathological outcomes. Rather, a range of possible responses, including growth and maturation as well as negative affect and psychopathology, can occur.

Differences in these perspectives have affected the kind of questions asked and methodologies used to study women who have had abortions. Clinical case studies drawn from the experience of clinicians or those studying women who are self-selected because they have reported experiencing psychological distress following an abortion (Speckhard, 1987) have looked almost exclusively at indicators of psychological distress. Broader descriptive studies and research conducted from a stress and coping perspective have generally used more representative samples of women undergoing abortion, strengthening the generalizability of findings. In addition, a few studies have included both positive and negative outcomes, providing a fuller picture of the experiences of women undergoing induced abortion (Major & Cozzarelli, in press).

From the stress and coping perspective, an unwanted pregnancy is seen as an event that can be challenging or stressful. Stress has been defined as emerging from an interaction of the individual and the environment in situations that the person appraises as "taxing or exceeding his or her resources and endangering his or her well-being" (Lazarus & Folkman, 1984, p. 19). The circumstances surrounding conception (e.g., whether it was planned, whether the woman has adequate resources to care for a child, whether the male partner is supportive, whether there is an indication of genetic abnormality) in conjunction with a woman's psychological and social resources provide the context that will affect a woman's response to her pregnancy.

Termination of an unwanted pregnancy may reduce the stress engendered by the occurrence of the pregnancy and the associated events. At the same time, the abortion itself may be experienced as stressful. As with pregnancy, the circumstances surrounding abortion (the woman's feelings about the morality of abortion, support for abortion by the partner and others who are close to the woman, and the actual experience she has in obtaining the abortion) are likely to influence later responses.

Research on the impact of stressful life events has pointed to the importance of several variables that mediate or moderate the impact of such events on the individual. Among the key variables that have been identified are social support, attributions for the cause of the event, the meaning attached to the event, and the coping strategies used for dealing with the event. As will be seen below, all of these factors have been shown to play an important role in responses of women following induced abortion.

Methodological Critique

Before reviewing the literature on abortion, methodological shortcomings must be noted. Several authors (Adler, 1979; Dagg, 1991; Illsley & Hall, 1976) have identified biases in the abortion literature. Some biases arise from ideological viewpoints or assumptions inherent in particular theories and approaches. For example, Fingerer (1973) demonstrated the operation of such bias in traditional psychoanalytic theory. She asked postdoctoral psychology students in psychoanalytic training programs to predict responses of women following abortion. They predicted severe sequelae, significantly greater than those predicted by women before undergoing an abortion or by men and women who accompanied women to an abortion clinic. The responses predicted by the postdoctoral psychologists were significantly more negative than those actually reported by women following their abortions. The bias toward expecting severe negative responses inherent in a number of studies has been exacerbated by the inappropriate generalization of conclusions from clinical or case studies that are of limited scientific merit and tell little about the experience of the vast majority of abortion patients.

Limited operationalization of post-abortion responses has been problematic in many studies. A narrow set of research questions has been emphasized, focusing almost exclusively on pathological or negative outcomes (Illsley & Hall, 1976). In addition, outcome measures have often been of questionable reliability and validity. Some researchers have used interviews to assess the mental health of abortion patients. It often is not possible to judge the results in terms of accuracy, reliability, or validity. In other studies questionnaires have been used but have not been evaluated for their psychometric characteristics. For example, a single item rating postdecisional regret is not a valid measure of a psychological disorder. In yet other instances standardized instruments have been used, and results have been discussed in terms of statistical significance; however, what constitutes clinically meaningful differences in scores is not considered in the discussion.

The interpretation of research on postabortion experiences must consider the entire context of the abortion (see Adler, in press). This should include the reasons for the occurrence of the pregnancy, (e.g., whether pregnancy was intended or not, whether it was the result of rape, the hardship the pregnancy would pose), the circumstances under which a decision to terminate was made (e.g., as a result of diagnostic testing, whether it was made with the support of others), and the experience of the procedure itself (e.g., type of procedure, treatment by provider, experience with protesters). Given the variety of experiences associated with abortion, it is inappropriate to generalize from one abortion circumstance (e.g., a late abortion using saline induction) to another without adequate evidence that similar responses are found in different contexts. In part because of the complexity of the abortion experience, abortion researchers since 1973 have concentrated largely on testing conditional hypotheses about variables that may influence postabortion psychological responses within identified samples of women.

The varied quality of studies examining psychological responses of women following abortion makes it difficult to draw conclusions from the entire body of existing research literature. Many reports are clinical observations of small numbers of women (Friedman, Greenspan, & Mittleman, 1974; Hatcher, 1976); some provide no data, or data are inappropriately or inadequately analyzed (Freeman, 1978; Perez-Reyes & Falk, 1973). Some studies report responses of women having illegal or therapeutic abortions rather than legal, elective procedures. Some studies, particularly those that are retrospective, may have a mix of women who had illegal, therapeutic, and elective abortions that are not analyzed separately (e.g., Speckhard, 1987). Such case studies are useful for developing hypotheses about why abortion may be followed by psychological dysfunction or pathology, for example, in cases of coerced or late abortion. However, they do not have adequate samples for determining common or normative responses following abortion, nor are they able to sort out the causal dynamics that result in a given outcome, particularly if retrospective reporting is used and preabortion emotional state is not assessed.

Reviews of the early studies have appeared elsewhere (Adler, 1979; Shusterman, 1976). Here we examine findings from only the best scientific studies that reflect current legal abortion practices in the United States and provide quantitative measures of psychological responses following abortion. We did not use meta-analysis in reviewing those studies because the number of appropriate studies that would be used for any given analysis is so small.

Selection Criteria for This Review

Conclusions presented in this article regarding psychological responses following abortion are based on review of studies that met three minimum criteria: First, the study had to be empirical, involving collection of data subjected to statistical analysis and used a definable sample; Second, because the experience of illegal abortion or of having to qualify for legal abortion under restrictive conditions is likely to be more stressful than that of a legal abortion, samples of women studied had to have had their abortions under legal, nonrestrictive conditions. Third, the sample had to be of women in the United States. The studies reviewed have used samples drawn from a variety of settings: private abortion clinics (both for profit and nonprofit), university and other hospital-based clinics, and counseling and referral centers. Most of the samples are of mixed ethnicity, although some do not report on the ethnic characteristics of the sample.

Normative Responses to Abortion

The weight of the evidence is that legal abortion as a resolution to an unwanted pregnancy, particularly in the first trimester, does not create psychological hazards for most women undergoing the procedure (Adler, 1990). Studies that have used measures with clinically relevant norms have found means obtained by abortion patients following the procedure to be well within normal (i.e., nonpathological) bounds (Major, Mueller, & Hildebrandt, 1985). The incidence of severe negative responses has been low. Even in studies using ratings of distress rather than measures of severe psychological disorder, positive feelings have been reported to be felt relatively more strongly than are negative emotions.

A woman's responses to abortion are complex, and she may feel a mixture of positive and negative emotions. When women are asked to indicate which emotions they experience following first-trimester abortion, the most frequent response is to report feelings of relief and happiness (Lazarus, 1985). For example, in a sample of 292 patients studied two weeks postabortion by Lazarus (1985), 76 percent reported feeling happiness. The most frequently cited negative emotion, guilt, was reported by only 17 percent of the sample. Adler (1975) identified three separate factors accounting for variations in emotions experienced by 70 women over a two- to three-month period following a first trimester abortion. One

factor consisted of *positive* emotions, relief and happiness. This factor showed the strongest response over the three-month period; women indicated a mean intensity of 3.96 on a scale ranging from 1 (*not at all*) to 5 (*extremely*). The negative emotions fell into two separate factors. One, consisting of shame, guilt, and fear of disapproval, was termed *socially based* and seemed to reflect responses to having taken an action that could generate social disapproval. The second negative emotion factor consisted of regret, anxiety, depression, doubt, and anger. These emotions were termed *internally based* and seemed to relate to the loss of the pregnancy and the meaning it had for the woman. The mean intensity ratings on these two factors were 1.81 and 2.26, respectively.

Some researchers have obtained measures of psychological responses and functioning both before and after the abortion or at two points following abortion. Psychological distress has generally been found to drop from before the procedure to immediately afterward and from preabortion or immediately postabortion to several weeks afterward. Cohen and Roth (1984) found significant decreases from before to several hours after the procedure in measures of depression and anxiety and on scores on the Impact of Events Scale (Horowitz, Wilner, & Alvarez, 1979), an indicator of stress. In two longer follow-up studies, Major et al. (1985) and Mueller and Major (1989) found significant improvement in adjustment (Beck & Beck, 1972) among women three weeks following the abortion compared with their immediate postabortion scores.

Zabin, Hirsch, and Emerson (1989) obtained ratings of self-esteem, locus of control, and state and trait anxiety for a group of Black adolescents at the time they sought a pregnancy test and again one and two years later. They compared those who had a negative pregnancy test, those who had a positive test and subsequently carried to term, and those who had a positive test and subsequently terminated the pregnancy. This study is one of only three studies that compare responses following abortion and term birth. Comparisons across groups at the one- and two-year follow-ups showed no adverse effects of the abortion experience. In fact, the abortion group scored significantly lower on trait anxiety than did either the negative pregnancy or the childbearing group at the two-year follow-up. In addition, despite the absence of significant differences at baseline among the three groups, the abortion group showed more positive responses (Rosenberg, 1965) than did the negative pregnancy group at the two-year follow-up and showed a more internal orientation than did the childbearing group at both the one- and two-year follow-ups.

Athanasiou et al. (1973) compared responses of women after first- and second-trimester abortion and term birth. Women completed the Minnesota Multiphasic Personality Inventory [MMPI] (Hathaway & McKinley, 1951) and the Symptom Checklist [SCL] (Derogatis, Lipman, Covi, & Rickels, 1972) before the abortion or delivery, and again 13 to 16 months afterward. At follow-up, women who had experienced term birth had higher scores on the Paranoia subscale of the MMPI than did women in either abortion group. Women who experienced a first trimester suction abortion reported fewer somatic complaints on the SCL than did either the second trimester saline abortion or delivery patients. On all other comparisons, no significant differences emerged, leading the authors to remark that the three groups were "startlingly similar."

Similar findings regarding benign effects of abortion versus childbirth emerged in a study by Russo and Zierk (1992). These researchers examined the relationship of abortion and childbearing to self-esteem in a national sample of U.S. women interviewed annually from 1979 to 1987 in the National Longitudinal Study of Youth (Center For Human Resources Research, 1988). Those women who had previously had an abortion had slightly higher global self-esteem compared with women who had never had an abortion. This difference was greater when comparing women having had an abortion with women having

had unwanted births. Women who had experienced repeat abortions did not differ in self-esteem from women who had never had an abortion. The time elapsed since the abortion was not related to self-esteem. This study demonstrates that up to eight years following an abortion, no negative associations occur with self-esteem.

Who Has Negative Responses After Abortion?

The discussion above documents a relatively benign course for women following termination of a pregnancy. Yet some women experience distress and negative responses following abortion. What factors account for such responses? And to what extent are these factors similar to those that influence responses following other potentially stressful life events? With one exception (Mueller & Major, 1989), the evidence is correlational, relating characteristics of the woman or her situation to a variety of measures following abortion.

Demographic and social factors. Younger and unmarried women without children are relatively more likely than those who are older and who have already given birth to experience negative responses. So, too, are women whose culture or religion prohibits abortions and those who attend church more frequently (Adler, 1975; Osofsky & Osofsky, 1972).

Length of gestation and medical procedure. Procedures done in the first trimester of pregnancy carry lower risks of physical morbidity and psychological difficulties than do second-trimester procedures (Kaltreider, Goldsmith, & Margolis, 1979). The increased likelihood of more negative psychological response may have to do in part with the characteristics of the small percentage of women who delay until the second trimester. They are younger and more likely to be Black, nulliparous, and in unstable relationships (Bracken & Kasl, 1975)—characteristics that are associated with a higher likelihood of negative responses following first-trimester abortion (Adler, 1975). Women who delay into the second trimester may also be more conflicted about the pregnancy, have less social support for the abortion decision, or have fewer resources for dealing with the unwanted pregnancy and abortion.

The medical procedures used for second trimester abortions are themselves more likely to be experienced as stressful than are those used in the first trimester. In the second trimester, saline or prostaglandin induction are used; these involve a more prolonged and painful experience than the dilation and evacuation or dilation and curettage procedure used in early pregnancy. In comparisons made between second-trimester patients undergoing a saline procedure versus those who had dilation and evacuation, more favorable responses were shown by the latter (Kaltreider et al., 1979).

The decision process. A number of studies have examined the relationship between aspects of the woman's decision process regarding abortion and her emotional responses afterward. Most women do not have difficulty with the abortion decision (Bracken, 1978). For example, Osofsky et al. (1973) found that 12 percent of 100 first-trimester patients stated the decision to have an abortion was difficult, and 7 percent reported initial indecision regarding continuation or termination of the pregnancy. However, among 200 *second*-trimester patients in the study, 51 percent reported difficulty in deciding, and 36 percent reported initial indecision. Other correlates of difficult decisions or of ambivalent feelings are being married (Bracken, 1978) and being Catholic (Osofsky & Osofsky, 1972). Satisfaction beforehand with the decision to abort has been related to perceived support from significant others, a favorable opinion of the abortion option, generally favorable attitudes toward abortion, and more years of education (Bracken, Klerman, & Bracken, 1978; Eisen & Zellman, 1984; Shusterman, 1979).

Studies examining the relation between aspects of satisfaction with the abortion decision and postabortion emotional response consistently find that women who are satisfied with their choice or who report little difficulty in making the decision to abort, show more positive postabortion responses. Greater difficulty in making the decision has been associated with higher negative postabortion reactions (Shusterman, 1979), including feelings of guilt (Osofsky & Osofsky, 1972), anxiety (Bracken, 1978), and internally based negative emotions (e.g., regret and depression) but not positive or socially based negative emotions (Adler, 1975).

Women who initially want to be pregnant may react more negatively to abortion. Shusterman (1979) found an association between a woman's immediate affective response to learning that she was pregnant and her response to abortion. Major et al. (1985) examined the relation between meaningfulness and intentionality of the pregnancy and postabortion responses. Women who reported the pregnancy as "highly meaningful" to them reported more physical complaints immediately after and anticipated more negative consequences from the abortion than did women who reported their pregnancy to be less meaningful. Three weeks following the abortion, women who had indicated that they had no intention of becoming pregnant exhibited significantly fewer subclinical symptoms of depression than women who had indicated that they had some intention to conceive.

In summary, women who are satisfied with their choice or who report little difficulty in making their decision show more positive responses postabortion. Greater meaningfulness and intentionality of the pregnancy, in contrast, are associated with poorer abortion adjustment. Women who report greater difficulty in deciding to abort are more likely to be married or Catholic, to have negative attitudes toward abortion, and to perceive little social support for their decision.

Perceived social support. Both perceived and actual social support can act to buffer some adverse psychological effects of exposure to stressful life events (Cohen & Wills, 1985). Studies examining the relationship of perceived support from significant others with women's postabortion response suggest that postabortion responses will be more positive among women with greater support for the decision to terminate. Bracken, Hachamovitch, and Grossman (1974) studied women before a suction abortion and again one hour after the procedure. Whether or not the partner and parents actually knew about the abortion was unrelated to postabortion responses. However, higher levels of perceived or anticipated support were associated with more favorable reactions to the abortion. The role of the partner has similarly been found to be a significant predictor of psychological responses as has the role of parents (Robbins & DeLamater, 1985; Moseley et al., 1981). Robbins (1984) examined the role of the woman's relationship with her partner after the abortion among primarily Black single women who had abortions or delivered at the same hospital. Reporting a strong relationship with the partner six weeks following the abortion was related to negative change on the MMPI and to greater regret over the abortion among women who had aborted. At one year post-resolution, a strong relationship with the male partner was associated with feelings of regret among aborters but was unrelated to regret among deliverers.

Perceived social support may or may not accurately reflect actual support. Major et al. (1985) recorded whether women were or were not accompanied by a male partner on the day of their procedure. Accompanied women were significantly more depressed and reported more physical complaints immediately after the abortion than were women who were unaccompanied by a partner. Further analyses revealed that women who were accompanied were younger and expected to cope less well with the abortion. This study demonstrates the complexity of social support. It may be that women who were more distressed about the abortion expressed a greater need for their partners to accompany them to the clinic.

In summary, perceived support generally appears to contribute to more positive postabortion adjustment. However, the relationship of social support to postabortion responses may be mediated and moderated by other variables.

Attributions for pregnancy. Attributions for negative life events have been found to relate to subsequent psychological adjustment (Michela & Wood, 1986; Sweeney, Anderson, & Bailey, 1986). In relation to abortion, adjustment may be affected by the woman's attributions for why the pregnancy occurred. Major et al. (1985) asked women before abortion the extent to which their pregnancy was due to aspects of their own character, their own behavior, chance, the situation they were in at the time, or someone else. Women who blamed their pregnancy on their own character were significantly more depressed, anticipated more severe negative consequences from the abortion, and tended to have more negative moods immediately postabortion than did women who were not self-blamers. In addition, women who blamed their pregnancy on someone else anticipated more negative consequences from the abortion than did those who did not.

Coping expectancies. Coping expectancies appear to play a role in responses following abortion. Women indicated, before their abortion, how well they expected to cope with the abortion (Major et al., 1985). Women who expected beforehand to cope well were less depressed, had more positive moods, anticipated fewer negative consequences, and reported fewer physical complaints both immediately following the abortion and at a three-week follow-up compared with women who expected to cope less well. Belief in one's ability to cope has been found to be *causally* linked to postabortion emotional responses. An experimental study of counseling interventions documented that enhancing self-efficacy for coping, combined with a regular counseling session, was effective at lowering women's risk for depressive symptoms after abortion compared with standard abortion counseling alone (Mueller & Major, 1989).

Other factors related to postabortion responses. Several other factors have also been found to relate to postabortion responses. Alter (1984) examined the relation between sex-role orientation and psychological response two weeks after a first-trimester abortion. Controlling for demographic and support variables revealed that women whose self-descriptions were congruent with their descriptions of a career woman exhibited more positive responses than did women whose self and career woman descriptions were incongruent. Cohen and Roth's (1984) results revealed that both anxiety and depression significantly decreased from pre- to postabortion, that coping style was consistent across assessments, and that high deniers were significantly more depressed than low deniers at both time points. In addition, the use of approach strategies was associated with a greater decrease in anxiety from pre- to postabortion.

Conclusions

The best available studies on psychological responses following legal, nonrestrictive abortion in the United States suggest that severe negative reactions are infrequent. Some individual women may experience severe distress or psychopathology following abortion, but it is not clear whether these are causally linked to the abortion (Dagg, 1991). As former Surgeon General C. Everett Koop (1989) testified before Congress regarding his review of research on psychological effects of abortion, emotional responses may be overwhelming to a given individual, but the problem of the development of significant psychological problems related to abortion is "minuscule from a public health perspective" (p. 211). Studies that have included comparison groups of women who carry to term (Athanasiou et al., 1973; Zabin et al., 1989) suggest that the choice made by women regarding their pregnancy is the one that is most likely to be best for them. Women at higher risk for relatively more negative responses include those who are terminating pregnancies that are wanted and meaningful, who perceive a lack of support from their partner or parents for the abortion, who are more conflicted and less sure of their decision and coping abilities beforehand, who blame themselves for the pregnancy, and who delay until the second trimester.

For the vast majority of women, an abortion will be followed by a mixture of emotions, with a predominance of positive feelings. This holds immediately after abortion and for some time afterward. We do not know about very-long-term effects. However, the positive picture shown up to eight years after abortion makes it unlikely that more negative responses will emerge later. Studies of other stressful life events show that those who experience the most distress in the immediate aftermath of the event are most likely to experience longer term difficulties and that those who show little distress in this period are unlikely to develop problems later (Wortman & Silver, 1989).

The best studies available on psychological responses to unwanted pregnancy terminated by abortion in the United States suggest that severe negative reactions are rare, and they parallel those following other normal life stresses. The time of greatest distress is likely to be before the abortion. Despite methodological shortcomings of individual studies, the fact that studies using diverse samples, different measures of postabortion response, and different times of assessment come to very similar conclusions is persuasive evidence that abortion is usually psychologically benign.

Abortion is intertwined with diverse moral, religious, and ethical perspectives that will impinge on how a given woman will react to her choice of pregnancy resolution. Although making the decision to terminate an unwanted pregnancy is difficult, available psychological evidence suggests that women tend to cope successfully and go on with their lives.

References

Abeles, N. (1981). Proceedings of the American Psychological Association, Incorporated, for the year 1980. *American Psychologist, 36*, 552–586.

Adler, N.E. (1989). *The medical and psychological impact of abortion on women.* Testimony on behalf of the American Psychological Association before the Subcommittee on Human Resources and Intergovernmental Operations, Committee on Government Operations, U.S. House of Representatives, 101st Congress, 1st session. March 16, 1989.

Adler, N. E. (1979). Abortion: A social psychological perspective. *Journal of Social Issues, 35,* 100–119.

Adler, N. E. (1975). Emotional responses of women following therapeutic abortion. *American Journal of Orthopsychiatry, 45,* 446–454.

Adler, N. E. (in press). Unwanted pregnancy and abortion: Definitional and research issues. *Journal of Social Issues.*

Adler, N. E., David, H. P., Major, B. N., Roth, S. H., Russo, N. F., & Wyatt, G. E. (1990). Psychological responses after abortion. *Science, 248,* 41–43.

Alan Guttmacher Institute. (1982). Abortion in the U.S.: Two centuries of experience. *Issues in Brief, 2,* 1–4.

Alter, R. C. (1984). Abortion outcome as a function of sex-role identification. *Psychology of Women Quarterly, 8,* 211–233.

Athanasiou, R., Oppel, W., Michaelson, L., Unger, T., & Yager, M. (1973). Psychiatric sequelae to term birth and induced early and late abortion: A longitudinal study. *Family Planning Perspectives, 5,* 227–231.

Beck, A. T., & Beck, R. W. (1972). Screening depressed patients in family practice: A rapid technique. *Postgraduate Medicine, 52,* 81–85.

Bracken, M. B. (1978). A causal model of psychosomatic reactions to vacuum aspiration abortion. *Social Psychiatry, 13,* 135–145.

Bracken, M. B., Hachamovitch, M., & Grossman, G. (1974). The decision to abort and psychological sequelae. *Journal of Nervous and Mental Disease, 158,* 154–162.

Bracken, M. B., & Kasl, S. (1975). Delay in seeking induced abortion: A review and theoretical analysis. *American Journal of Obstetrics and Gynecology, 121,* 1008–1019.

Bracken, M. B., Klerman, L. V., & Bracken, M. B. (1978). Abortion, adoption or motherhood: An empirical study of decision-making during pregnancy. *American Journal of Obstetrics and Gynecology, 130,* 251–262.

Center for Human Resources Research. (1988). *NLS Handbook.* Columbus: Ohio State University.

Cohen, L., & Roth, S. (1984). Coping with abortion. *Journal of Human Stress, 10,* 140–145.

Cohen, S., & Wills, T. A. (1985). Stress, social support, and the buffering hypothesis. *Psychological Bulletin, 98,* 310–357.

Dagg, P. K. B. (1991). The psychological sequelae of therapeutic abortion—Denied and completed. *American Journal of Psychiatry, 148,* 578–585.

David, H. P. (1989). *The medical and psychological impact of abortion on women.* Testimony on behalf of the American Public Health Association before the Subcommittee on Human Resources and Intergovernmental Operations, Committee on Government Operations, U.S. House of Representatives, 101st Congress, 1st session, March 15, 1989.

Derogatis, L. R., Lipman, R. S., Covi, L., & Rickels, K. (1972). Factorial invariance of symptom dimensions in anxious and depressive neuroses. *Archives of General Psychiatry, 27,* 659–665.

Eisen, M., & Zellman, G. L. (1984). Factors predicting pregnancy resolution decision satisfaction of unmarried adolescents. *Journal of Genetic Psychology, 145,* 231–239.

Fingerer, M. (1973). Psychological sequelae of abortion: Anxiety and depression. *Journal of Community Psychology, 1,* 221–225.

Freeman, E. W. (1978). Abortion: Subjective attitudes and feelings. *Family Planning Perspectives, 10,* 150–155.

Friedman, C., Greenspan, R., & Mittleman, F. (1974). The decision making process and the outcome of therapeutic abortion. *American Journal of Psychiatry, 131,* 1332–1337.

Grimes, D. A. (1984). Second-trimester abortions in the United States. *Family Planning Perspectives, 16,* 260–266.

Hatcher, S. (1976). Understanding adolescent pregnancy and abortion. *Primary Care, 3,* 407–425.

Hathaway, S. R., & McKinley, J. C. (1951). *The Minnesota Multiphasic Personality Inventory* (Form R). New York: The Psychological Corporation.

Henshaw, S. K. (1987). Characteristics of U.S. women having abortions, 1982–1983. In S. K. Henshaw & J. Van Vort (Eds.), *Abortion services in the United States, each state and metropolitan area, 1984–1985.* New York: Alan Guttmacher Institute.

Henshaw, S. K., Forrest, J. D., & Van Vort, J. (1987). Abortion services in the United States, 1984 and 1985. *Family Planning Perspectives, 19,* 63–70.

Henshaw, S. K., Koonin, L. M., & Smith, J. C. (1991). Characteristics of U.S. women having abortions. *Family Planning Perspectives, 23,* 75–81.

Henshaw, S. K., & Wallisch, L. S. (1984). The Medicaid cutoff and abortion services for the poor. *Family Planning Perspectives, 16,* 170–172, 177–180.

Horowitz, M., Wilner, N., & Alvarez, W. (1979). Impact of Event Scale: A measure of subjective stress. *Psychosomatic Medicine, 41,* 209–218.

Illsley, R., & Hall, M. H. (1976). Psychological aspects of abortion: A review of issues and needed research. *Bulletin of the World Health Organization, 53,* 83–103.

Kaltreider, N. B., Goldsmith, S., & Margolis, A. (1979). The impact of mid-trimester abortion techniques on patients and staff. *American Journal of Obstetrics and Gynecology, 135,* 235–238.

Kochanek, K. (1990). Induced terminations of pregnancy: Reporting states, 1987. *Monthly Vital Statistics Report, 38,* 1–8.

Koop, C. E. (1989). *The federal role in determining the medical and psychological impact of abortions on women* (HR No. 101–392, p. 14). Testimony given to the Committee on Government Operations, U.S. House of Representatives, 101st Congress, 2nd session, December 11, 1989.

Lazarus, A. (1985). Psychiatric sequelae of legalized first trimester abortion. *Journal of Psychosomatic Obstetrics and Gynecology, 4,* 141–150.

Lazarus, R., & Folkman, S. (1984). *Stress, appraisal, and coping.* New York: Springer.

Major, B., & Cozzarelli, C. (in press). Psychosocial predictors of adjustment to abortion. *Journal of Social Issues.*

Major, B., Cozzarelli, C., Sciacchitano, A. M., Cooper, M. L., Testa, M., & Mueller, P. M. (1990). Perceived social support, self-efficacy, and adjustment to abortion. *Journal of Personality and Social Psychology, 59,* 452–463.

Major, B., Mueller, P., & Hildebrandt, K. (1985). Attributions, expectations and coping with abortion. *Journal of Personality and Social Psychology, 48,* 585–599.

Michela, J. L., & Wood, J. V. (1986). Causal attributions in health and illness. In P. C. Kendall (Ed.), *Advances in cognitive-behavioral research and therapy* (pp. 179–235). San Diego, CA: Academic Press.

Moseley, O. T., Follingstad, D. R., Harley, H., & Heckel, R. (1981). Psychological factors that predict reaction to abortion. *Journal of Clinical Psychology, 37,* 276–279.

Mueller, P., & Major, B. (1989). Self-blame, self-efficacy, and adjustment after abortion. *Journal of Personality and Social Psychology, 57,* 1059–1068.

Niswander, K. R., & Porto, M. (1986). Abortion practices in the United States: A medical viewpoint. In J. D. Butler & D. F. Walbert (Eds.), *Abortion, medicine, and the law* (pp. 248–265). New York: Facts on File Publications.

Osofsky, J. D., & Osofsky, H. J. (1972). The psychological reaction of patients to legalized abortion. *American Journal of Orthopsychiatry, 42,* 48–60.

Osofsky, J. D., Osofsky, H. J., & Rajan, R. (1973). Psychological effects of abortion: With emphasis upon immediate reactions and follow-up. In H. J. Osofsky & J. D. Osofsky (Eds.), *The abortion experience.* Hagerstown, MD: Harper & Row.

Packwood, B. (1986). The rise and fall of the Right-to-Life movement in Congress: Response to the Roe decision, 1973–83. In J. D. Butler & D. F. Walbert (Eds.), *Abortion, medicine, and the law* (pp. 3–22). New York: Facts on File Publications.

Perez-Reyes, M. G., & Falk, R. (1973). Follow-up after therapeutic abortion in early adolescence. *Archives of General Psychiatry, 28,* 120–126.

Robbins, J. M. (1984). Out of wedlock abortion and delivery: The importance of the male partner. *Social Problems, 31,* 334–350.

Robbins, J. M., & DeLamater, J. D. (1985). Support from significant others and loneliness following induced abortion. *Social Psychiatry, 20,* 92–99.

Roe v. Wade, 410 U.S. 705 (1973).

Rosenberg, M. (1965). *Society and the adolescent self-image.* Princeton, NJ: Princeton University Press.

Russo, N. F., & Zierk, K. L. (1992). Abortion, childbearing, and women's well-being. *Professional Psychology, 23,* 269–280.

Schwartz, R. A. (1986). Abortion on request: The psychiatric implications. In J. D. Butler & D. F. Walbert (Eds.), *Abortion, medicine, and the law* (pp. 323–340). New York: Facts on File Publications.

Shusterman, L. R. (1976). The psychosocial factors of the abortion experience: A critical review. *Psychology of Woman Quarterly, 19,* 79–106.

Shusterman, L. R. (1979). Predicting the psychological consequences of abortion. *Social Science and Medicine, 13A,* 683–689.

Speckhard, A. C. (1987). *The psycho-social aspects of stress following abortion.* Kansas City, MO: Sheed & Ward.

Sweeney, P. D., Anderson, K., & Bailey, S. (1986). Attributional style in depression: A meta-analytic review. *Journal of Personality and Social Psychology, 50,* 974–991.

Tietze, C., Forrest, J. D., & Henshaw, S. K. (1988). United States of America. In P. Sachdev (Ed.), *International handbook on abortion* (pp. 474–483). Westport, CT: Greenwood.

Tietze, C., & Henshaw, S. K. (1986). *Induced abortion: A world review: 1986* (6th ed.). New York: Alan Guttmacher Institute.

Torres, A., & Forrest, J. D. (1988). Why do women have abortions? *Family Planning Perspectives, 20,* 169–177.

Wilmoth, G. (1989). APA challenges Koop's abortion report. *Advancing the Public Interest,* Winter, 7.

Wortman, C. B., & Silver, R. C. (1989). The myths of coping with loss. *Journal of Counseling and Clinical Psychology, 57,* 349-357.

Zabin, L., Hirsch, M. B., & Emerson, M. R. (1989). When urban adolescents choose abortion: Effects on education, psychological status and subsequent pregnancy. *Family Planning Perspectives, 21,* 248–255.

Chapter 29
Sexual Intercourse During Menstruation and Sexually Transmitted Disease

Koray Tanfer
Sevgi O. Aral

Much of the recent increase in the prevalence of STDs can be attributed to the increasing rates of sexual permissiveness and, to some degree, an increasing likelihood of involvement with multiple sex partners. The more frequently a person engages in casual sex, the greater the risk. Despite this fact, almost one-half of college women rarely ask their new sex partners about their number of lifetime sex partners. And, among college men, condoms appear to be used less frequently as the number of lifetime sex partners increases.

Although casual sex, multiple sex partners, and condom nonusage are certainly risk markers for STDs, other behavioral risk factors have been identified in current studies. Physiological changes in women during the reproductive years, especially those related to the menstrual cycle and pregnancy, also are thought to affect the risk of STDs. As Tanfer and Aral investigate the prevalence of sexual intercourse during menses, and the association between this sexual behavior and the STD experience, some interesting new findings surface with implications for all sexually active women and men, single and married.

The likelihood of infection with sexually transmitted diseases (STD) is affected by behavioral risk factors and risk markers. Multiple dimensions of sexual behavior, such as age at first intercourse, the number of lifetime sex partners, partner recruitment patterns, frequency and timing of sexual intercourse, the prevalence of certain sexual practices, and prophylactic and hygienic practices including vaginal douching, tampon use, and contraception influence the risk for STD and their aftermath.[1] Physiological changes in women during the reproductive years also are thought to affect the risk of STD. Such changes are related primarily to the menstrual cycle, pregnancy, and contraceptive use.[2] The risk of upper tract infection in women appears to be influenced by the menstrual cycle. Evidence from clinical studies suggests that symptomatic gonococcal or chlamydial pelvic inflammatory disease occurs most frequently during the first week of the menstrual cycle.[3] One reason for the increased risk for infection appears to be the relative penetrability of the cervical mucous during menses: another reason is the reflux of potentially contaminated blood into the fallopian tubes during menstrual uterine contractions.[2] For gonococcal infection, two other factors may be responsible: iron, which is abundant in menstrual blood, may promote gonococcal growth, and the type of gonococcus that causes tubal infection may proliferate at the cervix during menstruation.[4]

The normal flora of the genital tract consists of organisms that play a significant role in defense against infection. These organisms are often highly susceptible to the local environment and hormonal influence. For instance, the symptoms of trichomoniasis have been noted to appear or escalate more frequently during or immediately after the menstrual period.[5]

Retrograde menstrual blood flow from the uterine cavity through the fallopian tubes has been demonstrated in the great majority of women with patent tubes. Hence, microorganisms might spread with such blood, contributing to the development of pelvic inflammatory disease.[3] Therefore, intercourse during the menstrual period may expedite the spread of gonococci from the cervix to the endometrium and fallopian tubes.[6] Further, associations with the menstrual period have been suggested for gonococcal and trichomonal infections of the lower genital tract.[4,7]

More recently, the presence of blood during vaginal intercourse has emerged as a risk factor for heterosexual transmission of human immunodeficiency virus (HIV) in some studies.[8] Because HIV has been found in menstrual fluids, intercourse during menses places male partners at increased risk for acquiring HIV through heterosexual intercourse.[9]

This article reports on the prevalence and distribution in the United States of sexual intercourse during menses, the net effects of individual characteristics on the distribution of this practice across population subgroups, and the empirical association between sexual behavior during menses and self-reported STD history. To our knowledge, these are the first population-based estimates of this behavior.

THE CURRENT STUDY

Method

The data are from the 1991 National Survey of Women, with a representative sample of 20- to 37-year-old women in the contiguous United States. The total sample consists of 1669 women; 728 black and 941 non-black. The survey response rate was 71 percent.

Two outcome variables were used: the *usual* practice of vaginal intercourse during menstruation and vaginal intercourse during the *last menses*. In addition, coital frequency and the life-time number of sex partners were included in the analyses to examine their association with the practice of sexual intercourse during menses and to control for their independent effects on the likelihood of STD infection. The STD outcome is based on self-reports of whether the respondent ever had any sexually transmitted infections. Data analysis was confined to women who had ever had vaginal intercourse.

Results

In 1991, 16 percent of the women in the sample reported that they had vaginal intercourse during their last menstrual period. The proportion of women reporting this practice was lowest among women who were affiliated with conservative Protestant denominations and most common among non-Christians and those with no religious affiliation.

The proportion of women who reported having vaginal intercourse during menses "usually" was 26 percent. Patterns of usual practice were similar to patterns of *recent* practice.

The likelihood of having had sexual intercourse during the *last* menses was significantly higher among white women, married and cohabiting women, women who had a regular sex partner, and women who lived in the western United States. The likelihood of sex during menses significantly increased with education, income, coital frequency, and the number of sex partners. Women who, on the average, had intercourse more than once a week and women who had a lifetime number of seven or more sex partners were considerably more likely to have had intercourse during their last menstrual period than women who had sex less frequently (once a week or less) and women who had fewer than seven lifetime partners.

The results from the usual behavior patterns of women regarding sex during menstruation were similar to those obtained from the analysis of the most recent behavior. Higher education, frequent intercourse, and multiple sex partners significantly increased the likelihood of intercourse during the menstrual period. No statistically significant effects were observed for race-ethnicity, religion, region, or income. In contrast to its effect on recent behavior, age was strongly related to the usual coital behavior during menstruation. Women younger than 35 years were significantly more likely to have intercourse during the menstrual period than women 35 years of age and older. In fact, the practice of this behavior seemed to increase with age until approximately age 35 years and to decline thereafter. Finally, married or cohabiting women were less likely to report usually having sexual intercourse during their menstrual period than were single women.

Last, we examined the relative risk of self-reported prior STD experience according to sexual behavior during menses. There are not sufficient numbers of positive responses for any single STD to permit an examination of a possible association between sex during menses and a specific STD, such as chlamydia or gonorrhea. These data show that the cumulative prevalence of self-reported STD experience was significantly higher among those who have sexual intercourse during their menses, as well as among those women who had intercourse during their last menstrual period. The odds of a prior STD experience are nearly three times as high among those who usually have intercourse during their menstrual period as among those who do not. Although neither the usual nor the most recent behavior of the women can be causally related to prior incidence of STD, the results confirm the postulated hypothesis that there is an association between intercourse during menses and STD infection.

Discussion

These findings have interesting implications regarding sexual behavior and the prevention of sexually transmitted infections. Although only approximately one-fourth of sexually active women in the United States represented by this sample generally engage in coital activity during their menstrual period, this practice was significantly more common among certain population groups. Notably, black women, older women, and less educated women were more likely to refrain from intercourse when they had menstrual bleeding. A number of cultural and normative factors regarding sexual hygiene and personal cleanliness may account for

these behavioral differences. This practice also appears to be more common among Catholic women than would be expected. It might be that, because the Catholic Church proscribes all birth control except natural family planning, sexual intercourse during the menstrual period is more common among Catholic women exactly because it conforms with the church doctrine on family planning. The low prevalence among conservative Protestants might be attributed to their strict adherence to the canons of the Old Testament, which specifically prohibit this practice. This is reflected in the regional variation of this practice as well, with lower prevalence in the south and midwest regions of the United States, where affiliation with conservative Protestant doctrines is more common. Further, intercourse during menstruation is associated closely with regular and frequent sexual intercourse and large number of sex partners—two behaviors that are among the principal components of the transmission dynamics of STD.[10]

It is apparent from these data that there is a strong association between the practice of sexual intercourse during menstruation and STD history. However, although at the individual level the data demonstrate a strong and statistically significant positive association between sexual intercourse during menstruation and self-reported STD history, this practice was more common among subgroups marked by low STD prevalence and incidence.[11] Further, this behavior is less prevalent in the South and Midwest regions, which are marked by higher STD rates, than it is in regions in which the STD rates are relatively lower.[11] There are two possible reasons for this seeming anomaly: First, it may be that the relationship between STD and sexual intercourse during menstruation is a spurious one caused by the correlation between coital frequency, partner accumulation, and sex during menses. After controlling for the potential effects of these two sexual behavior variables, intercourse during menstruation still is associated with more than a twofold increase in self-reported STD history. Second, it is possible that the positive relationship between

STD history and sexual intercourse during menstruation results, in part, from a reporting bias. We rely on self-reports of sexual behavior and STD history, and it is commonly accepted that such reporting is often subject to a social desirability bias. Our data suggest that nonconservative women who are open minded about their sexuality were more likely to report sex during menses than were more conservative women. In addition, perhaps these same women were more likely to report their past STD experiences. Further, it is likely that women among whom sex during menses was more common were also more likely to recognize STD symptoms and more likely to have had regular health care visits during which such symptoms were diagnosed.

Despite limitations, our data provide the first population-based evidence on the distribution of usual and recent sexual intercourse during menstruation by demographic, social, and behavioral characteristics. Moreover, such limitations notwithstanding, the data demonstrate a distinct association between sexual intercourse during menses and STD experience. Unless future studies are able to show that this practice does not increase the risk for any sexually transmitted pathogens, prevention strategies should at least inform sexually active persons about the risks of having unprotected vaginal intercourse during menstruation. Such prevention efforts should be focused particularly on persons who have large numbers of sex partners, who have sexual intercourse frequently, and on young women, white women, and on women with relatively higher levels of education and income.

References

1. Aral SO. Sexual behavior as a risk factor for sexually transmitted disease. In: Germain A, et al., eds. *Reproductive tract infections*. New York: Plenum Press, 1992:185–198.

2. Ehrhardt AA, Wasserheit JN. Age, gender, and sexual risk behaviors for sexually transmitted diseases in the United States. In: Wasserheit JN, Aral SO, Holmes KK, eds. *Research issues in human behavior and sexually transmitted diseases in the AIDS era*. Washington, DC: American Society for Microbiology, 1991:97–121.

3. Sweet RL, Blankfort-Doyle M, Robbie MO, Schacter J. The occurrence of chlamydial and gonococcal salpingitis during the menstrual cycle. *JAMA* 1986; 255:2062–2064.

4. James J, Swanson J. Color opacity colonial variants of *Neisseria gonorrhoea* and their relationship to the menstrual cycle. In: Brooks GF, Gotschlich EC, Holmes KK, Sawyer WD, Young FE, eds. *Immunobiology of Neisseria gonorrhoea*. Washington, DC: American Society for Microbiology, 1978:338–343.

5. Catterall RD. Trichomonal infection of the genital tract. *Med Clin North Am* 1972; 56:1203–1205.

6. Brunham RC, Holmes KK, Embree JE. Sexually transmitted diseases during pregnancy. In: Holmes KK, Mard PA, Sparling PF, et al, eds. *Sexually transmitted diseases*. 2nd ed. New York: McGraw-Hill, 1990:771–801.

7. Cohen MS, Weber RD, Mardh P-A. Genitourinary mucosal defenses. In: Holmes KK, Mard PA, Sparling PF, et al. eds. *Sexually transmitted diseases*. 2nd ed. New York: McGraw-Hill, 1990:117–127.

8. De Vincenzi I. Longitudinal study of human immunodeficiency virus transmission by heterosexual partners. *N Engl J Med* 1994; 331:341–346.

9. Alexander N. Sexual transmission of human immunodeficiency virus: Virus entry into the female genital tract. *Fertil Steril* 1990; 54:1–18.

10. Anderson RM. The transmission dynamics of sexually transmitted diseases: The behavioral component. In: Wasserheit JN, Aral SO, Holmes KK, et al., eds. *Research issues in human behavior and sexually transmitted diseases in the AIDS era*. Washington, DC: American Society for Microbiology; 1991:38–60.

11. Division of STD/HIV Prevention. *Sexually transmitted disease surveillance, 1993*. U.S. Department of Health and Human Services, Public Health Service. Atlanta: Centers for Disease Control. December 1994.

Chapter 30
Predominant Risk Factors for Genital Papillomavirus Infection

Robert D. Burk
Gloria Y. F. Ho
Leah Beardsley
Michele Lempa
Michael Peters
Robert Bierman

Human papillomavirus (HPV), believed to be the most common STD in the United States, has been identified as the major cause of cervical cancer, and to have a strong association with cancer of the vulva, vagina, anus, and/or penis. Commonly called genital warts, the virus primarily affects persons ages 15 to 40. These highly contagious warts are transmitted through direct bodily contact during vaginal, oral, or anal intercourse as well as through nongenital contact. The problem is magnified because many infected male sex partners have no visible signs of these warts, which may be only inside the urethra. Additionally, a partner may be a carrier of the virus, which has not as yet produced warts. Therefore, the most common form of transmission is by a person who is asymptomatic. Adding to the bad news, no accurate screening test is currently available for this STD.

Because of these somewhat sobering facts, the Burk et al. epidemiological study that examines certain sexual behavior and partner characteristics as risk factors for HPV is an important link in the chain of sexuality education needed by young persons today. The article may prove to be of special value for those who are already sexually active, especially those with multiple sex partners. The somewhat inconsistent findings of prior studies underscore the need for this carefully designed and well-executed piece of research, which, in spite of its acknowledged limitations, is an important addition to this anthology.

Cervical cancer is the second most common cancer in women worldwide and accounted for ~5000 deaths in the United States in 1994 [1]. Epidemiologic studies have identified human papillomavirus (HPV) as the major cause of cervical cancer and cervical dysplasia [2–4]. Infection of the female genital tract with HPV is now recognized as one of the most, if not the most, common sexually transmitted diseases (STDs) [5–7]. However, studies that have examined the role of sexual behavior as a risk factor for HPV infection have yielded inconsistent results. Potential explanations accounting for this discrepancy include limitations in population size, differences in sampling strategies, and varying sensitivity, specificity, and accuracy of HPV detection methods [8–10]. In addition, little is known about how the behavior of the male partner is related to the risk of female genital HPV infection.

THE CURRENT STUDY

This study sought to test the hypothesis that sexual behavior and partner characteristics are the major risk factors for HPV infection in young women. A cohort of predominantly young college women was recruited through advertisement in order to assemble a group with heterogeneous sexual behavior.

Subjects and Methods

Between September 1992 and March 1994, women students from a state university were invited to participate in a longitudinal study designed to investigate the natural history of HPV infection. Women were eligible if they fulfilled the following criteria: first or second year in college and/or planning to stay in the area for at least 2.5 years; not currently pregnant and without plans to become pregnant in the next 3 years; and never had a cervical biopsy or invasive treatment for cervical lesions.

The ethnic distribution of the participants was representative of the ethnic distribution of the total female undergraduate population (i.e., 70 percent white, 9 percent Asian, 11 percent black, 8 percent Hispanic, and 2 percent other). Characteristics of the eligible nonparticipants (n = 308) and participants (n = 598) who completed the telephone screening were compared. Compared with nonparticipants, participants were slightly older and had more lifetime male sex partners. Hence, this study sample could overestimate the HPV prevalence in the general female college population.

At the baseline visit, each subject completed a self-administered questionnaire that obtained information on demographic background, sexual history, characteristics of sex partners, smoking history, recreational drug and alcohol use, oral contraceptive usage, and pertinent medical history.

Detailed sexual behavior of the subjects in the 6-month period before the baseline visit was assessed. Two types of sex partners were distinguished in the questionnaire: regular partners were sex partners with whom subjects had ongoing sexual contact for >1 month, whereas casual partners were defined as partners with whom subjects had sex for <1 month, including "one-night stand" relationships. For each regular partner, subjects provided information on the partner's demographic and lifestyle characteristics, as well as the frequency of having different types of sex, such as vaginal, oral, and anal sex, with that particular partner.

A pelvic examination was done at the baseline visit [and] a Pap smear was obtained. Thus, 604 subjects were included in this analysis.

Results

Characteristics of Study Population

Mean age of the 604 study subjects was 20.0 years; 83 percent were recruited through advertisements in the mail, on bulletin boards, or in the campus newspaper and 17 percent through word of mouth. The majority of subjects were in the first (50.7 percent) or second (30.6 percent) year of college. The study population was predominantly white (57.1 percent), with 13.1 percent Hispanic, 12.1 percent black, 9.6 percent Asian, and 8.1 percent other ethnicities. Median annual family income was $40,000–$49,999. Most of the subjects were sexually experienced; of the 12.6 percent who denied having had vaginal intercourse, 5.1 percent had had oral and/or anal sex. Among the 87.4 percent who had vaginal intercourse, the median age of first coitus was 16, and the median number of lifetime male sex partners was 3. STDs were rare.

Characteristics of Subjects That Were Risk Factors for HPV Infection

HPV DNA was detected in 27.8 percent of 604 subjects. The subjects' demographic and behavioral characteristics were examined for their associations with HPV positivity. Prevalent HPV infection was strongly associated with the subject's demographic characteristics—age, ethnicity, and year in college; sexual behavior—experience with vaginal sex, number of lifetime male partners for vaginal sex, frequency of douching after sexual intercourse, concern of having been exposed to an STD, and sexual activities in the last 6 months as indicated by the number of male partners for vaginal sex, number of regular sex partners, and having had casual sex; and other lifestyle and behavior characteristics, including frequency of attending religious service and number of smokers in the household. Variables not significantly associated with HPV infection included annual family income, frequency of giving or receiving oral sex in the last 6 months, and having had anal intercourse in the last 6 months.

Black and Hispanic subjects were more likely to be HPV-positive than the other subjects, who were predominantly white. HPV positivity increased proportionately with lifetime as well as more recent (6 months) numbers of male sex partners. None of the lifestyle or behavioral risk factors identified were significant, except the numbers of smokers in the household. Subjects who lived with people who smoked were more likely to have HPV infection than those who did not.

Characteristics of Subjects' Male Sex Partners That Were Risk Factors for HPV Infection in Subjects

The following regular male partner's characteristics [were] independently associated with an increased risk of genital HPV infection in women: age 20 years, black or Hispanic ethnicity, currently not attending college, and increased number of lifetime female sex partners. Subjects who had sex with their regular partner under the influence of alcohol or drugs and those who had a sexual relationship with their partner for 12 months also had an increased risk of HPV.

The subject's age (21–23 years), ethnicity (black and Hispanic), number of smokers in subject's household, lifetime number of male sex partners, duration of the sexual relationship, whether subject's partner was currently in school, and lifetime number of partners of the subject's regular male partner were significant risk factors for HPV infection in the subject.

Discussion

HPV infection was detected in 27.8 percent of a population-based group of young women participating in a study advertised throughout a college campus. Increasing numbers of sex partners for either the female subject or her regular male partner were the predominant risk factors for HPV infection, providing compelling evidence for the sexual transmission of HPV infection mediated through sexual promiscuity.

Association between sexual behavior and female HPV infection in previous studies has not been reported consistently in the literature [10, 12]. For example, Rohan et al. [15] did not identify number of sex partners as a risk factor for genital HPV in a student health clinic population. The lack of association could be attributed, in part, to differences in sample collection [13–14], virus detection methods lacking adequate sensitivity and specificity [9], or population characteristics.

An important feature of this study was the establishment of the cohort through advertisement. This attracted a diverse spectrum of the female college population with greater heterogeneity in sexual behaviors than women attending the health service for gynecologic exams. This latter point is relevant since demonstration of sexual behavior as the quintessential risk factor for HPV is analytically a comparison between groups in a cohort. The importance of how a population has been recruited becomes relevant when interpreting risk factors for HPV infection. Populations that tend to be more homogeneous in their or their partners' level of sexual promiscuity will diminish findings on the relationship between sexual behavior and HPV.

Three studies have reported significant association with lifetime number of sex partners and HPV infection in young women [6, 11–12]. The Berkeley study [6, 11] reported 33 percent of 467 subjects with cervical HPV infection and 46 percent with HPV detected in the vulvar or cervical swab specimen. The New Mexico study [12] reported that 44.3 percent of 357 women attending the University Student Health Center for routine gynecologic care were HPV-positive on cervical swabs. In both studies, HPV positivity was independently correlated with increasing numbers of sex partners. Consistent with the higher prevalence of HPV detected in these latter two studies, two differences in the populations should be noted. In the current study, a population-based cohort was obtained by advertisement, in contrast to the Berkeley and New Mexico studies, which both re-cruited women coming in for gynecologic care. The mean age of the women in both studies was 23 years, 3 years older than the current population.

A population-based Swedish study [16] detected cervical HPV infection in 20 per-cent of 581 women who were 19–25 years old. Lifetime number of male sex partners was the only independent risk factor for cervical HPV infection and showed a linear trend, similar to the current report. More-over, in the Swedish study, 4 percent of 55 non-sexually active women were HPV-posi-tive compared to 33 percent of women with 5 lifetime sex partners.

Taken together, the three previous stud-ies [11–12, 16] and the current report all show a significant association with lifetime number of sex partners and HPV infection in young women.

The relationship between lifetime part-ners and prevalent HPV infection is not as dramatic in older populations of women, in whom recent numbers of sex partners is more strongly associated with HPV [10]. This may reflect differences in the sexual experience of college-aged women, whose lifetime number of sex partners reflects sexual encounters in the recent time pe-riod. In contrast, for women 30 years of age, the period of time encompassing num-bers of lifetime sex partners may span de-cades, thus accentuating differences be-tween recent and lifetime number of partners. Moreover, the differences in risk for prevalent HPV infection in distinct age groups of women from lifetime versus re-cent partners may reflect the transient na-ture of most cervical HPV infections [10, 18]. Discrepant with the predominant sex-ual transmission of HPV, however, is the de-tection of HPV in virginal or non-sexually active women, albeit at a much lower prev-alence.

The information on sexual behavior of the women in the current study indicates that cervical HPV infection is associated with vaginal intercourse and not oral or anal sex. Only lifetime and recent number of male vaginal sex partners remained sig-nificant, suggesting exposure to different

men as the predominant risk, in contrast to frequency of sex. Alternatively, these other risk factors may just be correlated with number of partners. Surprisingly, subjects who claimed to use condoms all of the time still had a relatively high rate of HPV infec-tion (25 percent). Thus, this study did not provide compelling evidence that condoms offer adequate protection from transmis-sion of HPV infection. In addition, subjects who believed they had been exposed to an STD had a higher prevalence of HPV than those not anticipating such a risk.

Only age, ethnicity, and number of smokers in the household were independ-ently associated with HPV. Similar age trends have been seen in other studies of college-aged women [11, 19]. These trends probably reflect the sexual behavior pat-terns of college-aged women who enter col-lege relatively sexually quiescent and be-come more sexually active as they expand their social networks in their upper years of college. In support of this notion, the preva-lence of HPV went from 25 percent in the first 2 years of college to 46 percent in the later years. Different ethnic groups display varying prevalences of HPV in college pop-ulations [11–12]. Similar to our findings, the Berkeley study identified being black as an independent risk factor for HPV infec-tion [11]. Hispanic women were at in-creased risk in our study but not in the New Mexico study [12]. Reasons for ethnic dif-ferences as risk factors for prevalent HPV infection may include genetic predisposi-tion for acquisition or persistence of HPV infection. Alternatively, different levels of endemic HPV may exist in given groups, thus yielding a higher risk of exposure to a group member. This later mechanism has been proposed as an important variable in the high rate of cervical cancer in Latin America [20]. Similarly, the unexpected in-dependent risk factor of a woman living in a household with smokers might be con-strued as placing the subject at risk through association with friends who engage in risky sexual behaviors [21].

This is the first report to investigate the behaviors of the regular male sex partners of women as risk factors for HPV infection in the women. The significant factors among male partners imparting risk to the subjects included older age, black and Hispanic ethnicity, educational status, increasing number of sex partners, a short-term relationship, frequent sex while intoxicated, rarely using seat belts, and less attendance at religious service. Taken together, these risk factors paint the picture of male partners of HPV-infected women as being more sexually promiscuous, as indicated by lifetime number of partners, duration of relationship, and frequency of sex. In addition, male partners of infected women exhibit characteristics of risk-taking behaviors, as evidenced by lack of seat belt use and substance abuse. These observations strengthen the importance of the "male factor" in HPV infection in women and are consistent with the recent observation of HPV type-specific concordance in sex partners [22]. The lifetime numbers of both female and male partners were independently associated with HPV in subjects, as was ethnicity, college status of partner, duration of sexual relationship, and number of smokers in household.

Certain limitations apply to this study. The cohort of women studied is relatively young and early in their sexual behavior patterns and thus is not likely representative of older women. The information on male partners was obtained from the subjects and may be biased by each subject's own sexual behaviors and assumptions concerning her partner. In addition, differences in geographic or ethnic variation of endemic HPV could be significant variables influencing risk factors for HPV infection.

In summary, our data suggest three main areas of risk for college-aged women to have an HPV infection. The first and most significant is sexual exposure through multiple male sex partners. The second is their partners' level of promiscuity as evidenced by his lifetime number of partners. Last, the probability of a woman having HPV infection was related to the prevalence of HPV in her social/sexual contact pool. Characteristics of contact groups appear to be associated with ethnicity, college status,

having short-term relationships, and living with persons who smoke.

References

1. Boring C, Squires TS, Tong T, Montgomery S. Cancer statistics, 1994. *CA Cancer J Clin* 1994;44:7–26.

2. Schiffman MH. Epidemiology of cervical human papillomavirus infections. *Curr Top Microbiol Immunol* 1994;186:55–81.

3. Koutsky LA, Holmes KK, Critchlow CW, et al. A cohort study of the risk of cervical intraepithelial neoplasia grade 2 or 3 in relation to papillomavirus infection. *N Engl J Med* 1992;327:1272–8.

4. Munoz N, Bosch FX, De Sanjose S, et al. The causal link between human papillomavirus and invasive cervical cancer: a population-based case-control study in Colombia and Spain. *Int J Cancer* 1992;52:743–9.

5. Kiviat NB, Koutsky LA, Paavonen JA, et al. Prevalence of genital papillomavirus infection among women attending a college student health clinic or a sexually transmitted disease clinic. *J Infect Dis* 1989;159:293–302.

6. Bauer HM, YiTing MS, Greer CE, et al. Genital human papillomavirus infection in female university students as determined by a PCR-based method. *JAMA* 1991;265:472–7.

7. Jamison JH, Kaplan DW, Hamman R, Eagar R, Beach R, Douglas JM Jr. Spectrum of genital human papillomavirus infection in a female adolescent population. *Sex Transm Dis* 1995;22:236–43.

8. Schiffman MH, Schatzkin A. Test reliability is critically important to molecular epidemiology: an example from studies of human papillomavirus infection and cervical neoplasia. *Cancer Res* 1994;54(suppl 7):1944s–7s.

9. Franco EL. Measurement errors in epidemiological studies of human papillomavirus and cervical cancer. *IARC Sci Publ* 1992;119:181–97.

10. Hildesheim A, Gravitt P, Schiffman MH, et al. Determinants of genital human papillomavirus infection in low-income women in Washington, DC. *Sex Transm Dis* 1993;20:279–85.

11. Ley C, Bauer HM, Reingold A, et al. Determinants of genital human papillomavirus infection in young women. *J Natl Cancer Inst* 1991;83:997–1003.

12. Wheeler CM, Parmenter CA, Hunt WC, et al. Determinants of genital human papillomavirus infection among cytologically normal women attending the University of New Mexico Student Health Center. *Sex Transm Dis* 1993;20:286–9.

13. Vermund SH, Schiffman MH, Goldberg GL, Ritter DB, Weltman A, Burk RD. Molecular diagnosis of genital human papillomavirus infection: comparison of the methods used to collect exfoliated cervical cells. *Am J Obstet Gynecol* 1989;160:304–8.

14. Goldberg GL, Vermund SH, Schiffman MH, Ritter DB, Spitzer C, Burk RD. Comparison of cytobrush and cervicovaginal lavage sampling methods for the detection of genital human papillomavirus. *Am J Obstet Gynecol* 1989;161:1669–72.

15. Rohan T, Mann V, McLaughlin J, et al. PCR-detected genital papillomavirus infection: prevalence and association with risk factors for cervical cancer. *Int J Cancer* 1991;49:856–60.

16. Karlsson R, Jonsson M, Edlund K, et al. Lifetime number of partners as the only independent risk factor for human papillomavirus infection: a population-based study. *Sex Transm Dis* 1995;22:119–27.

17. Rosenfeld WD, Rose E, Vemund SH, Schreiber K, Burk RD. Follow-up evaluation of human papillomavirus infection in adolescents. *J Pediatr* 1992;121:307–11.

18. Hildesheim A, Schiffman MH, Gravitt PE, et al. Persistence of type-specific human papillomavirus infection among cytologically normal women. *J Infect Dis* 1994;169:235–40.

19. Melkert PW, Hopman E, van den Brule AJ, et al. Prevalence of HPV in cytomorphologically normal cervical smears, as determined by the polymerase chain reaction, is age-dependent. *Int J Cancer* 1993;53:919–23.

20. Bosch FX, Munoz N, de Sanjose S, et al. Importance of human papillomavirus endemicity in the incidence of cervical cancer: an extension of the hypothesis on sexual behavior. *Cancer Epidemiol Biomarkers Prev* 1994;3:375–9.

21. Millstein SG, Moscicki AB. Sexually transmitted disease in female adolescents: effects of psychosocial factors and high risk behaviors. *J Adolesc Health* 1995;17:83–90.

22. Baken LA, Koutsky LA, Kuypers J, et al. Genital human papillomavirus infection among male and female sex partners: prevalence and type-specific concordance. *J Infect Dis* 1995;171:429–32.

Part VII

Sexual Orientation

The word *homosexuality* was coined in 1869 when Hungarian Karoly Benkert first used the term; but it was British sexologist Havelock Ellis who introduced its English usage in the 1880s and 1890s (Weeks, 1981). Thereafter, the medical model of homosexuality as a form of mental disease was prevalent until the mid-1950s, when Hooker's pioneer study of matched samples of heterosexuals and homosexuals found that there were no significant differences in psychological functioning between the groups. However, it was not until 20 years later in 1974, after a number of other studies found similar results, that the American Psychiatric Association removed "self-accepting homosexuality" from its list of mental disorders (Troiden, 1988).

The two basic perspectives of homosexuality in both popular and scientific thought are essentialism and social constructionism (Stein, 1992). The popular, widespread view of essentialism relates homosexuality to biological or psychological factors. Ascribing a genetic causal model, this perspective is embraced by many scholars and researchers as well. Conversely, social constructionists question the universality of such categories as homosexuality and heterosexuality, proposing instead that concepts of sexual orientation and practices have changed over time and that they vary across societies. Persons who subscribe to either of these positions can be pro-gay or anti-gay in their beliefs. Although social

constructionism was mainly developed by pro-gay intellectuals who denied the innateness of homosexuality, in a twist of fate, some of their arguments of denial have been embraced by the right-wing anti-gays who use this position to support the view that homosexuality is a choice and therefore, a sin (Laumann, Gagnon, Michael, & Michaels, 1994).

A recent Associated Press poll reports that more than half of Americans say that gay/lesbian couples should not be allowed to marry, but more than one-half indicate that gay/lesbian partners should have some of the same legal rights as married couples: inheritance, Social Security benefits, and health insurance. Who are the minority sanctioning same-sex marriages? According to this poll, supporters include women rather than men, Democrats rather than Republicans, young rather than old, and more of those who feel that gays are born with their sexual orientation than those who see it as a choice ("Just Over Half," 2000).

A difference in perspectives concerning the origin of homosexuality is at the heart of many issues. The Parents and Friends of Lesbians and Gays (Parents FLAG) support organization is firmly behind any research that implicates biology as the source of homosexuality, possibly because it assuages any guilt for responsibility that they might feel. Conversely, many lesbians and gays have a growing skepticism about the search for the cause(s) of homosexuality, believing such a search implies that homosexuality is deviant and, therefore, needs to be cured. University of California, Los Angeles psychologist Evelyn Hooker stated:

> Why do we want to know the cause? If we understood . . . and accept it as a given, then we come closer to the kinds of attitudes that will make it possible for homosexuals to live a decent life in society. (Gelman, Foote, Barrett, & Talbot, 1992:53)

One wonders if tolerance and acceptance of gays/lesbians would increase if we, without any reservations, could conclude that homosexuality is genetically linked. Or, if we discovered a homosexual gene, would pregnant women obtain an abortion if the fetus were gay or lesbian? Would these women echo the sentiments of the mother of an adult gay man, who in a *Newsweek* feature said, "Had I known that I was to have a gay child, I would probably not want to have a gay child" (Gelman et al., 1992:50). Hard questions without easy answers are on the horizon for twenty-first century pilgrims. The articles on sexual orientation in Part VII enable readers to assess just how far society has progressed in its attitudes about homosexuality and, perhaps, the distance they themselves have traveled in their own journey.

Pillard and Bailey's technical, well-written review of the behavioral genetics research on sexual orientation includes studies of twins, the hypothalamus gland, and evolutionary trends. To determine if homosexuality runs in families, the authors examine sibling, twin, and adoption concordance rates that are compatible with the hypothesis that genes account for at least one-half of any variable in sexual orientation. Supporting the essentialist perspective of the authors, research findings are presented about gender atypicality as a forerunner of adult homosexuality, an unresolved topic that has been in the research literature for over a century. In raising the issue of a reproductive disadvantage of a homosexual orientation, this psychiatrist and psychologist team offer an evolutionary slant different from the Byne selection that follows.

After considering the heritable component of sexual orientation, a number of important questions surface. For example, why do lesbians and gays have fewer children than heterosexuals? Why are women more often bisexual than men? Is the fact that gay men tend to be born later into the family a significant factor to be explored in studying sexual orientation? Why are more gays found in urban than in rural areas? Is it because of more tolerance or anonymity there, or are other factors operating? And, finally, does homosexuality run in families? This selection is guaranteed to raise more questions than answers about an important and timely topic.

Byne is well-qualified to counter the argument that human sexual orientation has a heritable component. As a neuroanatomist and psychiatrist at Mt. Sinai School of Medicine, he studies correlations between brain structure and behavior in health and disease. He does not deny that all mental phenomena have a biological substructure, but he questions the precise contribution that certain biological factors may have in the development of sexual orientation. Although somewhat technical, the selection clearly and succinctly reviews several widely acclaimed studies suggesting a biological basis for sexual orientation and draws surprising conclusions. Addressing what he believes to be incomplete or misleading findings, Byne makes a cogent case for controlled, carefully designed longitudinal studies. In order to properly debate the issue of the origin(s) of homosexuality, students will need the insights gained from this article as well as the previous one by Pillard and Bailey.

Today, four to eight million lesbian and gay families are rearing three to fourteen million children, figures that are admittedly estimates (Lowry, 1999). More precise numbers are difficult to discern for various reasons—some obvious, others obscure. Obviously, many homosexual parents choose to remain anonymous because of discrimination, which can lead to loss of employment, loss of child custody, ostracism, or antigay/lesbian violence. Others may be ambivalent about their homosexuality, making it impossible for researchers to accurately assess the number of lesbian and gay parents. For example, when Michael Huffington, the 1998 California Republican senatorial candidate, announced that he was gay, did his heterosexual family suddenly become a gay family? And, how might we best categorize families of bisexuals or transsexual/transgendered persons? Readers who wish to expand their knowledge beyond Golombok and Tasker's experimentally designed British study on these topics are referred to a recent article by therapists Ariel and McPherson (2000), who address a number of such issues in their work with lesbian and gay parents and their children.

Of the hot topics pertaining to homosexual parenting, psychological stability is perhaps the most debated. Do lesbian or gay parents differ from heterosexual parents in their ability to nurture their children? Some people apparently believe so. A Florida court in 1996 removed a child from her biological mother, who was a lesbian, and awarded custody to the child's father, who had been convicted of murdering his first wife. Moreover, the mother suddenly died when the case was being appealed (*Ward v. Ward*, 1996). Golombok and Tasker also contrast biological and psychological theories as they address the subject of parental influence on the sexual orientation of children. An excellent, easy-to-follow review of various explanations of the causes of sexual orientation precedes the research in this British study.

A number of years ago, psychotherapist Rollo May (1969), in his classic work, *Love and Will*, decried the *Playboy* mentality in our society that took the fig leaf from the genitals and placed it on the face, resulting in much bed-hopping but little intimacy. Savin-Williams' litany of poignant quotes by lesbian/gay youth emphasizes the role of society in institutionalizing such a reality among homosexual youth. But for heterosexual and homosexual youth, the underlying causes of sex without intimacy appear to differ. That is, the sexual promiscuity of

heterosexuals addressed by May had at least partial roots in society's changing sexual mores. Conversely, the plight of lesbian/gay youth in establishing intimacy seems more related to the failure of sexual mores to change at all.

The inherent problems for lesbians and gays in accomplishing the developmental tasks of youth that are dramatically and knowledgeably magnified by Savin-Williams may be novel ideas for the vast majority of readers, who themselves are heterosexuals. Probably few adults recognize the significant role that dating has played, or can play, in their lives by helping them to achieve their own developmental tasks. For example, dating not only affords recreation and a venue for selecting a life partner, but through interaction with others, persons are also socialized for various life roles, become more independent, and are better able to meet their status and ego needs (Adams, 1986). This offering will not only raise consciousness about the negativism that lesbian, gay, and bisexual youth are prone to experience in romantic relationships with same-sex partners, it will also move readers along their own path of decision making about the role that society needs to play in this real-life drama.

References

Adams, B. N. (1986). *The family: A sociological interpretation* (4th ed.). San Diego: Harcourt Brace Jovanovich.

Ariel, J., & McPherson, D. W. (2000). Therapy with lesbian and gay parents and their children. *Journal of Marital and Family Therapy, 26*, 421–432.

Gelman, D., Foote, D., Barrett, D., & Talbot, M. (1992, February 24). Born or bred? *Newsweek*, pp. 46–50, 52–53.

"Just over half in poll reject gay marriage." (2000, June 1). *Saint Paul Pioneer Press*, p. 13A.

Laumann, E. O., Gagnon, J. H., Michael, R. T., & Michaels, S. (1994). *The social organization of sexuality: Sexual practices in the United States*. Chicago: University of Chicago Press.

Lowry, J. (1999, March 7). Gay adoption backlash growing. *San Francisco Examiner*, p. A20.

May, R. (1969). *Love and will*. New York: Norton.

Stein, E. (Ed.). (1992). *Forms of desire: Sexual orientation and the social constructionist controversy*. New York: Routledge.

Troiden, R. R. (1988). *Gay and lesbian identity: A sociological analysis*. Dix Hills, NY: General Hall.

Ward v. Ward, No. 95-4184, 1996 Fla. App. LEXIS 9130 (Fla. Dis. Ct. App. Aug. 30, 1996).

Weeks, J. (1981). Discourse, desire, and deviance: Some problems in a history of homosexuality. In K. Plummer (Ed.), *The making of the modern homosexual* (pp. 76–111). London: Hutchinson. ✦

Chapter 31
Human Sexual Orientation Has a Heritable Component

Richard C. Pillard
J. Michael Bailey

Homosexuality, as a topic, was discussed previously in this book when Reiss and Reiss gave an excellent accounting of the homosexual revolution in 1969 that began at Stonewall Inn, a gay bar in Greenwich Village, and of the subsequent birth of the Gay Liberation Front. Another beginning article in Part I by Bullough detailed the history of Kinsey's work on the topic of homosexuality from a different vantage point. Now, in this overview of behavioral genetics research on homosexual and heterosexual orientation, Pillard, a psychiatrist, and Bailey, a psychologist, team up to explore the heritability component of human sexual orientation. Against a backdrop of data about female and male sexual orientation, they impose recent research findings suggesting that sexual orientation is, at least in part, genetically based. Whether confirming or confounding for the reader, their research is an important contribution to understanding this still debatable topic.

A powerful generalization about human sexual desire is that members of the two sexes are attracted to each other but attracted by different qualities. Traditionally, men seek youth and beauty in a woman (although the standard of beauty may vary with time and place), whereas women seek in a man good health, high status, and evidence of willingness to provide for children (Symons 1979). These generalizations are intuitively compatible with evolutionary theory. The healthy, the young (women), and the rich (men) are more likely to produce viable offspring and raise them to maturity than the sick, the old, and the poor. (One example of fecundity enhanced by wealth and status: the late King Sombhuza of Swaziland was reported to have over 600 children.)

For a given individual the selection of a mate may be an inexact marker of sexual attraction because in many societies the individual has limited mate choice and sometimes no choice at all. Community expectations and the social and political ambitions of the family often override individual desires. Also, atypical sexual desires result in censure and therefore may be effectively concealed. Nevertheless, heterosexual attraction, broadly speaking, must be the paradigmatic adaptation. Men and women attracted to one another sufficiently to copulate, pair bond, and raise children to self-sufficiency are a precondition for hominid evolution (Symons 1979).

The development and mechanisms of human sexual attraction have only recently become objects of study. Visual animals that we are, visual cues are doubtless important triggers of sexual response. Olfactory cues may also play a role in sexual attraction, although the nature of the cues and their relative strength remain in controversy (Kohl 1995). (It is interesting to note that blind persons report that they can be sexually attracted by a particular tone of voice.) Whatever cues attract men and women to each other, it is hard to escape the conclusion that they are more or less wired in, the product of an evolutionary history parallel to that of sexual reproduction itself.

Homosexuality, the sexual desire for a person of the same sex, is an interesting challenge to an evolutionary account of sexual attraction, one reason that psychosocial theories have been dominant. Homosexuality is not the only trait that poses the problem of the apparent selection of a reproductively disadvantageous trait. Schizophrenia is ubiquitous in humankind, too frequent to be the result of occasional mutations, and it is genetically influenced and results in decreased fecundity. What can one make of traits that seem so evidently to defeat the biological imperative of optimizing reproductive success?

Here, we present some background data about male and female sexual orientation and follow with some recent research that in our opinion suggests that sexual orientation has a genetic component. Finally, we comment on some possible explanations for the paradox presented by the persistence of a trait that appears inimical to reproductive success.

Phenotype

Sexual orientation refers to an individual's erotic desire for a member of his or her own sex (homosexuality), the opposite sex (heterosexuality), or both sexes (bisexuality). Recognition of one's orientation generally comes during adolescence, although some individuals are aware of sex-specific attractions in childhood. A homosexual orientation may be concealed for practical reasons, but by adulthood it is almost always a conscious and more or less permanent personality trait. Psychological constructs such as "unconscious" or "latent" homosexuality have use for some clinicians but have dropped out of the research literature.

The ascertainment of an individual's sexual orientation for research purposes is generally done by a questionnaire or a sexual history interview, ideally conducted by a clinician with experience in sex history interviewing. Alfred Kinsey and his colleagues pioneered sex history interviewing with volunteer subjects, and a detailed account of the technique and content of the interviews upon which their survey research was based has been published (Kinsey et al. 1948). The information collected in a sexual history interview may include data about sexual feelings and behavior during the life epochs: childhood, adolescence, adulthood, and old age. Other information is obtained as the research protocol dictates, for example, the timing of developmental milestones (puberty, first sexual experience, marriage, menopause, etc.), the presence of sexual dysfunctions, safer sex practices, and sexual traumas.

As with any psychometric assessment, it is important to ensure the validity and reliability of the measures, and considerable work has been done on this issue (Bogaert 1996; Catania et al. 1995). Some researchers use physiological measures, such as penile plethysmography (Miner et al. 1995) or a vaginal probe, to evaluate sexual responsiveness to stimuli, usually presented by slides or videos. In this way responses to different erotic situations can be compared. These techniques, besides being somewhat invasive, require expensive instrumentation and their validity has not been fully established. Questionnaire and interview responses can be valid and reliable indicators of sexual behavior; as one example, respondents' accounts of their sexual activity can predict the occurrence of sexually transmitted diseases. The studies cited make use of interviews and questionnaires to ascertain the sexual orientation of research subjects. Despite sources of error, such as volunteer bias, pressure to give socially desirable responses, differences in interviewer technique and questionnaire items, these data give as clear and consistent a picture of the frequency and direction of sexual feeling and behavior as can be obtained from interview data on almost any other topic of interest to behavioral science.

Frequency of Homosexual Orientation

Some commentators in the early sexology literature believed that homosexuality was increasing because of the corrupting influences of city life (von Krafft-Ebing 1901). What they probably observed was the urbanization of nineteenth-century Europe bringing to the cities gays and lesbians who recognized that the opportunities for discreet liaisons were maximized there. More recently, Laumann et al. (1994)

found that the percentage of gay men in large U.S. cities is much higher than that in rural areas. Some of this differential is the result of the migration of gays from country to city, but Laumann also found that gay men were disproportionately born in urban areas. This could result from environmental exposure, a reporting artifact (urban gays might be more candid about their orientation), or a genetic effect such that people with "gay genes" are more likely to be city dwellers.

Surveys of sexual orientation began with the Kinsey reports of 1948 and 1953 (Kinsey et al. 1948, 1953). With respect to sexual orientation, the Kinsey team estimated the *relative* amounts of heterosexual and homosexual behavior, placing each subject on a 7-point scale from 0 (completely heterosexual) to 6 (completely homosexual) with intermediate points to describe mixtures of the two. Kinsey's data led to the much-cited estimate that 1 in 10 men are "more or less exclusively homosexual." Kinsey's colleague, Gebhard (1972), recognized the overrepresentation of subsamples with unusually high rates of homosexuality. By adjusting the sample weightings, Gebhard concluded that only 3–4 percent of men and 1–2 percent of women in the United States are exclusively homosexual or virtually so.

The Kinsey group also found that the frequency of more or less exclusive homosexuality was about the same in older subjects as in younger subjects. More recent surveys, although on a smaller scale, give estimates close to those from the Kinsey survey (as adjusted by Gebhard) a half-century ago (Seidman and Rieder 1994; Laumann et al. 1994). Thus, despite differences in definition, methodology, and time frame, these surveys taken together suggest that the frequency of gay and lesbian behavior in the United States has remained stable over several generations in spite of the revolutionary changes in the social status of homosexuality. Although comparable data from other countries would be useful, few are available. Some recent surveys report a frequency of homosexual behavior in the 1–2 percent range (Sell et al. 1995).

Bisexuality occupies a controversial place in the literature (Fox 1996). Kinsey suggested that bisexuality was both common and normal. His graphic presentations using a cumulative frequency distribution make it difficult for the reader to recognize that he found more respondents toward the extreme homosexual end of the spectrum (5 and 6 on the Kinsey scale) than in the intermediate range. Diamond (1993) concluded from his own survey that "exclusive or predominantly exclusive homosexual activities are more common than bisexual activities" (p. 291). In our experience this bimodality is more evident among men, whereas bisexuality is relatively more common in women.

Bisexuality is also more frequently endorsed among the young. Adult subjects are usually unequivocally able to say which sex they prefer in a partner, that is, which sex most strongly engages their fantasies and desires. On the other hand, people engage in sexual relations with the non-preferred sex for any number of reasons, and therefore frequency counts of behavior alone, particularly if sampled over a stretch of time, often result in a pattern that appears more bisexual than would be the case if desire alone prompted behavior. By the time they reach their mid-twenties, most men and most women give a clear and unambiguous answer when asked, Would you rather have sex with a woman or a man?

Gender Atypicality

Gay men and to a lesser extent lesbian women are often labeled as gender atypical. The term "gender atypical" is chosen to avoid prejudging whether the behaviors at issue are typically those of the other sex or simply not typical of the assigned sex. For men atypicality is evidenced in childhood by association with girl playmates, preference for girls' toys and games, and avoidance of boyish rough-and-tumble play. In adulthood gay men often have preference for female-typical activities and vocations. Lesbian women recollect tomboy behavior in childhood and preference for boys' games and companionship. As adults, lesbians tend to adopt male-typical social and vocational roles more often than do heterosexual women.

Gender atypicality as a forerunner of adult homosexuality has been noted in the sexology literature for more than 100 years (Ulrichs 1994). It is a robust phenomenon confirmed in both prospective and retrospective studies (Bailey, Miller et al. 1993; Bailey and Zucker 1995; Bailey, Nothnagel et al. 1995; Green 1987; Phillips and Over 1995). Whitam found that gender atypicality is a culturally invariable childhood trait for gay men (Whitam 1983) and women (Whitam and Mathy 1991) in such diverse cultures as Brazil, Peru, Guatemala, and the Philippines.

Of course there are many possible kinds of gender atypicality and many ways that a child or adult can feel and behave atypically. Nevertheless, comparing the gender behavior of gays and heterosexuals makes clear that this trait is not simply a matter of feeling lonely, isolated, different, or depressed. The feelings and behaviors are often strikingly and specifically those of the other sex (Pillard 1991).

Gender typical and atypical behaviors emerge in children at similar ages, around 2 to 4 years. Observers of gender-atypical children at play are struck by the pervasive and tenacious nature of this trait. Moreover, some gender-atypical children even look different. Zucker and his colleagues gave photographs of prepubertal gender-typical and gender-atypical boys (Zucker et al. 1993) and girls (Fridell et al. 1996) to raters blind to the child's behavior status. Raters described gender-atypical boys as "cuter," "prettier," and "more attractive" than the gender-typical boys and described the converse for the atypical girls. Apparently, in addition to their behavior, something in the physiognomy of these children marks them already in childhood as gender atypical. What we know about the natural history of this trait suggests that a larger than expected percentage will become gay and lesbian adults. A theory of the development of sexual orientation must take account of the robust and frequently replicated data on the coincidence of atypical

behavior in early childhood followed by same-sex attraction in adolescence and adulthood [for an alternative view, see Bem (1996)].

With the onset of adolescence same-sex or opposite-sex attractions become prominent in the gay or lesbian adult-to-be, but some measure of gender atypicality usually remains. Standard personality tests often include so-called masculinity-femininity (M-F) scales purporting to reflect the degree to which an individual matches the "maleness" or "femaleness" typical of his or her sex. Most such items are transparent: "I think I would like the work of a nurse" or "I like to read *Popular Mechanics* magazine" obviously will have different endorsement rates for the two sexes. What is surprising is how large the differences are, how consistent they are across cultures, and how little they have changed over time despite the profound changes in available gender appropriate activities and role models (Gough et al. 1968). The endorsement of female-typical pursuits and interests by gay men found by Terman and Miles (1936) on their M-F scale can be replicated today, again despite profound changes in the roles and social status of women and of gays.

Are gays and lesbians also atypical in other domains in which the sexes differ, such as patterns of cognitive abilities, brain lateralization, or incidence of physical and mental illness? These questions have not been well studied, and results are uneven (Bogaert and Blanchard 1996; Hall and Kimura 1995; Reite et al. 1995). Furthermore, there are at least some traits on which gender atypicality seems to be minimal or absent; for example, gay men tend not to show a female-typical interest in child care (Stringer and Grygier 1976).

The research just cited naturally led investigators seeking neuroanatomical correlates of sexual orientation to look at the hypothalamus, because it subserves reproductive functions, and at nuclei within the hypothalamus known to be gender dimorphic. Two recent articles reported differences between gay and heterosexual men in the size of hypothalamic nuclei. LeVay (1991) found that gay men have a smaller anterior hypothalamic nucleus, which is also smaller in women than in men. However, Swaab and Hoffman (1990) found that gay men have a larger suprachiasmatic nucleus, although it is *not* gender dimorphic. It thus appears that homosexual attraction and gender atypicality are more complex than simply a skewed mix of typically masculine and feminine qualities.

Birth Order

Blanchard and Bogaert (1996) have recently reported that gay men tend to be born later in the sibship, and this trend is accounted for by the presence of older brothers but not older sisters. A psychosocial explanation for this observation certainly seems plausible. Perhaps having an older brother stimulates homosexual attraction, perhaps the family's reaction to a younger brother is such as to bend him in a homosexual direction. There are also purely biological possibilities; for example, placental cells invade the uterine endometrium, and it is now known that protein fragments from these cells may remain in the maternal system for many years. Their effect (if any) is unknown, but their existence raises the possibility of an influence on later gestations (Blanchard and Bogaert 1996).

Familial Aggregation of Male and Female Sexual Orientation

Characteristics of interest to the behavioral geneticist generally run in families; familial aggregation suggests but does not prove a genetic contribution to the trait. Sexologists a half-century ago observed that sexual orientation may be familial (Hirschfeld 1936), but systematic research on the issue is relatively recent. Pillard and Weinrich (1986) used newspaper and radio advertisements to recruit subjects for studies of "personality, sexual behavior, and mental abilities." Some ads were placed in papers with a mostly gay readership to enrich the participation of the minority orientation and were written to be candid yet to conceal the specific hypotheses of the study. Volunteers were interviewed and given psychological tests; then permission was requested to recruit their sibs. A large number of sibs were enrolled and (to avoid bias) interviewed.

Pillard and Weinrich's (1986) primary finding was that nonheterosexual males (2–6 on the Kinsey scale) had an excess of nonheterosexual brothers (22 percent), whereas heterosexual males (0 or 1 on the Kinsey scale) had only 4 percent nonheterosexual brothers, close to the population average. We use the term "nonheterosexual" to highlight another finding: The few males who were bisexual (2–4 on the Kinsey scale) had as many gay brothers as did males who were exclusively gay. Individuals who had "more than occasional" gay contacts, even if most of their contacts were heterosexual, shared the tendency toward familial aggregation as strongly as did the exclusive homosexuals. An additional finding was that probands [brothers] were able to accurately report their sibs' orientation so long as they made the assessment with a high degree of confidence.

To summarize, we note that nonheterosexual males have from 2 to 5 times as many nonheterosexual brothers as do heterosexual males. The heterosexual males, in turn, have rates of nonheterosexuality among their brothers that are about equal to the population frequency, based on other large survey studies. Nonheterosexual women also appear to have more nonheterosexual sisters than do heterosexual women, although the familiality estimates for women vary more widely.

There is a trend for nonheterosexual men to have more nonheterosexual sisters [however, this was not found by Pillard and Weinrich (1986)], whereas nonheterosexual women tend to have more nonheterosexual brothers. However, the estimates varied considerably, leaving open the important issue of cofamiliality of male and female homosexuality.

Family trees with the systematically ascertained sexual orientation of parents, children, and other relatives of gay and lesbian probands are rarely published. Pillard et al. (1982) noted that, when males reported other gay or lesbian relatives, they usually came from the maternal side of the family, an observation also made by Hamer et al. (1993). This pattern suggests that some male homosexuality may be X-chromosome linked, an issue more fully discussed by Pattatucci (1998).

Female and Male Twins and Adoptees

The traditional method used by behavioral geneticists to disentangle genetic and environmental components of trait variance is the comparison of concordance between monozygotic (MZ) twins, dizygotic (DZ) twins, and adopted siblings (i.e., biologically unrelated individuals) reared together. If the influence of genes is paramount, MZ twins will be frequently concordant, whereas DZ twins will have the same concordance as nontwin siblings (in the absence of a congenital factor). Adopted siblings, sharing the family's environment but not their genes, will share the trait no more often than an average sample of the population.

Several twin studies of sexual orientation have been conducted recently. Bailey and Pillard (1991) and Bailey, Pillard et al. (1993) recruited two kinds of gay males: those with twins and those with adopted brothers or sisters. Males were interviewed concerning the sexual orientation of their co-twin or adopted sib, who was contacted where possible. Males were generally accurate in assessing their sibling's sexual orientation. In the male sample 56 MZ twins were ascertained, 52 percent of whom were concordant for a nonheterosexual orientation, 54 DZ twins were ascertained, 22 percent of whom were concordant [the same as for nontwin brothers according to Pillard and Weinrich (1986)], and 57 adopted male sibs were ascertained, 11 percent of whom were concordant with the gay male sib.

The female study yielded concordance rates of 48 percent for MZ twins, 16 percent for DZ twins, and 6 percent for adopted sisters. Heritability estimates for women were likewise substantial. However, more recent data obtained by Bailey et al. (1996) on twins from an Australian twin registry showed little difference in concordance rates between female MZ and DZ twins and thus gave essentially zero heritability for females. This result may be due to the different manner in which the twins were recruited.

Neither age of first recognition of gay or lesbian feelings, extreme Kinsey scale score, nor extent of childhood gender atypicality related to genetic liability for a homosexual orientation. However, both male and female *concordant* MZ twin pairs were also highly similar in their gender atypicality scores, suggesting a genetic basis for this trait. Whitam et al. (1993) reported somewhat higher concordance rates for both MZ and DZ twins. They also reported three sets of triplets. One set consisted of an MZ male pair, concordant for homosexuality, and a heterosexual sister. A second set of three sisters consisted of an MZ pair, both lesbian, and a DZ heterosexual sister. The third set consisted of three MZ brothers, all gay.

The few available examples of MZ twins *raised apart* (Eckert et al. 1986; Whitam et al. 1993) show a degree of concordance, at least for males, similar to the cited observations of MZ twins raised together. Concordance in several male MZ pairs reared apart extended to an interesting variety of personality traits as well.

The conclusion that sexual orientation has a heritable component depends on a set of assumptions, which we now examine. The primary assumption is that volunteer bias does not distort the outcome. Probands [subjects] for the twin studies were obtained through advertisements in gay-oriented publications. It may be that persons who read these publications and who volunteer for a study are systematically different from the larger population of gay twins or siblings. This possibility can be tested by comparing volunteer data with those from a captive sample, such as from a clinic, or with subjects randomly drawn from a census tract or phone book.

There may also be a systematic concordant-dependent bias; that is, twins or sibs

Sell, R.L., J.A. Wells, and D. Wypij. 1995. The prevalence of homosexual behavior and attraction in the United States, the United Kingdom, and France: Results of national population-based samples. *Arch. Sex. Behav.* 24:235–248.

Stringer, P., and T. Grygier. 1976. Male homosexuality, psychiatric patient status, and psychological masculinity and femininity. *Arch. Sex. Behav.* 5:15–27.

Swaab, D.F., and M.A. Hoffman. 1990. An enlarged suprachiasmatic nucleus in homosexual men. *Brain Res.* 537:141–148.

Symons, D. 1979. *The Evolution of Human Sexuality*. New York: Oxford University Press.

Terman, L.A., and C. Miles. 1936. *Sex and Personality: Studies in Masculinity and Femininity*. New York: McGraw-Hill.

Ulrichs, K.H. 1994. *The Riddle of "Man-Manly" Love: The Pioneering Work on Male Homosexuality*, M.A. Lombardi-Nash, trans. Buffalo, NY: Prometheus Books.

von Krafft-Ebing, R. 1901. *Psychopathia Sexualis*, 3d ed., translation of 10th German ed. Chicago, IL: W.T. Keener.

Weinrich, J.D. 1987. *Sexual Landscapes*. New York: Scribner's.

Whitam, F.L. 1983. Culturally invariable properties of male homosexuality: Tentative conclusions from cross-cultural research. *Arch. Sex. Behav.* 22:207–226.

Whitam, F.L., and R.M. Mathy. 1991. Childhood cross-gender behavior of homosexual females in Brazil, Peru, the Philippines, and the United States. *Arch. Sex. Behav.* 20:151–170.

Whitam, F.L., M. Diamond, and J. Martin. 1993. Homosexual orientation in twins: A report of 61 pairs and three triplet sets. *Arch. Sex. Behav.* 22:187–206.

Zucker, K., J. Wild, S. Bradley et al. 1993. Physical attractiveness of boys with gender identity disorder. *Arch. Sex. Behav.* 22:23–36.

Chapter 32

Why We Cannot Conclude Sexual Orientation Is a Biological Phenomenon

William M. Byne

After reading the previous article, claiming that human sexual orientation has a heritable component, readers will be challenged to broaden their conclusions by the Byne selection, which presents counterarguments to a number of scientific studies. For example, are the often quoted LeVay research findings focused more clearly by evidence that the medication used to treat AIDS causes change in the size of the hypothalamus gland? And what conclusions can be drawn from the information that the hormone profiles of gays and lesbians are reportedly indistinguishable from those of heterosexuals? These and other intriguing facts raise issues without answers. But the author, a medical researcher of brain structures and behavior, asks far more penetrating questions. Does biology simply provide a slate of neural circuitry upon which sexual orientation is inscribed by experience? Or do biological factors influence sexual orientation only indirectly by affecting personality variables that influence the environment in social relationships which in turn shape sexual orientation? Students, like more learned scholars, will be unable to answer the questions decisively after finishing this offering, but they will be farther along the path of scientific thought about this matter.

I would like to challenge [the following statement]: "Sexual orientation is primarily a biological phenomenon," from three different perspectives. First, we have to ask whether sexual orientation is a unitary phenomenon that can be accounted for by a single explanation. If, as seems more likely, there are multiple pathways to the same endpoint of relative sexual attraction to men or to women, then biology might play a greater or lesser role for different individuals depending on the idiosyncrasies of their individual developmental pathways. [To say that]: "Sexual orientation is primarily a biological phenomenon," fails to anticipate the need for analysis at such a level of complexity.

Second, what do we mean when we assert that sexual orientation is "primarily biological"? All psychological phenomena are primarily biological in the sense that they cannot exist in the absence of the biological activity of a living brain. "Primarily biological" must mean something else— perhaps, that biological factors are more important than psychosocial or experiential factors. But the processes integral to experience, namely perception, internalization, association, and assimilation, are themselves inextricably enmeshed with biology. How, then, can biological and experiential factors be teased apart, and what are the units of measurement that would allow them to be individually quantified and weighed against one another in order to determine which is more important? I believe that it would be more productive to explore the pathways through which biological and experiential factors might interact, than to argue about the primacy of one set of factors over the other.

The final perspective from which I wish to challenge the debate statement is to address the weakness of the biological database itself. Much of the commonly offered biological evidence has yet to be replicated or has to be discounted because it has failed replication (Byne, 1995, 1996; Byne & Parsons, 1993; Fausto-Sterling, 1992). Even the replicable data are often uninterpretable because of confounded experimental designs (Byne, 1995; Fausto-Sterling, 1992). Beyond these difficulties the research to date has produced purely correlational data. Correlations, no matter how robust, cannot demonstrate that sexual orientation is primarily biological in the absence of adequately controlled longitudinal studies that delineate the intermediate causal mechanisms (Byne, 1996)

Much of the research is premised on assumptions of questionable validity. Most biological research that addresses sexual orientation seeks to demonstrate that the brains of homosexuals are in some ways like those of the other sex (Byne & Parsons, 1993). The rationale behind this research is as follows: First, sexual orientation is assumed to be a unitary brain function that is sexually dimorphic. By sexually dimorphic, I mean that it takes two forms and differs between heterosexual men and heterosexual women. Researchers then seek to define two archetypes for the human brain: One of these they suggest would be shared by gay men and heterosexual women and would drive sexual attraction to men, while the other would be shared by heterosexual men and lesbians and would drive sexual attraction to women. Even a cursory review of human sexuality in historical and cross-cultural perspective suggests that these assumptions are culture bound and inadequate (Boswell, 1980; Ford & Beach, 1951).

Without questioning the validity of these assumptions, some researchers propose that the differentiation of these two archetypes is accomplished prenatally in response to sex differences in exposure to particular hormones (Allen & Gorski, 1992; Gladue et al., 1984; LeVay, 1991). This prenatal hormonal hypothesis draws upon animal research showing that a sexually receptive female mating posture called lordosis can be elicited from male rodents that were deprived of androgens during a critical period of brain development. Conversely, females that were experimentally treated with androgens during that same period fail to show lordosis in adulthood, but will show increased levels of male-typical mounting behavior (Goy & McEwen, 1980).

There are major problems in extrapolating from these findings to sexual orientation in humans. First, in the paradigm of the neuroendocrine laboratory, the male rat that shows lordosis [bending backward] when mounted by another male is considered the homosexual. But it is important to note that lordosis is little more than a reflex, and that the male that displays lordosis when mounted by another male will also display the posture if its back is stroked by a researcher. We cannot infer much about the sexual motivation of the male that exhibits this posture. Ironically, however, the animal that does display sexual motivation—the male that mounts another male—escapes scientific scrutiny and labeling as does the female that displays lordosis when mounted by another female. Some researchers have begun to acknowledge the problem of equating behaviors in rodents with sexual orientation, and have begun to employ a variety of strategies to actually assess partner preference in animals (Paredes & Baum, 1995).

But even these studies may have no relevance to human sexual orientation. This is because in order for the genetic male to behave as a female, with respect to either partner preference or lordosis behavior, he must be exposed to extreme hormonal abnormalities that are unlikely to occur outside the neuroendocrine laboratory. Not only must he be castrated as a neonate, depriving him of androgens, but in order to activate the display of female-typical behaviors and preferences, he must also be injected with estrogens in adulthood (Paredes & Baum, 1995).

It is difficult to see how this situation has any bearing on human sexual orientation when healthy gay men and lesbians have hormonal profiles that are indistinguishable from those of their heterosexual counterparts. Nor do the vast majority of homosexuals exhibit physical stigmata indicative of sexually atypical prenatal hormone levels (Meyer-Bahlburg, 1984).

However, if it proves to be replicable, Simon LeVay's report (1991) concerning the third interstitial nucleus of the anterior hypothalamus could be considered as evidence that some homosexual men experienced low androgen levels prenatally. Specifically, LeVay reported that the third nucleus is smaller in women and gay men than in presumed heterosexual men. The third nucleus in humans closely resembles a structure which, in rats, is much larger in males than in females. In rats, the size of this structure which is known as the sexually dimorphic nucleus of the preoptic area is primarily determined by perinatal hormones (Gorski et al., 1978).

LeVay's report that the size of the third nucleus varies with sexual orientation has been faulted for a number of technical reasons, such as small sample size, inadequate assessment of sexual orientation, and the reliance on the brains of gay subjects with AIDS. The small sample size really isn't a problem. In fact, statistical power analysis suggests that differences as large as those he reported could be detected with even smaller sample sizes. Also, by adding to uncontrolled variance, poor sexual histories would decrease rather than increase the probability of detecting statistically significant differences.

Unfortunately, there has been little discussion of the hormonal abnormalities associated with AIDS and the possible impact of such abnormalities on LeVay's findings. HIV-related hormonal abnormalities need to be taken into account because in some species the size of sexually dimorphic hypothalamic nuclei varies with the amount of testosterone in the adult animal's bloodstream (Commins & Yahr, 1984). Whether or not the nucleus is present is related to prenatal hormonal status. However, if an adult male is castrated, the size of his nucleus will decrease by half. This shrinkage can be prevented by the administration of testosterone, suggesting that testosterone is necessary to maintain the size of the nucleus in the mature animal (Commins & Yahr, 1984).

These findings are potentially highly relevant to LeVay's report because the testes fail in HIV infection and testosterone levels decline. Furthermore, some drugs used commonly to treat the opportunistic infections of AIDS also decrease testosterone

levels and the side effects of other medications may elevate estrogen levels (Croxson et al., 1989). Thus, it is entirely possible that the effects on the size of the third nucleus that LeVay attributed to sexual orientation were actually due to some hormonal abnormality resulting from AIDS or its treatment. His inclusion of a few heterosexual men who died with AIDS did not adequately control for this possibility.

In interpreting his study, LeVay (1991) has suggested that the third interstitial nucleus is involved in the "generation of male-typical sexual behavior." But this suggestion is made on the basis of an imprecise reading of the literature. While he is technically correct when he writes that lesions in the region of the rat's sexually dimorphic nucleus disrupt male sexual behavior, the effective lesion site lies above, not within, that nucleus (Arendash & Gorski, 1983). Furthermore, Gary Arendash and Roger Gorski at UCLA have shown that the sexually dimorphic nucleus can be destroyed on both sides of the brain without any effect on mounting behavior (Arendash & Gorski, 1983).

LeVay and Hamer (1994) conclude that similarly placed lesions in male rhesus monkeys cause them to become "completely sexually indifferent to females." But what the paper they cite actually shows is quite different. While dorsally placed medial preoptic lesions did decrease mounting, they by no means eliminated it (Slimp et al., 1978). Moreover, the males in this study pressed a lever for access to females more frequently following the lesions than before. So contrary to LeVay's interpretation, one cannot conclude that the lesioned males were sexually indifferent to females.

In another highly publicized neuroanatomical study, Laura Allen and Roger Gorski reported that the anterior commissure is larger in women and homosexual men than in presumed heterosexual men (Allen & Gorski, 1992). The major problem for this study is that the only other group to study the anterior commissure for sexual dimorphism found a sex difference but in the opposite direction (Demeter et al., 1988).

To summarize so far, then, the neuro-endocrinological and neuroanatomical evidence does not allow one to resolve that sexual orientation is primarily biological, and as I will now show, the same can be said about the genetic evidence.

Until only two years ago, the evidence that heritable factors influence sexual orientation consisted only of reports that homosexuality tends to run in families and that identical twins are more likely to share the same sexual orientation than are fraternal twins (Byne & Parsons, 1993). Such studies are not helpful in distinguishing between biological and environmental influences because related individuals share environmental variables as well as genes. Adoption studies are necessary to avoid this confound.

One of the recent heritability studies did include an adoption component, and this suggested a significant environmental contribution to the development of sexual orientation (Bailey & Pillard, 1991). This study included not only identical and fraternal twins, but also the unrelated adopted brothers of the gay probands [subjects]. If there were no environmental effect on sexual orientation, then the rate of homosexuality among the adopted brothers should be equal to the base rate of homosexuality in the population, which recent studies place at somewhere between 2 and 5 percent (Hamer et al., 1993). The fact that the observed concordance rate was 11 percent—that is 2 to 5 times higher than expected—suggests a major environmental contribution—especially when we consider that the rate of homosexuality in the non-twin biological brothers was only 9 percent in the study of Bailey and Pillard (1991), and 13.5 percent in a study by Dean Hamer et al. (1993). If the concordance rate for homosexuality among non-twin brothers is the same whether or not the brothers are biologically related, the concordance cannot be explained genetically.

Of all the recent biological studies, the genetic linkage study by Dean Hamer's group (Hamer et al., 1993) is the most complex conceptually, and the most likely to be misinterpreted, especially by those unfamiliar with the rationale of linkage studies. While this study did suggest that homosexuality may be linked to the X-chromosome in at least one cohort of men, the study did not uncover any particular genetic sequence associated with homosexuality as is commonly believed.

The verdict is still out as to whether or not Hamer's study can be independently replicated. Recent work done by George Ebers's group in London, Ontario, raises doubt. This group is convinced that sexual orientation is genetically determined and is currently screening approximately 10 markers a day distributed across the human genome. While they are confident that they will eventually establish a genetic linkage for homosexuality, they are equally confident that it will not be to the X-chromosome. To date, their family studies based on over 200 gay probands have failed to show any evidence of X linkage (Ebers, personal communication).

In closing, we are a long way from understanding the factors that contribute to sexual orientation. Even if the size of certain brain structures does turn out to be correlated with sexual orientation, current understanding of the brain is inadequate to explain how such quantitative differences could produce qualitative differences in a psychological phenomenon as complex as sexual orientation. Similarly, confirmation of genetic linkage would make clear neither precisely what is inherited nor how the heritable factor influences sexual orientation. For instance, would the heritable factor influence the organization of hypothetical neural circuits that mediate sexual orientation? Or would it act more indirectly, perhaps influencing temperamental variants that in turn influence how one interacts with the environment in constructing the social relationships and experiences from which sexual orientation emerges (Byne, 1996)? The existing biological data are equally compatible with both scenarios, and certainly do not allow us to resolve that sexual orientation is primarily biological.

As research into the biology of sexual orientation proceeds, we should ask why we as a society are so emotionally invested in its outcome. Will it—or should it—make any difference in the way we perceive ourselves and others or in the way we live our lives and allow others to live theirs? Perhaps the answers to the most salient questions in this debate reside not in the biology of human brains, but within the cultures those brains have created.

References

Allen, L. S., & Gorski, R. A. (1992). Sexual orientation and the size of the anterior commissure in the human brain. *Proceedings of the National Academy of Sciences, USA, 89*, 7199–7202.

Arendash, G. W., & Gorski, R. A. (1983). Effects of discrete lesions of the sexually dimorphic nucleus of the preoptic area or other medial preoptic regions on the sexual behavior of male rats. *Brain Research Bulletin, 10*, 147–154.

Bailey, J. M., & Pillard, R. C. (1991). A genetic study of male sexual orientation. *Archives of General Psychiatry, 48*, 1089–1096.

Boswell, J. (1980). *Social tolerance, Christianity, and homosexuality*. Chicago, IL: University of Chicago Press.

Byne, W. (1995). Science and belief: Psychobiological research on sexual orientation. *Journal of Homosexuality 28*, 303–344.

Byne, W. (1996). Biology and homosexuality: Implications of neuroendocrinological and neuroanatomical studies. In R. P. Cabaj & T. S. Stein (Eds.) *Textbook of homosexuality and mental health* (pp. 129–146). Washington, DC: American Psychiatric.

Byne, W., & Parsons, B. (1993). Sexual orientation: The biological theories reappraised. *Archives of General Psychiatry, 50*, 228–239.

Commins, D., & Yahr, P. (1984). Adult testosterone levels influence the morphology of a sexually dimorphic area in the Mongolian gerbil brain. *Journal of Comparative Neurology, 224*, 132–140.

Croxson, T. S., Chapman, W. E., Miller, L. K., Levit, C. D., Senie, R., & Zumoff, B. (1989). Changes in the hypothalamic-pituitary-gonadal axis in human immunodeficiency virus-infected men. *Journal of Clinical Endocrinology and Metabolism, 89*, 317–321.

Demeter, S., Ringo, J. L., & Doty, R. W. (1988). Morphometric analysis of the human corpus callosum and anterior commissure. *Human Neurobiol, 6*, 219–226.

Fausto-Sterling, A. (1992). *Myths of gender: Biological theories about women and men*. New York: Basic Books.

Ford, C. S., & Beach, F. A. (1951). *Patterns of sexual behavior*. New York: Harper and Bros.

Gladue, B. A., Green, R., & Hellman, R. E. (1984). Neuroendocrine response to estrogen and sexual orientation. *Science, 225*, 1496–1499.

Gorski, R. A., Gordon, J. H., Shryne, J. E., & Southam, A. M. (1978). Evidence for a morphological sex difference in the medical preoptic area of the rat brain. *Brain Research, 148*, 333–346.

Goy, R. W., & McEwen, B. S. (1980). *Sexual differentiation of the brain*. Cambridge, MA: MIT Press.

Hamer, D. H., Hu, S., Magnuson, V. L., Hu, N., & Pattatucci, A. M. L. (1993). A linkage between DNA markers on the X chromosome and male sexual orientation. *Science, 261*, 321–327.

LeVay, S. (1991). A difference in hypothalamic structure between heterosexual and homosexual men. *Science, 253*, 1034–1037.

LeVay, S., & Hamer, D. (1994). Evidence for a biological influence in male homosexuality. *Scientific American, 270*, 44–49.

Meyer-Bahlburg, H. F. L. (1984). Psychoendocrine research on sexual orientation: Current status and future options. *Progress in Brain Research, 71*, 375–397.

Paredes, R. G., & Baum, M. J. (1995). Altered sexual partner preference in male ferrets given excitotoxic lesions of the preoptic area/anterior hypothalamus. *Journal of Neuroscience, 15*, 6619–6630.

Slimp, J. C., Hart, B. L., & Goy, R. W. (1978). Heterosexual, autosexual, and social behavior of adult male rhesus monkeys with medial preoptic anterior hypothalamic lesions. *Brain Res, 142*, 105–122.

Chapter 33
Do Parents Influence the Sexual Orientation of Their Children?

Susan E. Golombok
Fiona L. Tasker

A *subject of major interest to many students is whether having a homosexual parent will predispose a person to a lesbian or gay identity. Golombok and Tasker investigate family environment as a causative factor in sexual orientation, identifying several factors that may influence whether children grow up to be heterosexual or homosexual. With one exception, they go a step beyond other investigations of adult daughters of lesbian mothers, which have focused on children rather than on adults and have failed to address sexual orientation.*

In addition, use of a comparison group of heterosexual parents definitely differentiates this research design from other such studies. But most important is its prospective nature, an approach that allows data about the sexual orientation of young adults reared by lesbian mothers to be examined. Thus, we receive a rare glimpse into the process through which childhood family characteristics and experiences may influence sexual orientation during the transition to adult life. Readers are cautioned, however, to interpret the data with care because respondent attrition in the follow-up stage of the study substantially reduced the sample size. This ambitious piece of research, which challenges readers with far from staid conclusions or "pat" answers, *may inspire or incite, yet it definitely will inform.*

Opinion varies among biological and psychological theorists regarding the extent to which it is possible for parents to influence the sexual orientation of their children. From a purely biological perspective, parents should make little difference. In contrast, psychoanalytic theorists believe that relationships with parents in childhood are central to the development of sexual orientation in adult life. Research on adults raised in lesbian families provides an opportunity to test theoretical assumptions about the role of parents in their children's sexual orientation; if parents are influential in whether their children grow up to be heterosexual, lesbian, or gay, then it might be expected that lesbian parents would be more likely than heterosexual parents to have lesbian daughters and gay sons. With the exception of Gottman's (1990) investigation of adult daughters of lesbian mothers in which actual sexual behavior was not reported, research on lesbian families has focused on children rather than adults, and sexual orientation has not been assessed (Golombok, Spencer, & Rutter, 1983; Green, Mandel, Hotvedt, Gray, & Smith, 1986; Patterson, 1992).

From the existing literature, it seems that no single factor determines whether a person will identify as heterosexual or homosexual. The current view is that there are a variety of influences, from the prenatal period onward, which may shape development in one direction or the other. Studies of gay men with twin brothers (Bailey & Pillard, 1991) and lesbian women with twin sisters (Bailey, Pillard, Neale, & Agyei, 1993) have found that a significantly greater proportion of monozygotic than dizygotic co-twins were gay or lesbian. The greater concordance between identical than nonidentical twin pairs indicates a genetic link to homosexuality, although this does not mean that a homosexual (or heterosexual) orientation is dependent on a specific genetic pattern. The identification of a genetic marker for male homosexuality has recently been reported by Hamer, Hu, Magnuson, Hu, and Pattatucci (1993). Of 40 pairs of brothers, both of whom were homosexual, 33 pairs were found to have a marker in a small region of the X chromosome, suggesting that there may be a specific gene, yet to be located, which is linked to male homosexuality. However, the presence of this gene, if it exists, would not necessarily determine a homosexual orientation, and not all homosexual men would necessarily possess the gene (the marker was not found in 7 pairs of brothers). Instead, it may be one of many factors that influence development along a homosexual rather than a heterosexual course.

Gonadal hormone levels may constitute another such factor. Although no consistent differences in gonadal hormone levels between heterosexual and homosexual adults have been identified (Meyer-Bahlburg, 1984), there is evidence to suggest that the prenatal hormonal environment may play some part in the development of sexual orientation. Studies of women with congenital adrenal hyperplasia (CAH), a genetically transmitted disorder in which malfunctioning adrenal glands produce high levels of androgens from the prenatal period onward, have found that these women were more likely to consider themselves to be bisexual or lesbian than were women who do not have the disorder, suggesting that raised levels of androgens prenatally may be associated with a lesbian sexual orientation (Dittman, Kappes, & Kappes, 1992; Money, Schwartz, & Lewis, 1984). In addition, a significantly greater proportion of women exposed in utero to the synthetic estrogen diethylstilbestrol (DES), an androgen derivative, reported bisexual or lesbian responsiveness compared with both unexposed women from the same clinic and their unexposed sisters (Ehrhardt et al., 1985). It is important to note, however, that most of the women with CAH, and most of the women prenatally exposed to DES, were heterosexual despite their atypical endocrine history.

On the basis of this research, together with animal research which has demon-strated that gonadal hormones influence the development of sex-typed behavior and sex differences in brain morphology (Goy & McEwen, 1980), it has been proposed that prenatal gonadal hormones may act on the human brain to facilitate development as heterosexual or homosexual (Hines & Green, 1990; Money, 1988). However, the mechanisms involved in the link between prenatal gonadal hormones, sex differences in brain morphology, and sexual orientation have not been established (Byne & Parsons, 1993). Although an anatomical difference in the hypothalamus of homosexual and heterosexual men has recently been identified (LeVay, 1991), the reason for this difference, and how it may influence sexual orientation, remains unknown.

A number of investigations point to a relationship between nonconventional gender role behavior in childhood and adult homosexuality. In retrospective studies, differences in childhood gender role behavior have been found between homosexual and heterosexual men (Bell, Weinberg, & Hammersmith, 1981; Whitam, 1977) and between lesbian and heterosexual women (Bell et al., 1981; Whitam & Mathy, 1991), with homosexual men and lesbian women consistently reporting greater involvement in cross-gender activities. Prospective studies of boys with gender identity disorder (American Psychiatric Association, 1994)—children who express a strong desire to be the other sex and characteristically engage in cross-gender behavior including a marked preference for friends of the other sex—have shown that more than two thirds of the children develop a bisexual or homosexual orientation in adulthood (Green, 1987). Nevertheless, the identification of a link between cross-gender behavior in childhood and homosexuality in adulthood does not mean that all or even most adults who identify as homosexual were nonconventional in their gender role behavior as children. A substantial proportion of gay and lesbian adults who participated in the retrospective studies reported no or few cross-gender behaviors in childhood, and the prospective studies examined gay men who had been referred in childhood to a clinic because of marked cross-gender behavior and thus were not representative of the general population of adult homosexual men. Investigations of parental influences on childhood gender nonconformity have failed to identify a clear and consistent association between the two, either for boys (Roberts, Green, Williams, & Goodman, 1987) or for girls (Green, Williams, & Goodman, 1982). However, to the extent that sexual orientation results from complex interactions between the individual and the social environment, studies that have demonstrated a link between boyhood cross-gender behavior and adult homosexuality suggest that feminine boys, and possibly masculine girls, in lesbian families may be more likely than their counterparts in heterosexual families to develop a sexual orientation toward partners of the same sex.

From the perspective of classical social learning theory, the two processes that are important for children's gender development are differential reinforcement and the modeling of same-sex individuals, particularly same-sex parents (Bandura, 1977; Lytton & Romney, 1991; Mischel, 1966). Although social learning theorists have focused on the development of gender role behavior rather than on sexual orientation, insofar as sexual orientation results from social learning, the processes of reinforcement and modeling would also apply. From this viewpoint, it could be expected that different patterns of reinforcement may be operating in lesbian than in heterosexual families, such that young people in lesbian families would be less likely to be discouraged from embarking upon lesbian or gay relationships. With respect to modeling, contemporary social learning theorists now believe that it is the modeling of gender stereotypes, rather than same-sex parents, that promotes gender development (Bandura, 1986; Perry & Bussey, 1979). Thus, girls would no longer be expected to adopt a lesbian identity simply by observing and imitating their lesbian mother. But by virtue of their nontraditional family, the sons and daughters of lesbian mothers may hold less rigid stereotypes about what con-

stitutes acceptable male and female sexual behavior than their peers in heterosexual families, and they may be more open to involvement in lesbian or gay relationships themselves. Thus, from a social learning theory perspective, children's sexual orientation may be influenced by attitudes toward sexuality in the family in which they are raised.

In examining the cognitive mechanisms involved in gender development, cognitive developmental theorists, like social learning theorists, have focused on the acquisition of sex-typed behavior rather than on sexual orientation (Kohlberg, 1966; Martin, 1993). Cognitive developmental explanations of gender development emphasize that children actively construct for themselves, from the gendered world around them, what it means to be male or female, and they adopt behaviors and characteristics that they perceive as being consistent with their own sex. Again, gender stereotypes, rather than parents, are viewed as being the primary source of gender-related information. To the extent that cognitive processes are contributing to the adoption of a heterosexual or homosexual orientation, it would seem that young people seek out information that is in line with their emerging sexual orientation, and they come to value and identify with those characteristics that are consistent with their view of themselves as heterosexual, lesbian, or gay. Cognitive developmental theorists would place less emphasis on the role of parental attitudes than on prevailing attitudes in the wider social environment. Thus, the social context of the family, within a wider community that is either accepting or rejecting of homosexuality, would be considered to facilitate or inhibit respectively young people's exploration of relationships with partners of the same sex as themselves.

Social constructionist theories start from the premise that sexual feelings are not essential qualities that the individual is born with or that are socialized by childhood experiences (Kitzinger, 1987; Simon & Gagnon, 1987). What these approaches have in common is an emphasis on the individual's active role, guided by his or her culture, in structuring reality and creating sexual meanings for particular acts. Sexual identity is considered to be constructed throughout the life course; the individual first becomes aware of cultural scenarios for sexual encounters and then develops internal fantasies associated with sexual arousal and interpersonal scripts for orchestrating specific sexual acts (Gagnon, 1990). Identification with significant others is believed to be important for enabling an individual either to neutralize a homosexual potential or to construct a homosexual identity. For example, heterosexual parents may respond negatively to what they perceive as children's same-gender sexual activity (Gagnon, 1977). Plummer (1975) suggested that awareness of others who identify as homosexual validates feelings of same-gender attraction that might otherwise go unnoticed or be denied. From a social constructionist perspective, therefore, children raised in lesbian families would be expected to be more likely than children in heterosexual families to adopt a lesbian or gay identity themselves as a result of their exposure to lesbian lifestyles, and often to gay lifestyles as well.

Although psychoanalytically oriented theorists hold the view that homosexuality arises from disturbed relationships with parents (Freud, 1920/1955, 1933; Socarides, 1978), empirical studies of the influence of parent-child relationships on the development of a gay or lesbian identity have produced inconclusive results. In a study of psychoanalysts' reports of the family relationships of their male homosexual patients, the fathers of gay men were described as hostile or distant and the mothers as close—binding, intimate, and dominant (Bieber et al., 1962). With a nonpatient sample, Evans (1969) also showed a similar pattern of a close mother and a detached father. However, Bene (1965) found no evidence that homosexual men who were not in therapy were more likely to have been overprotected by, overindulged by, or strongly attached to their mother than heterosexual men, and in a well-controlled large-scale study by

Siegelman (1974), no differences were identified in parental background between homosexual and heterosexual men who were low on neuroticism. Studies of the parents of lesbian women have similarly failed to produce consistent findings, although some investigations have reported mothers of lesbian women to be dominant and fathers to be inferior or weak (Bell et al., 1981; Newcombe, 1985).

Although existing research has failed to produce empirical evidence to demonstrate that parents' behavior influences the development of their children's sexual orientation, all of the studies to date have investigated heterosexual families. In addition, these studies have focused on the quality of parent-child relationships rather than on other aspects of the family environment. By investigating the sexual partner preferences of young adults who have grown up in a lesbian family, we hoped to examine the impact on sexual orientation of being raised by a lesbian mother, and thus to address the question of what influence, if any, parents may have in their children's development as heterosexual, lesbian, or gay. As data in this study were first collected from the families when the children were school age, this prospective investigation not only provides data on the sexual orientation of young adults raised by lesbian mothers, but it also allows an examination of the processes through which childhood family characteristics and experiences may influence the development of sexual orientation during the transition to adult life.

THE CURRENT STUDY
Method

Sample

Twenty-seven lesbian mothers and their 39 children and a control group of 27 heterosexual single mothers and their 39 children first participated in the study when the average age of the children was 9.5 years (Golombok et al., 1983). The two types of family were alike in that the children were being raised by women in the absence of a father in the household, but they differed with respect to the sexual orientation of the mother. The criteria for inclusion were that the lesbian mothers regarded themselves as predominantly or wholly lesbian in their sexual orientation and that their current or most recent sexual relationship was with a woman. The single-parent group was defined in terms of mothers whose most recent sexual relationship had been heterosexual but who did not have a male partner living with them at the time of the original study. The two groups were matched for the age and social class of the mothers, and all of the children had been conceived within a heterosexual relationship.

In 1992–1993, the children, who were 23.5 years old on average, were seen again. For ethical reasons, it was necessary to locate the mothers in the first instance to request permission to recontact their children. Fifty-one of the 54 mothers who participated in the original study were traced. The follow-up sample comprised 25 young adults raised in lesbian families (8 men and 17 women) and 21 young adults raised in heterosexual families (12 men and 9 women).

An examination of the demographic characteristics of the young people who participated at follow-up showed no statistically significant differences between those from lesbian and those from heterosexual single-parent homes with respect to age, gender, ethnicity, and educational qualifications. There were seven pairs of siblings in the lesbian group and five pairs of siblings in the heterosexual group. By the time of the follow-up study, all but one of the original group of heterosexual single mothers were reported by their children to have had at least one heterosexual relationship, and in most cases (18 out of 20), the new male partner had cohabited with the mother while the children were living at home. Likewise, all but one of the children in lesbian families reported that their mother had had at least one lesbian relationship, and in 22 out of 24 cases, their mother's female partner had resided with them. Thus, the large majority of children

in both groups had lived in a stepfamily during their adolescent years.

Measures

Data on the young adults' sexual orientation were gathered in the follow-up study by using a semistructured interview with a standardized coding scheme that had been developed specifically for the present investigation (Tasker & Golombok, in press). Each man and woman was interviewed either at home or at the university by a female interviewer (Fiona Tasker). The psychosexual history section of the interview commenced with questions on experience of prepubertal sexual play with same-gender and opposite-gender children and about interest in other children's bodies and physical development during puberty. The men and women were then asked to recall their first crush and subsequent crushes from the beginning of puberty through to their first sexual relationship in order to establish the extent of same-gender and opposite-gender attraction. To further assess the presence or absence of same gender attraction, we asked the participants whether they had ever thought that they might be physically attracted to a friend of the same gender, and whether they had ever had sexual fantasies about someone of the same gender. A chronological sexual relationship history was then given by each interviewee detailing their age when the relationship began, the gender of their partner, the level of sexual contact, and the duration of the relationship. In addition, information was obtained regarding their current sexual identity as heterosexual, bisexual, lesbian, or gay.

Five variables relating to sexual orientation were derived from the interview material: (a) The presence of *same-gender attraction* was established from data on sexual object choice in crushes, fantasies, and sexual relationships from puberty onward. (b) *Consideration of lesbian or gay relationships* was rated according to whether participants had ever previously thought that they might experience same-gender attraction or relationships, or whether they thought it possible that they might do so in the future.

(c) *Same-gender sexual relationships* ranged from a single encounter involving only kissing to cohabitation lasting over 1 year. (d) For the variable *sexual identity*, men and women were categorized according to whether they identified as bisexual, lesbian, or gay and expressed a commitment to a bisexual, lesbian, or gay identity in the future. (e) A composite rating of *same-gender sexual interest* was made for each participant.

Family Characteristics

Using an adaptation of a standardized interview previously designed to assess family functioning (Quinton, Rutter, & Rowlands, 1976), we obtained data on characteristics of the lesbian family environment that may be hypothesized to influence the development of children's sexual orientation from the lesbian mothers in the initial study when the children were school age. The variables derived from the initial study were the following: (a) number of years the child had been raised in a heterosexual home, (b) the mother's warmth to the child, (c) the child's contact with his or her father, (d) the child's gender role behavior, (e) quality of the child's peer relationships, (f) quality of the mother's relationship with her current female partner, (g) the mother's relationship history, (h) the mother's openness in showing physical affection, (i) the mother's contentment with her sexual identity, (j) the mother's political involvement, (k) the mother's preference for the child's sexual orientation, and (l) the mother's attitude toward men. Comparable data from the initial study are not available for the young people raised in heterosexual families as it would not have been meaningful to ask the heterosexual mothers questions about lesbian relationships when they had not experienced any (e.g., about physical affection shown toward their female partner in front of the child).

Results

Sexual Orientation: Comparison Between Young Adults Raised in Lesbian and Heterosexual Families

There was no significant difference between adults raised in lesbian families and their peers from single-mother heterosexual households in the proportion who reported sexual attraction to someone of the same gender.

Distinct from the experience of same-gender attraction is consideration of having a lesbian or gay relationship. Significantly more of the young adults from lesbian family backgrounds stated that they had previously considered, or thought it a future possibility, that they might experience same-gender attraction or have a same-gender sexual relationship or both. Fourteen children of lesbian mothers reported this to be the case compared with 3 children of heterosexual mothers. Daughters of lesbian mothers were significantly more likely to consider that they might experience same-gender attraction or have a lesbian relationship than daughters of heterosexual mothers. There was no significant difference between sons from the two family types for this variable.

With respect to actual involvement in same-gender sexual relationships, there was a significant difference between groups such that young adults raised by lesbian mothers were more likely to have had a sexual relationship with someone of the same gender than young adults raised by heterosexual mothers. None of the children from heterosexual families had experienced a lesbian or gay relationship. In contrast, 6 children from lesbian families had become involved in one or more sexual relationships with a partner of the same gender. It was also found that all of the men and women from lesbian (as well as from heterosexual) backgrounds had experienced at least one opposite-gender sexual relationship.

In terms of sexual identity, the large majority of young adults with lesbian mothers identified as heterosexual. Only 2 young women from lesbian families identified as lesbian compared with none from heterosexual families. This group difference did not reach statistical significance.

Childhood Family Characteristics and Adult Sexual Orientation

To examine prospectively the processes that may result in the children of lesbian mothers being more likely to engage in same-gender relationships than those raised by heterosexual mothers, we correlated variables from the initial study relating to family characteristics with the overall rating of same-gender sexual interest for the group of young adults raised by lesbian mothers. Young adults whose mothers had reported greater openness in showing physical affection to their female partner when their children were school age and young adults whose mothers had reported a greater number of lesbian relationships when their children were school age were more likely to report same-gender sexual interest. No significant associations were found between same-gender sexual interest in adulthood and the number of years the child had been raised in a heterosexual household, the mother's warmth to the child, the child's contact with the father, the child's gender role behavior, the quality of the child's peer relationships, the quality of the mother's relationship with her female partner, the mother's contentment with her sexual identity, the mother's political involvement, or the mother's attitude toward men. Similarly, data obtained from the heterosexual mothers in the initial study on the mother's warmth to the child, the child's contact with the father, the child's gender role behavior, and the quality of the child's peer relationships showed no significant association between these variables and the overall rating of the young adults' same-gender sexual interest.

Discussion

The sample studied in the present investigation is unique in that it constitutes the first group of young people raised in lesbian families to be followed from childhood to adulthood. As information about childhood family environment was collected before the participants began to engage in sexual relationships, the findings relating to the characteristics of the lesbian and heterosexual families in which these young people grew up are not confounded by knowledge of their sexual orientation in adult life.

Although no significant difference was found between the proportions of young adults from lesbian and heterosexual families who reported feelings of attraction toward someone of the same gender, those who had grown up in a lesbian family were more likely to consider the possibility of having lesbian or gay relationships, and to actually do so. However, the commonly held assumption that children brought up by lesbian mothers will themselves grow up to be lesbian or gay is not supported by the findings of the study; the majority of children who grew up in lesbian families identified as heterosexual in adulthood, and there was no statistically significant difference between young adults from lesbian and heterosexual family backgrounds with respect to sexual orientation.

It is important to remember that this research was conducted with volunteer samples of lesbian and heterosexual families, thus the generalizability of the findings is reduced. It is not possible to recruit a representative sample of lesbian mothers given that many do not publicly declare their sexual identity. However, both the lesbian and heterosexual groups reflected a diversity of families nationwide, from different socioeconomic backgrounds, and with different political or apolitical perspectives. Although our interviewees may have been reluctant to admit to same-gender sexual preferences, if underreporting took place, it seems reasonable to assume that this would have been more prevalent among men and women from heterosexual homes, as young adults from lesbian families appeared to be more comfortable in discussing lesbian and gay issues in general. Because of limitations of sample size, data have been presented for more than one child per family, which could have inflated significance. However, the 2 daughters who identified as lesbian were from different families, and of the 6 young adults from lesbian families who reported a same-gender relationship, only 2 belonged to the same family, suggesting that the findings cannot be explained in this way. To definitively address the questions raised in this article, one would require a large-scale epidemiological study following children of lesbian and heterosexual parents from childhood to adulthood with respect to their family characteristics and sexual identity development.

The greater proportion of young adults from lesbian families than from heterosexual families who reported consideration of, and involvement in, same-gender sexual relationships suggests an association between childhood family environment and these aspects of sexual development. Moreover, the association found in lesbian families between the degree of openness and acceptance of lesbian and gay relationships and young adults' same-gender sexual interest indicates that family attitudes toward sexual orientation, that is, as accepting or rejecting of gay and lesbian lifestyles, constitute one of the many influences that may shape development in either a heterosexual or a homosexual direction. It seems that growing up in an accepting atmosphere enables individuals who are attracted to same-sex partners to pursue these relationships. This may facilitate the development of a lesbian or gay sexual orientation for some individuals. But, interestingly, the opportunity to explore same-sex relationships may, for others, confirm their heterosexual identity. In the present sample, 4 of the 6 young adults who had experienced same-gender sexual relationships identified as heterosexual in early adulthood. Although the findings suggest that daughters of lesbian mothers are more open to same-sex relationships than are sons, in the initial investigation, there was a higher ratio of sons to daughters in the lesbian group and a higher ratio of daughters to sons in the heterosexual group, which remained at the follow-up. Thus a higher proportion of women than men who reported consideration of, and involvement in,

same-sex relationships may reflect this sampling bias.

It is important to point out that the mothers and children who participated in the research were genetically related to each other, and thus it is not possible to disentangle the influence of genetic and social aspects of the parent-child relationship, that is, the influence of parental genetic material as opposed to parental behavior. It cannot be ruled out that the outcomes for these young people would have been the same had they been raised by parents who were genetically unrelated to them (e.g., adoptive parents). However, the results suggest that the group difference in same-gender sexual interest is a consequence of the children's experiences with lesbian and heterosexual mothers while growing up, particularly in view of the finding that the childhood family environments of young adults from lesbian families who reported same-gender sexual interest were characterized by an openness and acceptance of a lesbian lifestyle. It should be noted that the young adults raised in lesbian households were no more likely than those from heterosexual households to experience mental health problems, and both groups obtained scores on standardized measures of emotional well-being that did not differ significantly from those of general population samples (Tasker & Golombok, in press).

Although not inconsistent with biological theories that propose that sexual orientation results from interactions between prenatal factors and postnatal experience (Money, 1988), the findings of this investigation are also compatible with social-cognitive and social constructionist explanations of the psychological mechanisms involved in gender development. What these latter theories have in common is the view that sexual orientation is influenced, to some extent at least, by social norms. From this perspective, if children grow up in an atmosphere of positive attitudes toward homosexuality, they would be expected to be more open to involvement in gay or lesbian relationships themselves. Different aspects of sexual orientation may be influenced to a greater or lesser degree by experiential factors such that sexual experimentation with same-gender partners may be more dependent on a conducive family environment than the development of a lesbian or gay identity. It is worth noting that none of the sons or daughters of lesbian mothers in the present investigation showed marked childhood cross-gender behavior of the type associated with a later lesbian or gay identity. In addition, no difference in childhood role behavior was found between young adults who reported same-gender sexual interest and those who did not.

Whereas there is no evidence from the present investigation to suggest that parents have a determining influence on the sexual orientation of their children, the findings do indicate that by creating a climate of acceptance or rejection of homosexuality within the family, parents may have some impact on their children's sexual experimentation as heterosexual, lesbian, or gay.

Growing attention has been paid in recent years to the social context of families and to the processes through which social environments affect family relationships. It is important to remember that the young adults in this study were born at a time when there was less social acceptance of lesbian women and gay men. As Gagnon (1990) pointed out, young people are now better informed about lesbian and gay lifestyles and know about lesbian and gay possibilities at an earlier age. How the changing social climate may influence exploration of same-gender relationships remains open to speculation. It is conceivable, however, that children born at the present time to heterosexual parents who are accepting of lesbian and gay relationships will be just as open to same-sex exploration in adulthood as their counterparts from lesbian families are today.

References

American Psychiatric Association. (1994). *Diagnostic and statistical manual of mental disorders* (4th ed.). Washington, DC: Author.

Bailey, J. M., & Pillard, R. C. (1991). A genetic study of male sexual orientation. *Archives of General Psychiatry, 48,* 1089–1096.

Bailey, J. M., Pillard, R. C., Neale, M. C., & Agyei, Y. (1993). Heritable factors influence sexual orientation in women. *Archives of General Psychiatry, 50,* 217–223.

Bandura, A. (1977). *Social learning theory.* Englewood Cliffs, NJ: Prentice Hall.

Bandura, A. (1986). *Social foundations of thought and action: A social cognitive theory.* Englewood Cliffs, NJ: Prentice Hall.

Bell, A. P., Weinberg, M. S., & Hammersmith, S. K. (1981). *Sexual preference: Its development in men and women.* Bloomington: Indiana University Press.

Bene, E. (1965). On the genesis of male homosexuality: An attempt at clarifying the role of the parents. *British Journal of Psychiatry, 111,* 803–813.

Bieber, I., Dain, H., Dince, P., Drellick, M., Grand, H., Gondlack, R., Kremer, R., Rifkin, A., Wilber, C., & Bieber, T. (1962). *Homosexuality: A psychoanalytic study.* New York: Basic Books.

Byne, W., & Parsons, B. (1993). Human sexual orientation: The biologic theories reappraised. *Archives of General Psychiatry, 50,* 228–239.

Dittman, R. W., Kappes, M. E., & Kappes, M. H. (1992). Sexual behavior in adolescent and adult females with congenital adrenal hyperplasia. *Psychoneuroendocrinology, 17,* 1–18.

Ehrhardt, A. A., Meyer-Bahlburg, H. F. L., Rosen, L., Feldman, L., Verdiano, N., Zimmerman, I., & McEwen, B. (1985). Sexual orientation after prenatal exposure to exogenous estrogen. *Archives of Sexual Behavior, 14,* 57–77.

Evans, R. (1969). Childhood parental relationships of homosexual men. *Journal of Consulting and Clinical Psychology, 33,* 129–135.

Freud, S. (1933). *Psychology of women: New introductory lectures on psychoanalysis.* London: Hogarth Press.

Freud, S. (1955). Beyond the pleasure principle. In J. Strachey (Ed.), *The standard edition of the complete works of Sigmund Freud* (Vol. 18, pp. 3–68). London: Hogarth Press. (Original work published 1920.)

Gagnon, J. H. (1977). *Human sexuality.* Glenview, IL: Scott Foresman.

Gagnon, J. H. (1990). Gender preference in erotic relations: The Kinsey scale and sexual scripts. In D. P. McWhirter, S. A. Sanders, & J. M. Reinisch (Eds.), *Homosexuality/hetero-*

sexuality: Concepts of sexual orientation (pp. 177–207). Oxford, England: Oxford University Press.

Golombok, S., Spencer, A., & Rutter, M. (1983). Children in lesbian and single-parent households: Psychosexual and psychiatric appraisal. *Journal of Child Psychological Psychiatry, 24,* 551–572.

Gottman, J. S. (1990). Children of gay and lesbian parents. In F. W. Bozett & M. B. Sussman (Eds.), *Homosexuality and family relations* (pp. 177–196). New York: Harrington Park.

Goy, R. W., & McEwen, B. S. (1980). *Sexual differentiation in the brain.* Cambridge, MA: MIT Press.

Green, R. (1987). *The "sissy boy syndrome" and the development of homosexuality.* New Haven, CT: Yale University Press.

Green, R., Mandel, J., Hotvedt, M., Gray, J., & Smith, L. (1986). Lesbian mothers and their children: A comparison with solo parent heterosexual mothers and their children. *Archives of Sexual Behavior, 15,* 167–184.

Green, R., Williams, K., & Goodman, M. (1982). Ninety-nine "tomboys" and "nontomboys": Behavioral contrasts and demographic similarities. *Archives of Sexual Behavior, 11,* 247–266.

Hamer, D., Hu, S., Magnuson, V., Hu, N., & Pattatucci, A. (1993). A linkage between DNA markers on the X-chromosome and male sexual orientation. *Science, 261,* 321–327.

Hines, M., & Green, R. (1990). Human hormonal and neural correlates of sex-typed behaviors. *Review of Psychiatry, 10,* 536–555.

Kitzinger, C. (1987). *The social construction of lesbianism.* London: Sage.

Kohlberg, L. (1966). A cognitive-developmental analysis of children's sex-role concepts and attitudes. In E. E. Maccoby (Ed.), *The development of sex differences* (pp. 82–173). Stanford, CA: Stanford University Press.

LeVay, S. (1991). A difference in hypothalamic structure between heterosexual and homosexual men. *Science, 253,* 1034–1037.

Lytton, H., & Romney, D. M. (1991). Parents' differential socialization of boys and girls: A meta-analysis. *Psychological Bulletin, 109,* 267–296.

Martin, C. L. (1993). New directions for assessing children's gender knowledge. *Developmental Review, 13,* 184–204.

Meyer-Bahlburg, H. F. L. (1984). Psychoendocrine research on sexual orientation: Current status and future options. *Progress in Brain Research, 61,* 375–398.

Mischel, W. (1966). A social learning view of sex differences in behavior. In E. E. Maccoby (Ed.), *The development of sex differences* (pp. 56–81). Stanford, CA: Stanford University Press.

Money, J. (1988). *Gay, straight or in-between: The sexology of erotic orientation.* New York: Oxford University Press.

Money, J., Schwartz, M., & Lewis, V. (1984). Adult heterosexual status and fetal hormonal masculinization and demasculinization: 46, XX congenital virilizing adrenal hyperplasia and 46, XY androgen-insensitivity syndrome compared. *Psychoneuroendocrinology, 9,* 405–414.

Newcombe, M. (1985). The role of perceived relative parent personality in the development of heterosexuals, homosexuals, and transvestites. *Archives of Sexual Behavior, 14,* 147–164.

Patterson, C. (1992). Children of lesbian and gay parents. *Child Development, 63,* 1025–1042.

Perry, D. G., & Bussey, K. (1979). The social learning theory of sex difference: Imitation is alive and well. *Journal of Personality and Social Psychology, 37,* 1699–1712.

Plummer, K. (1975). *Sexual stigma: An interactionist account.* London: Routledge & Kegan Paul.

Quinton, D., Rutter, M., & Rowlands, O. (1976). An evaluation of an interview assessment of marriage. *Psychological Medicine, 6,* 577–586.

Roberts, C. W., Green, R., Williams, K., & Goodman, M. (1987). Boyhood gender identity development: A statistical contract of two family groups. *Developmental Psychology, 23,* 544–557.

Siegelman, M. (1974). Parental background of male homosexuals and heterosexuals. *Archives of Sexual Behavior, 6,* 89–96.

Simon, W., & Gagnon, J. H. (1987). A sexual scripts approach. In J. H. Geer & W. T. O'Donahue (Eds.), *Theories of human sexuality* (pp. 363–383). London: Plenum Press.

Socarides, C. W. (1978). *Homosexuality.* New York: Jason Aronson.

Tasker, F., & Golombok, S. (in press). *Growing up in a lesbian family.* New York: Guilford Press.

Whitam, F. (1977). Childhood indicators of male homosexuality. *Archives of Sexual Behavior, 6,* 89–96.

Whitam, F., & Mathy, R. (1991). Childhood cross-gender behavior of homosexual females in Brazil, Peru, the Philippines and the United States. *Archives of Sexual Behavior, 20,* 151–170.

Chapter 34
Dating and Romantic Relationships Among Gay, Lesbian, and Bisexual Youths

Ritch C. Savin-Williams

The Savin-Williams article will be a revelation to many heterosexual students who think of homosexuality in terms of sexual behavior. The brief, poignant quotes add a clear description of the unhappiness experienced by gay/lesbian youth who feel deprived of romantic/love relationships so naturally formed by their heterosexual friends. Although the author stops short of labeling such homosexual youth as developmentally delayed, this assumption could possibly be made from the stories presented that detail the separation of a youth's homoerotic passion from socially sanctioned heterosexual dating. Students with a background in adolescent development will be most likely to understand the possible effects of these nuances in the gay/lesbian youths' growing up experiences. The fact that the termination of a close homosexual relationship for one college man was more stressful than revealing his sexual orientation to his parents portrays in bold relief the significance of a partnered relationship.

One of the limitations of the article is the failure to differentiate the circumstances for bisexual youth from those of homosexual youth. Nevertheless, the article is guaranteed to provoke a lively class discussion for stu-

dents who feel safe enough to venture into largely uncharted territory.

The Importance of Dating and Romance

According to Scarf (1987), the developmental significance of an intimate relationship is to help us "contact archaic, dimly perceived and yet powerfully meaningful aspects of our inner selves" (p. 79). We desire closeness within the context of a trusting, intimate relationship. Attachment theory posits that humans are prewired for loving and developing strongly felt emotional attachments (Bowlby, 1973). When established, we experience safety, security, and nurturance. Early attachments, including those in infancy, are thought to circumscribe an internal blueprint that profoundly affects future relationships, such as the establishment of intimate friendships and romances in adolescence and adulthood (Hazan & Shaver, 1987).

Developmentally, dating is a means by which romantic relationships are practiced, pursued, and established. It serves a number of important functions, such as entertainment, recreation, and socialization, that assist participants in developing appropriate means of interacting. It also enhances peer group status and facilitates the selection of a mate (Skipper & Nass, 1966). Adolescents who are most confident in their dating abilities begin dating during early adolescence, date frequently, are satisfied with their dating, and are most likely to become involved in a "committed" dating relationship (Herold, 1979).

The establishment of romantic relationships is important for youths regardless of sexual orientation. Isay (1989) noted that falling in love was a critical factor in helping his gay clients feel comfortable with their gay identity and that "the self-affirming value of a mutual relationship over time cannot be overemphasized" (p. 50). Browning (1987) regarded lesbian love relationships as an opportunity to enhance:

. . . the development of the individual's adult identity by validating her personhood, reinforcing that she deserves to receive and give love. A relationship can also be a source of tremendous emotional support as the woman explores her goals, values, and relationship to the world. (p. 51)

Because dating experience increases the likelihood that an intimate romantic relationship will evolve, the absence of this opportunity may have long-term repercussions. Malyon (1981) noted some of the reverberations:

Their most charged sexual desires are usually seen as perverted, and their deepest feelings of psychological attachment are regarded as unacceptable. This social disapproval interferes with the preintimacy involvement that fosters the evolution of maturity and self-respect in the domain of object relations. (p. 326)

Culture's Devaluation of Same-Sex Relationships

Relatively speaking, our culture is far more willing to turn a blind eye to sexual than to romantic relationships among same-sex adolescent partners. Same-sex activity may appear "temporary," an experiment, a phase, or a perverted source of fun. But falling in love with someone of the same gender and maintaining a sustained emotional involvement with that person implies an irreversible deviancy at worst and a bad decision at best. In our homes, schools, religious institutions, and media, we teach that intense relationships after early adolescence among members of the same sex "should" raise the concern of good parents, good friends, and good teachers. One result is that youths of all sexual orientations may become frightened of developing close friendships with same-sex peers. They fear that these friendships will be viewed as sexually intimate.

It is hardly surprising that a sexual-minority adolescent can easily become "the loneliest person . . . in the typical high school of today" (Norton, 1976:376):

For the homosexual-identified student, high school is often a lonely place where, from every vantage point, there are couples: couples holding hands as they enter school; couples dissolving into an endless wet kiss between school bells; couples exchanging rings with ephemeral vows of devotion and love. (Sears, 1991:326–327)

The separation of a youth's homoerotic passion from the socially sanctioned act of heterosexual dating can generate self-doubt, anger, and resentment, and can ultimately retard or distort the development of interpersonal intimacy during the adolescent years. Thus, many youths never consider same-sex dating to be a reasonable option, except in their fantasies. Scientific and clinical writings that ignore same-sex romance and dating among youth contribute to this conspiracy of silence. Sexual-minority youth struggle with issues of identity and intimacy because important impediments rooted in our cultural values and attitudes deter them from dating those they love and instead mandate that they date those they cannot love.

Empirical Studies of Same-Sex Romantic Relationships Among Youth

Until the last several years same-sex relationships among sexual-minority youths were seldom recognized in the empirical, scientific literature. With the recent visibility of gay, bisexual, and lesbian youths in the culture at large, social and behavioral scientists are beginning to conduct research focusing on various developmental processes of such youths, including their sexuality and intimacy.

Bisexual, lesbian, and gay youths, whether in Detroit, Minneapolis, Pennsylvania, New York, or the Netherlands, report that they desire to have long-lasting, committed same-sex romantic relationships in their future (D'Augelli, 1991; Sanders, 1980; Savin-Williams, 1990). According to Silverstein (1981), establishing a romantic relationship with a same-sex partner helps one to feel "chosen," to resolve issues of sexual identity, and to feel more complete. Indeed, those who are in a long-term love relationship generally have high levels of self-esteem and self-acceptance.[1]

Although there are few published studies of teens that focus primarily on their same-sex dating or romantic relationships, there are suggestive data that debunk the myth in our culture that gays, lesbians, and bisexuals neither want nor maintain steady, loving same-sex relationships. In two studies of gay and bisexual male youths, same-sex relationships are regarded as highly desirable. Among 29 Minnesota youths, 10 had a steady male partner at the time of the interview, 11 had been in a same-sex relationship, and, most tellingly, all but 2 hoped for a steady male partner in their future (Remafedi, 1987). For these youths, many of whom were living independently with friends or on the street, being in a long-term relationship was considered to be an ideal state. With a college-age sample of 61 males, D'Augelli (1991) reported similar results. One half of his sample was "partnered," and their most troubling mental health concern was termination of a close relationship, ranking just ahead of telling parents about their homosexuality.

The difficulty, however, is to maintain a visible same-sex romance in high school. Sears (1991) interviewed 36 Southern late adolescent and young adult lesbians, gays, and bisexuals. He discovered that although nearly everyone had heterosexually dated in high school, very few dated a member of the same sex during that time. Because of concerns about secrecy and the lack of social support, most same-sex romances involved little emotional commitment and were of short duration. None were overt.

Research with over 300 gay, bisexual, and lesbian youths between the ages of 14 and 23 years (Savin-Williams, 1990) supports the finding that sexual-minority youths have romantic relationships during adolescence and young adulthood. Almost 90 percent of the females and two thirds of the males reported that they have had a romantic relationship. Of the total number of romances listed, 60 percent were with same-sex partners. The male youths were

slightly more likely than lesbian and bisexual female youths to begin their romantic career with a same-sex, rather than an opposite-sex partner.

In the same study, the lesbians and bisexual females who had a high proportion of same-sex romances were most likely to be "out" to others. However, their self-esteem level was essentially the same as those who had a high percentage of heterosexual relationships. If she began same-sex dating early, during adolescence, then a lesbian or bisexual female also tended to be in a current relationship and to experience long-lasting romances. Gay and bisexual male youths who had a large percentage of adolescent romantic relationships with boys had high self-esteem. They were more likely to be publicly "out" to friends and family if they had had a large number of romances. Boys who initiated same-sex romances at an early age were more likely to report that they have had long-term and multiple same-sex relationships.

The findings from these studies are admittedly sparse and do not provide the depth and insight that are needed to help us better understand the experience of being in a same-sex romantic relationship. They do illustrate that youths have same-sex romances while in high school. Where there is desire, some youths will find a way. Sexually active same-sex friendships may evolve into romantic relationships (Savin-Williams, 1995), and those most publicly out are most likely to have had adolescent same-sex romances. Certainly, most lesbian, gay, and bisexual youths value the importance of a same-sex, lifelong, committed relationship in their adult years.

Perhaps the primary issue is not the absence of same-sex romances during adolescence, but the hidden nature of the romances. They are seldom recognized and rarely supported or celebrated. The research data offer little information regarding the psychological impact of not being involved in a same-sex romantic relationship or of having to hide such a relationship when it exists. For this, one must turn to stories of the personal struggles of adolescents.

Personal Struggles

Youths who have same-sex romances during their adolescence face a severe struggle to have these relationships acknowledged and supported. Gibson (1989) noted the troubling contradictions:

> The first romantic involvements of lesbian and gay male youth are a source of great joy to them in affirming their sexual identity, providing them with support, and assuring them that they too can experience love. However, society places extreme hardships on these relationships that make them difficult to establish and maintain. (p. 130)

A significant number of youths, perhaps those feeling most insecure regarding their sexual identity, may fantasize about being sexually intimate with a same-sex partner but have little hope that it could in fact become a reality. One youth, Lawrence, reported this feeling in his coming-out story:

> While growing up, love was something I watched other people experience and enjoy. . . . The countless men I secretly loved and fantasized about were only in private, empty dreams in which love was never returned. I seemed to be the only person in the world with no need for love and companionship. . . . Throughout high school and college I had no way to meet people of the same sex and sexual orientation. These were more years of isolation and secrecy. I saw what other guys my age did, listened to what they said and how they felt. I was expected to be part of a world with which I had nothing in common. (Curtis, 1988:109–110)

A young lesbian, Diane, recalled that "love of women was never a possibility that I even realized could be. You loved your mother and your aunts, and you had girlfriends for a while. Someday, though, you would always meet a man" (Stanley & Wolfe, 1980:47). Girls dated boys and not other girls. Because she did not want to date boys, she did not date.

Another youth knew he had homoerotic attractions, but he never fathomed that they could be expressed to the boy that he most admired, his high school soccer teammate. It took alcohol and the right situation:

> I knew I was checking out the guys in the shower after soccer practice. I thought of myself as hetero who had the urge for males. I fought it, said it was a phase. And then it happened.

> Derek was my best friend. After soccer practice the fall of our junior year we celebrated both making the "A" team by getting really drunk. We were just fooling around and suddenly our pants were off. I was so scared I stayed out of school for three days but we kept being friends and nothing was said until a year later when I came out to everyone and he came up to me with these tears and asked if he made me homosexual. (Savin-Williams, 1995)

It is never easy for youths to directly confront the mores of peers whose values and attitudes are routinely supported by the culture. Nearly all youths know implicitly the rules of socially appropriate behavior and the consequences of nonconformity. This single, most influential barrier to same-sex dating, the threat posed by peers, can have severe repercussions. The penalty for crossing the line of "normalcy" can result in emotional and physical pain.

Peer Harassment as a Barrier to Dating

Price (1982) concluded, "Adolescents can be very cruel to others who are different, who do not conform to the expectations of the peer group" (p. 472). Very little has changed in the last decade. For example, 17-year-old actor Ryan Phillippe worried about the consequences on his family and friends if he played a gay teen on ABC's soap opera *One Life to Live* (Gable, 1992:3D). David Ruffin, 19, of Ferndale, Michigan, explained why he boycotted his high school senior prom: "The kids could tell I was different from them, and I think I was different because I was gay. And when you're dealing with young people, different means not cool" (Bruni, 1992:10A).

Unlike heterosexual dating, little social advantage, such as peer popularity or acceptance, is gained by holding hands and kissing a same-sex peer in school hallways, shopping malls, or synagogues. Lies are spun to protect secrets and to avoid peer harassment. One lesbian youth, Kim, felt that she had to be an actress around her friends. She lied to friends by creating "Andrew" when she was dating "Andrea" over the weekend (Bruni, 1992).

To avoid harassment, sexual minority adolescents may monitor their interpersonal interactions. They may wonder, "Am I standing too close?" or "Do I appear too happy to see him(her)?" (Anderson, 1987). Hetrick and Martin (1987) found that youths are often apprehensive to show "friendship for a friend of the same sex for fear of being misunderstood or giving away their secretly held sexual orientation" (p. 31). If erotic desires become aroused and threaten expression, youths may seek to terminate same-sex friendships rather than risk revealing their secret. For many adolescents, especially bisexual youths, relationships with the other sex may be easier to develop. The appeal of such relationships is that the youths will be viewed by peers as heterosexual, thus peer acceptance will be enhanced and the threat of harassment and rejection will be reduced. The result is that some sexual-minority youths feel inherently "fake" and they therefore retreat from becoming intimate with others. Although they may meet the implicit and explicit demands of their culture, it is at a cost—their sense of authenticity.

Faking It: Heterosexual Sex and Dating

Retrospective data from gay, bisexual, and lesbian adults reveal the extent to which heterosexual dating and sex are commonplace during the adolescent and young adult years (Bell & Weinberg, 1978; Schafer, 1976; Troiden & Goode, 1980). These might be one-night stands, brief romances, or long-term relationships. Across various studies, nearly two-thirds of gay men and three-quarters of lesbians report

having had heterosexual sex in their past. Motivations include fun, curiosity, denial of homoerotic feelings, and pressure to conform to society's insistence on heterosexual norms and behaviors. Even though heterosexual sex often results in a low level of sexual gratification, it is deemed a necessary sacrifice to meet the expectations of peers and, by extension, receive their approval. Only later, as adults, when they have the opportunity to compare these heterosexual relationships with same-sex ones do they fully realize that which they had missed during their younger years.

Several studies with lesbian, bisexual, and gay adolescents document the extent to which they are sexually involved with opposite-sex partners. Few gay and bisexual [male] youth had *extensive* sexual contact with females, even among those who began heterosexual sex at an early age. Sex with one or two girls was usually considered "quite enough." Not infrequently these girls were best friends who expressed a romantic or sexual interest in the gay boys. The male youths liked the girls, but they preferred friendships rather than sexual relations. One youth expressed this dilemma:

> She was a year older and we had been friends for a long time before beginning dating. It was a date with the full thing: dinner, theater, alcohol, making out, sex. At her house and I think we both came during intercourse. I was disappointed because it was such hard work—not physically I mean but emotionally. Later on in my masturbation my fantasies were never of her. We did it once more in high school and then once more when we were in college. I labeled it love but not sexual love. I really wanted them to occur together. It all ended when I labeled myself gay. (Savin-Williams, 1995)

An even greater percentage of lesbian and bisexual female adolescents engaged in heterosexual sexual experiences—2 of every 3 (Herdt & Boxer, 1993), 3 of every 4 (Sears, 1991), and 8 of 10 (Savin-Williams, 1990). Heterosexual activity began as early as second grade and as late as senior year in high school. Few of these girls, however, had extensive sex with boys—usually with two or three boys within the context of dating. Eighteen-year-old Kimba noted that she went through a heterosexual stage:

> . . . trying to figure out what was so great about guys sexually. I still don't understand. I guess that, for straights, it is like it is for me when I am with a woman. . . . I experimented in whatever ways I thought would make a difference, but it was no go. My closest friends are guys; there is caring and closeness between us. (Heron, 1983:82)

Georgina also tried to follow a heterosexual script:

> In sixth and seventh grades you start wearing makeup, you start getting your hair cut, you start liking boys—you start thinking about letting them "French kiss" you. I did all those major things. But, I still didn't feel very satisfied with myself. I remember I never really wanted to be intimate with any guy. I always wanted to be their best friend. (Sears, 1991:327)

One young lesbian, Lisa, found herself "having sex with boys to prove I wasn't gay. Maybe I was even trying to prove it to myself! I didn't enjoy having sex with boys" (Heron, 1983:76). These three lesbian youths forfeited a sense of authenticity, intimacy, and love because they were taught that emotional intimacy can only be achieved with members of the other sex.

The reasons sexual-minority adolescents gave as to why they engaged in heterosexual sex were similar to those reported in retrospective studies by adults. The youths needed to test whether their heterosexual attractions were as strong as their homoerotic ones—thus attempting to disconfirm their homosexuality—and to mask their homosexuality so as to win peer- and self-acceptance and to avoid peer rejection. Many youths believed that they could not really know whether they were lesbian, gay, bisexual, or heterosexual without first experiencing heterosexual sex. For many, however, heterosexual activities consisted of sex without feelings that they tried to enjoy without much success (Herdt & Boxer, 1993). Heterosexual sex felt unnatural because it lacked the desired emotional intensity. One young gay youth reported:

> We'd been dating for three months. I was 15 and she, a year or so older. We had petted previously and so she planned this event. We attempted intercourse in her barn, but I was too nervous. I didn't feel good afterwards because it was not successful. We did it every week for a month or so. It was fun but it wasn't a big deal. But then I did not have a great lust or drive. This was just normal I guess. It gave me something to do to tell the other guys who were always bragging. (Savin-Williams, 1995)

Similarly, Kimberly always had a steady heterosexual relationship: "It was like I was just going through the motions. It was expected of me, so I did it. I'd kiss him or embrace him but it was like I was just there. He was probably enjoying it, but I wasn't" (Sears, 1991:327).

Jacob, an African American adolescent, dated the prettiest girls in his school in order to maintain his image: "It was more like President Reagan entertaining heads of state. It's expected of you when you're in a certain position" (Sears, 1991:126–127). Another Southern male youth, Grant, used "group dates" to reinforce his heterosexual image. Rumors that he was gay were squelched because his jock friends came to his defense: "He's not a fag. He has a girl-friend" (Sears, 1991:328).

These and other personal stories of youths vividly recount the use of heterosexual sex and dating as a cover for an emerging same-sex or bisexual identity. Dating provides opportunities to temporarily "pass" as straight until the meaning of homoerotic feelings are resolved or youths find a safe haven to be lesbian or gay. Heterosexual sex and dating may be less pleasurable than same-sex encounters, but many sexual-minority youths feel that the former are the only safe, acceptable options.

Impediments and Consequences

The difficulties inherent in dating same-sex partners during adolescence are monumental. First is the fundamental difficulty of finding a suitable partner. The vast majority of lesbian, bisexual, and gay youths are closeted, not out to themselves, let alone to others. A second barrier is the consequences of same-sex dating, such as verbal and physical harassment from peers. A third impediment is the lack of public recognition or "celebration" of those who are romantically involved with a member of the same gender. Thus, same-sex dating remains hidden and mysterious, something that is either ridiculed, condemned, or ignored.

The consequences of an exclusively heterosexually oriented atmosphere in the peer social world can be severe and enduring. An adolescent may feel isolated and socially excluded from the world of peers. Sex with others of the same gender may be associated exclusively with anonymous, guilt-ridden encounters, handicapping the ability to develop healthy intimate relationships in adulthood. Denied the opportunity for romantic involvement with someone of the same sex, a youth may suffer impaired self-esteem that reinforces the belief that one is unworthy of love, affection, and intimacy. One youth, Rick, even doubted his ability to love:

> When I started my senior year, I was still unclear about my sexuality. I had dated women with increasing frequency, but never felt love for any of them. I discovered that I could perform sexually with a woman, but heterosexual experiences were not satisfying emotionally. I felt neither love nor emotional oneness with women. Indeed, I had concluded that I was incapable of human love. (Heron, 1983:95–96)

If youths are to take advantage of opportunities to explore their erotic sexuality, it is sometimes, at least for males, confined to clandestine sexual encounters, void of romance, affection, and intimacy but replete with misgivings, anonymity, and guilt.

> Ted was 21 and me, 16. It was New Year's Eve and it was a swimming pool party at my rich friend's house. Not sure why Ted was there but he really came on to me, even putting his arm around me in front of everyone. I wasn't ready for that but I liked it. New Year's Day, every time Ted looked at me I looked away because I thought it was obvious that we had had sex. It did clarify things for me. It didn't feel like I was cheating on [my girlfriend] Beth because the sex felt so different, so right. (Savin-Williams, 1995)

A gay youth may have genital contact with another boy without ever kissing him because to do so would be too meaningful. Remafedi (1990) found this escape from intimacy to be very damaging: "Without appropriate opportunities for peer dating and socialization, gay youth frequently eschew intimacy altogether and resort to transient and anonymous sexual encounters with adults" (p. 1173). One consequence is the increased risk for contracting sexually transmitted diseases, including HIV. This is particularly risky for youths who turn to prostitution to meet their intimacy needs (Coleman, 1989).

When youths eventually match their erotic and intimacy needs, they may be surprised with the results. This was Jacob's experience (Sears, 1991) when he fell in love with Warren, an African American senior who also sang in the choir. Sex quickly evolved into "an emotional thing." Jacob explained: "He got to the point of telling me he loved me. That was the first time anybody ever said any thing like that. It was kind of hard to believe that even after sex there are really feelings" (p. 127).

Equally common, however, especially among closeted youths, is that lesbian, bisexual, and gay teens may experience a poverty of intimacy in their lives and considerable social and emotional isolation. One youth, Grant, enjoyed occasional sex with a star football player, but he was devastated by the subsequent exclusion the athlete meted out to him: "We would see each other and barely speak but after school we'd see each other a lot. He had his image that he had to keep up and, since it was rumored that I was gay, he didn't want to get a close identity with me" (Sears, 1991:330).

Largely because of negative peer prohibitions and the lack of social support and recognition, same-sex romances that are initiated have difficulty flourishing. Irwin met Benji in the eighth grade and was immediately attracted to him (Sears, 1991). They shared interests in music and academics and enjoyed long conversations, playing music, and riding in the countryside. Eventually, their attractions for each other were expressed and a romantic, sexual relationship began. Although Irwin was in love with Benji, their relationship soon ended because it was no match for the social pressures and personal goals that conflicted with Irwin being in a same-sex relationship.

Georgina's relationship with Kay began dramatically with intense feelings that were at times ambivalent for both of them. At one point she overheard Kay praying, "Dear Lord, forgive me for the way I am" (Sears, 1991:333). Georgina's parents demanded that she end her "friendship" with Kay. Georgina told classmates they were just "good friends" and began dating boys as a cover. Despite her love for Kay, the relationship ended when Georgina's boyfriend told her that no one liked her because she hung around "that dyke, Kay." In retropect, Georgina wished: "If everybody would have accepted everybody, I would have stayed with Kay" (p. 334).

Given this situation, lesbian, bisexual, and gay youths in same-sex relationships may place unreasonable and ultimately destructive demands on each other. For example, they may expect that the relationship will resolve all fears of loneliness and isolation and validate all aspects of their personal identity (Browning, 1987).

A Success Story

A vivid account of how a same-sex romantic relationship can empower a youth is depicted in the seminal autobiography of Aaron Fricke (1981), *Reflections of a Rock Lobster*. He fell in love with a classmate, Paul:

> With Paul's help, I started to challenge all the prejudice I had encountered during 16 1/2 years of life. Sure, it was scary to think that half my classmates might hate me if they knew my secret, but from Paul's example I knew it was possi-

ble to one day be strong and face them without apprehension. (Fricke, 1981:44)

Through Paul, Aaron became more resilient and self-confident:

> His strengths were my strengths. . . . I realized that my feelings for him were unlike anything I had felt before. The sense of camaraderie was familiar from other friendships; the deep spiritual love I felt for Paul was new. So was the openness, the sense of communication with another. (Fricke, 1981:45)

Life gained significance. He wrote poems. He planned a future. He learned to express both kindness and strength. Aaron was in love, with another boy. But no guidelines or models existed on how best to express these feelings:

> Heterosexuals learn early in life what behavior is expected of them. They get practice in their early teens having crushes, talking to their friends about their feelings, going on first dates and to chaperoned parties, and figuring out their feelings. Paul and I hadn't gotten all that practice; our relationship was formed without much of a model to base it on. It was the first time either of us had been in love like this and we spent much of our time just figuring out what that meant for us. (Fricke, 1981:46)

Eventually, after a court case that received national attention, Aaron won the right to take Paul to the senior prom as his date. This victory was relatively minor compared to the self-respect, authenticity, and pride in being gay that their relationship won for each of them.

Final Reflections

As a clinical and developmental psychologist, I find it disheartening to observe our culture ignoring and condemning sexual-minority youth. One consequence is that myths and stereotypes are perpetuated that interfere with or prevent youths from developing intimate same-sex relationships with those to whom they are erotically and emotionally attracted. Separating passion from affection, engaging in sex with strangers in impersonal and sometimes unsafe places, and finding alienation rather than intimacy in those relationships are not conducive to psychological health. In one study the most common reason given for initial suicide attempts by lesbians and gay men was relationship problems (Bell & Weinberg, 1978).

A youth's limited ability to meet other bisexual, lesbian, and gay adolescents compounds a sense of isolation and alienation. Crushes may develop on "unknowing friends, teachers, and peers. These are often cases of unrequited love with the youth never revealing their true feelings" (Gibson, 1989:131).

Sexual-minority youths need the validation of those around them as they attempt to develop a personal integrity and to discover those similar to themselves. How long can gay, bisexual, and lesbian adolescents maintain their charades before they encounter difficulty separating the pretensions from the realities? Many "use" heterosexual dating to blind themselves and others. By so doing they attempt to disconfirm to themselves the growing encroachment of their homoerotic attractions while escaping derogatory name calling and gaining peer status and prestige. The incidence of heterosexual sex and relationships in the adolescence of gay men and lesbians attests to these desires.

Future generations of adolescents will no doubt find it easier to establish same-sex relationships. This is due in part to the dramatic increase in the visibility that adult same-sex relationships have received during the last few years. Domestic partnership ordinances in several cities and counties, victories for spousal equivalency rights in businesses, court cases addressing adoption by lesbian couples and challenges to marriage laws by several male couples, the dramatic story of the life partnership of Karen Thompson and Sharon Kowalski, and the "marriage" of former Mr. Universe Bob Paris to male Supermodel Rod Jackson raise public awareness of same-sex romantic relationships. Even Ann Landers (1992) is spreading the word. In a column, an 18-year-old gay teen from Santa Barbara requested that girls quit hitting on him because, as he explained, "I have a very special friend who is a student at the local university . . . and [we] are very happy with each other" (Landers, 1992:2B).

A decade after Aaron Fricke fought for and won the right to take his boyfriend to the prom, a dozen lesbian, gay, and bisexual youths in the Detroit–Ann Arbor area arranged to have their own prom. Most felt excluded from the traditional high school prom, which they considered "a final, bitter postscript to painful years of feeling left out" (Bruni, 1992:10A). Seventeen-year-old Brenda said, "I want to feel rich for one moment. I want to feel all glamorous, just for one night" (Bruni, 1992:10A). Going to the "Fantasy" prom was a celebration that created a sense of pride, a connection with other sexual-minority teens, and a chance to dance—"two girls together, unguarded and unashamed, in the middle of a room filled with teenagers just like them" (Bruni, 1992:10A). One year later, I attended this prom with my life partner and the number of youths in attendance had increased sixfold.

We need to listen to youths such as Aaron, Diane, and Georgina, to hear their concerns, insights, and solutions. Most of all, we need to end the invisibility of same-sex romantic relationships. It is easily within our power to enhance the well-being of millions of youths, including "Billy Joe," a character in a famous Bobbie Gentry song. If Billy Joe had seen an option to a heterosexual life style, he might have considered an alternative to ending his life by jumping off the Tallahatchie Bridge.

Note

1. The causal pathway, however, is unclear (Savin-Williams, 1990). That is, being in a same-sex romance may build positive self-regard, but it may also be true that those with high self-esteem are more likely to form love relationships and to stay in them.

References

Anderson, D. (1987). Family and peer relations of gay adolescents. In S. C. Geinstein (Ed.), *Adolescent psychiatry: Developmental and clinical studies: Vol. 14* (pp. 162–178). Chicago: The University of Chicago Press.

Bell, A. P., & Weinberg, M. S. (1978). *Homosexualities: A study of diversity among men and women*. New York: Simon & Schuster.

Bowlby, J. (1973). *Attachment and loss: Vol. 2. Separation*. New York: Basic Books.

Browning, C. (1987). Therapeutic issues and intervention strategies with young adult lesbian clients: A developmental approach. *Journal of Homosexuality, 14*, 45–52.

Bruni, F. (1992, May 22). A prom night of their own to dance, laugh, reminisce. *Detroit Free Press*, pp. 1A, 10A.

Coleman, E. (1989). The development of male prostitution activity among gay and bisexual adolescents. *Journal of Homosexuality, 17*, 131–149.

Curtis, W. (Ed.). (1988). *Revelations: A collection of gay male coming out stories*. Boston: Alyson.

D'Augelli, A. R. (1991). Gay men in college: Identity processes and adaptations. *Journal of College Student Development, 32*, 140–146.

Fricke, A. (1981). *Reflections of a rock lobster: A story about growing up gay*. Boston: Alyson.

Gable, D. (1992, June 2). "Life" story looks at roots of homophobia. *USA Today*, p. 3D.

Gibson, P. (1989). Gay male and lesbian youth suicide. In M. R. Feinleib (Ed.), *Report of the secretary's task force on youth suicide, Vol. 3: Prevention and interventions in youth suicide (3-110-3-142)*. Rockville, MD: U.S. Department of Health and Human Services.

Hazan, C., & Shaver, P. (1987). Romantic love conceptualized as an attachment process. *Journal of Personality and Social Psychology, 52*, 511–524.

Herdt, G., & Boxer, A. (1993). *Children of horizons: How gay and lesbian teens are leading a new way out of the closet*. Boston: Beacon.

Herold, E. S. (1979). Variables influencing the dating adjustment of university students. *Journal of Youth and Adolescence, 8*, 73–79.

Heron, A. (Ed.). (1983). *One teenager in ten*. Boston: Alyson.

Hetrick, E. S., & Martin, A. D. (1987). Developmental issues and their resolution for gay and lesbian adolescents. *Journal of Homosexuality, 14*, 25–44.

Isay, R. A. (1989). *Being homosexual: Gay men and their development*. New York: Avon.

Landers, A. (1992, May 26). Gay teen tired of advances from sexually aggressive girls. *Detroit Free Press*, p. 2B.

Malyon, A. K. (1981). The homosexual adolescent: Developmental issues and social bias. *Child Welfare, 60*, 321–330.

Norton, J. L. (1976). The homosexual and counseling. *Personnel and Guidance Journal, 54*, 374–377.

Price, J. H. (1982). High school students' attitudes toward homosexuality. *Journal of School Health, 52*, 469–474.

Remafedi, G. (1987). Male homosexuality: The adolescent's perspective. *Pediatrics, 79*, 326–330.

Remafedi, G. (1990). Fundamental issues in the care of homosexual youth. *Adolescent Medicine, 74*, 1169–1179.

Sanders, G. (1980). Homosexualities in the Netherlands. *Alternative Lifestyles, 3*, 278–311.

Savin-Williams, R. C. (1990). *Gay and lesbian youth: Expressions of identity*. New York: Hemisphere.

Savin-Williams, R. C. (1994). Dating those you can't love and loving those you can't date. In R. Montemayor, G. R. Adams, & T. P. Gullotta (Eds.), *Personal relationships during adolescence: Vol 6. Advances in adolescent development* (pp. 196–215). Newbury Park, CA: Sage.

Savin-Williams, R. C. (1995). *Sex and sexual identity among gay and bisexual males*. Manuscript in preparation, Cornell University, Ithaca, NY.

Scarf, M. (1987). *Intimate partners: Patterns in love and marriage*. New York: Random House.

Schafer, S. (1976). Sexual and social problems of lesbians. *Journal of Sex Research, 12*, 50–69.

Sears, J. T. (1991). *Growing up gay in the South: Race, gender, and journeys of the spirit*. New York: Harrington Park Press.

Silverstein, C. (1981). *Man to man: Gay couples in America*. New York: William Morrow.

Skipper, J. K., Jr., & Nass, G. (1966). Dating behavior: A framework for analysis and an illustration. *Journal of Marriage and the Family, 27*, 412–420.

Stanley, J. P., & Wolfe, S. J. (Eds.). (1980). *The coming out stories*. New York: Persephone.

Troiden, R. R., & Goode, E. (1980). Variables related to the acquisition of a gay identity. *Journal of Homosexuality, 5*, 383–392.

Adapted from Ritch C. Savin-Williams, "Dating and Romantic Relationships Among Gay, Lesbian, and Bisexual Youths." In R. C. Savin-Williams & K. M. Cohen (Eds.), *The Lives of Lesbians, Gays, and Bisexuals: Children to Adults* (pp. 166–180). Copyright © 1996 by Harcourt, Inc. Reprinted by permission of the publisher. ✦

Part VIII

Sexual Victimization

As illustrated by the topics in Part VIII, sexual victimization can run the gamut, ranging from child sexual abuse to cybersex. The one variable inherent in all victimization, however, is power and its misuse. Even though all sexual relationships include an element of power, when this power is shared, partners are empowered and relationships strengthened. Conversely, coercive sexuality is characterized by a clash of personal power (Carroll & Wolpe, 1996). Whether evidenced in child sexual abuse, sexual aggression, sexual harassment, or cybersex, an unequal power structure inevitably results in harm.

All adults in our society are called upon to play a role in stemming the tide of sexual victimization. For example, when underage children or adolescents are victims of sexual abuse, laws mandate that any person with knowledge of the incident must play the role of reporter. Once the abuse becomes known to the authorities, if verified, the role of medical and mental health professionals is assessment and, eventually, the role of the therapist is to address healing (Faller, 1995). Legal roles are also part of the sexual victimization picture as evidenced by various state laws and institutional policies pertaining to sexual aggression and sexual harassment in occupational, educational, medical, and therapeutic settings. But the laws and roles involved in the protection against sexual victimization are not always clear-cut or embraced by everyone. As readers will see, some people question whether or not the government should have any role at all in the bedroom.

A number of models of sexual abuse have been advanced, but a comprehensive theory of sexual aggression has yet to be proposed. Such a theoretical vacuum exists in spite of the fact that almost one-half of Americans are affected by this serious social problem as either victims or perpetrators (Laumann, Gagnon, Michael, & Michaels, 1994). Moreover, viewing sexual aggression as only a societal problem ignores the horrendous personal emotional pain experienced by millions. Thus, sexual aggression should be considered a broad mix of social processes and interpersonal relationships.

Any theoretical model for child sexual abuse must differentiate among the possible immediate causes of sexual abuse, which lie in the psychology of the abuser and interpersonal relationships, those social factors and values that make children more or less likely to be victimized (Glaser & Frosh, 1988). Sexual victimization of the young can arise from outside factors (e.g.; child and adolescent sex rings, pornography, adolescent runaways, and juvenile prostitution) or from inside factors (e.g., incest, a family affair). The Finkelhor, Hotaling, Lewis, and Smith retrospective research clarifies a number of these concepts.

The Hall, Windover, and Maramba exploration of numerous types of sexual aggression provides a well-developed review of empirical research in the general population, even though the article's focus is on Asian Americans. This study raises many questions. Is the low rate of sexual aggression among Asian Americans because this group is less likely than others to experience developmental, motivational, and situational risk factors? In the Asian culture, does the emphasis on self-control of sexual and aggressive behavior serve as a protective factor? In this population, what are the relative roles of internal and external factors? These and other such queries can be more factually answered after reading the Hall et al. offering.

Nice women don't say "yes," and real men don't say "no." For more than a decade, Charlene Muehlenhard (1988) has maintained a research interest in the controversial topic of sexual scripting. The concept of stereotypes has also involved a number of other researchers studying gender and cultural differences in communication about sexual intercourse. Readers intrigued by the Muehlenhard and Rodgers selection are referred to the Sprecher, Hatfield, Cortese, Potapova, and Levitskaya (1994) research that added yet another dimension to this issue when they investigated the reverse of token resistance, saying "yes" when meaning "no."

If in fact token resistance, as defined by the authors, is a "scripted refusal," it is prudent to ask more about the phenomenon of sexual scripts. Accordingly, many women are reluctant to acknowledge their desire for sexual intercourse, lacking psychological permission to do so because of social norms dictating that "nice girls" should avoid engaging in sexual intercourse before marriage. But what is the basis of such sexual scripts? To answer that question, we must begin at the beginning. When in the first years of life, children discover their genitals, parents begin the long process of imparting their sexual attitudes and behaviors to their offspring. Other family members, and eventually peers, soon join the parade of values. Regardless of whether these and successive sexual experiences in the culture in which they are reared relay positive or negative sexual messages, by adulthood, everyone has fairly well-established sexual attitudes and ways of interacting sexually. This personal model is called a sexual script. The Muehlenhard and Rodgers selection leads students into yet uncharted waters in search of answers to ongoing communication dilemmas that occur when sexual scripts collide.

A team of mental health professionals who addressed the linkages between mental health, sexual harassment, and generalized workplace abuse among women and men in a university setting draw surprising conclusions. Their findings may challenge some well-established but unfounded perceptions about sexual harassment. Readers whose interests are piqued about the subject of this carefully designed and executed empirical study are referred to a lively exchange about this issue by Catharine Stimpson (1996), Graduate Dean at Rutgers University, and Gretchen Morgenson (1996), Senior Editor at *Forbes* magazine. Stimpson proposed that sexual harassment has reached epidemic proportions that will remain as long as men remain in power and control. Morgenson presented the flip side of the coin, arguing that statistics on the prevalence of sexual harassment are grossly exaggerated by "consultants" who make a good living instituting corporate antiharassment programs. The authors defend their positions with substantial information that should augment the more academic offering by Richman and her research team. This latter selection is a quick read about an issue not so quickly resolved.

Although printing, photography, and radio were early forms of transmitting sexually explicit materials, in the 1980s, inexpensive pornographic videocassettes were introduced, and by the 1990s, interactive hardcore CD-ROMs hit the market. Should society take steps to control the dissemination of what some have called "sexual barbarism" and "criminal perversion" on the 5,000 online newsgroups and equally numerous chat rooms on the Internet? The affirmative side of this debate has been ably argued by social commentators, while others have countered the question with assertions that Americans living in the land of the free should be able to decide for themselves which cyberspace communities they wish to frequent (Francoeur, 1996). Cybersex is apparently not a problem of limited proportions or one to be easily solved. In August 1999, 31 percent of the total Internet users visited an adult website (Leone & Beilsmith, 1999).

When Cooper, Delmonico, and Burg empirically examined the characteristics and usage patterns of individuals who use the Internet for sexual purposes, they analyzed an already existing database, which the lead author had constructed. Besides delineating the differences between users, abusers, and compulsives, the authors raise a number of pragmatic issues. For example, deceit is apparently alive and well in the *dotcom* world, where misrepresentations of age and race seem to occur with increasing frequency. One particularly disturbing example of age misrepresentation involves the fraudulent attempts by adults to contact young persons to arrange meetings for sexual purposes. It has been estimated that two-thirds of all visitors to children's web sites are adults posing as children in order to engage in cybersex (Allgeier & Allgeier, 2000).

"Gender bending" is a newly coined term describing another ploy used in cybersex. Although seemingly innocuous, it can prove to be deadly. For example, Kenny Wayne Lockwood, 32, was found dead in his cell, October 14, 2000, from suicide, concluding a bizarre news story that began when Lockwood was charged with capital murder in the death of Kenny Kujawa, a 20-year-old Texas A&M University student. The two had met through an Internet chat room in which Lockwood is alleged to have posed as a woman named "Kelly." Authorities believe that after Kujawa traveled to San Antonio to meet "Kelly," Lockwood killed Kujawa after the ruse was uncovered. Even though Kujawa's body was not found until weeks later, his family continued to receive e-mail, claiming that he was alive and well (Miller, 2000).

References

Allgeier, E. R., & Allgeier, A. R. (2000). *Sexual interactions* (5th ed.). Boston: Houghton Mifflin.

Carroll, J. L., & Wolpe, P. R. (1996). *Sexuality and gender in society*. New York: HarperCollins.

Faller, K. C. (1995). Assessment and treatment in child sexual abuse. In G. A. Rekers (Ed.), *Handbook of child and adolescent sexual problems* (pp. 209–231). New York: Lexington.

Francoeur, R. T. (1996). Should sex be banned on the Internet? In R. T. Francoeur (Ed.), *Taking sides: Clashing views on controversial issues in human sexuality* (5th ed., pp. 286–287). Guilford, CT: Duskin/Brown and Benchmark.

Glaser, D., & Frosh, S. (1988). *Child and sexual abuse*. Chicago: Dorsey.

Laumann, E. O., Gagnon, J. H., Michael, R. T., & Michaels, S. (1994). *The social organization of sexuality: Sexual practices in the United States*. Chicago: University of Chicago Press.

Leone, S., & Beilsmith, M. (1999, February). *Monthly report on Internet growth*. Washington, DC: Media Metrix.

Miller, A. (2000, November 1). Autopsy in jail suicide details cause of death. *San Marcos Record*, pp. 1–2.

Morgenson, G. (1996). May I have the pleasure. In R. T. Francoeur (Ed.), *Taking sides: Clashing views on controversial issues in human sexuality* (5th ed., pp. 279–283). Guilford, CT: Duskin/Brown and Benchmark.

Muehlenhard, C. L. (1988). "Nice women" don't say yes and "real men" don't say no: How miscommunication and the double standard can cause sexual problems. *Women and Therapy, 7*, 95–108.

Sprecher, S., Hatfield, E., Cortese, A., Potapova, E., & Levitskaya, A. (1994). Token resistance to sexual intercourse: College students' dating experiences in three countries. *Journal of Sex Research, 31*, 125–132.

Stimpson, C. (1996). Over-reaching: Sexual harassment and education. In R. T. Francoeur (Ed.), *Taking sides: Clashing views on controversial issues in human sexuality* (5th ed., pp. 274–278). Guilford, CT: Duskin/Brown and Benchmark. ✦

Chapter 35
Sexual Abuse in a National Survey of Adult Men and Women

David Finkelhor
Gerald Hotaling
I. A. Lewis
Christine Smith

will challenge the thinking of all students about a compelling topic so important to the well-being of society.

The Finkelhor et al. widely cited research, based on a national probability sample, is regarded by many professionals as the "gold standard" concerning the prevalence of child sexual abuse in the United States. Although the data, collected in 1985, are fifteen years old, they have assumed a life of their own, analogous in a lesser way to the Kinsey work. Those familiar with the Laumann et al. findings concerning persons who under the age of 18 were sexually abused will note a significantly larger percentage reported in this earlier study of a decade ago. Many questions could be raised by such differences. Are fewer reported cases of child sexual abuse in the later study a function of the research design or data collection techniques? Or is it safe to assume that actually there is less child sexual abuse today than formerly? Although the answers to those questions do not appear in this selection, the carefully reported findings on this important topic do furnish information with which students can form a hypothesis concerning such issues. The strong predictors of child sexual abuse found in this study may not be as surprising for students of family studies or child development as for those less familiar with the myriad effects of an unhappy family life. Nevertheless, this selection

Much of the important scientific knowledge about the nature, prevalence, and impact of child sexual abuse has come from community surveys of adults, reporting on their histories of abuse (Finkelhor, 1984; Russell, 1986). The revelations of these studies have suggested that even larger studies and ones using nationally representative samples could provide additional, valuable answers to questions about prevalence and risk factors. This paper reports on a large, national survey on the subject of sexual abuse and presents its findings concerning prevalence and risk factors.

THE CURRENT STUDY
Methodology

The survey was conducted in late July 1985. The *Los Angeles Times* Poll, a highly respected and experienced survey research organization, interviewed a sample of 2,626 American men and women 18 years of age or older, over the phone. The sampling frame was all residential telephones in the U.S., including the states of Alaska and Hawaii. The sample of 1,145 men and 1,481 women were questioned for approximately a half hour on topics related to sexual abuse—their attitude toward the problem, their own experiences, and their opinions about what should be done. The sample conformed in all respects to census demographics for the United States as a whole and to demographics for other similar telephone surveys. The refusal rate was 24 percent.

A history of sexual abuse was elicited through responses to four questions:

1. When you were a child (age 18 or under), can you remember having any experience you would now consider sexual abuse—like someone trying or succeeding in having any kind of sexual

intercourse with you, or anything like that?

2. When you were a child, can you remember any kind of experience that you would now consider sexual abuse involving someone touching you, or grabbing you, or kissing you, or rubbing up against your body either in a public place or private—or anything like that?

3. When you were a child, can you remember any kind of experience that you would now consider sexual abuse involving someone taking nude photographs of you, or someone exhibiting parts of their body to you, or someone performing some sex act in your presence—or anything like that?

4. When you were a child, can you remember any kind of experience that you would now consider sexual abuse involving oral sex or sodomy—or anything like that?

These screening questions are more comprehensive than some that have been used in earlier surveys, but they also have some problems, in part because they allow for a partially undefined interpretation of sexual abuse. Experiences some researchers might define as abuse could be left out because the respondent did not consider them as abuse. Other experiences of a minor nature that many researchers would exclude could have been counted because of a respondent's broad interpretation of the phrase "anything like that." Unfortunately, no subsequent questions were asked about the sexual acts that could have been used to exclude experiences that did not meet researchers' criteria.

On the other hand, these screening questions are an improvement over surveys which asked only a single broad question about a history of abuse. Comparison among studies has shown that respondents disclose more experiences when they are given multiple opportunities to disclose and a variety of cues about the kinds of events researchers are interested in as opposed to a single screening question (Peters, Wyatt, & Finkelhor, 1986).

Findings

Prevalence and Characteristics

The responses to the four screening questions are shown in Table 35.1. If we count as a victim anyone who answered yes to any one of the four questions, a history of sexual abuse was disclosed by 27 percent of the women and 16 percent of the men. More information on the nature of these experiences appears in Tables 35.2 and 35.3. The median age of abuse was 9.9 for boys and 9.6 for girls, with the victimization of 22 percent of the boys and 23 percent of the girls occurring before age 8. Boys were more likely to be abused by strangers, whereas girls were more likely to be abused by family members. Of the girl victims, 6 percent were abused by a father or stepfather. Half the offenders were seen by the victims to be authority figures. Both men and women reported that most of their abuse was perpetrated by men: 83 percent of the offenders against boys and 98 percent of the offenders against girls. Most of the offenders were 10 or more years older than their victims, but boys were more likely to be abused by younger offenders, most of whom were older adolescents. Very little of the abuse was by peers. Of the male victims, 62 percent and 49 percent of the female victims said they had experienced actual or attempted intercourse. Force was used in only 15 percent of the incidents to boys and 19 percent of the incidents to girls. A majority of the experiences were one-time events, and there was no significant gender difference in the percentage of experiences lasting more than a year. However, boys were somewhat more likely never to have disclosed the experience to anyone.

Overall, the description of abuse experiences from this national survey conforms to findings from other surveys (see Finkelhor, 1987; Russell, 1986) with two main exceptions. There was an unusually large amount of actual or attempted intercourse (49 percent of girls in this survey

Table 35.1

Types of Sexual Abuse

Type of Abuse	Men[*] %	Women[*] %
Sexual intercourse	9.5	14.6
Touch, Grab, Kiss	4.5	19.6
Exhibition, Nude Photos, Performing		
Photos	—	0.1
Exhibition	1.0	3.2
Performing	0.3	0.3
Other	0.3	0.1
Oral Sex, Sodomy	0.4	0.1

* Men (*n* = 1145); Women (*n* = 1481).

Table 35.2

Age of Sexual Abuse Victim

Age of Victim	Men[*] %	Women[*] %
Age at Time of Abuse		
0-6	12	14
7	10	9
8	12	11
9	6	7
10	11	15
11	7	8
12	11	14
13	11	8
14	8	4
15	3	2
16-18	6	6
Don't know	3	2
Median	**9.9**	**9.6**

* Men (*n* = 1145); Women (*n* = 1481).

Table 35.3

Characteristics of Sexual Abuse Perpetrators

Characteristics of Perpetrators	Men[*] %	Women[*] %
Gender of Perpetrator		
Male	83	98
Female	17	1
Age Difference		
3 years or less	3	4
4 to 10 years	34	19
10 years or more	61	72
Don't know	2	5
Relationship to Perpetrator		
Stranger	40	21
Known	31	33
Friend	13	8
Cousin	5	5
Uncle/Aunt	5	14
Sibling	1	2
Grandparent	0	2
Stepparent	0	3
Natural/parent	0	3
Other	5	9
Authority figure	49	49

* Men (*n* = 1145); Women (*n* = 1481).

compared to only 20 percent in Russell's survey) and an unusually small amount of coercion (only 19 percent of the incidents to girls in this survey compared to 41 percent in Russell). Both of these differences are probably due to quirks of particular survey questions. The question on coercion introduced a bias; it asked, "Did this person use any kind of force when this happened; for example, did this person strike you or use a weapon or threaten to harm you in any way or to restrain you by physical strength." Because force is illustrated in this question with examples of very serious force, victims who were bullied, intimidated or felt that the act was against their wishes may have been reluctant to say yes. Half or more of victims in other surveys (Finkelhor, 1979) report force or coercion. We are inclined to discount the findings from this survey on intercourse and force.

Risk Factors

Men and women were more likely to have been victimized if they reported that their family life had been unhappy, if their predominant family situation had been one without one of their natural parents, or if they were currently living in the Pacific region. Men, in addition, were at higher risk if their family came from English or Scandinavian ancestry. Women were at higher risk if they received an inadequate sex education. Older women were also at lower risk compared to younger women. Aside from these factors, other possible background characteristics such as race, parents' education, and having few friends were not related to victimization.

Unhappy Family Life

Growing up in an unhappy family appeared to be the most powerful risk factor for abuse. Both men and women who described their families this way were more than twice as likely to be abused. It is easy to understand why a child from an unhappy family might be vulnerable to the manipulations of an abuser who was offering affection or companionship to trick a child.

However, it is also possible that the causal relationship might be reversed. Some victims may have been describing their family life as an unhappy one because they were abused there or because they could never confide their secret there. To test for this, we repeated the analysis twice: first, for victims of extra-familial abuse only; and second, only for victims who had disclosed their abuse to a family member (girls only—there were too few boys who had disclosed).

An unhappy family life was still a strong predictor of abuse. This suggests that un-

happy family life is a true risk factor and not simply a distorted perception that a victim develops as a result of having been abused. Moreover, an unhappy family life may contribute to the risk for abuse outside as well as inside the family for two reasons (Finkelhor & Baron, 1986): first, children in such families probably receive poorer supervision when out of the home; and, such children, who may have particularly strong needs for positive attention and affection, may be more vulnerable to the ploys of nonfamily perpetrators who offer attention and affection as a lure.

Living Without a Natural Parent

Separation from a natural parent for a major portion of one's childhood was a risk factor in this study as in a number of other studies (Bagley & Ramsay, 1986; Finkelhor, 1979; Russell, 1986). Interestingly, girls showed markedly higher risk under all family circumstances except that of living with two natural parents and particularly when living alone with father or with two non-natural parents. Moreover, this higher risk held for all types of sexual abuse, not just the intrafamily type. Boys, in contrast, were primarily at risk only in two family constellations: when they lived with their mothers alone or with two non-natural parents. It would seem that almost any long-term disruption of the natural parent situation is risky for girls but not so for boys. Moreover, the transition from a single mother alone to a single mother with stepfather increases the risk for girls but not for boys.

Region

This first national survey of sexual abuse showed a markedly higher rate of abuse for Pacific states (California, Oregon, Washington, Alaska, and Hawaii). The rate in California for women was particularly high (42 percent). Several explanations are possible. First, Westerners may have been more candid about disclosing sexual abuse. California is one of the places where the social movement originated that first drew attention to the problem of sexual abuse. It is the state with the most advanced system of prevention and treatment (as evidenced by recent legislation mandating sexual abuse prevention for all school children). Moreover, Californians at the time of the survey had been barraged by news coverage of the notorious McMartin preschool abuse case. People there may be much more knowledgeable and comfortable about the subject and thus more prepared to disclose histories.

A second plausible explanation: There may be more abuse going on in the West. The West is and has been the frontier, perhaps attracting deviance. There is more sexual assault and other violence reported to the police in the West, a disproportion not necessarily explained by readiness to report (Baron & Straus, 1984). The West is also reputed to have a different ethic in regard to sex which may affect the prevalence of sexual abuse. The only problem here is that one study (Wyatt & Peters, 1986) looking into this hypothesis failed to find more abuse among those Californians raised in California than those raised elsewhere.

A third explanation may be that the West may tend to attract a disproportionate number of adult victims. Many people who suffered sexual abuse in childhood would justifiably feel alienated from their family and community and seek to settle elsewhere, away from the bad memories. Where have people in this country traditionally gone when they wanted to get away from a past? The West. So it is not clear whether being from the West puts someone at greater risk. But the issue needs further research.

Ethnicity

Men who reported English or Scandinavian heritage were at higher risk for abuse. The explanation for this is not clear. Associations between ethnicity and abuse have been found in a previous study (Finkelhor, 1979), but not these particular ethnicities.

Age

This national survey shows significantly lower rates of abuse for women over 60 and significantly higher rates for women 40 to 49, with a similar nonsignificant trend appearent for the men. This is additional fuel for the debate over the existence of historical trends or cohort effects. Also, Russell (1986) in a survey almost 10 years earlier did find lower rates among the oldest cohort of women and higher rates for a cohort then in their 30s.

One of the issues in the cohort debate concerns whether differences are real or reflect greater willingness among some age groups either to remember or report candidly on their experiences. Lower rates among older respondents could stem from memory loss about events that happened a long time earlier or greater embarrassment due to the values of an earlier historical era. However, Russell (1986) found the cohort effects for only some types of victimization, suggesting that the rate differences were real.

Addressing the element of embarrassment, the *Los Angeles Times* survey itself asked a question about the level of comfort in discussing the subject of sexual abuse. Respondents were asked early in the survey how much difficulty they had discussing the subject of sexual abuse. Only 23 percent claimed some, little, or great difficulty. The rest said hardly any at all. Surprisingly it was the youngest, not the oldest cohort, that had the highest level of discomfort. Moreover, it was only among the women of this youngest cohort that reporting an experience bore any relationship to level of discomfort. Women of this age who said they had had difficulty discussing sexual abuse revealed about one-third fewer experiences of abuse. Among the older groups of both men and women, there were no significant differences in rates between those with difficulty discussing sexual abuse and those without. This suggests that embarrassment is not a factor in the lower rates of the oldest group, although it is still possible that memory loss could be.

The *Los Angeles Times* survey does argue against the idea that there has been a precipitous rise in the amount of abuse in the very recent past, for example, in the wake of the "sexual revolution" of the 1960s. That is, the rates for the youngest cohorts (those growing up in the 1960s and 70s) are not higher than their immediate predecessors. The particularly higher risk in the age 40 to 49 cohort may be associated with women who had childhoods interrupted by World War II. It was a time when many fathers were gone from their families and returned after long absence. Separation from a natural father has been shown to be a risk factor both in this study and a number of other studies (Parker & Parker, 1986; Russell, 1986). In the current study, the cohorts do not vary significantly in the types of families (single parent, stepfather, etc.) reported by women. But the survey asked only about predominant family type during all of childhood, not about periods of significant absences.

Inadequate Sex Education

Women who described the sex education they received as inadequate were at higher risk for abuse. Adequate sex education may well protect children because it gives specific sexual abuse prevention information, like the kind advocated by prevention education programs (Finkelhor, 1986). Or it may be that inadequately educated children have unfulfilled curiosity about sex, a vulnerability which potential perpetrators can more easily manipulate. However, it is also possible that the causal order is reversed here. A child who has been abused could readily conclude that she had not received adequate sex education to help her avoid becoming a victim.

Conclusion

This first national prevalence study of sexual abuse does not itself break much new ground in its findings about the prevalence, nature, or risk factors for sexual abuse, but it does confirm much of what other more local studies have determined. A history of sexual abuse can be found in the backgrounds of an important fraction of men and women in the general population. Most of these experiences are at the hands of a person known to the child. Many of the victims never disclosed about the experiences to anyone, and children at risk were often ones from troubled families

whose parents left home, were sick, or died. Having these findings confirmed on a national level adds weight to what we already know. Some problems with methodology however, particularly the imprecision of the screening questions, do caution against relying on findings from this study alone in absence of supporting evidence from other research. Replications with other large samples are needed. Perhaps the two most interesting new findings seem to be the disproportion of disclosures from victims in California and those born in 1936–1945.

References

Badgley, R., Allard, H., McCormick, N., Proudfoot, P., Fortin, D., Ogilvie, D., Rae-Grant, Q., Celinas, P., Pepin, L., & Sutherland, S. Committee on Sexual Offenses Against Children and Youth. (1984). *Sexual offenses against children* (Vol. 1). Ottawa: Canadian Government Publishing Centre.

Bagley, C., & Ramsey, R. (1986). Sexual abuse in childhood: Psychosocial outcomes and implications for social work practice. *Journal of Social Work and Human Sexuality, 4,* 33–47.

Baron, L., & Straus, M. (1984). Sexual stratification, pornography, and rape in the United States. In N. Malamuth and E. Donnerstein (Eds.), *Pornography and sexual aggression.* Orlando FL: Academic Press.

Finkelhor, D. (1979). *Sexually victimized children.* New York: Free Press.

Finkelhor, D. (1984). *Child sexual abuse: New theory and research.* New York: Free Press.

Finkelhor, D. (1986). *Sourcebook on child sexual abuse.* Newbury Park CA: Sage.

Finkelhor, D. (1987). The sexual abuse of children: Current research reviewed. *Psychiatric Annals: The Journal of Continuing Psychiatric Education, 17,* 233–241.

Finkelhor, D., & Baron, L. (1986). High-risk children. In D. Finkelhor and Associates (Eds.), *Sourcebook on child sexual abuse.* Newbury Park CA: Sage.

Parker, H., & Parker, S. (1986). Father-daughter sexual abuse: An emerging perspective. *American Journal of Orthopsychiatry, 56,* 531–549.

Peters, S., Wyatt, G., & Finkelhor, D. (1986). Prevalence. In D. Finkelhor and Associates (Eds.), *Sourcebook on child sexual abuse.* Newbury Park CA: Sage.

Russell, D. (1986). *The secret trauma: Incest in the lives of girls and women.* New York: Basic Books.

Wyatt, G. & Peters, S. (1986). Issues in the definition of child sexual abuse in prevalence research. *Child Abuse & Neglect 10,* 231–240.

Chapter 36
Sexual Aggression Among Asian Americans

Gordon C. Nagayama Hall
Amy K. Windover
Gloria Gia Maramba

Some students may wonder why they need to read an article about sexual aggression among Asian Americans, because perpetration and victimization rates are lower for this group than all others. The answer is twofold. First, the unique patriarchal aspects of Asian cultures may place some of this population at more risk for sexual victimization or perpetration of sexually aggressive behavior than other groups. If so, special interventions that counteract these cultural aspects could further reduce that risk. Second, in setting the stage for their subject, the authors offer an excellent review of empirical findings concerning the risk factors for sexual aggression among both perpetrators and victims in the general population.

Touching on factors of childhood sexual abuse, peer influence, date rape, and re-victimization, this well-written piece enlightens readers who seek to determine if indeed there is a fine line or a vast chasm between normal and abnormal sexual behavior. The section on prevention and interventions with both women and men happens to focus on Asian Americans. But, in reality, it also casts a broader net, reviewing programs of risk reduction that appear to have positive results within the general population. An added bonus for students is the excellent list of references on the important topic of sexual aggression.

Existing research suggests that sexual aggression is a serious societal problem that affects as many as 1 in 4 Americans in terms of perpetration or victimization (Koss, Gidycz, & Wisniewski, 1987). Most of the available information on sexual aggression is applicable to European American populations. However, there is some evidence of differential rates of sexual aggression in ethnic minority populations. Lower rates of sexual aggression in ethnic minority groups may suggest that there are protective factors against sexual aggression within these groups that may not exist in European American groups.

Sexually aggressive behavior is relatively infrequent among Asian Americans. This is a consistent finding in both official data and in anonymous self-report data among perpetrators and victims (Federal Bureau of Investigation [FBI], 1994; Koss et al., 1987). Yet the reasons for this low frequency of sexual aggression are poorly understood. Most sexual aggression involves male perpetrators and female victims, which are the focus of this article.

General Risk Factors for Sexual Aggression

Perpetrator Risk Factors

Past sexually aggressive behavior is the best single predictor of future sexually aggressive behavior (Quinsey, Rice, & Harris, 1995). For men who are not sexually aggressive, the appraised threats of sexual aggression, including legal or societal sanctions against it, constitute a threshold that prevents them from engaging in sexually aggressive behavior (Hall, 1996). However, men who are sexually aggressive violate this threshold because the appraised threats of sexual aggression do not outweigh its appraised benefits, such as power and sexual gratification. Men who have violated this threshold are at greater risk to become sexually aggressive again than men who have not violated the threshold, because this threshold is weakened.

Why do some men violate the threshold against sexually aggressive behavior? Sexually aggressive males may experience different developmental patterns than males who are not sexually aggressive. Some developmental risk factors include poverty, parental neglect, physical or sexual abuse, a family criminal history, academic difficulties, and interpersonal difficulties (Hall, 1996; Hall & Hirschman, 1991). These factors create a general risk for antisocial behavior. The developmental variables most specifically associated with sexually aggressive behavior involve heterosexual relationships. Sexually aggressive males tend to initiate coitus earlier than men who are not sexually aggressive (Malamuth, Linz, Heavey, Barnes, & Acker, 1995). Initiation of coitus before a person is developmentally capable of establishing the emotional relationships that provide a context for sex may increase a male's risk of perpetrating sexual aggression because he comes to view females as sex objects rather than as people (Hall, 1996).

Sexually aggressive males also tend to have more sexual partners than males who are not sexually aggressive (Malamuth et al., 1995). Promiscuous men often have an impersonal approach to sex in which the partner may be devalued and objectified (Malamuth et al., 1995). When the primary or sole purpose of sex is personal gratification, the needs of the partner are less relevant, and the likelihood of using coercion to meet personal needs may increase. Objectification of females may lead to short-lived sexual relationships and a failure to establish nonsexual friendships with peer females (Hall & Barongan, 1997).

What causes men who have been sexually aggressive once to persist in sexually aggressive behavior? Forced sexual intercourse is often accompanied by the perpetrator's physiological sexual arousal, which may be highly reinforcing. The more times this type of conditioning occurs, the greater the likelihood that a male will be sexually aroused by sexually aggressive behavior (Marshall & Barbaree, 1984). Another effect of perpetrating sexual aggression on multiple occasions is a desensitization to the negative effects of sexual aggression. For some men coercive behaviors may come to be viewed as necessary and excusable components of having sex with someone who refuses (Hall, 1996). Other males who have multiple shortlived sexual relationships with females may become angry toward women because these relationships tend to be neither lasting nor satisfying (Gold & Clegg, 1990). Sexual aggression is the behavior that becomes an expression of this anger (Malamuth et al., 1995).

Sexually aggressive men become sexually aggressive under certain circumstances but not under others (Hall, 1996). For example, 21 percent of a group of nonaggressive undergraduate men reported some likelihood that they would force a woman into sexual acts, and another 14 percent also reported some likelihood that they would rape if they could be assured of not being caught (Malamuth, 1988). Extreme reductions in sanctions against rape occasionally occur, such as in times of war, and some nonaggressive men do become sexually aggressive. However, sanctions against rape are generally weak relative to sanctions against other crimes (Koss, 1993). Thus, the relatively low likelihood of punishment for sexually aggressive behavior may disinhibit sexual aggression among some men. Another implication of Malamuth's (1988) data is that sanctions against sexual aggression deter most men from engaging in it.

Peers may have a greater influence over sexual behavior than other influences, e.g., parents, schools (Rodgers & Rowe, 1993). The availability of opposite-gender peers who are willing to engage in sexual behavior creates the opportunity for sexual aggression to occur (Himelein, 1995), and the presence of sexually active same-gender peers, who may model the message that sexual activity is acceptable, is associated both with sexual activity and risk for sexual aggression (Vicary, Klingaman, & Harkness, 1995). Moreover, the presence of male peers who approve of sexually coercive behavior may increase a male's risk of engaging in sexually aggressive behavior (DeKeseredy & Kelly, 1995).

Sexually aggressive men often report that they used alcohol while they were sexually aggressive (Seto & Barbaree, 1995). However, alcohol may be used as an excuse for being sexually aggressive, and it is unlikely that alcohol use has a causal role in sexually aggressive behavior. More likely, alcohol use may disinhibit sexually aggressive impulses among some men (Seto & Barbaree, 1995).

In summary, a male's history of sexually aggressive behavior is associated with his likelihood of engaging in sexually aggressive behavior in the future. Developmental sexual factors, including early initiation of coitus and promiscuous sexual activity, may facilitate physiological, cognitive, and affective motivational factors for perpetrating sexually aggressive behavior. The likelihood that these motivational factors will influence a male to engage in sexually aggressive behavior may be mediated by situational factors. Among males who are motivated to become sexually aggressive, the likelihood of engaging in sexual aggression may be a function of perceived sanctions against sexually aggressive behavior, peer support for such behavior (i.e., availability of peer sexual partners, peer approval of sexual aggression), and alcohol use.

Victim Risk Factors

Victims of sexual aggression are not responsible for being sexually victimized. Most victims do not knowingly place themselves in situations in which they are likely to be sexually abused. However, potential victims' amount of contact with perpetrators comprises a risk factor for sexual victimization.

In a national sample of 32 colleges, Koss and Dinero (1989) found that the strongest predictors of sexual victimization among women were past sexual abuse, sexual activity, alcohol use, and sexual attitudes . . . [factors that] may appear to be under a woman's control. Thus women may appear to be responsible for these behaviors. However, many women who engage in behaviors associated with risk for being sexually victimized, such as having multiple sexual partners or drinking alcohol before engaging in sexual behavior, are not seeking to be sexually victimized. Moreover, such behaviors are risky only when they occur in the presence of a perpetrator. A woman who has multiple partners who are not perpetrators or who drinks on a date with a man who is not a perpetrator is not at increased risk for sexual victimization. Even when women engage in behaviors that may be associated with risk for sexual victimization, it is the perpetrator's decision to become sexually aggressive (Hall, 1996). Thus, women who happen to have sex with a perpetrator are not responsible for being sexually victimized.

A history of being sexually abused is associated with additional sexual victimization among females (Messman & Long, 1996). In a community sample, 21 percent of women who were not abused during childhood experienced sexual victimization involving physical contact during adulthood, whereas 56 percent of women who were sexually victimized during childhood experienced sexual victimization involving physical contact during adulthood (Wyatt, Guthrie, & Notgrass, 1992). Sexual victimization during childhood or adolescence is a risk factor for future sexual abuse insofar as the victim has come into contact with a pool of perpetrators, or at least one perpetrator from this pool, and is at risk for future sexual victimization any time she comes into contact with someone from this pool.

The increased risk of sexual re-victimization for victims of sexual abuse may exist in part because some women who have been previously sexually abused may begin to engage in indiscriminate sexual behavior in an effort to seek intimacy (Briere & Runtz, 1993). Sexual abuse of female children also may result in these victims' sexualized behaviors, including having an earlier first coitus, multiple sex partners, and brief sexual relationships that may place them at risk for additonal sexual abuse (Kendall-Tackett, Williams, & Finkelhor, 1993). Females who engage in indiscriminate sexual behavior may be perceived by perpetrators as more likely to engage in sex and may be targeted as potential victims more so than females who have more limited sexual contact (Himelein, 1995).

Data are conflicting on personality factors associated with risk for being sexually victimized once versus multiple times. Although there is evidence that single- and multiple-incident victims do not differ on personality characteristics (Wyatt et al., 1992), other evidence suggests that they do (Gidycz, Coble, Latham, & Layman, 1993). In a 9-month prospective study with a large sample of college women, a direct relationship was found between personality factors and additional sexual victimization among women who had been previously sexually victimized (Gidycz et al., 1993). Women who experienced greater levels of depression and anxiety after sexual victimization were more likely to be sexually re-victimized than were sexually victimized women who experienced less depression and anxiety (Gidycz et al., 1993). However, this association between victim personality factors and additional victimization was only partially supported in a follow-up study (Gidycz, Hanson, & Layman, 1995).

A second risk factor in Koss and Dinero's (1989) study for being sexually victimized was . . . [related to] sexual activity variables, including age at first coitus and number of sexual partners (Himelein, 1995; Vicary et al., 1995). Sexual activity is a situational variable that may increase contact with perpetrators. The greater the number of sexual partners, the greater the likelihood that a woman will come into contact with a perpetrator (Buss & Schmitt, 1993).

Although Koss and Dinero (1989) reported that sexual attitudes differentiated victims and nonvictims, three of the four items that composed Koss and Dinero's sexual attitudes variable involved questions about whether women had engaged in kissing, petting, and sexual intercourse. Thus, this variable appears to be more of a sexual behavior variable than an attitudinal one. Most rape victims and nonvictims do not differ on personality characteristics, including gender role attitudes and rape-supportive beliefs (Sorenson, Siegel, Golding, & Stein, 1991).

Alcohol use by females has been consistently associated with sexual victimization (Abbey, Ross, McDuffie, & McAuslan, 1996). It is possible that some victims may blame their victimization on their drinking behavior in a manner similar to the way perpetrators blame alcohol for their sexually aggressive behavior. However, the primary risk of female alcohol use may be that it is perceived by perpetrators as an excuse for becoming sexually aggressive (Koss & Dinero, 1989).

In summary, developmental factors that increase the likelihood of contact with peer or nonpeer perpetrators, including amount of sexual activity (e.g., early initiation of coitus, multiple sex partners) and sexual victimization, increase risk for sexual victimization during adulthood. The likelihood of adult sexual victimization is mediated by situational variables, including number of sexual partners and alcohol use, that may activate a perpetrator's cognitive distortions about the justifiability of becoming sexually aggressive. There do not appear to be specific personality characteristics of attitudes associated with women's risk for sexual victimization.

Risk and Protective Factors Among Asian Americans

Risk Factors

Women often have a subordinate status in Asian cultures (Ho, 1990). Some Asian American women may view themselves as responsible for being sexually victimized (Yoshihama, Parekh, & Boyington, 1991), and women who believe that women are to blame for rape may be at risk for being sexually victimized themselves (Muehlenhard & MacNaughton, 1988). Asian American women may be viewed by perpetrators as particularly vulnerable for these reasons. Moreover, stereotypes of Asian American women held by Asians and non-Asians are that they are exotic, sexual creatures. Some Asian American women may not want to report abuse to authorities because they blame themselves for what happened, feel that they will bring disgrace to their families, or fear that they or the perpetrator will face discriminatory or even brutal treatment by social service agencies when the perpetrator is Asian American (Yoshihama et al., 1991). Moreover, the Asian American community may also ostracize the woman if she reports being sexually victimized. Asian American women are less likely to report dating violence to police than are Latina and African American women, although Asian American women are not less likely to report dating violence to police than are European American women (Miller & Simpson, 1991).

Insofar as the percentage of non-Asian men who are sexually aggressive is greater than the percentage of Asian American men who are sexually aggressive (Koss et al., 1987), Asian American women who date non-Asian men may be at increased risk for being sexually victimized. Asian American women who date non-Asians may be more sexually active than Asian American women who exclusively date Asian American men (Huang & Uba, 1992). Opportunities for sexual behavior also create opportunities for sexually aggressive behavior. Some non-Asian men may deliberately choose to sexually victimize Asian American women because of their perceived vulnerability and relatively low likelihood of reporting sexual aggression. Immigrant women and those who have limited English language skills may be particularly vulnerable. However, because surveys typically have not assessed the ethnicity of perpetrator and victim (Cochran, Mays, & Leung, 1991; Koss et al., 1987), the prevalence of interracial sexual aggression among Asian Americans is unknown.

In summary, the patriarchal aspects of Asian cultures may create a risk for sexual aggression. Because they are often subordinated, some Asian American women may submit to sexually aggressive behavior and may be unwilling to report it to authorities. The perceived vulnerability of Asian American women may be attractive to perpetrators. Asian American men may be at risk to be sexually aggressive against those who appear to be members of out-groups. Nevertheless, very few Asian American men perpetrate sexual aggression, and very few Asian American women are sexually victimized. The reasons for this infrequency of sexual aggression among Asian Americans are unknown.

Protective Factors

Unlike the emphasis on individualism in mainstream American culture, American cultures having non-Western origins often emphasize collective values (Hill, Soriano, Chen, & LaFromboise, 1994). Whereas there tends to be a consensus about cultural norms and sanctions against violating these norms in collectivist cultures, there are often multiple, sometimes conflicting, cultural norms for which violation is often not punished in individualist cultures. Interpersonal conflict and violence tend to be minimal in cultures with collectivist orientations, because individual goals are subordinated to those of the group, social support is high, and competitiveness is low. Crime levels and collectivist influences are inversely associated (Triandis, 1995). In the United States, arrest rates for violent crimes perpetrated by Asian Americans are about one-third the rate of the numbers of Asian Americans in the population (American Psychological Association Commission on Violence and Youth, 1993).

The largest and most representative national survey of sexually aggressive behavior, in which participants' identities were anonymous, suggests differences in prevalence rates of sexual aggression across ethnic groups during adulthood (Koss et al., 1987). Prevalence rates of rape in Koss et al.'s (1987) study were significantly lower for Asian American women (7 percent) than for women in other groups (European American = 16 percent, Asian American = 10 percent, Latina = 12 percent, Native American = 40 percent). These findings are consistent with other multi-ethnic studies of self-reported rates of rape among college women (Urquiza & Goodlin-Jones, 1994: European American = 26 percent, Native American = 38 percent, Latina = 18 percent, Asian American = 11 percent). Moreover, few Asian American men perpetrate rape relative to most other groups.

It is possible that Asian Americans have narrower definitions of rape and other sexually aggressive behaviors than do other non-Asian groups (Mori, Bernat, Glenn, Selle, & Zarate, 1995). For example, a narrow definition would define rape as occurring only when physical force is involved. Such a definition would exclude rapes in which threats (e.g., with a weapon) or psychological coercion are involved. Koss et al.'s (1987) study avoided such definitional problems to some extent with the use of specific descriptions of sexually aggressive behaviors instead of terms such as *rape* or *sexual aggression.*

It is possible that the lower reporting of sexually aggressive behavior among Asian Americans is a function of social desirability (Urquiza & Goodlin-Jones, 1994). Russell (1984) suggested that Asian women may be less likely than non-Asian women to disclose intimate information. Nevertheless, among Asian Americans who were sexually active, there were no significant differences in sexual behaviors between those who were U.S. born and foreign born (Cochran et al., 1991). Moreover, there were also few differences between Asian Americans who were sexually active and members of other ethnic groups who were sexually active (Cochran et al., 1991). It is possible that social desirability is less influential for the responses of sexually active people than it is for those who are not sexually active.

Perhaps there are specific aspects of Asian American culture that serve as protective factors against sexually aggressive behavior (Hall & Barongan, 1997). The high value placed on self-control among Asian Americans (Uba, 1994) may prevent the development of the impulse dyscontrol associated with sexually aggressive behavior (Baumeister, Smart, & Boden, 1996). In Asian cultures, in which the self is not separate from others, any behavior that upsets group interdependence is not approved of (Markus & Kitayama, 1994). Deviant behavior may result in loss of face or the threat or loss of one's social integrity (Sue & Morishima, 1982). Loss of face may be a more important mediator of behavior among Asian Americans than among European Americans.

In collectivist cultures, the most important relationships are vertical, e.g., parent-child (Triandis, Bontempo, Villateal, Asai, & Lucca, 1988). Thus, parents may have more influence over their children's behavior than peers have. Age at first coitus is delayed among adolescents who perceive their parents as more influential than peers (Wyatt, 1989). Delaying coitus may limit opportunities to become a perpetrator or victim of sexual aggression.

Other-focused emotions, including empathy, tend to be more common in collectivist cultures than in individualistic cultures, in which ego-focused emotions, including anger, may be more common. The cognitions of collectivists tend to be directed toward the needs of the in-group, whereas cognitions among individualists tend to be directed toward personal needs (Triandis, 1995). Thus, sexual aggression by Asian Americans against other Asian Americans would be deterred by empathy, which may reduce the likelihood of the development of cognitive distortions about victims (Hall, 1996).

In a multi-ethnic sample of college students, 47 percent of Asian Americans were sexually active versus 72 percent of European Americans, 84 percent of African Americans, and 59 percent of Latinos (Cochran et al., 1991). These percentages are consistent with the percentages of sexually active college students by ethnic group in other samples (Huang & Uba, 1992). In some traditional Asian families, dating for females may be unacceptable until a certain age or until their education is completed (Yoshihama et al., 1991). Thus, some Asian American women may have limited contact with men, particularly in situations in which sexual aggression is likely to occur (e.g., dating, sexual situations). Huang and Uba (1992) speculated that Chinese Americans may delay sexual intercourse because they want to wait until they are certain that there is adequate emotional commitment, which also was found to be the primary reason for maintaining virginity among European Americans (Sprecher & Regan, 1996).

The collectivist aspects of Asian cultures may also contribute to lower rates of sexual activities among Asian Americans. Romantic relationships for Asian Americans may occur within the context of interconnectedness of larger social networks (Dion & Dion, 1993). Thus, relational aspects of romance may be emphasized over sexual aspects. Indeed, Asians tend to be more friendship oriented in their romantic relationships than do people of European ancestry (Dion & Dion, 1993).

Unlike non-Asian American groups, in which males tend to be more sexually experienced than females (Rodgers & Rowe, 1993), there is evidence to suggest that Asian American men have less sexual experience than Asian American women (Huang & Uba, 1992). The absence of opportunities for having sex may deter Asian American men from being sexually active more than it deters Asian American women (Huang & Uba, 1992). Stereotypes of Asian men are generally negative (Huang & Uba, 1992). Many Asian Americans may perceive themselves as unassertive and socially unskilled (Zane, Sue, Hu, & Kwon, 1991). Self-perceptions of shyness have also been found to be associated with virginity among European American males (Sprecher & Regan, 1996). Peer norms may also influence Asian Americans' behavior. The majority of Asian American college students are virgins (Huang & Uba, 1992). This may create less peer pressure toward compulsory heterosexual behavior among Asian Americans (Hall, 1996).

Having non-Asian sexual partners also affects Asian Americans' sexual behavior. Whereas approximately one third of Chinese Americans who dated only Asians and Asian Americans had experienced coitus, nearly two thirds of those who dated European Americans had done so (Huang & Uba, 1992). The greater sexual activity of Asian American females relative to Asian American males may be a function of Asian American females' greater sexual access to non-Asians. Greater contact among Asian American women with non-Asian men who may be more sexually aggressive than Asian American men may place these women at greater risk for becoming sexually victimized.

Alcohol use in dating situations is associated with risk for becoming a perpetrator or victim of sexual aggression. There is consistent evidence of lower rates of alcohol and drug use among Asian American men and women (Gillmore et al., 1991), which may reduce risk for sexual aggression in dating situations.

In summary, Asian Americans may have less involvement as perpetrators and victims of sexual aggression because of cultural influences. A cultural emphasis on impulse control may limit Asian Americans' sexual behavior. Limited sexual behavior decreases opportunities for sexual aggression to occur during development or adulthood. This emphasis on impulse control may make Asian American males unlikely to develop physiological, cognitive, and affective motivations to become sexually aggressive. Asian American peer support for promiscuous sexual behavior and for sexual aggression may be very limited. Alcohol use, which is a risk factor for sexual aggression, is relatively limited among Asian Americans.

Preventive Interventions

Interventions With Women

Most interventions for victims of sexual aggression have focused on the traumatic effects of victimization. For example, the diagnosis and treatment of posttraumatic stress in sexual assault victims has been extensively examined (Foa, Rothbaum, & Steketee, 1993). However, ameliorating the effects of sexual victimization does not necessarily reduce the likelihood of being revictimized.

One effective method of preventing additional sexual aggression is the incarceration of men who have previously been sexually aggressive and are at the highest risk to become sexually aggressive again. Incarceration of sexually aggressive men is contingent on these men being reported to authorities. Unfortunately, Asian American women may be less likely to report incidents of sexual aggression to authorities than are non-Asians because of a tendency not to identify sexually aggressive acts as such (Mills & Granoff, 1992). Moreover, more than European Americans, Asian Americans tend to view victims as being more responsible for the sexual aggression and generally tend to hold negative attitudes toward victims (Mori et al., 1995). Thus, preventive interventions with Asian American women should emphasize that any violation of consent constitutes sexual aggression and that perpetrators are solely responsible for engaging in sexually aggressive acts.

Non-Asian men tend to be more sexually active and more sexually aggressive than Asian American men (Huang & Uba, 1992; Koss et al., 1987). Asian American women may benefit from knowing that non-Asian men may have differing expectations of sexual behavior in a relationship than they may have. Moreover, an awareness of stereotypes of Asian women as both sexual and submissive may help Asian American women to avoid or confront Asian and non-Asian men who believe these stereotypes.

There is empirical evidence that women can reduce their risk of being sexually victimized by becoming aware of risk factors and by changing their behavior. Hanson and Gidycz (1993) designed a program for college women to (a) increase awareness of sexual assault, (b) dispel common myths about rape, (c) educate participants about social forces that foster a rape-supportive environment, (d) teach practical strategies for preventing rape, (e) change dating behaviors associated with acquaintance rape (alcohol consumption while on a date), and (f) foster effective sexual communication. Only 6 percent of college women who participated in an acquaintance-rape prevention program were sexually victimized over a 9-week period following the program, whereas 14 percent of college women who did not participate in the program were sexually victimized (Hanson & Gidycz, 1993). However, sexual victimization rates among college women who had previously been sexually victimized did not significantly differ between women who did and did not participate in the program, with re-

victimization rates ranging from 10 percent to 44 percent.

It is unclear why Hanson and Gidycz's (1993) program did not reduce the sexual victimization rates of women who had been previously sexually victimized. It is possible that these women did not have the resources to make changes in their behaviors and lifestyles that would prevent further victimization. It also is possible that perpetrators may perceive women who have been previously sexually victimized as more vulnerable than nonvictimized women.

Primary prevention with women who have not been sexually victimized may be more effective than tertiary prevention involving sexually victimized women. Moreover, many sexually victimized women, including Asian Americans, do not receive interventions because of their unwillingness to disclose their victimization to authorities or to mental health professionals (Koss, 1993). Thus, prevention programs that broadly target women may reach victims who would not otherwise receive interventions.

Interventions With Men

Perpetrators are responsible for sexually aggressive behavior, and effective prevention methods targeted at perpetrators or potential perpetrators would reduce the necessity of victim intervention programs (Hall, 1996; Hanson & Gidycz, 1993). Asian American men appear to be at lower risk than other groups for perpetrating sexual aggression (Koss et al., 1987; Mills & Granoff, 1992). However, Asian American men who perceive women as an out-group or who perceive women's role as being subservient to men may be at risk to become sexually aggressive. Thus, modifying cognitive distortions about women may be important in prevention programs for Asian American men.

There exists empirical evidence that men's attitudes concerning sexual aggression can be modified by means of primary and secondary prevention. Programs to enhance victim empathy that involve participation have been demonstrated to reduce cognitive distortions about sexual aggression (Gilbert, Heesacker, & Gannon, 1991; Schewe & O'Donohue, 1993). In one study, men who participated in a prevention program reported that they were less likely to commit rape than were men who did not participate in the program (Schewe & O'Donohue, 1993). However, the effectiveness of primary prevention programs in reducing actual sexually aggressive behavior is unknown.

Conclusion

Rates of perpetration of sexual aggression and sexual victimization are lower among Asian Americans than among other groups. These lower rates may be associated with a lower prevalence of risk factors among Asian Americans that are associated with perpetration and victimization. Moreover, Asian cultural restraints on sexual and impulsive behavior may serve as protective factors. However, there have not been empirical investigations of the role of culture in the low rates of Asian American sexual aggression. Research is necessary to determine the relative contributions of cultural, developmental, motivational, and situational factors in perpetration and victimization among Asian Americans.

References

Abbey, A., Ross, L. T., McDuffie, D., & McAuslan, P. (1996). Alcohol and dating risk factors for sexual assault among college women. *Psychology of Women Quarterly, 20*, 147–169.

American Psychological Association Commission on Violence and Youth. (1993). *Violence and youth: Psychology's response.* Washington, DC: American Psychological Association.

Baumeister, R. F., Smart, L., & Boden, J. M. (1996). Relation of threatened egotism to violence and aggression: The dark side of high self-esteem. *Psychological Review, 103*, 5–33.

Briere, J., & Runtz, M. (1993). Childhood sexual abuse: Long-term sequelae and implications for psychological assessment. *Journal of Interpersonal Violence, 8*, 312–330.

Buss, D. M., & Schmitt, D. P. (1993). Sexual strategies theory: A contextual evolutionary analysis of human mating. *Psychological Review, 100*, 204–232.

Cochran, S. D., Mays, V. M., & Leung, L. (1991). Sexual practices of heterosexual Asian American young adults. Implications for risk of HIV infection. *Archives of Sexual Behavior, 20*, 381–391.

DeKeseredy, W. S., & Kelly, K. (1995). Sexual abuse in Canadian university and college dating relationships: The contribution of male peer support. *Journal of Family Violence, 10*, 41–53.

Dion, K. L., & Dion, K. K. (1993). Gender and ethnocultural comparisons in styles of love. *Psychology of Women Quarterly, 17*, 463–473.

Federal Bureau of Investigation. (1994). *Uniform crime reports for the United States, 1993.* Washington, DC: U.S. Government Printing Office.

Foa, E. B., Rothbaum, B. O., & Steketee, G. S. (1993). Treatment of rape victims. *Journal of Interpersonal Violence, 8*, 256–276.

Gidycz, C. A., Coble, C. N., Latham, L., & Layman, M. J. (1993). Sexual assault experience in adulthood and prior victimization experiences. *Psychology of Women Quarterly, 17*, 151–168.

Gidycz, C. A., Hanson, K., & Layman, M. J. (1995). A prospective analysis of the relationships among sexual assault experiences: An extension of previous findings. *Psychology of Women Quarterly, 19*, 5–29.

Gilbert, B. J., Heesacker, M., & Gannon, L. J. (1991). Changing the sexual aggression-supportive attitudes of men: A psychoeducational intervention. *Journal of Counseling Psychology, 38*, 197–203.

Gillmore, M. R., Hawkins, J. D., Catalano, R. F., Day, L. E., Moore, M., & Abbott, R. (1991). Structure of problem behaviors in preadolescence. *Journal of Consulting and Clinical Psychology, 59*, 499–506.

Gold, S. R., & Clegg, C. L. (1990). Sexual fantasies of college students with coercive experiences and coercive attitudes. *Journal of Interpersonal Violence, 5*, 464–473.

Hall, G. C. N. (1996). *Theory-based assessment, treatment, and prevention of sexual aggression.* New York: Oxford University Press.

Hall, G. C. N., & Barongan, C. (1997). Prevention of sexual aggression: Sociocultural risk and protective factors. *American Psychologist, 52*, 5–14.

Hall, G. C. N., & Hirschman, R. (1991). Toward a theory of sexual aggression: A quadripartite model. *Journal of Consulting and Clinical Psychology, 59*, 662–669.

Hanson, K. A., & Gidycz, C. A. (1993). Evaluation of a sexual assault prevention program. *Journal of Consulting and Clinical Psychology, 61*, 1046–1052.

Hill, H. M., Soriano, F. I., Chen, S. A., & LaFromboise, T. D. (1994). Sociocultural factors in the etiology and prevention of violence among ethnic minority youth. In L. D. Eron, J. H. Gentry, & P. Schlegel (Eds.), *Reason to hope: A psychosocial perspective on violence and youth* (pp. 59–97). Washington, DC: American Psychological Association.

Himelein, M. J. (1995). Risk factors for sexual victimization in dating: A longitudinal study of college women. *Psychology of Women Quarterly, 19*, 31–48.

Ho, C. K. (1990). An analysis of domestic violence in Asian American communities: A multicultural approach to counseling. *Women and Therapy, 9*, 129–150.

Huang, K., & Uba, L. (1992). Premarital sexual behavior among Chinese college students in the United States. *Archives of Sexual Behavior, 21*, 227–240.

Kendall-Tackett, K. A., Williams, L. M., & Finkelhor, D. (1993). Impact of sexual abuse on children: A review and synthesis of recent empirical studies. *Psychological Bulletin, 113*, 164–180.

Koss, M. P. (1993). Rape: Scope, impact, interventions, and public policy responses. *American Psychologist, 48*, 1062–1069.

Koss, M. P., & Dinero, T. E. (1989). Discriminant analysis of risk factors for sexual victimization among a national sample of college women. *Journal of Consulting and Clinical Psychology, 57*, 242–250.

Koss, M. P., Gidycz, C. A., & Wisniewski, N. (1987). The scope of rape: Incidence and prevalence of sexual aggression and victimization in a national sample of higher education students. *Journal of Consulting and Clinical Psychology, 55*, 162–170.

Malamuth, N. M. (1988). A multidimensional approach to sexual aggression: Combining measures of past behavior and present likelihood. In R. A. Prentky & V. L. Quinsey (Eds.), *Human sexual aggression: Current perspectives* (pp. 123–132). New York: New York Academy of Sciences.

Malamuth, N. M., Linz, D., Heavey, C. L., Barnes, G., & Acker, M. (1995). Using the confluence model of sexual aggression to predict men's conflict with women: A 10-year follow-up study. *Journal of Personality and Social Psychology, 69*, 353–369.

Markus, H. R., & Kitayama, S. (1994). The cultural construction of self and emotion: Implications for social behavior. In S. Kitayama & H. R. Markus (Eds.), *Emotion and culture: Empirical studies of mutual influence* (pp. 89–130). Washington, DC: American Psychological Association.

Marshall, W. L., & Barbaree, H. E. (1984). A behavioral view of rape. *International Journal of Law and Psychiatry, 7*, 51–77.

Messman, T. L., & Long, P. J. (1996). Child sexual abuse and its relationship to revictimization in adult women: A review. *Clinical Psychology Review, 16*, 397–420.

Miller, S. L., & Simpson, S. S. (1991). Courtship violence and social control: Does gender matter? *Law and Society Review, 25*, 335–365.

Mills, C. S., & Granoff, B. J. (1992). Date and acquaintance rape among a sample of college students. *Social Work, 37*, 504–509.

Mori, L., Bernat, J. A., Glenn, P. A., Selle, L. L., & Zarate, M. G. (1995). Attitudes toward rape: Gender and ethnic differences across Asian and Caucasian college students. *Sex Roles, 32*, 457–467.

Muehlenhard, C. L., & MacNaughton, J. S. (1988). Women's beliefs about women who "lead men on." *Journal of Social and Clinical Psychology, 7*, 65–79.

Quinsey, V. L., Rice, M. E., & Harris, G. T. (1995). Actuarial prediction of sexual recidivism. *Journal of Interpersonal Violence, 10*, 85–105.

Rodgers, J. L., & Rowe, D. C. (1993). Social contagion and adolescent sexual behavior: A developmental EMOSA model. *Psychological Review, 100*, 479–510.

Russell, D. E. H. (1984). *Sexual exploitation: Rape, child sexual abuse, and workplace harassment.* Beverly Hills, CA: Sage.

Schewe, P., & O'Donohue, W. (1993). Rape prevention: Methodological problems and new directions. *Clinical Psychology Review, 13*, 667–682.

Seto, M. C., & Barbaree, H. E. (1995). The role of alcohol in sexual aggression. *Clinical Psychology Review, 15*, 545–566.

Sorenson, S. B., Siegel, J. M., Golding, J. M., & Stein, J. A. (1991). Repeated sexual victimization. *Violence and Victims, 6*, 299–308.

Sprecher, S., & Regan, P. C. (1996). College virgins: How men and women perceive their sexual status. *Journal of Sex Research, 33*, 3–15.

Sue, D. W., & Sue, D. (1990). *Counseling the culturally different: Theory and practice* (2nd ed.). New York: Wiley.

Sue, S., & Morishima, J. (1982). *The mental health of Asian Americans.* San Francisco: Jossey-Bass.

Triandis, H. C. (1995). *Individualism and collectivism.* Boulder, CO: Westview.

Triandis, H. C., Bontempo, R., Villareal, M. J., Asai, M., & Lucca, N. (1988). Individualism and collectivism: Cross-cultural perspectives on self-ingroup relationships. *Journal of Personality and Social Psychology, 54,* 323–338.

Uba, L. (1994). *Asian Americans: Personality patterns, identity, and mental health.* New York: Guilford Press.

Urquiza, A. J., & Goodlin-Jones, B. L. (1994). Child sexual abuse and adult re-victimization with women of color. *Violence and Victims, 9,* 223–232.

Vicary, J. R., Klingaman, L. R., & Harkness, W. L. (1995). Risk factors associated with date rape and sexual assault of adolescent girls. *Journal of Adolescence, 18,* 289–306.

Wyatt, G. E. (1989). Reexamining factors predicting Afro-American and White American women's age at first coitus. *Archives of Sexual Behavior, 18,* 271–298.

Wyatt, G. E., Guthrie, D., & Notgrass, C. M. (1992). Differential effects of women's child sexual abuse and subsequent sexual revictimization. *Journal of Consulting and Clinical Psychology, 60,* 167–173.

Yoshihama, M., Parekh, A. L., & Boyington, D. (1991). Dating violence in Asian/Pacific communities. In B. Levy (Ed.), *Dating violence: Young women at risk* (pp. 184–195). Seattle: Seal Press.

Zane, N. W. S., Sue, S., Hu, L., & Kwon, J. (1991). Asian-American assertion: A social learning analysis of cultural differences. *Journal of Counseling Psychology, 38,* 63–70.

Chapter 37
Token Resistance to Sex: New Perspectives on an Old Stereotype

Charlene L. Muehlenhard
Carie S. Rodgers

This intriguing, easy-to-follow study contains candid respondent narratives guaranteed to evoke thoughtful reader reactions. The fact that Muehlenhard, a feminist psychologist, is a noted authority on the issue of token resistance (i.e., "does no mean yes" or "do nice girls say no") can quickly be confirmed with a perusal of the article's bibliography. Although sexuality researchers typically only use survey responses in their data collection, this contribution is unique in its use of first person case studies.

Sexually active students will probably ask themselves several questions after reading this selection. Have I ever said "no" when I really wanted to have sexual intercourse and intended to do so? What role, if any, has the "swept away" phenomenon played in my sexual intercourse experience? Has male domination been a factor in instances when, as a female, I said "no" and meant "no," but sexual intercourse followed? What are the implications of implied consent versus verbal consent to have sexual intercourse? Being clear about one's own sexual intercourse experience or one's intentions for eventually engaging in sexual intercourse will add a dimension of reason that can take the "mis" out of miscommunication for women and men. A not-to-be-missed article.

The traditional sexual script dictates that women "are not supposed to indicate directly their sexual interest or engage freely in sexuality," and that men are supposed to "take the initiative even when a woman indicates verbally that she is unwilling to have sex (presumably because of the male belief that a woman's initial resistance is only token)" (Check & Malamuth, 1983, p. 344). This script incorporates the idea of "token resistance," which can be defined as refusing or resisting sexual activity while intending to engage in that activity. The traditional sexual script perpetuates the belief that women's refusals of sexual advances are often insincere and need not be taken seriously.

Popular culture has a long history of perpetuating the idea that women say "no" when they mean yes. This idea appeared in Louisa May Alcott's *Little Women* (1868–1869/1968) and in Jane Austen's (1813/1931) *Pride and Prejudice*. Many popular movies and television programs, as well as pornography, have incorporated the theme of token resistance (Cowan, Lee, Levy, & Snyder, 1988; Warshaw, 1994). There is both anecdotal and laboratory evidence that some men do not believe women's refusals. Anecdotally, women have reported cases of attempted and completed rape in which the male perpetrator seemed to believe that their resistance was insincere (Warshaw, 1994). In one laboratory study, men read a scenario in which a modestly dressed woman said "no" to her date's sexual advances three times and tried to move away (Muehlenhard, Linton, Felts, & Andrews, 1985). When the men were asked to rate how much the woman wanted to have sexual intercourse, their mean rating was 4.5 on a scale of 1 to 9. Further evidence came from the men's ratings of how justified the woman's date was in having sexual intercourse with her under these circumstances (rape-justifiability ratings) and how likely they themselves would be to behave similarly (self-likelihood ratings). Men's initial rape-justifiability and self-likelihood ratings decreased significantly when they were instructed to assume that the woman really meant no when she said "no," suggesting that the men had not initially believed her refusals. In another study, men watched a videotaped depiction of a woman and man on a date. Even when the woman told the man that she did not want to do "anything more than kiss," many men indicated that it was likely that she wanted to engage in petting and sexual intercourse (Muehlenhard, Andrews, & Beal, 1996). When asked directly, men have estimated that between 31 and 45 percent (B. A. Hunter & Shotland, 1994) of women have engaged in token resistance to sex.

Previous research has shown that some women do, in fact, report having experienced the following situation, which has commonly been used as an operational definition of token resistance to sexual intercourse:

> You were with a guy who wanted to engage in sexual intercourse and you wanted to also, but for some reason you indicated that you didn't want to, although you had every intention to and were willing to engage in sexual intercourse. In other words, you indicated "no" and you meant "yes." (Muehlenhard & Hollabaugh, 1988, p. 874)

The percentages of U.S. and Japanese college women in various studies who reported engaging in token resistance to sexual intercourse, as described previously, have been surprisingly consistent, ranging between 37 and 40 percent (Muehlenhard & McCoy, 1991; Shotland & Hunter, 1995; Sprecher, Hatfield, Cortese, Potapova, & Levitskaya, 1994). The highest prevalence—59 percent—was found by Sprecher et al. (1994) in a sample of Russian women using a questionnaire translated into Russian; this higher prevalence might reflect cultural differences or might have involved subtle but important changes in the meaning of the question when it was translated. Taken together, these results suggest that a substantial minority of women have—at least once—indicated no to sex when they meant yes.

Shotland and Hunter (1995) challenged this conclusion. They suggested that many of the women in these studies had really meant no when they indicated no; later, however, the women may have agreed to participate in sexual intercourse without ever actually saying "yes." Due to memory consolidation, some of these women may have recalled indicating no while meaning yes. Some research findings support this conclusion. For example, in one study, some of the women reported engaging in token resistance out of fear of pregnancy or sexually transmitted diseases (STDs) (Muehlenhard & Hollabaugh, 1988). Shotland and Hunter (1995) pointed out that these concerns are not addressed by engaging in token resistance; having refused prior to sexual intercourse does nothing to protect women from pregnancy or STDs. These fears are reasons for indicating no and meaning no, however. In another study, women who reported having engaged in token resistance reported feeling significantly more negative about the incident when it resulted in sexual intercourse than when it did not (Muehlenhard & McCoy, 1991). This seems inconsistent with the definition of token resistance used on the questionnaire: "He wanted to engage in sexual intercourse and *you wanted to also*" (p. 451, italics added). Shotland and Hunter (1995) found that, in situations in which women reported engaging in token resistance, most (83 percent) reported having more than one sexual intention during the situation, saying "no" and meaning either no or maybe prior to saying "no" and meaning yes.

Perhaps Shotland and Hunter's (1995) memory consolidation hypothesis is correct. Alternatively, it may be that the research participants did not realize that situations such as indicating no but changing their minds or indicating "no" and meaning no even though in some ways they wanted to engage in sex did not fit the definition of token resistance. We conducted the present study to investigate these issues.

The stereotype is that women—and only women—engage in token resistance. If men engage in this behavior, token resistance can no longer be viewed as a gender-specific behavior in which women are stereotyped as manipulative teases. In fact, some researchers have found that significantly more men than women reported having engaged in token resistance to sexual intercourse (Sprecher et al., 1994). Others, however, have reported no gender differences in this behavior (B. A. Hunter & Shotland, 1994). Thus, we also investigated whether men engage in token resistance. Most studies of token resistance, with one exception (O'Sullivan & Allgeier, 1994), have investigated token resistance to heterosexual intercourse. In the present study, we gave respondents the opportunity to report token resistance to any type of sexual activity, rather than limiting their reports to sexual intercourse. Instead of describing a situation and asking respondents merely to indicate whether they had or had not experienced such a situation, we asked them to describe what took place in their own words. By allowing respondents to relay their own accounts, we hoped to learn whether they meant "yes" when they indicated "no," or whether they changed their intentions as the situation progressed, or whether they never meant "yes" at all. They could also report situations involving homosexual as well as heterosexual behavior.

Method

Respondents were 65 female and 64 male introductory psychology students at the University of Kansas. Their mean age was 18.9 for the women and 19.4 for the men. Most (90.7 percent), of the participants were White/European/European American.

Respondents were asked about their experiences in three situations. The first situation (Situation A) was as follows:

> You were with a guy [for women's questionnaires]/girl [for men's questionnaires] you had never had sexual intercourse with before. He/she wanted to engage in sexual intercourse, and you wanted to also, but for some reason you indicated that you didn't want to, although you had every intention to and were willing to engage in sexual intercourse. In other words, you indicated "no" and you meant "yes."

The second situation (Situation B) was identical except that it began, "You were with a guy/girl you had previously had sexual intercourse with." The third situation (Situation C) was gender neutral and included any sexual activity with a new or previous partner. It read,

> You were with someone who wanted to engage in some type of sexual activity (such as kissing, or caressing, or oral sex, etc.) with you, and you wanted to also, but for some reason you indicated that you didn't want to, although you had every intention to and were willing to engage in sexual activity. In other words, you indicated "no" and you meant "yes."

Respondents were asked to indicate how many times they had been involved in each situation. If they had been involved in all three situations, they were asked to pick two to describe. If they had been in only one situation, they were asked to describe that situation and then make up a fictitious situation and describe it. If they had never been in any of the situations, they were asked to make up two situations and describe both. They checked blanks indicating whether each situation was real or imagined. We disregarded the fictitious narratives during the analyses.

Respondents were asked to describe the two situations in detail. They were then asked to list reasons why they had wanted to engage in sexual intercourse or sexual activity, reasons why they had not wanted to engage in sexual intercourse or activity (if any), and whether these reasons had changed over time. They were asked why they had said "no" when they meant "yes." Other questions involved their and their partner's feelings immediately after the situation and currently, long-term effects on their relationship, whether they would do anything differently if they could replay the situation, whether they had been using alcohol or drugs, and if so what effect they thought this had had. All the questions were open-ended.

Results

Frequency of Token Resistance

Contrary to the stereotype, women were not more likely than men to report token resistance; in fact, there was a trend in which more men (82.5 percent) than women (67.7 percent) reported having engaged in token resistance in at least one situation. Significantly more men than women reported having engaged in token resistance in situations involving sexual intercourse (Situations A and/or B). Broken down by situation, significantly more men than women endorsed Situation A (sexual intercourse with a new partner); there was a similar trend for Situation C (any type of sexual activity). The only situation not endorsed more often by men than by women was Situation B (sexual intercourse with a previous partner).

Qualitative Descriptions: Evidence of Misinterpretation

Respondents' qualitative descriptions of their experiences cast doubt on the percentages reported in the previous section. Respondents' narratives often indicated that they had misinterpreted our questions.

Confusion about desires and intentions. Many respondents described situations in which they wanted to engage in sexual intercourse or other sexual activity but did not intend to do so; they indicated no and meant no. They seemed to have disregarded the phrase "you had every intention to and were willing to engage in sexual intercourse/sexual activity." For example, one woman wrote the following:

I met a fellow at an amusement park. I ended up spending most of the day with him. At the end of the day he wanted to have sex in the woods. During the day we had kissed and hugged—it was the romance of it! Anyhow that night I wanted to also. I like sex and I liked him but the whole thing wrong was that I really didn't know him or his sexual past. Those two things were too large of a negative and so although my body wanted him my mind knew better. Besides I feel that if you're going to have sex just because your body says it wants

to—it won't be half as good as when your heart, soul, mind, and body say yes. By the way, we didn't have sex! (#209A)

A male respondent relayed the following:

I was with a woman that I had a past relationship with several years ago. We had been intimate numerous times throughout the course of our relationship. We went out together on a date, "no strings attached" and with no obligations to each other. Late in the evening, after returning to her apartment she wanted to engage in sexual intercourse. I was feeling fairly aroused and decided it would be a pleasant experience except; both her roommates were home in their separate rooms, she was obviously a bit intoxicated, as was I, and third, neither I, nor she, had any birth control device. Confusing because I had not been with her in a monogamous relationship for over two years, I was unsure about her sexual habits and decided not to "do the nasty." We slept together that night without engaging in intercourse. The following morning we both agreed it was the best thing not to have done it. (#130B)

One woman described a situation in which she was attracted to a man but said "no" to sexual intercourse. Her experience meets the legal definition of rape in Kansas:

. . . I was very sexually attracted to a guy in my senior class. We went to homecoming together. After the dance, we got plowed and one thing led to another. I can remember him being on top of me and hearing myself say "No." Then I remember saying, "We're really gonna do this, aren't we?" However, I did not put up any sort of fight. . . .

Why did you indicate no when you meant yes? I'm not sure that I ever really meant yes, but I am sure that my no was pretty pathetic. If the guy can't understand a simple no, how would you convince him with a definite NO! (#224A)

All three of these respondents reported being attracted to the other person, but none of them intended to engage in intercourse. These narratives did not meet our definition because the respondents said "no" and meant no.

Confusion about indicating 'no' and meaning 'yes' simultaneously. Some respondents did not seem to understand that we were asking them about situations in which they indicated no and meant yes simultaneously. They reported indicating no while meaning no but changing their minds. For example:

> We had been dating for a month and on previous occasions I had not allowed intercourse to occur. I knew he wanted to, but something was holding me back. He wanted to talk about it, which I found difficult. When you're not for sure what you're thinking it is difficult to express to someone else. I told him I wasn't secure enough in our relationship and he asked what I meant by this. He wanted clarification on any vague answers I gave. He commented that women don't always express what they are thinking. He said he hated using the word "special," but felt this would be something special shared between us. It was the next progression in our relationship. I told him that for me if I agreed to sleep with him, it would be an exclusive relationship. He wondered if I wanted to date around or if I was seeing other people. I wanted to sleep with him, but I didn't know how he viewed the relationship. With an understanding that our relationship is exclusive, I felt more secure. I didn't really say "no" and mean yes, we both knew I wanted to say "yes" but couldn't. After our discussion I changed my mind. (#208A)

Confusion about what sexual activity was refused and what sexual activity was intended. In some cases the sexual activity that respondents indicated no to was not the same sexual activity that they intended to engage in. They may have said "no" to sexual activity in one situation while intending to engage in sexual activity in a different situation. One man reported the following:

> I had been after a girl in my math class since the beginning of the year. I liked her emotionally as well as sexually. I saw her at a party and we were both very

drunk. After some small talk we went to a bedroom and started to mess around. She seemed very horny and I probably could have fucked her. But I thought if I fucked her now she would probably think I used her and would never talk to me again. So in order to start taking her out and fuck more often I didn't screw her that night. (#157A)

In this narrative, he reported indicating no to sexual intercourse on that night and intending to have sexual intercourse with her later. This did not meet our definition of token resistance.

Other misunderstandings of the definition. Respondents also misunderstood other aspects of our definition. In some cases, their partner had not wanted to engage in sexual activity:

> We had just got back from a bar. We went to this creek that had a 15-foot waterfall. We began kissing and caressing. She said she'd better stop because she was two years older than me. I indicated that I agreed when I didn't care how much older she was.
>
> *Why did you indicate no when you meant yes?* Because I didn't want to make her mad or force her to do any sexual activity. (#105C)

In other cases, the respondent had indicated "yes" and meant "yes" but felt reservations afterwards:

> One night stand—We were at my apartment and had been drinking. My roommate had brought back two women of which I had not met. We all got drunk and I started mashing with the girl. We later moved to the bedroom where she proceeded with fellatio. We never saw each other again. I loved it but felt kind of lost like I shouldn't have done it afterwards. (#104C)

Other misinterpretations involved indicating no and meaning no without ever wanting to engage in sex, indicating yes and meaning yes but being interrupted, indicating and feeling ambivalence, and having a partner misinterpret the respondent's behavior to mean no.

Raters' Coding of the Narratives

Because of the large number of women and men who misinterpreted our questions, we coded each narrative as to whether it met our definition of token resistance. Raters coded each narrative as token resistance or not token resistance according to the following criteria:

1. For a situation to be coded as token resistance, the respondent actually had to plan or intend to engage in sexual intercourse or other sexual activity.

2. For a narrative to be coded as token resistance, the act of indicating no and the intention to engage in sexual activity had to occur simultaneously.

3. The sexual activity that was refused and the sexual activity that a respondent intended to engage in had to be the same activity in the same situation.

4. For some of the criteria, we relied on the respondent's own interpretation of the situation.

Narratives were coded by two female and three male undergraduates, with each narrative being coded by one female and one male rater.

Of the 177 nonfictitious narratives respondents wrote as examples of token resistance, only 20 (11.3 percent) were coded as meeting our definition. For Situation A (heterosexual intercourse with a new partner), only 5.0 percent ($n = 1$) of the women's and 2.8 percent ($n = 1$) of the men's nonfictitious narratives met our definition. For Situation B (heterosexual intercourse with a previous partner), these percentages were 34.6 percent ($n = 9$) for women and 26.1 percent ($n = 6$) for men; for Situation C (any sexual activity with a new or previous partner of either gender), these percentages were 4.8 percent ($n = 1$) for women and 7.1 percent ($n = 2$) for men.

It was not possible to calculate the percentage of the entire sample who had actually engaged in token resistance to sex. Nevertheless, it is likely that the percentages of women and men who initially reported engaging in token resistance were extreme overestimates.

Themes Emerging From the Narratives

All the narratives that fit our definition of token resistance involved heterosexual interactions. We identified five major themes: moral concerns and discomfort about sex, adding interest to a relationship, wanting not to be taken for granted, testing a partner's response, and power and control over the other person.

Moral concerns and discomfort about sex. Two of the narratives, both written by women, reflected concerns about being "good." This example involved a new partner:

> I was with my boyfriend at my house, in my room, in the middle of the night. He had come over to my house and snuck in. He was there for a long time and we talked. Then we were kissing and one thing just led to another. We had talked about sexual intercourse many times before but the topic of conversation didn't come up that night until I said "no." Once I said "no," he wouldn't engage in sexual intercourse. I thought and felt I should say "no" because I was unsure if it was the right thing to morally do, yet I had every intention of participating in sexual intercourse that night. After I said "no" we talked about our situation, the circumstances of the moment, and what we had been raised believing.
>
> *Why did you indicate no when you meant yes?* It was what a "good girl" would say. (#230A)

Adding interest to an ongoing relationship. Contrary to the stereotype, most of the narratives that met our definition of token resistance took place in the context of an ongoing sexual relationship. Five women and one man wrote about adding interest to an ongoing relationship. Most reported positive consequences, and most thought that their partner was aware of the game they were playing. One woman reported that both she and her boyfriend said "no" when meaning yes:

The guy was a boyfriend of mine that I dated for two years. Throughout the relationship there were many times we would play around and joke about sex. I would say "no," even though I really wanted and intended to and he would either continue making advances or performing foreplay until I said "yes" or he would tease me by stopping any activity we were doing and would say he didn't want to fool around or have sex either. It was all in good fun. (#261B)

Thus, token resistance was sometimes used—successfully or unsuccessfully—to prevent a sexual encounter from becoming routine or to prevent sex from moving directly to intercourse.

Wanting not to be taken for granted. Token resistance in an ongoing relationship sometimes involved wanting not to be taken for granted. One woman described wanting to alter the routine in which she consented whenever her boyfriend initiated:

This happened once or twice with my boyfriend—we've been dating for about two years. Sometimes I feel like he takes me for granted, that he has most of the control over where we go, what we do, etc., etc. We were in my room, looking for a certain record he needed right then. Before he had said he had to hurry, but suddenly he pulled me close to him and started kissing me. I laughed and felt happy but at the same time I'm thinking—before he was so rushed—he always gets his way. So when he pulled me to the floor I said "No! You don't have time and neither do I, besides my roommate will be home any minute." But he knew I wanted him and I knew he would keep on trying to persuade me so I think it was more like a game—we both enjoyed it!

Why did you indicate no when you meant yes? I think I wanted it to be my decision not his. Mostly, he initiates and I consent. However sometimes that makes me feel like it's only his decision—he expects me to consent! (#234B)

Testing a partner's response. Two respondents, one woman and one man, reported engaging in token resistance to test their partners. For example:

I have been seeing the same guy for almost three years. At times I have every intention of having intercourse with him and end up saying "no." I think some of the time I just want to see what his reaction will be. I start wondering what our relationship would be like without sex, so I feel guilty sometimes when we do. He has told me that it makes him feel as though he's making me do something I have no desire to do. This is not the case. I have the same intentions, but I want to be sure that he cares for me beyond sex.

Why did you indicate no when you meant yes? To test him. I wanted to see if he would take the time out to show a true interest in my feelings. (#212B)

Thus, this respondent wanted information about how her partner would react to her refusal and whether their relationship was based on more than sex.

Power and control over the other person. Five narratives—four narratives written by three different men and one narrative written by a woman—reflected a desire for power over the other person. These narratives ranged from innocuous to manipulative and hostile. A woman wrote the following about an ongoing sexual relationship:

A guy who I was madly in lust for named _____ was my first. _____ and I didn't have a real relationship other than sexual and friendliness. He was always going out with other girls so when we had sex it was a big secret. I couldn't go out with him because he was my older brother's friend. Anyway it seems that _____ would always have to persuade me into having sex. I always wanted to be with him. Although the sex part was not really important. I knew when I would see him that we would end up together. Being in a room and having him there with me kissing and touching me, I knew I would be all over him. However, at times I would say "No _____" "No!" He would continue to persuade me. Sometimes he was unable. I think I said no because I like the fact that I was in control. I would tease him and that would make him want more and more.

Why did you indicate no when you meant yes? I think I said no to tease the guy so he would want more. (#213B)

Some of the narratives seemed more hostile. For example:

I met this girl at a bar. I didn't know who she was and I had never seen her before. When I met her we were both drunk it seemed. We started talking and then she wanted me to sit next to her. At this point I had a feeling that she wanted to get "fresh" with me. This turned me on and right away I thought about having sexual intercourse. As the night narrowed down I was thinking about how she really wants to "get busy." I wanted to just take her right away and do what a male and female do best—FUCK! Then I remembered about playing the role of the inexperienced one. One thing led to another, she agreed to come to my place for the night. Boom—I knew I had her then. Now all I had to do was pretend like I didn't want to for some kind of stupid reason. I always thought that would get a girl more anxious and ready for me. It's worked most of the time. When I'm fucking them I then let them feel the wrath of what I wanted from the beginning. (#101A)

Discussion

According to the stereotype, most women—and only women—engage in token resistance to sex, saying "no" when they mean yes. According to the stereotype, this occurs primarily in new sexual relationships because women do not want to appear "easy" or are playing "hard to get" (Muehlenhard, 1988; Muehlenhard & McCoy, 1991). The present study challenged all these assumptions. In the present study, more men than women initially reported engaging in token resistance, although most of the men's and women's narratives were coded as not meeting our definition. The percentages of women and men who wrote nonfictitious narratives meeting our definition did not differ significantly. Thus, based on the present study, it

seems likely that, consistent with recent studies, men as well as women engage in token resistance to sex, but that, in this and other studies, many of the men as well as the women who report engaging in token resistance may have misunderstood the question.

The occurrence of token resistance in ongoing relationships also contradicts the stereotype that women play "hard to get" primarily with new partners. In fact, in a study of how token resistance relates to the sexual double standard, Muehlenhard and McCoy (1991) investigated only situations involving new partners. The present results suggest that individuals in ongoing relationships sometimes use token resistance for various reason.

Reasons for Saying 'No' When Meaning 'Yes'

Moral concerns and discomfort about sex. Two women mentioned such concerns. Even though both expressed intentions to engage in sexual activity, they expressed reservations. One mentioned that she had been "brought up [to think that sex] was wrong," and that she was "unsure if it was the right thing to morally do" (#230A); the other mentioned feeling "embarrassed" and "apprehensive" and trying to block out thoughts of her parents (#204B). Both mentioned wanting to behave like a "good girl." In some instances, token resistance may be a way to handle feelings of guilt. If this makes someone feel better, it may serve a useful function. These narratives seemed closest to the sexual script in which women "are not supposed to indicate directly their sexual interest or engage freely in sexuality" (Check & Malamuth, 1983, p. 344). These narratives, however, seem to reflect sincere reservations rather than concerns merely about appearing too eager.

In this study, no men mentioned moral concerns or discomfort. This might be because boys generally do not grow up internalizing "the complex of reluctances and ambivalences about sex that makes up that part of classical femininity" (A. Hunter, 1992, p. 377). Interestingly, several men mentioned not wanting to appear too eager for sex. Typically, these men expressed concern that the woman would think they were interested only in sex, when in fact they were interested in a relationship.

Adding interest to an ongoing relationship. Adding interest to an ongoing relationship was a common theme. "Apparently any continuously repetitious behavior will become boring, even sex" (Hendrick & Hendrick, 1992, p. 134). For some women saying "no" seemed to be a way to encourage sexual activity other than intercourse (sometimes called "foreplay"). For example, "I'd say no and he'd do things to me to make me say yes like kiss, fondle, or the things he knew drove me crazy" (#214B). Women are frequently dissatisfied with fast, goal-directed penile-vaginal intercourse (Crooks & Baur, 1993). Token resistance can be a way for some women to obtain sexual pleasure from sexual behaviors other than intercourse. It can be a way to resist "the dominant assumption that heterosexual intercourse (coitus) is synonymous with 'real' sex" (Gavey, 1992).

Men can be dissatisfied with goal-oriented sex as well (Zilbergeld, 1992). They may be less likely to use token resistance in such situations, however; to the extent that men "run the show," they are likely to have other ways of getting the sexual behaviors they want.

Wanting not to be taken for granted. The traditional sexual script assigns the role of initiation to men and assigns the responsibility for regulating sexual activity to women (Crooks & Baur, 1993). "According to this script, males had positive control in a sexual encounter (using any available strategy to initiate sex), while females had negative control (using any available strategy to avoid having sex)" (McCormick, Brannigan, & LaPlante, 1984, p. 310). If a man makes a sexual advance, then a woman's only decision is whether to go along with it.

In this context, a woman's options are reduced to consenting or not consenting "in response to something that is *being done to her*" (Gavey, 1992, p. 337, italics in the original). If a woman in this situation always consents, she in effect has no control at all.

Even if she has become sexually aroused, agreeing to have sex can be seen as being "had by someone who knows how to arouse the traitor body" (A. Hunter, 1992, p. 376). Not automatically agreeing whenever her partner makes an advance that arouses her can be a way for a woman to gain some control over a situation that she did not initiate. Refusing occasionally may give her some degree of control—even if she intends eventually to say "yes."

Conversely, the traditional sexual script dictates that men take advantage of every sexual opportunity, responding automatically to any sexual stimulus (Zilbergeld, 1992). This pressure can be a burden for men.

Testing a partner's response. Another theme involved testing a partner. One woman reported saying "no" to her partner "to see if he would take the time out to show a true interest in my feelings" (#212B). This is consistent with the stereotype of men's "being only after one thing" (Hunter, 1992). Many men espouse norms in which the goal is to obtain sex with many different women by lying, getting them intoxicated, or—if necessary—using physical coercion (Muehlenhard & Falcon, 1990). In this context, token resistance could allow a woman to evaluate whether her partner is interested in her for anything other than sex.

Power and control. "In our culture, male eroticism is wedded to power" (Griffin, 1971, p. 29). This culture perpetuates the idea that "sex would lose its sexiness if it no longer included the element of the 'hunt'" (Hunter, 1992, p. 376). Some theorists have described the "cultural and political meanings attached to penile penetration of women (being 'had,' 'possessed,' 'taken,' 'fucked')" [Kitzinger, Wilkinson, & Perkins, 1992, p. 313]. Consistent with this construction of heterosexual sex, several men described how they used token resistance to control women. Interestingly, despite the stereotype of the sly, manipulative woman, in this study the most consciously manipulative narratives were written by men. Only one woman wrote a narrative coded as reflecting power and control. She described teasing a man she "was madly in lust for" in order to "make him want more and more" (#213B).

In summary, respondents who reported token resistance seemed to have many motivations. Many of the narratives were understandable in the context of the traditional sexual script and the construction of sexuality in our society. However, others indicated that many people do not act in accordance with this traditional script.

Conceptual Issues in Defining Token Resistance

It was often difficult to judge whether a situation corresponded to our definition. One reason for this difficulty was that any one act may have multiple motivations. Another reason was that the concepts involved in the definition, such as wanting and intending, are themselves complex.

Researchers often ask whether someone did or did not want to engage in a particular sexual act. Conceptualizing sex as either wanted or unwanted is too simplistic in several ways. First, wanting is not an all-or-nothing state; there are degrees of wanting. Second, there are many dimensions along which a sexual act can be wanted or unwanted. This concept is exemplified by the statement, "although my body wanted him my mind knew better" (#209A). Physiological sexual arousal, emotional comfort, and so forth can be regarded as separate dimensions, with a sexual act being more or less wanted on each dimension. Third, sexual acts can have consequences. A person could want the sexual act but not want the consequences (e.g., disease, a reputation as "promiscuous"). Conversely, a person could not want the sexual act but want the consequences (e.g., pleasing the partner). Finally, all of the above can change over time as individuals become more or less sexually aroused, as they and their partner interact, and so forth. Thus, when researchers ask respondents to think of a situation in which they were with someone "who wanted to engage in sexual intercourse and you wanted to also," we are asking them to reduce a highly complex situation to a black-and-white decision about whether they did or did not want to engage in the be-

havior. Respondents often described ambivalence in which sexual behaviors were neither totally wanted with no reservations nor totally unwanted with no desire to engage in them.

Intentions are also complex. Intentions are partly a function of what a person wants, which is complex. Intentions vary over time. Sometimes people engage in behaviors spontaneously, without ever really intending to do so. Intentions are often contingent on circumstances. For example, if a man says to a woman, "I intend to have sex with you tonight," this might seem frightening to her, as if he intends to engage in sex with her regardless of her desires. When people speak of intentions to engage in sexual intercourse, these intentions are usually contingent on the other person's desires at the time, their own desires at the time, events occurring between the time of the intention and the time of the act, and so forth. When researchers ask people to think about situations in which "you had every intention to and were willing to engage in sexual intercourse," we are not asking about simple all-or-none phenomena.

Another conceptual question involves what is necessary for someone to indicate "no." According to the traditional sexual script, sex is something that men initiate; if men do not initiate, then nothing will happen (Gavey, 1992). This may result in gender asymmetry in the conceptualization of token resistance. A man might think—perhaps correctly—that nothing will happen unless he makes it happen. In this case, he might equate doing nothing with indicating that he did not want to engage in sex. In the present study, for example, when asked why he indicated no, one man wrote, "It really didn't come to that. I just didn't act on the situation. She was naked but I didn't act" (#106A). Conversely, a woman might think—perhaps correctly—that, even if she does nothing, the man may still initiate; he might interpret her lack of resistance as consent. Thus, for a man, doing nothing might be interpreted as indicating no, whereas for a woman, doing nothing might be interpreted as indicating yes. For a woman, indicating no might mean actively refusing—something that a man might find unnecessary.

An additional source of gender asymmetry in token resistance involves the component of the definition stating that the other person "wanted to engage in sexual intercourse." Given the script that women "are not supposed to indicate directly their sexual interest" (Check & Malamuth, 1983, p. 344), men are probably less likely than women to be in a situation in which their partner is openly expressing desire for sexual intercourse.

Methodological Issues in Defining Token Resistance

Compared with previous studies, in this study larger percentages of both men and women initially reported engaging in token resistance to sexual intercourse. These discrepancies may have occurred because, unlike previous studies, we asked respondents about two different situations involving sexual intercourse, one specifying a new partner and one specifying a previous partner, thus providing respondents with more memory cues. Consistent with this line of reasoning, in studies of child sexual abuse and rape, multiple screening questions asking about different circumstances to prompt respondents' memories generally elicit higher prevalence rates than do single, more general screening questions (Koss, 1993). In addition, rather than asking respondents whether they had been involved in various situations, we asked them how many times they had been involved in various situations, which might have had a normalizing effect.

In some studies (Muehlenhard & Hollabaugh, 1988; Shotland & Hunter, 1995), respondents were first asked whether they had ever indicated no to sex when they meant no, even though in a way they wanted to engage in sex; next they were asked whether they had said "no" when they meant maybe; finally they were asked whether they had said "no" when they meant yes. Asking questions in this sequence might help respondents distinguish between saying "no" and meaning yes and saying "no" and meaning no or maybe, thus

decreasing the number of "false positives"—reports of token resistance based solely on confusion about the definition. In addition, in the present study follow-up questions such as "Why did you indicate no when you meant yes?" seemed helpful in clarifying whether respondents understood the definition.

Limitations

Our sample size, though adequate for a qualitative analysis, was too small to answer some questions, such as whether there are significant gender differences in token resistance. Additionally, percentages based on small samples are less stable than those based on larger samples. Our sample consisted of fairly young, mostly White/European American college students. Although this was similar to samples used in most previous studies and thus was appropriate for questioning the results of those studies, these results would not necessarily generalize to other groups.

Conclusions

Most women and most men initially reported having engaged in token resistance, although their narratives indicated that in most of these instances they had said "no" and meant no. The definition of token resistance specified on our questionnaire was identical or virtually identical to those used in other studies (Muehlenhard & McCoy, 1991; Shotland & Hunter, 1991; Sprecher et al., 1994); thus, it seems likely that many respondents in previous studies had also misunderstood the definition. Consequently, it seems likely that the percentages reported in previous studies overestimated the actual prevalence of token resistance.

Although the definition of token resistance used in this and other studies seems clear to us, apparently it was unclear to respondents. Confusion between saying "no" and meaning yes versus saying "no" and meaning no even though in some ways one would like to say "yes" is likely to perpetuate the myth that women's refusals need not be taken seriously. Although both women and men sometimes engage in token resistance to sex, most do not. All refusals should be taken seriously. Engaging in sex with someone who does not consent is rape.

References

Alcott, L. M. (1968). *Little Women*. Boston: Little, Brown. (Original work published in 1868–1869.)

Austen, J. (1931). *Pride and Prejudice*. New York: Grossett & Dunlap. (Original work published in 1813.)

Check, J. V., & Malamuth, N. M. (1983). Sex role stereotyping and reactions to depictions of stranger versus acquaintance rape. *Journal of Personality and Social Psychology, 45,* 344–356.

Cowan, G., Lee, C., Levy, D., & Snyder, D. (1988). Dominance and inequality in X-rated videocassettes. *Psychology of Women Quarterly, 12,* 299–311.

Crooks, R., & Baur, K. (1993). *Our sexuality* (5th ed.). Redwood City, CA: Benjamin/ Cummings.

Gavey, N. (1992). Technologies and effects of heterosexual coercion. *Feminism and Psychology, 2,* 325–351.

Griffin, S. (1971). Rape: The all-American crime. *Ramparts, 10,* 26–35.

Hendrick, S., & Hendrick, C. (1992). *Liking, loving, & relating*. Pacific Grove, CA: Brooks/ Cole.

Hunter, A. (1992). Same door, different closet: A heterosexual sissy's coming-out party. *Feminism and Psychology, 2,* 367–385.

Hunter, B. A., & Shotland, R. L. (1994). *"Token resistance" and compliance to sexual intercourse: Similarities and differences in men's and women's behavior*. Manuscript submitted for publication.

Kitzinger, C., Wilkinson, S., & Perkins, R. (1992). Theorizing heterosexuality. *Feminism and Psychology, 2,* 293–324.

Koss, M. P. (1993). Detecting the scope of rape: A review of prevalence research methods. *Journal of Interpersonal Violence, 8,* 198–222.

McCormick, N. B., Brannigan, G. C., & LaPlante, M. N. (1984). Social desirability in the bedroom: Role of approval motivation in sexual relationships. *Sex Roles, 11,* 303–314.

Muehlenhard, C. L. (1988). "Nice women" don't say yes and "real men" don't say no: How miscommunication and the sexual double standard can cause sexual problems. *Women and Therapy, 7,* 95–108.

Muehlenhard, C. L., Andrews, S. L., & Beal, G. K. (1996). Beyond "just saying no": Dealing with men's unwanted sexual advances in heterosexual dating contexts. *Journal of Psychology and Human Sexuality, 8,* 141–168.

Muehlenhard, C. L., & Falcon, P. L. (1990). Men's heterosocial skill and attitudes toward women as predictors of verbal sexual coercion and forceful rape. *Sex Roles, 23,* 241–259.

Muehlenhard, C. L., & Hollabaugh, L. C. (1988). Do women sometimes say no when they mean yes? The prevalence and correlates of women's token resistance to sex. *Journal of Personality and Social Psychology, 54,* 872–879.

Muehlenhard, C. L., Linton, M. A., Felts, A. S., & Andrews, S. L. (1985, June). Men's attitudes toward the justifiability of date rape: Intervening variables and possible solutions. In E. R. Allgeier (Chair), *Sexual coercion: Political issues and empirical findings*. Presented at the Midcontinent Meeting of the Society for the Scientific Study of Sex, Chicago.

Muehlenhard, C. L., & McCoy, M. L. (1991). Double standard/double bind: The sexual double standard and women's communication about sex. *Psychology of Women Quarterly, 15,* 447–461.

O'Sullivan, L. F., & Allgeier, E. R. (1994). Dissembling a stereotype: Gender differences in the use of token resistance. *Journal of Applied Social Psychology, 24,* 1035–1055.

Shotland, R. L., & Hunter, B. A. (1995). Women's "token resistant" and compliant sexual behaviors are related to uncertain sexual intentions and rape. *Personality and Social Psychology Bulletin, 21,* 226–236.

Sprecher, S., Hatfield, E., Cortese, A., Potapova, E., & Levitskaya, A. (1994). Token resistance to sexual intercourse and consent to unwanted sexual intercourse: College students' dating experiences in three countries. *Journal of Sex Research, 31,* 125–132.

Warshaw, R. (1994). *I never called it rape* (2nd ed.). New York: Harper & Row.

Zilbergeld, B. (1992). *The new male sexuality*. New York: Bantam.

Chapter 38
Sexual Harassment and Generalized Workplace Abuse

Judith A. Richman
Kathleen M. Rospenda
Stephanie J. Nawyn
Joseph A. Flaherty
Michael Fendrich
Melinda L. Drum
Timothy P. Johnson

Sexual harassment remains an often misunderstood and ill-defined concept, although the Federal Equal Opportunity Commission has operationalized its definition into two categories: "sexual harassment" and "hostile environment harassment." From "catcalls" by street crews to corporate boardroom overtures, no place seems immune to sexual harassment, not even the Oval Office. Typically, corporate human resource units react very quickly to complaints of sexual harassment, real or imagined, for fear of litigation by employees or federal intervention resulting in civil penalties.

In academic circles, policies at many institutions address sexual harassment. For example, dating between faculty and students may be prohibited, even in the absence of direct supervision or authority over students by professors. And, certainly, most schools offer faculty and staff training seminars to update their understanding of sexual harassment. The following selection describes sexual harassment and generalized workplace abuse in four occupational groups in a university setting. It is impressive because the hypotheses were derived from psychiatric epidemiological research on differential exposure to, and mental health consequences of, social stressors. The use of sophisticated instruments of measurement is noteworthy, as are the surprising conclusions offered about the relative incidence of sexual harassment compared to generalized workplace abuse. Students will find information from this selection even more valuable once they themselves become professionals in the world of work.

Research showing high rates of sexual harassment in work and educational institutions,[1–3] along with high-profile cases in the media, has established sexual harassment as a major social problem. Studies addressing the deleterious mental health consequences of sexual harassment also suggest that it has substantial public health implications.[1,4–5] Less attention has been directed to more generalized interpersonally abusive workplace experiences, since epidemiologic studies of workplace stressors have generally emphasized task-related aspects of work.[6–7] By contrast, organizational behavior studies focus greater attention on interpersonal interactions, and epidemiologic research has linked conflictual workplace interactions with psychiatric morbidity.[8]

Sexual harassment encompasses unwanted sexual advances, requests for sexual favors, and other verbal or physical conduct of a sexual nature.[9] *Quid pro quo* sexual harassment occurs when advances involve threats, bribery, or conditions of employment. Hostile-environment sexual harassment exists when harassment affects the target's ability to perform his or her job or when it creates an intimidating, hostile, or offensive working environment.[9]

Studies have shown substantial rates of sexual harassment: 42 percent among female federal workers,[10] 53 percent among female workers in the general population,[1] and 50 percent among female university students.[2] Mental health consequences include anger, depression, anxiety, and substance use and abuse.[1,4–5,11–12] Most studies have addressed situations involving a female target and thus have neglected victimization of men.[13] One study, however, suggested that men's experiences with sexual harassment are less distressful in nature because men have greater power in society.[14] Other researchers have pointed to additional sources of inequality that are inherent in hierarchies of power.[15] Consequently, men in lower-status occupational positions may be less protected from harassment than men in higher positions.

A smaller body of research has suggested that other types of degrading workplace interactions not explicitly involving gender are also highly prevalent and associated with deleterious outcomes. These involve psychologically demeaning and physically aggressive modes of interaction.[4,12] Björkqvist et al.[16] linked these experiences with symptomatic distress. Studies involving American medical trainees have shown similar linkages.[4,12]

THE CURRENT STUDY

This report studies the prevalence and mental health correlates of sexual harassment and generalized workplace abuse among men and women in 4 university occupational groups. It was hypothesized that (1) women's presumed greater exposure to sexual harassment would be complicated by a high level of victimization among lower-status men and women, (2) generalized abuse would be experienced by both genders, and (3) exposure to generalized abuse would vary inversely with hierarchical status. Exposure to harassment and abuse was hypothesized to relate to varied deleterious outcomes. These hypotheses were derived from psychiatric epidemiologic research on differential exposure to, and mental health consequences of, social stressors.[17]

Methods

Sampling

Data were obtained from a mail survey of employees of an urban American university. Occupational groups included faculty, graduate student workers and trainees (research and teaching assistants, medical residents, and postdoctoral fellows), clerical and secretarial workers, and service and maintenance workers.

Data Collection

Questionnaires were mailed to respondents' homes. The final sample of 2492 employees (52 percent response rate) included 1336 females (55 percent response rate) and 1156 males (48 percent response rate). The lower than desired response rates are reflective of the fact that the questionnaires were self-administered and contained highly sensitive material and identifiers for subsequent tracking.[18] Comparisons of the final sample with known characteristics of the total population revealed an acceptable match in terms of race and gender composition within each occupational stratum.

Measures

Sexual harassment was measured by a modified version of the Sexual Experiences Questionnaire.[19] This questionnaire included 19 items that behaviorally depict 3 types of sexual harassment. The first type, gender harassment, encompasses crude sexual comments or comments that demean the target's gender. Second, unwanted sexual attention comprises unwanted touching and repeated requests for dates. Third, sexual coercion involves demands for sexual favors that imply job-related consequences. An additional item assesses sexual assault.

Respondents rated each experience as occurring never, once, or more than once in their current job during the past year. Generalized workplace abuse was measured by a 29-item instrument, [which] assesses 5 dimensions of abuse: verbal aggression, disrespectful behavior, isolation/exclusion, threats/bribes, and physical aggression. Verbal aggression consists of hostile verbal exchanges involving yelling or swearing. Disrespectful behavior encompasses demeaning experiences such as being humiliated publicly or being talked down to. Isolation/exclusion involves having one's work contributions ignored or being excluded from important work activities. Threats or bribes encompass subtle or obvious bribes to do things deemed wrong or threats of retaliation for failing to do such things. Physical aggression involves being hit, pushed, or grabbed. Experiences were rated similarly to the Sexual Experiences Questionnaire ratings. With both instruments, experiences were scored positively only if they occurred more than once, with the exception of sexual coercion, sexual assault, and physical aggression (which were scored positively if they happened once, given their severity). Respondents were categorized as harassed or abused on the basis of these rules.

Depressive symptomatology occurring during the past week was measured by 7 items from the Center for Epidemiological Studies Depression Scale.[20–21] Anxiety during the past week was measured by the 9-item tension-anxiety factor of the Profile of Mood States.[22] Hostility during the past week was measured by the 6-item hostility dimension of the Symptom Checklist 90 Revised.[23]

Alcohol consumption was assessed for (1) frequency ("During the last 30 days, about how many days did you drink any type of alcoholic beverage?") and (2) quantity ("When you drank any type of alcoholic beverage during the last 30 days, how many drinks did you usually have per day?"). Frequency of heavy episodic drinking and drinking to intoxication were [also] measured: (1) "During the last 12 months, how often did you have 6 or more drinks of wine, beer, or liquor in a single day?" and (2) "About how often in the last 12 months did you drink enough to feel drunk, that is, where drinking noticeably affected your thinking, talking, and behavior?"

Escapist motives for drinking were assessed by 5 items tapping usual motives: to feel less tense, to escape, to cheer up, to forget things, and to forget worries. Interpersonal stress motives were measured by: to overcome feelings of inferiority, to get over being irritated or resentful, and to feel more confident in relating to others. Problem drinking was assessed by the Michigan Alcoholism Screening Test,[24] a 24-item instrument that screens for alcohol abuse or dependence. A drug inventory assessed past-year use of prescription drugs (tranquilizers, antidepressants, and sedatives), illicit drugs (marijuana/ hashish, cocaine, heroin, and psychedelics), and cigarettes.

Results

While faculty and student workers encompassed approximately equal proportions of females and males, the clerical group was disproportionately female and the service group was disproportionately male. Student workers were disproportionately younger than other groups, as expected. Faculty were disproportionately White, while clerical and service workers were disproportionately Black and student workers were predominantly White or Asian. Most faculty and student workers had graduate or professional degrees, as expected, while most other workers were high school graduates.

Prevalence of Sexual Harassment and Generalized Workplace Abuse

In the service and clerical groups, males experienced significantly higher rates of sexual harassment in general, and gender harassment in particular, while in the faculty group, females experienced significantly higher rates than males. Male service and clerical groups experienced more sexual harassment overall, and gender harassment in particular, than the other male groups. For sexual and gender harassment, there were no significant group differences in prevalence of harassment for women.

For generalized abuse, the major gender difference was that female faculty experienced higher rates of overall generalized workplace abuse, and of several of its subcomponents, than did male faculty. Male clerical and student workers, however, experienced more threats and bribes than their female counterparts. Physical aggression was experienced most frequently by male and female service workers and, to a lesser extent, clerical workers. Contrasts in the differential prevalence of sexual harassment and generalized abuse show that, across occupational groups, both genders are far more likely to experience generalized abuse than sexual harassment. More than half of the respondents in each gender/occupational group reported experiencing some form of generalized abuse.

Linkages Between Sexual Harassment, Generalized Workplace Abuse, and Mental Health

Linkages of harassment and abuse [exist] with depression, anxiety, hostility, frequency of drinking, and escapist drinking motives, and linkages also [exist] with heavy episodic drinking, drinking to intoxication, prescription drug use, and cigarette use. Neither harassment nor abuse was significantly related to quantity of drinking, interpersonal stress motives, problem-related drinking, or illicit substance abuse for men or women.

The relationships between harassment and abuse and each measure of symptomatic distress are highly significant and consistent for both genders. By contrast, the relationships with drinking outcomes and drug use are more variable. For women, (1) both harassment (in the form of unwanted attention) and abuse relate to frequency of drinking; (2) harassment relates to escapist drinking motives, drinking to intoxication, and prescription drug use; (3) abuse relates to cigarette use; and (4) neither harassment nor abuse relates to heavy episodic drinking. For men, (1) both harassment and abuse relate to heavy episodic drinking and prescription drug use; (2) harassment and abuse in the form of disrespectful behavior relate to drinking to intoxication; and (3) abuse in the form of threats or bribes relates to frequency of drinking.

Discussion

Men and women across occupational groups perceive substantial degrees of exposure to both sexual harassment and generalized workplace abuse. While sexual harassment, but not generalized workplace abuse, is illegal in the United States, the data demonstrate that generalized abuse is experienced far more frequently and is associated with deleterious outcomes in victims. Since sexual harassment and generalized workplace abuse are intercorrelated, it is possible that generalized workplace abuse may include more subtle forms of sexual harassment. For intervention and prevention purposes, legal definitions of workplace harassment could usefully broaden the domain of relevant experiences to regulate more adequately mental welfare in the workplace, as in Scandinavian countries.[17]

The data highlight the public health significance of both sexual harassment and generalized workplace abuse, which are significantly associated with a diverse range of negative mental health outcomes. Moreover, these patterns hold for both men and women. Although the strength of associations between harassment and abuse on the one hand and mental health outcomes on the other ranges from small to substantial, there is an overall pattern of negative mental health outcomes. Moreover, interpersonal stressors in the workplace may have delayed effects on mental health. The range of outcomes encompassing distress and possible self-medication with alcohol and cigarettes suggests that harassment and abuse may create an emotional climate of self-soothing behaviors in victims that, over time, leads to serious psychopathology such as problem drinking in individuals who tend to self-medicate when distressed.

Despite the dominant social construction of sexual harassment as a form of female victimization, both genders were shown to be subject to sexual harassment (mainly gender harassment) as well as to generalized workplace abuse. Moreover, the data show an interaction between gender and occupational status in the differential exposure to sexual harassment and generalized abuse in the studied population. While men were shown to be more subject to sexual harassment than women in the 2 lower-status occupations, faculty women were more exposed than faculty men and no less exposed than women in the lower-status groups. Thus, women are at greatest risk of harassment and abuse in the high occupational group and men are at greatest risk in the low occupational groups. Finally, variability in powerlessness may exist within occupational groups (e.g., female faculty are generally in lower ranks than male faculty).

This study involved one particular workplace setting, an ethnically diverse urban American university, and readers should be cautioned about making generalizations to other organizations and environments. While the gender and race composition of the sample generally corresponds to that of the occupational strata of the total population, the maintenance and service group as a whole was the most underrepresented. Moreover, the extent to which personal experiences with harassment and abuse affected willingness to participate in the study is unknown. Future replications of this study, encompassing other organizational settings and understudied groups, are needed to address the extent to which the prevalence and consequences of sexual harassment and generalized workplace abuse are generalizable to the broader labor force.

The data presented here were cross-sectional in nature. It is uncertain to what extent harassment and abuse predict deleterious mental health outcomes or to what extent individuals with mental health problems are differentially prone to evoke problematic workplace interactions. Alternatively, individuals with mental health problems may differentially perceive interactions as harassing or abusive.

References

1. Gutek BA. *Sex and the Workplace*. San Francisco, Calif: Jossey-Bass; 1985.

2. Fitzgerald LF, Shullman SL, Bailey N, et al. The incidence and dimensions of sexual harassment in academia and the workplace. *J Vocational Behav*. 1988; 32:152–175.

3. Koss MP, Goodman LA, Browne A, Fitzgerald LF, Keita GP, Russo NF. *No Safe Haven: Male Violence Against Women at Home, at Work, and in the Community*. Washington, DC: American Psychological Association; 1994.

4. Richman JA, Flaherty JA, Rospenda KM, Christensen M. Mental health consequences and correlates of medical student abuse. *JAMA*. 1992; 267:692–694.

5. Schneider KT, Swan S, Fitzgerald LF. Job-related and psychological effects of sexual harassment in the workplace: empirical evidence from two organizations. *J Appl Psychol*. 1997; 82:401–415.

6. Kohn ML, Schooler C. *Work and Personality: An Inquiry Into the Impact of Social Stratification*. Norwood, NJ: Ablex Publishing Corporation; 1983.

7. Karasek R, Theorell T. *Healthy Work: Stress, Productivity and the Reconstruction of Working Life*. New York, NY: Basic Books; 1990.

8. Romanov K, Appelberg K, Honkasalo M, Koskenvuo M. Recent interpersonal conflict at work and psychiatric morbidity: a prospective study of 15,530 employees aged 24–64. *J Psychosom Res*. 1996; 40:169–176.

9. Equal Employment Opportunity Commission (1980) (codified at 29 CFR § 1604. 11).

10. *Sexual Harassment of Federal Workers: Is It a Problem?* Washington, DC: US Merit Systems Protection Board; 1981.

11. Fitzgerald LF, Drasgow F, Hulin CL, Gelfand MJ, Magley VJ. Antecedents and consequences of sexual harassment in organizations: a test of an integrated model. *J Appl Psychol*. 1997; 82:578–589.

12. Richman JA, Flaherty JA, Rospenda KM. Perceived workplace harassment experiences and problem drinking among physicians: broadening the stress/alienation paradigm. *Addiction*. 1996; 91:391–403.

13. Vaux A. Paradigmatic assumptions in sexual harassment research: being guided without being misled. *J Vocational Behav*. 1993; 42:116–135

14. Berdahl JL, Magley VJ, Waldo CR. The sexual harassment of men? Exploring the concept with theory and data. *Psychol Women Q*. 1996; 20:527–547.

15. Rospenda KM, Richman JA, Nawyn SJ. Doing power: the confluence of gender, race, and class in contrapower sexual harassment. *Gender Soc.* 1998; 12:40–60.

16. Björkqvist K, Österman K, Hjelt-Bäck M. Aggression among university employees. *Aggressive Behav.* 1994; 20:173–184.

17. Mirowsky J, Ross CE. *Social Causes of Psychological Distress.* New York, NY: Aldine de Gruyter; 1989.

18. Sudman S, Bradburn N. Improving mailed questionnaire design. In: Lockhart DC, ed. *Making Effective Use of Mailed Questionnaires.* San Francisco, Calif: Jossey-Bass; 1984:33–47.

19. Fitzgerald LF. Sexual harassment: the definition and measurement of a construct. In: Paluch MA, ed. *Ivory Power: Sexual Harassment on Campus.* Albany: State University of New York Press; 1990:21–44.

20. Mirowsky J, Ross CE. Control or defense? Depression and the sense of control over good and bad outcomes. *J Health Soc Behav.* 1990; 31:71–86.

21. Radloff LS. The CES-D Scale: a self-report depression scale for research in the general population. *Appl Psychol Meas.* 1977; 1:385–401.

22. McNair DM, Lorr M, Droppleman L. *Profile of Mood States.* San Diego, Calif: Educational and Industrial Testing Service; 1981.

23. Derogatis LR. *SCL-90-R.* Baltimore, Md: Clinical Psychometric Research; 1975.

24. Selzer ML. The Michigan Alcoholism Screening Test: the quest for a new diagnostic instrument. *Am J Psychiatry.* 1971; 121:1653–1658.

Chapter 39
Cybersex Users, Abusers, and Compulsives

Al Cooper
David L. Delmonico
Ron Burg

Triple-A Engine and gender bending are just two of the concepts that may be new to students who read the Cooper, Delmonico, and Burg account of cybersex. The pursuit of sexual interests on the Internet is apparently big, and sometimes risky, business. Not only can online websites be used to indulge in personal sexual pleasures, but various Internet modalities, such as e-mail, news groups, and chat rooms, can also serve illegal purposes. Although the authors mention several examples of Internet use for healthy sexual expression, their emphasis is clearly on its unhealthy use by abusers and compulsives. Thus, this empirical study differentiates usage patterns of abusers and compulsives from those of other users, which is not typical of most other cybersex studies conducted on the basis of anecdotal data from clinical files.

It is a good guess that the Internet or so-called "Superhighway" as a new venue for sexual exploration is not only here to stay, but will also, without doubt, continue to grow. Because most states have some legislation in place to regulate printed pornography, it is reasonable to conclude that questions of regulation now on the horizon for cybersex will become more pressing. Thus, the most valuable part of this article for students may be the detailed recommendations for needed research, public education, and professional training for clinicians, all of which can improve their odds of making considered, informed decisions about cybersex issues.

Introduction

Given its burgeoning growth and wide accessibility, the Internet or World Wide Web (WWW) is altering patterns of social communication and interpersonal relationships. An estimated 9 to 15 million people access the Internet each day at a rate which is growing by an estimated 25 percent every three months. Internet users spend an average of about 9.8 hours per week visiting the more than 200 million web sites now in existence (*Computerworld*, 1998). An estimated 94 million individuals will have access to the Internet in the year 2001.

Sexuality is one aspect of human social behavior that is being dramatically impacted by the Internet. In fact, sex is reported to be the most frequently searched topic on the Internet (Freeman-Longo & Blanchard, 1998), and the pursuit of sexual interests on the Internet, or "cybersex," is a remarkably common activity for users. In April 1998, approximately nine million users (15 percent of the online population) accessed one of the top five "adult" web sites (Cooper, Scherer, Boies, & Gordon, 1999). This does not include the numerous other adult web sites, nor other Internet modalities which can be used for sexual pursuits (e.g., e-mail, news groups, and chat rooms). A sampling of online users in August 1999 found that 31 percent of the total online population visited an adult web site (Leone & Beilsmith, 1999). Cooper (1998a) suggested that there are three primary factors which "turbocharge" online sexuality and make it such an attractive venue for sexual pursuits. He called these the "Triple-A Engine," and they include accessibility (i.e., millions of sites available 24 hours a day, 7 days a week), affordability (i.e., competition on the WWW keeps all prices low and there are a host of ways to get "free" sex), and anonymity (i.e., people perceive their communications to be anonymous).

Clearly the Internet can be used for healthy sexual expression. For example, the Internet offers the opportunity for the formation of online or virtual communities where isolated or disenfranchised individuals (e.g., gay males and lesbians) can communicate with each other around sexual topics of shared interest (Cooper, Boies, Maheu, & Greenfield, 1999). Newman (1997) noted the educational potential of the Internet, citing the greater availability of information about sexuality and the potential for more candid discussions of sexuality online. The Internet may also be used to find romantic partners. In addition, the Internet may allow for sexual experimentation in a forum that seems "safer," possibly facilitating identity exploration and development (Leiblum, 1997).

At the same time, some researchers have suggested that the use of the Internet for sexual purposes may be counterproductive to normal, healthy sexual development in certain individuals. Van Gelder (1985) warned of the potential for the Internet to be used as a means of obtaining child pornography, for contacting children for sexual purposes, and for assuming false identities in sexually oriented communications. Durkin and Bryant (1995) studied criminal and deviant use of the Internet and posited that the instant gratification of online communication provided a reinforcement for the operationalization of sexual fantasies that would otherwise be extinguished. Others have noted the danger of individuals neglecting their real-world relationships by spending increasing amounts of time engaged in "pseudointimate" online relationships. Anonymity, accessibility, and affordability (Triple-A Engine) seem to increase the chances that the Internet will become problematic for those who either already have a problem with sexual compulsivity or those who have psychological vulnerabilities rendering them at risk for developing such compulsivity. Researchers investigating the addictive potential of the Internet—with regard to both sexual and nonsexual use—have noted correlations between time spent online and negative consequences reported by users (Cooper, Scherer et al., 1999; Young & Rogers, 1998).

Indeed, the Internet, like other technologies, has both costs and benefits. Some investigators have argued the importance of online sexual behavior as a continuum extending from adaptive to problematic (Cooper, Scherer et al., 1999; Leiblum, 1997). Cooper, Putnam, Planchon, and Boies (1999), in their recent survey of 9,177 Internet users, found that while 43 percent of the respondents spent less than one hour per week in online sexual pursuits, at the same time approximately 8 percent spent 11 hours or more per week engaged in such activity. These data suggested that the majority of users who pursued sexual interests on the Internet were capable of limiting the time spent in these activities to reasonable levels but that some were having clear problems. Cooper, Putnam, et al. (1999) put forth a theoretical model based on this "continuum model" describing three categories of people who use the Internet for sexual pursuits. These include *recreational users* who access online sexual material more out of curiosity or for entertainment purposes and are not typically seen as having problems associated with their online sexual behavior. Next there are *sexual compulsive users* who, due to a propensity for pathological sexual expression, use the Internet as one forum for their sexual activities. And finally there are the *at-risk users* who, if it were not for the availability of the Internet, may never have developed a problem with online sexuality. For these people the power of anonymity, accessibility, and affordability (Triple-A Engine) interacts with certain underlying personality factors of at-risk users and leads to patterns and behaviors that, without intervention, may develop into online sexually compulsive behavior. Delmonico (1997) suggests that issues such as isolation and fantasy contribute to at-risk users becoming sexually compulsive.

As Internet usage continues to increase, more and more clinicians are encountering patients whose presenting problem either stems from or is manifestly online sexual compulsivity. As the public and professional awareness of cybersex usage is raised, it becomes increasingly important to understand, assess, and treat this phenomenon. Cooper, Boies et al. (1999) examined Internet sexual behavior through the use of an online survey which asked web site visitors about their online sexual behavior. One focus area was the amount of time individuals reported spending online. Respondents [who] reported engaging in online activity 11 hours or more per week reported higher levels of distress around their online pursuits than other respondents. And, [they] seemed representative of those individuals whose online sexual activity was problematic and potentially compulsive.

Because the amount of time spent online represents only one dimension upon which to identify individuals who may be sexually compulsive it was decided that it would be valuable to expand the criteria to include some of the others factors generally accepted as important dimensions on which to identify sexual compulsivity. These include increased appetite, desire, or tolerance (contributing to increased time engaged in the activity); harm to self or others; denial or minimization of negative consequences; repeated attempts to stop or limit sexual behavior; repetition of behavior despite negative consequences; behavior interfering with social, academic, occupational, or recreational activities; obsession with the activity; and compulsion or loss of freedom in choosing whether to engage in a behavior (Cooper, 1998b; Carnes, 1991; Goodman, 1999; Schneider, 1994).

The Current Study

The purpose of this study was to increase our understanding of online sexual compulsivity by using refined criteria for sexual compulsivity to identify the cybersex compulsives in the sample. As was mentioned earlier the original study based group assignment on the number of reported hours spent online for sexual pursuits, while this study used scores from the Kalichman Sexual Compulsivity Scale (SCS) (Kalichman, Johnson, Adair, Rompa, Multhauf, & Kelly, 1994) combined with time online, in order to identify the group of users displaying cybersex compulsivity.

Methods

This study was a more in-depth analysis of survey data that had been previously collected by the lead author in a 1998 study. The following personal demographics were gathered: age, gender, occupational status, sexual orientation, relational status, and the total weekly amount of time individuals go online. Individuals were asked to report the weekly number of hours they go online for sexual pursuits using a ratio scale. They were also asked to indicate where they go online (home, work, both, or other) and what medium they most use online (e.g., e-mail, chat room, news groups, or WWW). In addition, respondents were asked to rate the frequency of specific sexual pursuits behaviors, their preoccupation with being online, some of the feelings they experience while online, and the degree to which they present themselves differently than the way they actually are. Three questions were designed to assess self-perception of deleterious effects on the respondents' lives: whether respondents keep the time spent online a secret, how it interferes with their lives, and what aspect of their lives are jeopardized, if any, by their behavior.

A *Sexual Compulsivity Scale*, developed by Kalichman et al. (1994), [was] included as part of the survey. Further, a *Sexual Sensation Seeking Scale* (SSSS) developed by Kalichman et al. (1994), assessing the propensity to engage in novel or risky sexual behaviors, [was used]. Finally, a *Nonsexual Sensation Seeking Scale* (NSSS), developed to assess thrill and adventure seeking, experience seeking, disinhibition, and susceptibility to boredom, [also was included].

In the original study, a 59-item survey was made available via the *MSNBC* web site in March and April 1998 for a period of seven weeks. Informed consent was provided, as well as information about confidentiality and anonymity with regard to survey responses. In addition to the regular *MSNBC* audience, a variety of major television and radio networks and newspaper interviews helped promote wider participation in the study. All surveys were completed interactively via the web site and submitted electronically. The data analyses were performed on the sample of 9,265 respondents.

The Kalichman SCS was used to divide the sample into four groups. The four groups were nonsexually compulsive (NC), moderate SCS score (MSCS), sexually compulsive (SC), and cybersexually compulsive (CC). There continues to be debate over the most appropriate terms to use in identifying those with compulsive sexual behaviors. Suggestions include nonparaphilia-related disorders (Kafka, 1993), sexual impulsivity (Barth & Kinder, 1987), sexual compulsion (Coleman, 1986), and sexual addiction (Carnes, 1983). There is still not a clearly agreed upon definition, classification, or label. However, the resolution of this controversy is beyond the scope of this article and for both consistency and simplicity we will utilize the term "sexual compulsivity."

A total of 83.5 percent of the subjects fell into [the] *Nonsexually Compulsive* (NC) category. The scores for the *Moderate SCS Score* (MSCS) group are such that members of this group are likely to have some degree of difficulties with sexual behaviors (and may in fact be sexually compulsive). A total of 10.9 percent of the subjects fell into this category, [while a] total of 4.6 percent of the subjects fell into the *Sexually Compulsive* (SC) category. Only 1 percent of the subjects fell into the *Cybersex Compulsive* (CC) category, [those] who reported spending more than 11 hours per week in online sexual pursuits. These are the individuals who are not only assessed as sexually compulsive (as measured by the SCS), but who seem to use the Internet as an important part of their sexual acting out, much like a drug addict who has a "drug of choice."

Results

Upon examination, the cybersex compulsive group appeared significantly different from the other three groups (see Table 39.1). A significant gender shift was noted in the cybersex compulsive group in that women were more likely to be included in this group. Heterosexuals are less likely to be in the cybersex compulsive group, whereas homosexuals and bisexuals are more highly represented in that group, relative to the other three groups. Married respondents [were] less likely to be in the cybersex compulsive group, and respondents who were both single and dating more likely to be in the cybersex compulsive group.

Time Spent Online

The nonsexually compulsive group, the moderate SCS score group, and the sexually compulsive group all reported spending approximately 15 to 25 total hours per week online overall. The cybersex compulsives reported spending an estimated average of about 35 to 45 total hours per week online overall. Similarly, the amount of time spent pursuing sexual material online is estimated at about 1 to 10 hours per week for the nonsexually compulsive group, the moderate SCS score group, and the sexually compulsive group, while the cybersex compulsives reported spending an estimated average of about 15 to 25 hours per week pursuing online sexual material. Thus, the cybersex compulsive group was overall online more than the other groups.

Occupation

The groups were also analyzed by occupation. Subjects were divided into one of five occupational categories: professional (combining the categories professional, management, educator, and health care provider on the survey), computer field, student, at-home (homemakers and the unemployed), and other. Students appear more likely to be members of the cybersex compulsive group, whereas professionals and those in the computer field appear less likely to be in the cybersex compulsive group.

Location

While groups differed on their reported location, one finding of particular interest was that nearly 6 percent of the

Table 39.1

Demographic Characteristics by Group

Variable	Nonsexually Compulsive (*n* = 7,738) (83.5%)	Moderate Sexually Compulsive (*n* = 1,007) (10.9%)	Sexually Compulsive (*n* = 424) (4.6%)	Cybersex Compulsive (*n* = 96) (1.0%)
Age (mean)	35.3	33.4	32.6	33.5
Gender (percent)				
Male	86	89	88	79
Female	14	11	12	21
Orientation (percent)				
Heterosexual	87	86	85	63
Gay/Lesbian	7	5	6	16
Bisexual	6	9	9	21
Relationship (percent)				
Married	47	49	49	38
Committed	17	15	16	15
Single/Dating	18	17	12	26
Single/Not Dating	18	19	23	21

nonsexually compulsive subjects reported pursuing sexual material solely from work. These numbers increased across groups; 7 percent of the moderate SCS score group and 8 percent of the sexually compulsive subjects reported work being the only place they went online for sexual purposes. (The numbers of subjects using their work computers for some part of their cybersex activities are actually higher, in that these numbers do not include those who reported using both their work and home computers to access sexual materials.)

The data suggest that regardless of the degree of sexual compulsivity, 6 percent of employees use their work computer for sexual purposes about 1 to 10 hours per week. Location of cybersex activities was further examined by gender, but gender did not appear to play a major role in determining use location. About 78 percent of males report using only their home computers for sexual pursuits and 6 percent reported using only

their work computers. Similarly, 84 percent of females report using only their home computer, and 4 percent reported using only their work computer for sexual pursuits.

Online Behaviors

Delmonico (1997) suggested that there are three main categories of cybersex activity: pornography exchange, real-time discussions, and compact disk (CD-ROM) distribution. Previous literature has suggested that there are significant gender differences associated with the online medium used (Cooper, Scherer et al., 1999).

Females tend to prefer chat rooms to other mediums and use the WWW as their second choice of online medium. Males prefer the WWW, with chat rooms as their second choice for the medium to engage in sexual pursuits. In looking at the cybersex compulsive group, the data generally supported the gender differences in online sexual pursuits with 70 percent of the female cybersex compulsives preferring chat rooms. Male cybersex compulsives tended to be more divided throughout the mediums; however, chat room and WWW usage continued to rank as their favored mediums. Females were significantly lower in their use of e-mail, which, as the most visible modality, may point up their desire to hide this type of behavior.

It is also interesting to note that no females in the sexually compulsive group or the cybersex compulsive group reported using newsgroups for sexual pursuits. Sexually-related newsgroups are primarily for the exchange of erotic pictures and stories and are more comparable to e-mail than to chat rooms. This finding supported other literature that suggests women tend to desire cybersex in the context of a "relationship" rather than simply viewing erotic images or text (Cooper, Scherer et al., 1999).

Gender Bending

A trend suggested by the media is the changing of demographic information while online for sexual pursuits. In fact, the practice is thought to be so widespread that the term "gender bending" has been used to describe individuals who switch gender while engaged in online sexual pursuits. Despite popular beliefs, only 5 percent of the entire sample reported having ever changed their gender while online. However, the data suggested that it is common for people to misrepresent their age, with 48 percent of the subjects reporting they changed their age "occasionally" and 23 percent reporting they changed their age "often" or "too often." Surprisingly, 38 percent of the entire sample reported changing their race while online.

Secrecy

Nonsexually compulsive individuals were less likely to keep their cybersex activities a secret from others, as compared to the sexual compulsives and cybersex compulsives. Sixty-eight percent of the nonsexually compulsive group reported keeping their online sex time a secret from others and about 84 percent of the other groups reported the same. However, it is

also apparent that, in general, keeping cybersex activities secret is important to subjects regardless of group assignment. This is not surprising as other sexual activities, whether or not compulsive, are also likely to be kept secret.

Interfering or Jeopardizing Aspects of Life

Overall, 32 percent of the entire sample identified at least one area of their life that has been negatively affected by their online sexual pursuits (e.g., personal, occupational, social, or recreational). When asked about jeopardizing a life area, 21 percent of all respondents reported that their online sexual pursuits had jeopardized an area of their life. In terms of ranking life areas, interference was reported most often in their personal life and relationships as the most common area jeopardized by online sexual pursuits. Overall, these data corroborate earlier findings (Cooper, Scherer et al., 1999) that the majority of Internet users engage in sexual pursuits in ways that do not lead to difficulties in their lives, while a small but significant minority find that their activities create a great deal of problems.

Sensation Seeking

In addition to the Kalichman SCS, there were also scales which measured Sexual Sensation Seeking (SSS) and Nonsexual Sensation Seeking (NSS) behavior. On the SSS factor, all groups were significantly different from one another, except that the sexually compulsive group was found not to be significantly different from the cybersex compulsive group. Both the sexually compulsive and the cybersex compulsive groups were significantly higher than the nonsexually compulsive and the moderate SCS score group. With respect to NSS scores, the nonsexually compulsive group was found to be significantly lower than all other groups, while the other three groups did not significantly differ from one another.

Time Online for Sexual Pursuits (TOS)

In the original study, respondents were separated into 1 of 3 groups in the data analysis: low users, whose TOS was less than one hour per week; moderate users, whose TOS was 1 to 10 hours per week; and high users, with a TOS of 11 or more hours per week. Of the 734 subjects with a TOS of 11 or more hours per week, only 96 were in the cybersex compulsive group. Four hundred ninety-four of the subjects with TOS of 11 or more hours per week were in the nonsexually compulsive group, and 144 were in the moderate SCS score group.

Though the 638 subjects in the high-user, noncybersex compulsive (HU/NC) category had low to moderate SCS scores, we wondered whether there was evidence that their being online 11 hours or more per week engaged in sexual pursuits either interfered with or jeopardized any aspects of their lives. When asked about interference with life areas, 54 percent of the HU/NC group reported experiencing no problems with life areas. However, 42 percent identified at least one life area affected, and 4 percent reported all five life areas were affected by their online cybersex use. When asked about jeopardizing life areas, 72 percent of the HU/NC group reported experiencing no jeopardizing of life areas. However, 27 percent identified at least one life area to have been jeopardized, and 1 percent reported that all five life areas had been jeopardized by their online activity.

Discussion

When considering our findings the reader is reminded that there are limitations of this study and that there are few other studies in this area to date. Thus, until a body of empirical research and replicated results are established all findings in this area need to be viewed with caution. Respondents to the survey were self-selected, and, as with any such survey, the possibility of a self-selection bias exists. Also, the cybersex compulsives in the group were identified on the basis of self-reported TOS and SCS scores. Since the SCS is a self-report measure, and denial of symptoms or concern can be a hallmark of sexual compulsivity, it is likely that there were cybersex compulsives in the sample that were not identified. At the same time, the

large sample size and conservative statistical and methodological approach give us confidence that future research will corroborate many of our findings. Our study highlights the value of conducting online research in better understanding various facets of human sexuality. In addition, the dearth of almost any substantial research in the area of Internet sexuality make this study enormously important for those interested in an empirically based theoretical understanding, as well as clinical formulations, of online sexual compulsivity.

Though the focus of this article is sexually compulsive behavior on the Internet, it bears reiterating that one of our major findings was that for the vast majority of respondents, surfing the Internet for sexual pursuits did not lead to significant difficulties in their lives. This was supported by findings that for most of the respondents their online sexual activity neither interfered with nor jeopardized any aspect of their lives. At the same time, for approximately 1 percent of the sample (i.e., cybersex compulsives) online sexual activity is clearly problematic and seems to have major deleterious consequences in their lives. In this group, 82 percent reported that their cybersex activities interfered with some aspect of their lives, and 72 percent said it actually jeopardized some facet of their lives.

Portions of the high TOS, NC group may be comprised of those in the early stages of developing a cybersex compulsion and thus not yet experiencing the levels of distress reported by those subjects more deeply entrenched in their compulsivity. And finally, it is likely that some percentage of this group is made up of those with a high TOS who truly do not have a problem with their online sexuality. Possibly, this latter group may have an unusually highly developed level of self-discipline and awareness of the potential dangers associated with the abuse of the Internet for sexual reasons. They may also have both personality and demographic variables that somehow help protect them (e.g., marital status, being a little older, working with computers).

Homosexual and bisexual respondents were clearly over represented in the CC (homosexual—16 percent; bisexual—21 percent) versus the NC (homosexual—7 percent; bisexual—6 percent) group. This is an intriguing finding but we must be cautious not to allow for simplistic explanations and instead realize this elevation is likely the result of a number of factors in combination. One being that bisexuals and homosexuals use the Internet more often than their heterosexual counterparts for experimentation and the expression of a variety of sexual behaviors. This is not surprising and indeed is even adaptive as anonymity, accessibility, and affordability (Triple-A Engine) provide a sense of safety and ready access to partners. In addition, different sexual norms and expectations, conflicted feelings about various aspects of homosexuality, as well as other cultural factors might lead to elevations on the SCS when in fact the respondent is not sexually compulsive.

While the above cultural and contextual factors cannot be underestimated it should, at the same time, not be lost that gay and bisexual subjects in the cybersex compulsive group did in fact report highly elevated SCS scores, as well as significant distress relative to other respondents. Thus, it is possible to acknowledge discrimination, societal repression, and different cultural norms and still remain concerned that many of these people may not be in control of their sexual behaviors.

Homosexuals and bisexuals (as well as other sexually disenfranchised groups) may be more at risk for online sexual compulsivity. The Internet has a number of potentially advantageous dimensions for these populations, in that it provides a venue for those who would otherwise be concerned about a host of negative repercussions to engage more freely in sexual pursuits. However, this freedom is a two-edged sword and can both enhance and damage the lives of those who avail themselves of it. Anonymity, accessibility, and affordability (Triple-A Engine) can pose a particular hazard for those users whose sexuality may have been suppressed and

limited all their lives when they suddenly find an infinite supply of sexual opportunities.

This danger is dramatically illustrated by the recent report (Nieves, 1999) of an alarming number of syphilis cases over a two-month period in San Francisco. The investigation found that all cases originated in the same San Francisco gay male chat room on America Online. Combined, these seven men had 99 sexual contacts in the prior two months, and five of the seven were HIV-positive. Although we cannot say with total confidence that these men were truly sexually compulsive, it is hard to deny that they were engaging in risky behavior and that their Internet activity played a role in this.

We also found that women tend to have more difficulties with online sexual compulsion. One explanation may be similar to that provided earlier if women are also thought of as a sexually disenfranchised population. Though the Internet offers women freedom from the constraints placed on their sexual expression by community standards and expectations regarding its "proper role" in their life, this freedom again cuts both ways, and carries with it increased risk for the development of problematic online sexual behaviors.

Another explanation is that men are less likely to self-identify as having a problem with online sexuality, while women are more willing to see these behaviors as problematic. This meshes with the fact that women are more likely to acknowledge a range of psychological difficulties. In this situation, they may be even less prone to denial since it is harder for a female to "normalize" excessive time on the Internet and/or because women are more likely to see using a computer for sexual pursuits as a problem.

Lesbians were found to present an interesting contrast to some of the earlier findings and explanations. Despite lesbians being both female and homosexual they were found to be underrepresented in the cybersex compulsive group. This result underscores the importance of considering lesbian sexuality as distinct from gay male sexuality in studies such as this, and raises the question as to what factors protect lesbians from developing cybersex compulsivity.

Another group less vulnerable to cybersex compulsion was those who were married. Reasons for this might be married people are either less likely to spend a great deal of time in cybersex pursuits, or perhaps simply less able to find the privacy to do so. Also plausible is that different dynamics lead a person to be either likely to get married or, alternatively, to develop an online sexual compulsion. Also of interest is that people who were both single and dating were more likely to be in the cybersex compulsive group. This makes intuitive sense when considering that people who are both single and dating are the subgroup most likely seeking sexual relationships, which might fuel a level of online sexual activity leading them to be more prone to problems with that behavior.

The location of cybersex activity and its prevalence at work were also striking. Although we did find that cybersex compulsives are more likely to use their work computers for cybersex activity, perhaps the most remarkable aspect of these findings was the extent to which subjects in all groups were apt to carry on cybersex activities at work. Even for the nonsexually compulsive group, 6 out of 100 employees reported their work computers to be the primary way they accessed sexual material. In addition, if we include respondents who reported using both work and home computers for sexual pursuits, then an amazing 20 percent of men and 12 percent of women are using their work computers for at least some portion of their online sexual activity. This corroborates data from other sources reporting that adult content sites are the fourth most visited category while at work (Leone & Beilsmith, 1999), and that 70 percent of all adult content traffic occurs during the 9-to-5 workday (Branwyn, 1999). Ignoring the financial implications associated with these data for the moment, it is still somewhat striking to find a trend in which subjects across all groups report engaging in a behavior involving significant risk if discovered.

Both male and female cybersex compulsives were more likely to use chat rooms. It may be that the particularly engaging nature of chat rooms may be a "slippery slope" for certain at-risk individuals in the development of their cybersex compulsivity; or that certain individuals who habituate to less powerful forms of online sexual activities over time gravitate to chat rooms; or that chat rooms are a transitional step from online sexual interactions to meeting and finding face-to-face partners. In any case, the use of chat rooms for sexual pursuits should be a red flag and something to which clinicians should pay particular attention.

In addition, subjects in the cybersex compulsive group differed from the other three groups with regard to time spent online. Cybersex compulsives spent, on average, nearly twice the amount of time in general online activities as the other groups. They also spent twice as much time pursuing sexual material as the other groups, and about half of their online time solely in pursuit of sexual materials.

Implications

Our findings indicate that the majority of Internet users surveyed engage in cybersex activities for 10 hours or less per week (and roughly half of this group for less than one hour per week). In general, these pursuits do not interfere with the respondents' lives. Nonetheless, there is a small group of users (approximately 1 percent) for whom online sexual activity has clearly become a compulsive behavior, as well as a larger group (17 percent) who give some strong indication of problems with their sexual behavior.

Several demographic variables came to light as putting an individual at an increased risk for cybersex compulsivity. The reader is cautioned to keep in mind that this does not mean that these groups have any monopoly on being at risk, but only that they may be at increased risk. Both women and gay men were more highly represented in the cybersex compulsive group, and we believe that the sexual disenfranchisement of these two groups may play a role in their increased risk. Surprisingly those working in the computer field were not found more in the cybersex compulsive group, and of the various occupational groups examined, only students emerged as at greater risk. The propensity to take risks both in sexual and nonsexual behavioral domains, consistent with previous research on other forms of sexual compulsivity, is also more common in cybersex compulsives. In addition, the use of chat rooms as well as the greater number of overall time online for sexual pursuits were both more frequently found for cybersex compulsives. [Cybersex compulsion] is a hidden public health hazard exploding, in part because very few are recognizing it as such or taking it seriously. Recommendations for learning more about this behavior are described.

Research

Research in this area needs to be conducted which investigates the relationship of cybersex compulsion to more traditional varieties of sexual compulsion and/or addiction. Carnes (1999) reported that 71 percent of sexual addicts reported experiencing trouble with some type of sexual activity on the Internet. Has the Internet "created" a new category of sexual compulsives, or has it simply provided the already existing sexual compulsive an additional way to act out their behavior? Understanding this relationship between sexual compulsion and cybersex may be the first step in developing effective treatment models.

Finally, a critical question that needs to be addressed is whether, and to what extent, online sexual compulsivity translates into or facilitates potentially damaging behavior offline. For example, the question of whether individuals who engage in online pedophilic pursuits are more or less likely to ultimately engage in these behaviors offline.

Public Education

The data find a clear need for a dramatic increase in broad-based educational efforts on issues of cybersex, as well as sexually compulsive behaviors in general. These educational efforts should be aimed at raising public awareness to facilitate the development of other preventive measures. In addition to this primary avenue of prevention, secondary and tertiary prevention should also be addressed. These prevention strategies would include the development of interventions for users prone to develop cybersex compulsivity as well as for individuals who are attempting to gain control over what they acknowledge to be problematic behaviors. One segment of this thrust would be to encourage seminars and focused discussions in schools, the workplace, and even in computer classes around both healthy and problematic uses of the Internet.

Enlisting the aid of the computer industry and Internet providers would provide the perfect time, place, and opportunity for those who profit from the public's interest in this technology to also take responsibility for warning users to the possible dangers. Clear warnings about the "potential hazards" of online sexuality could easily be delineated in their materials, analogous to that included with cigarettes, alcohol, firearms and other volitional activities that carry inherent risks (e.g., many gambling establishments participate in some level of public awareness of the difficulties that pathological gambling can pose to an individual and their family).

Finally, the most effective medium by which to reach and influence the greatest numbers of people in our society is by getting the attention of the media. Their commitment to additional in-depth and empirically based explorations (as opposed to highlighting prurient and sensationalistic hype) of these issues would be an invaluable way for rapidly raising the public's awareness and providing them with an increased ability to determine whether a loved one, an employee, or they themselves have a problem with cybersex.

Professional Training

There is little doubt that there need to be many more opportunities for therapists to participate in comprehensive trainings in the assessment and treatment of patients presenting with problems related to online sexual behaviors and cybersex compulsion. Though more professionals are able to identify the manifestations of general sexual compulsivity, there remains a lack of awareness and information about sexual compulsivity on the Internet. As technology continues to advance, clinicians need to increase their skills in assessing for cybersex compulsion and the constantly evolving ways that clients engage in sexual behaviors while online. Ways to enhance these skills might include reading articles (such as those in this journal), attending specific training at conferences, and/or taking relevant online continuing education courses.

Training will both need to help the therapists transfer extant knowledge and interventions from work with other sexual acting out problems to the online world, as well as identifying and developing methods specifically geared to cybersex issues. For example, one issue that was presented and supported in this research is the concept of the "Triple-A Engine" (Anonymity, Accessibility, and Affordability) which fuels cybersex compulsion (Cooper, 1998a). Clinicians may want to focus interventions on these Triple-A events in order to reduce the power of these factors in maintaining the cybersex cycle.

There is little doubt that use of the Internet will continue to explode. As people spend more time online and look to the Internet to fulfill an ever increasing amount of their sexual needs, the issues associated with online sexuality will become increasingly important and salient. We need to be involved in helping to educate the public, as well as other professionals, as to the ways that this new technology and venue can be used to enhance their lives and sexual relations, as well as to warn them as to the myriad ways that these modern day Sirens could, in fact, be luring them toward the rocks.

References

Barth, R. J., & Kinder, B. N. (1987). The mislabeling of sexual impulsivity. *The Journal of Sex and Marital Therapy, 13(1)*, 15–23.

Branwyn, G. (1999, March 12). How the porn sites do it. *The Industry Standard.* [Online]. *http://www.thestandard.net*

Carnes, P. (1983). *Out of the shadows: Understanding sexual addiction.* Minneapolis, MN: CompCare.

Carnes, P. J. (1991). *Don't call it love: Recovery from sexual addiction.* New York: Bantam Books.

Carnes, P. J. (1999). Editorial: Cybersex, sexual health, and the transformation of culture. *Sexual Addiction & Compulsivity, 6(2)*, 77–78.

Coleman, E. (1986). Sexual compulsion vs. addiction: The debate continues. *SIECUS Report, 14(6)*, 7–11.

Computerworld. (1998). *Commerce by numbers—Internet population* [Online]. *http://www.computerworld.com/home/Emmerce.nsf/All/pop*

Cooper, A. (1998a). Sexuality and the Internet: Surfing into the new millennium. *CyberPsychology & Behavior, 1(2)*, 181–187.

Cooper, A. (1998b). Sexually compulsive behavior. *Contemporary Sexuality, 32(4)*, 1–3.

Cooper, A., Boies, S., Maheu, M., & Greenfield, D. (1999). Sexuality and the Internet: The next sexual revolution. In F. Muscarella & L. Szuchman (Eds.), *The psychological science of sexuality: A research-based approach* (pp. 519–545). New York: Wiley.

Cooper, A., Putnam, D. E., Planchon, L. A., & Boies, S. C. (1999). Online sexual compulsivity: Getting tangled in the net. *Sexual Addiction & Compulsivity, 6(2)*, 79–104.

Cooper, A., Scherer, C., Boies, S. C., & Gordon, B. (1999). Sexuality on the Internet: From sexual exploration to pathological expression. *Professional Psychology: Research and Practice, 30(2)*, 154–164.

Delmonico, D. L. (1997). Cybersex: High tech sex addiction. *Sexual Addiction & Compulsivity, 4(2)*, 159–167.

Durkin, K. F., & Bryant, C. D. (1995). "Log on to sex": Some notes on the carnal computer and erotic cyberspace as an emerging research frontier. *Deviant Behavior: An Interdisciplinary Journal, 16*, 179–200.

Freeman-Longo, R. E., & Blanchard, G. T. (1998). *Sexual abuse in America: Epidemic of the 21st century.* Brandon, VT: Safer Society Press.

Goodman, A. (1999). *Sexual addiction: An integrated approach.* Madison, WI: International Universities Press.

Kafka, M. P. (1993). Update on paraphilias and paraphilia-related disorders. *Currents in Affective Illness, 12(6),* 4–8.

Kalichman, S. C., Johnson, R. R., Adair, V., Rompa, D., Multhauf, K., & Kelly, J. A. (1994). Sexual sensation seeking: Scaled development and predicting AIDS-risk behavior among homosexually active men. *Journal of Personality Assessment, 62,* 385–397.

Leiblum, S. R. (1997). Sex and the net: Clinical implications. *Journal of Sex Education and Therapy, 22(1),* 21–28.

Leone, S., & Beilsmith, M. (1999, February). *Monthly Report on Internet Growth.* Washington, DC: Media Metrix.

Newman, B. (1997). The use of online services to encourage exploration of egodystonic sexual interests. *Journal of Sex Education and Therapy, 22(1),* 45–48.

Nieves, E. (1999, August 25). Privacy questions raised in cases of syphilis linked to chat room. *New York Times,* p. 1.

Schneider, J. P. (1994). Sex addiction: Controversy within mainstream addiction medicine, diagnosis based on the DSM-III-R and physician case histories. *Sexual Addiction & Compulsivity, 1(1),* 19–44.

Van Gelder, L. (1985, October). The strange case of the electronic lover. *Ms.,* pp. 94, 99, 101–104, 117, 123–124.

Young, K. S., & Rogers, R. C. (1998). The relationship between depression and Internet addiction. *Cyberpsychology & Behavior, 1(1),* 25–28.

Part IX

Legal and Educational Issues

With changes in technology making pornography "easier to order into the home than pizza" and court decisions that offer broad legal protection to vendors, selling sex has become a $10 billion industry in the United States (Egan, 2000). Meanwhile, the "crazy aunt in the attic" phenomenon has been spawned, "everyone knows she is there but no one is talking about her!" It seems that legal issues about sexuality and money have become silent partners. American Telephone and Telegraph, Time Warner, General Motors, Marriot International, and the Hilton Corporation are all corporations with a big financial stake in the adult video film market, but all remain low-key about pornography profits. With market players of such magnitude, it is logical to question the relationship of economic factors to laws that have been or could be effected, especially those pertaining to sexual behavior and sexual exploitation. Part IX flushes out significant questions related to both legal and educational issues surrounding sexuality.

Responding to an embarrassed 21-year-old whose girlfriend had joked about the size of his penis, Drew Pinsky, M.D., a.k.a. Dr. Love, the key player on *Loveline*—a popular Los Angeles-based radio and television show—clarified that size is not a crucial factor in sexual satisfaction for women. The caller on this nighttime call-in radio program was admonished to reframe the issue by recognizing the fact that he was in a relationship with an abusive partner. Dr. Drew's chief mission is to change what he views as the culture of "broken down interpersonal relationships" that lack intimacy (Barovick, 1998). A fifteen-year veteran of an alternative approach to sexuality education, Pinsky is countering what he terms the "abdication of parenting ethos" of the 1970s. He views his show as a "sheep in wolf's clothing," discouraging sexual activity and encouraging responsibility and connection. He believes this is in stark contrast to the rest of the media force, which often depicts sex as a simple physical act, without an emotional component. In what some see as a "bad news" milieu, Pinsky's good news is that young teens today are more inquisitive and realistic about sexuality than their predecessors. Such good news is long overdue. Stodghill's exposé of teen sexual behavior, circa 2000, that realistically describes how America's youth really do learn about sex is an important piece of the sexuality puzzle.

An overwhelming majority of parents in a survey by the Kaiser Family Foundation, a health research organization, wanted schools to provide more, not less, sexuality education once their children reach the teenage years. They endorsed teaching about abstinence, avoiding pregnancy, sexually transmitted diseases, abortion, and sexual orientation. By contrast, an apparent gap exists between what parents want and what schools deliver. A large majority of parents indicated that sex education should last one-half a semester or more and over one-half thought classes should not be coeducational. Typically, however, classes do include girls and boys and last only one or two class sessions within a general course in health education (Schemo, 2000).

The lines of the polarized debate between advocates of a conservative approach to sexuality education and a more liberal one may be blurring, as indicated by a national survey conducted by the Alan Guttmacher Institute. Of all school districts, twenty-three percent currently require schools to teach abstinence until marriage and discuss contraception only in the context of its shortcomings. But, even among the one-third of parents who say schools should teach abstinence until marriage, a substantial number also want schools to arm their children with information about obtaining and using condoms, contraception, and abortion, in case they do become sexually active (Schemo, 2000). Is it any wonder that educators in the trenches often refer to our culture as sexually schizophrenic?

American ambivalence is illustrated by the case of the "Conservative Britains and Liberal Americans." The British inaugurated the nationwide, "Don't Die of Ignorance" campaign after England had diagnosed only a few cases of AIDS. In the United States, it took six years and thousands of cases of AIDS before the president even uttered the word in public.

> . . . [W]hile the British aim earnestly to protect their young from ignorance, we misguided Americans have [enlisted ignorance] in the fight! While the British motto might well be "Just Say Know!," we offer, in place of the power of knowledge, "Just Say No." And who are the "we"? We are the same adult community who can be seen saying "yes" all day long in those endless television images, contradicting ourselves in the eyes of our young with every change of channels. (Roffman, 1992:7)

Straight talk is urged by experts in the field of sexuality education as an antidote to such adult "doublespeak." Taking our cue from the sensible British, we might instead say:

> We love you and want you to be safe. The best way to do that is to abstain [from] any potentially risky behavior. Next best is to protect yourself and others as best you can. Here's how . . . . (Roffman, 1992:7)

Not only sexuality education but also legal issues are critically related to the sexual health of Americans. To understand how legal issues impact sexuality, one must be somewhat knowledgeable about legislative and legal processes. Basically, the levels of jurisdiction throughout the country begin at local levels, progressing from city, to county, to state, and to federal government, each with its own legal code. Additionally, even the military has a legal code of its own. All laws are subject to the provisions of the Constitution of the United States and, likewise, laws governing sexuality at any level cannot be inconsistent with the next highest level of governance. The law charts included in the Daley, Orenstein, and Wong article will intrigue students curious about their state sexuality laws and how such laws compare with those in other states.

The report that looks at sexuality laws and the sexual rights of citizens has been compiled by the public policy arm of the Sexuality Information and Education Council of the United States (SIECUS). A nonprofit voluntary health organization, SIECUS was founded in 1964 to help people understand, appreciate, and use their sexuality in a responsible and informed manner (Carroll & Wolpe, 1996). This interdisciplinary organization, the brainchild of a lawyer, a sociologist, a family life educator, and a physician, is the premier sexuality information center in the United States. Mary Calderone, the first female physician in the state of New York, was a cofounder and the first Executive Director. It is of note that prior to the founding of SIECUS, two female physicians were also the driving forces in similar health education movements in their own countries, one in Sweden and one in Denmark (Moore,

1986). Before the early 1950s, when Agentha Braestrup, M.D., spearheaded the establishment of the Danish system of sexuality education and family planning, a medical prescription was required to purchase a condom at the corner drugstore. Indeed, the Danes have "come a long way."

After reading the articles in Part IX, readers will be more aware that legal and educational issues pertaining to sexuality in this new millennium cannot be adequately solved with archaic strategies. Pouring "new wine into old wineskins" will not work. But, neither can workable solutions be secured without some form of wineskins. Whether these are called norms, mores, or values, a judicious mix of old and new is required: change must be balanced with continuity.

References

Barovick, H. (1998, June 15). Dr. Drew, after hours guru. *Time*, p. 59.

Carroll, J. L., & Wolpe, P. R. (1996). *Sexuality and gender in society*. New York: HarperCollins.

Egan, T. (2000, October 23). U.S. corporations finding sex sells. *Austin-American Statesman*, pp. A1, A8.

Koch, P. B. (1998). Sexual knowledge and education. In R. T. Francoeur, P. B. Koch, & D. L. Weiss (Eds.), *Sexuality in America: Understanding our sexual values and behavior* (pp. 70–88). New York: Continuum.

Moore, N. B. (1986). Cross-cultural perspectives: Family life education as a forum for strengthening families. In M. B. Sussman (Ed.), *Charybdis Complex* (pp. 91–115). New York: Haworth.

Roffman, D. M. (1992). Common sense and nonsense about sex education. *Family Life Matters*, pp. 2, 7.

Schemo, D. J. (2000, October 4). Survey finds parents favor more detailed sex education. *New York Times*, pp. 1A, 23A. ✦

Chapter 40
Where'd You Learn That?

Ron Stodghill II

Stodghill addresses educational issues about sexuality and American youth who are in the middle of their own sexual revolution, a situation leaving many parents feeling confused and, perhaps, powerless. This exploration of the question, "How does young sexual experimentation begin?" is at once entertaining and alarming. It would be easy for readers to reminisce and say, "The more things change, the more they stay the same." But reality asserts otherwise. In a day when children and young persons, ages 6 to 18, spend more time watching television than they spend in the classroom, changing paradigms of sexuality education are in play.

Sources cited by the author from which teenagers today learn about sexuality are, in order, peers—45 percent, television—29 percent, parents—7 percent, and sexuality education—3 percent. Even with new sexuality paradigms, some things have not changed: teenagers are not always logical. The increasing use of oral sex and anal intercourse among teenagers to avoid an unintended pregnancy flies in the face of reason, ignoring the fact that these practices offer no protection against sexually transmitted diseases. And, even though growing numbers of teens are knowledgeable about the mechanics of sex, the author asks, "What about their emotional health and social behavior?" An engaging topic presented in a compelling manner, this is a selection that students will not want to miss.

The cute little couple looked as if they should be sauntering through Great Adven-ture or waiting in line for tokens at the local arcade. Instead, the 14-year-olds walked purposefully into the Teen Center in suburban Salt Lake City, Utah. They didn't mince words about their reason for stopping in. For quite some time, usually after school and on weekends, the boy and girl had tried to heighten their arousal during sex. Flustered yet determined, the pair wanted advice on the necessary steps that might lead them to a more fulfilling orgasm. His face showing all the desperation of a lost tourist, the boy spoke for both of them when he asked frankly, "How do we get to the G-spot?"

Whoa. Teen Center nurse Patti Towle admits she was taken aback by the inquiry. She couldn't exactly provide a road map. Even more, the destination was a bit scandalous for a couple of ninth-graders in the heart of Mormon country. But these kids had clearly already gone further sexually than many adults, so Towle didn't waste time preaching the gospel of abstinence. She gave her young adventurers some reading material on the subject, including the classic women's health book *Our Bodies, Ourselves*, to help bring them closer in bed. She also brought up the question of whether a G-spot even exists. As her visitors were leaving, Towle offered them more freebies: "I sent them out the door with a billion condoms."

G-spots. Orgasms. Condoms. We all know kids say and do the darndest things, but how they have changed! One teacher recalls a 10-year-old raising his hand to ask her to define oral sex. He was quickly followed by an 8-year-old girl behind him who asked, "Oh, yeah, and what's anal sex?" These are the easy questions. Rhonda Sheared, who teaches sex education in Pinellas County, Fla., was asked by middle school students about the sound *kweif*, which the kids say is the noise a vagina makes during or after sex. "And how do you keep it from making this noise?"

There is more troubling behavior in Denver. School officials were forced to institute a sexual-harassment policy owing to a sharp rise in lewd language, groping, pinching and bra-snapping incidents among sixth-, seventh-, and eighth-graders. Sex among kids in Pensacola, Fla., became so pervasive that students of a private Christian junior high school are now asked to sign cards vowing not to have sex until they marry. But the cards don't mean anything, says a 14-year-old boy at the school. "It's broken promises."

It's easy enough to blame everything on television and entertainment, even the news. At a Denver middle school, boys rationalize their actions this way: "If the President can do it, why can't we?" White House sex scandals are one thing, but how can anyone avoid Viagra and virility? Or public discussions of sexually transmitted diseases like AIDS and herpes? Young girls have lip-synched often enough to Alanis Morissette's big hit of a couple of years ago, *You Oughta Know,* to have found the sex nestled in the lyric. But it's more than just movies and television and news. Adolescent curiosity about sex is fed by a pandemic openness about it—in the schoolyard, on the bus, at home when no adult is watching. Just eavesdrop at the mall one afternoon, and you'll hear enough pubescent sexcapades to pen the next few episodes of *Dawson's Creek,* the most explicit show on teen sexuality, on the *WB* network. Parents, always the last to keep up, are now almost totally pre-empted. Chris (not his real name), 13, says his parents talked to him about sex when he was 12 but he had been indoctrinated earlier by a 17-year-old cousin. In any case, he gets his full share of information from the tube. "You name the show, and I've heard about it. *Jerry Springer, MTV, Dawson's Creek, HBO After Midnight* . . . " Stephanie, 16, of North Lauderdale, Fla., who first had sex when she was 14, claims to have slept with five boyfriends and is considered a sex expert by her friends. She says, "You can learn a lot about sex from cable. It's all mad-sex stuff. If you're feeling steamy and hot, there's only one thing you want to do. As long as you're using a condom, what's wrong with it? Kids have hormones too."

In these steamy times, it is becoming largely irrelevant whether adults approve of kids' sowing their oats—or knowing so much about the technicalities of the dissemination. American adolescents are in the midst of their own kind of sexual revolution—one that has left many parents feeling confused, frightened and almost powerless. Parents can search all they want for common ground with today's kids, trying to draw parallels between contemporary carnal knowledge and an earlier generation's free-love crusades, but the two movements are quite different. A desire to break out of the old-fashioned strictures fueled the '60s movement, and its participants made sexual freedom a kind of new religion. That sort of reverence has been replaced by a more consumerist attitude. In a 1972 cover story, *Time* declared, "Teenagers generally are woefully ignorant about sex." Ignorance is no longer the rule. As a weary junior high counselor in Salt Lake City puts it, "Teens today are almost nonchalant about sex. It's like we've been to the moon too many times."

The good news about their precocious knowledge of the mechanics of sex is that a growing number of teens know how to protect themselves, at least physically. But what about their emotional health and social behavior? That's a more troublesome picture. Many parents and teachers—as well as some thoughtful teenagers—worry about the desecration of love and the subversion of mature relationships. Says Debra Haffner, President of the Sexuality Information and Education Council of the United States: "We should not confuse kids' pseudo-sophistication about sexuality and their ability to use the language with their understanding of who they are as sexual young people or their ability to make good decisions."

One ugly side effect is a presumption among many adolescent boys that sex is an entitlement—an attitude that fosters a breakdown of respect for oneself and others. Says a seventh-grade girl: "The guy will ask you up front. If you turn him down, you're a bitch. But if you do it, you're a ho. The guys are after us all the time, in the halls, everywhere. You scream, 'Don't touch me!' but it doesn't do any good." A Rhode Island Rape Center study of 1,700 sixth- and ninth-graders found 65 percent of boys and 57 percent of girls believing it acceptable for a male to force a female to have sex if they've been dating for six months.

Parents who are aware of this cultural revolution seem mostly torn between two approaches: preaching abstinence or suggesting prophylactics—and thus condoning sex. Says Cory Hollis, 37, a father of three in the Salt Lake City area: "I don't want to see my teenage son ruin his life. But if he's going to do it, I told him that I'd go out and get him the condoms myself." Most parents seem too squeamish to get into the subtleties of instilling sexual ethics. Nor are schools up to the job of moralizing. Kids say they accept their teachers' admonitions to have safe sex but tune out other stuff. "The personal-development classes are a joke," says Sarah, 16, of Pensacola. "Even the teacher looks uncomfortable. There is no way anybody is going to ask a serious question." Says Shana, a 13-year-old from Denver: "A lot of it is old and boring. They'll talk about not having sex before marriage, but no one listens."

Shana says she is glad "sex isn't so taboo now, I mean with all the teenage pregnancies." But she also says that "it's creepy and kind of scary that it seems to be happening so early, and all this talk about it." She adds, "Girls are jumping too quickly. They figure if they can fall in love in a month, then they can have sex in a month too." When she tried discouraging a classmate from having sex for the first time, the friend turned to her and said, "My God, Shana. It's just sex."

Three powerful forces have shaped today's child prodigies: a prosperous information age that increasingly promotes products and entertains audiences by titillation; aggressive public-policy initiatives that loudly preach sexual responsibility, further desensitizing kids to the subject; and the decline of two-parent households, which leaves adolescents with little supervision. Thus kids are not only bombarded with messages about sex—many of them contradictory—but also have more private time to engage in it than did previous generations. Today more than half of the females and three-quarters of the males ages

15 to 19 have experienced sexual intercourse, according to the Commission on Adolescent Sexual Health. And while the average age at first intercourse has come down only a year since 1970 (currently it's 17 for girls and 16 for boys), speed is of the essence for the new generation. Says Haffner: "If kids today are going to do more than kiss, they tend to move very quickly toward sexual intercourse."

The remarkable—and in ways lamentable—product of youthful promiscuity and higher sexual IQ is the degree to which kids learn to navigate the complex hypersexual world that reaches out seductively to them at every turn. One of the most positive results: the incidence of sexually transmitted diseases and of teenage pregnancy is declining. Over the past few years, kids have managed to chip away at the teenage birthrate, which in 1991 peaked at 62.1 births per 1,000 females. Since then the birthrate has dropped 12 percent, to 54.7. Surveys suggest that as many as two-thirds of teenagers now use condoms, a proportion that is three times as high as reported in the 1970s. "We're clearly starting to make progress," says Dr. John Santelli, a physician with the Centers for Disease Control and Prevention's Division of Adolescent and School Health. "And the key statistics bear that out." Even if they've had sex, many kids are learning to put off having more till later; they are also making condom use during intercourse nonnegotiable; and, remarkably, the fleeting pleasures of lust may even be wising up some of them to a greater appreciation of love.

For better or worse, sex-filled television helps shape young opinion. In Chicago, Ryan, an 11-year-old girl, intently watches a scene from one of her favorite TV dramas, *Dawson's Creek*. She listens as the character Jen, who lost her virginity at 12 while drunk, confesses to her new love, Dawson, "Sex doesn't equal happiness. I can't apologize for my past." Ryan is quick to defend Jen. "I think she was young, but if I were Dawson, I would believe she had changed. She acts totally different now." But Ryan is shocked by an episode of her other favorite show, *Buffy the Vampire Slayer*, in which

Angel, a male vampire, "turned bad" after having sex with the 17-year-old Buffy. "That kinda annoyed me," says Ryan. "What would have happened if she had had a baby? Her whole life would have been thrown out the window." As for the fallen Angel: "I am so mad! I'm going to take all my pictures of him down now."

And then there's real-life television. *MTV's Loveline*, an hour-long Q-and-A show featuring sex guru Drew Pinsky, is drawing raves among teens for its informative sexual content. Pinsky seems to be almost idolized by some youths. "Dr. Drew has some excellent advice," says Keri, an eighth-grader in Denver. "It's not just sex, its real life. Society makes you say you've got to look at shows like *Baywatch*, but I'm sick of blond bimbos."

With so much talk of sex in the air, the extinction of the hapless, sexually naive kid seems an inevitability. Indeed, kids today as young as seven to ten are picking up the first details of sex even in Saturday-morning cartoons. Brett, a 14-year-old in Denver, says it doesn't matter to him whether his parents chat with him about sex or not because he gets so much from TV. Whenever he's curious about something sexual, he channel surfs his way to certainty. "If you watch TV, they've got everything you want to know," he says. "That's how I learned to kiss, when I was eight. And the girl told me, 'Oh, you sure know how to do it.'"

Even if kids don't watch certain television shows, they know the programs exist and are bedazzled by the forbidden. From schoolyard word of mouth, eight-year-old Jeff in Chicago has heard all about the foul-mouthed kids in the raunchily plotted *South Park*, and even though he has never seen the show, he can describe certain episodes in detail. (He is also familiar with the AIDS theme of the musical *Rent* because he's heard the CD over and over.) Argentina, 16, in Detroit, says, "TV makes sex look like this big game." Her friend Michael, 17, adds, "They make sex look like Monopoly or something. You have to do it in order to get to the next level."

Child experts say that by the time many kids hit adolescence, they have reached a point where they aren't particularly obsessed with sex but have grown to accept the notion that solid courtships—or at least strong physical attractions—potentially lead to sexual intercourse. Instead of denying it they get an early start preparing for it—and playing and perceiving the roles prescribed for them. In Nashville, 10-year-old Brantley whispers about a classmate, "There's this girl I know, she's nine years old, and she already shaves her legs and plucks her eyebrows, and I've heard she's had sex. She even has bigger boobs than my mom!"

The playacting can eventually lead to discipline problems at school. Alan Skriloff, Assistant Superintendent of Personnel and Curriculum for New Jersey's North Brunswick School System, notes that there has been an increase in mock-sexual behavior in buses carrying students to school. He insists there have been no incidents of sexual assault but, he says, "we've dealt with kids simulating sexual intercourse and simulating masturbation. It's very disturbing to the other children and to the parents, obviously." Though Skriloff says that girls are often the initiators of such conduct, in most school districts the aggressors are usually boys.

Nan Stein, a senior researcher at the Wesley College Center for Research on Women, believes sexual violence and harassment is on the rise in schools, and she says, "It's happening between kids who are dating or want to be dating or used to date." Linda Osmundson, Executive Director of the Center Against Spouse Abuse in St. Petersburg, Fla., notes that "it seems to be coming down to younger and younger girls who feel that if they don't pair up with these guys, they'll have no position in their lives. They are pressured into lots of sexual activity." In this process of socialization, "no" is becoming less and less an option.

In such a world, schools focus on teaching scientific realism rather than virginity. Sex-ed teachers tread lightly on the moral questions of sexual intimacy while going heavy on the risk of pregnancy or a sexually transmitted disease. Indeed, health educators in some school districts complain that teaching abstinence to kids today is getting to be a futile exercise. Using less final terms like "postpone" or "delay" helps draw some kids in, but semantics often isn't the problem. In a Florida survey, the state found that 75 percent of kids had experienced sexual intercourse by the time they reached 12th grade, with some 20 percent of the kids having had six or more sexual partners. Rick Colonno, father of a 16-year-old son and 14-year-old daughter in Arvada, Colo., views sex ed in schools as a necessary evil to fill the void that exists in many homes. Still, he's bothered by what he sees as a subliminal endorsement of sex by authorities. "What they're doing," he says, "is preparing you for sex and then saying, 'But don't have it.'"

With breathtaking pragmatism, kids look for ways to pursue their sex life while avoiding pregnancy or disease. Rhonda Sheared, the Florida sex-ed teacher, says a growing number of kids are asking questions about oral and anal sex because they've discovered that it allows them to be sexually active without risking pregnancy. As part of the Pinellas County program, students in middle and high school write questions anonymously, and, as Sheared says, "they're always looking for the loophole."

A verbatim sampling of some questions:

- "Can you get AIDS from fingering a girl if you have no cuts? Through your fingernails?"
- "Can you gets AIDS from '69'?"
- "If you shave your vagina or penis, can that get rid of crabs?"
- "If yellowish stuff comes out of a girl, does it mean you have herpes, or can it just happen if your period is due, along with abdominal pains?"
- "When sperm hits the air, does it die or stay alive for 10 days?"

Ideally, most kids say, they would prefer their parents do the tutoring, but they realize that's unlikely. For years psychologists and sociologists have warned about a new generation gap, one created not so much by different morals and social outlooks as by career-driven parents, the economic neces-sity of two incomes leaving parents little time for talks with their children. Recent studies indicate that many teens think parents are the most accurate source of information and would like to talk to them more about sex and sexual ethics but can't get their attention long enough. Shana sees the conundrum this way: "Parents haven't set boundaries, but they are expecting them."

Some parents are working harder to counsel their kids on sex. Cathy Wolf, 29, of North Wales, Pa., says she grew up learning about sex largely from her friends and from reading controversial books. Open-minded and proactive, she says she has returned to a book she once sought out for advice, Judy Blume's novel *Are You There God? It's Me, Margaret*, and is reading it to her two boys, 8 and 11. The novel discusses the awkwardness of adolescence, including sexual stirrings. "That book was forbidden to me as a kid," Wolf says. "I'm hoping to give them a different perspective about sex, to expose them to this kind of subject matter before they find out about it themselves." Movies and television are a prod and a challenge to Wolf. In *Grease*, which is rated PG and was recently re-released, the character Rizzo "says something about 'sloppy seconds,' you know, the fact that a guy wouldn't want to do it with a girl who had just done it with another guy. There's also another point where they talk about condoms."

Most kids, though, lament that their parents aren't much help at all on sexual matters. They either avoid the subject, miss the mark by starting the discussion too long before or after the sexual encounter, or just plain stonewall them. "I was nine when I asked my mother the Big Question," says Michael, in Detroit. "I'll never forget. She took out her driver's license and pointed to the line about male or female. 'That is sex,' she said." Laurel, a 17-year-old in Murfreesboro, Tenn., wishes her parents had taken more time with her to shed light on the subject. When she was six and her sister was nine, "my mom sat us down, and we had the sex talk," Laurel says. "But when I was 10, we moved in with my dad, and he never talked about it. He would leave the room if a commercial for a feminine product came on TV." And when her sister finally had sex, at 16, even her mother's vaunted openness crumbled. "She talked to my mom about it and ended up feeling like a whore because even though my mom always said we could talk to her about anything, she didn't want to hear that her daughter had slept with a boy."

Part of the problem for many adults is that they aren't quite sure how they feel about teenage sex. A third of adults think adolescent sexual activity is wrong, while a majority of adults think it's O.K. and, under certain conditions, normal, healthy behavior, according to the Alan Guttmacher Institute, a nonprofit, reproductive-health research group. In one breath, parents say they perceive it as a public-health issue and want more information about sexual behavior and its consequences, easier access to contraceptives, and more material in the media about responsible human and sexual interaction. And in the next breath, they claim it's a moral issue to be resolved through preaching abstinence and the virtues of virginity and getting the trash off TV. "You start out talking about condoms in this country, and you end up fighting about the future of the American family," says Sarah Brown, Director of the Campaign Against Teen Pregnancy. "Teens just end up frozen like a deer in headlights."

Not all kids are happy with television's usurping the role of village griot. Many say they've become bored by—and even resent—sexual themes that seem pointless and even a distraction from the information or entertainment they're seeking. "It's like everywhere," says Ryan, a 13-year-old seventh-grader in Denver, "even in *Skateboarding* [magazine]. It's become so normal it doesn't even affect you. On TV, out of nowhere, they'll begin talking about masturbation." Another Ryan, 13, in the eighth grade at the same school, agrees: "There's sex in the cartoons and messed-up people on the talk shows—'My lover sleeping with my best friend.' I can remember the jumping condom ads. There's just too much of it all."

Many kids are torn between living up to a moral code espoused by their church and parents and trying to stay true to the swirling laissez-faire. Experience is making many sadder but wiser. The shame, anger or even indifference stirred by early sex can lead to prolonged abstinence. Chandra, a 17-year-old in Detroit, says she had sex with a boyfriend of two years for the first time at 15 despite her mother's constant pleas against it. She says she wishes she had heeded her mother's advice. "One day I just decided to do it," she says. "Afterward, I was kind of mad that I let it happen. And I was sad because I knew my mother wouldn't have approved." Chandra stopped dating the boy more than a year ago and hasn't had sex since. "It would have to be someone I really cared about," she says. "I've had sex before, but I'm not a slut."

With little guidance from grownups, teens have had to discover for themselves that the ubiquitous sexual messages must be tempered with caution and responsibility. It is quite clear, even to the most sexually experienced youngsters, just how dangerous a little information can be. Stephanie in North Lauderdale, who lost her virginity two years ago, watches with concern as her seven-year-old sister moves beyond fuzzy thoughts of romance inspired by *Cinderella* or *Aladdin* into sexual curiosity. "She's always talking about pee-pees, and she sees somebody on TV kissing and hugging or something, and she says, 'Oh, they had sex.' I think she's going to find out about this stuff before I did." She pauses. "We don't tell my sister anything," she says, "but she's not a naive child."

Adapted from Ron Stodghill II. "Where'd You Learn That?" *Time*, 1998, June 15, pp. 52–59. Copyright © 1998, Time Inc. Reprinted by permission. ✦

Chapter 41
Sexual Knowledge and Education

Patricia Barthalow Koch

The trajectory of sexuality education in the United States traced by Koch provokes a déjà vu experience for those familiar with its current status—contentious! Concerns that surround the trend toward adolescent sexual involvement at increasingly younger ages inevitably extend to the related issue of sexuality education. Although the need for sexuality education has been well acknowledged for decades, the list of attending unresolved questions remains long and ominous. Who is the actual sexuality educator? Who should it be? What should be taught and when? These are only a few queries that fuel the debate.

In spite of blatant sexual themes in today's television programs, movies, and popular music, most young people as well as many adults in the United States are ill-informed about sexual matters. And, apparently, sexual intercourse itself cannot be used as an index of sexual acumen. Otherwise, why would the United States continue to be noted among industrialized countries for having the highest percentage of sexually active teenagers, and among those teenagers, the highest rate of sexually transmitted diseases and unintended pregnancies?

Why do teenagers and society not learn from experience? The answer may be twofold. First, experience is not the only teacher. Adults who set the parameters for sexuality education in our society need to understand that persons learn about sexuality the same way that they learn about anything else. Learning occurs not only through experience, but also through didactic instruction and modeling from significant others, whether parents, peers, celebrities, or media myths. Second, those who make decisions about sexuality education appear to ignore the large body of knowledge available from research and theory concerning the significance of developmental and socio-cultural factors in learning. By now, it should be common knowledge that sexuality education is not as simple and direct as imparting information at a given time. Sexuality has been shown to be a multidimensional developmental process that begins for individuals at birth and extends to death. And physiological facts are but one important facet of sexuality education. Psychological and social-cultural dimensions are also a part of the equation.

Koch's review of the history of sexuality education will certainly raise questions for students about their own sexuality education. Additionally, readers may ask themselves about their role in improving sexual health in our society, now and in the future. As a professional or a parent or just as an informed citizen, we all have a stake in this crucial game of life.

According to the National Coalition to Support Sexuality Education,

> Sexuality education is a lifelong process of acquiring information and forming attitudes, beliefs, and values about identity, relationships, and intimacy. It encompasses sexual development, reproductive health, interpersonal relationships, affection, intimacy, body image, and gender roles [among other topics]. Sexuality education seeks to assist children [people] in understanding a positive view of sexuality, provide them with information and skills about taking care of their sexual health, and help them to acquire skills to make decisions now and in the future. (SIECUS 1992)

A Brief History of American Sexuality Education

Sexuality education in the United States has always been marked by tension between maintaining the status quo of the "acceptable" expression of individual sexuality, and change as precipitated by the economic, social, and political events of the time. The major loci for sexuality education have shifted from the family and the community (in earlier times being more influenced by religion, and in modern times, by consumerism and the media), to schools. Much of the education has been developed by and targeted towards middle-class whites. The two major movements to formalize sexuality education in the United States were spearheaded for the advancement of either "social protection" or "social justice." Throughout history, the goals, content, and methodologies of sexuality education in these two movements have often been in opposition to one another.

According to D'Emilio and Freedman (1988), young people in colonial America learned about sexuality through two primary mechanisms. In these agrarian communities, observation of sexual activity among animals was common. Observation of sexual activity among adults was also common, since families lived in small, often-unpartitioned dwellings, where it was not unusual for adults and children to sleep together. Second, more formal moral instruction about the role of sexuality in people's lives came from parents and clergy, with lawmakers endorsing the religious doctrines. The major message was that sexual activity ought to be limited to marriage and aimed at procreation. However, within the marital relationship, both the man and woman were entitled to experience pleasure during the procreative act.

Ministers throughout the colonies invoked biblical injunctions against extra-marital and nonprocreative sexual acts, while colonial statutes in both New England and the Chesapeake area outlawed fornication, rape, sodomy, adultery, and sometimes incest, prescribing corporal or capital punishment, fines, and in some cases, banishment for sexual transgressors. Together, these moral authorities attempted to socialize youth to channel sexual desires toward marriage (D'Emilio and Freedmen 1988).

After the War for American Independence, small autonomous rural communities gave way to more-commercialized areas, and church and state regulation of

morality began to decline. Individual responsibility and choice became more emphasized. Thus, instruction on sexuality changed from community (external) control to individual (internal) control. For example, between the 1830s and 1870s, information about contraceptive devices and abortion techniques circulated widely through printed matter (pamphlets, circulars, and books) and lectures. However, peer education was the primary source of sexuality education, with more "educated" people, especially women, passing along their knowledge to friends and family members.

Increasing secularization and the rise of the medical profession spawned a health-reform movement in the 1830s that emphasized a quest for physical, as well as spiritual, perfection. With advances in publishing and literacy, a prolific sexual-advice literature, written by doctors and health reformers of both genders, emerged. The central message was that men and women had to control and channel their sexual desires toward procreative, marital relations. "Properly channeled sexual relations promised to contribute to individual health, marital intimacy and even spiritual joy" (D'Emilio and Freedman 1988). The popularity of these materials demonstrated Americans' need for and interest in sexuality education. Much of the self-help and medical-advice literature directed at men emphasized the dangers of masturbation. Women were taught that they had more sexual passion than men, and their role was to help men to control their sexual drives. In other words, a standard of female "purity" was the major theme of the sexuality education of the time.

Studies of women's sexuality conducted in the early 1900s provide insight into the sources of sexual information for women during the nineteenth century. Katharine B. Davis (1929) studied one-thousand women (three-quarters born before 1890) and Dr. Clelia Mosher (1980) surveyed forty-five women (four-fifths born between 1850 and 1880). Over 40 percent of the women in Davis' study and half in Mosher's reported that they received less-than-adequate instruction about sex before marriage.

In the later nineteenth century, a combined health and social-reform movement developed that attempted to control the content of and access to sexuality education. Middle-class reformers organized voluntary associations, such as the Women's Christian Temperance Union (WCTU), to address issues, including prostitution and obscenity. The social-purity movement in the late nineteenth century added the demand for female equality and a single sexual standard to the earlier moral-reform movements. The WCTU spearheaded a sex-education campaign through the White Cross to help men resist sexual temptation. Social-purity leaders authored marital advice books that recognized women's sexual desires and stressed that women could enjoy intercourse only if they really wanted it. Women's rights and social-purity advocates issued the first formal call for sex education in America. They argued that women should teach children about sex: "Show your sons and daughters the sanctities and the terrors of this awful power of sex, its capacities to bless or curse its owner" (D'Emilio and Freedman 1988, 155). They demanded a public discourse of sexuality that emphasized love and reproductive responsibility rather than lust.

An example of the restricted character of sexuality education at the time was the enactment of the 1873 Comstock Law for the "Suppression of Trade in, and Circulation of Obscene Literature and Articles of Immoral Use." This revision of the federal postal law forbade the mailing of information or advertisements about contraception and abortion, as well as any material about sexuality. The Comstock Law was in effect until being overturned by a federal appeals court in 1936 in a decision about contraception: *United States v. Dow Package*.

The turn of the century ushered in a more "progressive" era fueled by industrial capitalism. Progressive reform provoked by the middle class called upon government and social institutions, including schools, to intervene in social and economic issues, such as sex education. One of the major movements for sex education was the social-hygiene movement spearheaded by Dr. Prince Morrow to prevent the spread of syphilis and gonorrhea. In 1905, he formed the Society of Sanitary and Moral Prophylaxis in New York City, later renamed the American Social Hygiene Association. This society was joined by the WCTU, YMCA, state boards of health, and the National Education Association in an "unrelenting campaign of education to wipe out the ignorance and the prejudices that allowed venereal diseases to infect the nation" (D'Emilio and Freedman 1988, 205).

They held public meetings and conferences, published and distributed written materials, and endorsed sex education in the public schools. While insisting on frank and open discussions of sexual-health matters, they promulgated the traditional emphasis of sexuality in marriage for reproductive purposes and the avoidance of erotic temptation (like masturbation). More conservative Americans considered such openness to be offensive. Former President Howard Taft described sex education as "full of danger if carried on in general public schools" (D'Emilio and Freedman 1988, 207). Not until after 1920 would these activists see any progress towards the goal of having some basic sex (reproductive) instruction integrated into any school curriculum.

The early 1900s found American minds being expanded by the writings of Sigmund Freud and Havelock Ellis, among others. These psychologists helped popularize the notion of sexuality as a marker of self-identity and a force permeating one's life, which, if repressed, risks negative consequences. In addition, socialist and feminist ideologies in the industrial economy created an environment fertile for the demand of birth-control information and services. These events spearheaded the second major movement for sexuality education, which was based on social-justice issues, particularly for women and the poor. In 1912, Margaret Sanger began a series of articles on female sexuality for a New York newspaper, which was confiscated by postal officials for violating the Comstock anti-obscenity law. Later, to challenge the constitutionality of this law, she published her own magazine, *The Woman Rebel,* filled with information about birth control. She was charged with nine counts of violating the law, with a penalty of forty-five years in prison, after writing and distributing a pamphlet, *Family Limitation.* To avoid prosecution, she fled to Europe; but in her absence, efforts mounted to distribute birth-control information. By early 1915, activists had distributed over 100,000 copies of *Family Limitation,* and a movement for community sexuality education was solidified. Public sentiment in favor of the right to such information was so strong that charges were dropped against Sanger when she returned to America. Community education about and access to birth control, particularly for middle-class women, began to become accepted, if not expected, as a matter of public health, as well as an issue of female equality (social justice).

Premarital experience became more common among the white middle class, beginning in the 1920s and accelerating as youth became more autonomous from their families (through automobiles, attendance at college, participation in more leisure activities like movies, and war experiences). Dating, necking, and petting among young peers became a norm. "Where adults might see flagrantly loose behavior, young people themselves had constructed a set of norms that regulated their activity while allowing the accumulation of experience and sexual learning" (D'Emilio and Freedman 1988, 261).

Courses on marriage and the family and (sexual) hygiene were being introduced into the college curriculum. Marriage manuals began to emphasize sexual expression and pleasure, rather than sexual control and reproduction, with more explicit instructions as to how to achieve satisfying sexual relationships (such as "foreplay" and "simultaneous orgasm"). By the end of the 1930s, many marriage manuals were focusing on sexual "techniques." [By the late 1940s], scientific reports, such as *Sex-*

ual Behavior in the Human Male by Alfred Kinsey and his associates (1948) and the corresponding *Sexual Behavior in the Human Female* (1953), were major popular works primarily read by the middle class. These books [that] provided sexuality education about the types and frequencies of various sexual expressions among white Americans to more than a quarter of a million people are considered landmarks in sexuality education.

As scientific information on sexuality became readily available to the American public, more-explicit presentation of sexual material in printed and audiovisual media became possible through the courts' decisions narrowing the definition of obscenity. The proliferation of such sexually explicit materials was encouraged by the expansion of the consumer-oriented economy. [As] advertising was developing into a major industry, beginning in the 1920s, sex was used to sell everything from cars to toothpaste.

In 1953, Hugh Hefner published the first issue of *Playboy,* whose trademark was a female "Playmate of the Month" displayed in a glossy nude centerfold. The early *Playboy* philosophy suggested males should "enjoy the pleasures the female has to offer without becoming emotionally involved" (D'Emilio and Freedman 1988). By the end of the 1950s, *Playboy* had a circulation of 1 million, with the readership peaking at 6 million by the early 1970s. Many a man identified *Playboy* as his first, and perhaps most influential, source of sex education.

By the 1970s, sex manuals had taken the place of marital advice manuals. Popular books like the *Joy of Sex* (1972) by Dr. Alex Comfort encouraged sexual experimentation by illustrating sexual techniques. Sexual references became even more prolific in the mainstream media. For example, the ratio of sexual references per page tripled between 1950 and 1980 in magazines, including *Reader's Digest, Time,* and *Newsweek.* In addition, Masters and Johnson's groundbreaking book, *Human Sexual Response,* emphasizing that women's sexual desires and responses were equal to those of men, was published in 1966. Yet, even with the explicit and abundant presentation of sexuality in the popular media, parents were still not likely to provide sexuality education to their children, nor were the schools.

In 1964, a lawyer, a sociologist, a clergyman, a family life educator, a public health educator, and a physician came together to form the Sex Information and Education Council of the United States (SIECUS). SIECUS is a nonprofit voluntary health organization with the aim to help people understand, appreciate, and use their sexuality in a responsible and informed manner. Dr. Mary Calderone was a co-founder and the first Executive Director. SIECUS soon became known all over the country as a source of information on human sexuality and sex education.

This private initiative for sexuality education was followed by a governmental one in 1966 when the Office of Education of the federal Department of Health, Education, and Welfare announced its newly developed policy:

> Family life and sex education as an integral part of the curriculum from pre-school to college and adult levels; it will support training for teachers . . . it will aid programs designed to help parents . . . it will support research and development in all aspects of family life and sex education. (Haffner 1989, 1)

In 1967, the American Association of Sex Educators and Counselors was formed to bring together professionals from all disciplines who were teaching and counseling about human sexuality. The organization later expanded to include therapists, and is known today as the American Association of Sex Educators, Counselors, and Therapists (AASECT). Opposition to sexuality education from conservative political and religious groups grew quickly. In 1968, the Christian Crusade published, "Is the Schoolhouse the Proper Place to Teach Raw Sex?" and the John Birch Society was calling sex education a "Communist plot." In response, over 150 public leaders joined the National Committee for Responsible Family Life and Sex Education.

In 1970, Maryland became the first state to mandate family-life and human development education at all levels in their public schools. However, the new "purity" movement by conservatives was under way, coordinating over 300 organizations throughout the country to oppose sex education in the public schools. Several states passed anti-sexuality education mandates, with Louisiana [having] barred sex education altogether in 1968. By the late 1970s, only half-a-dozen states had mandated sex education into their schools, and implementation in the local classrooms was limited.

In 1972, AASECT began developing training standards and competency criteria for certification of sexuality educators, counselors, and therapists. AASECT also has developed a code of ethics for professionals working in these fields.

In 1979, the federal government through the Department of Health, Education, and Welfare conducted a national analysis of sex-education programs in the United States. The researchers calculated that less than 10 percent of all students were receiving instruction about sexuality in their high schools. The report's overall conclusion stated:

> Comprehensive programs must include far more than discussions of reproduction. They should cover other topics such as contraception, numerous sexual activities, the emotional and social aspects of sexual activity, values clarification, and decision making and communication skills. In addition to being concerned with the imparting of knowledge, they should also focus on the clarifying of values, the raising of self-esteem, and the developing of personal and social skills. (Kirby, Atter, and Scales 1979, 1)

When AIDS burst upon the scene in the 1980s, education with the goal of "social protection" from this deadly disease was targeted for inclusion in public-school curricula. In a relatively short time, most states came to require, or at least recommend, that AIDS education be included in school curricula. The number of states mandating or recommending AIDS education surpassed those mandating or recommending sexuality education. Today, policies and curricula addressing **AIDS** tend to be much more specific and detailed than those dealing with other aspects of sexuality education, including pregnancy prevention. This may lead to students receiving a narrow and negative view of human sexuality (e.g., "sex kills!").

Throughout this time, SIECUS remained committed to comprehensive sexuality education, as emphasized in its mission statement: "SIECUS affirms that sexuality is a natural and healthy part of living and advocates the right of individuals to make responsible sexual choices" (Haffner 1989, 4). In 1989, SIECUS convened a national colloquium on the future of sexuality education, "Sex Education 2000," to which sixty-five national organizations sent representatives. Thirteen specific goals for the year 2000 were set forth as follows:

1. Sexuality education will be viewed as a community-wide responsibility.

2. All parents will receive assistance in providing sexuality education for their child(ren).

3. All schools will provide sexuality education for children and youth.

4. All religious institutions serving youth will provide sexuality education.

5. All national youth-serving agencies will implement sexuality education programs and policies.

6. The media will assume a more proactive role in sexuality education.

7. Federal policies and programs will support sexuality education.

8. Each state will have policies for school-based sexuality education and assure that mandates are implemented on a local level.

9. Guidelines, materials, strategies, and support for sexuality education will be available at the community level.

10. All teachers and group leaders providing sexuality education to youth will receive appropriate training.

11. Methodologies will be developed to evaluate sexuality education programs.

12. Broad support for sexuality education will be activated.

13. In order to realize the overall goal of comprehensive sexuality education for all children and youth, SIECUS calls upon national organizations to join together as a national coalition to support sexuality education. (SIECUS 1990)

To aid in the attainment of the third goal of providing comprehensive sexuality education in the schools, a national task force with SIECUS's leadership published *Guidelines for Comprehensive Sexuality Education, Kindergarten Through 12th Grade* in 1991. These guidelines, based on six key concepts, provide a framework to create new sexuality-education programs or improve existing ones. The guidelines are based on values related to human sexuality that reflect the beliefs of most communities in a pluralistic society. They represent a starting point for curriculum development at the local level. Currently, another task force is working to help providers of preschool education incorporate the beginnings of comprehensive sexuality education into their programs. In 1994, SIECUS also launched an international initiative in order to disseminate information on comprehensive sexuality education to the international community and to aid in the development of specific international efforts in this area.

Yet, in light of progress that has been made, challenges to sexuality programs from conservative organizations have become more frequent, more organized, and more successful than ever before (Sedway 1992). These nationally organized groups, including Eagle Forum, Focus on the Family, American Family Association, and Citizens for Excellence in Education, target local school programs that do not conform to their specific ideology. They attempt to control what others can read or learn, not just in sexuality education (which now is the major target), but in all areas of public education, including science (with the teaching of creationism), history, and literature (with censorship of many classics in children's literature). Although these groups represent a minority of parents in a school district, through well-organized national support, they often effectively use a variety of intimidating tactics to prevent the establishment of sexuality education programs altogether or establish abstinence-only ones. Their tactics include personal attacks on persons supporting comprehensive sexuality education, threatening and sometimes pursuing costly litigation against school districts, and flooding school boards with misinformation, among other strategies. The greater impact of this anti-sexuality-education campaign on education, in general, and American society, overall, has been poignantly described:

> In another sense, the continuing series of attacks aimed at public education must be viewed in the context of the larger battle—what has come to be known as a "Cultural Civil War"—over free expression. Motion pictures, television programs, fine art, music lyrics, and even political speech have all come under assault in recent years from many of the same religious right leaders behind attacks on school programs. At stake in attacks on schoolbooks and programs is students' exposure to a broad spectrum of ideas in the classroom—in essence, their freedom to learn. And when the freedom to learn is threatened in sexuality education, students are denied information that can save their lives. (Sedway 1992, 13-14)

Current Status of Sexuality Education

Youth-Serving Agencies

National youth-serving agencies (YSAs) in the United States provide sexuality education to over two million youths each year. Over the past two decades, YSAs began developing such programs, primarily in response to the problems of adolescent pregnancy and HIV/AIDS.

Second only to schools in the number of youth they serve, youth-serving agencies are excellent providers of sexuality education programs, both because they work with large numbers of youth, including many underserved youth, and because they provide an environment that is informal and conducive to creative and experiential learning. (Dietz 1989/1990, 16)

For example, the American Red Cross reaches over 1 million youth each year in the U.S. with their "AIDS Prevention Program," "Black Youth Project," and "AIDS Prevention Program for Hispanic Youth and Families." The Boys Clubs of America have developed a substance abuse/pregnancy prevention program, called "Smart Moves." The Girls Clubs of America have a primary commitment to providing health promotion, sexuality education, and pregnancy-prevention services to its members and reaches over 200,000 youth each year. The Girl Scouts of the U.S.A. developed a curriculum, "Decision for Your Life: Preventing Teenage Pregnancy," that focuses on the consequences of teen parenthood and the development of communication, decision-making, assertiveness, and values-clarification skills. In addition to the national efforts of YSAs, many local affiliates have designed their own programs to meet the needs of their local communities in culturally sensitive ways. For example, the National 4-H Council estimates that most state extension offices have developed their own programs to reduce teenage pregnancy in their areas.

Schools

More than 85 percent of the American public approve of sexuality education being provided in the schools, compared with 76 percent in 1975 and 69 percent in 1965 (Kenney, Guardado, and Brown 1989). Today, roughly 60 percent of teenagers receive at least some sex education in schools, although only a third receive a somewhat "comprehensive" program.

Each state can mandate or require that sexuality education and/or AIDS education be provided in the local school districts. Short of mandating such educational programs, states may simply recommend that the school districts within their boundaries offer education on sexuality, in general, and/or more specific AIDS education.

Although the majority of states either mandate or recommend sexuality and AIDS education, this does not guarantee that local school districts are implementing the suggested curricula. Inconsistencies in and lack of implementation of these curricula result from absence of provisions for mandate enforcement, lax regulations regarding compliance, diversity in program objectives, restrictions on course content, lack of provisions for teacher training, and insufficient evaluation.

In an evaluation of the thirty-four state-recommended AIDS-education curricula, 32 percent were found to be accurate in basic concepts and presentation. The majority (85 percent) emphasized abstinence and "just say no" skills, whereas only 9 percent covered safe sex as a preventative practice. There was no mention of homosexuality in over one-third of the curricula. In 38 percent, homosexuals were identified as the "cause" of AIDS. The Utah curriculum was especially negative and restrictive:

> Utah's teachers are not free to discuss the "intricacies of intercourse, sexual stimulation, erotic behavior"; the acceptance of or advocacy of homosexuality as a desirable or acceptable sexual adjustment or lifestyle; the advocacy or encouragement of contraceptive methods or devices by unmarried minors; and the acceptance or advocacy of "free sex," promiscuity, or the so-called "new morality." This section of their curriculum is replete with warnings of legal violations for instructors crossing prohibition lines; their guidelines indicate that with parental consent it is possible to discuss condom use at any grade level, but without it, such discussions are Class B misdemeanors. (Di Mauro 1989–90, 6)

In recent years, well-organized conservative organizations throughout the United States have been promoting the adoption of their own abstinence-only curricula in the public schools. Since 1985, the Illinois Committee on the Status of Women has re-

ceived $1.7 million in state and federal funds to promote such a curriculum, called *Sex Respect*. They have been successful in having *Sex Respect* adopted in over 1,600 school systems, even though this curriculum is designed to proselytize a particular conservative sexual-value system. The *Sex Respect* curriculum has been criticized because it:

> (1) substitutes biased opinion for fact; (2) conveys insufficient and inaccurate information; (3) relies on scare tactics; (4) ignores realities of life for many students; (5) reinforces gender stereotypes; (6) lacks respect for cultural and economic differences; (7) presents one side of controversial issues; (8) fails to meaningfully involve parents; [and] (9) is marketed using inadequate evaluations. (Trudell and Whatley 1991, 125)

Careful scientific evaluation of over forty sexuality- and AIDS-education curricula commissioned separately by the Centers for Disease Control and the World Health Organization resulted in the following conclusions:

1. Comprehensive sexuality and HIV/AIDS-education programs do not hasten the onset of intercourse nor increase the number of partners or frequency of intercourse.

2. Skill-based programs can delay the onset of sexual intercourse and increase the use of contraception, condoms, and other safer-sex practices among sexually experienced youth.

3. Programs that promote both the postponement of sexual intercourse and safer-sex practices are more effective than abstinence-only programs, like *Sex Respect* (Haffner 1994).

References

Davis, K. B. 1929. *Factors in the Sex Life of Twenty-Two Hundred Women*. New York: Harper and Row.

D'Emilio, J., and E. B. Freedman. 1988. *Intimate Matters: A History of Sexuality in America*. New York: Harper and Row.

Dietz, P. 1989/1990. (December/January). "Youth-Serving Agencies as Effective Providers of Sexuality Education." *SIECUS Report,* 18: 16–20.

Di Mauro, D. 1989/1990. (December/January). "Sexuality Education 1990: A Review of State Sexuality and AIDS Education Curricula." *SIECUS Report,* 18: 1–9.

Haffner, D. W. 1989. (March/April). "SIECUS: 25 Years of Commitment to Sexual Health and Education." *SIECUS Report,* 17: 1–6.

——. 1994. (August/September). "The Good News about Sexuality Education." *SIECUS Reports,* 17–18.

Kenney, A., S. Guardado, and L. Brown. 1989. "Sex Education and AIDS Education in the Schools: What States and Large School Districts Are Doing." *Family Planning Perspectives,* 21: 56–64.

Kinsey, A. C., W. Pomeroy, and C. Martin. 1948. *Sexual Behavior in the Human Male.* Philadelphia: Saunders.

Kinsey, A. C., W. Pomeroy, C. Martin, and P. Gebhard. 1953. *Sexual Behavior in the Human Female.* Philadelphia: Saunders.

Kirby, D., J. Atter, and P. Scales. 1979. *An Analysis of U.S. Sex Education Programs and Evaluation Methods: Executive Summary.* Atlanta, GA: U.S. Department of Health, Education, and Welfare.

Mosher, Clelia Duel. 1980. *The Mosher Survey: Sexual Attitudes of Forty-Five Victorian Women.* James Mahood and Kristine Wenberg, eds. New York: Arno Press.

Sedway, M. 1992. (February/March). "Far Right Takes Aim at Sexuality Education." *SIECUS Report,* 20(3): 13–19.

Sexuality Education in America: A State-by-State Review. 1995. Washington, DC: NARAL/The NARAL Foundation.

SIECUS. 1990. *Sex Education 2000. A Call to Action.* New York: SIECUS.

SIECUS Fact Sheet # 2. 1992. National Coalition to Support Sexuality Education.

Trudell, B., and M. Whatley. 1991. "Sex Respect: A Problematic Public School Sexuality Curriculum." *Journal of Sex Education and Therapy,* 17: 125–140.

Chapter 42
SIECUS Looks at States' Sexuality Laws and the Sexual Rights of Citizens

Daniel Daley
Susie Orenstein
Vivian Wong

Should the government be in the bedroom of consenting adults? What is the appropriate role for the legal system to play in supporting the sexual health and sexual rights of citizens? Questions such as these have sparked controversy for well over a century since the United States Congress passed an anti-obscenity bill, the first law of its kind. Not as amorphous today, queries are less philosophical and more pragmatic. Where do individual rights (i.e., the rights of a woman to an abortion) intersect with the rights of a fetus? Or, do we violate individual rights (i.e., of parents) if sexuality education is mandated by states? What about release time for "non-believers of sexuality education"?

The SIECUS Public Policy Staff has assembled an excellent accounting of current sexuality laws in American culture. In charts especially prepared for this anthology, seven areas of sexuality are compared on a state-by-state basis: sexuality education, contraceptive services, abortion services, HIV/AIDS infection, sexual orientation, sexual behaviors, and sexual exploitation. A perusal of these analyses will confirm that these United States are far from united about the topic of sexuality. This is a short treatment of the subject, but vital information for anyone concerned about promoting sexual health for self and others.

A basic tenet of our nation is that all Americans are equal under the law. But state laws vary. An American in one state enjoys different rights and privileges than an American in another state a mile away. So reality has a dash of George Orwell's *Animal Farm*—some citizens are more equal than others. Unfortunately, this is also true of laws governing intimate issues such as sexuality.

Most Americans don't give much consideration to the government's decision making concerning their sexual lives. They generally agree that sexual behavior is private and that what they do in their bedrooms is their own business. They may even think that sexuality-related laws are enacted for other people—not themselves. As a result, most Americans don't consider a state's laws on sexuality and sexual rights when deciding where to live or visit. Perhaps if they saw how the patchwork of laws come together to describe sexual rights in their state, they would.

SIECUS advocates for the right of individuals to make responsible sexual choices. This broader right is composed of a variety of specific rights—the right to information, the right to sexual health services, the right to engage in sexual behaviors in private with another consenting adult, the right to live according to one's sexual orientation, and the right to obtain and use materials that have a sexual theme or content. SIECUS believes that it is important to look at states' sexuality-related laws in total rather than by a single issue. SIECUS has, therefore, compiled information on state laws on a variety of sexuality-related topics. This is the first in an ongoing effort. Current research and analysis on the laws of each of the 50 states is broad and somewhat limited. Not every law in every state has been recently researched or interpreted. Not every issue has been addressed by state legislatures. SIECUS will continue to look at sexuality-related laws and will keep you informed of its findings.

Analysis of Categories

For this analysis, SIECUS is designating states' laws as (1) supportive of sexual health and sexual rights ("S"); (2) unsupportive of sexual health and sexual rights ("U"); or (3) neither supportive nor unsupportive of sexual health and sexual rights, [i.e., neutral] ("N"). These designations were determined by comparing the content of laws with SIECUS' position on the issue. In some cases, the absence of a state law is designated with an "NL" for no law. In other cases, the absence of a state law was interpreted as supportive or unsupportive depending on its impact on sexual rights.

In determining a state's overall supportiveness of sexual health and sexual rights, SIECUS counted each "S" as one point, each "U" as minus one point, and each "N" as no point. If a state's point total was positive, SIECUS termed it supportive or S; if it was negative, SIECUS termed it unsupportive or U; if it was zero, SIECUS termed it N for neither supportive nor unsupportive. NLs did not affect a score.

Sexuality Education

SIECUS believes that all people have the right to comprehensive sexuality education that addresses the biological, sociocultural, psychological, and spiritual dimensions of sexuality. Comprehensive school-based sexuality education that is appropriate to a student's age, developmental level, and cultural background is an important part of preparing young people for adulthood and is a critical component in promoting sexual health.

Opponents of comprehensive sexuality education once attempted to ban sexuality education outright. When that strategy proved unsuccessful, they tried to restrict the content and scope of such education. Even so, many states continue to mandate comprehensive sexuality education and HIV/AIDS education for their students.

While these mandates provide a legal basis for program implementation, they do not necessarily result in programs in every school. The enforcement of such mandates has not been determined or evaluated.

SIECUS believes that state mandates are supportive of sexual health and sexual rights (S); and that the absence of a state mandate is unsupportive of sexual health and sexual rights (U). As for content requirements, states that only require the teaching of abstinence without information about contraception and disease prevention were assigned unsupportive (U) status. States that require the teaching of abstinence with the inclusion of contraception and disease prevention information were assigned a supportive (S) status (see Table 42.1).

Overall, the majority of states and the District of Columbia are supportive of educating young people about sexuality issues. But there are some significant caveats. States are likely to focus on HIV/STD-prevention education rather than on overall sexuality education. They are also likely to remain silent on contraceptive and disease prevention information other than abstinence.[1]

Contraceptive Services

SIECUS believes that all people should have ready access to comprehensive contraceptive information, education, and services, regardless of age, gender, or income. While parents should be involved in their children's contraceptive decisions, each person has the right to confidentiality and privacy when receiving such information, counseling and services. SIECUS supports adolescent access to low-cost prescription and nonprescription methods through public funding and private insurance coverage.

SIECUS examined information on laws concerning insurance coverage for contraceptive services and parental consent or notice or minors' access to contraceptive services. SIECUS also included information on state funds for contraceptive services,

Table 42.1

Sexuality Education

	AL	AK	AZ	AR	CA	CO	CT	DE	DC	FL	GA	HI	ID	IL	IN	IA	KS	KY	LA	ME	MD	MA	MI	MN	MS	MO
Sexuality Education Mandate	S	U	U	S	S	U	U	S	S	S	S	S	U	S	U	S	S	U	U	S	U	U	U	S	U	U
STD/HIV Education Mandate	S	U	U	S	S	S	S	S	S	S	S	S	S	S	S	S	S	S	U	S	U	U	S	S	S	S
Mandate Includes Contraception	NL	U	NL	U	NL	S	NL	NL		S	S	S	NL	U	U	NL	NL	U	NL	NL	NL	U	NL	NL	NL	NL
Mandate Includes Disease Prevention	S	NL	S	NL	S	NL	NL	NL		S	S	S	NL	S	U	NL	NL	NL	NL	NL	NL	U	S	NL	NL	NL
Composite Score	S	U	U	S	S	N	N	S	S	S	S	S	U	S	U	S	S	U	U	S	U	U	S	S	U	N

	MT	NE	NV	NH	NJ	NM	NY	NC	ND	OH	OK	OR	PA	RI	SC	SD	TN	TX	UT	VT	VA	WA	WV	WI	WY
Sexuality Education Mandate	U	U	S	U	S	U	U	S	U	U	S	U	U	S	S	U	U	U	S	S	S	S	S	S	U
STD/HIV Education Mandate	U	U	S	U	S	S	S	S	U	S	U	U	S	S	S	U	S	U	S	S	S	S	S	S	S
Mandate Includes Contraception	NL	NL	NL	NL	S	NL	NL	S	NL	S	U	NL	NL	S	S	NL	S	S	U	S	NL	S	NL	NL	NL
Mandate Includes Disease Prevention	NL	NL	NL	NL	S	S	NL	NL	S	S	S	S	S	S	S	NL	NL	S	S	S	S	S	NL	NL	U
Composite Score	U	U	S	S	S	S	S	S	U	S	N	U	S	S	S	U	S	S	N	S	S	N	S	N	U

Source: National Abortion and Reproductive Rights Action League, *A State-by-State Review of Abortion and Reproductive Rights* (NARAL Foundation, Washington, DC, January 1998).

KEY

S	= Supportive
U	= Unsupportive
NL	= No Law
N	= Neutral

TOTALS

Sexuality Education Mandate: S = 20; U = 31
STD/HIV Education Mandate: S = 36; U = 15
Mandate Includes Contraception: S = 13; U = 10; NL = 28
Mandate Includes Disease Prevention: S = 22; U = 3; NL = 26
Composite Score: S = 27; U = 14; N = 10

and considered states that used any amount of state funds as supportive (S).

SIECUS believes states that require coverage for contraceptive services in private insurance are supportive of sexual health and sexual rights (S) because it removes financial barriers. Two states—Montana and West Virginia—stand alone in requiring health maintenance organizations to provide, as a part of preventative services, voluntary family planning (see Table 42.2).

Studies have confirmed that adolescents are likely to delay or avoid seeking care when parental consent or notice is mandated for family planning services. SIECUS considers such mandates as unsupportive of sexual health and sexual rights (U). States that have no law explicitly authorizing minors' ability to consent for contraceptive services are designated as having no law (NL). States that explicitly authorize the minor to make contraceptive decisions were considered supportive of sexual health and sexual rights (S).[2]

Abortion Services

SIECUS believes that every woman, regardless of age or income, should have the right to obtain an abortion under safe, legal, confidential, and dignified conditions as well as at a reasonable cost. She should also have full knowledge of alternatives, and should be able to obtain complete, unbiased information and counseling on the nature, consequences, and risks associated with abortion, pregnancy, and childbirth.

SIECUS believes in public funding and mandated insurance coverage for abortion services. It also believes that parental consent laws, late-term bans, and waiting periods have a negative impact on reproductive health and rights. Clinic anti-violence and harassment laws promote safer access to such services and help to eliminate unconscionable attempts to undermine women's reproductive health rights.

For this issue, SIECUS examined a wide variety of topics because abortion is heavily legislated. These subjects included public funding, mandated insurance, parental consent, waiting periods, abortion procedure bans, and violence against abortion service providers. In many cases, states have placed a variety of conditions upon abortion services (see Table 42.3).

While the U.S. Supreme Court ruled in Roe versus Wade that a woman has a fundamental right to terminate a pregnancy, opponents of the procedure have sought to limit access. SIECUS rated states which have enacted laws to limit such access as unsupportive of sexual health and sexual rights (U).

Public funding for abortion. The patchwork of state laws concerning public funding for abortion services is complex. As a result of the Hyde Amendment, the use of federal Medicaid funds for abortion is prohibited except in cases where the woman's life is in danger. The amendment was expanded in 1993 to include situations where the pregnancy resulted from rape or incest. Each state establishes its own abortion funding policy related to state revenues. Fifteen states fund abortion in their state medical assistance programs in all or most circumstances, [and] SIECUS termed them supportive (S). States which fund abortions only in highly restricted situations, such as life endangerment, rape, or incest, or those that do not fund abortions at all, were termed as unsupportive (U).

Private insurance coverage. SIECUS termed unsupportive (U) those states that ban insurance coverage for abortion unless women pay an extra premium. It gave the same rating to states that prevent access to insurance coverage for abortion in some circumstances in which public funds are used or public employees are insured. SIECUS termed states that mandated insurance coverage as supportive (S) and states that didn't have laws as no law (NL).

Abortion procedure bans. States are now considering bans on abortion procedures carried out in the second and third trimesters called "Dilation and Extraction" (D&E) and dubbed by opponents as a "partial-birth abortion." These bans prevent a physician from exercising discretion to determine the most appropriate procedure. Some courts have held that such bans are

Table 42.2

Contraceptive Services

	AL	AK	AZ	AR	CA	CO	CT	DE	DC	FL	GA	HI	ID	IL	IN	IA	KS	KY	LA	ME	MD	MA	MI	MN	MS	MO
State Funding	S	S	U	S	S	S	S	S	NL	S	S	NL	U	S	U	S	U	S	S	S	S	S	S	S	S	S
Insurance Coverage	U	S	NL	U	U	U	U	U	U	U	U	U	U	U	NL	U	U	U	U	NL	U	U	NL	U	S	U
Parental Consent/Notice	NL	S	U	S	S	NL	S	S	NL	S	S	S	NL	NL	NL	S	NL	S	S	NL	NL	NL	NL	NL	S	NL
Composite Score	N	S	N	S	S	N	S	N	N	N	N	S	N	U	S	U	N	S	N	N	N	N	N	N	S	N

	MT	NE	NV	NH	NJ	NM	NY	NC	ND	OH	OK	OR	PA	RI	SC	SD	TN	TX	UT	VT	VA	WA	WV	WI	WY
State Funding	S	U	U	S	S	S	S	S	NL	S	S	U	S	U	S	S	NL	S	U	S	S	S	U	S	U
Insurance Coverage	U	S	U	U	U	U	U	U	U	U	U	U	U	U	U	U	U	U	U	U	U	U	S	U	U
Parental Consent/Notice	S	NL	NL	NL	S	S	S	NL	NL	NL	NL	NL	S	NL	NL	NL	NL	S	NL	NL	S	NL	NL	S	NL
Composite Score	S	U	U	S	S	S	S	N	N	S	N	U	U	U	S	N	N	S	N	N	S	N	U	S	U

Source: "Teenagers' Right to Consent to Reproductive Health Care," *Issues in Brief* (Alan Guttmacher Institute, New York, 1997); "Public Funding for Contraceptive Sterilization and Abortion Services, 1994." *Family Planning Perspectives*, 28(4), July–August 1996.

KEY
S = Supportive
U = Unsupportive
NL = No Law
N = Neutral

TOTALS
State Funding: S = 37; U = 10; NL = 4
Insurance Coverage: S = 2; U = 49
Parental Consent/Notice: S = 24; NL = 27
Composite Score: S = 21; U = 13; N = 17

Table 42.3

Abortion Services

	AL	AK	AZ	AR	CA	CO	CT	DE	DC	FL	GA	HI	ID	IL	IN	IA	KS	KY	LA	ME	MD	MA	MI	MN	MS	MO
Public Funding	U	S	U[2]	U[2]	S	U[2]	S	U[2]	U[2]	U	U	S	U	U	U[2]	U[3]	U[2]	U[2]	U[2]	U[2]	S	S	U[2]	S	U[1]	U[2]
Mandated Insurance	NL	NL	NL	NL	U	NL	NL	NL	NL	NL	NL	NL	U	NL	NL	NL	NL	U	NL	NL	NL	NL	U	NL	NL	U
Parental Consent	U	U	NL	NL	U	S	U	NL	U	U	U	U	U	U	U	U	U	U	U	U	S	U	U	U	U	S
Waiting Periods	S	U	S	S	S	S	S	S	S	S	S	S	U	S	S	S	S	U	S	S	S	S	S	S	S	S
Procedure Bans	U[6]	U[7]	U[7]	U[7]	NL	NL	NL	NL	NL	U[5]	U[6]	NL	U[7]	NL	U[7]	NL	NL	U[5]	U[7]	NL	NL	NL	U[7]	NL	NL	NL
Anti-Violence Laws	NL	NL	NL	NL	S	S	S	NL	NL	S	NL	NL	NL	NL	S	NL	NL	NL	S	S	S	S	NL	NL	NL	NL
Composite Score	U	U	U	U	S	S	S	U	U	S	U	U	U	U	U	U	U	U	U	S	S	S	U	S	U	U

	MT	NE	NV	NH	NJ	NM	NY	NC	ND	OH	OK	OR	PA	RI	SC	SD	TN	TX	UT	VT	VA	WA	WV	WI	WY
Public Funding	S	U[2]	U[2]	S	U[3]	S	U[2]	U[2]	U[2]	U[2]	U	U	U	U	NL	U	U[2]	U[2]	U[2]	S	U[3]	S	U	U	U[2]
Mandated Insurance	NL	U	NL	NL	NL	NL	NL	NL	U	NL	NL	U	NL	NL	U	NL	NL	U	NL	NL	NL	NL	NL	NL	U
Parental Consent	S	U	S	S	S	S	U	S	U	S	U	S	U	S	S	U	U	S	U	NL	U	NL	U	S	U
Waiting Periods	S	S	S	S	S	U	S	S	U	S	S	U	U	S	S	S	S	S	S	S	S	NL	U	S	U
Procedure Bans	U[7]	NL	NL	U[7]	NL	NL	NL	U[7]	U	U	U[7]	NL	U[7]	NL	U	U	NL	U[4]	NL	NL	U[5]	NL	U	U	NL
Anti-Violence Laws	NL	S	NL	S	S	S	S	S	NL	NL	NL	S	S	NL	NL	S	NL	S	NL	S	S	S	NL	NL	S
Composite Score	S	U	U	S	S	U	S	U	U	U	U	S	U	U	U	U	U	U	U	N	U	S	U	S	U

Source: National Abortion and Reproductive Rights Action League, *A State-by-State Review of Abortion and Reproductive Rights* (NARAL Foundation, Washington, DC, January 1998).

1. Provide funding for abortions only when the woman's life is endangered.
2. Cover abortions for life endangerment, rape, and incest.
3. Cover abortions for life endangerment, rape, incest, and certain health circumstances.
4. "Partial-birth" abortion bans are in effect.*
5. "Partial-birth" abortion bans are scheduled to go into effect.*
6. "Partial-birth" abortion bans are partially in effect.*
7. "Partial-birth" abortion bans are blocked by state or federal court.*
* Information current as of 1998.

TOTALS

Public Funding: S = 15; U = 36
Mandated Insurance: U = 11; NL = 40
Parental Consent: S = 19; U = 31; NL = 1
Waiting Periods: S = 37; U = 14
Procedure Bans: U = 26; NL = 25
Anti-Violence Laws: S = 16; U = 26; NL = 35
Composite Score: S = 21; U = 26; N = 4

KEY

S = Supportive
U = Unsupportive
NL = No Law
N = Neutral

unconstitutional because they fail to provide an exception to the ban when protecting a woman's health. SIECUS rated states where abortion procedure bans are in effect, are scheduled to go into effect, or are partially in effect as unsupportive (U). States with no bans are indicated with no law (NL).

Provider violence and harassment. A nationwide campaign of blockades, harassment, and violence has impeded women's access to abortion services. SIECUS rated states which have enacted laws to protect medical personnel and women seeking services as supportive of sexual rights (S). States not offering these protections are rated unsupportive (U).

When examined as a whole, state-level protection for abortion rights reflects the public ambivalence about abortion. SIECUS found many states unsupportive because of public funding and restrictions on late-term abortions. This is troublesome because these issues address the most vulnerable populations. Also troubling is the lack of state efforts to protect its citizens from harassment and violence at legal medical facilities. Only 15 states and the District of Columbia do so.[3]

HIV/AIDS Infection

SIECUS believes that HIV testing should occur only with informed consent and that case reporting should utilize unique or coded identifiers to insure the privacy and confidentiality of the individual. Every state should provide, anonymous testing. SIECUS compiled information on state laws related to HIV testing options and HIV infection reporting (see Table 42.4). Name-reporting is currently a contentious issue and many state legislatures may soon consider it.

SIECUS assigned an unsupportive (U) rating to states that use a names-based reporting system because it compromises confidentiality and is, in turn, a disincentive to testing. States that have a system of reporting that is not names-based were designated as supportive (S). States with no reporting requirements were assigned no law

(NL). States offering anonymous and confidential testing sites were considered supportive (S), whereas states offering only confidential sites were termed neither (N) supportive or unsupportive, [i.e., neutral].

It appears that states are not aggressively pursuing HIV/AIDS policies that protect the privacy of individuals. States are relatively evenly divided among supportive, unsupportive, and neither. SIECUS acknowledges, however, that these two issues are in transition, and that other indicators, such as state appropriations, may prove a more definitive indication of support for HIV/AIDS prevention and treatment.[4]

Sexual Orientation

SIECUS believes that individuals have the right to accept, acknowledge, and live in accordance with their sexual orientation, whether bisexual, heterosexual, gay, or lesbian. The legal system should guarantee everyone's civil rights and protection. Prejudice and discrimination based on sexual orientation is unconscionable. SIECUS has reviewed state statutes relating to sexual orientation in such areas as workplace discrimination, public school discrimination, and the adoption of children by same-sex partners (see Table 42.5).

SIECUS rated states as supportive of sexual health and sexual rights if they ban discrimination on the basis of sexual orientation in the workplace and in the public school setting. It rated states without such laws as unsupportive (U) because there are no current federal protections to offset the lack of state law. It also rated states that restrict the family formation of same-sex couples as unsupportive (U).

It is clear that state laws addressing sexual orientation are the most unsupportive of sexual health and sexual rights of any covered in this article. In fact, it is the only category in which most states received unsupportive ratings.[5]

Sexual Behaviors

Sodomy laws were first initiated by religious institutions as "crimes against na-

Table 42.4

HIV/AIDS

	AL	AK	AZ	AR	CA	CO	CT	DE	DC	FL	GA	HI	ID	IL	IN	IA	KS	KY	LA	ME	MD	MA	MI	MN	MS	MO
HIV Infection Surveillance	U	NL	U	U	NL	U	U[1]	NL	U	S	NL	U	S	U	S	S	S	U	S	U	NL	U	U	S	NL	S
HIV Testing Options	NL	S	S	S	S	S	S	S	S	S	NL	S	S	S	S	S	S	S	S	S	NL	S	S	S	NL	S
Composite Score	N	S	N	N	N	N	U	N	N	S	N	N	S	N	S	S	S	N	S	N	N	N	N	S	N	S

	MT	NE	NV	NH	NJ	NM	NY	NC	ND	OH	OK	OR	PA	RI	SC	SD	TN	TX	UT	VT	VA	WA	WV	WI	WY
HIV Infection Surveillance	S	U	U	U	NL	U	U	U	U	U	U[2]	U	U	U	NL	U[3]	U	U	NL	U[4]	U	U	U	U	U
HIV Testing Options	S	S	NL	S	S	S	S	NL	S	S	S	S	S	NL	NL	NL	S	S	S	S	S	S	S	S	NL
Composite Score	S	U	U	U	U	U	U	S	U	U	U	S	S	S	S	S	S	S	N	N	N	N	N	N	N

Source: *Guide to Information and Resources on HIV Testing Document B053* (U.S. Centers for Disease Control and Prevention, National AIDS Clearinghouse, Atlanta, May 1997); "HIV Infection Surveillance," *AIDS Action Alerts* (U.S. Centers for Disease Control and Prevention, National AIDS Clearinghouse, Atlanta, February 1998).

1. Requires reports of HIV in children under 13 years of age by names; reports of HIV infections not required for adults/adolescents 13 years of age or older
2. Requires reports of HIV infection in children under six years of age.
3. Requires reports of HIV in children under 13 years of age by name; requires anonymous reports for adults/adolescents 13 years of age or older.
4. Requires named reporting of symptomatic HIV infection and AIDS.

TOTALS

HIV Infection Surveillance: S = 9; U = 33; NL = 9
HIV Testing Options: S = 41; NL = 10
Composite Score: S = 18; U = 10; N = 23

KEY

S = Supportive
U = Unsupportive
NL = No Law
N = Neutral

Table 42.5

Sexual Orientation

	AL	AK	AZ	AR	CA	CO	CT	DE	DC	FL	GA	HI	ID	IL	IN	IA	KS	KY	LA	ME	MD	MA	MI	MN	MS	MO
Workplace Discrimination	U	U	U	U	S	U	S	S	S	U	U	S	U	U	U	U	U	U	U	U	U	S	S	S	U	U
Public School Discrimination	U	U	U	U	S	U	S	U	U	U	U	S	U	U	U	U	U	U	U	U	U	S	U	S	U	U
Family Formation	NL	NL	NL	NL	NL	NL	NL	NL	NL	U	NL	NL	NL	NL	NL	NL	NL	NL	NL	NL	NL	NL	NL	NL	NL	NL
Composite Score	U	U	U	U	S	U	S	U	N	U	U	S	U	U	U	U	U	U	U	N	U	S	U	S	U	U

	MT	NE	NV	NH	NJ	NM	NY	NC	ND	OH	OK	OR	PA	RI	SC	SD	TN	TX	UT	VT	VA	WA	WV	WI	WY
Workplace Discrimination	U	U	S	U	S	U	U	U	U	U	U	U	U	S	U	U	U	U	U¹	U	U	U	U	S	U
Public School Discrimination	U	U	U	U	U	U	U	U	U	U	U	U	U	U	U	U	U	U	U¹	U	U	U	U	S	U
Family Formation	NL	NL	U	NL	NL	NL	NL	NL	NL	NL	NL	NL	NL	NL	NL	NL	NL	NL	NL	NL	NL	NL	NL	NL	NL
Composite Score	U	U	S	N	U	N	U	U	U	U	U	U	U	N	U	U	U	U	U	N	U	U	U	N	U

Source: *State and Local Laws Protecting Lesbians and Gay Men Against Workplace Discrimination, Overview of Lesbian and Gay Parenting*
(American Civil Liberties Union, New York, 1998).

1. Laws passed to prohibit gay student organizations from meeting on school campuses. These laws are being challenged in the courts (as of 1998).

TOTALS
Workplace Discrimination: S = 11; U = 40
Public School Discrimination: S = 2; U = 49
Family Formation: U = 2; NL = 49
Composite Score: S = 3; U = 40; N = 8

KEY
S = Supportive
U = Unsupportive
NL = No Law
N = Neutral

ture" and were later enforced by English common law in the sixteenth century. While intended to forbid anal intercourse, the definition of sodomy has broadened to include contact between the mouth and genitals. The U.S. Supreme Court ruled in *Bowers versus Hardwick* in 1986 that the Constitution allows states to criminalize sodomy. Prosecution is almost entirely limited to sexual conduct in a public place and penalties range from $200 fines to 20 years imprisonment.

Sodomy laws are now in less than half of all the states (see Table 42.6). Six states ban these sexual acts exclusively between people of the same sex (AR, KS, MD, MO, OK, TX). Fifteen states ban these sexual acts between gays and heterosexuals alike (AL, AZ, FL, GA, ID, LA, MI, MA, MN, MS, NC, RI, SC, UT, VA). All other states currently have no sodomy laws.[6]

SIECUS rated states with a sodomy law as unsupportive (U) and those with no sodomy law as supportive (S) of sexual health and sexual rights, because, in most cases, these states have taken legislative action to repeal archaic sodomy laws.

Sexual Exploitation

SIECUS believes that sexual relationships should be consensual between partners who are developmentally, physically, and emotionally capable of understanding the relationship. It believes that coerced and exploitative sexual acts and behaviors—such as rape, incest, sexual relations between adults and children, sexual abuse, and sexual harassment—are always reprehensible and should be outlawed.

SIECUS has examined laws addressing sexual exploitation through rape and sexual assault; child pornography; child prostitution; and sexual harassment in the schools. SIECUS also gathered information on state laws regarding the use of computers to exploit children and proliferate child pornography (see Table 42.7).

Sexual assault and rape. Sexual assault is any nonconsensual sexual act forced by one or more individuals upon another. The legal term *sexual assault* encompasses rape

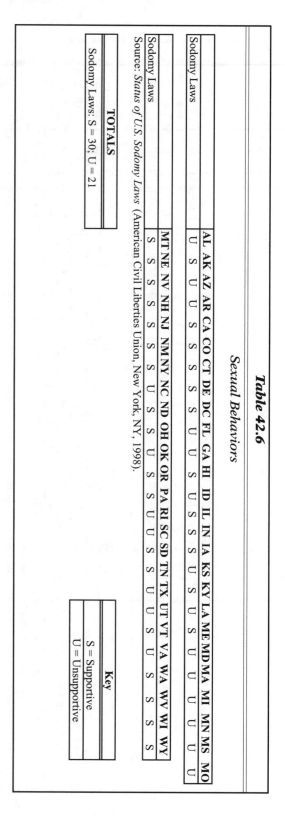

Table 42.6

Sexual Behaviors

	AL	AK	AZ	AR	CA	CO	CT	DE	DC	FL	GA	HI	ID	IL	IN	IA	KS	KY	LA	ME	MD	MA	MI	MN	MS	MO
Sodomy Laws	U	U	S	S	S	U	S	S	U	U	U	S	U	S	U	U	S	S	U	U	U	U	U	U	U	U

	MT	NE	NV	NH	NJ	NM	NY	NC	ND	OH	OK	OR	PA	RI	SC	SD	TN	TX	UT	VT	VA	WA	WV	WI	WY
Sodomy Laws	S	S	S	S	S	S	S	U	S	S	U	S	S	U	U	S	U	U	U	S	U	S	S	S	S

TOTALS
Sodomy Laws: S = 30; U = 21

Key
S = Supportive
U = Unsupportive

Source: *Status of U.S. Sodomy Laws* (American Civil Liberties Union, New York, NY, 1998).

Table 42.7

Sexual Exploitation

	AL	AK	AZ	AR	CA	CO	CT	DE	DC	FL	GA	HI	ID	IL	IN	IA	KS	KY	LA	ME	MD	MA	MI	MN	MS	MO
Rape and Sexual Assault	S	S	S	S	S	S	S	S	S	S	S	S	S	S	S	S	S	S	S	S	S	S	S	S	S	S
Child Pornography	S	S	S	S	S	S	S	S	S	S	S	S	S	S	S	S	S	S	S	S	S	S	S	S	S	S
Child Prostitution	S	S	S	S	S	S	S	S	U	S	S	S	S	S	S	S	S	S	S	S	S	U	S	S	S	U
Computer Crimes	U	U	U	U	S	U	S	U	U	U	S	U	S	U	U	S	U	U	U	U	U	U	U	U	S	U
Sexual Harassment in School Setting	U	U	U	U	S	U	S	U	U	S	U	U	U	U	U	U	U	U	U	U	S	U	S	U	U	U
Composite Score	S	S	S	S	S	S	S	S	S	S	S	S	S	S	S	S	S	S	S	S	S	S	S	S	S	U

	MT	NE	NV	NH	NJ	NM	NY	NC	ND	OH	OK	OR	PA	RI	SC	SD	TN	TX	UT	VT	VA	WA	WV	WI	WY
Rape and Sexual Assault	S	S	S	S	S	S	S	S	S	S	S	S	S	S	S	S	S	S	S	S	S	S	S	S	S
Child Pornography	S	S	S	S	S	S	S	S	S	S	S	S	S	S	S	S	S	S	S	S	S	S	S	S	U
Child Prostitution	S	S	S	S	S	S	S	S	S	S	S	U	S	S	S	U	S	S	S	S	S	S	S	S	S
Computer Crimes	S	U	S	U	U	U	S	U	U	U	U	U	U	U	S	U	S	U	U	U	S	U	U	U	U
Sexual Harassment in School Setting	U	U	U	S	U	S	U	U	U	U	U	U	U	U	S	U	U	U	U	S	U	U	U	U	U
Composite Score	S	S	S	S	S	S	S	S	S	S	S	S	S	S	S	S	S	S	S	S	S	S	S	S	U

Key
S = Supportive
U = Unsupportive

Source: *State Laws Prohibiting Sexual Harassment and Sexual Discrimination in Education* (National Organization of Women, Washington, 1996); *Child Abuse and Neglect State Statute Series, Volume V—Crime* (National Clearinghouse on Child Abuse and Neglect, Washington, DC, December 1996).

TOTALS
Rape and Sexual Assault: S = 51; U = 0
Child Pornography: S = 49; U = 2
Child Prostitution: S = 44; U = 7
Computer Crimes: S = 12; U = 39
Sexual Harassment in Schools: S = 8; U = 43
Composite Score: S = 48; U = 3

(forced vaginal intercourse), sodomy (forced anal or oral intercourse), incest, molestation, sexual battery or any unwanted touching of the sexual parts of the body. It is a felony in every state to engage in sexual penetration/intercourse where the offender causes the victim's submission through physical force. Most states also consider it a felony if the victim is incapable of consent due to physical or mental incapacitation. States prohibiting sexual assault and rape were assigned a supportive (S) rating.

Child pornography. Virtually all states have statutes on the solicitation, promotion, dissemination, or displaying of obscene matter containing a visual representation of a minor. These states legislate that sexual exploitation is committed if the child is induced to engage in any explicit sexual conduct for a commercial purpose. The definition of a minor ranges from 16 to 18 years of age depending on the state. Penalties for such crimes range from felonies to misdemeanors. States that have laws prohibiting child pornography were assigned a supportive (S) rating while states without child pornography laws were viewed as unsupportive (U).

Child prostitution. Child prostitution statutes address the inducing or employing of a child to work as a prostitute. The crime generally involves the persuasion, arrangement, or coercion of a minor for the exchange of money to provide acts such as sexual intercourse or sodomy. Most states categorize prostitution as a felony, with prison terms of three to 10 years, plus fines. While the severity of the penalties vary, states with laws prohibiting child prostitution received a supportive (S) rating and those states without child prostitution laws received an unsupportive (U) rating.

Computer-related exploitation of children. Individuals have used computers to disseminate child pornography and to meet children to solicit sexual acts. Many states have passed laws to forbid the transmission, production, and possession of computerized child pornography. Such laws make it unlawful to photograph, display, distribute, or sell pictures of minors engaged in sexual conduct via computers. Some states have also criminalized the dissemination of a minor's name for the purposes of soliciting sexual conduct. States that have passed such legislation have received a supportive (S) rating, and because of the seriousness of the issue, states without such legislation were assigned an unsupportive (U) rating rather than no law (NL).

Sexual harassment. Sexual harassment is generally an issue decided by the courts rather than state legislatures. There is currently no compilation of states' statutes on sexual harassment, in general, or in the workplace. However, state laws on sexual harassment and discrimination in schools include statutes that address unwanted sexual advances or inappropriate sexual conduct. Many states require schools to adopt policies that prohibit sexual harassment in elementary, secondary, and postsecondary schools. SIECUS views such states as supportive (S) and states that do not have such laws as unsupportive (U).

More than in any other sexuality-related category of law, a clear majority of states determined that sexual exploitation is serious enough to merit government intervention, especially when it concerns children.[7]

Conclusion: Work Ahead

When the seven categories in this article are viewed collectively, most states were supportive of sexual rights and sexual health. Specifically: 28 states and the District of Columbia were supportive, 17 states were unsupportive of sexual rights in general, and five were somewhere between supportive and unsupportive in their policies (see Table 42.8). No state demonstrated support in every category. On the other hand, no state had exclusively unsupportive laws. There is no definitive regional trend, although states along the West Coast and in the Northeast create small pockets of overall support.

In many ways, the overview of state sexuality-related laws reflects the broad ambivalence about sexuality in America's culture. State laws are generally more focused on

Table 42.8

Overview

	AL	AK	AZ	AR	CA	CO	CT	DE	DC	FL	GA	HI	ID	IL	IN	IA	KS	KY	LA	ME	MD	MA	MI	MN	MS	MO
Sexuality Education	S	N	U	U	S	N	S	S	S	S	S	N	S	S	U	S	S	U	U	S	U	N	S	S	N	N
Contraceptive Services	N	S	U	S	U	N	S	N	S	N	S	S	N	U	U	U	U	S	S	U	S	N	N	S	S	N
Abortion Services	U	S	S	U	S	U	S	U	S	U	U	S	U	U	U	U	U	N	S	S	S	S	U	U	U	U
HIV/AIDS	U	S	N	N	N	S	N	N	N	N	S	S	S	N	S	N	N	S	N	N	S	N	N	N	U	N
Sexual Orientation	U	U	U	N	U	N	U	N	N	U	U	U	U	U	U	U	U	U	U	U	S	U	N	U	U	U
Sexual Behaviors	U	S	U	U	S	S	S	S	S	S	S	S	S	S	S	S	S	S	U	U	U	U	U	U	S	U
Sexual Exploitation	S	S	S	S	S	S	S	U	S	S	S	S	S	S	S	S	S	S	S	S	S	S	S	S	S	U
Total Composite Score	U	S	U	N	S	U	S	S	S	S	N	S	U	S	S	N	S	S	S	S	S	U	U	S	U	U

	MT	NE	NV	NH	NJ	NM	NY	NC	ND	OH	OK	OR	PA	RI	SC	SD	TN	TX	UT	VT	VA	WA	WV	WI	WY
Sexuality Education	U	U	S	N	S	S	S	S	U	S	U	N	S	S	S	S	S	S	N	S	N	S	S	N	U
Contraceptive Services	S	U	U	N	S	S	S	S	U	U	N	S	N	U	U	U	S	U	U	S	N	S	N	N	U
Abortion Services	S	U	S	S	S	S	S	U	U	S	N	U	U	U	U	S	U	S	S	U	S	S	S	S	U
HIV/AIDS	S	N	N	U	N	N	N	N	U	N	N	N	S	S	U	U	N	N	U	N	N	N	N	N	U
Sexual Orientation	U	U	U	N	N	U	U	U	U	U	U	U	U	U	U	U	U	U	U	S	N	N	U	N	U
Sexual Behaviors	S	S	S	S	S	S	S	S	S	S	S	S	U	S	U	U	S	S	S	S	S	S	S	S	S
Sexual Exploitation	S	S	S	S	S	S	S	S	S	S	S	S	S	S	S	S	S	S	U	S	S	S	S	S	S
Total Composite Score	S	U	S	S	S	S	S	S	U	S	N	U	U	U	S	U	U	S	U	S	S	S	S	S	U

KEY

S = Supportive
U = Unsupportive
N = Neutral

OVERVIEW

Composite Score: S = 29; U = 17; N = 5

putting restrictions or stipulations on sexual decisions than on affirming sexual rights and healthy sexual decision making. From the perspective of state laws, sexuality is still something from which the citizens must be protected.

States have a clear consensus on protecting citizens from sexual harm. Nearly every state makes activities such as rape, child pornography, and child prostitution illegal. For other issues, states have no consensus even though some have enacted laws. For issues such as abortion and sexuality education, state laws articulate a wide variety of views. For these issues in particular, sexual rights are often governed by political considerations rather than public health and civil liberties concerns. Still, in many cases, the absence of laws speaks loudly. For sensitive and emerging issues, such as discrimination based on sexual orientation and sexual harassment, states have yet to pass laws that would protect their citizens from harm.

Although this collection of state sexuality laws indicates that states generally support sexual health and sexual rights, even this preliminary overview attests that every state has work to do in developing state laws to support sexual rights and sexual health. SIECUS will continue to expand the scope and depth of information that it makes available on state laws and policies. This article is its preliminary examination of these issues. SIECUS will post these and subsequent findings on a state policy section of its Web page (www.siecus.org). Advocates of sexual rights will want to check it regularly as state laws change.

References

1. *A State-by-State Review of Abortion and Reproductive Rights,* National Abortion and Reproductive Rights Action League (NARAL Foundation, Washington, DC, January 1998).

2. T. Sollom, et al., "Public Funding for Contraceptive, Sterilization, and Abortion Services, 1994," *Family Planning Perspectives,* vol. 28, no. 4, July–August 1996; R. Posner and K. Silbaugh, *A Guide to America's Sex Laws* (Chicago, University of Chicago,

1996); *Teenagers' Right to Consent* (The Alan Guttmacher Institute, Washington, DC, 1997).

3. *A State-by-State Review of Abortion and Reproductive Rights. NARAL Foundation* (National Abortion and Reproductive Rights Action League, Washington, DC, January 1998); "Late Term Abortions: Legal Consideration," *Issues in Brief* (The Alan Guttmacher Institute, New York, NY, January 1997); "So-Called Partial Birth Abortions," *Issues in Brief* (The Alan Guttmacher Institute, New York, NY, April 1998); *The Appropriations Process and Discriminatory Abortion Funding Restriction* (National Abortion and Reproductive Rights Action League, Washington, DC, 1998); *Constitutional Analysis of H.R. 1122* (National Abortion and Reproductive Rights Action League, Washington, DC, 1998); *Mandatory Waiting Periods and the Freedom to Choose* (National Abortion and Reproductive Rights Action League, Washington, DC, 1998).

4. *HIV Surveillance and Name Reporting: A Public Health Case for Protecting Civil Liberties* (American Civil Liberties Union, New York, NY, 1997); "HIV Infection Surveillance," *AIDS Action Alerts* (AIDS Action Council, Washington, DC, February 1998); *Guide to Information and Resources on HIV Testing, Document #B053* (U.S. Centers for Disease Control and Prevention, National AIDS Clearinghouse, Atlanta, GA, May 1997).

5. *Hostile Climate: A State-by-State Report on Anti-Gay Activity* (People for the American Way, Washington, DC, 1997); *Measuring Up: Assessing State Policies to Promote Adolescent Sexual and Reproductive Health* (Advocates for Youth, Washington, DC, 1998); *Overview on Lesbian and Gay Parenting* (American Civil Liberties Union, New York, NY, May 1998); *State and Local Laws Protecting Lesbians and Gay Men Against Workplace Discrimination* (American Civil Liberties Union, New York, NY, November 1997).

6. *Status of U.S. Sodomy Laws* (American Civil Liberties Union, New York, NY, 1998).

7. *Child Abuse and Neglect State Statutes Series. Volume V—Crimes* (National Clearinghouse on Child Abuse and Neglect, Washington, DC, December 1996); *State Laws Prohibiting Sexual Harassment and Sexual Discrimination in Education* (National Organization for Women); R. Posner and K. Silbaugh, *A*

Guide to America's Sex Laws (Chicago, University of Chicago, 1996).

Adapted from Daniel Daley, Susie Orenstein, & Vivian Wong, "States' Sexuality Laws and the Sexual Rights of Citizens." *SIECUS Report*, 26(6), August/September 1998, pp. 4–15. Copyright © 1998, Sexuality Information and Education Council of the U.S. (SIECUS). Reprinted by permission. ✦